California real estate principles

California
real estate principles

fourth edition

Hyman Maxwell Berston, Ph.D.
Professor of Business and Real Estate
City College of San Francisco

1983   **RICHARD D. IRWIN, INC.**
Homewood, Illinois 60430

ISBN 0–256–02725–0
Library of Congress Catalog Card No. 82–84269
Printed in the United States of America

1 2 3 4 5 6 7 8 9 0 K 0 9 8 7 6 5 4 3

Preface

California Real Estate Principles has been designed for use as a textbook in real estate principles classes and as a reference and guide for the real estate licensee, and any individual interested in California real estate. The material presented offers a firm foundation for the acquisition of a California real estate license and provides an excellent basis for advanced study. An appendix contains a sample real estate license examination with 150 multiple choice questions and answers. More than 30 years as a practicing Realtor® and teacher of real estate subjects has convinced the author that education is the key ingredient to success in the real estate profession.

Since its publication in 1971, *California Real Estate Principles* has been adopted for use in 75 collegiate institutions and schools in California, as well as in schools and colleges in other states. This revision thoroughly updates all of the material with respect to content, illustrations, various tables, and real estate forms presented.

In addition to the material which must be included in any study of real estate principles, the important forms commonly used in everyday real estate transactions are illustrated and discussed, and individual chapters also include such areas as real estate mathematics, income tax aspects, developments and subdivisions, real estate brokerage, and property insurance. An appendix contains an extensive listing of definitions of various words and phrases used in real estate and in building construction.

The individual chapters contain questions for classroom discussion and a number of multiple choice questions. It is important that the student become familiar with this type of question since the California real estate license examinations consist entirely of multiple choice questions. An appendix contains the answers to the 168 multiple choice chapter questions.

Acknowledgments

The author wishes to thank sincerely the numerous coordinators, real estate instructors, and licensees throughout the state who aided in the preparation of this revised edition. Preceding the actual work on the revision, questionnaires were sent to these individuals asking for comments and suggestions. The response was excellent and any improvement in this edition is directly attributable to this response. The author also received suggestions from students and real estate licensees who have used the text in the classroom. Additional help has also been provided by the California Department of Real Estate, National Association of Realtors®, California Association of Realtors®, California Association of Real Estate Teachers, and Title Insurance and Trust Company.

A very special thank you to my wife Bertie, and to my children—Debbie, Marilyn, Susan, Emanuel, and Judith—for their love and support while Father was locked in the study preparing and typing the revision.

H. M. BERSTON

Contents

List of illustrations

Introduction

Approximately 10 to 15 percent of the employment opportunities in the United States are to be found in the real estate business and its related activities. The business consists of the activities of private individuals and corporations, and the public activities of federal, state, and local governmental agencies.

The private segment of the real estate business is that of agency and brokerage practice, which involves selling, leasing, management, loan, and business opportunity brokerage. In addition, real estate licensees may be engaged in related activities, such as construction, modernization of existing structures, and land development and subdividing. Besides improving land by creating lots and bringing in utilities, the developer may also construct homes and commercial buildings and, on a larger scale, may create an entire community.

In addition to those individuals engaged in real estate brokerage activities, the real estate licensee must work with such specialists as surveyors, engineers, financial institutions that furnish the necessary funds, title companies, architects, contractors, pest control operators, attorneys, accountants, and other individuals whose special skills are necessary.

Government at all levels influences the real estate business, and numerous agencies and departments play a part. In the area of taxation are the administration of real property tax laws, valuation of real estate for tax purposes, assessment practices, and collection of real estate taxes. The management area involves acquisition, sales and leasing, and management of governmental lands and properties and public housing. Laws regulating the use of real estate involve building, health, zoning, and fire, electrical, and plumbing codes, while other areas include real estate licensing and real estate laws. The area of financing includes the Federal Housing Authority, Veterans Administration, and state veterans programs.

There are numerous employment opportunities available to the real estate principles student. In addition to the employment positions available in real estate brokerage firms, the student should investigate opportunities in banks, savings and loan associations, insurance companies, business and corporate real estate departments, and city, county, state, and federal governmental agencies.

Although numerous employment opportunities exist, the key to success is education, and California presently leads the nation in real estate education and research. At present, a number of community colleges offer courses in real estate, have established a Real Estate Certificate Program, and offer the Associate in Arts degree with a specialization in real estate. The University of California and the California State Universities offer numerous courses, and a student may obtain a B.S., M.S., or M.B.A. degree with a specialization in real estate. In addition, courses are offered by private schools, colleges, and universities, the California Association of Realtors®, local real estate boards, and in adult classes sponsored by local school districts.

H.M.B.

The nature of real property

1

In any study of the principles of real estate, the beginning must be a definition of the term *real property*. The terms *real estate* and *real property* are used interchangeably and mean the same thing.

There are various approaches to our definition. A geologist may define real property as the solid material of the earth and its component parts; an attorney may think of real property not only as a portion of the earth's surface but also as a group of rights that an owner has, such as possession, use, and disposition, subject of course to a number of legal restrictions, including zoning ordinances, building and health codes, taxation, and other governmental rules and regulations governing real property. However, most persons think of real property as a certain piece of land together with the buildings, fences, trees, and shrubs that belong to it.

REAL PROPERTY DEFINED

For our purposes, the best approach to the definition of real property is to say that it is first the surface of the land and certain things affixed to it by nature or man; second, that which lies beneath the surface; and third, the air space above the surface.

On the surface

Real estate is first of all the land, be it valley, mountain, or desert, and in addition it is *(a)* growing things affixed to the land by roots, *(b)* water, and *(c)* things embedded in and resting upon the land.

a. Growing things affixed to the land by roots are divided into classes. "Fructus naturales" is the term given to trees, shrubs, vines, perennial bushes, grasses, etc., which do not require annual cultivation and are a product of nature alone. They are considered to be a part of the land to which they are attached and are considered to be real property until they are severed, when they become personal property. It is possible for fructus naturales to be owned separately from the land. An example would be a stand of timber that an owner may convey to another, or a piece of land that may be purchased with the rights to the timber on the land reserved to another person.

"Fructus industriales" is the term given to crops such as wheat, lettuce, corn, and various other vegetables that are the result of annual labor. These crops are generally classified as personal property. A crop growing on trees or vines is also fructus industriales but here we have an example of both real and personal property. The apples sold from the tree would be personal property but the tree itself remains real property. Since growing crops are generally classified as personal property, they may be mortgaged separately from the land, and the Civil Code sets forth the provisions by which this may be done.

b. The availability of water and its tremendous importance to the economy of this state is an ever-continuing topic of discussion. A considerable body of law has developed concerning underground and surface water and related water rights, and the general principle behind these laws is that of conservation.

The California law recognizes this principle by establishing the policy that individual water rights are normally limited to taking only such amount of water as is reasonably required for beneficial

1

use. Surface water rights are dependent to some extent upon whether or not the surface water is flowing in a defined channel. A defined channel is any natural watercourse, even though dry during a good portion of the year, and when water is flowing in such a defined channel a landowner may not obstruct or direct it. When water flows across the surface of the earth without being contained in any clearly defined channel, the landowner below may not obstruct it in such a manner as to flood the owner above; by the same measure the landowner above may not divert or by artificial structures concentrate such waters upon the landowner below.

"Riparian rights" is the term used to denote the rights that an owner has to water adjoining or forming the boundary of his land. Basically, the property owner has the right to the use and enjoyment of the water, but only to the extent that it is fair and equitable with regard to adjoining landowners. A lake or pond that is entirely within the boundaries of one's land belongs wholly to him. Owners of property that touches upon a lake or navigable stream generally own to the low water mark or to a point midway between the low and high tide marks. Where the boundary is a nonnavigable stream, the owner generally owns to the center of the stream. How the size of a landowner's piece of property may be increased or decreased by the force of water will be discussed in Chapter 3.

c. Things embedded in and resting upon the land will complete our definition of real property on the surface of the earth. Thus, in addition to the land itself, real property includes that which is affixed to the land, and Section 660 of the Civil Code states that an item is deemed to be affixed to land when it is attached to it by roots, as in the case of trees and shrubs, or embedded in it, as in the case of walls, or permanently resting upon it, as in the case of buildings. This section also goes on to state that items of personal property that are permanently attached to that which is already permanent, immediately become real property themselves. For example, a homeowner purchases a quantity of roofing shingles at a neighborhood lumber yard. The shingles at this point are personal property. But when they are nailed onto the roof of the house they are considered to be real property. They have been permanently attached to that (the house) which is already permanent. Items of personal property that become real property will be treated in the discussion of fixtures later in this chapter.

That which is incidental or appurtenant to the land is also considered to be real property. *Appurtenant* means belonging to, and includes anything that by right is used with the real property for its benefit. A common type of appurtenance is stock in a mutual water company. When such stock is appurtenant to the land, its ownership may not be transferred unless the land is transferred with it.

Beneath the surface

Ownership of a piece of land generally includes all metals, ores, and other minerals that are stationary and also minerals such as oil and gas that may be nonstationary. Minerals mined in various parts of California include gold, silver, mercury, tungsten, borax, magnesium, and manganese.

A landowner may retain ownership of the land but may convey to another the right to the minerals as is often done in mineral, oil, and gas leases. Conversely, an owner may sell the land but retain the ownership of and the right to the minerals. Ownership of mineral rights generally includes certain pre-agreed-upon rights of entry upon the surface for the removal of the minerals.

There are several laws relating to the drilling for and production of gas and oil. The California courts have generally held that these substances, since they may shift and move beneath the surface of the earth, must be reduced to possession before there is absolute ownership. This is commonly referred to as the rule of capture, which means that a landowner has the right to drill wells on his land and to retain whatever substances are brought to the surface. It often occurs that oil being produced by a well on one owner's land not only comes from beneath this land but may in part shift over from beneath the land of an adjoining landowner. Even so, the owner of the well is entitled to whatever his well produces, and the owner of the adjoining land will have to sink his own wells, called offset wells, in order to capture the oil or gas that he may be losing. Most landowners who cannot afford the expense of drilling operations give leases to oil companies and then merely receive royalties for any gas or oil produced.

Water on the surface of the land has already been discussed, but there is also a vast amount of underground water and waters percolating through the soil. These waters are generally classified as real property, and the overlying landowner has the right to their use. In California, since water may be quite scarce in certain areas, the courts have held that any water not needed for a reasonable use by the overlying property owner may in certain instances be appropriated for public use. In many areas the availability of water through a public utility or from surface supply is such that the need for appropriation of underground waters is unnecessary and the landowner is free of any restrictions on the use of such waters.

Air space above the surface

The owner of a piece of land also owns the air space above it, and it would seem reasonable to conclude that just as one may own beneath the surface downward to the center of the earth, one also owns upward from the surface unto the heavens. The courts, however, have modified this definition of the ownership of air space to include only that portion the landowner can use or reasonably needs. The courts have held that above a certain height air space is a public thoroughfare, and thus airliners may fly across land at certain elevations without having to obtain permission from the landowners below.

In the same way that a landowner may lease or sell rights in oil or minerals beneath the surface of his land, so may he lease or sell air rights above his land. There are many illustrations of such uses. The Merchandise Mart in Chicago, for example, is built over the tracks of the Chicago and Northwestern Railroad. The building is supported upon steel columns. Only the columns rest upon the ground, while the building begins a sufficient number of feet above the surface so that the trains run on the surface of the earth beneath the building itself. In New York City the Pan American Building occupies air space above Grand Central Station. The shortage of construction sites in many of our large cities has led to an increasing awareness of the potential use of air space above existing structures or roadways.

Another example relating to air rights can be seen in the purchase of a condominium apartment. The purchaser of a condominium located on the eighth floor of the building would receive a deed giving him absolute ownership of the apartment, which in effect would be a rectangular space in the air. In addition the purchaser would receive a share of the ownership, along with all the other condominium apartment owners, in the outside walls of the building and the land upon which it stands.

FIXTURES

A fixture is an item that was once classified as personal property but has since become classified as real property, generally by virtue of its attachment in, on, or to that which is already real property.

The California legislature has by statute defined a fixture by declaring that a thing is affixed to the land when it is attached to it by roots, as in the case of trees, vines, or shrubs, or embedded in it, as in the case of walls, or permanently resting upon it, as in the case of buildings, or permanently attached to what is thus permanent, as by means of cement, plaster, nails, bolts, or screws. The courts have further utilized five general tests to determine whether an item of personal property is or is not a fixture. These are: (1) the intention of the parties, (2) the method of attachment, (3) the adaption of the item to the real property, (4) the existence of an agreement between the parties involved, and (5) the relationship between the parties involved.

1. The intention of the parties. The intention of the party or parties incorporating the personal property into the land or building is considered the most important test. If it is clear that the attachment was intended to be a permanent one, then the item so attached is a fixture and is considered to be real property. In most homes without modern kitchens the stove is free-standing, and its only means of attachment is at the connection to the gas pipe. Such an attachment is not considered permanent since the stove can easily be moved by unscrewing the gas pipe connection, and so this stove would be considered an item of personal property. In most newer and more modern homes, the kitchen is generally a "built in" one in which the sink, counters, stove, dishwasher, and cabinets are constructed and attached in a permanent manner, and the intention is quite clear that these items are fixtures.

2. The method of attachment. The method by which items are incorporated into the land or a building are important indicators. Thus, when the attachment is by cement and plaster, for example, the items so attached are generally fixtures. If an item is so attached to a building that its removal would damage the property, as in the case of plumbing or electrical wiring, then these items are considered to be fixtures and become real property. A fancy Persian carpet that is merely lying on the floor of a living room is an item of personal property, but carpeting in a basement den that is secured to the floor by means of an adhesive is permanently attached and is a fixture.

3. The adaption of the item to the real property. The adaption of an item to real property generally tends to show the intention of the annexing party, and if it is an item that is essential to the ordinary and convenient use of the building, or is an integral part of the building itself, then it is considered to be a fixture. The character of the article is also important in that one which has been specifically designed or custom-made for adaption to a particular building will generally be deemed a fixture.

4. The existence of an agreement between the parties involved. In many cases, problems that might have arisen with regard to certain items are solved by the existence of an agreement between the parties that clearly classifies and defines certain items as either personal property or fixtures. Such agreements are generally found in connection with trade fixtures, which are discussed later in this chapter.

5. The relationship between the parties involved. The relationship between the parties involved in a dispute regarding a particular article may be the decisive factor in defining it as a fixture or as personal property. As between a buyer and seller, in the absence of an agreement to the contrary, articles affixed to the land are regarded as fixtures and go to the buyer. The same is generally true as between a buyer and a lender, so that buyers and lenders inspecting property in contemplation of purchase or loan are justified in assuming that whatever is attached to the land or building and is essential for its use is a fixture. As between landlord and tenant, again in the absence of an agreement to the contrary, the basic rule is that an article attached in such a way as to become a fixture belongs to the landlord even though it may have been affixed by the tenant. The general exception to this rule is with regard to trade fixtures.

Trade fixtures

Trade fixtures are articles affixed by a tenant for the purpose of his trade or business. A tenant may remove from the premises anything he has affixed thereto for the purposes of trade, manufacture, ornament, or domestic use if the removal can be effected without injury to the premises. This exception does not generally apply if the item has, by the manner in which it is affixed, become

an integral part of the premises. It is very important that the property owner and the tenant have a clear agreement regarding trade fixtures, and this agreement should be incorporated into the provisions of their lease.

PERSONAL PROPERTY

While our definition of real property has been a lengthy one, the definition of personal property is quite simple. The Civil Code defines personal property by stating that every kind of property that is not real property is personal property.

SIGNIFICANCE OF DISTINCTION BETWEEN REAL AND PERSONAL PROPERTY

A further distinction between real and personal property is that real property is immovable, permanent, and fixed, while personal property is easily movable and is not to any degree in as fixed and permanent a position as real property. Another important distinction with regard to these two classes of property is the different rules of law with respect to their ownership.

Method of transfer

In a sale of real property, the transfer of title can be made only by an instrument in writing. Sales of personal property, unless of a large amount ($5,000 or more in California), normally are not required to be in writing, and title usually passes by delivery of possession. A written instrument, when used in connection with the transfer of personal property, is generally a bill of sale.

The California Commercial Code establishes special requirements for written evidence of a contract for the sale of certain types of personal property, such as sale of goods, securities, or security agreements.

Laws governing acquisition and transfer

Acquisition and transfer of title to land is governed exclusively by the laws of the state in which the property is located. Some minor exceptions exist with regard to federal lands or to real property involved in bankruptcy proceedings. California law controls the effect of instruments relating to real property in this state and also to distribution of real property of a decedent to the heirs or devisees. Personal property is governed by the laws of the place of residence of the owner regardless of the actual location of the personal property.

Recordation

The state has provided by law a system for recording documents or instruments affecting the title or interest in real property, and the law supposes that such instruments will be recorded, thus giving what is termed constructive notice to anyone who may search the records. It is common practice in California for instruments to be recorded in connection with the acquisition or sale of real property by the escrow officer prior to close of an escrow and transfer of title to the property.

With respect to personal property, written instruments, if used, are generally not required to be recorded. Such instruments may be recorded if the parties wish to do so, but recordation is not generally required, so the ownership or condition of title to personal property cannot usually be determined from the public records. The main instrument recorded in connection with personal property is a security agreement, formerly known as a chattel mortgage, by which personal property is pledged as security for a debt.

In addition to the foregoing, the distinction between real and personal property is important with respect to certain matters of taxation wherein real and personal property are taxed in a different manner, in condemnation actions where not only the land but also buildings and fixtures must be considered in arriving at an estimate of value, and in connection with certain judicial sales and judgment liens. The subject of recordation is treated in detail at the end of Chapter 4.

LAND DESCRIPTION

Since real estate is unlike other kinds of property in that it is immobile and in a fixed position, adequate proof that it belongs to the owner is essential. Generally one can describe a piece of property well enough for someone to find it. We may give the street name and number or may say that it is located across the street from a well-known building or landmark. While such descriptions will enable a person to find the property, the real estate broker and others involved in the sale and transfer of property must know the correct "legal description" of the property. Several methods of land description are in common use, often depending upon the type of parcel in question. The most common methods are (a) Lot, Block, and Tract, (b) U.S. Government Survey into Townships and Sections, and (c) Metes and Bounds Descriptions.

Lot and block description

The "lot, block, and tract" method of describing property is the general practice where land has been surveyed and subdivided into parcels and a map of this subdivision recorded in the office of the county recorder in the county in which the land is situated (Figure 1–1).

If, in conveying a property in question, the legally phrased official description of the property is the lot, block, and tract type, it might read as follows:

Lot 6 in Block 2 of Tract number 7594, in the city of Los Gatos, county of Santa Clara, state of California, as per map recorded in Book 77, Page 48, of maps, in the office of the recorder of said county.

On the official map of the area of which this lot is a part, the exact location will be shown as follows:

TRACT 7594 BLOCK 2 LOT 6
In the city of Los Gatos, county of Santa Clara, state of California, being a subdivision of part of Rancho Arguello, recorded in Patents 1–370.

To the property owner, this is much more than merely 170 Cedar Avenue, Los Gatos, California, or "Lot 6, Block 2, Tract 7594," but only by some legal designation like this is the property unmistakeably identified in legal documents. If we fit the property above into its surrounding area, it would look like Figure 1–2. It is interesting to know how the precise location of this lot was determined so that its legal description distinguishes it from all other land anywhere in the world. This calls for a brief review of certain basic practices in land measurement and location description.

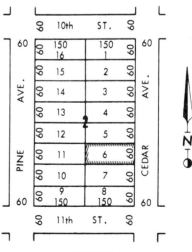

FIGURE 1–1

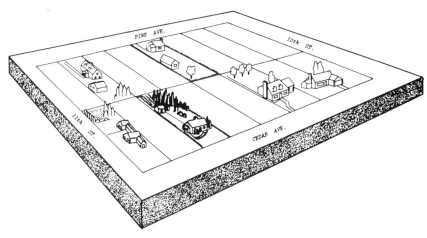

FIGURE 1–2

Where is California?

A ship at sea gives its position in terms of latitude and longitude. Similarly, the exact "world location" of any point on land may be so stated, naming the east-west line and the north-south line that cross at that spot. Using such points as starting places and measuring in stated directions, descriptions of land areas of any shape and size are developed.

Latitude is measured on east-west lines called parallels that encircle the earth parallel to and counting from the equator (0°). Longitude is measured on north-south lines called meridians that run between the poles and count from the one called the prime meridian (0°), which runs through Greenwich, England, a suburb of London.

Government surveys

Looking at a globe of the world, one finds it circled with but a few parallels of latitude and meridians of longitude, perhaps no more than at every 15 degrees. On a local map every degree line may be shown. Even so, degree lines are too distant from each other to be used alone in referring easily to the location of a small area such as a piece of real estate. For this reason, conveniently located markers have been established, and their precise latitude and longitude have been indicated so that there are practical starting points for surveys whenever any land is to be located and measured. The entire area of the United States has been surveyed by the U.S. government, and official reference points, usually called monuments, have been established and placed throughout the nation.

California survey lines

In California, as in many other states, certain "base lines" and meridians called by local names have been designated, from which measurements within the state are generally taken. Pictured in Figure 1–3 are California's three principal meridians and base lines: Humboldt, Mount Diablo, and San Bernardino. Base lines coordinate with meridians, and map makers call their intersections "coordinates."

What is a township?

A standard township is a 6-mile-square area consisting of 36 square miles of land. As used here, the term *township* has no connection with townsite or town. East-west rows of townships are called "tiers" and north-south columns of townships are called "ranges."

The above principal meridians and base lines are referred to, in specifying the location of California land areas, when the description includes reference to the township in which the property lies. Townships are given numerical identities with relation to their position north or south of the local base line, and east or west of the local meridian.

Thus, "Township 2S, Range 2E, S.B.M.," is an abbreviated form for designating that township which is at the intersection of the second tier of townships south of the San Bernardino base line and the second range of townships east of the San Bernardino Meridian. This township is shown in Figure 1–4, and is also shown divided into sections.

FIGURE 1-3

What is a section?

The next smaller unit than a township is an area one mile square, called a section. Townships consist of 36 sections, 6 sections wide by 6 sections long. A township is 36 square miles and a section is 1 mile square. The standard method of numbering a township's sections is to begin in the northeast corner, following a back-and-forth course through the township to the last unit in the southeast corner.

Let us now divide a section of land still further. It is, as we have stated, 1 mile square. A square mile is 5,280 feet square and contains 640 acres. A half section is 320 acres and a quarter section is 160 acres. In most areas where land holdings are thought of not in "city lot" size but in the number of acres, the common unit of measure-

ment is the section. An individual may be said to own two sections, or a half section, or a quarter section of land. A person who owns timberland or ranchland would probably refer to his land either by acres or in relation to a section.

California real estate license examinations have regularly contained problems or questions that require an applicant to locate some portion of land within a section. Parts of a section are described by compass references in conjunction with a statement of the size of the portion. Figure 1–5 shows a section (Section 22) divided into various portions.

In Figure 1–5, the division is first into quarter sections, each quarter containing 160 acres. The four quarters are referred to as the NW ¼ (northwest quarter), NE ¼, SE ¼, and SW ¼. Each quarter may be further divided in quarters so that

	FIRST	STANDARD	PARALLEL	NORTH
T.4N. R.2W.	T.4N. R.1W.	T.4N. R.1E.	T.4N. R.2E.	T.4N. R.3E.
T.3N. R.2W.				
T.2N. R.2W.				
T.1N. R.2W.				
T.1S. R.2W.				
T.2S. R.2W.				

SAN BERNARDINO MERIDIAN LINE

SAN BERNARDINO BASE LINE

FIGURE 1–4

there would be the SW ¼ of the NW ¼ of Section 22, or the SE ¼ of the NE ¼ of Section 22. A quarter section might be divided in half so that there would be a N ½ of the NW ¼ of Section 22.

In Figure 1–5, the land enclosed within the shaded line could be identified as "the W ½ of the NE ¼, and the SE ¼ of the NE ¼ of Section 22, situated in the county of Riverside, state of California." It amounts to 120 acres of land.

Area of an acre

An acre is 1/640 of a square mile, or section; it contains 43,560 square feet. A square piece of land of 1 acre in area is 208.71 feet on each side (208 feet 8½ inches). Thus, a lot that measures 200 feet by 200 feet is almost 1 acre in area. Many subdivisions offer the purchaser a 50 × 100 foot lot; 8 of these lots would fit into an acre of land.

Metes and bounds descriptions

Legal descriptions by metes and bounds are often used, metes meaning measurements and

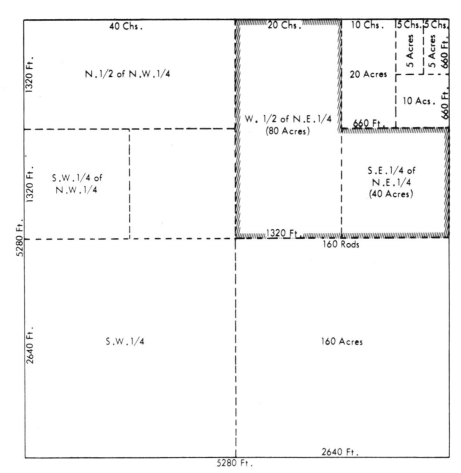

FIGURE 1–5

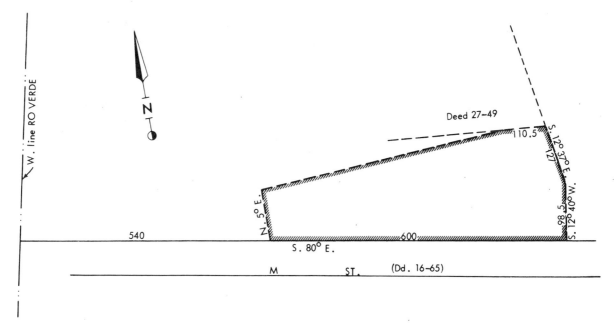

FIGURE 1-6

bounds meaning boundaries—so many units of measurement, usually feet, along such-and-such boundary line. Many times this type of description is lengthy and unintelligible to anyone but a civil engineer or surveyor, as it deals quite often with angles and measured distances from objects that are sometimes not permanent.

A metes and bounds description of the parcel of land illustrated in Figure 1–6 would be as follows:

That portion of the Rancho Verde in the county of San Bernardino, state of California, described as follows: Beginning at a point in the north line of "M" Street as conveyed to said county by deed recorded in Book 16, Page 65 of Deeds in the office of the recorder of San Bernardino County, distant along said line south 80° east 540 feet from the west line of said ranch; thence north 5° east 100 feet; thence northeasterly in a direct line to a point in the south line of land described in deed recorded in Book 27, Page 49 of said deed records distant westerly 110.5 feet from the southeast corner of said land; thence easterly along said south line 110.5 feet to said southeast corner; thence along the prolongation of the east line of said land south 12° 37′ east 127 feet; thence south 12° 40′ west 98.5 feet to a point in the north line of "M" Street distant easterly 600 feet from the point of beginning; thence north 80° west 600 feet to the point of beginning.

In addition to the lot, block, and tract type of description, a fairly simple type of metes and bounds description is often used by attorneys and others who are advertising a piece of property for public sale. The following description is of Lot 6, Block 2, Tract 7594, which was illustrated previously in Figure 1–1.

Commencing at a point on the northwest corner of the intersection of 11th Street and Cedar Avenue, distant therefrom 120 feet north along the westerly line of Cedar Avenue to point of beginning. Thence at a right angle 150 feet west; thence at a right angle 60 feet north; thence at a right angle 150 feet east; thence at a right angle 60 feet south to the point of beginning.

Locating tracts on a township plat

A township plat is shown in Figure 1–7. It will be noted that each numbered section is divided into quarters of quarter sections, each small square representing the location of 40 acres of land. Three examples of descriptions are given below, and their respective locations are shown on the township plat.

1. Beginning at the NE corner of SW ¼ of Section 17, thence southeasterly to the NW corner of the SE ¼ of Section 21, thence southwesterly to the SE corner of the NW ¼ of Section 29, thence northwesterly to the SW corner of the NE ¼ of Section 19, thence northeasterly back to the point of beginning.

2. The SE ¼ of the NE ¼ of the SE ¼, and the S ½ of the SE ¼ of Section 10; the SW ¼ of the NW ¼ of the SW ¼, and the SW ¼ of the SW ¼ of Section 11; the E ½ of the NE ¼ of Section 15; and the NW ¼ of Section 14, excepting the SE ¼ thereof.

3. Beginning at the NW corner of the SE ¼ of the NE ¼ of Section 27, thence due east 3,960 feet, thence due south 3,960 feet, then due west 7,920 feet, thence northeasterly in a straight line to the point of beginning.

Common measurements

A review of the more common types of measurements with respect to land discloses that:

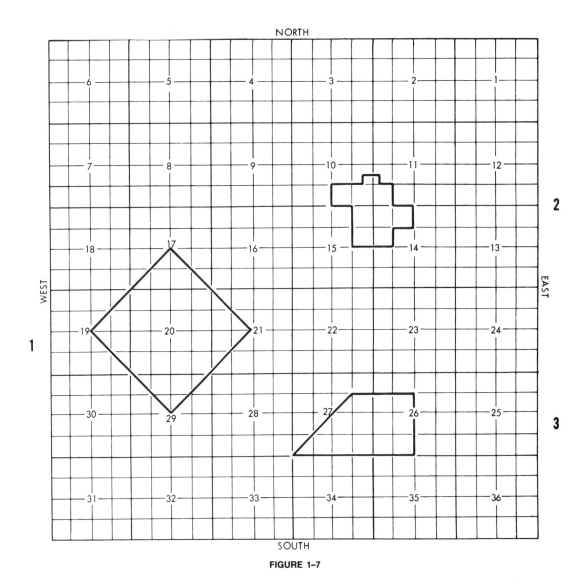

FIGURE 1-7

A square acre is 208.71 feet × 208.71 feet.

An acre is 43,560 square feet.

A linear mile is 5,280 feet.

A square mile contains 640 acres.

A section is 1 square mile.

A township is 6 miles square and contains 36 square miles.

A commercial acre is a term used by developers to refer to an acre of subdivided land after subtracting the area devoted to streets, sidewalks, and any other required public dedications.

CALIFORNIA LAND USES

The state of California has an area of 158,693 square miles, which includes 100,071,040 acres of land, 1,492,480 acres of inland water, and 44,160 acres of coastal water, according to the California Statistical Abstract. Approximately 42 percent of the land, or 42,416,000 acres, is forest land—17,345,000 acres are used commercially to produce industrial wood crops; 1,255,000 acres are productive public forest that has been withdrawn from timber utilization through statute or administrative regulation; and 23,816,000 acres are not productive and are incapable of yielding industrial wood crops.

Approximately 12 percent of the land or 11,815,000 acres, is used for the growth and cultivation of crops; 2 percent or 2,200,000 acres is urban and suburban land classified as residential; and the remainder of the land, 44 percent or 43,754,000 acres, is unclassified and not used for production of crops or for residential purposes.

The population of California was 24 million in 1982 and is expected to reach 28 million in 1990. The ownership of land in California is as follows:

Ownership	Acres	Percent of Total
Federal	44,904,000	45
State	2,332,000	2
Local	2,050,000	2
Private	50,785,000	51
Total	100,071,000	100

Federal lands are divided among the departments of Agriculture, Defense, Interior, and Transportation, and other governmental agencies. The State land belongs to the departments of Conservation, Fish and Game, Parks and Recreation, State Reclamation, Water Resources, and the Division of State Lands, the State Comptroller, and the Department of Public Works. Local ownership includes cities, counties, school districts, community college districts, and special districts.

Private ownership is limited to slightly more than 51 million acres of the state, mostly coastal and valley areas. Of the total privately owned land, about 78 percent is farm land, 17 percent is forest land, and 4.25 percent is urban and suburban land used mainly for residential purposes. Ninety percent of the state's population lives on approximately 2.5 percent of California's land area and 80 percent of the state's population resides or is employed in 12 of the state's 58 counties.

QUESTIONS FOR DISCUSSION

1. What is the basic difference between real and personal property?
2. What problems may arise in attempting to classify growing things affixed to the earth by roots?
3. Why is conservation so important with respect to water rights?
4. How might an item change from real to personal property?
5. In what instances may the value of real estate derive from other than the land surface?
6. Name some items in your own place of residence that would be classified as fixtures.
7. Name some items that in one house might be classified as personal property while in another house might be classified as fixtures.
8. What are the basic differences that may be encountered in the transfer of title to real property as against personal property?
9. How would you describe the property in which you reside using a metes and bounds description?
10. Why might more problems arise with boundary lines being incorrectly shown on a survey of land located in a city as against land in the country?

MULTIPLE CHOICE QUESTIONS

1-1. A term which refers to water rights is: *(a)* township, *(b)* fixtures, *(c)* riparian, *(d)* public utility.
1-2. The number of square feet in an acre is *(a)* 180, *(b)* 43,560, *(c)* 5,280, *(d)* 320.
1-3. A standard section contains: *(a)* 640 acres, *(b)* 180 acres, *(c)* 640 acres and is 6 miles square, *(d)* 20 square miles.
1-4. A township is: *(a)* 3 miles square, *(b)* 6 square miles, *(c)* 6 miles square, *(d)* none of these.
1-5. A metes and bounds description generally contains: *(a)* square feet, *(b)* block number, *(c)* measurements and boundaries, *(d)* street address.
1-6. The W ½ of a section contains: *(a)* 320 acres, *(b)* 180 acres, *(c)* 40 acres, *(d)* none of these.
1-7. Which of the following is most likely not classified as real property: *(a)* producing grape vines, *(b)* fences, *(c)* farm tractors, *(d)* recreational buildings.
1-8. Which of the following is not a test used to determine fixtures: *(a)* method of attachment, *(b)* intention of the parties, *(c)* adaption to the property, *(d)* none of these.

Titles and estates

2

In the previous chapter the distinction between real and personal property was discussed. All property has an owner, either the federal, state, or local government, or a private institution or private parties. The ownership interest that a person has in real property is called an estate, and this chapter will deal with the various types of estates and with the different methods of taking title to real property. The following chapter will then discuss acquisition, that is, the various ways in which one may acquire real property.

TYPES OF ESTATES

The word *estate* is used to express the degree, quantity, nature, duration, or extent of an interest in land. Estates are generally classified according to the extent of their duration. The two main categories are freehold estates and less-than-freehold estates. Freehold estates are those that provide the owner with the highest type of interest and derive from the feudal society of medieval England and the landholding of a freeman under this system. Such estates exist for an indefinite period of time measured usually by the life of some individual. Less-than-freehold estates are for a predetermined or fixed period of time and are commonly referred to as leasehold estates. Freehold estates are (1) estates in fee and (2) life estates. Less-than-freehold estates are (1) estates for years, (2) estates from period to period, (3) estates at will, and (4) estates at sufferance.

Estates in fee

An estate in fee is also commonly referred to as a fee, fee simple, or fee simple absolute. The owner of such an estate has an absolute ownership of indefinite duration, and as long as he acts within the law he may do as he wishes with his land. He may dispose of it by sale or gift or keep it during his lifetime and have it ultimately pass to his heirs. A fee estate is the type normally transferred in a typical sale of real property, and in California a fee estate is presumed to have been conveyed whenever there is a grant of real property unless the grant clearly states that a lesser estate was intended.

It is possible, although not often done, to separate a given parcel of land into more than one fee estate. Thus, one person may have the exclusive and unlimited right to minerals below the surface of the ground and another person may have all the rights to the surface and the air above it. Generally, however, the owner of the land would retain the fee estate and merely sell the right to another to remove the minerals or perhaps any oil or gas beneath the surface.

Defeasibility of a fee estate. When the owner of a fee estate holds it without any qualification he has a fee estate that is absolute, and this is the usual way in which real property is held. Under certain circumstances, however, a person who grants a piece of property to another may impose a condition or a limitation that may cause the fee estate to be defeated, undone, or revoked. When a condition is imposed it is either a condition precedent or a condition subsequent, and a limitation may either be a special limitation or an executory limitation.

Condition precedent and subsequent. An example of a condition precedent would be the offering by a land developer of a portion of land to a municipality provided that its board of supervisors within a certain period of time passes a resolution to construct and equip a children's playground thereon. If the supervisors do not pass such a resolution within the time specified, title to the land will not pass and it will remain the property of the developer. Thus, where there is a condition precedent, it is generally understood that title will not pass until the condition has been met.

With respect to a condition subsequent, the title actually passes but if there is a breach of the condition the former owner has the right to reenter and terminate the estate that had been granted, and the ownership will revert to him. This interest is often termed a reversionary interest. A common example of a condition subsequent has to do with the use to which the property may be put as in the case of one who grants land to a college with the condition that it be used only for the construction of educational facilities, or to a county on condition that it be used only for park and recreational purposes.

Special or executory limitation. Unlike an estate with a condition subsequent where the former owner, upon a breach of the condition, has the right to regain the estate if he wishes to exercise it, an estate given with a special limitation automatically terminates upon the occurrence of a stated event. No special act is required of the former owner to effect the termination since it occurs automatically. An estate subject to such a limitation is generally referred to as a determinable fee, and the reversionary interest is called the possibility of reverter. An example of an estate on special limitation would be the conveying of a piece of real property by a parent to an unmarried child for "so long as" she shall remain unmarried. Words generally found in such conveyances include "so long as," "until," "during," or "while." An estate given with an executory limitation also automatically terminates upon the occurrence of a stated event, but instead of reverting to the former owner the estate vests in another person. Using the preceding example, Parent A could convey to Child B for so long as B remains unmarried, then to Child C. Thus if B were ever to marry, the land would automatically pass to C rather than revert to A.

Life estates

A life estate is a freehold estate in real property that is limited in its duration to the life of the person holding it or to the life or lives of another person or persons. The life estate is granted either by deed or will. No special wording is needed so long as the grantor makes clear his intention that the grantee is to receive only a life estate. A common reason for the creation of a life estate is the desire of the grantor to provide some degree of security or a place of residence for the lifetime of the grantee. The following are different examples of the creation of a life estate.

1. Arthur owns a country home that he no longer uses, and wishes to provide for his aged brother Ben, who is a widower. Thus A would convey to B for his lifetime, with the real property reverting to A upon the expiration of B.

2. If brother Ben is married and Arthur's intention is to take care of both brother Ben and his wife Cora, then the conveyance would be to B and C jointly during their joint lifetimes, and to the survivor of them during the period of the balance of the survivor's life, and upon expiration of the survivor the estate shall revert to A.

3. It is possible to grant a life estate measured by the life of a third person. A could convey to B for the life of a third person C. Upon the expiration of C the life estate would terminate and the property revert to A. Should B expire before C there would no longer be a life tenant and the property would revert to A.

In the preceding examples we have assumed that the person making the conveyance, A, wished to have the estate eventually revert to him. If A, after making the conveyance, were to be the first to expire, then the estate would revert to his heirs. It is possible, if the person making the conveyance wishes to do so, to have the estate ultimately go to someone else whom he names. William wishes to grant a life estate to his sister Sarah, and upon her expiration, to his daughter Diane. W would then grant to S with the remainder to D.

Another common situation is that of a person who wishes to deed a piece of property to another but be guaranteed the use of the property for his lifetime. For example, Eleanor is a widow who wishes to give her house to daughter Dorothy, but wants to be sure that Dorothy does not sell the house after she acquires title. To guard against this, Eleanor would convey to Dorothy but would reserve to herself a life estate.

Interest and duties of the life tenant. The grantee of a life estate has the right of possession just as if he were the owner in fee, and he has the right to all rents and profits from the land while his life estate endures. He must keep buildings in repair and pay taxes and routine annual

14

charges as well as a just proportion of extraordinary assessments. Although he does not have to make payments on the principal of any encumbrances on the property, he must pay the current interest charges and must act reasonably with reference to the use of the land so as not to cause harm to the owners of succeeding interests.

Unless the conveyance by which he received the life estate prevents him from doing so, the life tenant may encumber the estate, lease it, or sell it. He cannot, however, create any interest in the property that will extend beyond the life used to measure the estate. One who unknowingly deals with a life tenant thinking him to be an owner in fee may find to his dismay that whatever interests in the property he thinks he may possess suddenly cease to exist upon the expiration of the life tenant.

Future interests. The term *future interests* or *future estates* refers to the right that a person has at the present time to an interest in real property that will not result in possession until some future time. These future estates are classified generally as either reversions or remainders. Examples of such estates were given in connection with the preceding discussion of life estates.

Less-than-freehold estates

Less-than-freehold estates consist of what are today more commonly called leases or leaseholds. Leasehold estates are possessory interests in land but are not real property; instead, they are classified as personal property and are often referred to as a "chattel real." A chattel is an item of personal property and is a term used to denote personal property. The holder of a leasehold has the right to use, possess, and enjoy the realty for a specified period of time, but title to the property remains with the owner of the property.

The four fundamental types of leaseholds, based on the length of their duration, are *(a)* estate for years, *(b)* estate from period to period, *(c)* estate at will, and *(d)* estate at sufferance. A thorough discussion of leaseholds will be found in Chapter 10, Landlord and Tenant, which is more properly the place for coverage of this subject.

THE METHODS OF TAKING TITLE TO REAL PROPERTY—OWNERSHIP

Examining the nature of estates in real property brings us to a discussion of the methods of holding title to real property as evidence of ownership. Basically, property is owned either by an individual or by two or more persons.

Sole ownership

Sole ownership, also commonly referred to as separate ownership, single ownership, or severalty ownership, simply means ownership by a single individual. This person is said to have ownership in severalty as against two or more persons, who would be termed co-owners. The term *several* is misleading since it seems to denote more than one person but it is a legal term meaning that sole ownership is severed from all other forms of ownership.

An individual who is a sole owner enjoys all of the rights and benefits of his property, as well as being subject to the accompanying burdens such as payment of taxes, repayment of a loan in connection with the purchase, and other liabilities that may arise during the term of ownership.

Co-ownership

Co-ownership, also known as joint ownership, concurrent ownership, or multiple ownership, is a form of ownership in which the title to the real property is vested in two or more persons. The four main types of co-ownership recognized in California are *(a)* joint tenancy, *(b)* tenancy in common, *(c)* community property, and *(d)* tenancy in partnership. In addition to these, there are some additional forms of co-ownership that will be discussed.

Joint tenancy

Joint tenancy means the joint ownership of a single estate by two or more persons with right of survivorship, all of the joint tenants owning an equal interest and having equal rights in the property.

Creation of a joint tenancy. A joint tenancy may be created either by will or by deed. Four unities are necessary in order to create a joint tenancy—title, time, interest, and possession. Thus the joint tenancy must be created by one and the same instrument, executed and delivered at one and the same time, and conveying equal interests to the recipients who must hold undivided possession. The effect of this requirement is the establishment of complete equality among the persons who are to be joint tenants.

Whether the instrument used in the creation of the joint tenancy is a will or a deed, the intention of the party or parties to create the joint tenancy must be without doubt and the language used must be clear and explicit. A deed which states that a grant is being made "to A and B" or "to A and B jointly" would not suffice; instead, the grant should be "to A and B as joint tenants" or "to A and B in joint tenancy." In many instances the words "with right of survivorship" are also inserted, although legally they are not necessary for the valid creation of the joint tenancy. It would, however, leave no doubt as to the intention of the grantor that the grantees are to take title as joint tenants, if the phrase used was "to A and B as joint tenants with right of survivorship."

The Civil Code establishes procedures for the creation of a joint tenancy:

1. By a title created by a simple will or transfer, when expressly declared to be a joint tenancy. This is the most common way in which a joint tenancy is created. When a husband and wife purchase property in California, the deed is generally prepared to show them taking title as joint tenants, and many title companies use a form of deed that is clearly labeled a "Joint Tenancy Grant Deed."

2. By transfer from a sole owner to himself and others. It often happens that an owner in severalty wishes to place the name of another on record as a joint tenant with himself. He would be able to do so by preparing a deed in which he would grant from himself to himself and another person as joint tenants. It would seem here that one of the four unities necessary for the valid creation of a joint tenancy, namely that of title, is being violated since one of the joint tenants already had an ownership interest. However, California law allows this one exception to the unities rule and a sole owner may create a joint tenancy by a conveyance from himself to himself and others.

3. By transfer from joint tenants to themselves and others, or from persons holding title as tenants in common to themselves and others. Since there is no limit to the number of persons who may be co-owners, persons already holding title as joint tenants may add the names of others and thus increase the number of joint tenants. Persons holding title as tenants in common, a method explained later in this chapter, may also add others in a manner that will cause all persons involved to be joint tenants.

4. By transfers from a husband and wife when holding title as community property or otherwise, to themselves, or to themselves and others. A husband and wife who hold title to property other than as joint tenants may create a joint tenancy should they desire to, and may add others as joint tenants with them.

5. By transfer to executors of an estate or to trustees of a trust where it is desired to have such persons hold title as joint tenants.

Rights and duties of joint tenants. Joint tenants have equal rights so far as the use and possession of their property is concerned, and they share equally in the rents, issues, and profits of the property. Property taxes, loan payments, and expenses of maintenance are generally apportioned equally among them.

Where all of the joint tenants occupy the property, as might be the case with a farm or ranch, each would be exercising his right of possession and would be contributing to the productivity and maintenance and be clearly entitled to his share of profits or other benefits. Where none of the joint tenants resides upon the property, for instance an apartment house or commercial building, they would share in the rental receipts after deductions for taxes, maintenance, and other necessary payments and expenses.

Occasionally, however, only one or more of the joint tenants may be occupying and/or contributing to the production of the property while other joint tenants are not. Unless there is an agreement to the contrary, the former do not have to pay rent to the others and are entitled to any profits derived solely from their own skill and labor.

While one joint tenant may not generally bind the other joint tenants by any agreement relating to the property which he may enter into, he may dispose of his interest by entering into a contract of sale, the usual result of such an action being a termination of the joint tenancy as discussed below.

Termination of the joint tenancy. If any of the essential unities necessary for the creation of the joint tenancy is destroyed, then the joint tenancy will cease to exist and either a tenancy in common or ownership in severalty will come into being. The joint tenancy is only permanent so long as the individual joint tenants wish it to be so, and it may be terminated or modified at any time.

A joint tenant may convey his interest to another and thus cause a severance of the joint tenancy as regards his interest. If A and B are joint tenants and A sells his interest to C, then the joint tenancy is severed and B and C hold title as tenants in common. If A, B, and C are joint tenants and C conveys his interest to D, then A and B own a two-thirds share in the property as joint tenants and D owns a one-third interest as a tenant in common. If there are only two joint tenants, A and B, and A conveys his interest to B, then B becomes a sole owner or what is referred to as an owner in severalty.

Where the joint owners wish a severance of the joint tenancy and all are agreeable to this, the co-ownership of the property would cease and each would own an equal share in severalty. Quite often, some of the joint tenants wish a severance while others do not, with the result that those wishing the severance will go into court and ask that the estate be partitioned. A court proceeding by which co-owners seek to sever their joint ownership is known as a partition action.

An involuntary transfer of title will also cause severance of a joint tenancy. Assume that A and B are in business and hold title to a piece of property as joint tenants. If either A or B goes into bankruptcy, title to the property of the person in bankruptcy will automatically be transferred to a trustee in bankruptcy under the Bankruptcy Act, and this will have the effect of severing the joint tenancy. If, in a divorce action, a court orders joint tenancy property sold and the proceeds divided between the joint tenants, the joint tenancy will cease to exist.

There are certain common acts of joint tenants which will not cause a severance of the joint tenancy. If A and B hold title to a property as joint tenants and A executes a lease to C, the joint tenancy will not be severed, since C is entitled only to A's right of possession for the term of the lease. Assume that instead of a lease, A grants an easement to C. The joint tenancy remains in effect, and if A expires before B, then B will take the property free and clear of the easement.

There are also certain occurrences that initially will not sever the joint tenancy but may eventually result in severance. A mortgage or deed of trust executed against the interest of one joint tenant creates only a lien against his interest, but if subsequently the mortgage or deed of trust is foreclosed, the foreclosure or trustee's sale would have the effect of severing the joint tenancy. If a judgment is obtained against a joint tenant, it has no effect upon the joint tenancy. If, however, a writ of execution is later obtained ordering the sale of the joint tenant's interest to satisfy the judgment, this will have the effect of severing the joint tenancy.

Survivorship. The most distinctive, and to many the most important, feature of joint tenancy is the right of survivorship. A joint tenant cannot will his interest in the property, since immediately upon his expiration the title vests in the surviving joint tenant or tenants. Thus there is no testamentary disposition of joint tenancy property since it is not a part of the estate of the deceased joint tenant. The surviving joint tenant takes the estate free from any creditor's claim or debts against the deceased joint tenant, and this includes a judgment lien, tax lien, or a deed of trust against the decedent's interest. It is possible under certain circumstances for an inheritance tax to be due upon the expiration of a joint tenant, and this will be discussed later in the chapter.

A lengthy probate proceeding is unnecessary, since joint tenancy property is not subject to probate; however, it is necessary to establish the fact that a joint tenant has expired so that the official records in the county recorder's office may be changed to show title vesting in the remaining joint tenant. A standard form of affidavit is used in which the deceased joint tenant is identified for this purpose. The affidavit, together with a certificate issued by the local county department of public health registry office, is filed with the county recorder. After this has been done, any title search of the property affected will disclose the expiration of the deceased joint tenant and thus give notice that title is now with the remaining joint tenant or joint tenants if more than one survive.

Advantages and disadvantages. There are both advantages and disadvantages to joint tenancy. To what degree one or the other may be in evidence depends upon the particular circumstances in any given case. The main advantages are generally the right of survivorship, the elimination of probate proceedings, and taking of title by the surviving joint tenant free from any claims or debts against the deceased joint tenant.

What may be an advantage in one situation may be a disadvantage in another, depending upon the particular parties involved. Let us assume that an elderly widowed parent presently holding title in severalty to the home in which the parent resides decides that it would be a good idea to make an adult child a joint tenant so that upon the expiration of the parent, the property would automatically pass to the child. If the child is a mature and responsible adult, the action by the parent in establishing the joint tenancy may in time result in the desired effect. However, suppose that the child is irresponsible and goes heavily into debt, with the result that the creditors obtain a judgment and force an execution that results in a sale of the property. Also, in the event that the joint tenants argue or disagree, one of them may petition the court for a partition of the property. For this reason, many individuals choose to leave an interest in property by will, since a will can always be changed should the desire to do so arise.

Many think that in certain cases the most serious disadvantage to the creation of a joint tenancy may lie in the area of taxation, especially the effect of the joint tenancy with regard to income, gift, inheritance, and estate taxes, both on the federal and state level. This is a complicated area for discussion and often has to do with joint tenancy and community property laws in connection with property held by a husband and wife. Chapters 16 and 17, which deal with the taxation of real estate, will discuss these matters in detail.

The foregoing discussion of joint tenancy should leave the reader aware of the many problems that may arise when dealing with a person who is a joint tenant. If one enters into a transaction, be it either as a tenant, buyer, or creditor, and the other party is a joint tenant, it may be wise to make sure that the other joint tenant or tenants are aware of what is occurring and perhaps become parties to any agreements that may be entered into for the proper protection of all concerned.

Tenancy in common

A tenancy in common exists when two or more persons have undivided interests in the same property. It is created whenever an instrument conveying an interest in real or personal property to two or more persons does not specify that the interest is acquired by them in joint tenancy, partnership, or as community property. When property is deeded to a married couple and no particular method is specified, the presumption is community property.

If the instrument by which the tenants in common acquire title does not specify their respective interests, the presumption is that the interests are equal; thus, if a parent deeds a piece of property to two children without specifying their respective interests, each will be regarded as having received an undivided one-half interest in the property. Interests of tenants in common need not be equal and may be any fraction of the whole; thus, one party may own one third and another two

thirds, or in the case of three co-owners, one may own one half and each of the others one fourth.

Unity of possession. Unlike joint tenancy, a tenancy in common does not require unity of title, time, or interest, but only that of possession. Each owner has a right to possession, and except by agreement between themselves, none can exclude the others nor claim any specific portion for himself. A cotenant in possession of the property is not responsible for the payment of rent to the other cotenant or cotenants, but if the cotenant in possession receives rents from other third parties, he must divide such rents with the other tenants in common in proportion to the shares owned in the property. Payments or expenditures made in connection with the property, such as taxes or necessary repairs, must be distributed among the tenants in common in the same proportion as their shares of ownership. The same is true with respect to improvements made upon the property, but only if all of the cotenants have agreed to the improvements. If one cotenant makes improvements without the consent of the other or others, he will be responsible for the cost.

Transfer of interests. A tenant in common may sell, mortgage, or otherwise convey his interest in the property as he wishes, and the new owner simply becomes a tenant in common with the other cotenants. At times it may be impractical for a cotenant to sell his fractional interest in a piece of property. Let us assume that three brothers or tenants in common each own a one-third interest in a house, and one of the brothers wishes to convert his interest into cash. It would probably be extremely difficult to find someone who would want to purchase his one-third of the house, and his only chance to convert his interest to cash would probably be to sell it to one or both of the other brothers. If no such agreement could be reached, the result would probably be what is referred to as a "partition action," where one of the tenants in common files a partition action in court asking the court to effect a sale of the property and divide the proceeds among the cotenants.

Upon the expiration of a tenant in common, there is no automatic right of survivorship in the remaining cotenants, and the interest of the decedent passes to his heirs or devisees, who simply take his place as tenants in common with the other cotenants. For example, A, B, and C as tenants in common each own a one-third interest in a piece of property. A expires and leaves his interest to Y and Z. B, C, Y, and Z are now tenants in common, with B and C each owning one third and Y and Z one sixth of the property.

A lease entered into by a tenant in common and a third-party lessee will not allow the lessee to exclude the other cotenants from their possessory rights in the property, and is only valid as against the interest of the lessor cotenant. In order for a lessee to acquire a lease of the whole property, each of the tenants in common would have to participate as a party to the lease.

A married couple who are tenants in common with other persons may hold their fractional portion of the ownership as other than tenants in common. A and B are husband and wife and own a one-half interest in a property as tenants in common with C, a single woman who owns the other one-half interest. A and B could hold their one-half interest as joint tenants, while C would, as a sole owner, hold her one-half interest in severalty. Upon the expiration of either A or B, the surviving spouse would immediately take title to the one-half interest and would continue to hold as a tenant in common with C. They would be tenants in common, with each holding their respective one-half interests as a sole owner, in severalty.

Community property

Community property basically consists of all property acquired by a husband and wife, or either, during a valid marriage, other than specific types of separate property. California's community property laws may be traced back to their origins in the old Spanish and Mexican rules on marital property. Under the 1848 Treaty of Guadalupe Hidalgo, which ended the U.S. war with Mexico and by which California became a part of the United States, existing property rights of Mexicans were to be respected. Accordingly, the prevailing Spanish laws governing the property of husband and wife were incorporated into California's legal structure by enactment of the first legislature of the state and were known as common property laws. The term *common property* became *community property,* and at present there are seven community property states—Arizona, California, Idaho, Louisiana, Nevada, New Mexico, Texas, and Washington.

The Civil Code of California states that all property acquired by husband and wife after marriage is community property, with the following exceptions regarded as separate property:

a. All property owned by either husband or wife before marriage.

b. All property acquired by either spouse during marriage by gift or inheritance (bequest, devise, or descent).

c. All rents and profits from separate property, proceeds from the sale of separate property, and property acquired with the rents and profits of separate property, or proceeds from the sale of separate property.

d. The earnings and profits of the wife from her own business as a sole trader.

e. Earnings and accumulations of the wife, and of her minor children who are in her custody or live with her while she is living separate and apart from her husband.

f. Earnings and accumulations of each party after rendition of a court decree of separate maintenance.

g. Money damages awarded to either spouse in a civil action for personal injuries.

The preceding definitions of what constitutes separate property are quite important to remember, since many persons are of the opinion that property owned by either spouse before marriage automatically becomes community property upon marriage. Such is definitely not the case, and property owned before marriage remains separate property after marriage as long as it is clearly identifiable and is not converted into community property.

Before her marriage to B, A had a separate savings account. The money in her account and the interest it earns will remain her separate property. She may take some of the money from the savings account and purchase shares of stock in her name, and these shares will also be considered her separate property. Let us assume, however, that after the marriage A and B open a joint savings account and A takes the money out of her former account and puts it into the new joint savings account. The law now considers her as having made a gift of separate property to the community, and these funds will now be considered community property.

B owned a building that was one-third paid for at the time of his marriage to A. After the marriage, B puts his wife's name on the deed. This building will now be part separate and part community. As the building increases in value over the years, that fractional portion derived from the husband's equity at the time of marriage will remain the husband's separate property, while the remainder will be community property.

Presumption of community property. California court decisions have led to certain presumptions that may be made with regard to determining the character of property. These presumptions will generally be conclusive, but the law allows the presumption to be controverted if sufficient evidence to do so is presented. It is therefore very important that adequate records be kept with regard to the acquisition, method of taking and holding title, and the intent of the spouses.

The basic presumption is that all property acquired by husband and wife after marriage is community property, with the exceptions of what constitutes separate property given previously. This basic presumption may also at times be overcome by the husband's and wife's taking title other than as community property, that is, as joint tenants or as tenants in common. Even though property is held by the spouses as joint tenants or as tenants in common, the presumption of community property may not be overcome unless it can be clearly shown that such was the intent of the parties involved. A husband and wife may take title to property as joint tenants in order to avoid probate proceedings upon the expiration of one of them rather than to avoid the presumption of community property.

Property conveyed to a married man in his name alone is presumed to be community property, and the burden of proof is upon the husband to show that the property is in fact his separate property if he so claims. However, property conveyed to a married woman in her name alone is presumed to be her separate property. If community property funds are used to make improvements to or maintain the separate property of the wife, the improvements made or monies expended become part of the separate property. If, however, community funds are used with regard to the husband's separate property, the wife gains an interest in the property to the extent of her share of the funds used.

Community property management and liability for debts. The law presently gives husband and wife co-equal control and management of community property. An exception exists if one of the spouses manages a community personal property business without assistance from the other spouse. In such cases, the managing spouse has full control and management of the business. The California Civil Code states that the respective interests of husband and wife in community property during the continuance of the marriage are present, existing, and equal interests. In managing and controlling community personal property, neither spouse may give it away without the written consent of the other spouse. Neither spouse may make a gift without the consent of the other. Neither spouse may sell, convey, or encumber the furniture, furnishings, or fittings of the home, or the clothing or wearing apparel of the other spouse or minor children, unless the other spouse consents in writing. With reference to community real property, similarly the husband or wife may not give it away or convey it without valuable consideration, unless the other spouse consents in writing. The wife must, personally or by authorized agent, join with the husband in executing any instrument by which community real property or any interest therein is sold, conveyed, or encumbered, or leased for a period longer than one year.

As to the liability for debts of the community property, the Civil Code makes community property liable for all debts of either spouse after marriage. If a creditor obtains a money judgment against the husband or wife and has it recorded, it is a lien upon all of the community real property.

Cohabitation. In certain cases of unmarried individuals who live together (cohabitation) the California courts have held that certain property rights and obligations may be created as the result of such cohabitation. Such individuals may find it wise to consult an attorney and prepare a contractual agreement with respect to any previously owned property and property acquired during their cohabitation.

Disposition of community property. When a husband and wife desire to convey community real property to another person or persons, they will both enter into the agreement for such conveyance and as grantors will both sign a deed conveying title to the grantee or grantees as the case may be. When a husband or wife desires to convey to the other his or her community interest in property, the deed executed should contain a recital that it is the grantor's intention to vest the title to the property described as the separate property of the grantee. To convert property held other than as community property into community property, a deed executed by both husband and wife as grantors to themselves "as community property" is sufficient.

Each spouse has the right to dispose of his or her one half of the community property by will.

Upon the expiration of the husband, one half of the community property will automatically belong to the wife, and if he has willed her his half, she will receive all of the community property. One who expires without leaving a will is said to have expired intestate, and under the California rules of intestate succession the surviving spouse will receive the decedent's half of the community property. If the wife expires without leaving a will, the husband will receive her half of the community property. At this point we should recall our previous discussion of joint tenancy property and remember that property held as joint tenants is not subject to testamentary disposition, that is, it cannot be left by will. Upon the expiration of a joint tenant, the property automatically passes to the surviving joint tenant. Thus, there may be a considerable difference in the disposition of property upon the expiration of one of the spouses, depending upon whether title was held by them as "community property" or as "joint tenants." California law now provides that if a spouse expires without a will, or by will confers his or her interest in community property to the surviving spouse, such property after 40 days from date of expiration may be sold or otherwise dealt with by the surviving spouse without the necessity of probate with respect to the property. This law will eliminate the necessity for probate sale procedures in a great number of estates.

The reader is referred to Chapter 3, Acquisition and Transfer of Real Property, for steps in a probate sale of real property, and to Chapter 16, Taxation of Real Property, for a discussion of certain problems that arise in connection with community property and joint tenancy property with regard to probate and inheritance taxes.

Rather than a divorce state, California is now a marriage dissolution state. The basis for dissolution of marriage is either irreconcilable differences between the spouses or incurable insanity of a spouse. The terms *divorce, separate maintenance,* and *annulment* have been replaced with *dissolution, legal separation,* and *nullity.* The general rule regarding division of community property in the event of a dissolution is to divide the property equally between the spouses. There are a few exceptions to the general rule, but even in these the court attempts to make a substantially equal distribution. Where the major portion of the community property is a going business, the court at its discretion may award the business to the spouse who is running it and award the other spouse a half interest in cash, a greater share of

other community property, or a larger support allowance. If a spouse has deliberately wasted or spent community funds, the other spouse may be granted a larger share of the remaining community property. The court may award all of the community property to a spouse if the other spouse is guilty of desertion and cannot be located, and the value of the community property is less than $5,000.

Tenancy in partnership

The California Corporations Code defines a partnership as an association of two or more persons to carry on as co-owners a business for profit. Each partnership that transacts business in California under a fictitious name, or a designation not showing the surnames of the partners, must file a certificate stating the names and residences of the partners with the county clerk.

The Uniform Partnership Act, which has been adopted in 43 states including California, states that a partnership may acquire title to property in the partnership name, and title so acquired can be conveyed only in the partnership name. Every partner is an agent of the partnership for the purpose of its business, and the act of every partner, including the execution in the partnership name of any instrument, is generally binding upon the partnership as a whole. A tenancy in partnership exists when two or more persons, as partners, own property for partnership purposes, and some of the more important features of a tenancy in partnership are the following.

a. A partner has an equal right with other partners to possession of specific partnership property for partnership purposes only, and generally has no other rights of possession except by special agreement between the partners.

b. A partner's rights in specific partnership property are not assignable except in connection with the assignment of rights of all the partners in the same property.

c. A partner's rights in specific partnership property are not subject to attachment or execution of a judgment based upon a claim exclusively against him as an individual, but must be based upon a claim against the partnership itself.

d. If a member of the partnership expires, his rights in partnership real property vest in the surviving partner or partners. The heirs of the decedent are entitled to the value of his interest in the partnership at time of expiration. This value of the interest in the partnership is considered to be personal property and is included in the estate of the decedent.

An examination of the Uniform Partnership Act will disclose many exceptions and additions to the general features outlined above, in addition to presenting a detailed explanation of the partnership form for those who may be interested in the subject.

Corporate ownership

A corporation is often referred to as a legal person or entity. This entity exists with separate rights and liabilities distinct from its shareholders, and may hold real or personal property in its corporate name. A domestic corporation is one created by the laws of a particular state. Thus, a corporation incorporated in and formed under the laws of the state of California would be known as a domestic corporation. A foreign corporation is one incorporated in a state other than California or in another country. A foreign corporation may transact business within the state of California, but must obtain from the California secretary of state a certificate of qualification to do intrastate business in California, and is of course subject to certain conditions and limitations prescribed by the state of California.

A corporation, usually through the issuance of resolutions by its board of directors, may acquire, lease, and convey property and may encumber it by borrowing funds and putting the property up as security. The corporation may enter into contracts or do any acts incidental to the transaction of its business, and may become a party to a mortgage or deed of trust.

Nonprofit corporation. In addition to corporations formed for the purpose of engaging in business and commerce for profit, there are many that are nonprofit and that do not contemplate the distribution of gains, profits, or dividends to their members. Examples are religious, charitable, social, benevolent, and educational nonprofit corporations. These corporations do not issue shares of stock, but instead have what are termed memberships. The nonprofit corporation may also perform the same acts with regard to property as mentioned previously for the profit corporation.

Unincorporated association. There are certain organizations and associations that are not incorporated and that may not engage in property transactions in the name of the organization or association unless this is done in the name of a specific individual or individuals as trustees for the group. Exceptions to this rule include fraternal societies and labor unions, which by law may buy, own, and sell real and personal property necessary for the business purposes and objectives of the organization. Whenever this is done, the authority of the specific individual trustees to perform such acts should be established by inspection of the charter and bylaws of the organization.

Additional ownership methods

In addition to the methods of ownership discussed previously, there are a number of others that occur with sufficient frequency to warrant discussion here. They are trusts, syndicates and joint ventures, real estate investment trusts, cooperatives and condominiums, and stock cooperative projects.

Trusts. There are various types of trusts, depending on how and by whom they are created. The basic idea of a trust is the holding of property by one person called the trustee for the benefit of another person called the beneficiary. A person creating a trust is called the trustor, and a trust is generally formed so that someone who has the ability and knowledge to properly manage and take care of property (the trustee) will perform such a function for the benefit of a person or persons (beneficiaries) who do not have the experience or are unable for one reason or another to do so for themselves. Anyone who is legally able to contract may create a trust and may give a wide range of powers to the trustee for the benefit of the beneficiary. The legal title is vested in the trustee, and the beneficiary is said to have an equitable title. Any person having the capacity to take and hold title to property may be a trustee, and anyone who is capable of taking an interest in property, such as an adult, minor, or charitable institution or organization, may be a beneficiary.

An express trust is one created by a trustor in writing, and may take the form of a declaration of trust or a deed stating that the property is to be held in trust. Trusts are commonly created by will for the purpose of conserving property for the benefit of the surviving spouse and/or children, and such trusts are referred to as testamentary trusts. A trust created by an individual during his or her lifetime is known as an inter vivos trust, and has been used as a means of reducing the payment of taxes, since federal gift taxes are lower than federal estate taxes. Another benefit may be the shifting of property income from a parent in a high tax bracket to a child in a much lower tax bracket. A detailed explanation and treatment of the complex subject of trusts may be found in the California Civil Code.

Syndicates and joint ventures. A real estate syndicate generally consists of a group of persons who come together for the purpose of raising capital in order to invest in real property either for income purposes, resale at a profit, or both. Syndicates are usually interested in large and more expensive pieces of property, such as vacant land for development or improved properties for investment or for speculation.

The syndicate may consist of a few members, but quite often the membership is larger in order to accumulate the funds necessary for large-scale activities. The participants may range from individuals to corporations, and each member's interest is usually limited to a fixed share or percentage under a partnership arrangement. Quite often the syndicate may be formed by a real estate broker who has obtained an option for the purchase of the property involved, or for the acquisition of a leasehold interest in a particular piece of real property. The broker, as organizer of the syndicate, may receive his share of interest in the organization as compensation for his work in organizing the group, and may also be a monetary investor as are the other members. The syndicate may hold property in a number of ways, such as tenants in common or as partners, but whatever form of ownership is decided upon, it is generally dependent upon income tax considerations as they affect the participants.

The limited partnership, formed for a specific and limited purpose, is often used by syndicates because it avoids the dual tax situation confronting the corporation that pays taxes on profits before their distribution and whose stockholders in turn pay a tax on dividends received on their shares. While using the partnership arrangement may result in a loss of some of the operative advantages of a corporation, the tax advantages are the prime consideration. Not only is there avoidance of double taxation, but also an important benefit results from the fact that depreciation deductions pass directly to the individual investors.

A joint venture may resemble a syndicate in some ways, but whereas a syndicate is usually intended to continue in business for a continuous and indefinite period of time, the joint venture is formed for a single transaction or a single series of transactions, and thus exists for a very limited time. The participants in a joint venture are part-

ners, and the partnership form is employed in the formation of the joint venture. An example would be that of a real estate broker, a property owner, and a building contractor, who form a joint venture for the purpose of erecting a building and effecting its sale.

California Real Estate Syndicate Act. The Real Estate Syndicate Act, a part of the Real Estate Law and California Administrative Code, became effective on January 2, 1970. The real estate commissioner was given jurisdiction over syndicates with fewer than 100 participants and where a public offering was made of investment opportunities by the syndicate.

Effective January 1, 1978, the Real Estate Syndicate Act was repealed, and administration of offerings of all real estate syndicate interests was transferred to the California Department of Corporations. Real estate brokers who engage in any syndicate transactions where the syndicate has fewer than 100 participants are excluded from having to obtain any special approval or license from the California Department of Corporations. However, real estate brokers must be aware of, and not violate, any of the rules and regulations of the Corporations Code involving the sale, exchange, or trade of real estate syndicate interests.

The rules and regulations of the Department of Corporations are intended to ensure that the syndicator transacts business fairly and honestly, and that when participations in the syndicate are issued to investors the procedures used will be fair, just, and equitable. In order to effect this aim, a permit must be obtained before syndicate interests may be sold or offered for sale. An application for a permit to offer or sell such interests must be made on a form provided by the corporations commissioner. Before and after the issuance of a permit the corporations commissioner will investigate in detail the offering of the syndicate and will review all advertising matter to be presented to prospective investors. The corporations commissioner has the authority to deny a permit; and after having issued a permit, if any violations of the law occur, a cease-and-desist order may be issued.

The syndicate may be formed as a general or limited partnership, joint venture, or unincorporated or incorporated association, but whatever form is used the rights and duties of the participants will be governed by the terms of the syndicate agreement or contract and the applicable laws, rules, and regulations. Syndicates are becoming very popular for attracting the funds of large investors and also individuals who are not knowledgeable in real estate and do not wish to participate in management decisions but do wish to invest funds.

Real estate investment trusts. The real estate investment trust, often referred to as a REIT, is a direct descendant of the so-called "Massachusetts Trusts" of the late 19th century, which were weakened in their investor appeal by U.S. Supreme Court decisions holding them to be taxable, at corporate rates, on all net income. Investors, not wanting to have their profits diminished by taxes on the trusts, turned to stock investment companies instead because such companies were not taxed on earnings distributed to shareholders. In 1960, however, the law was changed to equalize this differential between the real estate investment trust and the stock company. The trust is now taxed only on retained earnings, so that if the trust distributes 90 percent or more of its ordinary income to its stockholders, it goes virtually untaxed. The investors find themselves in the same position with respect to taxation of earnings as direct investors in real estate or in real estate mortgages.

Some of the other advantages that real estate investment trusts now share with stock investment companies are: (1) both enable small investors to pool their individual funds to take advantage of big investment opportunities, (2) both offer the financial ability to obtain expert management and legal counsel, (3) both offer the added safety and probability of higher returns from widely diversified investment projects, (4) both are usually regulated by state and federal regulatory agencies, and in California the corporations commissioner supervises such institutions.

The REITs now differ from stock investment companies primarily in that the trust invests in real estate and real estate mortgages exclusively, while the stock company, as its name implies, concerns itself with stock and securities. The real estate investment trust is an unincorporated trust or association of investors, and generally one or more trustees manages the affairs of the trust.

Cooperatives and condominiums. The cooperative method of owning real property may be applied to various types of real property, but its most common use has been with respect to community apartment projects, or cooperative apartments as they are sometimes called. The ownership of the property is generally vested in a stock or membership corporation controlled by the individual apartment owners as a group. When one

purchases an apartment he receives stock or membership rights, and an undivided interest is conveyed, coupled with the right to occupy a certain unit or apartment. The operation, maintenance, and control of the property is usually exercised by a governing board elected by the individual owners, and the expenses incurred are divided proportionately and are often referred to as monthly assessments.

The individual apartment owner may be properly considered as both an owner and a tenant. The ownership aspect is in the possession of the stock or membership certificate that he received at time of purchase, and the tenancy aspect arises from his right to occupy a certain apartment that is given in the form of a lease. An owner who wishes to sell his apartment cannot generally do so without the consent of the other co-owners, since most cooperatives are formed with the provision that the stock or membership and the lease cannot be transferred without the approval of the governing board or majority of the members. This procedure must be used in a fair and equitable manner, and not as a basis for discrimination against a prospective buyer because of his race, color, or creed.

The condominium method of ownership resembles that of the cooperative but there is one major difference: the owner of a condominium owns his unit in fee simple and is a tenant in common with other owners as regards the common areas of the building such as the halls, elevators, driveways, and the building site. The purchaser of a condominium owns the air space in which his unit is situated in fee simple, has a deed thereto, gets a separate tax assessment, and may apply for and acquire a title insurance policy on his property. In addition to this, he has an undivided interest in common in other defined common areas of the whole property. As with the cooperative, the management function is usually performed by an elected governing board. Monthly assessments are made to cover the expense of maintaining the common areas. Sale of the condominium unit does not require the approval of the other owners, since title to the unit is held in fee simple, and the interest that the owner has in the common areas is an easement which passes to a new owner when he takes title to a unit. Cooperatives and condominiums are further treated in Chapter 19, which deals with subdivisions.

Stock cooperative project. A stock cooperative is a corporation that is formed or availed of primarily for the purpose of holding title to improved real property, either in fee simple or under a leasehold for a term of years. An essential element is that all or substantially all of the shareholders of such corporations receive a right of exclusive occupancy of a portion of the real property. The title is held by the corporation and the right of occupancy is transferrable only concurrently with the transfer of a share or shares of stock in the corporation held by the person having such right of occupancy. Most stock cooperative projects are of the apartment house type, and operate with a board of directors. Many of these projects also provide community recreation facilities for the benefit of the members.

Another type of cooperative project is known as a sales type cooperative project. Each individual purchaser becomes a stockholder in a cooperative housing corporation that is organized for the purpose of financing and constructing the entire project of dwellings on individual lots. The buyer is an investor and does not receive title to an individual lot until after completion of the entire project. Individual loans are made on each improved lot, and the corporation is dissolved following delivery of deeds to all of the various lots in the project.

HISTORICAL BACKGROUND OF LAND TITLES IN CALIFORNIA

Having discussed the various types of estates and different methods of taking title to real property, it would be appropriate at this point to consider the historical background of land titles in California under Spanish, Mexican, and American rule.

Spanish rule

The state of California has one of the most unique and picturesque histories of any state in the Union. From the time in 1513 when Vasco Nuñez de Balboa first looked upon the Pacific Ocean, claiming it and the shores washed by it for the King of Spain, until 1822, the lands that are now California were part of the Spanish realm. During this period of Spanish rule the local government was of a patriarchal nature with little regard for formal civil law. Military law prevailed, as presidios and army garrison towns were established to maintain Spanish dominion over the vast and varied but sparsely populated territory. As instruments for spreading the Christian faith

among the California Indians, and for the purpose of providing supplies for the military posts, 21 missions were established. All land in California was held in the name of the King of Spain and, indeed, technically it belonged to him.

At the time of the American Revolution, California was under the civil law of Spanish rule, and the use of land could be acquired only by political or military agencies of the King of Spain. Their rights to the use of the land were not, however, grants of an absolute fee title. Several rancho grants were made by the Spanish monarchs, but these were strictly for limited grazing and agricultural purposes.

Mexican rule

In 1822, Mexico, then a territorial possession of Spain, established its independence. Inspired by the stories of fabulous wealth in California, the Mexican government encouraged the colonization of California. Governors were given absolute discretion in the selection of the persons who could receive grants of land. An applicant for land filed his petition with the governor, and, if approved, received a decree that was referred to the legislative department for ratification. Upon such approval a formal grant of the land petitioned for was made. The governor was empowered to recognize grants and possessory rights formerly made by the Spanish government.

American rule

From the time of Mexican independence in 1822, until the year 1846, when the Mexican War broke out, there were approximately 675 grants of land made in California. In the latter years of this period several grants were made in evident anticipation of American occupation. Curious in nature, and of vague description, these grants later became the basis of many judicial contests of titles to California land, some of them even in recent years.

In 1848 the Treaty of Guadalùpe Hidalgo ended the war with Mexico. California became a possession of the United States, subject to a treaty provision that existing property rights of Mexicans should be "inviolably respected." Thereupon, confusion of land titles and property rights became rampant. To remedy the situation, Congress in 1851 passed an act providing for the appointment of a board of land commissioners to which all claims to private land in California were to be submitted. All titles and claims of title of every nature were to be determined by this commission. Claims to land titles rejected by this commission were appealable to the U.S. District Court and to the U.S. Supreme Court. Claims that were eventually approved by the commission or the courts were discharged by the United States giving grants of land, called patents, to the claimants who were entitled to them. The process of clearing titles was quite lengthy, often taking from 12 to 17 years. The process was further complicated by the many adventurous immigrants from the East, called "squatters," who arrived and settled upon the land without previous ownership rights.

In addition to the privately owned rancho land grants under Spanish and Mexican law, each organized city, or pueblo as it was then called, received 4 square leagues of land without necessity of any formal government grant. A square league under the old Spanish law consisted of approximately 4,400 acres, and so sizable areas were involved.

Upon admission of California into the Union in 1850, the state became owner of all lands lying under navigable streams and lakes, and above ordinary high tide line. The ownership passed from the United States without the formality of a grant. The state owns the tidelands in trust for the people, for such purposes as navigation, recreation, and fisheries. Generally speaking, the state cannot transfer these lands absolutely to private owners, although substantial revenues have been realized from the sale of oil and gas rights thereon.

The United States retained certain paramount rights in the territory involved. Thus the federal government kept as public lands all those not specifically confirmed as Mexican or Spanish grants, tidelands, cities, or towns. Thereafter, title to public lands was acquired only by specific grants from the United States government. Much of this land has since been granted to the state for educational purposes and state parks, and large grants were made to railroad companies as an inducement for the construction of transportation facilities. Nevertheless, of the state's total land area of some 100,071,000 acres, the federal government still owns approximately 45 percent.

Although California inherited from Spain and Mexico certain laws governing the estates of real property, the basic principles now employed were derived from England's common law, and in the absence of some constitutional or statutory provisions specifically applicable, the common law prevails. Under the Spanish and Mexican rule of California there were no registry or recording laws with respect to real property, and one of the first acts of the California legislature after its formation was to adopt a recording system patterned after that of the original American colonies. Recordation is discussed in detail in the latter part of Chapter 4, Principle Instruments of Transfer—Deeds.

QUESTIONS FOR DISCUSSION

1. Of what importance is extent of duration with respect to freehold and less-than-freehold estates?
2. What type of estate is generally presumed to pass, in California, upon a grant of real property?
3. Discuss the various reasons for the creation of a life estate.
4. What is the dominant feature of a joint tenancy, and how may it be created?
5. Discuss the advantages and disadvantages of a joint tenancy.
6. How may a tenancy in common differ from a joint tenancy with respect to size of interest held?
7. How may an individual be a joint tenant and a tenant in common at the same time?
8. Discuss the important factors in keeping separate property from becoming community property after marriage.
9. Discuss the presumption of community property by the courts.
10. Is a surviving spouse always entitled to all community property?
11. In whom do the rights to partnership real property generally vest upon the expiration of one of the partners?
12. Why may a corporation hold title to real property in the corporate name?
13. What are some of the reasons for the creation of a trust?
14. What is the major difference between the cooperative and condominium methods of ownership?
15. When were recording laws first introduced in California?

MULTIPLE CHOICE QUESTIONS

2-1. An example of a freehold estate is: (a) a lease for three years, (b) a lease for less than a year, (c) a fee simple, (d) a tenancy at will.
2-2. Prior to Mexican independence, California belonged to: (a) American settlers, (b) France, (c) King of Spain, (d) none of these.
2-3. Property acquired by a husband or wife by gift is: (a) community property, (b) automatically owned by them as tenants in common, (c) separate property, (d) none of these.
2-4. Automatic right of survivorship is associated with: (a) tenants in common, (b) severalty ownership, (c) community property, (d) joint tenancy.
2-5. The holding of property by an individual for the

benefit of another individual is a: *(a)* leasehold, *(b)* joint venture, *(c)* condominium, *(d)* trust.

2–6. In a typical sale of real property in California, the type of estate transferred is: *(a)* community property, *(b)* corporate ownership, *(c)* a fee, *(d)* none of these.

2–7. California law presumes that real property pur-chased by a husband and wife is: *(a)* tenancy in common, *(b)* community property, *(c)* tenancy in partnership, *(d)* joint tenancy.

2–8. The cooperative method of owning real property is generally found with respect to: *(a)* community apartments, *(b)* partnerships, *(c)* commercial properties, *(d)* leaseholds.

3   Acquisition and transfer of real property

This chapter will deal with the various methods by which real property is acquired or transferred, and the following chapter will deal with the deed, a document most commonly used as an instrument for the transfer of title to real property. While virtually all individuals may acquire title to real property, many classes, such as minors, incompetents, and convicts deprived of certain civil rights, may not convey their property without certain special procedures such as a guardianship proceeding, and must have court approval of such acts. The capability of individuals to contract will be discussed in Chapter 8, Elements of Contracts.

Most persons are not aware of the various methods of acquiring title to real property and think only in terms of purchasing property or inheriting it, since these are the two methods that occur most frequently. The California Civil Code declares that property may be acquired by *(a)* will, *(b)* succession, *(c)* accession, *(d)* occupancy, and *(e)* transfer.

BY WILL

Property acquired by an individual during his or her lifetime may be disposed of to designated beneficiaries effective upon the expiration of the individual. The instrument used to achieve this disposition is called a will. The person who makes the will is called the testator if a male, and the testatrix if a female. After the maker of the will expires, the individual is termed deceased, and is often referred to as the decedent. A person named in a will to acquire property is a beneficiary, and there are different terms commonly used to denote the type of property that has been willed. Money is termed a legacy, personal property is a bequest, and real property is a devise. Although the person receiving property in a will is generally called the beneficiary regardless of the type of property involved, there are various legal terms for the beneficiary such as an heir or a devisee. The beneficiary who receives a gift of real property by will is also called a devisee, and one who receives a gift of money or other personal property is termed a legatee.

The distinguishing feature between a will and other instruments creating property interests, such as a deed or contract, is that the will becomes effective only upon the expiration of the maker. Until then, the maker of the will does not divest himself of any rights in the property, and the beneficiaries do not have any rights to the property vested in them. One who leaves a will is said to have expired testate, while one who does not leave a will is said to have expired intestate. The person who prepares a will has obviously done so in order to make adequate provision for the disposition of his property, but the person who expires intestate may have to have the court decide what is to be done with his property. In making a decision, the court is guided by the rules of intestate succession contained in the probate code that governs the disposition of such property, and that will be discussed later in this chapter. In many cases, the absence of a will does not pose any particular problem regarding the disposition of the property of the decedent. As was pointed out in the previous chapter, the community property of one who expires intestate automatically passes to the surviving spouse, and if property is held in joint tenancy it automatically passes to the surviving joint tenant and cannot in any case be the subject of a testamentary disposition by will.

Probating the will

The right to dispose of property by will is a statutory right, and the probate code states that every person of sound mind over the age of 18 years may dispose of his or her property by will. The testator, when preparing the will, usually names someone who is to have the responsibility for carrying out the provisions of the will. An executor is a person specifically named by the testator in the will to carry out his wishes and administer the estate. An administrator is appointed by the court to administer an estate when the decedent has not left a will or has not named an executor in the will. An administrator may also be appointed by the court if the named executor is unable for one reason or another to perform the function expected of him; he is then called an administrator with the will annexed. The executor is usually a relative of the decedent, an attorney, or the trust department of a bank.

Upon the expiration of the testator, the executor or person in possession of the will should deliver it to the clerk of the probate court, and the probate procedure will commence with a "petition for probate." The main purposes of probate proceedings are (a) to determine the extent and amount of the estate by preparing an inventory and preparing an appraisal of value, (b) to give the necessary six month's notice to creditors who may have claims to file against the estate, (c) to manage the estate during the probate period, (d) to provide for possible sale of real property by the executor or administrator subject to court approval, and (e) to make final distribution of the remaining assets of the estate to beneficiaries entitled to receive them as provided for in the will.

Types of wills

The three types of will permitted by law in California are (a) a witnessed or formal will, (b) a holographic will, and (c) a nuncupative will.

Witnessed will. A witnessed will, or formal will as it is often called, is one that is prepared in writing, signed by the testator, and witnessed by persons capable of acting in this capacity. The document should be quite clear as to its content and meaning and should not contain any ambiguities that may later serve to cloud the true intent of the testator. The will should be dated and signed by the testator at the bottom of the document and in the presence of those persons who are also to affix their signatures as witnesses. In California, two witnesses are required, but it is common for three to be used. The purpose in doing this is to better ensure the availability of at least two witnesses should they be needed to testify at the time the will is admitted to probate. It may also be a wise precaution that all of the witnesses not be elderly persons. Generally, anyone may serve as a witness, since his function is merely to acknowledge that the testator did execute and sign the will in his presence, and the only serious restriction on a qualified witness is that he should not have any interest in the will he is witnessing. If a witness is also a named beneficiary under the will, this may lead to a charge of undue influence by other beneficiaries or individuals, and subsequent lengthy litigation.

The testator and witnesses should all sign in the presence of each other, and the testator must declare, for all to hear, that the will being signed is indeed his will. Such a statement must be made since the document itself is usually never prepared in the presence of the witnesses but in another place, for instance the office of the testator's attorney.

Holographic will. While a witnessed or formal will is usually prepared on appropriate legal size paper and the content is typewritten, the distinguishing feature of a holographic will is that the entire document is written, dated, and signed in the handwriting of the testator. If any portion of the document is printed or typewritten this will generally invalidate a holographic will, since it must all be in the testator's handwriting. The other important feature of the holographic will is that no witnesses are required, since the testator's handwriting is proof of the genuineness of the document. Such a will may dispose of any property disposable under a witnessed or formal will, and no particular form is necessary so long as the document shows the intent of the testator, and clearly identifies the specific property and individual beneficiaries.

Nuncupative will. A nuncupative will, or oral will as it is sometimes called, is not in writing. It is an oral statement made in the presence of two witnesses by a member of the armed forces who is in imminent peril or has been severely wounded, or by any individual in an accident or other situation who has sustained an injury that is critical. According to the probate code, a nuncupative will may only be used for disposal of personal property not exceeding $1,000 in value, and the statement made by the decedent must be reduced to writing by either of the witnesses within 30 days and offered for probate not later than six months from the date of expiration of the decedent.

Revocation and codicils

A will may be revoked at any time by the testator and passes no rights to others until his expiration. Because of this, a will is called an ambulatory instrument, meaning that it may be revoked at any time. It need not be notarized and is not recorded.

If the testator wishes to make an addition to the will or revise a portion of it, he may do so by an instrument called a codicil. The same formal procedures are required for the preparation of the codicil as were required for the will, although a holographic codicil may be attached to a witnessed will. If the changes desired by the testator are quite lengthy or complex, it may be best to revoke the old will and prepare an entirely new document.

BY SUCCESSION

A person who expires without leaving any type of will is said to have expired intestate, and the decedent's property will be distributed according to the statutes of succession, or as they are often called, the statutes of intestate succession. The probate code contains these statutes that will govern the distribution of the decedent's separate property, since community property vests in the surviving spouse and joint tenancy property in the surviving joint tenant or joint tenants.

The distribution of the separate property is as follows:

a. If the decedent leaves a surviving spouse and one child, the property goes one half to each.
b. If there is a surviving spouse and more than one child, the property goes one third to the surviving spouse and the remaining two thirds is divided equally among the children.
c. If the decedent leaves no surviving spouse but one or more children, the property is divided equally among the surviving children.
d. If one of the decedent's children is also deceased but there are grandchildren, then the grandchildren divide the share that the parent would have received.

e. If the decedent leaves a surviving spouse but no children, then the property goes one half to the surviving spouse and one half to the parents of the deceased spouse.
f. If the decedent leaves a surviving spouse but no children or parents, then the property goes one half to the surviving spouse and one half is distributed equally among the decedent's surviving brothers and sisters or decedents of deceased brothers and sisters.

Many other rules exist for varying situations that may include even more distant relatives of the deceased than those mentioned above, such as uncles, aunts, cousins, and others. Other clarifications are made with respect to situations arising from remarriage and the rights of children who may be natural, legally adopted, step-children, or illegitimate. If the decedent leaves no heirs who can be located, his property will eventually pass to the State of California and is said to escheat to the state.

BY ACCESSION

Accession basically means the right of a property owner to any increase in the property he owns, whether caused by man or by nature. The various ways in which this may occur are through (a) accretion, reliction, and avulsion, and (b) addition of fixtures and improvements in error.

Accretion, reliction, and avulsion

Accretion is the gradual addition of land by the action of the water in a river, bay, or stream. Minute particles of sand, earth, and other materials are washed up and deposited along the bank. This material, called alluvion, causes an increase in the land. Dredging operations must often be performed in certain waterways because of the amount of material deposited by moving waters.

Reliction is the increase in land above the water line that results when water subsides, as with a change in tide or permanent drop in the water level.

Avulsion occurs when water in a river or stream violently tears away a portion of the bank and deposits it elsewhere. This may occur during a storm, flood, or sudden runoff of water due to melting snows.

An addition to land by accretion or reliction immediately becomes a part of the particular land and belongs to its owner. Earth deposited by avulsion, however, may be reclaimed by the owner of the land from which it was torn away at any time within one year from the date of occurrence; if not reclaimed it becomes the property of the owner upon whose land it has been deposited. While land that has been deposited and added by avulsion has been suddenly or violently torn away, that which is added by accretion has been steadily but very slowly removed from its course. The removal of the soil in this manner by water is termed erosion. A loss by erosion is permanent and may not be regained by the owner of land that is eroded; all that he may do is attempt in some manner to stop the erosion process, if possible.

Addition of fixtures

The acquisition of title by addition of fixtures may occur when a person affixes his property to that of another in such a manner that it becomes a permanent fixture. In the absence of a prior agreement to remove the fixture, it generally becomes a part of the property to which it has become affixed and belongs to the owner of that property. The subject of fixtures, their creation, and to whom they belong, is covered in Chapter 1 and also in Chapter 10, which deals with landlord and tenant relationships.

Prior to 1953 there was no compensation for the innocent person who mistakenly improved someone else's property, but the California legislature in 1953 amended the Civil Code to provide that in certain instances one who affixes improvements to the land of another, and did so in good faith believing that he had a right to do so, may remove the improvements made in error upon payment of damages to the owner of the property or to persons who have acquired an interest in the property in reliance on such improvements.

The Uniform Commercial Code covers the broad area of accession with regard to personal property wherein many problems arise regarding security interests, conversion, and confusion of goods.

BY OCCUPANCY

Title to real property and certain lesser rights may be acquired through occupancy by (a) adverse possession, (b) prescription, and (c) abandonment.

Adverse possession

Any person who is legally capable of owning property may acquire by adverse possession the title to any real estate that is not devoted to public use or owned by any governmental agency. The basic principle involved is the taking of possession of the land for a given period of time by a person who is not the actual owner. In order for such a person to eventually acquire legal title to the property, the possession must be (a) actual possession, open and notorious, (b) hostile to the true owner's title, (c) under claim of right or color of title, (d) continuous and uninterrupted for a period of at least five years, and that (e) the adverse possessor, called the claimant, must have paid all taxes and assessments levied against the property during this five-year period.

Actual possession, open and notorious. Although the claimant may do so, he does not actually have to reside on the property, but he must by certain physical acts show his intention of holding and possessing the land. Such acts may be the fencing or enclosing of the land, but this must be coupled with an actual use in some manner such as making improvements on the land or cultivation for agricultural purposes. The claimant may also hold possession through someone acting for him, such as an agent or a tenant. The open and notorious provision means that the claim of possession must not be kept a secret. It must be such that any person inspecting the property would be aware that someone was in possession and claiming a right to it.

Hostile to the true owner's title. The possession must actually be hostile to the true owner and must be exclusive possession. It cannot be any possession or use to which the owner has agreed or consented, nor can it be concurrent with that of the title owner or an agent or tenant of the title owner.

Under claim of right or color of title. The actions of the claimant must be such as to give the impression that he has the absolute right to the possession of the property. He cannot be there with any permission from the true owner, and his claim of right, or claim of ownership as it is often called, must be in opposition to the title to which his possession is adverse.

Possession under a color of title results when the claimant takes possession under an instrument that purportedly conveys title to him but is in effect an instrument defective or void in some way, resulting in title not having been properly conveyed. Possession under a color of title may or may not exist, but it is not a requirement nor essential to obtaining title by adverse possession. A claim of right or claim of ownership on the part of the adverse possessor is the necessary ingredient, whether coupled with a color of title or not. One advantage that results if an adverse possessor claim title under color of title in addition to claim of right is that he will, if he completes all the adverse possession requirements, receive title to all of the real property described in the defective instrument even though he actually possessed or used only a portion of the described property. Where the claim of right is not coupled with a color of title, the claimant will only receive title to that real property that he has actually possessed and used.

Continuous and uninterrupted for five years. In California, the statutory period for the acquisition of title by adverse possession is five years. If at any time during the five-year period the true owner, his agent, or anyone acting in such capacity enters upon the property and tells the adverse possessor that he is trespassing, the statutory period is broken. Such notice to the adverse possessor may also be communicated in writing. The prescription period having been broken, the chance to obtain title by adverse is lost to the claimant. The true owner would probably initiate court action to remove the claimant, or if the owner wished to execute a lease, the former adverse possessor might remain on the property but with the status of an ordinary tenant.

Another interesting aspect of the five-year prescription period has to do with what is known as tacking. An adverse possessor, never having had any communication with the true owner, may have spent some time on the land and then pass possession on to another person who of course would also be an adverse possessor. The new claimant could "tack on" to the time already spent by the former claimant and when the five-year total is reached, the new claimant could claim title by adverse possession.

Payment of taxes and assessments. The claimant is responsible for payment of taxes and assessments on the property. While an adverse possessor may make these payments when they are due, he may also satisfy the requirement by paying any delinquent taxes that may be due.

Since the method of acquiring title by adverse possession exists, it is extremely important that any owner of real property must give sufficient attention to its management so that he is aware of the use to which it is being put and what rights any person or persons in possession actually have or may claim to have.

Prescription

In certain cases, a claimant may have satisfied all of the requirements specified above with regard to adverse possession with one exception: he has not been paying the taxes and assessments on the property. Where the taxes and assessments have been paid by the true owner but an adverse possessor satisfies all of the other requirements, the claimant may require an easement by prescription rather than title to the property. Such an easement would be the right to use the land of another, and will be discussed in Chapter 5 dealing with encumbrances, liens, and easements.

Abandonment

Abandonment occurs when a tenant who has a leasehold interest in real property abandons the premises, thus allowing the owner to reacquire possession and control of the premises.

BY TRANSFER

The most common method of acquiring property is by transfer. Property is acquired by transfer when, by an act of the individual parties or of a court of law, title to property is conveyed from one person to another. Transfer may be by (a) private grant, (b) public grant, (c) gift, or (d) alienation by operation of law or court action.

Private grant

Transfer of real property by private grant is the most common method used today. The principal instrument of transfer is the deed, and the various types of deeds will be discussed in Chapter 4. Whether the transfer of ownership is from a seller to a buyer as the result of a sale, or from an owner to another as the result of a gift, the private grant results in an owner's voluntarily conveying his ownership rights to another.

Public grant

During the early years of our country's history, the United States government, through law en-

32

acted by Congress, made public grants of land to settlers at low cost in order for the land to become occupied and cultivated.

The Preemption Act of 1841 allowed persons living on federal land who were known as "squatters" to preempt 160 acres at a cost of approximately $1.25 per acre. The Homestead Act was passed in 1862; vast stretches of land were opened for homesteading, whereby the head of a family or any person over 21 years of age could obtain 160 acres. A homesteader, in order to obtain the land, had to file a declaration of homestead with the county recorder or at a designated land office, giving a description of the land, date of claim, and a statement that he intended to occupy and improve it. A registration fee of approximately $25 had to accompany the document. After the homesteader had resided upon the land for a period of five years, the government issued him a document, called a patent, that conveyed the ownership to him.

The government also granted land to many groups for the establishment of cities and towns, to educational institutions, and to the railroads. Although very little land subject to such public grant remains today, it is still possible in a few places, such as Alaska, for one to homestead and obtain public lands.

Gift

An owner of property may voluntarily transfer it to another person without demanding or receiving any consideration. If the gift is one of real property, it would normally be conveyed by a deed, and consideration would not be necessary to its validity. Gifts of property and the California gift tax are discussed in Chapter 16.

An owner may gift real property for public use, known as public dedication. The most prevalent method is by statutory dedication, and this occurs in compliance with the Subdivision Map Act when the landowner records a map approved by local governmental officials in which certain areas are expressly dedicated to the public as, for example, streets and parks. A property owner may also execute a deed to a piece of property describing a boundary as being a street or avenue, and the public may accept this type of dedication by local ordinance or public use. Many land developers formally deed parcels of land to local governmental units giving them fee title in the land rather than what may merely be an easement.

Alienation by operation of law or court action

The most common method of transferring ownership of real property is by a voluntary gift or sale, and this is known as voluntary alienation. There are, however, many ways in which ownership may be transferred whether the owner wishes it or not, and this is known as involuntary alienation.

Statutes provide many ways in which ownership may be transferred involuntarily by operation of law or court action. The most common, which will be discussed below, are: (a) bankruptcy, (b) declaratory relief action, (c) eminent domain and condemnation, (d) estoppel, (e) execution sale or sheriff's sale, (f) forfeiture, (g) foreclosure and trustee's sale, (h) marriage, (i) partition action, (j) probate sale, (k) quiet title action, and (l) tax sale.

Bankruptcy. Property may often have to be sold in connection with a bankruptcy proceeding and will thus change ownership. The procedures involved are discussed in Chapter 5.

Declaratory relief action. A declaratory relief action or equity action is one in which the court expresses an opinion with regard to the rights and duties of persons involved in a controversy. The interpretation of a written instrument such as a deed, declaration of restrictions, or a homestead may be involved, and the parties are attempting to have their rights, duties, and responsibilities clarified with respect to the particular instrument. Any person desiring such a declaration by the court with respect to an instrument affecting real property may institute such an action.

Eminent domain and condemnation. Eminent domain is the right of the federal, state, or local government to take land for public use after fairly compensating the owner for the value of the property taken. The process by which this is accomplished is called condemnation, and is discussed further in Chapter 18, which deals with governmental controls.

Estoppel. A court of equity is often required to transfer title to real property if justice is to be done. Assume that a true owner of real property permits a friend of his to appear to the world as the owner of that particular property, and an innocent third person buys the land from the apparent owner without knowing that the true owner is someone else. Under the doctrine of equitable estoppel, the true owner, whose fraudulent action made this transaction possible, would be barred or "estopped" by the court from claiming any further ownership. Similarly, if a person has a lesser estate in real property than one that he purports to convey, or if he has a defective title in the land he conveys and he later acquires the full title or estate, the person to whom he made the conveyance will automatically receive the afteracquired title or estate by way of estoppel. This is a statutory rule under the California Civil Code.

Execution sale—Sheriff's sale. A sheriff's sale of real property is usually the result of a judgment obtained against the owner of the property and the court's subsequent issuance of a writ of execution. This writ directs the sheriff, or other officer whom the court may elect, to enforce the judgment against the property of the one against whom the judgment has been obtained. Attachment, judgment, and execution liens are discussed in Chapter 5.

Forfeiture. Forfeiture is an involuntary loss of an estate or interest in property by an act of law, usually as a consequence of some negligence, omission, or default of the owner. An owner, when granting title to another, may impose a certain condition in the deed, and if the condition is later breached by the grantee, the former owner (the grantor) has the power to terminate the estate and reacquire title. Similarly, the owner may impose a special limitation in his deed. If the stated event occurs, or the prescribed status fails to endure, the estate automatically terminates and the grantor or his successor has the title. In both of the above cases, the property would be reacquired by the grantor, who would bring an action to recover and no new consideration would be paid.

Forfeiture may also occur when a purchaser under a land contract or contract of sale breaches a condition of the agreement, or when a lessee under a lease breaches a condition of the lease.

Foreclosure and trustee's sale. Foreclosure is a legal procedure whereby real property, which has been pledged as security for a debt, is sold to pay the debt to the lender in the event the borrower defaults in his payments. Such sales most commonly occur with respect to defaults under a deed of trust or mortgage and also with regard to mechanic's liens. A detailed presentation of the procedures involved in such an action under a deed of trust or mortgage will be found in Chapter 12 dealing with instruments of finance, while the mechanic's lien is covered in Chapter 5.

Marriage. Under California law, although the wedding ceremony does not effect a transfer of title to property, subsequent earnings and acquisitions of husband and wife or either during marriage, and when not acquired as separate property, are community property. Each of the spouses has a present, existing, and equal interest in such property.

Partition action. A partition action may occur when a co-owner of property brings suit against the other co-owners requesting a severance of the respective interests. If the property cannot practically be divided physically, as is usually the case with real property such as a building, the court may order a sale, transfer title to the buyer, and then divide the proceeds among the former owners. This type of judicial proceeding is called a partition action.

Probate sale. The terms *probate sale, estate sale,* and *court sale* are used interchangeably by many persons. We are here concerned with real property that is being offered for sale as the result of the probate of an estate, and will use the term *probate sale.* In California the superior courts have jurisdiction over the probate and administration of estates. Although called the probate court, the department to which this function is assigned is actually not a separate court at all but merely a department of the superior court.

Notice of sale. A probate sale may be made under direction of the court by either an executor, administrator, guardian, or conservator. Executors and administrators were treated in our discussion of wills; a guardian is appointed by the court to administer the estate of a minor or incompetent; a conservator is one appointed to administer the estates of those who are unable to manage their affairs. As was mentioned in Chapter 2 with respect to community property, a surviving spouse may now sell such property without the necessity of its being included in probate proceedings.

Real property is usually sold in order to pay debts and expenses of administration, including attorney fees and court costs, and for the payment of taxes. The property may be sold either at public auction or by private sale, but since the idea is to get the best price obtainable for the property, it is almost always sold by publishing a notice of intended sale, or notice of sale as it is also called, and accepting bids for the property.

The notice of sale contains the following:

1. The date, time, and place of the sale; that is, when the bids will be opened.

2. A legal description of the property to be sold. Often, the street address will also be given for added ease in identifying the property.

3. The address at which bids for the property may be delivered prior to the date set for the sale and actual opening of the bids.

4. Rules to be observed in preparation of the bid. It is important that the provisions and conditions outlined in the notice be carefully followed, since a bid submitted that does not follow these guidelines may be rejected, even though it is the highest price offered.

5. Terms and conditions of the sale. The two most common are: *(a)* a certified or cashier's check in the amount of 10 percent of the offered purchase price must be included with the bid; *(b)* the offer must be all cash or terms acceptable to the estate, with the property to be purchased in its present as-is condition. Although the bid may be for all cash to the estate, the buyer is given sufficient time to arrange for adequate financing following acceptance of his bid.

6. A statement to the effect that the representative may reject any and all bids. Personal representative is the legal term often applied to an executor or administrator. If the bids opened on the day and time of the sale are considered by the representative to be too low, he may reject all the bids. A new notice of sale must then be published and the procedure repeated. The price offered for probate sale property must be at least 90 percent of the value of the property as set by the inheritance tax appraiser and/or the court. Usually bids submitted exceed this minimum amount, but in the event that none of the bids does, the sale will probably have to be repeated.

If the notice does not contain information about how the property may be inspected by prospective purchasers before the date of sale, this information can usually be obtained by contacting the representative. Quite often, the representative places a set of keys to the property, if vacant, in the office of a real estate broker in the vicinity of the property.

Sale and opening of bids. On the day, time, and place set for the sale in the published notice of sale, the bids are opened. Frequently this occurs at the office of an attorney or the trust department of a bank. The bid accepted at the time of the opening should be the highest net bid to the estate. That is, the representative should actually deduct from any bid submitted by a real estate broker the amount of the broker's commission if a commission is requested in the bid. If a broker is acting for himself rather than for a client, or if the bidder is a private party, no commission will be requested in the bid. Where payment of

a commission is necessary, it will be ordered by the court and paid out of the proceeds of the estate. Bids are usually made on a standard real estate purchase contract and receipt-for-deposit form commonly used by real estate brokers in the particular locality in which the sale is taking place, or on a form provided by the representative.

Court confirmation and issuance of deed. Upon accèpting a bid, the representative asks the court to set a date for confirmation of the bid. On the date set, the judge of the court, immediately prior to confirmation, asks if anyone in court wants to raise the bid in question. Any interested person or any broker representing a client may attend the court hearing, and at this point may step forward and raise the existing high bid. However, this first increased bid must exceed the accepted bid by 10 percent of the first $10,000 and by 5 percent of the excess. Any subsequent increase may be in any amount. If the person who submitted the original high bid at the time of the sale is present in court or has someone there acting for him, the result may be an auction-like affair. No distinction is now made between gross and net bids, and the judge finally accepts the highest amount at this time; if there is a commission to be paid the judge fixes the amount.

After confirming the sale, the court issues an order to the representative, who in turn executes a deed to the purchaser. The deed refers to the order confirming sale, and both the deed and order should be recorded in the office of the county recorder.

An executor or administrator of an estate can grant an exclusive right to sell listing to a real estate broker for a period not exceeding 90 days if prior court permission is obtained upon a showing of necessity and advantage to the estate. However, property sold pursuant to such an exclusive right to sell listing will still be subject to court confirmation and additional bidding at the time the confirmation hearing is held, and the commission on the sale will be the amount determined by the court.

Quiet title action. A quiet title action is a judicial proceeding arising from a claim or cloud against a title that may render it unmarketable or that may keep it from being insured by a title insurance company. An owner may bring such an action against an individual who claims an interest that will affect the title to the property, or the individual who claims the adverse interest may institute the action. The court will determine in whom title to the particular property in question actually vests, and will issue a decree so stating. Upon recordation of a certified copy of the decree, the title will have been quieted and the owner will now have a marketable and insurable title. A person claiming title by adverse possession would use this method to perfect his title against the owner of record. It may also be used when a lender has recorded a lien against the property of a borrower and later, when the borrower has repaid the loan, the parties have failed to record this fact. The lien would still show as a matter of record, even though the obligation for which the lien was filed had long ago been repaid and satisfied. The court action would remedy this situation and eliminate the lien.

Tax sale. When real property taxes have not been paid for a certain period of time, the property may be sold by the state, county, or city tax collector in order to satisfy the tax delinquency. A detailed treatment of the procedures involved will be found in Chapter 16, Taxation of Real Estate.

QUESTIONS FOR DISCUSSION

1. Discuss the various means by which the property of an individual who expires intestate might be distributed.
2. What are the differences among the three basic types of wills?
3. How may real estate be acquired by the movement of water?
4. What type of property would be most likely to be acquired by adverse possession?
5. Which of the required actions in the acquisition of property by adverse possession would be most difficult to satisfy?
6. What examples may be found in your own locality or area of property transferred by public grant?
7. Discuss the events that might culminate in an execution sale of real property.
8. Does a wedding ceremony itself effect a transfer of title to real property?
9. What are the most common reasons for the sale of real property during the probate of an estate?
10. Under what circumstances might a quiet title action be necessary?

MULTIPLE CHOICE QUESTIONS

3–1. Most real property is acquired by: (a) gift, (b) court order, (c) transfer, (d) prescriptive easement.
3–2. A handwritten will is: (a) holographic, (b) signed by witnesses, (c) nuncupative, (d) none of these.
3–3. The transfer of property without receipt of monetary consideration is generally by: (a) court action, (b) gift, (c) private grant, (d) none of these.
3–4. A suit by a co-owner against other co-owners requesting a severance of respective interests is: (a) private grant, (b) sale by sheriff, (c) partition action, (d) none of these.
3–5. A probate sale is administered by: (a) title company, (b) county clerk, (c) assessor, (d) superior court.
3–6. Property distributed according to the statutes of succession is most often: (a) community property, (b) tenancy in common, (c) separate property, (d) none of these.
3–7. The sale of property by a sheriff is usually the result of: (a) accretion, (b) addition of fixtures, (c) adverse possession, (d) judgment against owner.
3–8. An adverse possessor who satisfies all requirements except payment of real property taxes most often obtains: (a) public grant, (b) ownership by court order, (c) easement by prescription, (d) none of these.

Principal instruments of transfer—deeds

4

In California today, the most common method of transfer of title to real property is by a written instrument called a deed. When properly executed, delivered, and accepted, the title to real property passes from one person called the grantor to another person called the grantee. If two or more individuals are conveying title, they are known as grantors, and when two or more individuals receive the title, they are called the grantees. The law prescribes what a valid deed must contain, but does not specify an exact form of document that must be used. Through custom and usage, however, standardized printed forms of deeds have evolved in California and are now employed by title insurance companies, attorneys, and brokers.

Since most transfers of title to real property are voluntary transfers, the grant deed, quitclaim deed, and gift deed are most commonly used, and these as well as other forms of deeds will be discussed later.

REQUISITES OF A VALID DEED

The requisites of a valid deed in California are as follows.

1. It must be in writing. Under the statue of frauds, any transfer of interests in real property must be made by an instrument in writing.

2. The parties must be properly described. Since there are so many individuals with like or similar names, it is very important that the parties to a deed be identified as clearly as possible in order to avoid any later confusion as to true identity. The person who receives title to real property in a deed is the grantee. When, at some later date, this grantee conveys the title to another, he then becomes the grantor since he is now conveying the title. Any substantial variation between the name of the grantee in one instrument and the name of the grantor in the following instrument will, irrespective of the fact that identity may be shown by "off record" evidence, render the title defective and prevent the recorded deed from imparting constructive notice.

The full legal name should be used and the legal status of the individual should also be shown. A conveyance by a husband and wife may be shown as "James Arthur Smith and Mary Elizabeth Smith, husband and wife," the full legal names being used together with their legal status showing that they are husband and wife. A legal name consists of one personal or given name, and one surname or family name. The old common law recognized but one given name, and frequently disregarded middle names or initials. It is often stated that the insertion or omission of, or mistake or variance in, a middle name or initial is immaterial, and such name may be dropped and resumed or changed at pleasure. Now, however, the middle name or initial has become quite important, especially as a distinguishing identification of a person, and should certainly be used when the person is a party to a legal document.

Any person in whom the title of real estate is vested, who afterwards has his name changed, must, in any conveyance of real estate held, set forth the name in which he derived title. Although a person may assume a fictitious name in which to receive title, he must thereafter either transfer title in the identical name or refer to such former name. A common situation in which a person's name is changed is as the result of a marriage.

Thus, where a single woman receives title as Lynette Carter, and later marries, she should grant the property as "Lynette Taylor, who acquired title as Lynette Carter." Any document that does not comply with this provision does not impart constructive notice of the contents to subsequent purchasers and encumbrancers, although it is valid as between the parties thereto and those who have actual notice thereof.

A deed to a purely fictitious person is void, but a deed to an actual person under a fictitious name by which he is known, or which he assumes for the occasion, is valid. If the grantee is misnamed in the deed, the error can be corrected by a second deed to the same grantee under the true name. The grantee designated in the deed must be a natural person or legal entity capable of taking title to real property. A deed to a deceased person is void, since the grantee would not be capable of taking title, but a deed to "the heirs of William Brown, deceased" is sufficient and will pass title to them.

3. The parties must be competent to convey and capable of receiving the grant of the property. The law says that a competent person is one who is mentally and physically able to act for himself as prescribed by law, or who has legally been given the authority to act as an agent, executor, administrator, guardian, or the like. The grantee must be either a real person or a legal entity capable under the law of taking title. The basic legal principle involved is that while there must be someone legally capable of conveying title, there must also be someone legally capable of taking title. Thus a person cannot convey from himself to himself, but it is perfectly permissible for an individual to convey from himself to himself and others, and this is often done when one who holds title in severalty wishes to establish a joint tenancy relationship with another. A further discussion of the competency of individuals to execute instruments will be found in Chapter 8, Elements of Contracts.

4. The property conveyed must be adequately described. It is very important that the deed contain a clear and accurate description of the real property to be conveyed. If the description in the deed is sufficient to identify the property, the description is a good one, and will not be overturned by any minor error or inconsistency. The most common descriptive forms used are *(a)* lot, block, and tract, *(b)* metes and bounds, and *(c)* government survey or surveyor's report.

5. There must be a granting clause. A granting clause, or words of conveyance as they are commonly called, must be contained in the deed in order to pass title to the property. The words in a grant deed such as *grant, transfer,* or *convey,* or in a quitclaim deed the terms *quitclaim, remise,* or *release* are sufficient for the requirement of providing a granting clause.

6. The deed must be signed by the party or parties making the conveyance. A deed must be executed, that is, signed, by the grantor or grantors and should be dated. The grantor will usually affix his signature in the usual manner in which he signs his name, and the form of the name should be the same as that used to identify the grantor at the beginning of the deed form. If the grantor was identified as William Charles Hatcher, the signature should be William Charles Hatcher.

The Civil Code allows a signature to be made by mark. Where some condition exists that may prevent the grantor from signing a legible signature, a grantor may make a mark in the presence of two witnesses who must also affix their signatures to the document. One of the witnesses should write in the name of the grantor near the mark, and the deed should contain a brief statement explaining that this method of execution by mark was used. The same procedure is employed in the event that the grantor does not know how to write. Another type of situation that may arise is if the grantor can write his name, but in an alphabet other than that used in English. Here again, there should be two witnesses and one of the witnesses should write an explanatory statement near the signature, such as "the above is the signature of Takisura Okamoto, written in Japanese."

7. There must be delivery and acceptance. In order for a deed to transfer title to real property effectively, there must be a proper delivery and acceptance as prescribed by law. There must be a clear and honest intent on the part of the grantor to pass title to the grantee by the deed that the grantor has executed. Where a deed is obtained through duress or force, or as a result of some form of fraud, the deed may be voided.

There are various methods by which delivery may be effected. Manual delivery occurs when the grantor physically gives the deed to the grantee. A manual delivery may not always be sufficient to meet the requirements of the law. If, for instance, a grantor gives a deed to the named grantee merely for the purpose of having the grantee examine the document, but without the intent on the part of the grantor of actually having it take effect at that time, such an act will not constitute legal delivery. If a grantee manages to take a deed without the knowledge or consent of the grantor, and has it recorded, it will be void for want of proper delivery.

The delivery of the deed must be effective during the grantor's lifetime, and should not be used to take the place of a will. A deed that is delivered to a grantee with the condition that it is not to take effect until the expiration of the grantor is not valid, since the intent to pass title would not occur during the lifetime of the grantor. Under California law there is a presumption of delivery if the deed is in the possession of the grantee or if it has been recorded, but these are rebuttable rather than conclusive, since there may not have been a legal delivery.

In order for a deed to be valid, it cannot be delivered conditionally. An example would be where A, wishing to avoid ultimate probate proceedings with regard to his property, gives a deed to B, telling B that he is not to record it until the expiration of A. This is a conditional delivery, and not valid, since there was no intent on the part of the grantor to transfer title to B upon delivery of the deed. The one common exception in this regard is delivery of a deed to an escrow holder who holds the deed until close of escrow and is then obligated, as a trustee for both parties, to deliver the deed to the grantee.

In addition to delivery by the grantor, there must be a voluntary and unconditional acceptance on the part of the grantee. Although the grantee usually accepts the deed, the law does state that the grantee has the right to refuse acceptance and cannot be forced to accept if he does not wish to do so. Acceptance by the grantee is usually accomplished by certain words, acts, or conduct on his part that lead to the presumption of voluntary acceptance.

Recordation of the deed by the grantee would constitute proper acceptance, but it is interesting to note that if the grantor records the deed without the consent of the grantee, the grantee may still refuse acceptance, since it cannot be imposed upon him by recordation. Other instances in which acceptance may be presumed are when the grantee takes possession of the deed, takes possession of the real property, enters into a conveyance of the property to another, pays a consideration to the grantor, executes a mortgage or deed of trust on the property, or performs any other act on the part of the grantee that would be defined as that of an owner.

Consideration

In the voluntary conveyance between private individuals, a statement of consideration is not essential to the validity of the deed. In actual practice, however, deeds usually make mention of a consideration, since it gives presumptive evidence that something of value was given for the real property being conveyed. In most cases, the consideration is the purchase price paid for the property, but the exact amount is seldom shown on the deed itself. Most deeds contain a clause such as "for value received" or "for a valuable consideration, receipt of which is hereby acknowledged," immediately preceding the name of the grantor. In a gift deed, the consideration need not be a monetary one and instead may be shown as love and affection. The usual clause in the gift deed states "for and in consideration of the love and affection," and this is taken to be sufficient consideration for the conveyance in the gift deed.

An exception to the rule that a statement of consideration is not essential to the validity of the deed occurs with regard to conveyances made under a court order by a person such as an executor, administrator, guardian, trustee, and the like. Such conveyances must be evidenced by a consideration, as must those by an attorney-in-fact acting under a power of attorney, or a deed given in lieu of foreclosure under a deed of trust. Also, as was mentioned in our previous discussion of community property, a husband may not convey community real property without receiving a sufficient and valuable consideration unless agreed to by the wife in writing. The sufficiency of consideration is also an important factor in cases where one in debt makes a conveyance without sufficient consideration, which would be fraudulent against creditors.

Void and voidable deeds

Certain deeds are void at inception and pass no title to the grantee. Examples are deeds that are (a) from a grantor judicially declared incompetent to convey, (b) forgeries, (c) from a grantor under 18 years of age, (d) from a grantor entirely without understanding of the act, (e) executed in blank with the grantee's name later inserted without the grantor's authorization, (f) undelivered, stolen from the grantor, or delivered by an escrow officer without the authorization of the grantor, and (g) altered or changed in some way in escrow without the authorization of the grantor.

Certain other deeds are not void and can pass good title, but are voidable as the result of appropriate judicial proceedings. Examples of such deeds are *(a)* a deed from an incompetent grantor whose incapacity has not been judicially determined, *(b)* a deed procured by duress, undue influence, menace, mistake, or fraud, *(c)* a deed delivered by mistake, *(d)* a deed from an individual under 18 years of age and thus a minor, and *(e)* a deed unlawfully obtained by confidential relationships. When a deed is voidable, the general rule is that one who purchases from the grantee for a sufficient and valuable consideration receives a good title as against the original grantor.

There are certain persons who may not be able to either acquire or make a proper conveyance because of their legal status, such as certain classes of aliens, American Indians in certain cases, and persons convicted of a felony who have been deprived of their civil rights. Conveyances may be made by a person acting as an agent for the owner, for example when one is acting under a power of attorney. The duties and responsibilities of agents will be discussed in Chapter 7, Agency and the Real Estate Licensee.

Reservations, exceptions, and restrictions

Deeds may on occasion contain certain reservations and exceptions to the estate being conveyed, or make reference to restrictions that are already a matter of record or are being created at the time of the conveyance. A recital in a deed that excludes a portion of the property being granted is known as an exception. An example would be the granting by A to B of a 160-acre tract of land excepting therefrom a certain specified 10 acres. The land excepted must be clearly identified and described so that no doubt exists as to the parcel that the grantor is excepting from the grant.

A reservation in a deed is the acquisition by the grantor of some right or benefit that did not exist as a separate right prior to the conveyance. An example would be the granting of certain land to a grantee with a reservation creating an easement to cross a certain portion of the land in favor of the grantor.

A restriction is a type of encumbrance that may be imposed by deed and restricts the use of land in a particular way. Restrictions are treated in detail in Chapter 5, Liens and Encumbrances.

ACKNOWLEDGMENT

Before a deed can be recorded, it must be acknowledged. An acknowledgment is a formal declaration by a person who has executed an instrument that he did in fact execute the instrument and that such execution is his voluntary act and deed. The acknowledgment is made before a person authorized by law to take an acknowledgment, such as a notary public, who will prepare and attach to the instrument a certificate of acknowledgment form. An acknowledgment should not be confused with a verification. A verification is a sworn statement that the contents of a document are true, while an acknowledgment is a sworn statement from the person whose signature appears on the document that he did in fact execute and sign it.

Who may take an acknowledgment

The California Civil Code designates those persons who are authorized to take acknowledgments. In this state and within the city, county, city and county, or district for which the officer was selected or appointed, acknowledgment may be made before either a notary public, a judge of a municipal or justice court, a clerk of a court of record, a county recorder, a county clerk, a court commissioner, or before certain military officers who are authorized to take acknowledgments of persons serving in the military. An acknowledgment taken by a person who has a direct interest in the instrument, such as a grantee in a deed, is void.

Who may make an acknowledgment

The acknowledgment is made by the person whose rights and interests are being transferred or encumbered by the particular document—by the grantor in the case of a deed. The requirement of acknowledgment of certain instruments prior to recordation protects the property owner from unwarranted or unauthorized encumbrance of his property on the official records. Among such instruments, besides conveyances, mortgages, and trust deeds, are agreements for sale, option agreements, real estate purchase contract and receipt for deposit forms, commission receipts, or any affidavit which quotes or refers to these instruments.

Certificate of acknowledgment

Most printed forms of deeds, such as the grant deed illustrated in this chapter, have made the certificate of acknowledgment a part of the form itself and have it printed at the bottom of the document. Blank acknowledgment forms may also be obtained in most stationery stores, and after being properly filled out, they are attached to the particular instrument to be recorded. The form shows the place and date of the taking of the acknowledgment, the name of the person appearing and making the acknowledgment, and the signature of the person taking the acknowledgment attesting to the fact that it was made before him and that proper identity of the party appearing before him was established.

An acknowledgment taken outside this state, if not in accordance with the forms, provisions, and laws of this state, should have attached thereto a certificate of a clerk of the court of record of the county or district where the same was taken that the certificate of acknowledgment is in accordance with laws of the state in which it was taken and that the officer taking the same was authorized by law to do so and that his or her signature is true and genuine.

In California, a notary public is required to have a seal on which his name must appear, together with the county in which the notary is located, and also the words *notary public* and the state seal. The date of expiration of the notary's commission must also be shown. The seal used by the notary public must reproduce photographically, and notaries are allowed to use either a seal press or a rubber stamp seal.

The law now requires a notary public to keep a sequential journal of all official acts performed as a notary public. The journal must contain the following:

a. Date, time, and type of every official act.
b. Character of every instrument acknowledged or proved in the notary's presence.
c. The signature of every individual whose signature is being notarized by the notary.
d. Type of information used to verify the identity of the parties whose signatures are being acknowledged.
e. Amount of notary fee charged.

In addition, a notary public must provide, to any individual requesting it, a certified copy of any page from the journal, and can make a per-page charge to such individual. A notary public who has a direct financial or beneficial interest in a particular transaction is prevented from acting as a notary in it.

The most important responsibility of the person taking the acknowledgment is that he be satisfied as to the identity of the individual appearing before him. The acknowledgment should not be taken unless the person properly identifies himself, is personally known to the notary, or is identified by a credible witness. Although it is fairly standard practice for the person making the acknowledgment to actually affix his signature to the document in the presence of the notary, it is not a legal requirement. The document may have been signed elsewhere, and the signer need only acknowledge in the presence of the notary that he signed the document.

After a deed has been properly acknowledged, it may then be recorded. The subject of recordation, since it applies to many instruments other than deeds, will be treated separately at the end of this chapter.

TYPES OF DEEDS

The following section will discuss the various forms of deeds in use. In California these are basically grant deeds and quitclaim deeds, with certain forms given a name to indicate the context or situation in connection with which they are being used.

Grant deed

The grant deed is the most commonly used form to convey real property in real estate sales transactions in California. By use of the word "grant" on the deed, the Civil Code states that the grantor impliedly warrants *(a)* that previous to the time of execution of such conveyance, he has not conveyed the same estate, or any right, title, or interest therein, to any person other than the grantee, and *(b)* that at the time of execution of such conveyance the estate is free from encumbrances done, made, or suffered by the grantor, or any person claiming under him. Unless restrained by express terms contained in the conveyance, any after-acquired title of the grantor is also conveyed.

Although these protective covenants are contained in the deed, virtually all purchasers and lenders have come to insist on an accompanying policy of title insurance as a means of protecting their interests in connection with a conveyance of title. The grant deed is illustrated in Figure 4-1.

—— SPACE ABOVE THIS LINE FOR RECORDER'S USE ——

DOCUMENTARY TRANSFER TAX $ ....
☐ COMPUTED ON FULL VALUE OF PROPERTY CONVEYED, OR
☐ COMPUTED ON FULL VALUE LESS LIENS & ENCUMBRANCES
REMAINING THEREON AT TIME OF SALE.

Signature of declarant or agent determining tax — firm name

Grant Deed

THIS FORM FURNISHED BY TITLE INSURANCE AND TRUST COMPANY

TO 405 C

FOR A VALUABLE CONSIDERATION, receipt of which is hereby acknowledged,

William Seller and Mary Seller, husband and wife

hereby GRANT(S) to

Arthur Buyer and Janet Buyer, husband and wife, AS JOINT TENANTS,

the following described real property in the City of Los Angeles
County of Los Angeles , State of California:

BEGINNING at the point of intersection of the northerly line of Elm Street
with the easterly line of Hallock Street; running thence northerly along the
easterly line of Hallock Street 100 feet; thence at a right angle easterly 50
feet; thence at a right angle southerly 100 feet to the northerly line of Elm
Street; thence at a right angle westerly along said line of Elm Street 50 feet
to the point of beginning.

Being a portion of Lot 6 of the JOHNSON HEIGHTS SUBDIVISION, according to map
thereof filed July 1, 1927, in Book " O " of Maps, at Page 9, in the office of the
Recorder of the County of Los Angeles, State of California.

Dated _____ January 28, 19-- _____

(s) William Seller

(s) Mary Seller

STATE OF CALIFORNIA City and
COUNTY OF Los Angeles } SS.
On January 28, 19-- before me, the under-
signed, a Notary Public in and for said State, personally appeared
William Seller and Mary Seller
_____
_____
_____, known to me
to be the person S whose name S are subscribed to the within
instrument and acknowledged that they executed the same.
WITNESS my hand and official seal.

Signature (s) Margaret Notari

Margaret Notari
Name (Typed or Printed)

(This area for official notarial seal)

Title Order No._____ Escrow or Loan No._____

MAIL TAX STATEMENTS AS DIRECTED ABOVE

FIGURE 4–1

42

Quitclaim deed

The grantor in a quitclaim deed merely relinquishes any right or claim he has in the property. There are no implied covenants or warranties of any kind. The grantee acquires only what the grantor has; it may convey fee simple title or very little interest. It does not convey any afteracquired title.

A quitclaim deed is generally used to clear some "cloud on the title," which is an expression used to cover some minor defect that needs to be removed in order to perfect the title.

Gift deed

While a grantor may make a gift of property by using a grant or quitclaim deed, the gift deed is most commonly employed for this purpose. The basic difference in this form is that it makes clear that the consideration involved is one of love and affection rather than a monetary one, and love and affection as used in the gift deed legally constitute a good and valid consideration. The gift deed may not, however, be used to defraud creditors, and if put to this use by the grantor it will be set aside and voided by the courts.

Warranty deed

The warranty deed is seldom used in California, having been replaced by the grant deed, but is still in use in many other states. The warranty deed was in use before it became customary for the grantee to have the protection of a title insurance policy. The warranty deed contains express covenants of title, which in effect means that the grantor guarantees that the grantee is receiving a good title. Before the advent of title insurance companies, the only recourse a grantee had if the title proved to be defective was against the grantor because of the express warranties contained in the warranty deed. Now, however, a sounder and better protection is afforded the grantee by the large title insurance company, and so the common practice today is for the grantor to convey via a grant deed, and protection is provided by the title insurance policy.

Deed of trust or trust deed

The deed of trust, or trust deed as it is also called, is discussed in detail in Chapter 12, Real Estate Finance—Instruments of Finance. It is an instrument that is used to make real property the security for a loan, and thus protect the lender in the event that the borrower is unable to repay the loan.

Deed of reconveyance and trustee's deed

The deed of reconveyance is the instrument by which the trustee, under a deed of trust, conveys title to real property back to the borrower, when the money borrowed has been repaid to the lender. If the borrower cannot repay the loan and the lender orders the trustee to sell the property, the trustee will conduct a sale of the property and execute a trustee's deed to the person who acquires the property at the time of the sale. A detailed discussion of a trustee's sale, and also a mortgage foreclosure, will be found in Chapter 12.

Sheriff's deed

A sheriff's deed is a deed given to a purchaser upon the foreclosure of property, levied under a judgment for foreclosure on a mortgage, or of a money judgment against the owner of the property. This deed is given by court order, and the title conveyed is only that acquired by the state or the sheriff under the foreclosure.

There are many conveyances of rights and title in property that are the result of a court action or under the supervision of a court. Depending upon the circumstances and the person authorized to make the sale, there are numerous types of deeds given in addition to those discussed previously, such as a marshal's deed, executor's deed, guardian's deed, personal representative's deed, and commissioner's deed.

Patents

A patent is a document used by the federal or a state government to transfer title of public lands to private individuals. The form and content of a patent is similar to that of a deed, but is rarely used today since so little government land is now being granted.

RECORDATION

When California was administered by the Spanish and Mexican governments, there were no recording laws. After California became a state, one of the first acts of the state legislature was to adopt a recording system by which evidence of title or interest in real property could be collected in a convenient and safe public place.

Requisites for recordation

After being acknowledged, any instrument or judgment affecting the title to or possession of real property may be recorded. An instrument is defined as a document signed and delivered by one person to another, transferring the title to or creating a lien on property, or giving a right to a debt or duty.

Examples of such instruments are various deeds, mortgages, deeds of trust, leases, contracts of sale, and certain types of agreements between property owners that may affect their property. In addition to the foregoing, there are many other documents that have a direct effect on making the record title to real property complete, and may thus be recorded.

Although the documents mentioned above are usually recorded as a matter of course, failure to record does not render them ineffective or destroy their validity in most cases. Some documents, however, are not effective at all unless they are recorded. Among these are evidences of involuntary liens such as attachments, judgments, executions, and mechanic's liens; while others are a notice of completion, declaration of homestead, declaration of abandonment of homestead, revocation of a recorded power of attorney to convey or execute instruments affecting real property, and a notice of *lis pendens*, which gives notice that a legal action has been commenced regarding the property.

In addition to instruments that may or must be recorded, there are those that cannot be recorded. Examples would be documents that are not acknowledged, that do not contain an adequate description of the property, or that contain a mechanical defect or omission that will cause the recorder to reject the instrument for recordation.

Effect of recordation

The basic effect and purpose of recording is to give notice. In California there are two kinds of notice, actual and constructive. Actual notice is express information or actual knowledge of a fact, while constructive notice is notice imputed by law. Thus, recordation of instruments imparts constructive notice to subsequent purchasers and encumbrancers. A person is bound not only by what he actually knows about a piece of property, but also by what he would learn from a proper search of the records. The theory behind constructive notice is that subsequent purchasers, mortgagees, or beneficiaries under a deed of trust are considered to have notice of the contents of properly recorded instruments. Recordation gives protection to a purchaser who acquires property for a valuable consideration and without knowledge of a prior unrecorded conveyance. It gives protection to a purchaser, mortgagee, or beneficiary under a deed of trust who first records any instrument affecting the property, from subsequent purchasers or lenders who may later record an instrument affecting the property.

Let us assume that A conveys property to B, and thereafter conveys the same property to C; that is, he has sold the same property to two different buyers, each of whom has paid him a valuable consideration. If B failed to record immediately and C records first without any actual knowledge of the conveyance to B, then C's interest will prevail over that of B. If B had recorded immediately, this would have constituted the giving of constructive notice, and the subsequent purchase by C would not prevail over B's interest. Constructive notice by recordation had been given by B, and C would have found out about the conveyance if he had properly checked the records.

Recording a document that contains a defect or is invalid does not make it valid. The recording procedure merely gives notice that a document has been made a matter of public record. No one should assume that every instrument recorded is legally perfect. An instrument that is a forgery or fraudulent prior to recordation remains so after recordation. This is one of the reasons why virtually all real property transactions in California include a title search and the issuance of a policy of title insurance, which are discussed fully in Chapter 14.

It was mentioned previously that certain documents may be recorded but that failure to do so does not affect their validity. They are valid as between the parties to the agreement and those persons having actual notice of their existence. In addition, there are other types of unrecorded interests that may be disclosed by a physical inspection of the property. Possession of the property by someone other than the owner may indicate the possibility of an unrecorded contract of sale or lease; a pathway or road on the property may mean an unrecorded easement; and building materials on or about the premises may be the result of work done on the building for which someone may have the right to file a mechanic's lien. The law generally holds that a prospective purchaser who inspects property and finds such conditions has been put on notice that further inquiry is necessary to ascertain any unrecorded rights and interests that these conditions may indicate.

Actual recordation of an instrument

The instrument to be recorded is deposited at the office of the county recorder, in the county in which the property is located, with instructions to "file for record." The recorder must record the instrument without delay, and does this by endorsing on the instrument the proper filing number, the year, month, day, hour, and minute of its reception, and the fees required by law for recordation. The fees are generally minimal, amounting only to a few dollars. The recorder writes upon the instrument the book and page in which it is recorded, and after recordation is made, the instrument is returned to the party who left it to be recorded. There are various books in which different records are kept in the recorder's office, but most documents are recorded in books called "official records." The content of documents filed for recordation used to be written into the official records, but this has been replaced by photostating the documents, and in some counties they are stored on microfilm. Because of this, county recorders will now refuse to record any document that cannot be photographed clearly.

In addition, the recorder is required to maintain an index. These indexes are alphabetically arranged by grantor and grantee, showing the names of the parties, title of the instrument, date of filing, and recording reference. All documents recorded in the county recorder's office are accessible to the public and may be traced by use of the names indexes maintained.

The primary job of the county recorder is to record recordable documents, and he is not required to make a search of the records should an individual so request. However, most clerks in the county recorder's office will answer general questions and explain the use of the various indexes and location of different volumes that make up the official records to individuals who may wish to search the records and obtain information regarding a document on record.

A deed or instrument executed to convey title to real property will not be accepted for recordation until a name and address to which future tax statements may be mailed is noted across the bottom of the first page. This regulation is intended to help new property owners avoid penalty payments for overdue taxes caused by lack of mailing addresses.

When it is necessary to record a document written in a foreign language, such as Spanish, the recorder must permanently file the foreign language instrument with a certified translation to English attached.

Prior to January 1, 1968, federal documentary tax stamps were required to be affixed to recorded conveyances. Since the above date, federal stamps are no longer required and have been replaced by a real estate transfer tax that is levied by the individual counties in the state. Notice of payment is shown on the deed prior to recordation and applies when the consideration in the deed, exclusive of the value of any lien or encumbrance attaching to the property at the time of sale, exceeds $100. Tax is computed at the rate of 55 cents for each $500 or fraction thereof of the consideration or value of the property.

Although we have stated that the recordation of land takes place at the office of the county recorder in which the land is located, we should at this point take note of an interesting exception to this general rule. Information pertaining to certain federally owned lands, such as park lands, may be recorded with the Bureau of Land Management rather than the local county recorder, and thus a complete title search of such property should include a check with the Bureau of Land Management.

QUESTIONS FOR DISCUSSION

1. Why must a deed in California be in writing?
2. Under what circumstances might an individual be both a grantor and grantee in a deed?
3. May a grantor who is unable to sign his name in English execute a valid deed?
4. Discuss the difference between delivery and acceptance of a deed.
5. When might an acceptable consideration in a deed not be monetary?
6. What are some examples of deeds that are void at inception?
7. When might a deed be voidable?
8. Discuss the differences in a deed between a reservation, an exception, and a restriction.
9. What is the importance of acknowledgment with respect to a deed?

10. What implication does the word *grant* have in a deed?

11. Why are warranty deeds not commonly used in California?

12. When is a deed of reconveyance used?

13. A patent might be used in connection with the granting of what type of land?

14. Discuss the basic effect and purpose of recordation of an instrument.

15. What incorrect assumption is often made with respect to an instrument that has been recorded?

MULTIPLE CHOICE QUESTIONS

4–1. An acknowledgment is made by a: *(a)* notary public, *(b)* judge or clerk of a municipal court, *(c)* grantor, *(d)* title officer during an escrow.

4–2. The recording law was introduced into California by: *(a)* United States government, *(b)* Mexican government, *(c)* California legislature, *(d)* King of Spain.

4–3. Recordation of documents imparts: *(a)* legal validity, *(b)* court approval, *(c)* constructive notice, *(d)* none of these.

4–4. The most common type of deed used to transfer title to property in California is: *(a)* warranty, *(b)* sheriff, *(c)* gift, *(d)* grant.

4–5. A deed is executed when it is *(a)* in writing, *(b)* given to a grantee, *(c)* signed by a witness, *(d)* signed by grantor.

4–6. A recital in a deed which excludes a portion of the property being granted is: *(a)* an acknowledgment, *(b)* a patent, *(c)* a restriction, *(d)* none of these.

4–7. A sworn statement that the contents of a document are true is: *(a)* a contract, *(b)* a verification, *(c)* a judicial consideration, *(d)* an acknowledgment.

4–8. An instrument which transfers an interest in real property must be: *(a)* in writing, *(b)* a contract stating a monetary consideration, *(c)* approved by the county recorder, *(d)* witnessed by an escrow or title officer.

5 Liens and encumbrances

An encumbrance is anything that limits an owner's interest and enjoyment in his property. The rights that a landowner has may be affected by certain claims, rights, or interests in his property possessed by others. Encumbrances that make property security for the payment of a debt or discharge of an obligation are known as liens. There are additional forms of encumbrances, among them easements, which give to one individual the right to use and enjoy the property of another, within certain limits. The distinction is often made that liens affect the title to real property while other encumbrances affect use of the property.

First, we shall discuss those encumbrances that are liens, such as attachment, judgment, and execution liens, mechanic's liens, bankruptcy, taxes and special assessments, and trust deeds and mortgages. Then we will consider other encumbrances such as easements, homesteads, covenants, conditions, and restrictions, encroachments and party walls, and building codes and zoning laws.

Liens are often classified as being either voluntary or involuntary, and either specific or general. A voluntary lien is created with the acceptance of the property owner, and the most common example is a trust deed or mortgage which a buyer signs when purchasing a property. An involuntary lien is imposed by law and is generally contrary to the wishes of the property owner. Examples of involuntary liens are attachment, judgment, and execution liens, mechanic's liens, and tax liens. A specific lien is a lien against a specific piece of property such as a trust deed or lien for property taxes. A general lien, such as a judgment lien or lien for federal income taxes, applies to all property of an owner.

ATTACHMENT, JUDGMENT, AND EXECUTION LIENS

Attachment is the process by which real or personal property of a defendant in a lawsuit is seized and retained in the custody of the law as security for satisfaction of the judgment the plaintiff hopes to obtain in the pending litigation. The plaintiff obtains the lien before entry of judgment, and thus he is assured of availability of property of the defendant for eventual execution sale in satisfaction of his claim in the event that he actually obtains a judgment against the defendant as a result of the suit. The judgment may arise in connection with an action for payment of money upon an unsecured contract, for example, or in an unlawful detainer action to recover unsecured overdue rent, or in an action by the state or its political subdivisions for collection of taxes or money due upon any legal obligation or penalty.

The attachment is a lien upon all real property, attached for a period of three years after the date of levy, and may thereafter be ignored unless (1) an abstract of judgment has been recorded, (2) a levy of execution has been recorded, (3) the plaintiff or the defendant was in the military service at the end of the three-year period or was in military service within three months immediately preceding the end of such period, in which case the period is extended until three months after the discharge of such party from military service, or (4) a certified copy of a court order has been recorded, which may extend the period for up to two years.

The attachment may be released or discharged in various ways, such as (a) dismissal of the action, (b) recording the abstract of judgment obtained in the legal action, (c) by order of the court because of some defect in the proceedings, *(d)* by order of the plaintiff after the defendant settles the claim, *(e)* by a levying officer, for instance when a third party establishes his ownership of the property, *(f)* by the defendant's claiming legitimate exemption of the property from attachment, or *(g)* expiration of the defendant during the pendency of the action.

Property subject to and exempt from attachment

Generally, all real and personal property of the defendant within the state that is not exempt by law from execution may be attached. This includes not only real property, which would be disclosed by record as belonging to the defendant, but also realty he owns that may stand of record in the name of another.

With regard to such property, the writ of attachment must describe the property, the interest of the defendant in said property, and the name of the person holding the property according to the records. The lien will attach to any interest the defendant has in the property, whether or not such interest appears of record.

As a matter of public policy, certain property is exempt from attachment or execution when proper claim is made for exemption. One half of the earnings of the defendant or judgment debtor that are received for his personal services rendered at any time within 30 days next preceding the levy of attachment or execution, are exempt without even filing a claim for exemption. All such earnings are exempt if they are necessary for use of the debtor's family, residing in California, provided he does support them in whole or in part. However, if the debts involved were incurred by him, his wife, or family for the common necessaries of life, or were incurred for personal services rendered by any employee or former employee of the debtor, this 100 percent exemption does not apply.

The most important exemption with regard to real property is the homestead, and the formalities of declaration of homestead by the owner to obtain exemption are discussed later in this chapter. The Code of Civil Procedure lists certain other property exempt from attachment or execution. Among these are such items as shares of stock in a building and loan association up to the value of $1,000, a house trailer actually occupied by the defendant and his family up to a value of $40,000, one motor vehicle of a value not exceeding $500,

necessary household, table, and kitchen furniture, certain monies received from a governmental agency such as a pension or retirement and disability benefit, and certain farming utensils and equipment.

Judgment

A judgment is the final determination of the rights of the parties in an action or proceeding by a court of competent jurisdiction. There is always a possibility that either party will appeal and that the judgment might subsequently be reversed or amended, and so the judgment is not truly finalized until the time to appeal or seek other procedural legal relief has elapsed.

Judgments that may result in a lien against real property are those that *(a)* foreclose liens on the property and order the sale of such property in order to pay the amount of the judgment, *(b)* award money damages and impose a lien on property in order to obtain the money awarded, *(c)* result in a lien against a debtor's property in order to pay off the debt.

With regard to *a* above, if the sale of the property does not produce sufficient funds to satisfy the debt, a deficiency judgment may result. A deficiency judgment is one for the amount remaining due to mortgage or beneficiary after a foreclosure, and is discussed in detail in Chapter 12, Finance.

Creation of lien. A judgment does not automatically create a lien. However, as soon as a properly certified abstract of judgment or decree of any court of this state or any federal court of record is recorded with the recorder of any county, it becomes a lien upon all nonexempt real property of the judgment debtor located in that county. It extends, moreover, to all realty he may thereafter acquire before the expiration of the lien, which usually continues in effect for a period of 10 years from the date of entry of the judgment or decree.

Appeal from judgment. Appeal may be taken from any judgment of a superior court from which an appeal lies within 60 days from date of entry of the judgment, unless there has been filed a notice of motion for a new trial or a motion to vacate a judgment or to vacate and enter another and different judgment. Appeal may be taken from any judgment of a municipal court within 30 days after entry of judgment, unless there has been filed a notice of motion for a new trial or a motion to vacate a judgment or to vacate and enter another and different judgment. An appeal may be taken from a federal court judgment within 30 and, in certain cases, up to 60 days.

Termination of judgment lien. The lien of a judgment may be terminated by satisfaction of the judgment. Satisfaction of a judgment may be entered upon an execution returned satisfied, or upon an acknowledgment of satisfaction filed with the clerk of the court. Specific properties may be released by payment of certain portions of the judgment, in which case a partial release may be executed and acknowledged by the judgment creditor and filed. The lien of a judgment may also be terminated by an appeal taken from a money judgment and a stay bond filed. Upon an appeal from a judgment, a bond may be filed and must usually be double the amount named in the judgment. Finally, the lien may be terminated by granting of a new trial or the entry of an order of the court setting aside the judgment. Once the time for appeal has passed, the preceding orders will have the effect of terminating the judgment lien.

Execution

A writ of execution may be issued by a court at any time within 10 years of entry of a judgment, directing a sheriff or other officer appointed by the court to enforce a judgment against the property of a judgment debtor. It is the means of enforcement of the judgment obtained by the plaintiff in the legal action. When this judgment is a lien against the judgment debtor's real property, the writ of execution does not create a new lien but is merely the method of enforcing the judgment, and a sale under the judgment lien must be made during the statutory period of the judgment lien. However, where the judgment is not a lien upon the judgment debtor's real property, the execution is not only a method of enforcing the judgment but also creates a lien against the real property for up to one year from the date of its levy.

An execution is levied in the same manner as an attachment. It is recorded in the office of the county recorder and must contain a description of the real property against which it is levied. A similar notice is served upon the occupant of the property described, or if there is no occupant the notice is posted upon the property.

How discharged or released. A writ of execution may be discharged or released by *(a)* a sale of the property or a return of the writ wholly satisfied, *(b)* an order of the court vacating the

writ or a decree enjoining the enforcement of the writ of execution, *(c)* a satisfaction of the judgment or proceedings voiding the judgment, or *(d)* a release executed and recorded by the judgment creditor, his assignee or attorney, or by the court officer who levied the execution.

Execution or sheriff's sale. The issuance of a writ of execution will result in the sale of the real property of the judgment debtor in order to satisfy the judgment. Such a sale is known as an execution sale or a sheriff's sale. The property is sold at public auction, and the purchaser receives a certificate of sale from the officer of the court conducting the sale.

The law allows the judgment debtor a 12-month redemption period, and the debtor may remain in possession during this time. If the debtor does not redeem the property by paying back the purchase price and certain expenses incurred by the purchaser during the 12-month period, the officer of the court executes and delivers a deed to the buyer and the sale becomes final.

MECHANIC'S LIENS

Under California law, persons who furnish labor or materials for the construction or improvement of real property may file a lien upon the property affected if they are not compensated for their materials and/or services. The California Code of Civil Procedure specifies who may secure a mechanic's lien. Mechanics, materialmen, contractors, subcontractors, artisans, architects, machinists, builders, teamsters, and draymen are mentioned. However, the statute extends the right to all persons and laborers of every class who perform labor or bestow services or furnish materials or equipment that contribute to the construction, alteration, addition, or repair of any building or other structure or work of improvement upon the land. It includes grading and filling and landscaping of lots or tracts of land, as well as demolition and removal of buildings.

The work may have been done at the direction of the owner or of any other person acting by the authority of the owner. The statute states that every contractor, subcontractor, architect, builder, or other person in charge of the job is deemed to be an agent of the owner for purposes of the lien law. Charges for materials and services are usually paid when due, but if there is a default by the owner or contractor, the claimant must act promptly to exercise his lien rights. The following are the more important steps and procedures involved in connection with the filing of a mechanic's lien, termination of the lien, and preventive measures that may be taken by an owner so that he will not be responsible for work done and thus not subject to a lien.

Preliminary notice

A written preliminary notice should be given by the potential claimant to the owner, general contractor, or construction lender within 20 days of the first furnishing of labor, equipment, or material and must contain a statement that if all bills are not paid in full for the labor, equipment, or material furnished, the improved property may be subject to a mechanic's lien.

Commencement of work

The determination of when work commenced is an important factor. Fixing the exact time is crucial when questions of priority of claim arise, for instance between a mechanic's lien and a deed of trust. The California courts have generally held that work commences when materials are delivered and deposited upon the work site, when work is commenced upon the ground as in the digging for a foundation, or when work of any description is begun that everyone can readily observe and recognize.

Priority of mechanic's lien

A mechanic's lien generally has priority over any other lien, mortgage, deed of trust, or encumbrance that may have been attached to the real property subsequent to the time of commencement of work in connection with which the claimant has filed the mechanic's lien. The claimant may even have filed his mechanic's lien after a deed of trust has been recorded and the mechanic's lien will still have priority as long as it can be shown that work began before the recording of the deed of trust.

The holder of a mortgage or deed of trust may, however, file a bond with the county recorder and thus obtain priority over any lien claimants. The bond must be in an amount of not less than 75 percent of the principal amount of the mortgage or deed of trust, and its purpose is to assure payment of any judgment in suits that may be brought to foreclose mechanic's liens on the property. Where a mortgage or deed of trust in connection with a valid existing obligation is filed prior to commencement of work, the mortgage or deed of trust will take priority over any subsequent mechanic's liens that may be filed against the property.

Completion of work

Also important is the determination of the time when the work of improvement is completed. In establishing whether or not a given claim of lien has been filed within the proper time limit fixed by law, it is often necessary to be able to fix the time of completion to the exact day. Generally, any one of the following alternatives is recognized by the law as equivalent to completion:

a. Occupation or use by the owner or his agent, accompanied by cessation of labor thereon.
b. Acceptance by the owner or his agent of the work of improvement.
c. Cessation of labor thereon for a continuous period of 60 days.
d. Cessation of labor thereon for a continuous period of 30 days or more, if the owner files for record a prescribed notice of cessation.

Where a cessation of labor for the period described above is accepted by the owner or his agent as being equivalent to completion, a notice of cessation signed and verified by the owner or his agent may be filed in the office of the county recorder. If there has been a cessation of work for 60 days, all claimants have 90 days thereafter in which to file a lien. However, if the owner files a notice of cessation, an original contractor has 60 days and every other claimant 30 days in which to file a lien.

Notice of completion

Although cessation of work may be accepted as completion by an owner, the common situation that usually occurs is an actual completion of the work contracted for between the owner or his agent and the individual contractor responsible for doing the work. This will constitute the completion, and the owner will file a notice of completion rather than one of cessation of work. A notice of completion is shown in Figure 5–1.

When and by whom lien may be filed

A mechanic's lien may be filed by the original contractor within 60 days after a notice of completion has been filed. Any claimant, other than the

RECORDING REQUESTED BY

AND WHEN RECORDED MAIL TO

Name

Street
Address

City &
State

SPACE ABOVE THIS LINE FOR RECORDER'S USE

INDIVIDUAL FORM

Notice of Completion

Before execution, refer to title company requirements stated on reverse side.

TO 407 C

Notice is hereby given that:

1. The undersigned is owner of the interest or estate stated below in the property hereinafter described.
2. The full name of the undersigned is _____
3. The full address of the undersigned is _____
4. The nature of the title of the undersigned is: In fee. _____
   (If other than fee, strike "In fee" and insert, for example, "purchaser under contract of purchase," or "lessee".)
5. The full names and full addresses of all persons, if any, who hold title with the undersigned as joint tenants or as tenants in common are:

   NAMES   ADDRESSES

6. The names of the predecessors in interest of the undersigned, if the property was transferred subsequent to the commencement of the work of improvement herein referred to:

   NAMES   ADDRESSES

   (If no transfer made, insert "none".)

7. A work of improvement on the property hereinafter described was completed on _____
8. The name of the contractor, if any, for such work of improvement was _____

   (If no contractor for work of improvement as a whole, insert "none".)

9. The property on which said work of improvement was completed is in the City of _____
   _____, County of _____, State of California, and is described as follows:

10. The street address of said property is _____
    (If no street address has been officially assigned, insert "none".)

Dated: _____

Signature of
owner named
in paragraph 2 _____

(Also sign verification below at X)

STATE OF CALIFORNIA,
COUNTY OF_____ } SS.

The undersigned, being duly sworn, says: That __he is the owner of the aforesaid interest or estate in the property described in the foregoing notice; that __he has read the same, and knows the contents thereof, and that the facts stated therein are true.

SUBSCRIBED AND SWORN TO before me

Signature of
owner named
in paragraph 2 X_____

on _____

(Seal)

Signature_____

Name (Typed or Printed)
Notary Public in and for said State

DO NOT RECORD

Title Order No._____
Escrow or Loan No._____

FIGURE 5–1

original contractor, may file a mechanic's lien within 30 days after filing of a notice of completion. If a notice of completion is not recorded, then all persons have 90 days after completion of the work of improvement within which to file their claims of lien.

Effect and termination of the lien

A mechanic's lien is generally terminated by a voluntary release of the lien, usually as the result of payment of the debt. Even in the absence of such a release, the lien does not endure indefinitely. The law provides that a mechanic's lien will not bind any property for more than 90 days after filing of the lien or 90 days after the expiration of a credit, unless proper foreclosure proceedings are commenced by the claimant within that time.

Notice of nonresponsibility

An owner or any person having or claiming any interest in the real property may, within 10 days after obtaining knowledge or becoming aware of construction, alteration, or repair, give notice that he will not be responsible for the work being done. This notice is given by posting a notice of nonresponsibility in some conspicuous place on the property and recording a verified copy thereof. This notice must contain a description of the property, with the name and nature of title or interest of the person giving it and the name of the purchaser under the contract, if any, or the lessee, if known.

If such a notice is posted, the owner of the property or other interested person who recorded the notice will be protected against having his interest subjected to a mechanic's lien. A common situation is one in which a tenant or lessee orders work to be done upon the premises. If the tenant, for instance, has a painting contractor come in to paint the apartment and the owner of the building wants to make sure that he is not held responsible for payment, the owner would post and record the notice of nonresponsibility. In effect he would be telling the painting contractor that he can look only to the tenant for payment and will not later be able to file a mechanic's lien against the owner of the property in the event that he does not receive payment from the tenant. A discussion of maintenance and repairs by a tenant or lessee in relation to a mechanic's lien will be found in Chapter 10, Landlord and Tenant.

BANKRUPTCY

A bankruptcy proceeding is one initiated under the federal statutes whereby an insolvent debtor may be adjudged bankrupt by the court, which thereupon takes possession of his property and distributes the proceeds proportionately among his creditors. A voluntary bankruptcy occurs when a debtor files a petition for adjudication, an involuntary bankruptcy when the petition is filed by the requisite number of creditors.

An adjudication in bankruptcy brings the entire estate of the bankrupt owned by him at the date of filing the petition into the custody of the law. The purpose of the proceeding is to satisfy the claims of creditors and to permit the bankrupt to acquire new property free of such claims to the extent allowed by the Bankruptcy Act. Certain property may be exempt from such proceedings, such as that protected by the Homestead Law.

The title to all nonexempt property of the bankrupt is vested in a trustee, and it is the trustee's responsibility to turn these assets into cash and use this money, so far as it will go, to pay off creditors so much on each dollar owed by the bankrupt. Certain transfers made by the bankrupt within four months prior to bankruptcy, and certain fraudulent transfers made by and obligations incurred by the debtor within one year prior to the bankruptcy action, may be voided by the trustee and returned to the assets used to pay off the creditors. Outstanding valid liens on the property of the bankrupt are not affected by the bankruptcy proceeding, and title to the property passes to the trustee in bankruptcy subject to such liens.

When the bankruptcy proceedings are completed a discharge in bankruptcy results. With certain exceptions, such as tax liens, discharge in bankruptcy releases a bankrupt from all of his debts whether allowable in full or in part.

TAXES AND SPECIAL ASSESSMENTS

Land as the basis of taxation first drew the attention of a tax assessor in England some 600 years ago with regard to the assumption that taxes should be assessed in accordance with an individual's ability to pay. At that time the extent and quality of a man's agricultural holdings were a dependable index of his ability to pay taxes, as his income then was derived almost entirely from agricultural products. It followed, therefore, that land which an individual owned became a surface guide for determining the amount of tax levied. Another reason for the taxation of land is that it is so easily assessable and cannot be concealed from the taxing authorities.

Real property is thus assessed and taxed in order to obtain revenues for the support of governmental functions. In addition to the general taxes levied against real property on an annual basis, there are various types of special assessments that may be levied as the need arises. A thorough treatment of the subject of taxation of real estate will be found in Chapter 16.

TRUST DEEDS AND MORTGAGES

In most purchases of real property, the buyer must borrow a certain amount of money in order to effect the purchase. The lender will require some security for payment of the loan, and this is usually done by creating a lien against the property being purchased. Either a mortgage or a deed of trust may be used in order to create this lien. The result is that the property stands as security for repayment of the monies borrowed.

The mortgage is an instrument by which property is given as security for the repayment of a debt or obligation. In the event that the borrower defaults on his payments, that is, he is unable to make the payments, the mortgage may be foreclosed and such procedure is established and regulated by statute.

The deed of trust, or trust deed as it is commonly called, has virtually replaced the use of the mortgage in California. Under the trust deed, the borrower conveys title to a third person, called a trustee. Should the borrower default in his payments, the trustee has the right to act for the benefit of the lender and effect a sale of the property.

A thorough discussion of these instruments, as well as the promissory note, will be found in Chapter 12, which deals with instruments of real estate finance.

EASEMENTS

An easement is an interest that one person has in the land of another that gives him a right to use and enjoy that land, or a portion thereof, within certain definable limits. Easements are generally classified as (a) easements appurtenant, and (b) easements in gross.

Easements appurtenant

The term *appurtenant* means "belonging to," and thus an easement appurtenant belongs to the land receiving the benefit of the easement and cannot be separated from it; it is said to "run with the land." Where an easement appurtenant exists, there are two separate parcels of land under separate ownership. The parcel of land receiving the benefit of the easement is known as the "dominant tenement," and the parcel of land being used or enjoyed and over which the easement runs is known as the "servient tenement."

An easement appurtenant, even though not specifically mentioned in an instrument transferring title to the land that is the dominant tenement, passes automatically with the land. It may not be conveyed separately and apart from the land that it benefits.

The following is an example of an easement appurtenant: A owns 10 acres of land, a portion of which fronts upon a county road. A sells B a 2-acre portion of this land, the parcel sold being set back quite a distance from the road. In the deed conveying title, A grants B the right to cross over a certain portion of his land in order to gain entrance to, and exit from, the portion that B has purchased. The right created is an easement appurtenant to B's land, which is the dominant tenement, and gives B the right to cross over A's land, which is the servient tenement.

Easement in gross

It is possible to have an easement that is not appurtenant to a particular parcel of land. Thus A, who owns no land, may have a right of way over B's land. This is a personal interest that does not attach to any dominant tenement and must thus be expressly transferred. An easement in gross, like all easements, may not be revoked at the will of the owner of the servient estate. An example of an easement in gross would be the right given to a public utility company to erect poles and string wires over private lands, or the right given to a city to run sewer or water lines through private property.

Our discussion thus far has defined certain characteristics of easements, namely that they (a) are nonpossessory interests in land with a limited use or enjoyment, (b) may be created by a legal conveyance, (c) as interests in land are subject to the laws governing real property, (d) are interests that one person has in the land of another, and *(e)* are not revocable at will by the owner of the servient estate, although later in this chapter we shall discuss transfer and termination of easements.

Creation of easements

The Civil Code lists a number of reasons for which easements (or land burdens or servitudes, as they are also known) may be created, such as rights-of-way; rights of taking water, wood, minerals, and other things; right of transacting business or sports upon the land; right of receiving air, light, or heat from overland, or discharging the same upon or over land; right of receiving water from or discharging the same upon land; right of receiving more than natural support from adjacent land; right of flooding land; and right of using a wall as a party wall.

Easements, when attached to a dominant tenement, are considered appurtenant thereto and automatically pass upon transfer of the dominant tenement. Purchasers of a servient tenement usually take it subject to the easement, either because the easement is recorded or because it is apparent on the ground.

Easements are created in various ways and may arise by *(a)* express grant or reservation, *(b)* implied grant or reservation, *(c)* necessity, *(d)* estoppel, *(e)* condemnation, *(f)* dedication, *(g)* reference to maps, and *(h)* prescription.

Express grant or reservation. An easement may be given by an agreement or contract between the parties involved, or by an express grant or reservation contained in a deed. It must be remembered that an easement is an interest in land, and the instrument used should either be a deed or contain all of the requisites of a deed. It should be in writing, adequately describe the easement and its purpose and the land involved and subject to the easement, and identify the parties, and it should be executed and acknowledged by the grantor and delivered to the grantee. The example given previously of an easement appurtenant wherein A granted to B the right to cross over his land to reach the county road is an example of an easement by express grant, since the easement was created in a deed from A to B.

An easement by express reservation occurs when one conveys land but reserves an easement in the land conveyed. Example: A owns lots 1 and 2. He sells lot 2 to B but wants to continue using a road that crosses a portion of the lot. A's deed to B, conveying title to lot 2, will contain a clause stating that he reserves the right to use the road crossing over lot 2. A will thus have created an easement by reservation. The easement will be appurtenant to lot 1, the dominant tenement that receives the benefit of the easement, and lot 2 will be the survient tenement.

Implied grant or reservation. Quite often a piece of property may be conveyed with no mention at all of easements, and yet an easement will have been created by implied grant or reservation. Example: A purchases 10 acres of a 20-acre tract owned by B. At the time A inspected the property prior to purchase, it was evident that to reach the 10 acres he wished to purchase, A would have to use the existing road which ran through the property to be retained by B. A reasonably assumes that he will have the right to use the road and at the time of the sale does not question the fact that the deed prepared by B makes no mention of an easement.

In this situation, while it would have been better for an easement to be mentioned in the deed conveying the land from B to A, it makes no difference, for A has acquired an implied easement because of the circumstances. When an owner sells a portion of his land, or one of a number of adjacent lots that he owns, and there is an existing use that would constitute an easement if the portions were owned by different individuals, then, upon the sale of one of these parcels of land, an implied easement is created if there is none expressly granted.

Certain general conditions must usually exist for the creation of an implied easement: *(a)* the use in question must be reasonably obvious and apparent, for instance a road or other right of way (underground pipes or sewers are also included); *(b)* the use must have been in existence for a sufficient period of time to consider it permanent; *(c)* there must be separate ownership, that is, the parcels of land involved must become separately owned—an easement is a right obtained with regard to the property of another; and *(d)* the use must be a necessary one, beneficial to the land for which it is used. If the only way of reasonably obtaining water is through pipes that pass over adjacent land, this will be considered a necessary use. The same is true of a single road that provides the only means of leaving or entering the property, and interestingly enough, there may also be an implied right of entry, as with a conveyance of mineral rights to an individual that carries with it the implied right to enter upon the land to remove such minerals.

An easement by reservation occurs when an owner sells a portion of his property and retains a portion that will require an easement. Instead of conveying the right to minerals beneath his land, let us assume that an owner sells the land but reserves the mineral rights to himself and makes no mention of an easement. In this case, the former owner will be considered to have obtained an easement by reservation to allow him to remove the minerals. Another example would be that of an owner of a parcel of land who sells a portion of it and retains the rest. The only way to reach the highway from the land he has retained is over a small road that passes through a portion of the property that he sold. If the conditions mentioned previously for the creation of an implied easement exist, an easement by implied reservation arises in favor of the owner, who may then use the road that runs to the highway.

Necessity. An easement of necessity, unlike an implied easement, arises by operation of law and does not depend upon the existence of a prior use. The usual situation in which an easement of necessity is created occurs when a grantor conveys a portion of his land to a grantee, and the portion conveyed is completely surrounded by the land of the grantor and thus is landlocked. No road was in existence at the time of conveyance that might have led to an implied easement, and the grantee finds that he is truly landlocked and has no access to his property except over the land of the grantor. If such is the case, the grantee will have an easement over the land of the grantor by virtue of necessity. The easement will continue for as long as the necessity exists. If the grantee subsequently acquires an adjacent parcel of land that allows him access to a road, or if he enters into an agreement for an easement with another adjoining property owner, the easement originally acquired by necessity will cease. An easement by necessity may only be obtained by a grantee over the land of a grantor.

Estoppel. An easement by estoppel may be created when a property owner tells a prospective purchaser that certain easements exist for the benefit of the land offered for sale, and yet these easements are not mentioned in the actual conveyance of the property. The owner may describe certain roads or streets, or a driveway, all of which belong to the owner, and lead the purchaser to believe that he will have the use of them in con-

nection with his purchase and ownership of the property. Where such representations are made, and the purchaser buys the property acting upon them, the owner will later be estopped from denying such representations and the buyer will have obtained the right to these easements by estoppel.

Condemnation. Federal, state, or local government may acquire fee title to real property by condemnation under the power of eminent domain. This is often done in certain situations, for instance the taking of private property for freeway construction. Condemnation may also be employed to obtain easements rights for such purposes as a street, highway, telephone line, electric power line, or railroad right-of-way.

Dedication. A common situation in which an easement is created by dedication occurs when a developer or subdivider sets aside certain areas of land for public use. When a subdivision map that is recorded and accepted shows a parcel of land set aside as a park or playground, or certain streets, roads, or common-use areas, then these easements are created by dedication and are said to be statutory easements.

A common-law dedication may be created when an owner of land indicates by his acts or words that he wishes the public to be allowed the use of certain areas and the public in effect does so use them. A dedication is often defined as an appropriation of land for some public use that is accepted for such use by authorized public officials or the public.

Reference to maps. A good deal of land is sold by individuals engaged in land sales to buyers who are merely referred to a map or other descriptive literature concerning the property. Where the map shown to the buyer contains a diagram not only of the actual lots but also of areas within the tract that are designated as streets, avenues, roads, or the like, then, upon purchasing a parcel of land shown on the map, the buyer automatically acquires an easement to pass over the streets, avenues, and roads shown on the map. This right is acquired even though the deed does not specifically mention such easements.

Prescription. An easement by prescription and title acquired by adverse possession were discussed in detail in Chapter 3. It should be recalled that if an individual occupies the land of another openly and notoriously for a period of five years, pays the taxes on the property, and satisfies certain other requirements, the adverse possessor may ultimately acquire the title to such property. If he satisfies all of the requirements with the exception of paying the taxes on the property, he can acquire only an easement by prescription rather than the title.

Use and enjoyment of easements

The use of the term *profits* may be encountered in connection with a discussion of easements. While an easement is said to be the right to use and enjoy land, a profit is the right to take something from the land of another, such as water, timber, or minerals. The California code does not make a distinction here, but puts these together in listing what it terms as servitudes upon the land. These were mentioned previously in discussing creation of easements. It is thus important that in the creation of an easement, wherever possible an attempt be made to define clearly the purposes and uses to be contained in the easement. It is, of course, easier to accomplish this purpose in an easement that has been expressly created than in one created by implication.

An easement appurtenant may be used for the benefit of the dominant tenement only, and not for the benefit of any other parcel of land without the permission of the owner of the servient tenement. If the owner of the dominant tenement acquires additional land after the creation of the easement, such land does not have the right to the use of the easement unless agreed to by the owner of the servient tenement. If the owner of the dominant tenement knows at the time an easement is acquired that he may later acquire additional land that will need the benefit of the easement, such a provision can be incorporated into the instrument creating the easement.

The owner of the servient tenement, in the case of an easement of ingress and egress, has the right to use the portion of the road on his property as long as he does not interfere with the right of the owner of the dominant tenement to use it. When an easement right for a road across land is initially granted, certain restrictions may be contained in the instrument creating the easement. It may be established exclusively for the use of the owner of the servient tenement to later allow another individual to have easement rights over a portion of that part of the road that is on his land. When a road is used by both the landowner and the holder of the easement right, in equal proportions, they must usually share the cost of maintenance and repair that may be necessary. If only the owner of the dominant tenement uses the easement, he has the right to keep it in a reasonably usable condition. Also, if an easement for ingress and egress was originally created by grant, it can be used for all reasonable purposes, and is not restricted only to those that were reasonable at the time the grant was made. However, if the easement was acquired by prescription, its use is limited to that which was in effect when it was acquired.

Transfer of an easement

Easements appurtenant generally pass along with a conveyance of the land that it benefits. Therefore, when the dominant tenement is conveyed, the easement will pass with the land even though it may not be mentioned in the instrument of conveyance. Generally, however, the easement will be mentioned in the deed, agreement of sale, or other instrument used. The servient tenement is the one that is subject to the easement, and if the easement has been recorded, the grantee in a conveyance of the servient tenement will be deemed to have constructive notice of the easement and will acquire title to the land subject to the easement. It is important that the purchaser have actual or constructive notice. If the easement is unrecorded and a purchaser for value after inspecting the property would have no reason to assume that an easement exists, he may then take title without being subject to the easement.

If an easement in gross is transferred, the courts have held that it may not be so apportioned as to increase the burden on the servient tenement. The same basis applies with regard to an easement appurtenant, in that the dominant tenement cannot be divided or partitioned in such a way as to increase the burden of the land that is subject to the easement.

Termination of easements

There are a number of ways in which an easement may be terminated or extinguished. They are as follows.

Express release. Since an easement can be created by a written instrument, it can also be extinguished and terminated by a conveyance. This would occur where the easement holder, usually by the use of a quitclaim deed, releases his right to the easement to the owner of the servient tenement.

Merger of servient and dominant tenement. When the servient and dominant become merged into one ownership, the easement will cease to exist because the same individual now owns both parcels of land and an owner cannot have an easement in his own land since, by virtue of his ownership, he possesses the right to use the land. Merger often occurs when the owner of the servient tenement purchases the land belonging to the easement holder, or the easement holder purchases the parcel consisting of the servient tenement.

Termination of time limit or purpose. Where an easement has been created for a particular time limit, the easement will terminate at the end of the term for which it was established. An easement will also cease to exist if it was created for a particular purpose and the purpose ceases. An example was previously given of the purchaser of a landlocked parcel of land who could acquire an easement by necessity. If at some later date the county constructs a new road that touches upon this land and thus allows the owner a new means of ingress and egress, the purpose for which the easement by necessity was created will have ceased to exist and the easement will be terminated.

Abandonment or nonuse. An easement may be extinguished by abandonment if there is a clear intent on the part of the easement holder, as evidenced by his actions, to abandon the easement. For instance, where a railroad right-of-way exists and the company removes the rails and ties and discontinues the use, this would indicate an intention to abandon the easement. An easement created by grant or agreement cannot be terminated, because it is not used for a period of time, but an easement obtained by prescription will terminate if the easement is not used for the same amount of time as that which was required to create it.

Misuse or excessive use. Where an easement holder misuses the easement or uses it to an unreasonable excess, the general remedy is the obtaining of a court injunction against the continuance of such use. In certain cases, however, the courts have found that where an easement holder increases the burden of the servient tenement greatly and refuses to change this condition, the court will order a forfeiture of the easement and it will be thus terminated.

Destruction of the servient tenement. Where there is a destruction of the servient tenement, an easement may be extinguished. Such occurrences have to do with an easement involving a building when such building is subsequently destroyed.

Eminent domain and adverse possession. When a local, state, or federal government exercises the power of eminent domain over a parcel of land, this may also serve to terminate any easements that were in existence on the land acquired. In the same way that an easement by prescription can be created by adverse possession, it can also be extinguished by adverse possession. This is usually done by the owner of the servient tenement. An example would be when such an owner erects a fence across an easement road on his property and the easement holder, who owns the dominant tenement, takes no action to stop this condition for the length of the statutory prescriptive period, which is five years in California.

HOMESTEADS

In California a homestead consists of the family dwelling house, together with outbuildings, and the land on which they are situated. The dwelling may be in a condominium, planned development, stock cooperative, or community apartment project. When a declaration of a homestead has been filed in the county recorder's office by the claimant, in compliance with statutory regulations and requirements, the property becomes a homestead and is protected up to a specified amount against creditors. The homestead is protected from execution and forced sale except as otherwise provided by statute, and it remains so until conveyed or abandoned by a recorded instrument of abandonment.

The homestead discussed here is not to be confused with the term applying to filings on federal lands, whereby an individual acquires title to acreage by establishing residence or making improvements upon the land. The declaration of homestead, as considered here, applies to a special provision of the California law that permits a homeowner to protect his home from sale to satisfy his debts within certain limitations. Figure 5–2 illustrates a Declaration of Homestead.

Who may claim a homestead exemption

A homestead may be selected and claimed by (a) the head of the family, the homestead claim not to exceed $45,000 in actual cash value over and above all liens and encumbrances on the property at the time of any levy of execution; (b) by any person 65 years of age or over, the value of the homestead claim not exceeding $45,000 in actual cash value over and above all liens and

DECLARATION OF HOMESTEAD

(JOINT DECLARATION OF HUSBAND AND WIFE)

———◆———

_____ and _____
(Name of Husband)   (Name of Wife)

do severally certify and declare as follows:

(1) They are husband and wife.

(2) _____ is the head of a family, consisting of himself and wife
(Name of Husband)

and_____   _____

(3) They are now residing on the land and premises located in the City of_____

County of_____, State of California, and more particularly described as follows:

(4) They claim the land and premises hereinabove described together with the dwelling house thereon, and its appurtenances, as a Homestead.

(5) No former declaration of homestead has been made by them, or by either of them, except as follows:[1]

(6) The character of said property so sought to be homesteaded, and the improvements thereon may generally be described as follows:[2]

IN WITNESS WHEREOF, they have hereunto set their hands this_____day of _____, 19_____.

_____
(Husband)

Footnotes 1 and 2: See Reverse Side.

_____
(Wife)

STATE OF CALIFORNIA } ss.	STATE OF CALIFORNIA } ss.

STATE OF CALIFORNIA   } ss.

COUNTY OF_____

On_____, 19_____
before me, the undersigned, a Notary Public in and for said State,
personally appeared_____

_____

and_____

_____

known to me to be the persons whose names are subscribed to the within instrument, and severally acknowledged to me that they executed the same.

Witness my hand and official seal.

_____
Notary Public in and for said State.

STATE OF CALIFORNIA   } ss.

COUNTY OF_____

and_____
husband and wife, each, being first duly sworn, deposes and says:
That he/she is one of the declarants in the foregoing declaration of homestead; that he/she has read the foregoing declaration and knows the contents thereof. and that the matters therein stated are true of his/her own knowledge.

_____
(Husband)

_____
(Wife)

Subscribed and Sworn to before me on

_____, 19_____

_____
Notary Public in and for said State.

FIGURE 5–2

encumbrances; and *(c)* any other person, the value of the homestead not to exceed $30,000 in actual cash value over and above all liens and encumbrances. The dollar amount of homestead exemption applies to the homeowner's equity in the property, which is the difference between all liens having priority over the homestead and the market value of the property.

The law provides that the head of a family may be: either the husband or wife, when the claimant is a married person; the family includes every person who has been residing on the premises with either of them, and under their care and maintenance, *(a)* his or her minor child or minor grandchild or the minor child of his or her deceased wife or husband, *(b)* a minor brother or sister or a minor child of a deceased brother or sister, *(c)* a father, mother, grandfather, or grandmother either of himself or herself or of a deceased husband or wife, *(d)* an unmarried sister, or *(e)* any other relatives above-mentioned who have reached majority and are unable to take care of or support themselves.

Method of selection and property selected

The husband or any head of a family as above set forth, or the wife in case the husband has not made such selection, or any person other than the head of a family, must execute and acknowledge a declaration of homestead in the same manner as a grant deed of real property as acknowledged, and must record the same in the office of the recorder of the county in which the land is situated. If the land lies partly in two counties, then a duplicate of the declaration of homestead must be filed in each county. The date of recording the declaration is ineffective until it is recorded.

If the claimant of a homestead is married, the homestead may be selected from the community property or the separate property of the husband, or it may be selected from the property held by husband and wife as tenants in common or in joint tenancy, or from the separate property of the wife if she consents by making or joining in making the declaration of homestead. When the claimant is not married but is the head of a family as described earlier, the homestead may be selected from any of his or her property. If the claimant is an unmarried person other than the head of a family, the homestead may be selected from any of his or her property. Property includes any freehold title, interest, or estate that vests in the claim-

ant an immediate although not necessarily exclusive right of possession.

Requirements for valid declaration

There are certain requirements that are essential in the declaration of a homestead. All of these requirements must be observed, and the omission of any renders the homestead void. These requirements are:

1. A statement showing that the claimant is the head of a family, if such is the case; or, when the declaration is made by the wife, a statement that the husband has not made such declaration and that she, therefore, makes it for their joint benefit.
2. If the claimant is married, the name of the other spouse.
3. A statement that the claimant is residing on the premises and claims them as a homestead.
4. A description of the premises as would be valid in a deed.
5. An estimate of their actual cash value.

Even though the declaration may be sufficient in that it conforms to the statutory requirements, the homestead may be invalid in fact because the statements contained in the declaration are not true. From the records alone, the validity of a homestead cannot be finally determined. It is therefore necessary to obtain a judicial determination as to the truth of the statements contained in the declaration of an attaching or judgment creditor. An individual may have only one valid homestead at any particular time.

A valid homestead will defeat the following:

1. A money judgment which becomes a lien after the declaration of homestead has been recorded, and those state tax liens having the effect of a money judgment.
2. Attachments which have become liens subsequent to the recordation of the declaration of homestead.
3. Prior unrecorded mortgages and trust deeds, and in most cases subsequent mortgages and trust deeds not executed and acknowledged by both husband and wife as required by law.
4. An execution, provided that the declaration of homestead was recorded prior to the sale on execution and the judgment does not constitute a valid lien on the homestead.

A valid homestead will not defeat the following:

1. Judgments that became liens prior to the time the declaration of homestead was recorded.

2. Liens of mechanics, contractors, subcontractors, laborers, materialmen, artisans, architects, builders, or vendors upon the premises.
3. Mortgages and trust deeds executed and acknowledged by husband and wife or by an unmarried claimant.
4. Mortgages and trust deeds recorded before the declaration of homestead was recorded.
5. Federal tax liens.

When a valid execution for the enforcement of a judgment is levied upon the homestead, the judgment creditor may at any time within 60 days thereafter apply to the superior court of the county in which the homestead is situated for appointment of appraisers if he believes that the property homesteaded exceeds in value the homestead exemption plus the aggregate of all liens and encumbrances thereon. If the petition of the creditor satisfies the statutory requirements, the superior court judge will appoint appraisers who will report to the court the value of the homesteaded property, the amount of the liens and encumbrances, and their determination upon the matter of a division of the land claimed. If a division of the land is feasible, so much of the land, including the residence and outbuildings, as will amount in value to the homestead exemption over and above all liens and encumbrances is set off for the homestead claimant, and the execution may be enforced against the remainder of the land.

If it is impractical to divide the land and it appears that the land claimed as homestead exceeds in value, over and above all liens and encumbrances, the amount of the homestead exemption, the judge will make an order directing its sale under the execution. At such sale, no bid shall be received unless it exceeds the amount of the homestead exemption plus the aggregate amount of all liens and encumbrances on the property.

If the sale is made, the proceeds must be divided in the following order:

1. To the discharge of all liens and encumbrances, if any, on the property.
2. To the homestead claim and to the amount of the homestead exemption.

If the homestead is sold by the owner, the proceeds arising from such sale to the extent of the value allowed for his homestead exemption are exempt to such owner for a period of six months following the sale. This permits the owner to reinvest in another dwelling and declare a homestead thereon.

Termination of homestead

A declaration of homestead is usually terminated by *(a)* a sale of the homestead that results in a conveyance of the property, and *(b)* recordation of a declaration of abandonment. Where the homestead is for the benefit of a husband and wife, they must jointly execute the declaration of abandonment or the conveyance. If they do not jointly execute, they may each individually do so by separate instruments. The declaration of abandonment, or grant in the event of a conveyance, must be recorded, and becomes effective only upon recordation. A married person's separate homestead may be abandoned or conveyed by the individual claimant alone.

In the event of dissolution of marriage, a property settlement between the husband and wife may abandon the homestead, or by agreement it may be assigned to one of the parties. A homestead is not terminated by removal from the premises, a deed that is in fact a mortgage except as to innocent third parties who rely on the records, a transfer without consideration followed by a transfer, or a reconveyance to one of the spouses under a trust deed. Where a homestead had not been previously recorded, a probate court has the authority to select certain property from an estate and establish a probate homestead for the benefit of the surviving spouse, minor children, or both. The court may also be called upon to make certain decisions regarding a homestead upon the expiration or declared incompetence of one of the parties to a homestead.

COVENANTS, CONDITIONS, AND RESTRICTIONS

A common type of encumbrance is the restrictive covenant, which is a general term used to describe covenants, conditions, and restrictions that affect the use of land and are generally contained in deeds or other instruments. These restrictions are created by private owners, typically by appropriate clauses in deeds, or in agreements, or in general plans of entire subdivisions.

Method of creation

Restrictions usually assume the form of a covenant, or promise to do or not to do a certain thing. If breached, the remedy is an action for dollar damages, although a court of equity may often grant an injunction compelling compliance. Infrequently, a restriction may assume the form of a condition subsequent, but conditions subsequent may involve a reversion of title to the creator of the condition in case of breach. Because they may result in such forfeiture, the courts generally construe such conditions as covenants. To be enforceable, conditions must be clearly spelled out as such, and the person whose property is affected must have actual or constructive notice. Recordation is normally utilized, and this would, of course, give constructive notice.

Restrictions imposed by deeds, or in similar private contracts, may be drafted to restrict, for any legitimate purpose, the use or occupancy of land. The right to acquire and possess property includes the right to dispose of it or any part of it, and to impose upon the grant any reservations or conditions the grantor may deem proper, the only limitation being that the right not be exercised in a manner forbidden by law. Race restrictions, for example, are forbidden by law.

Restrictive subjects

Restrictions may validly cover a multitude of matters, including use for residential or business purposes; character of buildings, such as single-family or multiple units; cost or size of buildings, such as a provision that houses must cost more than $200,000 or contain a certain number of square feet; location of buildings, such as side lines of 10 feet and 20-foot setbacks; and even requirements for architectural approval of proposed homes or other buildings by a local group established for that purpose.

In contrast to zoning ordinances, private restrictions need not be promotive only of public health or general public welfare, but may be intended to create a particular type of neighborhood deemed desirable by the tract owner, and may be based solely on aesthetic conditions. The most common use of restrictions today is in new subdivisions. The original subdivider establishes uniform regulations as to occupancy, use, character, cost, and locations of buildings. He records a "declaration of restrictions" when the subdivision is first created. All original deeds contain a reference to the declaration. Thereafter, all lot owners, as among themselves, may enforce the restrictions against any one or all of the others. In some cases, when the land is originally subdivided, arrangement is made in the nature of a covenant whereby a perpetual property owners' association is formed. The association is governed by rules and regulations set forth in an agreement signed by all new lot purchasers. Such associations

are often given the power to amend tract restrictions from time to time to correspond with community growth. They may have the power to revise building restrictions pertaining to certain blocks of lots in the development, impose architectural restrictions, and make other authorized requirements and changes.

Term of restrictions

Restrictions may be originally established with the provision that they run for a certain number of years, at which time they are automatically extended for successive periods of time unless it is decided by a vote of a majority of the property owners to make a change in the restrictions as to content or term. Another method is to establish restrictions that either have a fixed termination date or a restriction that becomes effective upon recordation of a cancellation notice by a given percentage of the property owners.

Courts, under unusual circumstances, may sometimes refuse to enforce otherwise valid restrictions; for instance where the complainant himself has violated them, or where there has been a very material change over the years in the character or condition of the area.

Unless the language used in the deed indicates definitely that the grantor intended the conditions or restrictions to operate for the benefit of other lots or persons, the restrictions run to the grantor only, and a quitclaim deed from him or his heirs or assigns is a sufficient release. However, if the language used in the deed indicates definitely that the grantor intended the conditions or restrictions for the benefit of adjoining owners or, as is usually the case, for all of the lots and owners in the tract, then quitclaim deeds must be obtained from all owners of property having the benefit thereof, as well as from the grantor or his heirs or assigns, in order to release them.

Race restrictions

On May 3, 1948, the United States Supreme Court held that racially restrictive covenants could not be enforced in equity against black purchasers because such enforcement would constitute state action denying equal protection of the laws to blacks, in violation of the fourteenth amendment to the federal constitution. Later in the same month, the California Supreme Court referred to this decision and reversed the decisions of the several trial courts in the cases then before it that had undertaken to enforce such restrictive covenants.

In 1950 the insurance by the Federal Housing Administration or by the Veterans Administration of loans secured by mortgages or trust deeds was made subject to regulations designed to discourage the practice of restricting real property against sale or occupancy on the ground of race, color, or creed. In 1953 the United States Supreme Court held that a restrictive covenant could not be enforced at law by a suit for damages against a cocovenanter who broke the covenant.

Prior to 1948, California law provided that a provision in a deed against sale, lease, or rental of property to persons of an indicated race was regarded as a restraint on alienation and, therefore, invalid. However, a restriction on the use or occupancy of property by persons of an indicated race was recognized as valid. In 1961 the California legislature added Section 782 to the Civil Code to provide that any provision in any deed of real property in California, whether executed before or after the effective date of the section, that purports to restrict the right of any person to sell, lease, rent, use, or occupy the property to persons of a particular racial or ethnic group is not actionable at law and is void. Thus, race restrictions contained in any instruments of record are now void, while all the other restrictions remain valid.

ENCROACHMENTS AND PARTY WALLS

A portion of a building, a wall, or a fence that extends over a recognized boundary line onto the land of another is known as an encroachment. Adjoining owners of real property often find themselves involved with the real estate law because of encroachments. An encroachment may constitute a trespass or a nuisance, and relief is obtainable through an action at law.

The party encroaching on his neighbor may be doing so with legal justification, since he may have acquired an easement by implication or prescription, or he may have gained title to the encroached-upon land by adverse possession. If, however, the encroachment is wrongful, the party encroached upon may sue for damages and require removal of the encroaching structure. If the encroachment is only a few inches over the property boundary line, the cost of removal great, and the cause due to an excusable mistake, the courts will not usually require removal but may award dollar damages.

A party wall is one that is common to two buildings, usually straddles the boundary line between two adjoining pieces of land, and was erected by a builder in order to save the expense of building two separate walls for row-type buildings that adjoin each other. Each of the adjoining property owners generally owns the half of the wall resting on his land and has an easement for support as regards the other half. The use, care, and maintenance of the wall will usually be governed by what is known as a party-wall agreement. Such agreements generally provide that each owner is to have the use of the wall for support, or to contain a flue, electrical wiring, or a fireplace; and further, one owner cannot alter the wall in such a way as to deny the aforementioned uses to the other, unless there is agreement by both parties.

BUILDING CODES AND ZONING LAWS

Restrictions upon the use of land may be imposed by governmental regulation as well as by private contracts or agreements, and the governing authority of a city or county has the power to adopt building codes and zoning ordinances. These provide for regulation of basic construction, plumbing, heating, and electrical systems, and of health and safety factors in connection with improvements upon land. Such restrictions must be substantially related to the preservation or protection of public health, safety, morals, or general welfare. They must be uniform in operation for the general public, and cannot be discriminatory nor be created for the benefit of any particular group. Public authorities may enjoin or abate improvements or alterations that are in violation of such codes and ordinances. Chapter 18, Government Controls, will discuss these items further.

TITLE POLICY DISCLOSURES

Liens and encumbrances of record are shown in a title insurance policy. The policy illustrated in Chapter 15 shows liens and encumbrances for the specific property insured in connection with taxes, easements granted to utility companies, declaration of restrictions, and deed of trust.

QUESTIONS FOR DISCUSSION

1. What is the purpose of an attachment of real property?
2. What type of property may be exempt from attachment or execution?

62

3. Does a judgment automatically create a lien against real property?

4. How may a writ of execution be discharged?

5. Discuss the circumstances under which certain individuals may file a mechanic's lien.

6. What is the difference between a notice of cessation and a notice of completion?

7. How may an owner of real property use a notice of nonresponsibility for protection?

8. What types of debts are not released by a discharge in bankruptcy?

9. What is the difference between an easement appurtenant and an easement in gross?

10. What are some common reasons for the creation of easements?

11. What conditions must exist for an easement by implication to arise?

12. How might an easement be created by estoppel?

13. Discuss the methods by which an easement may be terminated.

14. Discuss what a valid homestead may and may not protect a homeowner against.

15. In what way may private restrictions be beneficial to the property involved?

MULTIPLE CHOICE QUESTIONS

5-1. An encumbrance that makes property security with respect to payment of a debt is: (a) a zoning law, (b) an easement, (c) a lien, (d) a homestead.

5-2. The right given a utility company to string wires across a number of private properties is an (a) easement appurtenant, (b) easement in gross, (c) encroachment, (d) appurtenant reservation.

5-3. The issuance of a writ of execution may result in: (a) an increase in property tax assessment, (b) the filing of a writ of attachment, (c) a sheriff's sale, (d) a mechanic's lien.

5-4. A homestead most often protects against a: (a) tax lien, (b) zoning restriction, (c) party-wall encroachment, (d) judgment.

5-5. Bankruptcy proceedings are regulated by: (a) state laws, (b) real estate law, (c) federal statutes, (d) none of these.

5-6. An example of an encroachment is a: (a) local building code, (b) portion of a building extending onto the property of an adjoining owner, (c) party-wall agreement, (d) restrictive covenant.

5-7. The owner of a dominant tenement: (a) must hold title as a tenant in common, (b) receives the benefits of an easement, (c) receives a preferential tenement tax rate, (d) acquires an easement by necessity.

5-8. Which of the following is a method of removing an easement from the records: (a) obtain a court attachment and deliver it to easement owner, (b) file a bankruptcy petition, (c) record a quitclaim deed signed by the easement owner, (d) record a note secured by a deed of trust.

6 Rights and duties accompanying ownership

Although California inherited from Spain and Mexico certain laws governing real property, the basic principles now employed were derived from the Common Law of England. The term *property* is generally used to indicate the physical aspect of real estate, but in the technical and historical legal sense, property refers to the rights and interests that the owner has in the thing owned. This "bundle of rights" concept applies to the ownership of both real and personal property, but we shall here be concerned only with real property. These rights include *(a)* possession and control, *(b)* use and enjoyment, and *(c)* disposition, all subject, of course, to compliance with applicable laws.

POSSESSION AND CONTROL

Ownership brings with it the right to possession and control of the property owned. The owner has the absolute right of possession and may exclude others from entering upon his property. No one has the right to enter upon his land without his permission, and if they do, they may be liable to the owner for damages because of their trespass. An owner may, of course, give some of the rights he has to others by agreement.

While the ownership interest remains with the owner, he may give a possessory interest to another, as in the case of a lease to a lessee; or he may give a security interest in the property to a lender by borrowing funds and placing the property as security for repayment of the loan.

USE AND ENJOYMENT

Another of the inherent rights of ownership is that of use and enjoyment. As long as the owner conforms to laws regulating use and enjoyment such as zoning regulations, building codes, and the like, he is in a position of being able to do as he wishes. The owner may improve vacant land by constructing buildings thereon, he may remove existing structures and replace them with others, he may plant trees and shrubs or grow and harvest certain crops, or if he wishes, the owner may leave the land in the same condition as when he acquired it. In addition to benefits accruing to the owner from his own use of the real property he owns, he may also receive profits and rents from tenants and others for allowing them the use of the property.

RIGHT OF DISPOSITION

The right of disposition as an owner wishes is another fundamental right. An owner may keep his property or he may transfer it as the result of a sale, he may dispose of it by will, by making a gift of it to another, or he may create a life estate in the property for the benefit of a particular individual. If he makes no provision for disposition, the property will pass to his heirs by the rules of intestate succession. While the owner is usually free to dispose of his property in any manner he wishes, the law requires that whatever instrument may be used in connection with the disposition conform to certain legal requirements regarding its preparation and execution.

RESPONSIBILITIES TO OTHERS

As the reader has already noted in previous chapters and will discover in many of the subsequent chapters, the study of real estate principles is to a very great extent a study of the "bundle of rights" described above. In the remainder of this chapter, we will discuss some of the responsibilities which an owner of real property has to adjoining landowners and other persons who may come upon his land.

Water

The responsibilities of a landowner with regard to water may be divided between water originating on or solely within the boundaries of his land, and water that passes through his property as in a stream or other watercourse.

An owner may use as he wishes any water contained entirely within the boundary of his property, as in a lake or pond. The same is true of waters arising through a natural spring from beneath the surface. He may also pump and use such underground water or water percolating beneath the soil. As was mentioned in Chapter 1, however, the basic principle behind California water laws is that of conservation, and so an owner may be prevented from taking any more water than he reasonably needs, or from wasting such waters.

An owner whose land is bounded by a watercourse or has a watercourse running through his property is subject to riparian rights and is termed a riparian owner. While he has a right to the reasonable use of the waters, this right is one that he holds in common with the other adjacent riparian owners. They are all entitled to the benefits accruing from these waters. *Potable* is a term which is used to refer to drinkable water. If a riparian owner does something that causes pollution to any water, he may be liable for damages to other owners through whose lands the polluted waters will flow. Such waters that normally flow across the land of various owners may not be diverted or stopped by a dam or other means by one owner so that they would be denied to the others who would normally receive them. An obstruction erected to divert potential flood waters, or for any other purpose, may cause damage to an adjacent owner's property by forcing the water to flow onto his land in unusual amounts or over portions of the property not normally covered by flowing waters.

Trees and hedges

Trees and hedges that grow directly on a boundary line are owned in common by the ad-

joining property owners, and neither should substantially cut or remove them without the agreement of the other. In many cases, however, the trees or other types of hedges or bushes grow entirely upon the land of one owner but project or hang over onto the land of another. It is fairly well established at law that an owner has the right to cut back to his boundary line any branches or roots that overhang or extend from an adjacent owner's property.

Lateral and subjacent support

Support of land is lateral when the supported and supporting lands are divided by a vertical plane; support is subjacent when the supported land is above and the supporting land is beneath it. A landowner is entitled to have his land supported in its natural state by the land that adjoins it, and thus no landowner should excavate on his land in any manner that may weaken the land of an adjoining owner so that it becomes loose and slides or falls into the excavation.

Before excavation is started, the person doing the excavating should determine the subsoil conditions by checking with others who have built in the same area, or by test borings. Many conditions may exist beneath the surface of the soil that would not be apparent from a mere inspection of the conditions and topography of the surface. A rock ledge beneath the surface may necessitate expensive removal. Where fill of any kind has been used, the foundation of an intended building should, if possible, extend through the fill to undisturbed soil. Some types of soil become semiplastic when wet and squeeze out from under the foundation footings, causing irregular settlement of the foundations. The water table or natural ground waters may exist close to the surface, particularly in areas near watercourses or lakes.

Under the common law, a property owner was absolutely liable for any damage caused to his neighbor's land as a result of excavations, but he was not liable for damage caused to any buildings. This rule of absolute liability has been somewhat modified by statute in California. Under these statutes, the excavator must not only use the utmost care in making the excavation, but must also notify the adjoining landowner prior to commencement of excavation. The notice must state the location of the intended excavation, the date and time the work is to be done, and also the depth of the excavation. In certain cases, the adjacent property owner must be given a 30-day period in which to make certain preparations for the protection of his property prior to commencement of work. If the excavation is to go below the depth of the foundation of the adjoining property owner's building, the excavator must provide adequate support for the building and will generally be liable for any substantial damage to the building as a result of his work.

The main basis on which one may be entitled to damages against an excavator is for failure to give adequate notice and negligence in performing the work. Negligence would result not only from the use of improper methods in performing the physical excavation itself, but also from lack of proper exercise of good judgment (as when one excavates during a time of year when heavy rains are likely), leaves the excavation open for an unnecessarily long period of time, or commences work without having made a preliminary study of the soil conditions in the work area.

Subjacent support has to do with the weakening of land above by the removal of land beneath. Such situations are commonly found with regard to construction of tunnels for highway and rapid transit systems. The governmental authority in charge of such construction, be it state, county, or city, is responsible for using the highest degree of care in connection with such construction, and will be liable to owners of property above such construction for any damage to their land or buildings as the result of any negligent practices.

Fences

Any type of barrier that serves to divide two parcels of land, be it constructed of wood, metal, or stone, and regardless of its particular design, may be termed a fence. In one case an owner may decide to leave his land unfenced, and in another he may desire to fence it in order to make known the boundaries of his property and provide privacy or to prevent livestock or other types of animals from wandering onto the lands of adjacent owners. Local statutes generally govern the erection and types of fences allowed in certain areas, and fences, once erected upon the land, are considered to be real property.

The responsibility for maintaining a fence that serves to divide the property of adjacent owners is a common problem. In the absence of a specific agreement between the owners, a fence that stands wholly upon the land of one owner is his responsibility, and where it stands exactly upon a boundary line, statutes generally require both owners to contribute equally to its maintenance. In the case of a typical wooden fence, the general rule is that it belongs to the owner of the land in which the support posts of the fence are embedded.

The height allowed is also generally governed by local statute, and the Civil Code states that a fence 10 feet or more in height may constitute a "spite fence," and if erected for no good purpose other than to annoy a neighbor, would probably be classified by the courts as a nuisance subject to correction as required by law.

Encroachment and party wall

An encroachment consists of a portion of a building or of a fixture such as a fence that projects from one parcel of land partly onto that of an adjoining parcel. A party wall is a wall erected on the boundary line between two parcels of land for the common use of buildings on both parcels. Both encroachments and party walls are treated in Chapter 5, Liens and Encumbrances.

Nuisances

The Civil Code defines a nuisance as something that is indecent or offensive to the senses, is injurious to health, or obstructs the free use of property. Where something interferes with the right that an owner has to the use and enjoyment of his property, it is generally termed a private nuisance. If it affects a great number of individuals, it may also be a public nuisance.

The basic test of an act creating a nuisance is whether or not it interferes with the right of another to use his property or is injurious to him, and an owner creating a nuisance is usually liable to others who may be so affected. Many statutes have been enacted during the last few years to control such nuisances as the emission of pollutants into the air or discharge of harmful substances into waterways. Examples of some common nuisances are undue noise, smoke, fumes, odors, noxious gases, pollution, obstruction of free passage, negligent spraying of poisonous chemicals, and other such dangerous conditions.

Liabilities to third persons

There are many ways in which a property owner may become liable to third persons for damages incurred in connection with his property, and it is the rare owner indeed who does not carry some form of public liability insurance protection. An owner's liability with regard to lessees and tenants will be considered in Chapter 10, Landlord and Tenant. Here we will discuss trespassers, licensees, and invitees.

Trespassers. A property owner owes the least duty of protection to a person who trespasses upon his land. A trespasser is one who enters upon, or remains on, the land of another without the owner's consent or permission. With a few exceptions that will be discussed subsequently, the general rule at law is that a landowner is not liable for any injuries or other mishaps that may occur to one who is trespassing upon the land. The trespasser is on the property without the permission of the owner and must bear the risk fully for any unsafe conditions that may exist. Even if an owner becomes aware that someone is trespassing on his land, the above rule still remains in effect. Two exceptions to the rule are with regard to malicious injury inflicted upon the trespasser and with respect to the doctrine of attractive nuisance when the trespasser is a child.

While the owner is generally under no liability for injury to a trespasser, he may become liable if he maliciously and intentionally harms a person he knows to be a trespasser. This does not mean that a landowner may not protect himself as in the case of an armed burglar who breaks into a building at night with the intention of committing a theft or other felony; what it does mean is that the owner may not create some condition that will intentionally injure the trespasser. An example would be the setting of a dangerous animal trap or a device that will automatically trigger a rifle or revolver.

Another exception to the rule that an owner has no affirmative duty of care to trespassers has to do with what are termed attractive nuisances. An attractive nuisance exists when a dangerous object or condition exists upon the lands that is particularly attractive to children who, because of their age, are not mature enough to understand, comprehend, and avoid the risk and dangers involved.

Examples of an attractive nuisance would be: buildings under construction, mechanical equipment and machinery, certain types of animals, swimming pools, and an abandoned well or mine. The landowner is merely under a duty to exercise ordinary care in such cases, and is not responsible for taking measures that would place an undue burden upon him. The degree of responsibility of the owner may vary depending upon whether he is totally unaware of anyone's trespassing, or does in fact know that children have been attracted to and do trespass upon his property. If an owner has taken reasonable precautions that constitute sufficient warning, an injury resulting to one who trespasses will not usually render the landowner liable for damages.

Licensees. When a person enters upon the property of another with the owner's consent and permission, such a person is classified not as a trespasser but as a licensee. The duty that an owner owes to a licensee is not much more than that owed to a trespasser, and a licensee under the law is generally said to assume the risk of any danger present and to be responsible for any injuries that may result. A further legal distinction with respect to a licensee is that his presence is not specifically beneficial to the owner or in connection with the owner's business or occupation; furthermore, the licensee has generally asked for permission to come onto the property, rather than having been initially invited or requested to enter the property by the owner. Since the licensee's entry onto the property is not for the benefit nor at the invitation of the owner, no liability for injury will usually attach to the owner so long as he has taken reasonable and ordinary care for the protection of persons who may enter upon the property.

Invitees. An invitee is a person who has been invited by the owner, either expressly or by implication, to enter the property for a business purpose. The implication is that the invitee's presence will result in mutual or business benefit to the property owner. An example of an invitee would be a customer in a store, a patron in a restaurant or theater, a painter or plumber who has come to perform some work, a guest in a hotel, a salesman delivering merchandise, or a motorist who drives into a service station to purchase gasoline.

The owner has a duty to exercise ordinary care in connection with the premises and to keep them in a safe condition. Any dangerous or hazardous conditions must be made known to the invitee, and the owner has a duty to inspect the premises periodically to ascertain their condition. A social guest is generally considered to be a licensee, and the principle at law seems to be that invitation is inferred when there is a mutual advantage or business interest, while a licensee is inferred when the object is mere pleasure or when benefit accrues only to the person entering and not to the owner.

Conditions outside the property boundaries. The previous discussion has concerned the liability of an owner for persons entering upon his land or buildings, that is, anywhere within the boundaries of his property. As to conditions existing outside the boundaries of his property, the owner is generally not liable. Local statutes and ordinances differ with regard to such areas, and in some instances a property owner may be responsible for maintenance of sidewalks and may be liable for injuries resulting from their unsafe condition.

QUESTIONS FOR DISCUSSION

1. How does the "bundle of rights" concept apply to real property?
2. Under what circumstances may a landowner generally use water on his property as he wishes?
3. What may a property owner do with respect to branches of a tree that project over a boundary fence and onto his property?
4. Under what conditions might a property owner who is excavating on his land be responsible for damage to buildings of an adjacent property owner?
5. When would both landowners be responsible for the maintenance of a boundary fence?
6. Give examples of various conditions in your own locality that might be correctly termed nuisances.
7. When might a property owner be liable for damages to a trespasser?
8. What examples can you give of conditions in your neighborhood that might be termed attractive nuisances?
9. What is the difference between a licensee and an invitee?
10. How might a property owner protect himself against a charge of negligence in connection with an attractive nuisance on his property?

MULTIPLE CHOICE QUESTIONS

6–1. The height and construction of fences are most often regulated by: (a) state law, (b) real estate law, (c) local ordinances, (d) state housing codes.
6–2. An example of an attractive nuisance is: (a) loud noises, (b) mechanical equipment, (c) smoke or fumes, (d) none of these.
6–3. A riparian owner: (a) is responsible for the repair and maintenance of fences on boundary lines, (b) must provide special lateral support for adjacent buildings, (c) has certain water rights in common with other owners, (d) none of these.
6–4. The type of interest given to a lessee by an owner is: (a) ownership, (b) security, (c) possessory, (d) riparian.
6–5. A property owner owes the least duty of protection to: (a) tenant, (b) invitee, (c) licensee, (d) trespasser.
6–6. If shrubs and branches from A's property extend onto B's property: (a) A and B become tenants in common, (b) A must trim the branches at B's request, (c) B has the right to trim the shrubs and branches back to the fence or other boundary line, (d) none of these.
6–7. A social guest is generally considered to be: (a) a licensee, (b) an invitee, (c) an agent, (d) a tenant.
6–8. The best protection a property owner has against possible liability to others is to: (a) post adequate signs, (b) install a burglar alarm, (c) carry adequate insurance and maintain safe premises, (d) install special locks.

Agency and the real estate licensee

7

Most real estate transactions in California today involve the use of a real estate broker or salesperson acting as an agent. The person for whom the licensee acts is called the principal. This principal generally seeks to buy property from or sell property to a third party. The California Civil Code defines an agent as one who represents another, called a principal, in dealings with third persons. This is known as an agency relationship, or simply an agency, and is governed by the law of agency, which regulates and sets forth the rights of the principal, agent, and third party.

Since our discussion of agency relationships will be in connection with the real estate licensee acting as an agent, let us begin by defining the real estate broker and real estate salesperson.

BROKER AND SALESPERSON DEFINED

The general public thinks of a real estate broker as an agent whose duty it is to bring a seller and buyer together, and thus negotiate the sale and/or purchase of real property. The California Business and Professions Code, Division 4, Real Estate, gives a much more detailed definition of a real estate broker. It defines him as a person who actually does, or offers or attempts to do, certain acts. These acts are done for others for a compensation or in expectation of a compensation, and are with regard to or in connection with real property.

The acts are defined as follows:

1. Sells or offers to sell; buys or offers to buy.
2. Solicits prospective sellers or purchasers.
3. Solicits or obtains listings.
4. Negotiates the purchase, sale, or exchange of real property.

5. Leases or rents, collects rents, or negotiates the sale, purchase, or exchange of leases.
6. Negotiates real property loans and deals with borrowers, lenders, or note holders in connection with real estate loans.
7. Buys, sells, or exchanges real property contracts or promissory notes secured by liens on real property.
8. Claims or collects an advance fee in connection with an advance fee listing to sell, lease, exchange, or rent real property or to obtain a loan thereon.
9. Collects payments or performs other functions in connection with real property contracts or promissory notes secured by liens on real property.
10. Assists in filing an application for the purchase or lease of, or in locating or entering on, lands owned by the state or federal government.

Real estate salesperson

A real estate salesperson is one who, for a compensation or in expectation of a compensation, is employed by a licensed real estate broker to do one or more of the acts set forth in the definition of a real estate broker above. While a person holding a real estate broker license may establish an office and operate independently on his own, a person holding a real estate salesperson license must work for and under the supervision of a licensed broker. The requirements for obtaining a real estate license will be discussed in the chapter dealing with real estate brokerage.

When license not required. The definition of a real estate broker and a real estate salesperson does not include the following, and a broker's license or salesperson's license does not have to be held by the following:

1. Anyone who directly performs any of the defined acts with reference to his own property, or a corporation which, through its regular officers who receive no special compensation therefore, performs any of the acts defined with regard to the corporation's own property.
2. Anyone holding a duly executed power of attorney from the owner.
3. Services rendered by an attorney-at-law in performing his duties as such attorney-at-law.
4. Any receiver, trustee in bankruptcy, or any person acting under the order of the court.
5. Any trustee selling under a deed of trust.

The above exceptions are the most common. For further details regarding exemptions from license requirements, the reader is referred to Section 10133.1, Real Estate Law, Division of Real Estate Reference Book.

While a person dealing with his own property does not have to be licensed, there is often a question as to how many transactions within a year may be engaged in before the owner is deemed to be a broker and thus fall under the licensing provisions. The following section from the Real Estate Law, Section 10131.1 should provide ample clarification as regards this point:

1. The acquisition for resale to the public, and not as an investment, of eight (8) or more real property sales contracts or promissory notes secured directly or collaterally by liens of real property during a calendar year, or
2. The sale to, or exchange with, the public of eight (8) or more real property sales contracts or promissory notes secured directly or collaterally by liens on real property during a calendar year.

The law further provides, however, that any transactions negotiated through a real estate licensee shall not be considered in determining whether a person is a broker and subject to the license requirement. This means that no matter how many pieces of property an individual may buy or sell within a year, as long as these transactions are negotiated through a real estate licensee, the individual will not have to obtain a license himself. Without a license, one cannot legally collect a commission or fee for performance of any of the acts defined as within the authority of the licensed salesman or broker. The reader is referred to Chapter 20 for additional discussion of the duties and responsibilities of a real estate licensee and the requirements for obtaining a real estate salesperson or real estate broker license.

Having defined a real estate broker and real estate salesperson and established the fact that they act as agents, we shall now turn to a discussion of the laws of agency. Although these laws apply to all types of agency relationships, our discussion will be mainly concerned with the real estate agent and the persons with whom he deals.

CREATION OF AGENCY

The agency relationship may be created by agreement, estoppel, and ratification.

Agreement

While the relationship of principal and agent may be created expressly or implied, with or without a contract, the status of real estate agent is created in California only by an express contract generally referred to as a listing. A listing agreement is an employment contract between a principal and a real estate licensee and creates the agency relationship. The various types and forms of listings are discussed in Chapter 9, Real Estate Contracts.

The statute of frauds requires contracts affecting any right, title, or interest in property to be in writing, and because of this the rule in California is that the agreement creating the agency relationship must also be in writing. Known as the *equal dignities rule,* it means simply that since the real estate agent will be authorized to enter into contracts that are required to be in writing, his authorization to act as an agent should also be created by a written instrument.

Any person having the capacity to contract may appoint an agent, and since the listing agreement is a contract, all of the essential elements of a contract must be present; there must be mutual assent, parties capable of contracting, a lawful object, and sufficient consideration. There is an exception to the consideration rule to the effect that where one gratuitously acts as an agent and a principal relies thereon, the agency may be held liable for failure to perform. This does not apply with respect to the listing agreement, since it is a bilateral contract and consideration must be present. The bilateral implication arises because there is a promise for a promise. The principal promises to sell the property under the terms and conditions in the listing and to pay the broker a commission when he procures a purchaser, and the broker promises in turn to use due diligence in finding a buyer for the property. The authority given the broker is governed by the terms in his contract, and it is important to remember that the filling in and signing of whatever form may be used creates a contractual relationship and that care must be exercised to ensure that the contract correctly expresses the intent of the parties.

Estoppel

An agency by estoppel may arise when one person makes it appear that another is his agent or has agency authority that he actually does not have. When a third party deals with this supposed agent in the belief that he actually represents a certain party, that party will be estopped, that is he will not be allowed to deny the supposed agency relationship. The individuals acting as principal and agent will be held liable as though the agency actually existed. This situation does not generally occur with regard to a real estate agent since his authority is required to be in writing.

Ratification

An agency by ratification may come about in two ways. When an agent performs unauthorized acts on behalf of his principal, and the principal upon finding out consents to these acts, he is said to have ratified them and assumes liability for them. The second instance is where one falsely purports to be the agent of another, and enters into an agreement on his behalf, without the knowledge or consent of the other person. If the supposed principal, upon finding out, accepts the benefits of the agreement, he will have created an agency by ratification and will be liable.

TYPES OF AGENTS AND AGENCY

This section will distinguish between various types of agents and agency and will discuss the difference among a special and general agent, actual and ostensible agency, and attorney-in-fact acting under a power of attorney, subagents and dual agency, and the classification of the licensee as an independent contractor or employee.

Special and general agents

An agent for a particular act or transaction is a special agent, while all others are general agents.

The distinction is in the scope of authority allowed and degree of powers conferred. The general agent usually has broad powers, whereas the special agent is more limited and is appointed for a particular transaction.

The relationship between a real estate agent and his client is that of principal and special agent. The acts of a special agent bind the principal only when they are strictly within the authority conferred in the employment contract between the two parties.

ACTUAL AND OSTENSIBLE AGENCY

A real estate agency is an actual agency since it comes into being as the result of an express written contract. An agency is ostensible when a principal either intentionally or unintentionally causes a third person to believe another to be the principal's agent. This situation was discussed previously in connection with agency by estoppel and ratification.

SUBAGENTS AND DUAL AGENCY

Unless a principal gives his agent the express or implied authorization to do so, the general rule is that an agency may not establish a new relationship of principal and agent between his own principal and a third person. If the original agent does attempt to shift his responsibilities to a subagent without proper authority from the principal, the principal has no connection with the purported subagent. Unless specifically forbidden by his principal to do so, an agent may delegate powers to another person when (a) the act is purely mechanical, (b) the act is something the agent cannot do himself and the subagent can lawfully perform, as in the taking of an acknowledgment by a notary, and (c) it is the general custom or usage to delegate such powers, as is the case in the real estate business with respect to real estate salespersons and cooperating brokers. Most listing contracts now in common use permit the listing broker to delegate much of the work of procuring a buyer to his salespersons and cooperating brokers, all of whom would be considered agents of the listing broker and not agents of the property owner. While the personal performance of the broker may not be required, he still remains liable for the details delegated to and executed by others.

Although the usual type of listing appoints one broker as exclusive agent, there is one type of listing agreement, called a multiple listing, in which the broker is expressly authorized to submit the listing to his multiple listing service and its real estate licensee members. The result is that a large number of licensees become subagents of the property owner, who may be liable for certain of their acts.

Attorney-in-fact

An attorney-in-fact is an individual appointed by an owner under an instrument called a power of attorney, and this agent may be given the power to do anything that the principal himself may do. These powers are granted under the express terms of the agreement and may be special, as where the attorney-in-fact is given authority to sell a specific piece of property for the owner, generally authorizing the agent to transfer or convey any property that the principal may own. A power of attorney must be acknowledged and recorded, and any person who may legally contract may give or act under a power of attorney. An attorney-in-fact should not be confused with an attorney-at-law, and with regard to our previous definition of a real estate broker it will be recalled that one acting under a power of attorney is exempt from the real estate licensing requirement.

Employee and independent contractor

An ordinary employee is one who is employed to render personal service to his employer and who, in rendering such service, remains entirely under the control and direction of his employer. An independent contractor, however, is one who does his work in his own way and is merely responsible for attaining a final result. The person hiring the independent contractor cannot tell him how to do his job, as is the case with an employee. An agent is generally distinguished from an employee or independent contractor, but with regard to real estate agents the classification of the individual agent may vary depending upon the particular circumstances.

The classification of a person as an agent, employee, or independent contractor is important with respect to two general areas. The first involves coverage under social security, unemployment insurance, and workman's compensation insurance. An employee is generally covered, while one who works for himself as an independent contractor may be without certain of these benefits.

The second area is with respect to liability, and while a real estate licensee is an agent, he may also be classified as either an independent contractor or an employee. While a principal is generally responsible for the acts of his agent, there are situations in which the principal may not be liable if the agent is an independent contractor. This liability finds its most notable illustrations in the cases involving automobile accidents of employees while driving on the employer's business. If the wrongdoer were an independent contractor, as a real estate broker is usually classified, the person who hired him is generally not held responsible for injuries caused by his negligence. Since a real estate salesperson is often considered to be an employee of the broker, virtually all brokers carry substantial public liability insurance covering all their salespersons and other office personnel.

Most real estate salespersons work for their brokers under an employment agreement called a broker-salesperson contract. Because of the importance of distinguishing whether the salesperson is an employee or an independent contractor, the employment agreement should be carefully prepared. The California Association of Realtors® makes available for use two different forms of broker-salesperson contract. The first, in which the status of the salesperson is to be that of an employee, contains a clause stating that the salesperson has no authority, either express or implied, to represent anything to a prospective purchaser unless it is in the listing agreement or unless he receives specific written instructions from the broker. The point here is that the salesperson is under the complete direction and control of the broker, and it will be recalled that this is one of the important points in the classification of an individual employee. The other form provided attempts to classify the salesperson as an independent contractor and states that the parties to the agreement are and shall remain independent contractors, and that the salesperson is under the control of the broker as to the result of the salesperson's work only, and not as to the means by which such result is accomplished.

AUTHORITY OF THE AGENT

The duties and authority of an agent are extensively covered in the Civil Code, which in part states that every agent has the authority to (a) do everything necessary or proper or usual in the ordinary course of business for effecting the purpose of his agency, and (b) make representations as to facts involved in the transaction in which he is engaged.

The broker is bound by the authority given him in his listing contract. The standard listing form, usually called an exclusive authorization and right to sell, confers upon the broker the authority to advertise the property and to solicit offers. It does not give the broker the actual right to sell the property or to enter into an agreement on behalf of the owner that would definitely obligate the owner to convey title. The broker merely obtains an offer from a prospective purchaser, and it is up to the owner to either accept or reject the offer. An agent may, if the owner wishes, be given the authority actually to sell and convey real property, but this is not usually the case in the normal real estate agency relationship.

Under certain conditions, the authority of an agent is broadened by an emergency, and he has the power to disobey instructions when it is clearly in the interest of his principal to do so and there is not time to communicate with his principal. The Civil Code further states that an agent can never have authority, either actual or ostensible, to do an act that is known or suspected by the person with whom he deals to be a fraud upon the principal. Unless specifically authorized, an agent has no authority to act in his own name unless it is in the usual course of business to do so.

No liability is incurred by the principal for acts of the agent beyond the scope of his actual or ostensible authority. However, a third party who deals with an agent and knows of the agency is under a duty to ascertain its scope. If the agent acts beyond his actual authority, and the conduct of the principal has not been such as to give him ostensible authority to do the act, the third party cannot hold the principal.

Authority to accept a deposit

The standard form of listing gives the broker the authority to accept a deposit from a prospective purchaser in connection with an offer the latter may make for the property. One of the greatest causes of complaint coming to the Real Estate Department arises out of deposits and the demand for their return by the party giving the deposit. It is important to remember that the deposit money never belongs to the broker. If the listing agreement does not authorize him to accept a deposit, and he does so, he then holds the deposit as the agent of the purchaser. If the listing agreement, as it usually does, gives the broker the authority to accept a deposit, he holds such money as the agent of the seller.

Since the deposit money does not belong to the broker, he must not commingle it with his own funds. This is not only a general principle of agency, but commingling is one of the specific grounds for discipline against a real estate licensee. Since the real estate agent must not commingle deposit money with his own, the law requires him to place all funds received on behalf of principals immediately in a special trust account or in a neutral escrow depository, or give the funds to the principal entitled to them. An additional discussion of the deposit will be found in connection with the deposit receipt and purchase contract covered in Chapter 9, Real Estate Contracts.

DUTIES—AGENT AND PRINCIPAL

Real estate licensees owe a definite loyalty and duty to their clients, and this is generally known as the fiduciary relationship. An agent is a fiduciary, and as such, he is bound in his relations with his principal to exercise the utmost good faith, loyalty, and honesty in executing the duties of his agency. The courts have regarded this relationship in the same general manner and strictness as that of a trustee and beneficiary. The Civil Code forbids a real estate agent from doing any act that a trustee is forbidden to do. The code provides that a trustee is bound to act in the highest respect toward his beneficiary and may not obtain any advantage therein over the beneficiary by the slightest misrepresentation, concealment, duress, or adverse pressure of any kind. The real estate agent, then, owes these duties not only to his principal but to all persons with whom he deals in his capacity as an agent.

Article 3 of the California Real Estate Law covers disciplinary action and contains Section 10176, which outlines the grounds for revocation or suspension of a real estate license. Some of the more important provisions of this section are as follows:

The Commissioner may, upon his own motion, and shall, upon the verified complaint in writing of any person, investigate the actions of any person engaged in the business or acting in the capacity of a real estate licensee within this state, and he may temporarily suspend or permanently revoke a real estate license at any time where the licensee, while a real estate licensee, in performing or attempting to perform any of the acts within the scope of this chapter, has been guilty of any of the following:

a. Making any substantial misrepresentation.
b. Making any false promises of a character likely to influence, persuade, or induce.

c. A continued and flagrant course of misrepresentation or making of false promises through real estate agents or salesmen.

d. Acting for more than one party in a transaction without the knowledge or consent of all parties thereto.

e. Commingling with his own money or property the money or other property of others that is received and held by him.

f. Claiming, demanding, or receiving a fee, compensation, or commission under any exclusive agreement authorizing or employing a licensee to perform any acts for compensation or commission where such agreement does not contain a definite, specified termination date.

g. The claiming or taking by a licensee of any secret or undisclosed amount of compensation, commission, or profit or the failure of a licensee to reveal to the employer of such licensee the full amount of such licensee's compensation, commission, or profit under an agreement authorizing or employing such licensee to do any acts for which a license is required under this chapter for compensation or commission prior to or coincident with the signing of an agreement evidencing the meeting of the minds of the contracting parties, regardless of the form of such agreement, whether evidenced by documents in an escrow or by any other or different procedure.

h. The use by a licensee of any provision allowing the licensee an option to purchase in an agreement authorizing or employing such licensee to sell, buy, or exchange real estate or a business opportunity unless, coincident with election to exercise such option to purchase, the licensee reveals in writing to the employer the full amount of the licensee's profit and obtains the written consent of the employer approving the amount of such profit.

i. Any other conduct, whether of the same or a different character than specified in this section, which constitutes fraud or dishonest dealing.

In addition to the prohibition against making any substantial or fraudulent misrepresentations in connection with his agency, the real estate licensee must constantly be aware of his duty to keep his principal informed of material facts, not act for more than one party in a transaction without the consent of both, and not make a secret profit for himself.

Disclosure of material facts

While an agent may do what is necessary or proper in order to carry out his duties, he must always be very careful this his principal has full knowledge of what the agent is doing and approves of his actions. The agent must not keep any secrets from his principal and must not do anything that would be against the best interest of his principal. There should always be full disclosure of facts between an agent and those whom he represents. Not only does failure to abide by these principals place the licensee in a position of jeopardizing his license, but the courts have held that the agent is not entitled to any profit from transactions in which he is guilty of violating these principles.

Although agents are obliged to fully disclose to a principal all material facts that might influence the principal's decision concerning any real estate transaction, they should be aware that the California Attorney General has stated that race, creed, or color is not a material fact and should not be disclosed, even though the furnishing of such information is at the request of the owner. A discussion of Fair Housing Laws will be found in Chapter 18.

Acting for more than one party to a transaction

In general, agents do not usually act for more than one party in a transaction; they do not represent opposing parties. In the real estate business, however, the licensee is often in a position of representing both the seller and the buyer. When such is the case, the licensee must make known to the parties that he is representing them both and owes to each party the same duty of utmost good faith, honesty, and loyalty in the transaction, and the same duty to disclose any material fact that would affect the judgment of either party. While the commission in a real estate transaction is usually paid by the seller, the licensee may receive a commission from both parties in a transaction, but only if they are both aware of this and consent to it.

Secret profits

The courts have held that an agent cannot acquire any secret interests adverse to his principal, and he cannot lawfully make a secret personal profit out of the subject of the agency. If an agent conceals his interest in the property sold or purchased, he is liable to those persons whom he rep-

74

resents for all secret profits made by him. An agent will have committed fraud if he represents to his principal that he obtained a certain selling price for a property but actually obtained a higher price than the one he disclosed.

A real estate agent must inform persons with whom he deals of any personal interest he may have or be acquiring in a transaction in which he acts as an agent. A licensee must disclose the amount of profit he makes in connection with a net listing or option listing. If a licensee uses a "dummy buyer" in an attempt to profit secretly, he will be guilty of fraudulent action. An example would be a broker who makes a low offer, usually through a dummy buyer, when the broker already has a higher offer from a legitimate buyer of whom the seller is not aware. When the dummy buyer, who is working for the broker, acquires the property, it is then sold to the real buyer whom the broker has waiting. The broker has, through fraud, made not only a commission but also a secret profit.

A real estate salesperson is responsible for the same fiduciary relationship and compliance with the laws of agency as the broker. If the salesperson fails to fulfill the duties of an agent to a client, and attempts through dummy transactions or through manipulations with other salespeople to gain a secret profit, these actions may not only result in loss of the salesperson's license but may place the broker in the same position as well. A broker and salesperson will also be violating the law when a broker sells property listed with him to a salesperson so that a second sale may be made at a profit without the knowledge of the owner.

Disclosure of licensee status

Quite often a real estate broker or salesperson will deal in property for his own account. The licensee will be acting as a principal and not as an agent. In the case of a licensee acting as a principal, the law does not require the licensee to disclose the fact that he has a real estate license. However, the Commissioner has repeatedly cautioned real estate licensees that it is in their best interest to disclose in writing that they are a real estate broker or real estate salesperson acting as a principal.

Commissioner's regulation 2727 requires all licensed salespersons to disclose principal transactions to their broker within five days from execution of the agreement or before completion of the transaction.

DUTIES—AGENT AND THIRD PARTIES

Many of the duties and responsibilities of the agent to persons with whom he deals have already been covered in the previous section. We will here be additionally concerned with the agent's duties and liabilities with regard to third persons in the area of torts, preparation of contracts, and warranty of authority.

Torts

Torts are private injuries or wrongs committed upon an individual's person or property arising from a breach of duty created by law rather than by contract. Even though he may have been acting in accordance with his principal's directions, the agent is always responsible for his own torts, fraudulent acts, or negligence. When an individual misrepresents his authority to act as agent for another, he may be liable in a court action to the third party who relies thereon to his detriment.

An agent is liable to his employer, the principal, for torts such as negligence, or for breach of contract by wrongfully abandoning the employment before the end of its term. The agent may also be liable to the principal for the acts of a subagent, as has been discussed previously.

Statements made by brokers and salespersons

Not only is an agent liable for fraudulent or negligent statements while negotiating a sale, but by virtue of the relationship of principal and agent, and regardless of the innocence of the principal, the principal may also be liable to third parties.

Real estate agents are constantly making statements to prospects concerning the property being offered for sale. Usually, one or more of the parties involved in the transaction may have erroneous impressions regarding the property. Such statements and impressions can be generally classified as follows:

1. Statements intended and understood as merely expressions of opinion.
2. Statements intended and understood to be part of the contract itself.
3. Mistakes.
4. Statements intended and understood as representations of fact.
5. Nondisclosure of material facts by silence.

A statement by the agent that the building he is offering for sale is "the best on the block" or that it is "very well constructed and in the best neighborhood in town" are examples of statements that are merely expressions of opinion. The prospective purchaser should recognize them as such, and these opinions would not place the licensee under any liability under the law.

Statements incorporated into the deposit receipt and real estate purchase contract become part of the contract itself. If these statements or promises were made in good faith, their falsity results only in breach of contract, and the licensee is not liable under the law. The statements, however, must have been made in good faith.

When the parties to a transaction merely form untrue conclusions with respect to the property, the case is usually one of mutual mistake. The contract may be rescinded, and the licensee would not ordinarily be liable under the law.

Thus, if there was good faith and honest intent on the part of the licensee, statements that fall under 1, 2, and 3 above usually will not place the licensee in a position of liability under the law. Litigation usually occurs with regard to statements that fall under 4 and 5.

Statements intended and understood as representations of fact that later prove to be false will fall under three general classifications.

Innocent misrepresentations. Such statements later found to be false permit recision of the contract, and ordinarily no liability attaches against the licensee.

Negligent misrepresentations. The broker's or salesperson's liability for negligent statements is considered to be a form of deceit. The liability can be enforced either by the injured party in a civil action for damage, or by the Commissioner in a disciplinary action to suspend or revoke the broker's or salesperson's license.

Fraudulent misrepresentations. This kind of statement is one made by a person who knows it to be false. This is clearly fraud, and not only subjects the licensee to both civil and disciplinary action but also may result in criminal action against him.

Our last classification is that of nondisclosure of material facts by silence. Liability for silence will result when the licensee has knowledge of facts that affect the property in question and knows that the prospective purchaser or seller is unaware of these facts.

When the principal supplies the agent with false information concerning a property, and the agent reasonably relies on this information and repeats it to a prospective purchaser, the agent will not be held liable.

The agent who makes such misrepresentations must show that they were made with the belief that they were true, and that the agent did, in fact, believe them to be true. Since the seller of a property may not always give the broker correct information, the broker or salesperson must be very cautious and thoroughly examine any information he feels is inadequate or suspicious in any way. If the information given the licensee is such that any responsible licensee would have cause to question it, then a licensee who does not do so may find himself open to liability when he passes this information on to others.

Warranty of authority and contracts

The agent generally acts with authority for the principal in the name of the principal, and will not usually be liable on a written contract made in the name of the principal.

When an agent acts without authority or in excess of authority, he may be held liable for breach of his implied warranty of authority. Where an agent enters into a contract with a third party and had no authority to do so, the remedy of the third party is on the warranty of authority.

While an agent warrants his authority to third persons with whom he may deal, he does not impliedly warrant his principal's capacity to contract, and if it turns out that the principal is incapable of legally contracting, the agent will not be liable so long as he can show that he was unaware of the principal's inability to contract. If, however, the agent expressly warrants his principal's capacity to contract, or fraudulently conceals the fact of the incapacity, he will put himself in a position of liability.

Where an agent acts for an undisclosed principal, the third party may hold either the agent or the principal if and when he discovers the principal's identity. In order to relieve himself from liability, the agent must disclose the name of the principal on the contract so that it is clear the third party intended to bind the principal and not the agent.

When negotiations are closed and the parties are ready to sign a contract, it is the general practice for the licensee to have filled in the necessary blanks in the form he uses. This procedure is a very important part of the licensee's duties, and the licensee is generally not in the position of unlawfully practicing law when he completes these forms. As long as he merely completes forms generally used by real estate agents in connection with their usual duties and business, he is not in violation of the law; however, the agent will be in violation of the law when he goes beyond this and attempts to give legal advice or construct contracts of his own that should properly be prepared by an attorney. Forms distributed to member brokers by their local real estate board or those prepared by the California Association of Realtors are most generally used; the licensee should fill in these forms with accuracy, completeness, and with language free from uncertainty.

DUTIES—PRINCIPAL AND THIRD PARTIES

Since an agent acts on behalf of his principal, the general rule at law is that the principal is responsible for the acts of his agent whether such agency is created by agreement, estoppel, or ratification. When an agent incurs liability for his acts as an agent on behalf of his principal, the principal will often be liable to a certain degree also. It was mentioned previously that in connection with false information supplied to an agent by the principal, the agent may or may not be liable depending upon the circumstances; but the principal, supplying information he knows to be false, most certainly will incur liability.

While a principal is generally not liable for the acts of an independent contractor, if the person claiming to be an independent contractor is a real estate licensee acting as an agent for the principal, this will have some bearing in certain cases upon the principal's degree of responsibility for his agent's acts.

It is interesting to note that the principal's liability to third persons for either his or his agent's fraudulent acts not only extends to the immediate buyer but may attach to subsequent purchasers as well. If a situation exists where a purchaser may legally enforce a claim for liability against a seller because of fraud, a third party who purchases the property from the original purchaser may instigate the legal action and enforce the claim for damages.

RIGHT OF AGENT TO COMPENSATION

For successfully performing the duties of his agency, the real estate broker is paid on a commission basis. Our discussion of the subject of compensation will include the form of compensation, a broker's right to be compensated, and how and when it is earned.

Form of compensation

The broker's compensation is called a commission and is based upon a percentage of the selling price of the property. If the broker negotiates a transaction other than a sales, for instance a lease or the rental of a dwelling unit, the broker's commission will be based on a percentage of the value of the lease or the amount of rent to be paid.

The amount of commission a broker may receive or the rate he may charge is not set by law and is strictly a matter to be agreed upon between the agent and his principal. The rate may vary depending upon the broker, geographical location, and type of property involved. Local custom and practices determine the rate charged by brokers in a particular area. Local real estate boards used to prescribe rates to be charged by their members, but certain questions raised in connection with the federal antitrust laws have resulted in discontinuance of this practice. It is not uncommon to find a rate of 10 percent used in connection with unimproved property and 6 percent for improved property. Quite often the 6 percent will apply to the first $50,000 or $100,000 of the purchase, with a lesser percentage applied to any excess in the amount. Since the actual selling price is usually lower than the price shown in the broker's listing contract, the rate of commission will apply to the actual selling price of the property.

Prerequisite conditions

Before an agent may maintain an action at law to receive payment of a commission, he must show (a) that he holds a valid real estate license as required by law, (b) that he is authorized by his principal in writing, and (c) that he has fully complied with the requirements of this written agreement with his principal. While a broker may initially become an agent for a seller or buyer without a written agreement, he may not collect a commission in a real estate transaction unless his authority is in writing. The written agreement is almost always in the form of a listing agreement, but may also come about only as the result of the buyer's and seller's entering into a purchase contract and deposit receipt agreement.

The real estate broker's most fundamental rights to compensation, however, are based upon his written listing contract. The broker is generally said to be entitled to his commission when he procures a buyer who is ready, willing, and able to purchase the property under the exact terms of the listing agreement or upon any other terms that may be acceptable to the seller. The broker is bound by the terms of his written contract, and there are variances in terms and conditions depending upon the form of listing used. This area will be discussed in detail in the section on listing forms in Chapter 9.

Procuring cause

The real estate agent must be the procuring cause of the sale, and procuring cause has been defined as the cause which originates a series of events that, without a break in their continuity, results in accomplishing the main objective of the employment. The broker must be the predominant motivating force and effective cause of bringing the buyer and seller together. Along these lines, the broker is often referred to as the originating cause from whence the real estate transaction finally results. The broker is generally entitled to the commission when he brings the buyer and seller together and they enter into a contract, even though the sale is actually never concluded. In certain cases, however, the broker is entitled to his commission only if and when the transaction is actually carried through to final completion and the property is conveyed from seller to buyer.

Ready, willing, and able buyer

A ready and willing buyer denotes one who makes an offer on the terms and conditions stated in the listing agreement or upon any other terms and conditions that are acceptable to the seller. He is said to be able when he has the financial capacity and is legally able to purchase the property. Having the ability to obtain the necessary funds at the proper time would constitute adequate financial capacity.

TERMINATION OF AGENCY

Under the Civil Code, an agency may be terminated by (1) acts of the parties, or (2) operation of law. Revocation by acts of the parties occurs when *(a)* the parties to the contract creating the agency relationship agree to terminate it, *(b)* the agent renounces the agency and withdraws as agent, and *(c)* the principal revokes the agency. Termination occurs by operation of law *(a)* when the agency is terminated by expiration of its term, *(b)* by extinction of its subject, and *(c)* by the

expiration or incapacity of either the principal or the agent.

A principal may revoke the agency relationship at any time by giving notice to the agent. The basic exception to this general rule is that the principal cannot terminate the agency by revocation where the agent's authority is coupled with an interest, as with a trustee under a deed of trust who has a title interest as well as a power of sale. Under the typical agency agreement between a broker and principal, the commission to be earned by the broker is not considered to be such an interest and thus the principal may revoke the agency at any time. If the agency was created by a recorded instrument containing a power to convey or execute instruments affecting the property, the revocation is ineffective unless the writing containing it is also acknowledged and recorded in the same place.

Under certain conditions, termination of the agency relationship by revocation may place the principal in a position of liability for breach of contract. In the exclusive authorization and right-to-sell listing, which is most generally used, the broker may be entitled to a commission if the principal revokes the agency and thus withdraws the property from the market at any time before the definite specified date of final and complete termination contained in the agreement.

The basis in law for allowing either party in the agency relationship to terminate the relationship, regardless of the fact that liability for breach of contract may or may not result, is that the agency relationship must be one of mutual trust between the agent and the principal, and should circumstances occur that cause this to not be the case, it would be impractical to force a continuance of the agency relationship upon the parties.

When a principal revokes an agency, he should give notice to third parties of whom he has knowledge who have dealt with the agent, since the former agent is still an ostensible agent to those persons who have not had notice of the revocation of the agency. With regard to the real estate agency, the principal does not usually know all of the third parties with whom the agent may have dealt during the agency, but since the real estate agent is seldom given the authority actually to execute a contract on behalf of the principal, notice to third parties of the termination of the agency relationship does not usually pose any particular problem.

In addition to termination of agency by acts of the parties, previously discussed, the termination may also result by operation of law. A common occurrence is the termination of agency by expiration of its term as stated in the agency contract. If a broker lists a property for sale and the property is subsequently destroyed, the agency is said to have been terminated by extinction of its subject, and where there is incapacity or expiration of either party to the agency relationship, a termination of the agency relationship will result.

QUESTIONS FOR DISCUSSION

1. A broker is defined as a person who performs certain acts with relation to real property. As an individual, list as many of these acts as you can that fall within an area with which you many have had some contact.
2. How does the equal dignities rule affect the real estate licensee?
3. Why would a real estate licensee seldom become an agent by estoppel or ratification?
4. When may an agent delegate powers to another?
5. Why might an owner appoint an attorney-in-fact to sell his property?
6. How does an independent contractor differ from an employee?
7. To whom may a deposit taken by a real estate licensee belong?
8. What is meant by the agent's fiduciary relationship?
9. Under what circumstances might a broker or salesperson be said to have earned a secret profit?
10. What are some examples of torts committed by an agent?
11. Can a real estate licensee be held liable for something he does not say?
12. Is a real estate licensee in California in the position of unlawfully practicing law when he completes commonly used real estate forms?
13. Why may a principal be liable for the fraudulent acts of his agent?
14. How is the rate of commission charged by a real estate broker determined?
15. What must an agent show before he may maintain an action at law to receive payment of a commission?
16. Why is the term *procuring cause* important to the real estate agent?
17. What constitutes a ready, willing, and able buyer?
18. By what instrument is the agency relationship between the broker and principal usually created?
19. How may an agency generally be terminated?
20. What term is generally used to denote the form of compensation received by the broker?

MULTIPLE CHOICE QUESTIONS

7-1. The individual who employs an agent is: *(a)* a trustee, *(b)* a broker, *(c)* a principal, *(d)* an attorney.
7-2. The duties and authority of an agent are found in the: *(a)* local ordinances, *(b)* California Civil Code, *(c)* housing codes, *(d)* none of these.
7-3. A real estate agency is generally: *(a)* actual, *(b)* an independent contractor, *(c)* ostensible, *(d)* a partnership.
7-4. A real estate licensee's most fundamental right to compensation is based on: *(a)* advertising the property, *(b)* showing the property to a prospective purchaser, *(c)* a written listing contract, *(d)* presenting an offer to a seller.
7-5. The compensation paid to a broker is generally: *(a)* a percentage of the asking price of the property, *(b)* an hourly rate of pay, *(c)* set by the real estate commissioner, *(d)* a percentage of the selling price of the property.
7-6. The best definition of who may appoint an agent is: *(a)* a property owner, *(b)* a real estate licensee, *(c)* any individual having the capacity to contract, *(d)* any individual at least 21 years of age and a citizen.
7-7. A real estate licensee must: *(a)* have the seller approve any advertising in connection with the sale of the property, *(b)* disclose to the seller any material facts in connection with the transaction, *(c)* show the property to prospective purchasers when the seller is present, *(d)* none of these.
7-8. A real estate licensee is said to be practicing law when: *(a)* preparing a standard listing contract, *(b)* preparing an offer, *(c)* giving advice with respect to methods of taking title to real property, *(d)* none of these.

8 Elements of contracts

In this chapter we will consider contracts in general and the rules governing their creation and operation. In the following chapter, we shall confine our discussion to those specific contracts that are used most frequently in the real estate business.

DEFINITION OF CONTRACT

The California Civil Code defines a contract as "an agreement to do or not to do a certain thing." The American Law Institute defines a contract as "a promise or a set of promises for the breach of which the law gives a remedy, or the performance of which the law in some way recognizes as a duty." Still another definition of a contract is "an agreement between two or more parties to do or not to do a certain thing, and supported by consideration." There are certain terms used to classify contracts with regard to manner of creation, content of the agreement, extent of performance, and legal effect.

Manner of creation

A contract may be either *express* or *implied.* In an express contract, the parties express their terms and intentions either orally or in writing. Listings, deposit receipts, leases, and the like are all express contracts. An implied contract is one in which the parties infer their intention to create a contract by acts and conduct. Examples of such conduct are daily occurrences: boarding a means of public transportation at the corner bus stop, entering a barbershop for a haircut, or wheeling a loaded shopping cart up to the check-out stand at the local supermarket.

Content of the agreement

A contract may be *bilateral* or *unilateral.* A bilateral contract is one in which the promise of one party is given in exchange for the promise of the other party. A offers to reshingle B's roof for $1,600 and B agrees to pay the price. A unilateral contract, however, is one in which a promise is given by one party to induce some actual performance by the other party. The latter is not bound to act, but if he acts, the former is obligated to keep his promise. Using our previous example, A offers to reshingle B's roof for $1,600, and B says he will think it over and let A know. B is under no obligation at this point, but if in a few days he calls A and tells him that he agrees to the price and to go ahead with the roofing job, A is obligated to perform.

Extent of performance

A contract may be *executory* or *executed.* In an executory contract, something remains to be done by one or both of the parties to the contract. In an executed contract, both of the parties have completely performed.

Legal effect

A contract may be classified as *void, voidable, unenforceable,* or *valid.* A void agreement is not a contract at all because it lacks legal effect, as does a contract by a minor under 18 relating to real property. A voidable contract is one that seems to be valid and enforceable but that may be rejected by one of the parties, for instance a contract that has been induced by fraud and may thus be voided by the innocent party. An unenforceable contract is valid, but for some reason cannot be proved or sued upon by one or both of the parties, for instance a contract that cannot be enforced because of the passage of time under the statute of limitations, which will be discussed later in this chapter. And finally, a valid contract has all the essential elements required by law and is one that is binding and enforceable upon the parties to the contract.

ESSENTIAL ELEMENTS OF CONTRACT

Under the Civil Code of California, it is essential to the existence of a contract that there be *(a)* parties capable of contracting, *(b)* the consent of the parties, *(c)* a lawful object, and *(d)* a sufficient consideration. In addition to these requirements, the statute of frauds requires that certain contracts must be in writing.

Parties capable of contracting

In order for a valid contract to exist, there must be two or more parties who have at least a limited legal capacity to contract. Generally everyone is fully capable of contracting, except persons who are subject to certain limitations, such as minors, persons of unsound mind, and persons deprived of civil rights.

Minors. A minor is any person under the age of 18. Anyone who has reached 18 years of age in California is considered to be an adult person for the purpose of entering into any transaction regarding real property.

A minor under the age of 18 cannot make a contract relating to real property and, in addition, it is undesirable to contract with a minor because a minor may generally disaffirm any such contracts during his minority or for a reasonable time after reaching majority by restoring consideration or its equivalent to the party from whom it was received.

Veterans under the age of 18 who would otherwise be classified as minors may be given an exception by the Veterans Administration and the California Veterans Program and be considered adults for the purpose of purchasing a home or farm under these programs.

A minor is also deemed incapable of appointing an agent, and thus such delegation of authority or power of attorney is void. For this reason, a real estate licensee could not serve as agent of a minor to buy or sell. The licensee can represent an adult in dealing with a minor, but the adult must be willing to hazard the possibility of having the contract voided by the minor. The licensee should attempt to ascertain, if possible, whether the other party is a minor and if so inform his client. Difficulty can be avoided by negotiating in real property with or for a minor only through a court appointed guardian and with court approval of the transaction.

Aliens. In California, resident or nonresident aliens have essentially the same property rights as citizens. The Civil Code provides that any person, whether citizen or alien, may take, hold, and dispose of property, real or personal, within the state of California. Certain federal laws, however, contain restrictions with respect to the property rights of aliens.

Incompetents. California law provides that after the incapacity of a person of unsound mind has been judicially determined, no contract can be made with him. A contract may be made, however, with a person who had been judicially declared incompetent but at a later date had been restored to capacity to contract by the court. A person entirely without understanding has no power to contract, regardless of whether or not such person has ever been judicially declared incompetent by a court. In dealing with incompetents concerning real property, proper procedure calls for appointment of a guardian and court approval of the acts of the guardian.

Persons deprived of civil rights. Persons falling within this classification are generally felons who have been imprisoned and thus deprived of their right to contract. In certain cases, the state parole board may give permission for a convict to enter into a valid contract.

Mutual consent

The second major requirement of a valid contract is that the parties who have capacity to contract shall properly and mutually consent or assent to be bound by the contract. This mutual consent is normally evidenced by an offer of one party and acceptance by the other party. Such action must be genuine and free, and if it is clouded or negated by such influences as fraud or mistake, the contract may be voidable at the option of one or both parties, depending upon the particular circumstances. These necessary elements will be considered in the following order: *(a)* the offer, *(b)* the acceptance, and *(c)* the reality or genuineness of assent.

The offer. An offer expresses the offeror's willingness to enter into a contract and must be communicated to the offeree. It must, moreover, manifest a contractual intention. Thus, a social invitation is not a legal offer that results in a binding contract when accepted, nor is the usual advertisement an offer, but rather merely an invitation to deal. Often some of the terms are left for future determination, or it is understood that the contract will not be deemed complete until reduced to writing. Sometimes not all the necessary signatures are obtained, or there may be a condition that must be met before the parties become obligated. In any of these situations, it is usually held that there have been only preliminary negotiations and a binding contract has not come into existence.

Further, the offer must be definite and certain in its terms. The offer must be nonillusory in character, that is, it must actually bind the offeror if it is accepted. An illusory offer would exist if it were stated in it that the offeror could cancel or withdraw at pleasure without reasonable notice. Another example would be an offer to buy that is "contingent upon the buyer's obtaining a loan acceptable to him." Such an offer would mean that the buyer could use any excuse he wished, true or not, in stating that he could not find a loan acceptable to him and thereby be released from performance under the contract. Such conditional clauses will be further covered in the following chapter in discussion of the deposit receipt.

Termination of offer. The hope of the offeror is that the other party will accept and a contract will be formed, but the offeror does not want nor need to wait indefinitely. His offer may be terminated in any one of a number of ways.

Lapse of time. The offer is revoked if the offeree fails to accept it within a prescribed period set by the offeror. Even if the offeror does not set a specific time limit, upon the lapse of a reasonable time without communication of acceptance by the offeree the offer may be considered to have been revoked. What is a reasonable time is a question of fact dependent upon the circumstances. The safest method, as is generally the case in real estate contracts, is to provide for a specific time for the offeree either to accept or reject.

Rejection by the offeree. An unequivocal rejection by the offeree ends the offer, but simple discussion and preliminary bargaining does not do so when it involves no more than inquiries or suggestions for different terms. Generally, however, if the offeree changes the terms of the offer,

he is said to have rejected the original offer and is now making a counteroffer that may be accepted or rejected by the original offeror.

Communication of notice of revocation. This can be done effectively any time before the other party has communicated his acceptance. Even if the person making the offer had said that he would keep the offer open for a stated period of time that has not yet elapsed, he can withdraw the offer before acceptance by the other party. An exception would be in the case of an option agreement between the parties. An option may be defined as an agreement to keep an offer open, or as a contract to make a contract. An option for the purchase of real property is discussed in the following chapter.

Failure of offeree to fulfill a condition. The failure of the offeree to fulfill a condition prescribed by the offeror may result in termination of the offer. If the offeree makes a qualified acceptance by changing one of the terms, it is, in effect, a counteroffer. The roles of the parties are thus exchanged, and the counteroffer itself may be terminated as may an original offer.

Additional methods. In addition to the previous methods, an offer is terminated if before acceptance either of the parties expires or is adjudged incompetent, the subject matter of the contract is destroyed, or an intervening illegality occurs that would make the proposed contract illegal to perform.

The acceptance. An acceptance is the proper assent by the offeree to the terms of the offer. Clearly the person to whom the offer is made must have knowledge of it before he can accept. Thus acceptance by anyone other than the offeree does not occur. Most contracts are bilateral, but interesting problems arise in connection with the less common unilateral variety where the offeror asks for action, not a promise. Normally when the requested act is performed by one having knowledge of the offer it is automatically accepted.

The acceptance must be absolute and unqualified, for if it modifies the terms of the offer in any material way, it becomes a counteroffer. As already noted, this terminates the original offer. Acceptance must also be expressed or communicated. Silence may amount to an acceptance when the circumstances or previous course of dealing places the party receiving the offer under a duty to act or be bound. Acceptance may be made by implication, as by the acceptance of a consideration tendered with an offer, and this constitutes an acceptance of the offer.

An offer must be accepted in the manner specified in the offer, but if no particular manner of acceptance is specified, then acceptance may be by any reasonable and usual means. With real estate contracts, since they are required to be in writing, the acceptance by the offeree is generally effected by his signing of the deposit receipt.

Genuine assent. The final requirement for mutual consent is that the offer and acceptance be genuine. The principal obstacles to such genuine or real assent are fraud, mistake, duress, menace, or undue influence. If any one of these obstacles is present, the contract may be voidable and a party to the alleged contract may seek recision, which in effect restores both parties to their former positions, or dollar damages or possible restructuring of the contract to make it correct.

Fraud. This may be actual or constructive in nature. The Civil Code lists five acts that would be deemed actual fraud when done by or with the connivance of a party to a contract with intent to induce another party to enter into the contract, or even simply to deceive such other party:

1. The suggestion, as a fact, of that which is not true, by one who does not believe it to be true.
2. The positive assertion, in a manner not warranted by the information of the person making it, of that which is not true though he believes it to be true.
3. The suppression of that which is true by one having knowledge or belief of the fact.
4. A promise made without any intention of performing it.
5. Any other act fitted or intended to deceive.

Constructive fraud, as defined in the Civil Code, may consist of:

1. Any breach of duty that, without an actual fraudulent intent, gains an advantage for the person in fault, or anyone claiming under him, by misleading another to his prejudice or to the prejudice of anyone claiming under him.
2. Such act or omission as the law specifically declares to be fraudulent without respect to actual fraud. The element of reliance is essential in an action claiming fraud.

A distinction should be made between fraud in the inception or execution, and fraud in the inducement of a contract. Where the promiser knows what he is signing, and his consent is induced by fraud, the contract is voidable by him; but if the fraud goes to the inception or execution of the agreement so that the promiser is deceived as to the nature of his act and actually does not know what he is signing, and does not intend to enter into a contract at all, it is void. Thus it is obvious that where the contract is voidable, it is binding until rescinded, while if the contract is void, a formal act of recision is not necessary.

When an individual signs a contract without reading it, and where the failure of the individual to familiarize himself with the contents of a written contract prior to its execution is solely carelessness or negligence, relief is denied. Where such failure or negligence is induced by the false representation and fraud of the other party to the contract, so that its provisions are different from those set out, the court, even in the absence of a fiduciary or confidential relationship between the parties, may reform the instrument to reflect the true agreement of the parties.

A party to a contract who has been guilty of fraud in its inducement does not relieve himself from the effects of his fraud by any stipulation in the contract, either that no representations have been made, or that any right that might be grounded upon them is waived. Such a stipulation or waiver will be ignored, because the fraud renders the whole agreement voidable, including the waiver provisions. Where the false representations are made by an agent, and the contract contains a recital limiting the agent's authority to make representations, the innocent principal may, by certain stipulations, relieve himself from liability in a court action for damages for fraud and deceit, but the defrauded third party may nevertheless rescind the contract. The guilty agent may, of course, be liable in damages for his wrongful act. The laws with regard to agency and the real estate licensee as an agent were covered in the previous chapter.

Mistake. Another possible obstacle to genuineness of assent that might make the contract either void or voidable is mistake. Mistakes are classified in the Civil Code as mistake of fact or mistake of law.

A mistake of fact is one consisting of ignorance or forgetfulness of a legal duty on the part of the person making it. Or it may consist in the mistaken belief in the existence of the thing material to the contract, or a belief in the past existence of such a thing that has not existed.

A mistake of law is described as one that arises from a misapprehension of the law by all parties involved, all supposing they knew and understood it, yet making substantially the same mistake. It may also be a misapprehension of the law by one party, of which the others are aware at the time of contracting, but which they do not rectify.

Where both parties are mistaken as to the identity of the subject matter of the contract, there can be no contract. Where the subject matter of the agreement has, unknown to the parties, already ceased to exist so that the performance of the contract would be impossible, there is no contract.

Mutual agreement as to the subject matter is the basis of the contract, and if the parties of the agreement consent thereto, a contract results, but it may be voidable where there is a substantial mistake as to some basic or material fact that induced the complaining party to enter into it. Negligence of the injured party does not in itself preclude release from mistakes, unless it is gross negligence, as where the individual simply fails to read the agreement. One who accepts or signs an instrument that appears to be a contract is deemed to assent to all of its terms and cannot escape liability on the ground that he has not read it. This is true only in the absence of such influences as fraud, undue influence, or duress.

Duress, menace, or undue influence. Sometimes a contract may be rendered voidable because it was entered into under the pressure of duress, menace, or undue influence. All three may in effect deprive an individual of the free exercise of his will, and so the law permits him to avoid the contract, and may also provide other remedies.

There are two kinds of duress: the duress of persons, where an individual is forced to perform an act against his will, and the duress of goods, which is the unlawful detention of the property of such person.

Menace consists of a threat to commit duress, but also includes threat of unlawful and violent injury to any of the persons to an agreement, or a threat of injury to the character of any such persons.

Undue influence consists in the use, by one in whom a confidence is reposed by another, or who holds a real or apparent authority over him, of such confidence or authority for the purpose of obtaining an unfair advantage. Undue influence is most frequently encountered in connection with contracts between persons in confidential relationships, where one party is justified in assuming the other party will not act contrary to the former's welfare. An example of relationships that usually fall within this rule are those of trustee and beneficiary, broker and principal, husband and wife, attorney and client, and the like.

In addition to our discussion of the laws of agency and the real estate licensee in the previous chapter, the reader should also refer to Chapter 20 for a discussion of fraudulent actions under the Real Estate Law that affect the real estate licensee and may be grounds for suspension or revocation of the agent's real estate license.

Lawful object

Assuming now that parties are capable of contracting and have properly manifested their consent through an offer and acceptance, the validity of their agreement might still be attacked on grounds of legality. The contract must be legal in its formation and operation, and both its consideration and object must be lawful.

The object refers to what the contract requires the parties to do or not to do. Where the contract has but a single object, and that object is unlawful in whole or in part, or is impossible of performance, the contract is void. If there are several distinct objects, the contract is normally valid as to those parts that are lawful. An object is not lawful if it is contrary to an express provision of the law, or contrary to the policy of express law, or otherwise contrary to good morals.

Thus, the objects and consideration of a contract must be legal and not violate some specific prohibition of the law. If such violation does occur, its effect upon the contract may depend upon the particular statute involved. Some of the more frequent types of situations in the real estate field involving statutory violations are the following:

a. Contracts of unlicensed "brokers" or "general contractors." Persons claiming to act in such capacity cannot enforce their contracts unless they can prove they are properly licensed by the state of California to act in their respective capacities.

b. Forfeiture clauses in deposit receipts, contracts of sale, and leases. Although a liquidated damages clause may be valid, it is a general principle of law that any arrangement whereby the money or property of one person may be retained by another without regard to actual damage is void because it is a penalty. The courts have generally refused to permit a seller to retain a buyer's deposit upon default by the latter except where such retention is based on a valid liquidated damages clause and the actual damages can be proven by the seller.

c. A contract calling for payment of interest in excess of limits set by California law may be usurious depending upon the identity of the lending entity and the purpose of the loan. If such a contract is usurious, that portion of the contract relating to the payment of such unlawful interest is void.

d. In addition to the preceding, real estate licensees must be careful to comply with the numerous regulatory measures incorporated in the Real Estate Law and Rules and Regulations of the Commissioner, and this area is discussed in Chapter 20. Not only may a violation of law affect the enforcement of a contract but it may also affect a broker's or salesperson's license and subject the violator to charges of criminal liability.

Sufficient consideration

Although an agreement meets all the requirements of a valid contract already discussed, it may fail because of lack of sufficient consideration. In general, every executory contract requires consideration. The consideration may be either a benefit conferred or agreed to be conferred upon the person making the promise or any other person, or a detriment endured or agreed to be endured. It may be an act of forbearance or a change in legal relations. It is the price bargained for and paid for a promise, and it may, of course, be a return promise.

If a valid consideration exists, the promise is binding. Ordinarily the nature of the consideration is reflected in the written agreement of the parties, and the consideration must have some value. However, there is no requirement of adequacy to make the contract enforceable; thus an option to purchase valuable property may be given for consideration of $1.00 or some other nominal sum. It is only in an action for specific performance that the amount is important, and in this event the equitable remedy will be denied unless an adequate consideration is proved. It is important to note here, however, that gross inadequacy of consideration may be a circumstance that, together with other facts, may tend to show fraud or undue influence. In a bilateral contract, a promise of one party is consideration for the promise of another.

THE STATUTE OF FRAUDS

The statute of frauds was first adopted in England in 1677 and became part of the English common law. It was subsequently introduced into this country and has been codified in California. The purpose was to prevent perjury, forgery, and dishonest conduct on the part of unscrupulous people in proving the existence and terms of certain important types of contract. Thus, most contracts, which by statute are required to be in writing, are referred to as coming under the statute of frauds.

The statute provides that certain contracts are invalid unless the same or some note or memorandum thereof is in writing and subscribed, that is, signed, by the party to be charged or by his agent. Under California's Civil Code, contracts that are required to be in writing are:

1. An agreement that by its terms is not to be performed within a year from the making thereof.

2. A special promise to answer for the debt, default, or failure of performance of another, except in the cases provided for in Section 2794 of the Civil Code.

3. An agreement made upon consideration of marriage, other than a mutual promise to marry.

4. An agreement for the leasing for a longer period than one year, or for the sale of real property, or of an interest therein; such agreement, if made by an agent of the party sought to be charged, is invalid unless the authority of the agent is in writing, subscribed by the party sought to be charged.

5. An agreement authorizing or employing an agent, broker, or any other person to purchase or sell real estate, or to lease real estate for a longer period than one year, or to procure, introduce, or find a purchaser or seller of real estate or a lessee or lessor of real estate where such lease is for a longer period than one year, for compensation or a commission.

6. An agreement which by its terms is not to be performed during the lifetime of the promiser, or an agreement to devise or bequeath any property, or to make any provision for any reason by will.

7. An agreement by a purchaser of real property to pay an indebtedness secured by a mortgage or deed of trust upon the property purchase, unless assumption of said indebtedness by the purchaser is specifically provided for in the conveyance of such property.

8. An agreement for the sale of personal property may be required to be in writing. Contracts for the sale of goods properly comes under a discussion of the uniform commercial code (U.C.C.), the entire code having been adopted and in effect in California.

Comments with regard to statute of frauds

A thorough discussion of the implications of the statute of frauds is more properly left to a textbook dealing with the law of contracts or real estate law. We will here mention only a few basic points of importance, and generally confine these to the real estate business and transactions therein.

If a contract is made orally, and such contract falls within the scope of the statute of frauds but fails to comply with it, such contract is not void or illegal but is merely unenforceable. If a party to an oral contract brings suit in court to enforce the contract, which under the statute of frauds should have been in writing, the defendant party may use the statute of frauds as a defense and the contract will be held to be unenforceable by the court.

The statute of frauds is a defense only, and cannot be the basis for an affirmative action; thus where a purchaser pays money under an oral contract for the sale of land, and the seller is willing to perform under the agreement, the purchaser cannot thereafter file suit to recover the money paid. If an oral contract that comes under the statute of frauds has been fully performed, the statute of frauds does not apply and neither party can use it as a basis for recision of the contract or recovery of consideration given.

The note or memorandum required by the statute of frauds may be in any form, since its purpose is simply evidence of the contract. In the real estate business a number of common forms are used, and these are illustrated throughout this text. The required writing may consist of anything from one of these standard forms to a series of statements made in letters between the parties involved. Whatever the form of the writing, the important point is that it must contain all the material terms of the contract clearly enough so that a court would be able to determine what the parties had agreed to. The writing must bear the signature or signatures of the party or parties to be held to the agreement.

Parol evidence rule. When a contract is expressed in a writing that is intended to be the complete and final expression of the rights and duties of the parties, parol evidence is not admissible as evidence. This is what the law calls the parol evidence rule. Parol evidence refers to prior oral or written negotiations or agreements of the parties, or even oral agreements made at the same time as the written contract. The parol evidence rule prohibits the introduction of any outside evidence, either oral or written, to vary or add to the terms of an integrated written instrument such as a will, deed, or contract unless it may be necessary to complete an ambiguous or incomplete document.

PERFORMANCE, DISCHARGE, AND BREACH OF CONTRACTS

Having considered the essential elements of a valid contract, we will now review some of the legal aspects of performance, discharge, and breach of contracts.

Timely, substantial, and satisfactory performance

Forms used in most real estate transactions either state that "time is of the essence," and/or state a specific time given for the performance of the agreement. By statute, if no time is specified for the performance of an act required to be performed, a reasonable time is allowed. What is reasonable depends upon the particular situation, but since time for performance is generally so important with respect to contractual obligations, it is best not to leave this area in doubt and to state time periods clearly whenever possible. In our discussion of the Real Estate Law and the Rules and Regulations of the Commissioner in Chapter 20, and of real estate contracts in Chapter 9, the reader will continually be made aware of the importance of the question of time.

Substantial performance has to do with the degree of performance with regard to the exact requirements in the contract. One who substantially performs will generally be able to enforce the contract should the matter have to be decided in court. Suppose you contract to have the exterior of your house painted and tell the contractor that you want it all white with the exception of the doors and window trim, which are to be dark green. After the job is completed, you refuse to pay on the basis that the green is a medium green rather than a dark green. Should the case have to come to court, you may be permitted some adjustment of price, but the court would probably find that there has been substantial performance of the contract.

In other cases there must be what is termed *satisfactory performance*. Where satisfaction is subjective, as in the purchase of a custom-made suit, the purchaser must be satisfied as to its appearance and fit. There must also be satisfactory performance where such performance can be measured by a clearly objective standard, as where a new thermostat is installed to operate the furnace automatically and the thermostat fails to function properly.

Assignment. A party to a contract may wish to drop out of the agreement without terminating the contract. This may often be done by either assigning the contract to another or by novation. Whether the contract is assignable depends upon its nature and terms. Ordinarily, either a bilateral or a unilateral contract is assignable unless it calls for some personal quality of the promiser or unless it expressly or impliedly denies the right to assign it. The contract may expressly provide that it shall not be assigned, or it may contain provisions that are equivalent to such expressed stipulations. The effect of assignment is generally to transfer to the assignee all of the interest of the assignor. Since an assignment carries with it all the rights of the assignor, the assignment of a note carries with it any incidental securities such as mortgage or other lien.

Novation. The substitution by agreement of a new obligation for an existing one is termed novation. The substitution may be a new obligation between the same parties and/or a new party. A novation requires an intent to discharge the old contract and, being a new contract, requires consideration and other essentials of a valid contract.

Discharge of contracts

In the matter of discharge of contracts we can quickly recognize two extremes: full performance of the contract, which is the usual case, and a breach of contract, which occurs when one of the parties fails to perform. Between these two extremes are a variety of possibilities, including the following methods of discharge of a contract.

Partial performance. As long as the parties to the contract agree, a partial performance by one party may be accepted by the other as fulfillment and discharge of the contract. If the dispute involves a debt or a claim, acceptance of partial performance must be evidenced by an expressed agreement in writing.

Substantial performance. This has been mentioned previously, and in certain cases will be accepted by the court as having discharged the contract.

Impossibility of performance. Impossibility of performance can often, but not always, be used by one party to a contract as a means of discharging his responsibilities under the contract. For ex-

ample, let us assume that A, a plumbing contractor with a number of men working for him, personally contracts with B at an agreed-upon price for the modernization of an old-fashioned bathroom in B's home. Thereafter, A informs B that he has sprained an ankle and will not be able to do the job. Even though A cannot personally perform, he will be held to the terms of the contract since he can easily have one of his employees perform the agreed-upon work.

There are, however, a number of situations in which the courts will allow a party to be discharged from his failure to perform on the basis that there is an impossibility of performance. The more common of these excuses for nonperformance are as follows:

1. Where the performance becomes illegal by the passage of a local ordinance or other type of law that would make it illegal for one or both of the parties to perform. One example would involve the type of commercial frustration described below.

2. Destruction of the subject matter or means for performance of the contract before the promiser has performed, or where such destruction makes continued performance impossible.

3. Commercial frustration is also an excuse for nonperformance, as where one leases a building for the manufacture of a highly flammable product and the city council thereafter passes an ordinance prohibiting the manufacture of such products within the city limits; the lessee could then be excused from the lease. In addition to illegality, some other condition might arise that would make it extremely unreasonable to force one of the parties to perform, and if there is no loss to the other party, performance will be excused. Also, where the obligation under the contract is strictly personal in nature, and the performance cannot be assigned or delegated to another, the inability of the promiser to perform will constitute discharge.

Agreement between the parties. If the original parties to a contract later agree to release each other from the obligations under the contract, it may be discharged in this manner. This can generally be accomplished only where there are no third parties involved whose rights may be violated by such agreement. An agreement to discharge a party to a contract must be supported by consideration, and while there are fewer problems where there has been little or no actual performance by the parties, there may be more when there has been full or virtually full performance under the terms of the contract. A revocation or repealing of a contract by mutual consent of the parties involved is often referred to as a mutual recision of the contract.

Release and alteration. If one of the parties to a contract materially alters it in any way without the knowledge of the other party, the party without knowledge of such alteration is discharged from performing under the contract. Once the parties have entered into an agreement, neither may make any changes in the terms without the agreement of the other. This is one of the reasons that the Real Estate Law requires a real estate licensee to provide a person signing an agreement of any type with a copy of the agreement at the time of the signing. If any change is secretly made later, the party or parties affected would thus have a copy of the authentic document in their possession.

Operation of law. Certain aspects of discharge by operation of law have been mentioned previously. Whenever any illegality occurs in connection with an agreement, it may serve to effect a discharge of the contract.

Acceptance of a breach of contract. Where there is a breach of contract, which is the failure of one of the parties to perform, the other party may merely accept the breach. We shall discuss breach, and remedies other than acceptance of the breach, after a review of the statute of limitations.

Discharge by statute of limitations

The statute of limitations as we know it today has evolved because of the historical refusal of the courts to grant a remedy to an individual who has delayed an unreasonable time before bringing suit. The statute of limitations, then, sets the time period after a cause of action has occurred during which a civil action seeking relief for a breach of contract can be commenced. An action is considered to have commenced when a complaint is formally filed.

It is therefore said that the running of the statute of limitations will bar any action seeking relief in the courts. A summary of some of the clauses that are of special interest to those in the real estate business are as follows.

Actions that must be brought within 90 days. Civil actions for the recovery of or conversion of personal property such as trunks, valises, or baggage alleged to have been left at a hotel, boarding house, lodging house, furnished apartment house, or furnished bungalow court shall be commenced within 90 days from the departure of the owner of said property.

Within six months. An action against an officer or officer de facto to recover any goods, wages, merchandise, or other property seized by any such officer in his official capacity as tax collector, or to recover the price or value of any such goods or other personal property, as well as for damage done to any person or property in making any such seizure must be commenced within six months; so must actions on claims against a county that have been rejected by the board of supervisors.

Within one year. An action for libel or slander, or for injury to or the expiration of one caused by the wrongful act or neglect of another, or by a depositor against a bank for the payment of a forged or raised check must be commenced within one year.

Within two years. An action upon a contract, obligation, or liability not founded upon an instrument in writing (other than open book accounts, accounts stated and open, and current and mutual accounts, where the limit is four years); or an action founded upon a contract, obligation, or liability evidenced by a certificate or abstract of guaranty of title of real property or by a policy of title insurance, provided that the cause of action of such contracts shall not be deemed to have accrued until the discovery of the loss or damage suffered by the aggrieved party thereunder must be commenced within two years.

Within three years. An action upon a liability created by statute other than a penalty of forfeiture; an action for trespass upon or injury to real property; an action for taking, detaining, or injuring any goods or chattels, including actions for the recovery of specific personal property; and an action for relief on the ground of fraud or mistake must begin within three years. Such cause of action is not to be deemed to have accrued until the discovery by the injured party of the facts constituting the fraud or mistake.

Within four years. An action upon any contract, obligation, or liability founded upon an instrument in writing except an option upon any bonds, notes, or debentures issued by any corporation or pursuant to permit of the commissioner of corporations, or upon any coupons issued with such bonds, notes, or debentures if they shall have been issued to or held by the public, in which case an additional two years are allowed.

Within five years. An action for intermediate profits and profits from the use of land during wrongful occupancy, and an action for the recovery of real property must be commenced within five years.

Within 10 years. An action upon a judgment or decree of any court of the United States or of any state within the United States must begin within 10 years.

Remedies for breach of contract

A contract may be discharged by simple acceptance of the breach. Thus, if one party fails to perform, the other may accept the contract as ended. He may do so for various reasons, either because he feels that damages recoverable are too limited to justify costly litigation, or because he considers the other party to be without sufficient assets to satisfy a judgment obtained against him.

If the victim of a breach, however, is not willing to accept the breach, various remedies are available, the most common being *(a)* unilateral recision, *(b)* action for dollar damages, or *(c)* action for specific performance.

Unilateral recision. Recision is available to a person who enters a contract without real or genuine assent because of fraud, mistake, duress, menace, or undue influence. Also, if the consideration for his obligation fails in whole or in part through the fault of the other party, or if such consideration becomes entirely void, or if it fails in a material respect before it is rendered to him, he may rescind. Recision may be adjudged on the application of the aggrieved party in either oral or written contracts, when the contract is unlawful for causes not apparent in the agreement or context of the document and the parties are not equally at fault, or when the public interest will be prejudiced by permitting it to stand. As has been previously mentioned, a minor or incompetent may generously rescind his contracts.

Mutual recision is a means of discharging a contract by agreement between the parties, but where one of the parties has breached the contract the other party who has been wronged may himself unilaterally rescind. He must, however, use reasonable diligence to comply with the following statutory rules:

1. He must rescind promptly, upon discovering the facts that entitle him to rescind, if he is free from duress, menace, undue influence, or inability and is aware of his right to rescind.

2. He must restore to the other party everything of value received from him under the contract, or he must offer to restore the same, upon condition that such other party shall do likewise, unless the latter is unable or refuses to do so.

If a court adjudges the recision, it may require the party to whom such relief is granted to make any compensation to the other that it deems correct. It should be noted, however, that a party having the right to rescind may himself accomplish a complete recision. The reader is referred to Chapter 12 for a discussion of an individual's right to rescind in connection with the truth-in-lending law.

Action for monetary damages. Where a breach of contract has been detrimental to an individual, he may often recover compensation therefore in money, which is called damages. He is entitled to interest thereon from the time his right to recover is vested, and if the contract stipulates a legal rate of interest, that rate remains chargeable after the breach as before and until superseded by a court order or other new obligation. The damages for breach of contract must be reasonable, and exemplary damages that serve to punish the defendant are not allowed. The detriment caused by the breach of an agreement to convey title or an interest in real property is deemed to be the price paid and the expenses properly incurred in examining the title and preparing the necessary papers, with interest thereon.

In certain contracts, the parties may anticipate the possibility of a breach, for example in a building contract the possible delay of completion beyond a promised date. The parties may specify in the contract the amount of damages to be paid in the event of the breach, and such damages are known as liquidated damages. They will be enforced by the courts provided the amount specified is not so excessive as to constitute a penalty, and provided it would be impractical or extremely difficult to fix the actual damage, and normally only if the contract expressly provides that liquidated damages shall be the only remedy available in the event of breach of the contract.

Specific performance. Another source of relief in the event of breach of contract is a suit for specific performance. In such action, the aggrieved party will ask the court to compel the other party to perform according to the provisions of the contractual agreement. If specific performance is to be ordered by the court, the remedy must be mutual. That is, neither party to an obligation can be compelled specifically to perform it unless the other party thereto has performed or is likewise compelled specifically to perform. To be entitled to use the equitable remedy of specific performance, a plaintiff must show that the contract is just and reasonable to the defendant. Further, specific performance cannot be enforced against a party to a contract if he has not received adequate consideration.

With respect to any community real property, the wife must join with the husband in executing any instrument by which such community real property or any interest therein is sold, conveyed or encumbered, or leased for a longer period than one year. Since an agreement to procure the consent of a wife cannot be specifically enforced, it is important to get the signature of the wife on the instrument. It frequently happens that this failure to procure the signature of the wife is cured by the seller's putting into escrow the deed signed by both husband and wife, or by the buyer's putting into escrow a deed of trust signed by both. Where this is done the original want of mutuality is cured, provided it is done before an attempt is made to withdraw from the contract by the other party. It is, however, unwise to rely on this possibility, and the signatures of both parties should be obtained when the instrument is prepared. However, the right of a purchaser in good faith without knowledge of the marriage relationship where the husband alone holds the record title to the real property may be established without the wife's signature. There are often owners of real property other than husband and wife. It is therefore necessary to get the signatures of all of the owners, since the buyer cannot compel specific performance of the contract as to one-half of the property where it is contemplated that the whole is to be sold.

Specific performance cannot be enforced against a party to a contract if his assent was obtained by misrepresentation, concealment, or any other unfair practice of any party to whom performance would become due under the contract. A buyer is always entitled to receive a merchantable title. Therefore, if the seller cannot give the buyer a title free from reasonable doubt, the seller cannot specifically enforce such an agreement. This does not mean that the title need be merchantable at the time the original agreement was executed, but it must be at the time it becomes the duty of the seller to convey. If there are encumbrances known to the parties, subject to which it is agreed the title will be conveyed, these encumbrances should be described in the contract and will not block specific performance. The condition in an agreement that a policy of title insurance shall be issued is the common protection against unknown liens or encumbrances at the time an agreement is initially entered into.

Courses of action as a result of nonperformance and breach of a contract in connection with the purchase of real property will be further discussed in the following chapter.

Third party beneficiaries. The situation often arises in which individuals who are not parties to a contract may acquire rights in it. Assignees are such persons, and the assignment of a contract was discussed previously. Another example of where a third party may benefit from a contract is where the contract is intended to confer a benefit upon such third party, who is termed a third party beneficiary. Thus, not only may the original parties to a contract enforce their rights in court, but third parties who acquire rights in the contract may also enforce their rights in court.

QUESTIONS FOR DISCUSSION

1. What problems may arise as the result of contracting with a minor?
2. May a real estate broker act as an agent for an individual under 18 years of age?
3. What is the difference between a bilateral and a unilateral contract?
4. Why are real estate contracts termed *express contracts?*
5. What are some methods by which an offer may be terminated?
6. Discuss the basic difference between an acceptance and a counteroffer.
7. How is acceptance usually effected with regard to a contract for the sale of real property?
8. What types of acts would be classified as actual fraud?
9. Give some examples of void, voidable, and unenforceable contracts.
10. Discuss the difference between duress, menace, and undue influence.
11. Give some examples of unlawful objects and consideration in a contract.
12. How might inadequacy of consideration in a real estate contract tend to show fraud?
13. What is the purpose of the statute of frauds?
14. What is the importance of a "time is of the essence" clause in a real estate contract?
15. How does satisfactory performance differ from substantial performance?
16. How might impossibility of performance arise with respect to a contract?
17. Of what effect is the statute of limitations?
18. What are some of the ways in which a contract may be discharged?

19. Discuss the remedies available as the result of a breach of contract.
20. How may an individual not a party to a contract acquire rights in it?

MULTIPLE CHOICE QUESTIONS

8–1. An offeror is an individual: *(a)* accepting an offer, *(b)* to whom an offer is given, *(c)* making the offer, *(d)* representing a purchaser.

8–2. Parol evidence refers to: *(a)* oral statements, *(b)* specific conditions in a purchase offer, *(c)* required signature of a parole officer, *(d)* none of these.

8–3. A contract to sell community property: *(a)* requires court approval, *(b)* must be signed by both husband and wife, *(c)* is valid if either spouse signs it, *(d)* must be prepared by a licensed real estate broker.

8–4. An executory contract: *(a)* is generally prepared by court order, *(b)* must contain a monetary consideration, *(c)* has yet to be completed by the parties, *(d)* generally contains a novation.

8–5. The statute of frauds specifies: *(a)* time allowed to file a court action, *(b)* types of fraudulent statements, *(c)* responsibilities of a real estate licensee in preparing contracts, *(d)* which contracts must be in writing.

8–6. A contract is usually enforceable if there is: *(a)* duress, *(b)* substantial breach, *(c)* substantial performance, *(d)* misrepresentation.

8–7. An example of an unlawful object is: *(a)* a listing contract, *(b)* an assignment clause in a contract, *(c)* an interest rate of 10 percent per annum, *(d)* a contract of an unlicensed general contractor.

8–8. An acceptance that slightly modifies an offer: *(a)* results in a legal contract, *(b)* is valid with respect to real property, *(c)* constitutes a ratification, *(d)* none of these.

Real estate contracts

9

In this chapter we shall discuss and illustrate examples of the most commonly used types of real estate contracts. These will include: *(a)* the listing agreement, *(b)* standard deposit receipt form, and real estate purchase contract and receipt for deposit form, *(c)* real estate exchange agreement, *(d)* option to purchase real estate, and *(e)* agreement of sale.

LISTING CONTRACTS

A listing is an employment contract that establishes the agency relationship between a broker (the agent) and a property owner (the principal) for the purpose of attempting to negotiate the sale or purchase of real property.

Generally speaking, a verbal agreement to pay a commission is not enforceable in court unless the broker has a written listing signed by the owner of the property. The listing must show the intention of the owner to pay a commission to the broker when he procures a buyer with whom the owner enters into an agreement for the purchase of the property.

There are a few exceptions to this general rule. Although no broker should make a practice of trying to sell a property without the protection of a properly executed listing form, the question arises as to whether or not a broker can collect a commission even though he was not working under a listing from the owner.

The courts have held that where the only agreement to pay a commission is contained in an agreement for the sale of the property between the seller and the buyer, the broker is entitled to a commission on performance of the provisions contained in the sales agreement. The requirement that a contract with a broker to .sell real property be in writing may also be satisfied by evidence that the buyers and sellers signed escrow instructions providing for payment of a commission out of money deposited in escrow, and that the escrow was satisfactorily completed.

It is important to remember that the subject of commission payable to the broker arises three times during the normal real estate transaction:

1. At the time the listing agreement is completed.
2. At the time the sales agreement is completed.
3. In the instructions prepared by the escrow officer, attorney, or whoever else may be acting in this capacity.

TYPES OF LISTINGS

Oral listing

As the name implies, an oral listing contains nothing in writing and, although used occasionally by some brokers, should be avoided as unsound business practice. When working on a property where there has been only an oral discussion between the licensee and property owner regarding the price, terms, commission, and so on, the licensee is putting forth time and expense without the protection of a written contract. Often a broker may talk to a prospect about a piece of property and even show him the property, only to find later that the buyer had subsequently contracted and purchased directly from the owner, thus eliminating the commission the broker would have earned.

Open listing

Open listings, and all listings to be discussed subsequently, are listings in writing. In an open listing, the seller may employ a number of brokers, each of whom will have an equal opportunity to sell the property and earn a commission. Under an open listing the commission is payable only to the first broker who procures a buyer with whom the seller enters into an agreement. An open listing may or may not contain a specified term, whereas all subsequent listings that will be discussed must contain a definite termination date.

The seller may sell the property himself and pay no commission, and he may withdraw the property from the market at any time he wants, since the open listing contains no definite term of employment. Open listings, which are sometimes referred to as nonexclusive listings, are used by builders, developers, attorneys, and others who do not want to be bound to any particular broker or set of specific requirements.

Exclusive-agency listing

In an exclusive-agency listing, one broker is designated as the exclusive agent by the property owner, and only this one broker has a listing for the sale of the property. The listing is for a specified term, but the owner still has the right to sell the property himself without having to pay a commission.

This type of listing is slightly better for the broker than the open listing in that it excludes other brokers. If another broker has a client who is interested in buying the property, he will have to contact the broker named in the listing and work with him. However, since the owner reserves the right to sell the property himself, another broker may bypass the broker who has the listing and attempt to reach some agreement with the owner in connection with a sale of the property.

Exclusive-right-to-sell listing

The exclusive-right-to-sell listing, also commonly referred to as an exclusive authorization and right-to-sell listing, is the one most commonly used by brokers throughout the United States. This listing gives the broker named the exclusive right to sell the property and excludes the owner from doing so without paying the broker a commission. The broker named in the listing thus becomes the sole agent, and if the property is sold by the owner or by anyone else during the term of the listing the broker is entitled to a commission. Most exclusive-right-to-sell listings contain the further provision that in the event the owner, after expiration of the listing, sells the property to a person or persons with whom the broker negotiated during the term of the listing, then the broker is still entitled to a commission.

This is the best type of listing not only for the broker but also for the property owner. By entering into this form of listing, the owner shows that he has complete confidence in the broker and is content to let the broker handle the entire transaction. In turn, the broker will certainly give the property his full attention, advertise it properly, and try to effect a sale in the shortest possible time. The broker named in the listing may, if he wishes, cooperate with other brokers who may have an interested buyer. This type of cooperation between two real estate firms, one with the property for sale and the other with an interested buyer, is practiced quite often. The owner pays the commission agreed on in the listing, and the cooperating brokers divide the commission between themselves as they wish, usually 50–50.

Multiple listing

A multiple listing is an exclusive-right-to-sell listing used by brokers who belong to a multiple-listing service or exchange. Under this arrangement brokers pool their listings so that a listing by any one broker who belongs to the multiple-listing service is made available to all of the other members of the organization. The initials MLS are commonly used to designate this type of listing and to indicate that a broker may be a member of a multiple-listing service. In some areas of the state an MLS broker must submit all his listings for distribution to fellow members, while in other areas a broker may use an MLS listing form for some properties but retain other properties on an exclusive listing within his office.

The broker who obtains the MLS listing has control over the negotiations, and other MLS members must work through him. The listing broker who sells the property himself earns the entire commission. If he must cooperate with another MLS broker, then the commission is divided by agreement between the brokers involved.

Net listing

A net listing allows the broker to receive as his commission any amount in excess of the selling price fixed by the seller. In the listings we have discussed previously, the commission has been stated as a fixed percent of the final selling price. In the net listing, the broker and seller agree on a specific price the seller will accept, and the broker receives whatever he is able to get over and above the amount the seller wants.

Net listings generally are not used to any great extent. They often give rise to a claim of unfairness by the seller, who will usually say that the net price agreed on was too low and that the broker should have known this and set a higher net amount for the seller to receive. In California, a broker must disclose to the seller the amount of his commission in connection with a net listing before the seller signs a sales agreement.

Option listing

An option listing gives the broker an option to purchase the property himself. When exercising this option, the broker is in a fiduciary position and must make a full disclosure of all outstanding offers to purchase and any other information in his possession. The reasoning behind this is quite obviously to be certain that the broker does not take unfair advantage of the seller. For example, a broker can wait until he finds a third party to whom he can make a profitable resale of the property and then exercise his option to purchase it. The seller here is not aware that the broker has a buyer waiting. Since the option under an option listing is usually exercised only after a period of time during which the broker is supposedly trying to sell the property in the normal way, it follows that the broker may not try too hard once he finds a buyer who is willing to pay a price well above the option price. The temptation is strong for an unethical broker to wait until he can exercise his option, buy the property, and then sell to the waiting buyer, thus making a good deal more than the normal commission. A variation of the option procedure is often used quite properly in connection with a guaranteed trade-in plan discussed in Chapter 21. Using this plan, the broker guarantees the buyer that he will sell the buyer's presently owned property within the usual amount of time given in a listing, or buy it from him for a preagreed-upon price if it is not sold.

With such a guarantee, the buyer will be able to negotiate and enter into a contract for the purchase of a new property.

ANALYSIS OF THE LISTING FORM

Although the exact wording and form of listings may vary somewhat throughout the state, they are basically the same as far as their major provisions are concerned. The example in Figure 9–1 is an exclusive-right-to-sell listing form prepared by the California Association of Realtors® (CAR). The numbered parts of the form in this illustration correspond to those of the explanations that follow.

1. *Right to sell.* The name of the real estate broker or of the real estate firm is entered here. Often, the listing form will be prepared by a licensed salesman rather than by the broker himself, and the salesman should be careful not to write in his own name at this point. It is the broker who is being appointed agent under the terms of the listing contract, and if the salesman is filling in the form he will sign his name at the bottom.

The term of the listing is entered, usually a term of 30, 60, or 90 days. Although 90 days is the most common, there is no set term. If the broker feels that a particular piece of property may take a longer than average time to sell, he may ask the owner for a longer period. The words *exclusive and irrevocable* are very important, since it is these words preceding the term that identify this as an exclusive-right-to-sell listing. The city and county in which the property is located are entered, and then a space is provided for entering the location of the property. This may be done in a variety of ways. Some brokers merely enter the street and number of the property, while others enter not only the mailing address but also the lot and block number of the property, which may be obtained from the owner's tax bill or from the county recorder's office. If the property is large in area, such as country or ranch property, the broker may enter the legal metes and bounds, or surveyor's description.

2. *Terms of sale.* The purchase price at which the property is being offered for sale is stated.

A space is provided for the specific terms under which the seller is offering the property to a prospective purchaser. These terms must be discussed in detail by the broker and the seller, and must be completely understood by both, since it is on these terms that the broker will offer the

EXCLUSIVE AUTHORIZATION AND RIGHT TO SELL

THIS IS INTENDED TO BE A LEGALLY BINDING AGREEMENT—READ IT CAREFULLY.

CALIFORNIA ASSOCIATION OF REALTORS® STANDARD FORM

1. **Right to Sell.** I hereby employ and grant _____Maxwell Realty Company_____
hereinafter called "Agent," the exclusive and irrevocable right commencing on _____March 9_____, 19 _--_ , and expiring at
midnight on _____June 9_____, 19 _--_ , to sell or exchange the real property situated in _____,
County of _____San Francisco_____, California described as follows:

_____Lot and improvements designated as Assessors Block 1833, Lot 3_____
_____commonly known as 828 Rockaway Avenue, San Francisco, California._____

2. **Terms of Sale.** The purchase price shall be $ _____153,000_____, to be paid in the following terms:

_____Sellers prefer all cash to sellers at close of escrow but may assist buyers_____
_____with some secondary financing._____

(a) The following items of personal property are to be included in the above-stated price:

_____Wall-to-wall carpeting and drapes presently in the premises._____

(b) Agent is hereby authorized to accept and hold on my behalf a deposit upon the purchase price.

(c) Evidence of title to the property shall be in the form of a California Land Title Association Standard Coverage Policy of Title Insurance in
the amount of the selling price to be paid for by _____buyers_____

(d) I warrant that I am the owner of the property or have the authority to execute this agreement. I hereby authorize a FOR SALE sign to be
placed on my property by Agent. I authorize the Agent named herein to cooperate with sub-agents.

**3. Notice: The amount or rate of real estate commissions is not fixed by law. They are set by each broker
individually and may be negotiable between the seller and broker.**

Compensation to Agent. I hereby agree to compensate Agent as follows:

(a) _____6_____ % of the selling price if the property is sold during the term hereof, or any extension thereof, by Agent,
on the terms herein set forth or any other price and terms I may accept, or through any other person, or by me, or _____6_____ %
of the price shown in 2, if said property is withdrawn from sale, transferred, conveyed, leased without the consent of Agent, or made unmarketable by
my voluntary act during the term hereof or any extension thereof.

(b) the compensation provided for in subparagraph (a) above if property is sold, conveyed or otherwise transferred within _____90_____
days after the termination of this authority or any extension thereof to anyone with whom Agent has had negotiations prior to final termination, provided I
have received notice in writing, including the names of the prospective purchasers, before or upon termination of this agreement or any extension
thereof. However, I shall not be obligated to pay the compensation provided for in subparagraph (a) if a valid listing agreement is entered into during the
term of said protection period with another licensed real estate broker and a sale, lease or exchange of the property is made during the term of said valid
listing agreement.

4. If action be instituted to enforce this agreement, the prevailing party shall receive reasonable attorney's fees and costs as fixed by the Court.

5. In the event of an exchange, permission is hereby given Agent to represent all parties and collect compensation or commissions from them,
provided there is full disclosure to all principals of such agency. Agent is authorized to divide with other agents such compensation or commissions in
any manner acceptable to them.

6. I agree to save and hold Agent harmless from all claims, disputes, litigation, and/or judgments arising from any incorrect information supplied by
me, or from any material fact known by me concerning the property which I fail to disclose.

7. This property is offered in compliance with state and federal anti-discrimination laws.

8. Other provisions:

9. I acknowledge that I have read and understand this Agreement, and that I have received a copy hereof.

Dated _____March 9_____, 19 _--_ _____San Francisco_____, California

_____(s) Sam Seller_____   _____(s) Virginia Seller_____
OWNER   OWNER

_____828 Rockaway Avenue_____   _____San Francisco, California 94118_____   _____363-7788_____
ADDRESS   CITY—STATE—PHONE

10. In consideration of the above, Agent agrees to use diligence in procuring a purchaser.

_____Maxwell Realty Company_____   _____800 Market Street, San Francisco, 94112_____
AGENT   ADDRESS—CITY

By _____(s) H. M. Maxwell_____   _____564-1919_____   _____March 9, 19--_____
         PHONE   DATE

FIGURE 9-1

property to the public. Included here are items relating to the financial arrangements and possible second loan to be carried back by the seller. Instead of noting specific terms, many brokers prefer to state, "All cash or other terms acceptable to seller." This does not bind the seller to accept any offer other than all cash and allows the seller to consider any other offer which may be made by the buyer.

a. Items of personal property, such as stove and refrigerator, which will be included in the purchase price are shown.

b. The agent is authorized to accept a deposit from a prospective purchaser. Most forms contain this provision to make it quite clear that any deposit money accepted by the broker is held for the benefit of the seller and does not belong to the agent.

c. A statement dealing with the issuance of a policy of title insurance and who shall pay for the policy is shown. In California it is customary for proof of title to be in the form of a title insurance policy prepared and issued by a title insurance company. The main purpose is to be certain the buyer receives a good marketable title, free of all liens and encumbrances except those he agrees to assume. Whether buyer or seller pays for the title insurance policy varies throughout the state and is discussed in detail in Chapter 15.

d. Seller warrants ownership of the property and agrees to permit the broker's sign to be affixed to the property. State law specifically allows placement of a sign on real property with respect to sale, rental, or exchange. The sign must be of a reasonable size as determined by the city or county having jurisdiction and must be permitted to show the name, address, and phone number of the owner or his agent.

3. *Compensation to agent.* The amount of the commission is set down as a percentage of the selling price and is also usually written out in the space provided.

a. A percentage figure should be given, since the selling price of the property usually will not be the asking price of the seller; thus a stated percentage can later be applied to the amount the property finally brings. The amount of the broker's commission is not fixed by law but is strictly a matter of agreement between the seller-principal and the broker-agent. Assembly Bill 802, effective July 1980 and added to the Business and Professions Code as Section 10147.5, requires that any printed or form agreement which fixes the compensation to be paid to a real estate licensee

for the sale of residential real property containing not more than four residential units shall contain the following statement in not less than 10-point boldface type immediately preceding any provisions of such agreement relating to compensation of the licensee: Notice: The amount or rate of real estate commissions is not fixed by law. They are set by each broker individually and may be negotiable between the seller and broker.

Since this is an exclusive-right-to-sell form, valid for a stated period of time, the seller agrees that should he sell the property himself during this time, withdraw it from the market, or lease or rent it, he will be responsible for the payment of a commission to the broker. The amount of the commission is based on the stated percentage as applied to the stated asking price on the listing.

b. A safety clause is provided which protects the broker's commission with respect to a common situation. A buyer has been shown the property by the broker, or has talked to the broker about a particular piece of property, and then goes to the owner and attempts to purchase directly from him. The owner and buyer may wait until the broker's listing has terminated and then deal with each other. In any event, the seller expects to avoid the need to pay the broker a commission and thus save the buyer some money by accepting a reduced amount for the property.

It is very important, therefore, that a broker or salesman keep complete and accurate records of the names of all persons with whom he comes into contact regarding the sale of a particular piece of property. Many licensees make it a practice to supply the seller with a list of such names in writing to be able to later show that they had negotiated with those persons named during the term of the listing.

4. This provision is common in most contracts and reminds the parties that in a lawsuit, attorneys' fees and court costs are generally added to any amounts the court may award.

5. The listing also gives the broker the exclusive and irrevocable right to act as agent in the exchange of the property, and this section deals with exchanges and cooperation with other real estate agents.

6. Although the owner agrees to hold the agent harmless from any liability or damages with respect to incorrect or missing information, the broker must be sure to obtain all relevant information about the property when securing the listing and not always rely completely upon facts supplied by the owner. In order to avoid an accusation of

negligence, the broker must be very careful with respect to statements made to clients and must conduct his own investigation with respect to the property.

7. This "civil rights" provision complies with requirements of federal and state law. The seller is made aware that racial discrimination is against the law.

8. Space is provided for insertion of additional provisions which may relate to any number of subjects, such as certain repairs to be made by the seller or the way in which the seller will give possession of the property at close of escrow.

9. The listing agreement must be dated and signed by the property owner. Since California is a community property state, it is important that both the husband and wife sign all documents pertaining to any real estate transaction. This may not be necessary where separate property is involved, but since most property held by husband and wife is community, the broker should be on the safe side and obtain both signatures.

The law requires that a copy of any document pertaining to the sale or purchase of real property must be given to those persons signing such a document.

10. The broker signs the agreement, or the name of the broker or the firm is entered and is followed by the signature of the licensed salesperson.

THE DEPOSIT RECEIPT

The form generally used in connection with the sale of real property in California has come to be known as the "deposit receipt." The California Association of Realtors® in conjunction with the California Bar Association (CBA) has developed and made available a form titled, "Real Estate Purchase Contract and Receipt for Deposit." In several states other than California, the state bar associations have brought charges of illegal practice of law against real estate brokers and brokers' organizations, basing the actions on the type of deposit receipts used, or on the way they were filled out, or both. In some states the right of the real estate agent to complete a deposit receipt form was jeopardized by court decisions on the actions brought. Compromise was achieved, usually based on the agreement that real estate licensees would use a stipulated form or forms or else subject themselves to a charge of unlawful practice of the law. It was to avert the development of any such situation in this state that the

CAR and CBA negotiated at length and agreed on content and preparation of the present form.

Deposit receipt as a contract

The deposit receipt is one of the most important forms used by the real estate licensee. It not only constitutes a receipt for a deposit to bind an offer by prospective purchasers, but when properly signed by the purchasers and accepted by the sellers and signed by them, it also becomes a contract for the purchase and sale of real property.

In addition to its contract purpose, the acceptance section at the bottom of the deposit receipt form also restates the obligation of the sellers to pay the real estate broker a specified sum as his commission. Although the sellers may have previously agreed to payment of a commission in the listing contract, the exact amount of the commission based on the actual agreed-on selling price is stated on the deposit receipt. Since the broker may be selling property for which he has no listing, he is protected by the properly completed deposit receipt, which will entitle him to his commission on completion of the transaction. The most protection regarding his commission is afforded the broker acting under a written listing agreement who subsequently obtains a completed deposit receipt. The broker acting under a written listing may be entitled to a commission even though the transaction is never consummated, while the broker who has only a deposit receipt will generally not receive a commission unless the transaction is actually completed.

As a contract, the deposit receipt is essentially like any other, and because it deals with real property it must be in writing and signed by the parties involved in order to be valid under the statute of frauds. There must be *(a)* parties capable of contracting, *(b)* their consent, that is, genuine offer and acceptance, *(c)* a lawful object, and *(d)* sufficient consideration.

In a real estate sales transaction, the seller usually states the price, terms, and conditions under which he is willing to sell the property when he completes the listing agreement with his broker, or even if he attempts to sell the property himself. These terms and conditions are known as his offer. When a prospective purchaser accepts these terms and conditions set forth by the seller, the result is a binding contract. Usually, however, the buyer does not completely accept the terms and conditions asked for by the seller, and instead makes his own offer to the seller.

It makes no difference whether the offer comes from the property seller or from the buyer; if negotiation finally leads to a definite offer on the one side and unconditional acceptance on the other side, a contract has been effected. All that is legally required to complete the contract for the sale of real property is to reduce the terms and conditions to writing and have the parties sign the contract. This is done on the deposit receipt form.

All forms such as deposit receipts, listing agreements, exchange agreements, and any other agreement for the sale or exchange of real property should contain the following provisions.

1. Date of the agreement.
2. Names and addresses of the parties to the contract.
3. Description of the property.
4. Consideration.
5. Reference to creation of new mortgages or trust deeds, if any.
6. References to existing mortgages or trust deeds, if any.
7. Any other provisions that may be required or requested by either party.
8. Date and place of closing.

PREPARING THE DEPOSIT RECEIPT

Different forms of deposit receipts are in use throughout the state. While they are basically the same, the phraseology of various sections of the form have been changed in certain parts of the state to conform more closely to the general practice in that particular area.

Although we will use the CAR Real Estate Purchase Contract and Receipt for Deposit as an illustration, it makes no difference which of the rather standardized deposit receipt forms is used, since they will all show the same general procedure.

1. The seller will provide the buyer with a deed.
2. A policy of title insurance will be issued.
3. The buyer will sign a note secured by a deed of trust for any money he may have to borrow in order to effect the purchase of the property.

All this will have occurred between the time the deposit receipt has been signed and accepted by the parties to the transaction and the successful completion of the transaction at close of escrow.

Throughout our discussion of deposit receipt preparation, we shall assume the most basic of all real estate transactions—the sale of a single-family residence. The parts of the deposit receipt form in Figure 9–2 correspond to those of the explanations which follow.

(a) Enter the name of the city or town in which the agreement is being filled out, and the current date, in the upper right corner of the deposit receipt.

(b) Received from. Enter the name(s) of the person(s) making the purchase offer. The name of the purchaser and legal status should be shown. Examples:

> Llewelyn Snyder and Marie Snyder (husband and wife).
> Julia Clark (a single woman).
> Paul Fisher (a married man).
> George Martin (a licensed real estate broker) and Elizabeth Martin (husband and wife).
> William McCarthy (a licensed real estate salesman) and Mabelline McCarthy (husband and wife).

The law does not require a real estate licensee to disclose to individuals with whom he may deal possession of a real estate license, as long as the licensee is acting as a principal and not as an agent in connection with the transaction.

Commissioner's Regulation 2727 states that a real estate salesman or a real estate broker acting in the capacity of a real estate salesperson who enters into an agreement as a principal involving the purchase or sale of real property while licensed to, or in the case of a broker/salesperson, while subject to the supervision of a broker, shall make a written disclosure of the fact of purchase or sale to the supervising broker within five days from execution of the agreement and before close of escrow. In other words, disclosure doesn't have to be to individuals with whom the licensee deals, but it must be to a supervising or employing broker.

These are only a few examples of the many possible. If the persons making the offer are related, always make clear the relationship. If one is married and the other is not, this also should be made clear.

> A single man or woman is one who has never been married.
> An unmarried man or woman is one who has been married but is now legally divorced, and the final divorce decree has been issued by the court, or whose marriage has been dissolved and a dissolution decree has been issued by the court.
> A married man or woman is a legally married person.
> A widow or widower is one who has lost a spouse and has not remarried.

CALIFORNIA ASSOCIATION OF REALTORS® STANDARD FORM

REAL ESTATE PURCHASE CONTRACT
AND RECEIPT FOR DEPOSIT

THIS IS MORE THAN A RECEIPT FOR MONEY. IT IS INTENDED TO BE A LEGALLY BINDING CONTRACT. READ IT CAREFULLY.

(A) _____ San Francisco , California. _____ March 25 , 19--

(B) Received from James A. Byar and Margaret Byar, husband and wife _____

(C) herein called Buyer, the sum of Fifteen hundred Dollars .... Dollars $ 1,500.
evidenced by cash ☐, cashier's check ☐, or _____ ☐, personal check ☒ payable to 1st American
Title Insurance Company , to be held uncashed until acceptance of this offer, as deposit on account of purchase price of

(D) One hundred fifty thousand Dollars .... Dollars $ 150,000.

(E) for the purchase of property, situated in City of San Francisco , County of San Francisco , California,
described as follows: 828 Rockaway Avenue, San Francisco, California 94118

1.   Buyer will deposit in escrow with 1st American Title Insurance Company the balance of purchase price as follows:

TERMS: $ 35,000. cash down payment, including deposit.

$ 115,000. 1st loan to be obtained by James and Margaret Byer from ABC Savings
and Loan Association. Interest not to exceed fifteen percent (15)
per annum, term of 30 years, with monthly payments including
principal and interest to be approximately $ 1,454.12.

$ 150,000. Purchase Price

CONDITIONS:
1. Subject to a structural pest control inspection report. Purchasers to pay
for cost of termite report and sellers for cost of any indicated corrective
work.

2. Wall-to-wall carpeting, window treatments, stove and refrigerator presently
in the premises are to remain and be included in the purchase price.

3. Parties to pay customary and usual closing costs.

Set forth above any terms and conditions of a factual nature applicable to this sale, such as financing, prior sale of other property, the matter of structural pest control inspection, repairs and personal property to be included in the sale.

2.   Deposit will ☒ will not ☐ be increased by $ 13,500. to $ 15,000. within 10 days of acceptance of this offer.

3.   Buyer does ☒ does not ☐ intend to occupy subject property as his residence.

4.   The supplements initialed below are incorporated as part of this agreement.

Other

X Structural Pest Control Certification Agreement   ____ Occupancy Agreement   ____ _____

____ Special Studies Zone Disclosure   ____ VA Amendment   ____ _____

____ Flood Insurance Disclosure   ____ FHA Amendment   ____ _____

5.   Buyer and Seller acknowledge receipt of a copy of this page, which constitutes Page 1 of 2 Pages.

X _____ (s)   James A. Byar _____   X _____ (s)   Sam Seller _____
BUYER   SELLER

X _____ (s)   Margaret Byar _____   X _____ (s)   Virginia Seller _____
BUYER   SELLER

A REAL ESTATE BROKER IS THE PERSON QUALIFIED TO ADVISE ON REAL ESTATE. IF YOU DESIRE LEGAL ADVICE CONSULT YOUR ATTORNEY.

FIGURE 9–2

REAL ESTATE PURCHASE CONTRACT AND RECEIPT FOR DEPOSIT
The following terms and conditions are hereby incorporated in and made a part of Buyer's Offer

6. Buyer and Seller shall deliver signed instructions to the escrow holder within _____10_____ days from Seller's acceptance which shall provide for closing within _____60_____ days from Seller's acceptance. Escrow fees to be paid as follows:
Buyer pays escrow fees.

7. Title is to be free of liens, encumbrances, easements, restrictions, rights and conditions of record or known to Seller, other than the following: (1) Current property taxes, (2) covenants, conditions, restrictions, and public utility easements of record, if any, provided the same do not adversely affect the continued use of the property for the purposes for which it is presently being used, unless reasonably disapproved by Buyer in writing within ___5___ days of receipt of a current preliminary title report furnished at ___buyers___ expense, and (3) _____
Seller shall furnish Buyer at _____buyers_____ expense a standard California Land Title Association policy issued by ___1st American Title___ Company, showing title vested in Buyer subject only to the above. If Seller (1) is unwilling or unable to eliminate any title matter disapproved by Buyer as above, Seller may terminate this agreement, or (2) fails to deliver title as above, Buyer may terminate this agreement; in either case, the deposit shall be returned to Buyer.

8. Property taxes, premiums on insurance acceptable to Buyer, rents, interest, and _____ shall be pro-rated as of (a) the date of recordation of deed; or (b) _____
Any bond or assessment which is a lien shall be ~~paid~~ by ___seller___ ___Seller___ shall pay cost of transfer taxes, if any.

9. Possession shall be delivered to Buyer (a) on close of escrow, or (b) not later than _____3_____ days after close of escrow or (c) _____

10. Unless otherwise designated in the escrow instructions of Buyer, title shall vest as follows: _____
James A. Byar and Margaret Byar, husband and wife, as joint tenants.
(The manner of taking title may have significant legal and tax consequences. Therefore, give this matter serious consideration.)

11. If Broker is a participant of a Board multiple listing service ("MLS"), the Broker is authorized to report the sale, its price, terms, and financing for the information, publication, dissemination, and use of the authorized Board members.

12. **If Buyer fails to complete said purchase as herein provided by reason of any default of Buyer, Seller shall be released from his obligation to sell the property to Buyer and may proceed against Buyer upon any claim or remedy which he may have in law or equity; provided, however, that by placing their initials here Buyer: (   ) Seller: (   ) agree that Seller shall retain the deposit as his liquidated damages. If the described property is a dwelling with no more than four units, one of which the Buyer intends to occupy as his residence, Seller shall retain as liquidated damages the deposit actually paid, or an amount therefrom, not more than 3% of the purchase price and promptly return any excess to Buyer.**

13. If the only controversy or claim between the parties arises out of or relates to the disposition of the Buyer's deposit, such controversy or claim shall at the election of the parties be decided by arbitration. Such arbitration shall be determined in accordance with the Rules of the American Arbitration Association, and judgment upon the award rendered by the Arbitrator(s) may be entered in any court having jurisdiction thereof. The provisions of Code of Civil Procedure Section 1283.05 shall be applicable to such arbitration.

14. In any action or proceeding arising out of this agreement, the prevailing party shall be entitled to reasonable attorney's fees and costs.

15. Time is of the essence. All modifications or extensions shall be in writing signed by the parties.

16. This constitutes an offer to purchase the described property. Unless acceptance is signed by Seller and the signed copy delivered to Buyer, in person or by mail to the address below, within _____2_____ days, this offer shall be deemed revoked and the deposit shall be returned. Buyer acknowledges receipt of a copy hereof.

(F)
Real Estate Broker ___Maxwell Realty Company___
By ___(s) H. M. Maxwell___
Address ___800 Market Street, S. F., 94112___
Telephone ___564-1919___

Buyer (s) ___James A. Byar___
(s) ___Margaret Byar___
Address ___88 Fulton Street, S.F.___
Telephone ___363-2288___

ACCEPTANCE

(G)
The undersigned Seller accepts and agrees to sell the property on the above terms and conditions. Seller has employed _____ ___Maxwell Realty Company___ as Broker(s) and agrees to pay for services the sum of ___Nine thousand___ Dollars ($ ___9,000.___), payable as follows:
(a) On recordation of the deed or other evidence of title, or (b) if completion of sale is prevented by default of Seller, upon Seller's default or (c) if completion of sale is prevented by default of Buyer, only if and when Seller collects damages from Buyer, by suit or otherwise and then in an amount not less than one-half of the damages recovered, but not to exceed the above fee, after first deducting title and escrow expenses and the expenses of collection, if any. In any action between Broker and Seller arising out of this agreement, the prevailing party shall be entitled to reasonable attorney's fees and costs. The undersigned acknowledges receipt of a copy and authorizes Broker(s) to deliver a signed copy to Buyer.

Dated: ___3/25/ --___ Telephone ___363-7788___
Address ___828 Rockaway Avenue, San Francisco___
Broker(s) agree to the foregoing. Broker ___Maxwell Realty Company___
Dated: ___3/25/--___ By ___(s) H. M. Maxwell___

Seller ___(s) Sam Seller___
Seller ___(s) Virginia Seller___
Broker _____
Dated: _____ By _____

Page ___2___ of ___2___ Pages

FIGURE 9–2 (concluded)

100

(c) The amount and form of the deposit. Enter the amount and form of the deposit the purchasers give the broker at the time the offer is made and to whom it is payable. The amount must be spelled out and also written numerically. Example: One thousand dollars. . . . . ($1,000.00). If a mistake is made and the two amounts differ, the amount spelled out will be deemed correct and will prevail. The deposit should be substantial enough to protect the seller in the event the buyer changes his mind after the seller has accepted the offer. The problem of obtaining a substantial deposit from the purchaser at the time the offer is made is a common one to the real estate licensee. In this regard, it is interesting to note that Section 2 of the purchase contract provides for a means of increasing the amount of deposit.

The form of the deposit may be cash, a personal check, a cashier's check, or anything of value acceptable to the seller. The deposit may also take the form of a promissory note when a check or cash is not immediately available. The broker should use a straight note form payable on demand to the broker with no interest. On the back of the note the broker should state that the note is being taken in conjunction with the deposit receipt in question and should describe the property involved.

(d) The offered price. Enter the amount being offered by the purchaser, both numerically and written out. Example: Ninety thousand dollars. . . . . ($90,000.00).

(e) Property description. There are various ways of identifying and stating the description of the property. The main thing to remember is that the description should be accurate and thorough enough to absolutely identify the specific property in question. Examples:

Lot and improvements commonly known as 828 Rockaway Avenue, San Francisco, California.

Assessors Block 1833, Lot 3, commonly known as 828 Rockaway Avenue, San Francisco, California.

Assessors Block 1833, Lot 3, commonly known as 828 Rockaway Avenue, San Francisco, California. Legally described as . . . (full legal description given if known).

Quite often, the legal description will have to be used, since the property may be an unimproved lot or country land without a street address or block and lot number.

1. Buyer will deposit in escrow with. Enter the name of the firm to act as escrow. It may be an escrow company, a bank, or a title insurance company, and it should be remembered that the de-termination of who will act as escrow is by agreement of the parties involved in the sale.

In northern California the escrow function is usually handled by the title insurance company. In southern California some brokers use the title company to perform the escrow function, while others use a separate escrow company, and the title company merely issues the policy of title insurance. A period of 30 to 60 days from the date of acceptance is usually allowed to complete the escrow and close the transaction.

Terms and conditions of the sale. In this area of the deposit receipt, the broker enters the terms and conditions of the sale. The broker writes in the word *terms,* and under it he includes in detail the means by which the buyer will compile the amount being offered as the purchase price. It will generally include some cash, a first loan, and perhaps a second loan. *Conditions* will include all matters, other than financing, that the parties want to be included on the deposit receipt.

Terms. The various ways in which a purchase may be financed will be treated in Chapters 12 and 13, dealing with real estate finance. Two of the more common ways in which the terms for the sale of the property at 828 Rockaway Avenue, San Francisco, might set forth on the deposit receipt are as follows.

Example 1—cash over conventional loan. All cash to seller as follows: Down payment of $35,000 cash, including the above deposit, subject to purchaser's obtaining a first loan secured by this property in the amount of $115,000 from ABC Savings and Loan Association, with interest at 15 percent per annum, for a term of 30 years, payable at approximately $1,454.12 per month.

Example 2—cash down payment plus first and second loans. Down payment of $15,000 cash including the above deposit, subject to purchaser's obtaining a first loan secured by this property in the amount of $112,500 from ABC Savings and Loan Association, with interest not to exceed 15 percent, for a term of 30 years, payable at approximately $1,422.50 per month. Purchaser to execute a note secured by a second deed of trust on this property, in favor of the seller, in the amount of $22,500 payable at $225 per month or more, including interest at 12 percent per annum, with the entire balance due 5 years from date of this note, or immediately on the sale or transfer of this property if prior to the due date.

There are numerous ways to state the terms of financing, depending on the method used, such as:

a. A down payment plus a conventional loan.

b. A down payment, a conventional first loan, and a second loan.

c. A down payment and assumption of an existing first loan.

d. A down payment and assumption of an existing first and second loan.

e. All cash to the seller—no loans.

f. A new, or assumption of an existing, FHA loan.

g. A new, or assumption of an existing, Veterans Administration (GI) loan.

h. A California Veterans Loan.

i. Exchange of property the buyer presently owns for the property being purchased, or a down payment and a note secured by a deed of trust on a property the buyer presently owns.

The broker must remember that at this point in the deposit receipt he must clearly and adequately state exactly how the purchaser plans to finance the purchase and obtain the necessary funds, which when totaled will equal the amount being offered to the seller.

Conditions. Having completed the description of terms, the licensee now enters the word *conditions* on the deposit receipt.

Termite report. A termite inspection is not required by law. A building may be sold "as is" by the seller, without any liability for any termite or dry rot conditions in the building, so long as the purchaser and seller agree to this condition. However, some savings and loan associations and other lending institutions require a termite report before they will complete the loan, while others do not. In most cases a termite inspection is required in connection with a government guaranteed or insured loan. Quite often the purchaser himself will insist on an inspection of the building. What must be made clear on the deposit receipt is (a) who will pay for the termite inspection (usually $75–150) and (b) who will pay for the corrective work that may be recommended in the report if it is decided that such work is to be done.

Effective October 1979, every time a pest control company makes an inspection of real property, the inspector must post a tag at the entrance of the attic, subarea, or garage giving the company name and date of inspection. If any corrective work is subsequently completed on the property, the company must post an additional tag in the same location.

The law requires that whenever a licensee is an agent in a transaction in which the delivery of a structural pest control inspection report, notice of work completed, or certification prescribed by Section 8519 of the Business and Professions Code is a condition of a contract effecting the transfer, the licensee shall (1) cause delivery of the appropriate documents to the transferee, (2) determine that the transferor has caused such delivery, or (3) advise the transferee that Section 1099 of the Civil Code requires that the appropriate documents be delivered to the transferee.

The licensee must maintain a record of the action taken by him to effect compliance with this regulation in accordance with Section 10148 of the Business and Professions Code.

The California Association of Realtors provides a structural pest control agreement, illustrated in Figure 9–3, which may be used in the event that the seller agrees to an inspection and to pay for any indicated corrections.

Licensees who do not choose to use the CAR termite form, may enter the following on the deposit receipt.

Property to be examined by a licensed pest control operator at the expense of the buyer; any work, to repair damage from infestation of wood-destroying organisms or to correct conditions that caused infestation, to be done at the expense of the seller; funds for such work to be held in escrow and disbursed on clearance by the inspection and delivery of a certificate of completion and termite clearance.

Sometimes the above wording is shortened and the following written in:

Seller to provide buyer with standard termite clearance. Buyer to pay for cost of inspection and seller for costs of correction.

We have so far been discussing a case in which the seller is willing to have an inspection of the property and pay for corrections needed. Now let us look at the other extreme, when (a) the seller does not want to pay for any work, and (b) the seller does not want to pay for any work and does not want to allow any inspection of his property.

a. Property is to be purchased in its present as-is condition, with seller not to be responsible for any corrective work whatsoever. Subject to buyer's approval of existing pest control inspection report issued by (name of pest control firm) and dated (date of report).

b. Property is to be purchased in its present as-is condition, with seller not to be responsible for any corrective work whatsoever, no pest control inspection report having been issued.

If the buyer is purchasing the property as is

STRUCTURAL PEST CONTROL CERTIFICATION AGREEMENT

California Association of Realtors Standard Form

This agreement is part of and is hereby incorporated in that "Real Estate Purchase Contract and Receipt for Deposit" between the parties hereof dated_____19____, pertaining to the property described as follows:

_____

_____

1. _____ agrees at his expense to furnish

                              Seller/Buyer

_____ within_____days from date

                              Buyer/Seller

of SELLER's approval of this agreement with a current written report of an inspection by a licensed Structural Pest Control Operator of the main building and all attached structures.

_____
(specify any additions or exceptions)

2. If no infestation or infection of wood destroying pests or organisms is found, the report shall include either in the form of an endorsement or as a separate written statement by the inspecting licensed Structural Pest Control Operator a CERTIFICATION to provide in accordance with B & P Code 8519(a): "This is to certify that the above property was inspected on _____ (date) in accordance with the Structural Pest Control Act and rules and regulations adopted pursuant thereto, and that no evidence of active infestation or infection was found".

3. All work recommended in said report to repair damage caused by infestation or infection of wood-destroying pests or organisms found and all work to correct conditions that caused such infestation or infection shall be done at the expense of SELLER.

_____
(specify any additions or exceptions)

Funds for work to be performed shall be held in escrow and disbursed upon receipt of a CERTIFICATION on the "Notice of Work Completed" to provide, in accordance with B & P Code 8519(b): "This is to certify that the property described herein is now free of evidence of active infestation or infection".

4. With the additions or exceptions, if any, noted below, BUYER agrees that any work to correct conditions usually deemed likely to lead to infestation or infection of wood-destroying pests or organisms, but where no evidence of existing infestation or infection is found with respect to such conditions, is NOT the responsibility of the SELLER, and that such work shall be done only if requested by BUYER and then at the expense of BUYER.

_____
(specify any additions or exceptions)

5. If inspection of inaccessible areas is recommended in the report, BUYER has the option of accepting and approving the report or requesting further inspection be made at the BUYER's expense. If further inspection is made and infestation, infection, or damage is found, repair of such damage and all work to correct conditions that caused such infestation or infection shall be at the expense of SELLER. If no infestation, infection or damage is found, any repairs to entry of the inaccessible areas shall be at the expense of BUYER.

6. _____ hereby selects the following licensed

                            Seller/Buyer

Structural Pest Control Operator to inspect the property: _____

SELLER consents to such inspection.

COPY OF REPORT TO BUYER

SELLER acknowledges his responsibility under Civil Code Section 1099 to deliver to BUYER as soon as practical before transfer of title or the execution of a real property sales contract as defined in Civil Code Section 2985 a copy of the inspection report, a "NOTICE OF WORK COMPLETED" OR A "CERTIFICATION pursuant to B & P Code 8519" as may be required.

SELLER directs _____

                            name of Broker

to deliver such copies of the above documents as may be required.

BUYER AND SELLER ACKNOWLEDGES RECEIPT OF A COPY OF THIS AGREEMENT WHICH INCORPORATES THE EXCERPTS FROM THE BUSINESS AND PROFESSIONS CODE AND THE CIVIL CODE printed on the reverse hereof.

Date Approved and Accepted	Date Approved and Accepted
BUYER	SELLER

- -

REQUEST FOR STRUCTURAL PEST CONTROL CERTIFICATION REPORT

To_____

        Name of Operator   Address of Operator

You are instructed to make a Structural Pest Control Inspection of the main building and all attached structures.

_____
(specify any additions or exceptions)

Located at_____

For purposes of clarification you are requested to identify and separate in your report as clearly as possible, your findings and recommendations as follows:

SECTION 1) Work recommended to repair damage caused by existing infestation or infection of wood-destroying pests or organisms and all work recommended to correct conditions that caused such infestation or infections.

SECTION 2) Work recommended to correct conditions usually deemed likely to lead to infestation or infection of wood-destroying pests or organisms, but where no evidence of active infestation or infection is found with respect to such conditions.

Your quotations for cost of any recommended work should be segregated as above and be as itemized as possible.

Inspection of inaccessible areas, if any, shall not be made without specific authorization.

If your report discloses no infestation or infection, you shall issue a CERTIFICATION to that effect in accordance with B & P Code 8519(a).

If your report discloses infestation and infection and you subsequently are requested to perform recommended work in whole or in part your NOTICE OF WORK COMPLETED shall contain a CERTIFICATION to that effect in accordance with B & P Code 8519(b) or (c), whichever is applicable.

The undersigned agrees to pay $_____ for your inspection and report in the above form, providing you deliver said report as indicated below on or before_____ 19_____.

Dated_____

Person ordering the report	Address	City	State	Zip	Phone

Copies to:

Name of listing Broker	Address	Other	Address
Name of selling Broker	Address	Other	Address

FIGURE 9–3

and without benefit of a report, the seller and the broker must exercise extreme caution not to make any representations one way or another concerning the condition of the property and the broker would probably be wise, in connection with the use of *b* above, to state also that the buyers have physically entered upon the property and observed its apparent condition. A seller or real estate licensee who is aware of any existing damage, and fails to tell the purchaser, will be liable at law for full cost of any corrective work necessary.

Another situation that may frequently occur is one in which the buyer wants to make his offer conditional on his acceptance of a subsequent termite report, or the seller wants his acceptance of an offer to be subject to his approval of a subsequent report. In these cases the licensee may write the following:

This offer is subject to a structural pest control inspection report acceptable to both the buyer and seller.

This is an extremely unwise condition to include in the deposit receipt, since in so doing the licensee has given the buyer or the seller a way of backing out of the transaction after receipt of the report. Although the termite report may not be the actual reason at all, either party may be able to use it as an excuse not to go through with the transaction.

Some licensees feel that when a piece of property is placed on the market it may be advantageous to have the property inspected and have a report issued before the receipt of an offer from a prospective buyer. If the property is newer, or appears to be in good condition, many brokers advise their principals to order a report as soon as possible. Knowing exactly what corrective measures may be needed, if any, and the cost involved, will make it much easier for the broker to negotiate with the prospective buyer.

Often, the seller does not want to obligate himself to pay for all the necessary work a report may show is needed, but at the same time does not insist that he be relieved of all responsibility in this regard. The seller is willing to obligate himself for an amount that seems reasonable to him. In such a case, the broker will word his entry on the deposit receipt so that it limits the seller's liability. The following is an example.

This offer is subject to a structural pest control inspection report. Buyer to pay for cost of the report (not to exceed $150), and seller to pay for indicated corrective work up to, but not in excess of, three thousand dollars ($3,000).

Personal property and fixtures. Another subject often treated under conditions on the deposit receipt relates to items included with the purchase aside from the land and the bare house itself. Anything the buyer assumes will be included in the purchase price but might in any way be in doubt should be put in writing on the deposit receipt. However, if too much personal property is included, the lender may reduce the amount of his loan, and thus a separate bill of sale is often used with respect to the personal property involved. The most common entry refers to carpeting and drapes, and so the following is often included.

All wall-to-wall carpeting and all drapes presently in the building shall remain and be included in the above purchase price.

In addition to the foregoing, we commonly find such entries as these.

The purchase price stated above shall also include the stove and refrigerator presently in the building.
All furnishings presently in the building are to be included for the above purchase price. These items are to be identified and listed separately on a bill of sale form, which shall be made a part of the escrow.

Anything affixed to a building with the intent that it be made a permanent part of the building is generally considered to be real property, and automatically goes with the building for the purchase price stated in the deposit receipt. Many times, however, there is a question about whether carpeting, drapes, a crystal chandelier in the entry hall or dining room, or other such items are to be automatically included in the purchase price. The buyer may think he is getting these items, while the seller may intend to remove some or all of them. It is obvious, then, that many kinds of items and fixtures may have to be mentioned in the deposit receipt in order to avoid future complications, which may delay the closing of the transaction. Fixtures are items of personal property attached or incorporated into the land or building in such a manner that they become real property and are then considered part of the land or building.

The courts in California have utilized several general tests to determine whether or not an item of personal property has become a fixture. The two most important are *(a)* the intention of the person attaching or incorporating the personal property into the land or building, and *(b)* the particular method by which the property is actually incorporated or attached, and the degree of damage that might result to the property were the item to be removed.

Closing costs. Another item often appearing under *conditions* on the deposit receipt relates to the closing costs to be paid by the buyer and/ or seller in connection with the sale and purchase of the property. The buyer especially should never be allowed to assume that the deposit he put down on the property will automatically take care of the closing costs. In most cases, the buyer will have a substantial amount of closing costs to pay and the licensee should explain to him, even before the offer is made, that a certain amount of money will be required for closing costs in connection with the purchase, and that this money will have to be deposited in escrow prior to closing of the transaction. The licensee should properly inform both the buyer and seller of the approximate amount of closing costs they may have. These costs will be discussed in Chapter 15 dealing with escrows, and generally include such items as the policy of title insurance, loan fees, and expenses as the result of insurance and tax prorations.

The following are examples of clauses that may be found on the deposit receipt in connection with closing costs.

Buyer and seller to pay normal and usual closing costs in connection with this transaction.

In addition to the down payment specified above, the buyer is to be responsible for the payment, in escrow, of approximately $2,500 for closing costs in connection with this sale and purchase.

Having completed our discussion of terms and conditions, let us now turn to the remaining printed portion of the deposit receipt (Figure 9–2).

2. If the purchaser gives the broker a small deposit at the time he makes the offer, it is general practice to have the deposit increased upon acceptance of the offer, usually to 10 percent of the purchase price. Thus, if a purchaser makes an offer of $170,000 on a property when conventional financing is planned, and gives the licensee $2,000 as a deposit at the time the offer is made, the purchaser will have to deposit an additional $15,000 at the time that the seller accepts the offer and signs the deposit receipt.

3. The statement by the purchaser with respect to intention to occupy is important to the bank or savings and loan association. A copy of the purchase contract is generally submitted along with the loan application, and with respect to the purchase of single-family residences, a number of

lenders are wary of speculators. Although intention not to occupy may merely signify an investment purchase, it can also mean a speculative purchase. A real estate licensee who falsifies such a disclosure is subject to disciplinary action by law.

4. Supplements incorporated as part of the purchase agreement are shown.

5. The law requires parties signing any document to be given a copy.

6. This clause provides spaces to state the number of days given to deliver escrow instructions and to close escrow. The payment of escrow fees is by local custom and is discussed in Chapter 15.

7. If a preliminary title search has not been made, it is difficult to know just what a search will disclose concerning the overall condition of the title. Certain restrictions may be disclosed that the purchaser does not wish to accept. Here we have a situation similar to that of termite inspection. A broker who has a preliminary title search before writing up the offer will know the condition of the title and can discuss it with the prospective purchaser when the offer is made. In most cases, however, it is only after an offer has been received and accepted by the seller that escrow is opened and a title search ordered to disclose the condition of the title that the seller has to convey.

If a seller is unable to convey a marketable title, or if the property is destroyed or substantially damaged prior to the actual transfer of title, the buyer is released from his contractual obligation and any deposits are returned.

The title company, and who will pay for the title policy are shown. This subject is discussed in greater detail in Chapter 15.

8. This clause merely indicates that, where necessary, there shall be a proration of items as of the date of transfer of title. The necessary prorations are done by the escrow officer, and the results are shown on the buyer's and seller's statements. The items most commonly involved are taxes, rents, interest, insurance premiums, and expenses for which the buyer and/or seller may now be responsible. The amount of any bond or assessment that is a lien against the property is generally paid by the seller, as are any existing delinquencies. The seller customarily pays for any transfer taxes.

9. In most cases, possession of the property passes from the seller to the buyer as of the close of escrow, since at this time recordation of the deed and other necessary documents takes place, and title passes to the buyer.

It is very important for the licensee to be certain that the seller understands this, since many times the seller thinks he has a reasonable amount of time after close of escrow in which to move out. A space is provided in the event that the seller is to be allowed a certain amount of days after close of escrow in which to move.

The licensee must remember that while it may be normal for the seller to be a bit hesitant and want some time in which to move, the buyer becomes the legal owner of the property as of close of escrow and recordation, and is responsible for his loan payments and taxes. In complete fairness to both buyer and seller, if occupancy is not given on close of escrow the deposit receipt should contain a condition stating *(a)* the exact number of days the seller has to remain on the property, and *(b)* an amount of rent (per day) the seller is to pay the buyer for these additional days beyond the close of escrow. The amount is the cost per day to the new owner for loan payment, insurance, and taxes.

If the buyer and seller agree, the escrow officer may be instructed to withhold from the seller's funds an amount equal to the entire rental for the agreed-to period of occupancy. When the escrow officer is later notified that the former owner has vacated the property, he will forward the amount of rental to the buyer. If the seller vacates before the full amount of time agreed on, the escrow officer will forward to the buyer what is due him and refund the difference to the seller.

10. This clause specifies the way in which the buyers wish to take title.

When the buyers ask the broker his opinion about how they should take title, the broker must remember that such advice may be regarded as practicing law, and the buyers should be advised to consult their attorney. This part of the deposit receipt form may then be left blank or the statement may be made that instructions are to follow and the information may later be given to the escrow officer.

11. If the broker is a member of multiple listing, the broker is given permission to disclose certain information about the transaction as required of members. However, the broker need not disclose any information in connection with the sale if the buyers and sellers wish such facts to be kept confidential.

12. California courts have held that clauses which provide for automatic retention or forfeiture of deposits are generally not valid. To conform with the California Liquidated Damage Law, effective July 1978, this new liquidated damage clause is provided should buyer and seller wish to use it. If the buyer and seller initial the appropriate places in the clause, the law provides that if the buyer fails to perform and there is a breach of contract, the seller may retain as liquidated damages, from the deposit actually paid, an amount not to exceed three percent of the purchase price of the property.

If the buyer and seller do not initial the appropriate places in the clause, it will not apply, and any disputes the parties may have with respect to the contract or deposit will have to be settled by instituting legal action.

13. If acceptable to the parties and retained in the purchase contract this clause provides that if a dispute is strictly with respect to disposition of buyer's deposit in event of a default, the matter shall be settled by arbitration in accordance with rules of the American Arbitration Association.

14. Standard clause contained in most contracts should legal action be necessary.

15. Time is of the essence of this contract. Most contracts contain a statement to the effect that time is of the essence. This phrase has its origin in the law, and simply means that the time requirements of the contract must be strictly adhered to.

16. The usual amount of time given the seller to consider and accept the offer is one to two days, although the time is flexible and depends upon the particular situation. Most responsible brokers agree that an offer should be presented to the seller as soon as possible. It must be remembered that the prospective purchaser may withdraw his offer at any time prior to acceptance by the seller.

(f) Space is provided for entering the name and address of the real estate firm and the signature of the licensee preparing the offer. A space is provided for the purchasers' signatures. If the purchasers are husband and wife, the licensee must obtain the signatures of both parties. A copy must be given to parties signing the contract.

(g) The acceptance portion contains space for entering the name of the broker or brokers involved, the total sum of commission to be paid, and conditions upon which payment of the commission is due. Condition *(c)* takes into account that the parties may not have initialed the liquidated damages clause and that a suit in court or other negotiations may be necessary.

In the event that the listing and selling brokers are different, space is provided for inserting the names of the cooperating brokers. If the sellers are husband and wife, the broker must obtain the signatures of both parties. As with the buyer, the seller must also be given a copy of this deposit receipt; it is the broker's responsibility to be sure that all parties who have signed the deposit receipt receive a copy. It is sufficient that husband and wife receive a single copy.

THE COUNTEROFFER

A broker who represents both the buyer and the seller may have a better chance of writing up an offer that is completely acceptable to the seller and requires no counteroffer. The broker who obtains the listing is often, but not always, in a position to know just what the sellers are willing to accept and can base his discussion with the prospective purchasers on these facts. The broker who represents only the buyers is, of course, trying to get the best deal possible for them, and the terms and conditions of the offer he prepares may often weigh heavily in favor of his clients. It is most advantageous if the selling broker and the listing broker are able to communicate satisfactorily with each other prior to preparation of the offer so that there will be a closer understanding of what is required to make the sale.

When all attempts to secure an acceptance of an offer have failed, the broker should certainly try to obtain a counteroffer from the seller. The counteroffer may be written on the reverse side of the original offer and begins with the following statement:

All conditions of the deposit receipt as stipulated on the reverse side are acceptable to the seller with the following exceptions:

The broker then lists the exceptions, which may include such items as the purchase price, financing, possession, or termite provisions. The counteroffer is then signed and dated by the seller. If the change in the original offer is minor, then the above method may be satisfactory, but if the changes are major ones or are extremely long, then the broker should prepare a separate counteroffer or make out an entirely new deposit receipt. It would contain the changes the seller wants, and the seller would sign his name in the acceptance section of the deposit receipt and enter the current date.

The deposit receipt can then be presented to the buyer, and if the buyer agrees to the changes he can sign his name, thus creating a completed deposit receipt and binding contract. Negotiations may continue back and forth for some time until there is a meeting of the minds and a complete deposit receipt. This may at times involve a number of counteroffers, but the effective licensee keeps trying as long as there is a chance for agreement between buyer and seller.

If another licensee brings in an offer during these negotiations, or if the listing broker receives an offer from a prospective purchaser, these offers must be presented to the seller for his consideration and possible acceptance. Thus, speed is of the essence in a real estate transaction, for while one licensee may be discussing some minor point with his client, another licensee will bring in just the offer the seller wants, and he will effect the sale.

NONPERFORMANCE

What happens if the deposit receipt is properly signed by all parties to the transaction and then one of them decides not to go through with the transaction as agreed? If the buyer fails to perform, the seller may do any of the following.

1. He may declare the contract void and return the buyer's deposit.
2. He may declare the contract void and refuse to return the buyer's deposit. The buyer, of course, may agree to a forfeit of his deposit or he may bring suit against the seller for a return of the deposit.
3. He may sue the buyer for specific performance or damages.

If the seller fails to perform, the buyer may do any of the following.

1. He may agree to termination of the contract and the return of his deposit.
2. He may agree to termination of the contract and allow the seller to retain his deposit, although this course of action would be highly unlikely.
3. He may sue the seller for specific performance or damages.

For all practical purposes, it may be correctly said that suits for specific performance rarely occur in everyday real estate transactions. The time and expense involved make this remedy impractical. Only in a very large and complex transaction will court action for specific performance occur.

REAL ESTATE EXCHANGE AGREEMENT FORM

Real estate exchanging has become one of the specialty areas within the real estate business and is discussed in detail in Chapter 21. There are various reasons for entering into an exchange, one of the more common being that if an owner sells his property he may have to pay a tax on the gain realized, but if he exchanges the property for another he may be able to defer payment of the taxes to a future date. Groups of licensees interested in exchanges exist on local, state, and national levels.

Licensees who qualify on the basis of certain education, examination, and experience requirements may qualify for the designation certified property exchanger (CPE). The National Institute of Real Estate Brokers sponsors the International Traders Club, which provides its members with printed materials and information regarding properties throughout the United States and Canada. The exchange agreement form is to the exchange as the deposit receipt form is to the usual sale of real property. The exchange agreement must be written in a clear and concise manner, and must be complete in all details necessary to the transaction. The agreement form will represent a legal contract when properly executed and signed by the parties involved.

For purposes of illustration we shall use the California Association of Realtors® exchange agreement form. The numbered parts of the CAR exchange form, Figure 9–4, correspond to the explanations that follow.

1. The names of the interested parties are entered. The legal status of the parties should also be clearly noted.

2. A complete description and address of the property should be given.

3. All liens and encumbrances known to exist against the property should be stated in detail. The terms, conditions, and balances of any loans against the property should be shown and, in addition, any tax liens that exist. The property may also be subject to certain covenants, conditions, and restrictions that the parties may wish to review prior to close of escrow.

Terms and conditions of an exchange

The broker must set forth clearly the terms and conditions of the exchange. He must specify in detail what is to be done or accomplished by each party to the exchange, since this will provide a pattern for the steps to be taken during the escrow. This section, which presents the details of the exchange, includes such items as:

a. How the equities of the properties involved in this exchange are to be equalized, which usually is accomplished by stating which party in the exchange must deposit cash in escrow and the amount of such deposit.

b. Any contingencies that are to be made a part of the agreement.

c. Mention of any rental statements that may have to be approved.

d. Provisions for refinancing either of the properties in the exchange.

e. Any trust deeds that may be involved and their terms and conditions.

Page two of the agreement contains various printed clauses.

1. The title company is named and number of days allowed in which to deliver escrow instructions is shown together with the number of days allowed for close of escrow. Space is provided for determining how escrow fee is to be paid. In the southern part of the state, escrow instructions are usually delivered within a few days of opening escrow. In other parts of the state, the time limit for both delivery of instructions and for close of escrow are the same.

The amount of time required may vary depending on the particular transaction and the location of the properties involved. Whether the parties involved shall pay for the escrow fee or title policy fee for the property acquired or conveyed is dependent on the general practice in the particular area.

2. A title clause is provided which refers to liens, encumbrances, easements, restrictions, rights, and conditions of record. Since the status of these matters is not usually known until a preliminary title search is issued, it is general practice to allow the parties to examine the preliminary title reports and then discuss any objections which may result.

The title company issuing the title policy is shown, and provision is made for payment of title policy fees.

3. A clause is provided to show how Richard and Wilma Arthur wish to take title to the property acquired. If there is doubt as to the proper method of acquiring title, the broker

CALIFORNIA ASSOCIATION OF REALTORS® STANDARD FORM

EXCHANGE AGREEMENT

THIS IS INTENDED TO BE A LEGALLY BINDING CONTRACT. READ IT CAREFULLY.

(A)   Richard Arthur and Wilma Arthur, husband and wife

herein called Arthur   , offers to exchange

the following described property, designated as Property No.   (A)   situated in Los Angeles

County of   Los Angeles   , State of California

(B)   Lot 23, Tract 5998, recorded in Book 21, Page 68 of Maps, commonly known as
        178 Harbor Way. Subject to (1) Current taxes, (2) Deed of Trust recorded in book 67,
(C)   page 57 O.R., Los Angeles County, with present balance of approximately $ 85,000.
        payable at $ 714.74 per month including interest at 9 ½ percent per annum,
        (3) Covenants, conditions, restrictions and easements of record.

for the following described property of   Philip Brown and Carol Brown, husband and wife
(A)

herein called Brown   designated as Property No. (B)

situated in   Lancaster

County of   Los Angeles   State of   California

(B)   Lot 19, Tract 338, recorded in Book 18, Page 93 of Maps, commonly known as
        826 La Habra Avenue. Subject to (1) Current taxes, (d) Deed of Trust recorded in book
        78, Page 20 O.R., Los Angeles County, with present balance of approximately $ 78,000
        payable at $ 670.15 per month including interest at 9 3/4 percent per annum,
        (3) Covenants, conditions, restrictions and easements of record.

Terms and Conditions of Exchange:

Value of Arthur property	$ 190,000	Value of Brown property	$ 200,000
Subject to loan balance of	85,000	Subject to loan balance of	78,000
Arthur's Equity is	$ 105,000	Brown's Equity is	$ 122,000

1. Difference in equities of approximately $ 17,000 to be adjusted by Arthur depositing in escrow the sum of $ 17,000. This amount to be paid to Brown on close of escrow.

2. If, at close of escrow, the loans of record are more or less than the approximate amounts shown, differences shall be adjusted in cash to the respective parties.

3. Arthur to take title to Brown property subject to existing loan, and Brown to take title to Arthur property subject to existing loan.

4. Both parties to furnish a termite report for their respective properties and to pay the cost of any corrective work indicated in the report. Funds to pay for said work to be deposited in escrow.

5. Possession and occupancy of both properties to be given within 15 days of close of escrow.

The supplements initialled below are incorporated as part of this agreement.

Other

__X__ Structural Pest Control Certification Agreement   _____ _____

_____ Special Studies Zone Disclosure   _____ _____

_____ Flood Insurance Disclosure   _____ _____

Both parties acknowledge receipt of a copy of this page. Page 1 of 3   Pages.

X _(s) Richard Arthur_____   X _(s) Philip Brown_____

X _(s) Wilma Arthur_____   X _(s) Carol Brown_____

**A REAL ESTATE BROKER IS THE PERSON QUALIFIED TO ADVISE ON REAL ESTATE. IF YOU DESIRE LEGAL OR TAX ADVICE,
CONSULT A COMPETENT PROFESSIONAL.**

For these forms, address California Association of Realtors®
505 Shatto Place, Los Angeles, California 90020
Copyright   1978, California Association of Realtors®   FORM E-11-1

FIGURE 9–4

EXCHANGE AGREEMENT

The following terms and conditions are hereby incorporated in and made a part of the offer.

1. The parties hereto shall deliver signed escrow instructions to U.S. Title Company
, escrow holder, within 5 days from acceptance, which shall provide for closing within 60 days from acceptance. Escrow fees shall be paid as follows: Each party agrees to pay escrow fee for property conveyed.

2. Title is to be free of liens, encumbrances, easements, restrictions, rights and conditions of record or known to the conveying party, other than the following: Respective parties to examine preliminary title reports and report any objections within 5 days of receipt.

Each party shall provide the other with (a) a standard California Land Title Association policy, or (b)
, issued by U.S. Title Company
to be paid for as follows: Property (A) Brown, and Property (B) Arthur
showing title vested in the acquiring party subject only to the above and to any liens or encumbrances to be recorded in accordance with this agreement. If the conveying party fails to deliver title as above, the acquiring party may terminate this agreement and shall be released from payment of any compensation to broker(s) for services rendered.

3. Unless otherwise designated in escrow instructions, title to the property acquired shall vest as follows: Richard Arthur and Wilma Arthur, husband and wife, as joint tenants
(The manner of taking title may have significant legal and tax consequences. Therefore, give this matter serious consideration.)

4. Property taxes, premiums on insurance acceptable to the party acquiring the property insured, rents, interest and
shall be prorated as of (a) the date of recordation of deed, or (b)
Any bond or assessment which is a lien on a party's property shall be paid or assumed as follows: None

5 (A). Possession of Property No. (A) shall be delivered (a) on close of escrow, or (b) not later than 15 days after close of escrow, or (c)

5 (B). Possession of Property No. (B) shall be delivered (a) on close of escrow, or (b) not later than 15 days after close of escrow, or (c)

6. If, as a part of this exchange, any property is to be sold to a third party, the original transferor shall indemnify and hold harmless the party conveying the property to the third party from all claims, liability, loss, damage and expenses including reasonable attorneys' fees and costs incurred by reason of any warranties or representations made by conveying party to the purchaser provided they conform to the warranties and representations made by the original tranferor either by this agreement or in any statement made or document delivered to the conveying party or to the designated escrow holder.

7. Each party warrants that he has no knowledge of the existence of any notices of violations of city, county or state building, zoning, fire and health codes, ordinances, or other governmental regulations filed or issued against his property.

8. Each party represents to the other that no tenant, if any, is entitled to any rebate, concession or other benefit except as set forth in rental agreements and leases, copies of which are to be exchanged or delivered within ----- days of acceptance. If such rental agreements or leases are not disapproved in writing within ----- days of receipt thereof, this condition shall be deemed waived.

9. Unless acceptance of this offer is signed by the other party hereto and the signed copy delivered to the undersigned, in person or by mail to the address below, within 5 days, this offer shall be deemed revoked.

10. Each party agrees that Ann Smith, Realtor, Los Angeles, representing Arthur and ABC broker
address Realty, Lancaster, representing Brown. , California
telephone can act as agent for, and may accept compensation for services from, each party herein. Broker is authorized to cooperate with other brokers and to divide such compensation as agreed by them.

11. It is the intention of the parties to the extent permitted by law, that the mutual conveyances agreed to herein will qualify as an "exchange" within the meaning of Section 1031 of the Internal Revenue Code of 1954 and Section 18081 of the California Revenue and Taxation Code. Failure to so qualify however, shall not affect the validity of this agreement.

12. Each party agrees to execute and deliver to escrow any instrument or to perform any act reasonably necessary to carry out the provisions of this agreement.

13. In any action or proceeding arising out of this agreement, the prevailing party shall be entitled to reasonable attorneys' fees and costs.

14. Time is of the essence of this agreement. All modifications or extensions shall be in writing signed by the parties.

Both parties acknowledge receipt of a copy of this page. Page 2 of 3 Pages.

X (s) Richard Arthur   X (s) Philip Brown

X (s) Wilma Arthur   X (s) Carol Brown

For these forms, address California Association of Realtors®
505 Shatto Place, Los Angeles, California 90020 (Revised 1978)
Copyright ©1978, California Association of Realtors®   FORM E-11-2

FIGURE 9-4 (continued)

EXCHANGE AGREEMENT

The following terms and conditions are hereby incorporated in and made a part of the offer.

If the other party hereto accepts the foregoing offer, I agree to pay to Ann Smith, Realtor
as broker for services rendered as follows: Nine Thousand Five Hundred Dollars ($ 9,500.)

payable (a) on recordation of deed or on delivery of a Real Property Contract as defined by Civil Code Section 2985; or (b) upon default if completion of the exchange is prevented by me; or (c)

In any action or proceeding arising out of this agreement, the prevailing party shall be entitled to reasonable attorney's fees and costs.

Receipt of a copy hereof is hereby acknowledged. Page 3 of 3 Pages.

Los Angeles , State California , Dated: July 2 , 19 --

Address: 178 Harbor Way   X (s) Richard Arthur
Los Angeles   X (s) Wilma Arthur
Telephone: 303-1123   X

Broker(s) agree to the foregoing.

Dated: July 2 , 19 --   Dated: , 19

Broker Ann Smith, Realtor   Broker

By (s) Ann Smith   By

ACCEPTANCE

The foregoing offer and agreement to exchange the properties upon the terms and conditions stated is hereby accepted and I agree
to pay ABC Realty Company 620 Center Lane, Lancaster, California

California, telephone 350-2329   as broker(s) for services rendered as follows:
Ten Thousand Five Hundred Dollars ($ 10,500.)

payable as follows: (a) on recordation of Deed or delivery of Real Property Sales Contract as defined by Civil Code Section 2985; (b) upon default if completion is prevented by me; or (c)

Unless otherwise designated in the escrow instructions, title to the property acquired shall vest as follows:
Philip Brown and Carol Brown, husband and wife, as community property
(The manner of taking title may have significant legal and tax consequences. Therefore, give this matter serious consideration.)
In any action or proceeding arising out of this agreement, the prevailing party shall be entitled to reasonable attorneys' fees and costs.

Receipt of a copy hereof is acknowledged and broker is authorized to deliver a signed copy to the other party named above. Page 3 of Pages.

Lancaster , State California , Dated: July 5 , 19 --

Address: 826 La Habra Avenue   X (s) Philip Brown
Lancaster, California   X (s) Carol Brown
Telephone: 350-7389   X

Broker(s) agree to the foregoing:

Dated: July 5 , 19 --   Dated: , 19

Broker ABC Realty Company   Broker

By (s) Virginia Marsh   By

For these forms, address California Association of Realtors®
505 Shatto Place, Los Angeles, California 90020
Copyright ©1978, California Association of Realtors®   FORM E-11-3

FIGURE 9–4 *(concluded)*

should be careful not to give any legal advice and should refer the parties to their attorney and tax advisor.

4. Any prorations which may be necessary are dealt with, and who shall pay for or assume any bond or assessment which may exist is determined.
5. Clauses 5(A) and 5(B) allow separate possession and occupancy provisions relating to each property. Space is provided for mention of a possible rental payment by either party who may wish to remain in possession of all of part of the premises after close of escrow.
6. Numbers 6, 7, and 8, are self-explanatory.
9. The amount of time to be allowed for acceptance of the offer is stated.
10. The broker or brokers representing the parties are shown. The clause allows a broker representing both parties to receive payment from both and allows cooperation between brokers if necessary.
11. An intent to exchange is shown. It is important that the parties clearly state that they are entering into a property exchange to legally defer federal and state taxes as allowed by law.
12. The parties agree to do whatever is necessary to expedite the transaction.
13. Numbers 13 and 14 are self-explanatory.

Page three of the agreement contains the agreement of offerors Richard and Wilma Arthur to pay their broker, Ann Smith, a commission. The exact amount of the commission to be received is shown. Commissions in a three-way or other type of multiple exchange may be quite complicated, and separate detailed instructions relating to the payment of commission may have to be executed by the parties. Richard and Wilma Arthur and their broker, Ann Smith, sign the agreement.

Acceptance

The offerees, Philip and Carol Brown, accept the offer to exchange and agree to pay their broker, ABC Realty Company, a commission. Title is to be vested in Philip Brown and Carol Brown, husband and wife, as community property. The Browns and Realtor Virginia Marsh sign the agreement.

When properly prepared by the broker and signed by all parties to the exchange, the exchange agreement will constitute a valid and binding le-

gal contract. This will allow the escrow officer to begin the escrow procedure. All parties to the exchange must perform as stated in the exchange agreement.

OPTION TO PURCHASE REAL ESTATE FORM

In our discussion of listings, it was stated that occasionally a broker may take a listing and also an option agreement. An option agreement is a separate form of contract, however, and may be used in a variety of situations independent of any listing agreement. An option is best defined as a contract to make a contract. An example of its use is as follows.

Nesbitt offers Fraden a piece of property at a price of $95,000. Fraden thinks the price is satisfactory and would like very much to purchase the property. However, he has made some prior business commitments and will need approximately 60 days before he can make a decision. Fraden thinks that someone else may purchase the property during this time, so he offers Nesbitt $1,000 for an option to purchase within 60 days at the price of $95,000.

Nesbitt agrees and signs an option agreement; he must now allow Fraden up to 60 days to exercise the option. Fraden has given Nesbitt a consideration in return for his promise to wait the required time, and the agreement is a valid contract between the two parties. A typical option agreement is illustrated in Figure 9–5.

Agreement of sale

The agreement-of-sale form is more commonly known as a *land contract*, and may also be referred to as an *installment and contract, contract of sale,* or *installment sale contract*. This form is basically an instrument of finance and is discussed in Chapter 12.

QUESTIONS FOR DISCUSSION

1. How might a broker collect a commission even though there is no listing agreement with the owner?
2. Why is the exclusive right-to-sell listing most commonly used by real estate brokers?
3. What is the most distinctive feature of a multiple listing?
4. Under what circumstances might a seller claim fraud in connection with the use of a net listing?
5. Why is the amount of commission generally set

Option
to Purchase Real Estate

San Francisco, California, ... July 3, ... 19......

For and in consideration of the sum of

One Thousand Dollars .... 1,000. ....($..................) Dollars

to seller in hand paid, the receipt of which is hereby acknowledged by said seller, to apply on the purchase price, the undersigned

Thomas Nesbitt

herein designated as the seller, hereby grants the right and option to purchase and agrees to sell to

Jules Fraden

herein designated as the purchaser, or his assigns, at any time within .... 60 ..... days from the date hereof, the following described property in the City and County of San Francisco, State of California, to wit:

Lot and improvements designated as Block 986, Lot 8, Forest Hill Tract,

as recorded April 23, 1910, Book 7, Page 19 of Maps, City and County of

San Francisco, State of California.

Commonly known as 180 Santa Maria Avenue, San Francisco, California.

For the purchase price of

Ninety-five Thousand Dollars .... ($.......95,000.........) Dollars

lawful money of the United States of America, payable as follows:

Cash to seller within 30 days from date of exercise of option.

If said purchaser elects to purchase said property at the price and on the terms herein set forth, and within the time specified, the said purchaser shall give said seller due notice in writing and shall pay an additional sum of $.......8,500:.......... for account of said seller to.......Western Title Insurance Company, Golden Gate Branch.....................................

said sum to apply on the purchase price, whereupon thirty (30) days after the exercising of this option shall be allowed said purchaser to examine title to said property and report any valid objection thereto, if any, to said seller. If no such objection to title is reported, the balance of the purchase price shall be paid by said purchaser at or before the expiration of said time and said seller shall thereupon deliver a properly executed and acknowledged grant deed to said property. If such objection to title is reported, then said seller shall use due diligence to remove same within ninety (90) days thereafter and if it is so removed the balance of the purchase price shall be paid within five (5) days after such objection has been removed and upon delivery of said deed as hereinabove provided; but if such objection to title cannot be removed within the time allowed, all rights and obligations hereunder, at the election of the purchaser, shall terminate and end and all payments made hereunder shall be returned to the purchaser unless said purchaser elects to buy the said property subject to such defect in title.

If said purchaser does not give said seller written notice of intention to complete the purchase of said property on or before the date of expiration of this option or does not make the additional payment on account of purchase price as herein provided, then seller shall be released from all obligation hereunder and all rights hereunder, legal and equitable, of said purchaser shall cease and the consideration hereinabove receipted for by seller shall be retained by said seller as liquidated and agreed damages.

All notices required hereunder to be given said seller shall comply herewith if posted U. S. Registered Mail addressed to said seller at .... 180 Santa Maria Avenue, San Francisco, California. ....

Taxes for the fiscal year ending June 30, following the date hereof, rents and insurance shall be pro-rated as of the date of recordation of deed.

Subject to any zoning and set back ordinances of the City and County of San Francisco.

In this agreement, the masculine includes the feminine and neuter, and the singular includes the plural.

Time is of the essence of this agreement.

Witness: Seller:

....   (s) Thomas Nesbitt
                                           ....

....

                                           Purchaser:

....   (s) Jules Fraden
                                           ....

....

FIGURE 9–5

down as a percentage in the listing agreement rather than as a specific amount of money?

6. Discuss the importance of keeping accurate records of prospective clients with whom the broker may come into contact with respect to one of his listings.

7. Discuss the importance of the term *diligence*, as used in a listing, in connection with the procuring of a purchaser.

8. What is the importance of the deposit-receipt form in addition to evidencing the receipt of a deposit?

9. What is the difference between a single man, an unmarried man, and a widower?

10. In addition to cash, what are some other acceptable forms of a deposit?

11. Is a termite report required by state law in connection with the sale of real property?

12. Discuss the advantages or disadvantages of ordering a termite inspection before a purchase offer is received.

13. What problems may arise with regard to the classification of certain items as fixtures in connection with the sale of real property?

14. Discuss the usual closing costs for which each of the parties may be liable in your particular locality.

15. What problems may arise in connection with occupancy of a property by the buyer?

16. Why should an interested purchaser not delay unduly in considering a counteroffer received from the seller?

17. Discuss what a buyer or seller may do in the event of nonperformance by either.

18. Discuss the various circumstances in which an option agreement may be used.

19. How may an exchange be said to be doubly profitable to a real estate broker?

20. What are some of the main advantages to an exchange rather than a sale of real property?

MULTIPLE CHOICE QUESTIONS

9–1. A written listing that allows a number of brokers to act as agent is: *(a)* net, *(b)* oral, *(c)* open, *(d)* none of these.

9–2. The listing that affords a broker the greatest amount of protection is: *(a)* exclusive agency, *(b)* exclusive right to sell, *(c)* open, *(d)* oral.

9–3. A deposit receipt: *(a)* is a contract for the purchase of real property, *(b)* must include a clause specifying a termite report, *(c)* is legally considered a listing until accepted by a seller, *(d)* must contain a notary stamp.

9–4. A property description in a purchase agreement must: *(a)* show the proper zoning classification, *(b)* show metes and bounds measurements, *(c)* be sufficient to clearly identify the property, *(d)* contain a legal street address.

9–5. With respect to a buyer taking possession of purchased property: *(a)* broker determines possession, *(b)* time of possession is set by law, *(c)* must be given when escrow closes, *(d)* strictly be agreement between buyer and seller.

9–6. If seller accepts an offer and buyer refuses to perform: *(a)* deposit must be retained by seller, *(b)* deposit belongs to broker, *(c)* seller may order escrow officer to return deposit, *(d)* none of these.

9–7. If an offer is rejected by a seller, the broker will usually try to obtain: *(a)* ratification, *(b)* option agreement, *(c)* counteroffer, *(d)* listing extension.

9–8. The method by which buyers take title to real property: *(a)* is set by local ordinances, *(b)* must be shown on the purchase contract, *(c)* generally is shown in the listing, *(d)* none of these.

Landlord and tenant

The landlord and tenant relationship arises when an owner of real property agrees to give another the temporary use and possession of it in return for a consideration, called *rent*. While the terms *landlord* and *tenant* apply to all rental situations, it is more correct to use the terms *lessor* and *lessee* when there is a written lease in connection with the rental. Generally, however, the owner of the property is referred to as *owner, lessor,* or *landlord,* while the person doing the renting is called the *tenant* or the *lessee.*

ORIGIN OF LEASES

The old English law made a distinction between freehold estates and less-than-freehold estates. It is from the less-than-freehold estates classification that leases as we know them today are derived. The main feature of a leasehold estate is the degree of possession the lessee (tenant) has in the land and/or building of the lessor (owner).

During the term of the lease the lessor has parted with his right of exclusive possession and has merely the basic title to the property, called *reversion.* A lease is usually referred to as a leasehold estate and is normally considered to be a form of personal property.

TYPES OF LEASEHOLD ESTATES

There are four basic types of leases, distinguished by the length of their duration: (1) tenancy for years, (2) periodic tenancy, (3) tenancy at will, and (4) tenancy at sufferance.

Tenancy for years

This is the most common type of leasehold. The tenancy for years is for a fixed period of time, agreed on by the lessor and lessee. The name may be misleading, since the lease does not have to be for an even amount of years but, rather, for any agreed-on period of time. It may be for a number of years, months, or weeks. Under this type of lease, the lessee has the right to exclusive possession for a fixed period of time agreed to by both parties and usually shown on the lease agreement itself.

Periodic tenancy

A periodic tenancy is created by the lessor and lessee to continue for successive periods of the same length, unless sooner terminated by notice. This type of tenancy does not terminate merely by the passing of time but, instead, is deemed to be renewed at the end of each of the periods by which the payment of rent is determined.

A periodic tenancy may be created when a lease runs out and the lessee remains and pays rent, which is accepted by the lessor. In this case, the tenancy is not usually renewed for the term of the original lease but, rather, for the amount of time equal to the time between rent payments.

The most common type of periodic tenancy is a tenancy from month to month. In the absence of any agreement respecting the length of time or the rent, the tenancy is presumed to be monthly. A periodic tenancy is usually terminated by giving a 30-day notice to the tenant if the rent is paid on a monthly basis, or a notice equal to whatever number of days usually elapses between the payments of rent.

Tenancy at will

A tenancy at will is created by agreement between the parties involved, but has no fixed term and is terminable at the will of either party. Originally no notice had to be given to terminate this type of tenancy, but today most states require that some form of notice be given.

Tenancy at sufferance

A tenant at sufferance is one who originally had lawful possession but whose right to remain on the premises has now passed. A tenant who receives a Three Day Notice To Pay Rent or Vacate, or a 30 day notice to vacate certain premises, and does not respond to the owner within a specified time, becomes a tenant at sufferance. If, the owner of the property accepts a payment of rent from the tenant at sufferance, this type of tenancy usually ceases, and the person in possession becomes either a tenant at will or a periodic tenant.

LESSEE AND LICENSEE

Our discussion throughout this chapter deals with relationship between an owner and a tenant or lessee, rather than between an owner and a licensee. A lessee has a contractual relationship with the owner; he has a form of leasehold estate that gives him a possessory right in the property.

A license is a personal privilege, and the licensee merely is given permission to be on the property that is in the possession of another. A licensee does not have any legal estate with regard to the property, and whatever acts he performs thereon would be a trespass were it not for the license given him to perform these acts. A license is not assignable and may be revoked at any time. The responsibilities that an owner owes to a licensee were discussed in Chapter 6.

REQUIREMENTS FOR CREATION OF A LEASE

A lease is a contract and is generally required to be in writing if its term is one year or more. As a practical matter, it is wise business procedure to have all leases in writing, regardless of the term, to avoid any misunderstanding between the parties involved.

The lease should contain the names of the parties, description of the property, amount of the rent, and length of time the lease will continue. In addition, there are usually many special conditions and clauses on the standard form.

The lessor must sign the lease and deliver it to the lessee. While it does not have to be signed by the lessee, it is common practice for the lessee to sign a copy and return it to the lessor. When the lessee enters into possession of the property and pays his rent, he automatically signifies his intent to agree to and abide by the provisions in the lease, even though he may not have signed and returned a copy of the lease.

As in any other contract, both parties to the lease are bound by the conditions in it, and any change in these terms and conditions must be agreed to by the parties involved. The lease may be recorded in the county where the property is located if the signature of the lessor is acknowledged, usually by a notary public, and such recordation will give constructive notice to all of the existence of the lease and the property involved.

RIGHTS AND OBLIGATIONS OF THE PARTIES

The rights and obligations of the parties to a lease are varied and at times quite complex, and should be adequately covered by the provisions to be found in the lease agreement. Some of the more important subjects to be covered, no matter how simple or complicated the form of the lease may be, are: (1) duration, (2) rent, (3) maintenance and improvements, (4) liability, (5) transfer by lessee, (6) termination, (7) special conditions and provisions. These will be discussed in connection with the following analysis of a standard lease form.

ANALYSIS OF LEASE FORM

We shall use as an example of a standard lease the form prepared by the California Association of Realtors® which is illustrated in Figure 10–1. The CAR Residential Lease uses the terms *landlord* and *tenant*, but in our discussion we shall continue to use the more traditionally accepted terms *lessor* and *lessee* in connection with a lease agreement. A few of the lease provisions are self-explanatory and excluded from our discussion.

1. The city and date are entered, together with the name of the lessor and lessee followed by the address, location, and description of the property being leased. Any items such as furniture, appliances, and special fixtures are shown.

RESIDENTIAL LEASE

THIS IS INTENDED TO BE A LEGALLY BINDING AGREEMENT – READ IT CAREFULLY

CALIFORNIA ASSOCIATION OF REALTORS® STANDARD FORM

_____ , California _____ 19 ____
_____ _____ , Landlord, and
_____ , Tenant, agree as follows:

    1. Landlord leases to Tenant and Tenant hires from Landlord those premises described as: ___ _____ _____
_____
_____

together with the following furniture, and appliances, if any, and fixtures: _____
_____

(Insert "as shown on Exhibit A attached hereto" and attach the exhibit if the list is extensive.)

    2. The term of this lease shall be for a period of _____ months; _____ years
commencing _____ 19 _____ and terminating _____ 19___ .

    3. Tenant is to pay a total rent of $ _____ , payable as follows: _____
_____
_____
_____
_____

The rent shall be paid at _____
or at any address designated by the Landlord in writing.

    4. $ _____ as security has been deposited. Landlord may use therefrom such amounts as are reasonably necessary to remedy Tenant's defaults in the payment of rent, to repair damages caused by Tenant, and to clean the premises upon termination of tenancy. If used toward rent or damages during the term of tenancy, Tenant agrees to reinstate said total security deposit upon five days written notice delivered to Tenant in person or by mailing. Balance of security deposit, if any, shall be mailed to Tenant at last known address within 14 days of surrender of premises.

    5. Tenant agrees to pay for all utilities and services based upon occupancy of the premises and the following charges: _____
_____
_____

except _____
which shall be paid for by Landlord.

    6. Tenant has examined the premises and all furniture, furnishings and appliances if any, and fixtures contained therein, and accepts the same as being clean, in good order, condition, and repair, with the following exceptions: _____
_____

    7. The premises are leased for use as a residence by the following named persons: _____
_____

No animal, bird, or pet except _____
shall be kept on or about the premises without Landlord's prior written consent.

    8. Any holding over at the expiration of this lease shall create a month to month tenancy at a monthly rent of $_____
payable in advance. All other terms and conditions herein shall remain in full force and effect.

    9. Tenant shall not disturb, annoy, endanger or interfere with other Tenants of the building or neighbors, nor use the premises for any unlawful purposes, nor violate any law or ordinance, nor commit waste or nuisance upon or about the premises.

    10. Tenant agrees to comply with all reasonable rules or regulations posted on the premises or delivered to Tenant by Landlord.

    11. Tenant shall keep the premises and furniture, furnishings and appliances, if any, and fixtures which are leased for his exclusive use in good order and condition and pay for any repairs to the property caused by Tenant's negligence or misuse or that of Tenant's invitees. Landlord shall otherwise maintain the property. Tenant's personal property is not insured by Landlord.

    12. Tenant shall not paint, wallpaper, nor make alterations to the property without Landlord's prior written consent.

    13. Upon not less than 24 hours advance notice, Tenant shall make the demised premises available during normal business hours to Landlord or his authorized agent or representative, for the purpose of entering (a) to make necessary agreed repairs, decorations, alterations or improvements or to supply necessary or agreed services, and (b) to show the premises to prospective or actual purchasers, mortgagees, tenants, workmen or contractors. In an emergency, Landlord, his agent or authorized representative may enter the premises at any time without securing prior permission from Tenant for the purpose of making corrections or repairs to alleviate such emergency.

    14. Tenant shall not let or sublet all or any part of the premises nor assign this lease or any interest in it without the prior written consent of Landlord.

    15. If Tenant abandons or vacates the premises, Landlord may at his option terminate this lease, and regain possession in the manner prescribed by law.

    16. If any legal action or proceeding be brought by either party to enforce any part of this lease, the prevailing party shall recover in addition to all other relief, reasonable attorney's fees and costs.

    17. Time is of the essence. The waiver by Landlord or Tenant of any breach shall not be construed to be a continuing waiver of any subsequent breach.

    18. Notice upon Tenant shall be served as provided by law. Notice upon Landlord may be served upon Manager of the demised premises

at _____ . Said Manager is authorized to accept service on behalf of Landlord.

    19. Within 10 days after written notice, Tenant agrees to execute and deliver a certificate as submitted by Landlord acknowledging that this agreement is unmodified and in full force and effect or in full force and effect as modified and stating the modifications. Failure to comply shall be deemed Tenant's acknowledgement that the certificate as submitted by Landlord is true and correct and may be relied upon by any lender or purchaser.

    20. The undersigned Tenant acknowledges having read the foregoing prior to execution and receipt of a copy hereof.

Landlord _____   _____ Tenant

Landlord _____   _____ Tenant

For these forms, address – California Association of Realtors®
505 Shatto Place, Los Angeles, California 90020

FIGURE 10–1

TENANT APPLICATION

Property Address: _____ Apt. No. _____

Name(s) of Applicant(s): _____

Other Name(s) used within last 3 years: _____

Names and Age of other Occupants: _____

_____

Pets (Number & Type): _____

Present Address: _____

    How long? _____ Reason for leaving: _____

    Name and Address of Owner or Owner's Agent: _____

Previous Address (Past 3 Years): _____

    How long? _____ Reason for leaving: _____

    Name and Address of Owner or Owner's Agent: _____

Previous Address (Past 3 Years): _____

    How long? _____ Reason for leaving: _____

    Name and Address of Owner or Owner's Agent: _____

Employment: Social Security Number_____ Drivers License Number _____

    Present Employer: _____ How long?_____

    Address: _____ Telephone: _____

    Employed as: _____ Salary: $ _____ per _____

Employment of any other Occupant: Social Security Number _____Drivers License Number_____

    Present Employer _____ How long?_____

    Address: _____ Telephone: _____

    Employed as: _____ Salary: $ _____ per _____

Other Income: $ _____ Source: _____

Credit References (2): _____

Credit Cards: Issuer_____ Acct. No. _____ Issuer_____ Acct. No. _____

_____

Automobile License No. _____ State of Registry: _____

    Make & Model: _____Year: _____ Color: _____

IN CASE OF EMERGENCY:

Name of Closest Relative: _____ Relationship: _____

    Address: _____ Telephone: _____

AUTHORIZATION TO VERIFY INFORMATION

I Authorize Landlord or his Authorized Agents to Verify the above information, including but not limited to obtaining a Cred
if this application is accepted I agree to execute the residential lease or rental agreement as set forth on the reverse side hereof

Date _____ 19 _____ Applicant: _____

Telephone No. _____ Applicant: _____

    RECEIPT FOR DEPOSIT

    The undersigned acknowledges receipt of $_____ in the form of ( ) Cash, ( ) Personal Check _____

    or ( ) _____ payable to _____ as deposit on the above _____
    described property.

Date _____ Agent _____

FIGURE 10–1 (*concluded*)

2. The term of the lease is stated, showing the exact date of beginning and ending of lease duration. It is interesting to note that in California there are certain statutory restrictions in the leasing of real property with regard to the duration: *(a)* agricultural or horticultural lands cannot be leased for a longer period than 51 years; *(b)* the property of a minor or an incompetent person cannot be leased for a longer period than a probate court may authorize; *(c)* property situated within a city or town cannot be leased for a longer period than 99 years; *(d)* a lease of land for the purpose of effecting the production of minerals, oil, gas, or other hydrocarbon substances from other lands may be made for a period certain or determinable by any future event prescribed by the parties, but no such lease shall be enforceable after 99 years from the commencement of the term thereof. This refers to the lease of drill sites for slant drilling also.

Rent

3. Rent is the consideration paid by the tenant for use of the property. The lease should clearly state the amount of the rent in total, and then show when, where, how, and in what amounts the rent is to be paid to the lessor by the lessee.

Sometimes the lessor may ask the lessee for the first and last month's rent in advance at the time the lease is drawn up and signed by the parties. The Internal Revenue Service will consider this last month's rent as "prepaid rent," and the lessor must declare this as income in the year received. Many times, when the lessor collects an additional amount of rent in advance, the lessee may feel that should he decide to move from the premises, notice is unnecessary, since the lessor will keep the additional amount.

In order to avoid declaring this prepaid rent as income in the year received, or risking the lessee's moving without notice, the lessor should call the extra money a security deposit. If he does this, the money need not be declared as income, and the lessee will still be obligated to pay the last month's rent when it is due. The security deposit is then returned when the lease terminates.

Escalator clause. A number of leases and rental agreements now contain an escalator clause which allows an owner to increase the rent during the term of the lease if various costs such as a tax increase or the like are levied against the owner. Quite often, such rental increases are tied to a wholesale or consumer price index or other governmental cost-of-living indicator.

Security

4. The California legislature has resolved an area of confusion surrounding such terms in the landlord-tenant vocabulary as "cleaning deposit, rent guarantee and breakage fee" by including these terms in a single category to be called "Security."

Assembly Bill 94, effective January 1978, uses the single term *security* and defines it to mean any payment, fee, deposit or charge, including, but not limited to, an advance payment of rent, used or to be used for any purpose.

According to the new law a security may not be greater than the equivalent of two months' rent for unfurnished residential property (three months' rent for furnished residential property) in addition to any rent paid *in advance* for the first month's rent. When the term of the lease is six months or longer, larger initial deposits are permitted.

The new law provides, among other things, that the landlord may use the security to:

Compensate for a tenant's failure to pay rent.

Repair damages (other than ordinary wear and tear) to the property caused by the tenant.

Clean the property upon termination of the tenancy.

The landlord holds the security *for the tenant.* After the tenancy is terminated and the tenant has moved out, the landlord has two weeks in which to return any unused security and to explain in writing how the remainder was used.

If a landlord unjustifiably claims any portion of a security, the landlord may be liable to pay the tenant $200 in punitive damages, in addition to any actual damages. The landlord has the burden of proving the reasonableness of the amounts of the security not refunded to the former tenant.

The landlord may not attempt to avoid the provisions of this law by referring to the security furnished by the tenant as "nonrefundable." The law prohibits such characterization of a security and such action might be construed as a bad faith claim, subjecting the landlord to payment of damages.

If a landlord conveys rental real property to another person, the landlord can do one of two things with the security being held for tenants (a real estate broker negotiating the sale or exchange should inform the seller of seller's obligation and, if so instructed by the seller, the broker may act on behalf of the seller in fulfilling these obligations):

Transfer the security to the new owner/landlord and notify the tenant by personal delivery or certified mail of such transfer, setting forth any claims made against the security. The notice must include the new security holder's name, address, and telephone number. If personal delivery is made, the tenant must acknowledge receipt on the landlord's copy by signing his name.

Alternatively, the landlord may return the security to the tenant after making any lawful deductions and furnishing a written itemized accounting to the tenant.

5. Any type of premises may be leased on a rental basis that includes all or part of the utilities, or that has the lessee pay all of the utilities. Whatever the arrangement, it should be clearly stated in the lease. Many times, the lessor will pay for certain utilities, the most common being water, and the lessee will pay for others.

Liability for injury

6. Both the lessor or his agent, and the lessee, should carefully inspect the premises before the lease agreement is completed and signed by the parties. Such an inspection will disclose any items that are broken or not in proper working order and any conditions that may be likely to cause injury to the occupants.

Many leases contain a statement, commonly called an *exculpatory clause,* wherein the lessor attempts to avoid liability for injuries to any individuals who may be injured on the premises.

Even though the lease may contain a provision of this type, if it can be shown that the injury was due to negligence on the part of the lessor, and such negligence can be proven, the lessor probably will be held liable and have to pay damages.

Generally, when all the premises are leased the lessor is not liable for injuries to the tenant or others resulting from the defective condition of the premises. Such a condition results when the lessee leases an entire building from the lessor. Usually, however, a lessee is leasing only an apartment or a flat in a building containing other apartments or dwelling units. In such a condition, the owner of the building has a direct responsibility with regard to entrances, common hallways and stairs, and the elevator, if any. The lessee is responsible for injuries occurring within his own dwelling unit.

Practically speaking, it is almost impossible to find an owner of rental property who does not carry some form of public liability insurance and other coverages to afford him protection in such cases. The tenant usually carries protective insurance also, and quite often the lease is drawn to require the lessee to carry such insurance.

7. Identifying the specific tenants will keep additional individuals from moving into the premises without permission of the lessor. A restriction against pets will protect against the lessee who states that he has no pets but after moving into the premises decides to purchase a dog or cat. The lessor may allow certain types of pets such as tropical fish or canaries, and wish to avoid others such as cats, dogs, and rattlesnakes.

8. This section provides that if at termination of the lease term the tenant should remain in possession and the lessor should accept a rent payment, this does not constitute a renewal of the former lease, and the tenant is on a strictly month-to-month basis. It also allows the lessor to raise the rent if he wishes, or to leave the rent the same as it was during the term of the lease.

The lessor should always include such a provision in the lease to make clear what happens at the end of the lease if the tenant continues in possession. The tenant is then known as a "holdover tenant," and in many areas if the owner accepts rent from the former lessee after the lease has terminated, the period for which the lease was originally written is automatically renewed for the same period and on the same terms.

Maintenance and repairs

11–12. Except for normal wear and tear, the lessee is expected to keep the premises in good condition and not wilfully or negligently damage or destroy anything. In addition, any alterations require approval of the lessor.

The owner of a building must be very careful with respect to liability for any work done on the premises. If he has not ordered the work and does not want to be held responsible for payment, he must notify the person performing the work of this fact. This is usually done by the use of a written notice called a notice of nonresponsibility. Failure to do so may result in the owner's having to pay for work he did not order should the person performing the work file a mechanic's lien against the property. The lessor should have a very clear understanding with the lessee regarding this entire area of maintenance and repairs.

Entry of premises by lessor

13. The lessee is entitled to quiet possession and privacy. In addition to entry for purposes stated in this provision, the owner or his agent may wish to enter the premises in connection with delinquent rent payments or violation of a lease provision. The lessor must be extremely careful of his actions in this respect. Should he enter the premises and forceably evict the lessee, he may be open to a suit for any injury or damage to the lessee's personal effects, and may also be open to suit for any physical injury the lessee may claim. A later section in the chapter discusses remedies of the lessor and deals with eviction and unlawful detainer proceedings.

Assign or sublet

14. The lessee must not sublet or assign his leasehold rights without permission of the lessor. If the lessor gives the lessee permission to assign his right to another, the individual to whom the rights are assigned now assumes all the rights, duties, and responsibilities of the original lessee. If a lessee merely sublets the premises, the original lessee is still responsible to the lessor for payment of the rent. Generally, the sublessee pays the original lessee, and the original lessee must, in turn, pay the lessor.

15. The lessor must be sure that the lessee has not merely taken a vacation and that the premises have actually been abandoned by the lessee.

16. This provision states that in connection with any legal action by either party, the prevailing party is entitled to attorneys' fees and court costs. Any legal action in connection with the leasehold agreement must conform to specific applicable laws.

The lease we have been using as an illustration is relatively simple. It is not uncommon for certain leases to contain from a dozen to fifty or more separate provisions and conditions. The larger the property and the more complicated its use, the longer and more complex is the lease. A residential rental agreement for month-to-month tenancy is illustrated later in the chapter, since the use of monthly tenancy agreements are becoming increasingly popular.

TERMINATION OF THE LEASE

There are many ways and differing reasons for which a lease agreement may be terminated by one or both of the parties involved. The more common are the following:

Expiration of the term

A lease is most commonly terminated when the end of the term agreed on in the lease has been reached. A lease should have some specific provision concerning what is to occur at the end of the term. The lessee may be given an option to renew on the same terms and conditions, he may be given the right only to negotiate a new lease, or he may be given notice by the lessor that he is to surrender the premises.

By tenant for failure of owner to provide quiet possession

A lessee is entitled to quiet possession of the premises he has leased. He is entitled to reasonable privacy and enjoyment, and failure of the lessor to provide such conditions is ground for termination of the lease by the lessee. This is known as constructive eviction.

Although the lessee has the right to reasonable privacy, most leases give the lessor the right to enter and inspect the premises in order to make repairs and alterations that may be necessary, or for the purpose of showing the property to prospective tenants during the closing weeks of the lease.

By tenant for owner's refusal to repair

Under most lease forms, the lessee is responsible for keeping the premises in good normal repair and for making minor repairs that may be necessary. The lessor is generally responsible for any major repairs that must be made. He is further responsible for any major structural repairs needed and cannot allow the building to become so dilapidated that it is no longer fit for human occupancy. If an owner of a building refuses to make necessary repairs after being notified by the tenant, and the premises in question is a dwelling unit, the tenant may spend one month's rent for repairs, but beyond this he cannot usually force the lessor to act and may if he wishes abandon the premises, and he will not be held responsible for the payment of the rent or performance of other conditions in the lease.

The California Supreme Court recently held that there is a warranty of habitability inherent in every residential rental relationship; that the standard of the warranty is any building code or housing code materially affecting health or safety; and that tenants are permitted to raise this issue as a counterclaim in any action for possession for nonpayment of rent.

Eviction

Eviction is the dispossession of the tenant by the owner of the property. Actual eviction by law occurs after a lessor has brought action against the lessee, usually for failure to pay rent, and on receiving an order from the court has the lessee evicted. This will be discussed further in a subsequent section of this chapter dealing with remedies of the lessor.

Constructive eviction occurs when a lessee is denied quiet enjoyment or privacy, and therefore moves from the premises. Where there is an eviction by law, the lessee may be liable for any monetary damages suffered by the lessor. When a constructive eviction occurs, the lessee is usually not required to pay the rent remaining in the lease.

By either party on destruction of the premises

Should the premises be destroyed there is usually an automatic termination. If the damage is slight, however, the tenant may want to remain while the lessor makes the necessary repairs.

By either party on breach of a condition of the lease

Since violation of one of the conditions of the lease may result in termination, it is important that the lessor and lessee fully understand the provisions and terms of the lease they have signed.

By mutual agreement of the parties to the lease

Termination of the lease by mutual agreement is commonly called *surrender* and may be accomplished in two ways: (1) mutual agreement or (2) operation of law.

Termination accomplished by mutual agreement is quite a simple matter. Parties to a lease frequently agree to its termination. The main point is that such termination must be by mutual agreement, and one party cannot force the other to terminate without a good and valid reason if the party does not wish to do so.

Termination by operation of law is more complex, and is usually the result of court action. An example might be that of a lessee who moves out of an apartment without giving notice and is thus said to have abandoned the premises. The lessor subsequently reenters and takes possession. The lessor will then have a cause for court action and would probably bring suit to recover the remainder of the rent due under the terms of the lease. Generally, the lessor will attempt to re-lease the property, and will be allowed to recover only the actual amount he loses, plus any expenses incurred in repairing or cleaning the premises before leasing them again.

REMEDIES OF THE LESSOR

In our discussion thus far, we have touched on some of the remedies available to the lessor against the lessee. The same remedies are available as between a landlord and tenant when there is no lease and the tenancy is on a monthly basis. In such cases, the owner may recover possession of the premises by giving a 30-day notice to the tenant to vacate the premises.

The following is the legal process for eviction:

1. Three-day notice to pay rent or comply with a provision of the lease or rental agreement is given.
2. Complaint in unlawful detainer is filed with the Municipal Court Clerk and summons is issued.
3. Summons and complaint is served on tenant.
4. The tenant has the legal right to file a pleading in answer to the complaint, and in this event a trial will be held.

If the tenant does not file a pleading and answer to the complaint, the following action will be taken:

5. Default of tenant is taken.
6. Default judgment is received.
7. Municipal Court Clerk issues writ of possession.
8. Writ of possession, instruction to sheriff, and a court prescribed fee is delivered to the sheriff.
9. Sheriff evicts tenant and stores furnishings.

Although the lessor has these specific remedies at law, in practice it is better if litigation can be avoided. Court proceedings are expensive when one considers the attorney's fee, and if the sheriff must evict the tenant, further expenses accrue to the owner of the property. Even though the lessor may be entitled to recover these expenses from the lessee, it usually follows that one who cannot pay his rent, if this is the reason for the eviction, will also be unable to pay any judgment.

DUTIES OF THE LESSOR

Recent legislative enactments have substantially increased an owner's responsibility toward his tenants, and requires all rentals to be fit for human habitation. The basic items that must exist to meet the necessary standards are heating, plumbing, and effective weather protection. The premises must also be sanitary and in reasonably safe condition.

Utility shut-offs

The law now provides increased financial liability for owners who willfully cause any interruption of utilities to tenants, if the owner is acting with intent to evict a tenant. The owner can be liable for any expenses incurred by the tenant due to utility shut-offs.

Preventing access

An additional Civil Code section now makes it unlawful for an owner to prevent a tenant from gaining access to the property by locks being changed or any other such means. In addition, the owner cannot enter the premises and remove any of the tenant's belongings if the intent is to evict the tenant.

Retaliatory eviction

If an owner attempts to evict a tenant for making repairs and deducting any costs from the rent, or for reporting the owner to some governmental agency, it is referred to as retaliatory eviction. The law provides for a 180-day period during which no such eviction may take place. The owner is prohibited from raising rent or taking any eviction action for a period of 180 days following the date the tenant has exercised any legal rights or reported any violations.

Proper maintenance

While the law requires an owner to maintain property in a clean and safe condition, the tenant must also maintain properly and not cause any willful damage to the premises. The law excuses an owner from repairing damaged premises caused by any of the tenants.

ADDITIONAL CLAUSES FOR THE LEASE FORM

An example of a few additional lease provisions commonly found in lease and rental agreements are now presented for your information.

1. "Water beds are not allowed on the premises without the prior approval of the lessor." Some water beds hold over 200 gallons of water and weigh approximately 2,000 pounds, and excessive damage due to weight or water leakage may result.

2. "The roof and exterior walls of the premises are not subject to this lease, and exclusive rights to the use thereof are reserved by the lessor." Such a provision may be necessary when large outdoor signs or other advertising matter are affixed to the walls or on the roof, for which the owner receives additional income.

3. "No signs, advertisements, or notices shall be inscribed, painted, or affixed to the outside or inside of the premises without the express consent of the lessor." This is a typical provision, which allows the lessor to control an area that can often lead to problems. When a building is leased to a number of tenants for dwelling purposes, the lessor may not want tenants to erect signs of a commercial nature. Typical of these are such signs as "Alterations" or "Notary Public" or "Watch Repairing."

RENTAL DETERMINATION

There are various methods of determining the amount of rent to be charged under a lease. The common method with regard to residential dwelling units is to compare the unit being offered with other like units in the area and rents being charged for them. An owner will generally not be able to receive any amount in excess of that being charged for comparables in the immediate area.

With respect to business and commercial properties the same principal holds true, but there are different types of leases in use, such as the gross lease, the net lease, and the percentage lease. All of these derive their names from the method used in the rental determination.

Rent control laws have been enacted in various parts of the state and property owners should be aware of any such restrictions which may affect their property.

Gross lease

In this type of arrangement, the lessee pays to the lessor a fixed rate of rent at fixed periods of time, the same as is done with regard to residential leases. The lessor must pay the property taxes, the necessary insurance, the general upkeep, and the major repairs.

Net lease

Under a net lease, the lessee pays all the taxes, insurance, and other general expenses involved in the operation of the property, and the lessor receives a net rental figure.

Percentage lease

The amount of rent to be paid under a percentage lease is related to the gross amount of sales completed by the lessee. The percentage may be applied in various ways. The rent may be stated as a fixed amount, plus a percent applied to all gross sales in excess of a certain amount; some leases state a fixed amount, plus a percent of gross sales with a guaranteed minimum and maximum; or the lease may state the rent only in terms of a certain percent of the gross or net sales of the lessee. The most common practice is to specify a fixed amount of rent, plus a percentage agreement of some type.

Oil, gas, and mineral leases

In many parts of the country, real estate brokers specialize in leases that give rights to something contained under the surface of the land rather than on it. Large oil companies lease land they think contains gas or oil. The owner generally receives a flat fee or rental for allowing the company to drill on the land. Then, if the wells actually begin to produce, the owner will receive an additional amount commonly called a *royalty*.

Ground lease

A ground lease, as the name implies, is a lease for unimproved property for a term of years. Such a lease is often made in connection with a large commercial or recreational development, and the land is quite often used for garage or parking purposes. Such leases often provide for the erection of improvements by the lessee, and these improvements ultimately become the property of the lessor.

Farm lease

The farm lease is another type of specialized lease used in certain areas. The lessee will operate the farm and pay the lessor either a flat sum as rental or a percentage of the value of a future crop. Many times, there will be a flat sum specified as rent, and in addition a percentage of the value of crops that the lessee will ultimately market. Such arrangements can be adapted to virtually any agricultural or ranch property.

Sale-and-leaseback

Sale-and-leaseback arrangements are often used by large business concerns. A simple illustration is a firm that cannot find the kind of building or facility in the particular location it wants. If sufficient capital is available, it can have a building constructed and then enter into a sale-and-leaseback arrangement with an investor. The firm now has the kind of building it wants, it gets its investment back at the time of the sale, and it has a long-term lease for the use of the building. Since the former owner is now in the position of being a lessee, all rent payments plus maintenance and repair costs are tax deductible. The same arrangement can be used for an existing building on which a substantial amount of the allowable depreciation has already been taken by the owner.

The benefits to the investor should be an excellent long-term tenant and the depreciation allowance available as an offset against income. Sale-and-leaseback is also correctly classified as a form of financing device for the firm that utilizes this method. Sears, Roebuck and Co. has extensively used the sale-and-leaseback method in establishing new retail outlets and large insurance companies have been the purchasers.

A recapture provision may be incorporated into the agreement to allow the original owner to reacquire the property at the end of the lease term. Such an arrangement is quite complex, however, because of the effect of certain Internal Revenue Service tax rules and regulations.

LEASE-OPTION ARRANGEMENT

During a time when loans are not easily available, or when a purchaser does not have a sufficient

RESIDENTIAL RENTAL AGREEMENT

(Month To Month Tenancy)

THIS IS INTENDED TO BE A LEGALLY BINDING AGREEMENT — READ IT CAREFULLY

CALIFORNIA ASSOCIATION OF REALTORS® STANDARD FORM

_____ , California _____ 19 ____
_____ , Landlord, and
_____ , Tenant, agree as follows:

1. Landlord rents to Tenant and Tenant hires from Landlord those premises described as: _____
_____
_____

together with the following furniture, and appliances, if any, and fixtures: _____
_____
_____

(Insert "as shown on Exhibit A attached hereto" and attach the exhibit if the list is extensive.)

2. The term shall commence on _____ , 19 _____ , and shall continue from month to month. This rental agreement may be terminated at any time by either party by giving written notice 30 days in advance.

Tenant agrees to pay $ _____ rent per month payable in advance on the _____ day of each month and $ _____ representing prorated rent from date of possession.

3. The rent shall be paid at _____
or at any address designated by the Landlord in writing.

4. $ _____ as security has been deposited. Landlord may use therefrom such amounts as are reasonably necessary to remedy Tenant's defaults in the payment of rent, to repair damages caused by Tenant, and to clean the premises if necessary upon termination of tenancy. If used toward rent or damages during the term of tenancy, Tenant agrees to reinstate said total security deposit upon five days written notice delivered to Tenant in person or by mailing. Security deposit or balance thereof, if any, shall be mailed to Tenant at last known address within 14 days of surrender of premises.

5. Tenant agrees to pay for all utilities and services based upon occupancy of the premises and the following charges:
_____
except _____
which shall be paid for by Landlord.

6. Tenant has examined the premises and all furniture, furnishings and appliances if any, and fixtures contained therein, and accepts the same as being clean, in good order, condition, and repair, with the following exceptions: _____
_____

7. The premises are rented for use as a residence by the following named persons: _____
_____

No animal, bird, or pet except _____
shall be kept on or about the premises without Landlord's prior written consent.

8. Tenant shall not disturb, annoy, endanger or interfere with other Tenants of the building or neighbors, nor use the premises for any unlawful purposes, nor violate any law or ordinance, nor commit waste or nuisance upon or about the premises.

9. Tenant agrees to comply with all reasonable rules or regulations posted on the premises or delivered to Tenant by Landlord.

10. Tenant shall keep the premises and furniture, furnishings and appliances, if any, and fixtures which are rented for his exclusive use in good order and condition and pay for any repairs to the property caused by Tenant's negligence or misuse or that of Tenant's invitees. Landlord shall otherwise maintain the property. Tenant's personal property is not insured by Landlord.

11. Tenant shall not paint, wallpaper, nor make alterations to the property without Landlord's prior written consent.

12. Upon not less than 24 hours advance notice, Tenant shall make the demised premises available during normal business hours to Landlord or his authorized agent or representative, for the purpose of entering (a) to make necessary agreed repairs, decorations, alterations or improvements or to supply necessary or agreed services, and (b) to show the premises to prospective or actual purchasers, mortgagees, tenants, workmen or contractors. In an emergency, Landlord, his agent or authorized representative may enter the premises at any time without securing prior permission from Tenant for the purpose of making corrections or repairs to alleviate such emergency.

13. Tenant shall not let or sublet all or any part of the premises nor assign this agreement or any interest in it without the prior written consent of Landlord.

14. If Tenant abandons or vacates the premises, Landlord may at his option terminate this agreement, and regain possession in the manner prescribed by law.

15. If any legal action or proceeding be brought by either party to enforce any part of this agreement, the prevailing party shall recover in addition to all other relief, reasonable attorney's fees and costs.

16. Time is of the essence. The waiver by Landlord or Tenant of any breach shall not be construed to be a continuing waiver of any subsequent breach.

17. Notice upon Tenant shall be served as provided by law. Notice upon Landlord may be served upon Manager of the demised premises
_____
at _____ . Said Manager is authorized to accept service on behalf of Landlord.

18. Within 10 days after written notice, Tenant agrees to execute and deliver a certificate as submitted by Landlord acknowledging that this agreement is unmodified and in full force and effect or in full force and effect as modified and stating the modifications. Failure to comply shall be deemed Tenant's acknowledgement that the certificate as submitted by Landlord is true and correct and may be relied upon by any lender or purchaser.

19. The undersigned Tenant acknowledges having read the foregoing prior to execution and receipt of a copy hereof.

Landlord _____   _____ Tenant

Landlord _____   _____ Tenant

NO REPRESENTATION IS MADE AS TO THE LEGAL VALIDITY OF ANY PROVISION OR THE ADEQUACY OF ANY PROVISION IN ANY SPECIFIC TRANSACTION. A REAL ESTATE BROKER IS THE PERSON QUALIFIED TO ADVISE ON REAL ESTATE. IF YOU DESIRE LEGAL ADVICE CONSULT YOUR ATTORNEY.

For these forms, address — California Association of Realtors®
505 Shatto Place, Los Angeles, California 90020

FIGURE 10–2

down payment, a lease-option arrangement, or lease-purchase agreement as it is sometimes called, may be used. In this method, the prospective purchaser leases the property desired, with an option to purchase at a later date for an agreed-on price. Usually a certain amount of credit against the purchase will be given for rent paid before exercise of the option to purchase.

MONTHLY TENANCY AGREEMENT

Written agreements for a tenancy on a month-to-month basis are becoming increasingly popular throughout the country. Month-to-month agreements contain many of the provisions found in a standard residential lease and are used for apartments, flats, duplexes, and other common types of residential dwelling units. An example of such an agreement is the CAR residential rental agreement, which appears in Figure 10–2. The back of the form contains the same application material shown in Figure 10–1, the residential lease.

Basically, these agreements provide for a stated monthly rental, a cleaning charge, and often an initial deposit put up by the tenant at the time the agreement is signed. The cleaning charge is forfeited in part or whole by the tenant for property damage and/or cleaning required at the end of the agreement term. The deposit may also be forfeited if the tenant vacates the premises without giving the proper notice as set forth in the agreement.

The amount of the deposit may be more than, less than, or equal to the rent for one month. This depends on the custom in a particular area or on the desire of the landlord. It is only natural that such a form should have come into wide usage. If the tenant vacates an apartment or other dwelling unit before the end of the lease term under a standard lease, the lessor may then go to court to try to recover damages, if any. However, the lessor can usually only collect the actual amount of rent lost. In most cases, the property owner will try to rerent the premises as soon as possible, and will be able to do so within a month or two. Practically, then, it is usually unwise for the lessor to go to court over a tenant who skips out, since the fees the lessor will incur will more than offset the few months of rent he will be entitled to collect. In the month-to-month type of agreement, the deposit should be about enough to take care of any loss of this type incurred by the owner of the property from the time the ten-

ant leaves to the time the dwelling unit is rented to another tenant.

A monthly tenancy agreement may be quite simple, or it may be lengthy and contain many conditions and provisions. Many of the conditions discussed in connection with leases may be incorporated into the monthly tenancy agreement.

The law now provides that the name and usual address of the person authorized to manage the premises and of an owner or person authorized to act on behalf of the owner for receipt of notices, demands, and process, must be furnished in the lease or rental agreement; or, in the case of an oral rental agreement, be furnished in writing on demand of the tenant; or be posted in at least two conspicuous places on the premises, including every elevator.

A topic often discussed in connection with the rental and leasing of real property is that of the fair housing laws and possible discrimination in rentals. This area is covered in detail in Chapter 18, Governmental Controls.

QUESTIONS FOR DISCUSSION

1. What are the fundamental types of leasehold estates?
2. What is the difference between an assignment and a sublease?
3. Discuss some of the more important subjects generally covered in a lease or monthly tenancy agreement.
4. What are the reasons that a lessor may require a security deposit?
5. What are the duties of the lessor with regard to maintenance and repairs?
6. Discuss the different reasons for the termination of a lease.
7. What remedies are available to a lessor under a lease?
8. What are the general duties and responsibilities of the lessor and lessee under a lease?
9. Identify and discuss various types of leases.
10. If you were the owner of a building containing residential units, what clauses other than those mentioned in the chapter might you wish to incorporate into a lease or monthly tenancy agreement?

MULTIPLE CHOICE QUESTIONS

10–1. A type of lease that permits the lessee to purchase the property is: (a) residential, (b) percentage or net, (c) lease option, (d) tenancy agreement.

10–2. The most common type of leasehold is: (a) periodic tenancy, (b) rental agreement, (c) tenancy for years, (d) none of these.

10–3. The property owner in a lease agreement is: *(a)* broker, *(b)* lessor, *(c)* lessee, *(d)* tenant.

10–4. The manner in which the rent is to be paid is usually set by: *(a)* real estate law, *(b)* broker, *(c)* owner, *(d)* tenant.

10–5. Cancellation of a lease by mutual agreement is: *(a)* periodic tenancy, *(b)* result of court action, *(c)* recapture, *(d)* surrender.

10–6. A complaint in unlawful detainer has to do with: *(a)* preparation of a lease or rental agreement, *(b)* periodic rental payments, *(c)* tenant eviction, *(d)* maintenance of apartments.

10–7. Assignment of a lease generally requires: *(a)* payment of additional rent, *(b)* renegotiation of the lease agreement, *(c)* permission of lessor, *(d)* none of these.

10–8. The best protection to the parties in a rental situation is: *(a)* agreement in writing, *(b)* large rental deposit, *(c)* dealing directly with the owner, *(d)* real estate commissioner.

11 Real estate mathematics

Section 10153 of the California Real Estate Law states that licensees must have an appropriate knowledge of the English language, including reading, writing, and spelling, and must also have a good basic knowledge of elementary arithmetic. This knowledge must be sufficient to allow the licensee to correctly calculate and compute mathematical problems common to normal real estate transactions. The real estate salesperson and real estate broker examinations contain a number of practical problems of this nature. This chapter will review and illustrate the various types of mathematical problems that occur in everyday real estate transactions, and methods of solving them will be shown. Such problems include:

1. Calculation of interest.
2. Prorations, including such items as rent, taxes, and insurance.
3. Percentage problems involving commissions, profit and loss, net listings, capitalization, loan ratio, and discount.
4. Property tax.
5. Depreciation.
6. Amortization and calculation of the present value of a loan.
7. Area measurement.

INTEREST

Interest is an amount of money paid for the use of money. When one leases an apartment, he pays rent to the landlord for use of the apartment. In the same way, when one borrows money he pays for use of the money a rent or fee called *interest*.

Rate, or the rate of interest, is the amount being charged for use of money, expressed as a percentage per annum of the amount being borrowed. Principal is the amount of money that has been loaned by the lender and borrowed by the borrower. Time is the number of days, months, or years for which an amount of money has been borrowed and for which interest may be charged.

Simple and compound interest

Simple interest is the type charged by banks, savings and loan associations, insurance companies, and other lenders for the use of money borrowed from them. The principal and the interest of the loan may be repaid in several ways. The most common is for the borrower to make monthly amortized payments over a given period of time. Each payment applies toward paying off both the interest and the principal.

Simple interest is the type the borrower pays to the lender; compound interest is the type the lending institution pays to a depositor for money in a savings account. Compound interest may not be charged by lenders in California to persons who borrow money; it can be paid only to persons who put their money in savings accounts. Compound interest causes interest to be paid on interest. As an example, assume that a savings and loan association pays depositors interest at the end of each quarter, or four times a year. If a depositor does not withdraw any of his funds during the year, not only will he receive a rate of interest on the amount he originally deposited, but also at the end of each quarter the interest he receives will be added to the amount on deposit. Since the amount of interest paid at the end of each quarter is calculated on the amount on deposit, the depositor is actually receiving interest on interest, as well as on the original principal.

Computing time

The two most common methods of measuring time for interest computations are (1) 30-day month time and (2) exact time. Using the 30-day method, the year is divided into 12 30-day months, and 360 days is one year. Using the exact-time method, the year is represented by 365 days or, if a leap year, 366 days.

In computing interest, the time factor is represented by a fraction. The numerator represents the amount of days for which interest is to be charged, the denominator the number of days in the year—either 360 or 365. In calculating the number of days on which interest is to be charged, the days are counted from the day following creation of the obligation up to and including the last day. The rule is simplified by remembering to skip the first day and include the last day.

Assuming interest is to be calculated for 67 days, the fraction representing time would be 67/360 if the 360-day year is used, and 67/365 if an exact time year is used. The 360-day year, however, is the one used in real estate transactions, and it will be used in all subsequent examples.

Where the period of time is expressed in even years, the time factor will not be shown as a fraction, but rather as a whole number representing the actual years. Thus, in calculating the interest for a loan in which the time is 11 years, the time factor would be represented by 11. Where the period of time is expressed in even months, the time factor is shown as a fraction with a denominator of 12. Thus, for a loan of 7 months, the time factor fraction will be shown as 7/12. Where the period of time is to be expressed in days, the time factor fraction will show the amount of days as the numerator and 360 as the denominator. If the interest is to be calculated for 79 days, the time factor fraction will be shown as 79/360.

Interest formulas

Interest can be calculated by using the formula

$$I = PRT$$
Interest = Principal × Rate × Time.

1. What is the interest on a loan of $6,000 for 3 years at 11 percent? In calculating interest, the rate is expressed as a decimal. Solution:

Interest = $6,000 × .11 × 3
Interest = $1,980.

The $6,000 is first multiplied by .11, giving an answer of $660. The result is then multiplied by 3, giving an answer of $1,980.

2. What is the interest on a loan of $8,000 for 7 months at 15 percent? Solution:

Interest = $8,000 × .15 × 7/12
Interest = $700.

3. What is the interest on a loan of $30,000 at 16½ percent interest for 70 days? Solution:

Interest = $30,000 × .165 × 70/360
Interest = $962.50

Rate of interest may be found by use of the formula

$$R = \frac{I}{P \times T}$$
$$\text{Rate} = \frac{\text{Interest}}{\text{Principal} \times \text{Time}}.$$

1. If the amount of the loan is $20,000, the time is 3 years, and the interest charged is $6,000, what is the rate? Solution:

$$\text{Rate} = \frac{\$6,000}{\$20,000 \times 3} = \frac{\$6,000}{\$60,000} = \frac{1}{10} = 10\%.$$

(1/10 expressed as a percent is 10%).

2. Amount of loan is $12,000, interest is $1,190, and time is 7 months. What is the rate? Solution:

$$\text{Rate} = \frac{\$1,190}{\$12,000 \times 7/12} = \frac{\$1,190}{\$7,000} = .17 = 17\%.$$

Principal can be found by using the formula

$$P = \frac{I}{R \times T}$$
$$\text{Principal} = \frac{\text{Interest}}{\text{Rate} \times \text{Time}}.$$

1. What is the principal amount of a loan on which the interest is $11,875, the rate is 9½ percent, and the time is 5 years? Solution:

$$\text{Principal} = \frac{\$11,875}{.095 \times 5} = \frac{\$11,875}{.475} = \$25,000.$$

2. If the interest is $350, the rate is 12 percent, and the time is 5 months, what is the principal amount of the loan? Solution:

$$\text{Principal} = \frac{\$1,050}{12/100 \times 5/12} = \$21,000.$$

(Rate is usually stated as a decimal. However, in this problem the 12 percent rate is not expressed as .12 but is shown as the fraction 12/100 because the time, 5 months, is better expressed as 5/12 than as its decimal equivalent, 0.41⅔.)

3. What is the principal amount of the loan if the interest is $2,000, the rate is 16 percent, and the time is 3 months? Solution:

$$\text{Principal} = \frac{\$2,000}{.16 \times .25} = \$50,000$$

(In this problem, the time 3 months expressed fractionally is 3/12, which reduces to ¼. The decimal equivalent of ¼ is .25, so it is more convenient to express both the rate and the time as decimals.)

Time can be found by using the formula

$$T = \frac{I}{P \times R}$$

$$\text{Time} = \frac{\text{Interest}}{\text{Principal} \times \text{Rate}}.$$

1. What is the time on a loan of $70,000 when the rate is 11½ percent and the interest is $28,175? Solution:

$$\text{Time} = \frac{\$28,175}{\$70,000 \times .115} = 3½ \text{ years.}$$

60-day 6 percent method

Numerous shortcut methods for finding interest are available. One of the more common is the 60-day 6 percent method. The basis of this method is that 6 percent interest for 1 year equals 1 percent interest for 2 months, or 60 days. The 1 percent is easily found merely by moving the decimal point in the amount of the principal.

To find interest at 6 percent for 60 days, merely move the decimal point in the principal amount 2 places to the left. Example: What is the interest on $2,550 at 6 percent for 60 days? Solution: Moving the decimal point 2 places to the left in $2,550, we have $25.50, which is the amount of interest. We can check this answer by using the formula previously stated: $I = P \times R \times T$.

$$\text{Interest} = \$2,550 \times 0.06 \times 60/360 = \$25.50$$

With some practice, one can find the interest when the time period varies from 60 days and when the rate differs from 6 percent. Example: What is the interest on $2,550 at 6 percent for 150 days? Solution:

$25.50 interest for 60 days
  25.50 interest for 60 days more
  12.75 interest for 30 days (½ of the 60-day amount)
$63.75 interest at 6% for 150 days.

Example: What is the interest on $2,550 at 8 percent for 150 days? Solution: Calculation of the interest by the 60-day 6 percent method (preceding problem) gives us $63.75 as interest, but this is at 6 percent. To find the interest at 8 percent, we must realize that 8 percent is ⅓ more than 6 percent, so we take ⅓ of $63.75, which equals $21.25, and add it to the $63.75. Interest on $2,550 at 8 percent for 150 days equals

$63.75 (at 6%)
  21.25 (additional 2%)
$85.00 interest at 8%.

Interest tables

Although each of the preceding methods allows the licensee to calculate interest accurately, anyone who has occasion to make such calculations regularly should obtain a series of interest tables. Such tables supply a numerical multiplier to be used in determining interest on various amounts, for different periods of time, at different interest rates. The principal sum is multiplied by the appropriate multiplier, and the answer is the amount of interest. Table 11–1 is an example of an interest table. It shows the various amounts of interest per $1,000 at different rates of interest for from 1 to 30 days.

TABLE 11–1
Interest Figured on $1,000
(360 days to the year)

Days	12%	13%	14%	15%	16%
1	.333	.361	.389	.417	.444
2	.667	.722	.778	.833	.889
3	1.000	1.083	1.167	1.250	1.333
4	1.333	1.444	1.556	1.667	1.778
5	1.667	1.806	1.944	2.083	2.222
6	2.000	2.167	2.333	2.500	2.667
7	2.336	2.528	2.722	2.917	3.111
8	2.667	2.889	3.111	3.333	3.556
9	3.000	3.250	3.500	3.750	4.000
10	3.333	3.611	3.889	4.167	4.444
11	3.667	3.972	4.278	4.583	4.889
12	4.000	4.333	4.667	5.000	5.333
13	4.333	4.694	5.056	5.417	5.778
14	4.667	5.056	5.444	5.833	6.222
15	5.000	5.417	5.833	6.250	6.667
16	5.333	5.778	6.222	6.667	7.111
17	5.667	6.139	6.611	7.083	7.556
18	6.000	6.500	7.000	7.500	8.000
19	6.333	6.861	7.389	7.917	8.444
20	6.667	7.222	7.778	8.333	8.889
21	7.000	7.583	8.167	8.750	9.333
22	7.333	7.944	8.556	9.167	9.778
23	7.667	8.306	8.944	9.583	10.222
24	8.000	8.667	9.333	10.000	10.667
25	8.338	9.028	9.722	10.417	11.111
26	8.667	9.389	10.111	10.833	11.556
27	9.000	9.750	10.500	11.250	12.000
28	9.336	10.111	10.889	11.667	12.444
29	9.667	10.472	11.278	12.083	12.889
30	10.000	10.833	11.667	12.500	13.333
31st day	—	—	—	—	—

1. What is the amount interest on $1,000 at 12 percent for 20 days? Solution: A move to the right from 20 days to the 12 percent column reveals a figure of 6.667, which rounded off to the nearest cent equals 6.67. Thus, the interest on $1,000 at 12 percent for 20 days is 6.67.

2. What is the interest of $18,000 at 15 percent for 26 days? Solution: From the table we can determine that the interest for $1,000 at 15 percent for 26 days is $10.833, and we must multiply this number by 18 in order to arrive at the interest for $18,000.

$$18 \times \$10.833 = \$194.994 = \$194.99$$

Finding number of days

One of the many types of tables helpful to the licensee is a table that allows rapid calculation of the exact number of days between two dates. Table 11–2 is an example of a table that shows the number of days from any date in one month to the same date in another month.

1. How many days from February 12, 1983, to October 12, 1983? Solution: From February in the left column, move to the right and stop under October. The number shown is 242, so from February 12 to October 12 there are 242 days. If it were 1984, a leap year, an additional day would have to be added for February, making the total 243.

2. How many days from January 21, 1983, to November 26, 1983? Solution: From January in the left column, moving to the right to November, we find 304. Thus, from January 21 to November 21 there are 304 days. However, the problem asks for the time to November 26, so we must add the 5 days from the 21st to the 26th and arrive at a total of 309 days.

With some additional calculations, this same type of table can be used to determine the exact amount of days from a month and day in one year to a month and day in a subsequent year.

PRORATIONS

Proration generally takes place in escrow. Its purpose is to apportion income and expense items correctly between the parties to the sale. The more common items that usually need to be prorated are rents, taxes, insurance, and interest. Table 11–3 shows one of the many different types of proration tables employed in such calculations.

1. The sale of an apartment house involves a small store which rents for $700 per month, payable in advance on the first of each month. Escrow is to be closed on the 25th day of a 30-day month. How much of the month's rent is due to the seller and how much to the buyer? Solution: To find the value of 25 days of a 30-day month, refer to the left column (years, months, days) of the proration table. To the right of the number 25 we find the factor 0.8333 under the 30-day month column:

$$0.8333 \times \$700 = \$583.31.$$

Thus, the seller gets $583.31, and the buyer receives the remainder, $116.69.

2. Brennan purchases an apartment house on which the owner Hatcher has already collected the rents, amounting to $5,240. Escrow is to be closed on the 18th day of a 31-day month. How is the rent apportioned between Brennan and Hatcher? Solution: From the proration table, the factor of 0.5806 is given for the 18th day of a 31-day month.

$$0.5806 \times \$5,240 = \$3,042.34$$
$$\$5,240.00 - \$3,042.34 = \$2,197.66$$

Brennan, the buyer, is entitled to $3,042.34 of the $5,240.00 that Hatcher has already collected.

TABLE 11–2
Number of Days between Dates

From To	Jan.	Feb.	March	April	May	June	July	Aug.	Sept.	Oct.	Nov.	Dec.
January.......365		31	59	90	120	151	181	212	243	273	304	334
February......334	365		28	59	89	120	150	181	212	242	273	303
March.........306	337	365		31	61	92	122	153	184	214	245	275
April..........275	306	334	365		30	61	91	122	153	183	214	244
May...........245	276	304	335	365		31	61	92	123	153	184	214
June..........214	245	273	304	334	365		30	61	92	122	153	183
July...........184	215	243	274	304	335	365		31	62	92	123	153
August........153	184	212	243	273	304	334	365		31	61	92	122
September....122	153	181	212	242	273	303	334	365		30	61	91
October....... 92	123	151	182	212	243	273	304	335	365		31	61
November..... 61	92	120	151	181	212	242	273	304	334	365		30
December..... 31	62	90	121	151	182	212	243	274	304	335	365	

TABLE 11–3
Proration for Rents, Taxes, and Insurance

Number of Years, Months, and Days	Rents One Month Days to Month		Taxes and Insurance One Year		Insurance						Number of Years, Months, and Days
					Three Years			Five Years			
	30	31	Months	Days	Years	Months	Days	Years	Months	Days	
1	.0333	.0323	.0833	.0028	.3333	.0278	.0009	.2000	.0167	.0006	1
2	.0667	.0645	.1667	.0056	.6667	.0556	.0019	.4000	.0333	.0011	2
3	.1000	.0968	.2500	.0083	1.0000	.0833	.0028	.6000	.0500	.0017	3
4	.1333	.1290	.3333	.0111		.1111	.0037	.8000	.0667	.0022	4
5	.1667	.1613	.4167	.0139		.1389	.0046	1.0000	.0833	.0028	5
6	.2000	.1935	.5000	.0167		.1667	.0056		.1000	.0033	6
7	.2333	.2258	.5833	.0194		.1944	.0065		.1167	.0039	7
8	.2667	.2581	.6667	.0222		.2222	.0074		.1333	.0044	8
9	.3000	.2903	.7500	.0250		.2500	.0083		.1500	.0050	9
10	.3333	.3226	.8333	.0278		.2778	.0093		.1667	.0056	10
11	.3667	.3548	.9167	.0306		.3056	.0102		.1833	.0061	11
12	.4000	.3871	1.0000	.0333		.3333	.0111		.2000	.0067	12
13	.4333	.4194		.0361			.0120			.0072	13
14	.4667	.4516		.0389			.0130			.0078	14
15	.5000	.4839		.0417			.0139			.0083	15
16	.5333	.5161		.0444			.0148			.0089	16
17	.5667	.5484		.0472			.0157			.0094	17
18	.6000	.5806		.0500			.0167			.0100	18
19	.6333	.6129		.0528			.0176			.0106	19
20	.6667	.6452		.0556			.0185			.0111	20
21	.7000	.6774		.0583			.0194			.0117	21
22	.7333	.7097		.0611			.0204			.0122	22
23	.7667	.7419		.0639			.0213			.0128	23
24	.8000	.7742		.0667			.0222			.0133	24
25	.8333	.8065		.0694			.0231			.0139	25
26	.8667	.8387		.0722			.0241			.0144	26
27	.9000	.8710		.0750			.0250			.0150	27
28	.9333	.9032		.0778			.0259			.0156	28
29	.9667	.9355		.0806			.0269			.0161	29
30	1.0000	.9677		.0833			.0278			.0167	30
31		1.0000									31

3. Van Egri paid both installments of his property tax, amounting to $1,850, and sells his property with escrow to close on May 1. What is the tax proration? Solution: Taxes are paid for the fiscal year July 1 to June 30. The period from July 1 to May 1 is 10 months. The factor from the proration table, under the column Taxes and Insurance, is 0.8333.

$$0.8333 \times \$1.850 = \$1,541.6050 = \$1,541.61$$
$$\$1,850.00 - \$1,541.61 = \$308.39.$$

Van Egri, the seller, is credited with $308.39, and the buyer is charged the $308.39.

It is interesting to note that the factor used in this problem (0.8333) is the same as that used in the preceding example 1. In that example, 0.8333 represented the 25th day of a 30-day month. As a fraction, 25 days out of 30 is shown as 25/30, which reduces to 5/6. In this problem, 10 months out of 12 as a fraction is 10/12, which

reduces to 5/6. Obviously, 0.8333 is 5/6 represented decimally. (See Figure 11–1.)

4. Smith pays $570 as the premium on a three-year fire insurance policy. He sells his home 1 year and 17 days later. Assuming that the premium is to be prorated according to this time period, what must the buyer pay to Smith? Solution: From the proration table:

$$1 \text{ year} = 0.3333$$
$$17 \text{ days} = \underline{0.0157}$$
$$0.3940$$

1 year and 17 days = 0.3940 × $570 = $224.58
$570.00 − $224.58 = $345.42 (amount to be charged the buyer).

5. A five-year policy premium is $2,955. Find the value of 3 years, 5 months, and 16 days. Solution: From the proration table,

Numerators

Denom-inator	1	2	3	4	5	6	7	8	9	10	11	12	13	14	15
1.00 or 100%															
2	.50 / 50%														
3	.333 / $33\frac{1}{3}$%	.666 / $66\frac{2}{3}$%													
4	.25 / 25%	.50 / 50%	.75 / 75%												
5	.20 / 20%	.40 / 40%	.60 / 60%	.80 / 80%											
6	.166 / $16\frac{2}{3}$%	.333 / $33\frac{1}{3}$%	.50 / 50%	.666 / $66\frac{2}{3}$%	.833 / $83\frac{1}{3}$%										
7	.142 / $14\frac{2}{7}$%	.285 / $28\frac{4}{7}$%	.428 / $42\frac{6}{7}$%	.571 / $57\frac{1}{7}$%	.714 / $71\frac{3}{7}$%	.857 / $85\frac{5}{7}$%									
8	.125 / $12\frac{1}{2}$%	.25 / 25%	.375 / $37\frac{1}{2}$%	.50 / 50%	.625 / $62\frac{1}{2}$%	.75 / 75%	.875 / $87\frac{1}{2}$%								
9	.111 / $11\frac{1}{9}$%	.222 / $22\frac{2}{9}$%	.333 / $33\frac{1}{3}$%	.444 / $44\frac{4}{9}$%	.555 / $55\frac{5}{9}$%	.666 / $66\frac{2}{3}$%	.777 / $77\frac{7}{9}$%	.888 / $88\frac{8}{9}$%							
10	.10 / 10%	.20 / 20%	.30 / 30%	.40 / 40%	.50 / 50%	.60 / 60%	.70 / 70%	.80 / 80%	.90 / 90%						
11	.090 / $9\frac{1}{11}$%	.181 / $18\frac{2}{11}$%	.272 / $27\frac{3}{11}$%	.363 / $36\frac{4}{11}$%	.454 / $45\frac{5}{11}$%	.545 / $54\frac{6}{11}$%	.636 / $63\frac{7}{11}$%	.727 / $72\frac{8}{11}$%	.818 / $81\frac{9}{11}$%	.909 / $90\frac{10}{11}$%					
12	.083 / $8\frac{1}{3}$%	.166 / $16\frac{2}{3}$%	.25 / 25%	.333 / $33\frac{1}{3}$%	.416 / $41\frac{2}{3}$%	.50 / 50%	.583 / $58\frac{1}{3}$%	.666 / $66\frac{2}{3}$%	.75 / 75%	.833 / $83\frac{1}{3}$%	.916 / $91\frac{2}{3}$%				
13	.077 / $7\frac{9}{13}$%	.153 / $15\frac{5}{13}$%	.230 / $23\frac{1}{13}$%	.307 / $30\frac{10}{13}$%	.385 / $38\frac{6}{13}$%	.462 / $46\frac{2}{13}$%	.538 / $53\frac{11}{13}$%	.615 / $61\frac{7}{13}$%	.692 / $69\frac{3}{13}$%	.769 / $76\frac{12}{13}$%	.846 / $84\frac{8}{13}$%	.923 / $92\frac{4}{13}$%			
14	.071 / $7\frac{1}{7}$%	.142 / $14\frac{2}{7}$%	.214 / $21\frac{3}{7}$%	.285 / $28\frac{4}{7}$%	.357 / $35\frac{5}{7}$%	.428 / $42\frac{6}{7}$%	.50 / 50%	.571 / $57\frac{1}{7}$%	.642 / $64\frac{2}{7}$%	.714 / $71\frac{3}{7}$%	.786 / $78\frac{4}{7}$%	.857 / $85\frac{5}{7}$%	.929 / $92\frac{6}{7}$%		
15	.066 / $6\frac{2}{3}$%	.133 / $13\frac{1}{3}$%	.20 / 20%	.266 / $26\frac{2}{3}$%	.333 / $33\frac{1}{3}$%	.40 / 40%	.466 / $46\frac{2}{3}$%	.533 / $53\frac{1}{3}$%	.60 / 60%	.666 / $66\frac{2}{3}$%	.733 / $73\frac{1}{3}$%	.80 / 80%	.866 / $86\frac{2}{3}$%	.933 / $93\frac{1}{3}$%	
16	.062 / $6\frac{1}{4}$%	.125 / $12\frac{1}{2}$%	.1875 / $18\frac{3}{4}$%	.25 / 25%	.3125 / $31\frac{1}{4}$%	.375 / $37\frac{1}{2}$%	.4375 / $43\frac{3}{4}$%	.50 / 50%	.5625 / $56\frac{1}{4}$%	.625 / $62\frac{1}{2}$%	.6875 / $68\frac{3}{4}$%	.75 / 75%	.8125 / $81\frac{1}{4}$%	.875 / $87\frac{1}{2}$%	.9375 / $93\frac{3}{4}$%

FIGURE 11-1
Fraction, Decimal, and Percentage Equivalents

```
        3 years = 0.6000
        5 months = 0.0833
        16 days = 0.0089
                  0.6922

        0.6922 × $2,955. = $2,045.45
```

The value of 3 years, 5 months, and 16 days is $2,045.45.

The proration of interest enters into a real estate transaction in many ways. One of the most common is in the sale of a house when the buyer arranges for a new loan and the seller must pay off his old loan. When the lender sends his demand to the escrow officer with regard to the loan's being paid off, the seller will usually be charged for interest from the time of the last payment to the date of the close of escrow.

If the buyer assumes an existing loan, we may have a different situation. The interest portion of a monthly payment is usually for the month past. Thus if escrow closes on the 15th of the month, the seller will be charged for two weeks interest that will be credited to the buyer, since at the end of the month the buyer will make his payment, which will include interest for the entire preceding month.

PERCENTAGE

A great many of the problems encountered in everyday real estate practice are percentage problems. These are generally of three types, since there are three elements in percentage problems, and the problems usually involve finding one of the elements when given the other two. The elements are: (1) base, (2) rate, and (3) part (also referred to as percentage or portion).

The *base* is the principle amount and represents 100 percent.

The *rate* is the relationship between the base and a part of the base and is expressed as a percent.

The *part* of the base will vary in size, depending on the rate used, and may be more or less than the base.

The following formulas are used:

$$\text{Base} = \text{Part divided by rate} = B = \frac{P}{R}$$

$$\text{Rate} = \text{Part divided by base} = R = \frac{P}{B}$$

$$\text{Part} = \text{Rate times base} = P = R \times B$$

The following examples will illustrate the use of the formulas.

1. Lorvan receives $3,000, representing an 8 percent return on an investment. What amount has he invested? Solution: Part is $3,000, rate is 8 percent, base is unknown. Using the formula

$$B = \frac{P}{R}$$

$$B = \frac{\$3,000}{.08}$$

$$B = \$37,500$$

2. McNaughton sells a building for $280,000 and receives a commission of $19,600. What percent of the selling price is his commission? Solution: Base is $280,000, and part is $19,600. Using the formula

$$R = \frac{P}{B}$$

$$R = \frac{\$19,600}{\$280,000} = .07 = 7\% \text{ rate}$$

3. Szukalski tells Funke that he can expect a 12 percent return on his investment of $385,000. How much will Funke receive? Solution: Base is $385,000, and rate is 9 percent. Using the formula

$$P = R \times B$$
$$P = .09 \times \$385,000 = \$46,200$$

The following are examples of common types of percentage problems found in real estate practice.

Commissions

1. Salesperson Perez gets one half of the commission his firm receives on the sale of a building. If the building sells for $850,000 and the commission rate is 5 percent, Thomas's share is:

```
Commission = .05 × $850,000 = $42,500
$42,500 ÷ 2 = $21,250
```

2. Broker Lippitt sells a building for $286,500. He receives a commission of 6 percent of the first $100,000 and 5 percent of the balance of the selling price. How much does he get? Solution:

```
.06 × $100,000 = $ 6,000
.05 × $186,500 =   9,325
                 $15,325 Lippitt's total
                         commission
```

3. Salesperson Wagner's contract with broker Wong states that if Wagner lists and sells a property he is to receive 60 percent of the commission, less 10 percent for advertising expense. On the sale of a house at $128,500, what will Wagner receive? The commission rate is 6 percent of the selling price. Solution:

.06 × \$128,500 = \$7,710 commission on sale received by office.

.60 × \$7,710 = \$4,626 Wagner's share before advertising deduction.

.10 × \$4,626 = \$462.60 deduction for advertising expense.

\$4,626 − \$462.60 = \$4,163.40 Wagner's share of commission.

Profit and loss

1. Irene Anderson purchases a lot for \$5,000 and later sells it for \$8,000. What is her percent of profit on the original cost? Solution:

$$\$8,000 \text{ selling price}$$
$$\underline{-5,000 \text{ cost}}$$
$$\$3,000 \text{ profit}$$

Rate = Part (\$3,000) divided by base (\$5,000)
= .60 = 60%

2. Morris Green sells his house for \$120,000 and makes a profit of 25 percent based on the original cost. What was the cost? Solution: In this type of problem, the selling price represents the cost plus the profit. The cost is the base, which is always 100 percent, and to this is added 25 percent profit, so that the selling price of \$120,000 represents 125 percent.

$$B = \frac{P}{R} = B = \frac{\$120,000}{1.25} = \$96,000 \text{ original cost}$$

3. Louis Shaffer purchases 10 acres of land for \$200,000. He wants to sell the land and make a profit of 35 percent. For how much must he sell the property? Solution:

.35 × 200,000 = \$70,000 profit of 35%
\$200,000 cost plus \$70,000 desired profit
= \$270,000 selling price

Net listing

1. Joseph Calleja tells broker Travers that he wants to net \$141,000 on the sale of his property. For how much must Batmale sell the property in order to make a 6 percent commission in addition to the \$141,000 for Calleja? Solution: Since the selling price must include \$141,000 plus a 6 percent commission, the reader should realize that the \$141,000 must represent 94 percent. This, when added to the 6 percent commission, equals the selling price or 100 percent.

$$\text{Base (100\%)} = \frac{\$141,000 \text{ (part)}}{.94 \text{ (rate)}}$$
$$= \$150,000 \text{ selling price}$$

The \$150,000 selling price minus 6 percent commission of \$9,000 equals \$141,000 net to the seller. Because net listings may often lead to a misunderstanding between the broker and seller, it is usually better for the broker to calculate the selling price necessary to allow for a normal commission and then list the property in the regular way.

Capitalization

Capitalization of income is treated extensively in Chapter 14, dealing with appraisal and valuation.

1. Batmale wants to purchase an income property that shows a net yearly income of \$120,000. If he wants an 8 percent return on his total investment, how much should he pay for the building? Solution:

$$\frac{\$120,000 \text{ (net income)}}{.08 \text{ (8\% capitalization rate)}}$$
$$= \$1,500,000 \text{ purchase price}$$

2. Nesbitt purchases a building for \$425,000. The building shows a net yearly income of \$25,500. What is his rate of return? Solution:

$$R = \frac{\text{Net income}}{\text{Present value}} = \frac{\$25,500}{\$425,000} = .06 = 6\%$$

A capitalization table similar to the one shown in Table 11–4 is often used to simplify such problems. The rate of capitalization desired is selected, and the net income is multiplied by the factor which is shown on the table for the particular rate.

TABLE 11–4
Capitalization

Percent Rate	Factor	Percent Rate	Factor
7½	13.3	13	7.69
8	12.5	13½	7.40
8½	11.7	14	7.14
9	11.1	14½	6.90
9½	10.5	15	6.67
10	10.0	15½	6.45
10½	9.52	16	6.25
11	9.09	16½	6.06
11½	8.69	17	5.88
12	8.33	17½	5.71
12½	8.00	18	5.56

3. What should be the selling price for a building being sold on the basis of its net income of \$23,800, capitalized at 8 percent? Solution: From

the capitalization table, we find that the factor for 8 percent is 12.5; thus,

$$12.5 \times \$23,800 = \$297,500 \text{ selling price}$$

Loan ratio

A broker or salesman often must approximate the amount of first loan available on a property and the down payment that may be necessary by applying the same loan ratio he thinks the lender will use.

1. Broker Barry shows Mr. and Mrs. Katz a house priced at $135,000. He thinks he can get an 80 percent loan from ABC Savings and Loan Company. If the down payment is to be cash over loan, what will be the amount of the loan and the down payment? Solution:

$$.80 \times \$135,000 = \$108,000 \text{ loan}$$
$$\$135,000 - \$108,000 = \$27,000 \text{ down payment}$$

On conventional home financing, if the first loan is 75 or 80 percent of the selling price, a shortcut method may be employed to determine the amount of first loan and required down payment. For instance, an 80 percent first loan means 4/5 of the selling price with a down payment of 1/5. Dividing the selling price by five gives the down payment (1/5 = 20%), and subtracting this amount from the selling price gives the amount of the first loan (4/5 = 80%).

2. The selling price is $180,000. On the basis of an anticipated 80 percent first loan, what will be the loan and what will be the down payment? Solution:

$$\$180,000 \div 5 = \$36,000 \text{ down payment.}$$
$$\$180,000 - \$36,000 = \$144,000 \text{ first loan.}$$

Or the calculation may be made as follows:

5) $180,000 selling price
− 36,000 down payment
$144,000 first loan

Thus, five divided into $180,000 equals $36,000, and the $36,000 subtracted from the $180,000 gives $144,000.

3. The selling price is $168,000. On the basis of a 75 percent loan, what is the first loan and what is the required down payment? Here, 75 percent represents ¾, and the down payment is ¼. Solution:

$$\$168,000 \div 4 = \$42,000 \text{ down payment}$$
$$\$168,000 - \$42,000 = \$126,000 \text{ first loan}$$

or

4) $168,000 selling price
− 42,000 down payment
$126,000 first loan

Discount

1. A second note has been discounted 20 percent, and the amount of the discount is $1,200. What was the original amount of the note? Solution:

$$\frac{\$1,200}{.20} = \$6,000 \text{ original amount}$$

2. Conklin owns an old building in the city which he wants to convert to cash in order to purchase some country acreage. The building is free and clear. Misthos offers Conklin $95,000 on the following terms: Misthos will obtain a first loan of $60,000 from his bank, put down $20,000 in cash, and Conklin is to carry back a second loan of $15,000. Conklin agrees, and after close of escrow, he sells the note to Casey at a 25 percent discount. How much cash does Conklin now have for the purchase of the country property? Solution: Conklin received $80,000 plus a $15,000 note on the sale of his building. He discounts the note 25 percent:

$$\$15,000 \times .25 = \$3,750 \text{ discount}$$
$$\$15,000 - \$3,750 = \$11,250$$

The $80,000 from the building plus the $11,250 from the note equals $91,250 Conklin now has to invest.

PROPERTY TAX

1. Fernandez owns a 12-unit building with a 1976–77 full cash value of $180,000. If the assessor has allowed for a 2 percent yearly increase compound on the tax and adds 15 percent for bond payoff, what is Fernandez's 1980–81 tax amount? Solution:

$$.01 \times \$180,000 = \$1,800$$
(77–78) $1.02 \times \$1,800 = \$1,836$
(78–79) $1.02 \times \$1,836 = \$1,872.72$
(79–80) $1.02 \times \$1,872.72 = \$1,910.17$
(80–81) $1.02 \times \$1,910.17 = \$1,948.37$
$1.15 \times \$1,948.37 = \$2,240.62$

2. Miner receives a statement from the assessor showing an assessed valuation of $12,000 on her apartment house. If the assessor uses 24 percent of market value as the basis for his assessment, what value has been set on Miner's property? Solution:

$$\frac{\$12,000}{.24} = \$50,000 \text{ market value}$$

3. If a property was purchased in 1976 for $65,000, what will each installment of taxes for 1980–81 be with a 2 percent yearly increase compounded on the tax and a $70 homeowner's exemption? Solution:

$$.01 \times \$65,000 = \$650$$
$$(77\text{–}78)\ 1.02 \times \$650 = \$663.00$$
$$(78\text{–}79)\ 1.02 \times \$663 = \$676.26$$
$$(79\text{–}80)\ 1.02 \times \$676.26 = \$689.79$$
$$(80\text{–}81)\ 1.02 \times \$689.79 = \$703.59$$
$$\$703.59 - \$70.00 = \$633.59$$
$$\$633.59 \div 2 = \$316.80$$

DEPRECIATION

The reader is referred to Chapter 17, Income Tax and Real Estate, for an extensive discussion of depreciation.

1. As the result of an exchange, Scourkes receives an income property with a value of $850,000. Seventy-five percent of value is to be allotted to building and the remainder to land. Scourkes will use straight-line method of depreciation and a depreciable life of 30 years for the property. What will be the amount of depreciation? Solution:

$$.75 \times \$850,000 = \$637,500 \text{ basis for depreciation}$$
$$\$637,500 \div 30 = \$21,250 \text{ yearly depreciation}$$

2. Vincent's property has a depreciable basis of $156,000. He will use the Accelerated Cost Recovery System (ACRS) method of depreciation with a depreciable life of 15 years. What will be the first year's depreciation? Solution:

$$\$156,000 \div 15 = \$10,400$$
$$175\% = 1.75$$
$$1.75 \times \$10,400 = \$18,200 \text{ first year's depreciation}$$

3. In example 2, what will be Vincent's depreciation for the second year? Solution:

$$\$156,000 - \$18,200 \text{ (first year's depreciation)}$$
$$= \$137,800$$
$$\$137,800 \div 14 = \$9,842.86$$
$$1.75 \times \$9,842.86 = \$17,225 \text{ second year's depreciation}$$

AMORTIZATION

Real estate loans usually are repaid by an equal monthly payment over the term of the loan. The payment includes principal and interest, and the process is called amortization. All real estate licensees should have in their possession an *Equal Monthly Loan Amortization Payments* booklet. The booklet shows monthly payments necessary to amortize a loan in a given number of years at different rates of interest and for different amounts. The licensee can usually obtain a copy from his local bank or savings and loan association. Any interested individual can obtain a copy for a nominal fee by writing to the Financial Publishing Company, 82 Brookline Avenue, Boston, Massachusetts.

Table 11–5, reproduced from this booklet, shows the monthly payments necessary to amortize a loan at 15 percent interest per annum in amounts ranging from $100 to $100,000 with terms.

1. What is the monthly payment necessary to amortize a loan of $70,000 at 15 percent interest per annum for a term of 18 years? Solution: The amount shown in the "18 years" column (Table 11–5) for $70,000 is $939.19. This is the fixed monthly payment necessary to completely pay off the loan, including principal and interest, over a period of 18 years.

2. What is the monthly payment necessary to amortize a loan of $119,500 at 15 percent interest per annum for a term of 25 years? Solution:

$$\$100,000 \text{ at } 15\% \text{ for } 25 \text{ years} = \$1,280.84$$
$$\$19,000 \text{ at } 15\% \text{ for } 25 \text{ years} = \$\ \ 243.36$$
$$500 \text{ at } 15\% \text{ for } 25 \text{ years} = \underline{\qquad 6.41}$$
$$\text{Total payment required} = \$1,530.61$$

3. What will be the monthly payment necessary to amortize a loan of $275,000 at 15 percent interest per annum for a term of 30 years? Solution:

$$\text{Payment for } \$100,000 = \$1,264.45$$
$$\text{Payment for } 100,000 = 1,264.45$$
$$\text{Payment for } 75,000 = \underline{\quad 948.34}$$
$$\text{Total payment required} = \$3,477.24$$

Amortization schedule

For any loan, an amortization schedule can be constructed to show the allocation of each payment into interest and principal, and the balance outstanding after each payment has been made. This is done by (1) computing the interest on the previous balance, (2) deducting the interest from the payment, and (3) crediting the remainder as a repayment of principal. A schedule for any loan can be obtained from the Financial Publishing Company, Boston, Massachusetts.

Present balance of a loan

It is often necessary for the licensee to determine the present balance due on an outstanding

TABLE 11-5

15% **MONTHLY PAYMENT** NECESSARY TO AMORTIZE A LOAN

TERM AMOUNT	14 YEARS	15 YEARS	16 YEARS	17 YEARS	18 YEARS	19 YEARS
100	1.43	1.40	1.38	1.36	1.35	1.33
200	2.86	2.80	2.76	2.72	2.69	2.66
250	3.57	3.50	3.45	3.40	3.36	3.33
300	4.29	4.20	4.14	4.08	4.03	3.99
400	5.71	5.60	5.51	5.44	5.37	5.32
500	7.14	7.00	6.89	6.79	6.71	6.65
1000	14.28	14.00	13.77	13.58	13.42	13.29
2000	28.55	28.00	27.54	27.16	26.84	26.57
3000	42.82	41.99	41.31	40.74	40.26	39.85
4000	57.09	55.99	55.08	54.31	53.67	53.13
5000	71.36	69.98	68.84	67.89	67.09	66.41
6000	85.63	83.98	82.61	81.47	80.51	79.70
7000	99.90	97.98	96.38	95.04	93.92	92.98
8000	114.17	111.97	110.15	108.62	107.34	106.26
9000	128.44	125.97	123.91	122.20	120.76	119.54
10000	142.71	139.96	137.68	135.78	134.17	132.82
11000	156.98	153.96	151.45	149.35	147.59	146.11
12000	171.25	167.96	165.22	162.93	161.01	159.39
13000	185.52	181.95	178.99	176.51	174.42	172.67
14000	199.79	195.95	192.75	190.08	187.84	185.95
15000	214.06	209.94	206.52	203.66	201.26	199.23
16000	228.33	223.94	220.29	217.24	214.68	212.52
17000	242.60	237.93	234.06	230.81	228.09	225.80
18000	256.87	251.93	247.82	244.39	241.51	239.08
19000	271.14	265.93	261.59	257.97	254.93	252.36
20000	285.41	279.92	275.36	271.55	268.34	265.64
21000	299.68	293.92	289.13	285.12	281.76	278.93
22000	313.95	307.91	302.89	298.70	295.18	292.21
23000	328.22	321.91	316.66	312.28	308.59	305.49
24000	342.49	335.91	330.43	325.85	322.01	318.77
25000	356.76	349.90	344.20	339.43	335.43	332.05
26000	371.04	363.90	357.97	353.01	348.84	345.34
27000	385.31	377.89	371.73	366.58	362.26	358.62
28000	399.58	391.89	385.50	380.16	375.68	371.90
29000	413.85	405.89	399.27	393.74	389.10	385.18
30000	428.12	419.88	413.04	407.32	402.51	398.46
31000	442.39	433.88	426.80	420.89	415.93	411.75
32000	456.66	447.87	440.57	434.47	429.35	425.03
33000	470.93	461.87	454.34	448.05	442.76	438.31
34000	485.20	475.86	468.11	461.62	456.18	451.59
35000	499.47	489.86	481.87	475.20	469.60	464.87
36000	513.74	503.86	495.64	488.78	483.01	478.16
37000	528.01	517.85	509.41	502.35	496.43	491.44
38000	542.28	531.85	523.18	515.93	509.85	504.72
39000	556.55	545.84	536.95	529.51	523.26	518.00
40000	570.82	559.84	550.71	543.09	536.68	531.28
41000	585.09	573.84	564.48	556.66	550.10	544.57
42000	599.36	587.83	578.25	570.24	563.52	557.85
43000	613.63	601.83	592.02	583.82	576.93	571.13
44000	627.90	615.82	605.78	597.39	590.35	584.41
45000	642.17	629.82	619.55	610.97	603.77	597.69
50000	713.52	699.80	688.39	678.86	670.85	664.10
55000	784.88	769.78	757.23	746.74	737.93	730.51
60000	856.23	839.76	826.07	814.63	805.02	796.92
65000	927.58	909.74	894.91	882.51	872.10	863.33
70000	998.93	979.72	963.74	950.40	939.19	929.74
75000	1070.28	1049.70	1032.58	1018.28	1006.27	996.15
100000	1427.04	1399.59	1376.77	1357.71	1341.70	1328.20

MONTHLY PAYMENT NECESSARY TO AMORTIZE A LOAN **15%**

TERM AMOUNT	20 YEARS	22 YEARS	25 YEARS	30 YEARS	35 YEARS	40 YEARS
100	1.32	1.30	1.29	1.27	1.26	1.26
200	2.64	2.60	2.57	2.53	2.52	2.51
250	3.30	3.25	3.21	3.17	3.15	3.14
300	3.96	3.90	3.85	3.80	3.78	3.76
400	5.27	5.20	5.13	5.06	5.03	5.02
500	6.59	6.50	6.41	6.33	6.29	6.27
1000	13.17	12.99	12.81	12.65	12.57	12.54
2000	26.34	25.98	25.62	25.29	25.14	25.07
3000	39.51	38.97	38.43	37.94	37.71	37.60
4000	52.68	51.96	51.24	50.58	50.28	50.13
5000	65.84	64.95	64.05	63.23	62.85	62.67
6000	79.01	77.94	76.85	75.87	75.41	75.20
7000	92.18	90.93	89.66	88.52	87.98	87.73
8000	105.35	103.92	102.47	101.16	100.55	100.26
9000	118.52	116.91	115.28	113.80	113.12	112.80
10000	131.68	129.89	128.09	126.45	125.69	125.33
11000	144.85	142.88	140.90	139.09	138.25	137.86
12000	158.02	155.87	153.70	151.74	150.82	150.39
13000	171.19	168.86	166.51	164.38	163.39	162.92
14000	184.36	181.85	179.32	177.03	175.96	175.46
15000	197.52	194.84	192.13	189.67	188.53	187.99
16000	210.69	207.83	204.94	202.32	201.10	200.52
17000	223.86	220.82	217.75	214.96	213.66	213.05
18000	237.03	233.81	230.55	227.60	226.23	225.59
19000	250.20	246.80	243.36	240.25	238.80	238.12
20000	263.36	259.78	256.17	252.89	251.37	250.65
21000	276.53	272.77	268.98	265.54	263.94	263.18
22000	289.70	285.76	281.79	278.18	276.50	275.71
23000	302.87	298.75	294.60	290.83	289.07	288.25
24000	316.03	311.74	307.40	303.47	301.64	300.78
25000	329.20	324.73	320.21	316.12	314.21	313.31
26000	342.37	337.72	333.02	328.76	326.78	325.84
27000	355.54	350.71	345.83	341.40	339.34	338.38
28000	368.71	363.70	358.64	354.05	351.91	350.91
29000	381.87	376.69	371.45	366.69	364.48	363.44
30000	395.04	389.67	384.25	379.34	377.05	375.97
31000	408.21	402.66	397.06	391.98	389.62	388.50
32000	421.38	415.65	409.87	404.63	402.19	401.04
33000	434.55	428.64	422.68	417.27	414.75	413.57
34000	447.71	441.63	435.49	429.92	427.32	426.10
35000	460.88	454.62	448.30	442.56	439.89	438.63
36000	474.05	467.61	461.10	455.20	452.46	451.17
37000	487.22	480.60	473.91	467.85	465.03	463.70
38000	500.39	493.59	486.72	480.49	477.59	476.23
39000	513.55	506.58	499.53	493.14	490.16	488.76
40000	526.72	519.56	512.34	505.78	502.73	501.29
41000	539.89	532.55	525.15	518.43	515.30	513.83
42000	553.06	545.54	537.95	531.07	527.87	526.36
43000	566.22	558.53	550.76	543.72	540.43	538.89
44000	579.39	571.52	563.57	556.36	553.00	551.42
45000	592.56	584.51	576.38	569.00	565.57	563.96
50000	658.40	649.45	640.42	632.23	628.41	626.62
55000	724.24	714.40	704.46	695.45	691.25	689.28
60000	790.08	779.34	768.50	758.69	754.09	751.94
65000	855.92	844.29	832.54	821.89	816.93	814.60
70000	921.76	909.23	896.59	885.12	879.77	877.26
75000	987.60	974.18	960.63	948.34	942.61	939.92
100000	1316.79	1298.90	1280.84	1264.45	1256.82	1253.23

loan. He may want to know how much will be necessary to pay off the obligation or what is the present value of the owner's equity.

A call to the bank or savings and loan association usually is all that is needed to find out the balance of the first loan, and many lenders show the balance on the monthly or yearly statement sent to the borrower. Although the licensee may have to calculate the balance due on a first loan, it is usually with respect to second loans that such calculations become necessary.

Tables are available for this purpose. Table 11-6 shows a loan progress chart for the remaining balance per $1,000 on a loan at 12 percent interest per annum. The table assumes that amortized monthly payments have been made.

1. What is the present balance of a $5,000 loan at 12 percent interest per annum with a term of 10 years, 3 years after date of execution of the note? Solution: The age of the loan is 3 years, and the table shows that the balance per $1,000 on a 3-year-old loan originally written for 10 years is now $813. Thus, for a $5,000 loan amount, the balance due will be

$$5 \times \$813 = \$4,065$$

TABLE 11–6
Loan Progress Chart
(dollar balance remaining on a 12 percent loan of $1,000)

LOAN PROGRESS CHART

12% — Showing dollar balance remaining on a $1,000 loan

AGE OF LOAN	ORIGINAL TERM IN YEARS											AGE OF LOAN
	5	8	10	12	15	16	17	18	19	20	21	
1	845	921	945	960	975	978	981	983	985	987	989	1
2	670	831	883	915	946	953	959	964	969	973	976	2
3	473	731	813	865	914	925	935	943	950	956	962	3
4	250	617	734	808	877	894	907	919	929	938	946	4
5		489	645	744	837	858	877	892	906	917	928	5
6		345	545	672	790	818	842	862	879	894	907	6
7		183	432	590	738	773	802	828	849	868	884	7
8			305	499	680	722	758	789	815	838	858	8
9			161	395	614	665	708	745	777	805	829	9
10				279	540	600	652	696	735	767	796	10
11				148	456	528	589	641	686	725	759	11
12					361	446	518	573	632	677	717	12
13					255	353	437	509	571	624	670	13
14					135	249	347	430	501	563	617	14
15						132	245	341	424	495	557	15
16							130	240	336	418	489	16
17								127	237	332	413	17
18									126	234	328	18
19										124	231	19
20											123	20

AGE OF LOAN	ORIGINAL TERM IN YEARS											AGE OF LOAN
	22	23	24	25	26	27	28	29	30	35	40	
1	990	991	992	993	994	995	995	996	996	998	999	1
2	979	982	984	986	987	989	990	991	992	996	998	2
3	966	970	974	977	980	982	984	986	988	993	996	3
4	952	958	963	967	971	975	978	980	982	990	995	4
5	936	944	951	957	962	966	970	974	977	987	993	5
6	918	928	937	944	951	957	962	966	970	984	991	6
7	898	910	921	930	939	946	952	958	963	980	989	7
8	875	890	903	915	925	934	941	948	954	975	986	8
9	850	868	884	897	909	920	929	938	945	970	984	9
10	821	842	861	878	892	905	916	926	934	964	980	10
11	788	814	836	855	872	887	900	912	922	958	977	11
12	751	781	807	830	850	868	883	897	909	950	973	12
13	710	745	775	802	825	846	864	880	894	942	968	13
14	663	704	739	770	797	821	842	860	876	933	963	14
15	611	657	698	734	765	793	817	838	857	922	958	15
16	551	605	652	694	730	761	789	814	835	910	951	16
17	485	547	601	648	689	726	758	786	811	897	944	17
18	409	480	542	597	644	686	723	755	783	882	936	18
19	325	406	477	539	593	641	683	720	752	865	926	19
20	229	322	403	473	536	590	638	680	717	846	916	20
21	121	227	319	400	471	533	587	635	677	825	904	21
22		120	225	317	398	468	530	585	633	800	891	22
23			119	224	315	395	466	528	583	773	876	23
24				119	222	314	394	464	526	742	859	24
25					118	221	312	392	462	708	840	25
26						117	220	311	391	669	819	26
27							117	219	310	625	795	27
28								116	219	575	768	28
29									116	519	737	29
30										457	703	30
31										386	664	31
32										306	621	32
33										216	571	33
34										114	516	34
35											453	35

The balance due on a second loan for which the monthly payment has not been amortized can be found by using the *Equal Monthly Loan Amortization Payments* information shown in Table 11–7.

1. What is the present balance of a note executed five years ago in the amount of $6,000 at 9¾ percent interest per annum for a term of eight years? Payments have been $60 per month. Solution: From the 9¾ percent table, find the $6,000 amount and the payment closest to $60. This is found as $60.33 in the "17 years" column. Thus,

TABLE 11-7
Monthly Payments Necessary to Amortize a 9¾ Percent Loan
(term: 10–17 years)

9¾% MONTHLY PAYMENT NECESSARY TO AMORTIZE A LOAN

TERM AMOUNT	10 YEARS	11 YEARS	12 YEARS	13 YEARS	14 YEARS	15 YEARS	16 YEARS	17 YEARS
$ 100	1.31	1.24	1.19	1.14	1.10	1.06	1.04	1.01
200	2.62	2.48	2.37	2.27	2.19	2.12	2.07	2.02
300	3.93	3.72	3.55	3.40	3.28	3.18	3.10	3.02
400	5.24	4.96	4.73	4.54	4.38	4.24	4.13	4.03
500	6.54	6.19	5.91	5.67	5.47	5.30	5.16	5.03
600	7.85	7.43	7.09	6.80	6.56	6.36	6.19	6.04
700	9.16	8.67	8.27	7.94	7.66	7.42	7.22	7.04
800	10.47	9.91	9.45	9.07	8.75	8.48	8.25	8.05
900	11.77	11.15	10.63	10.20	9.84	9.54	9.28	9.05
1000	13.08	12.38	11.81	11.34	10.94	10.60	10.31	10.06
1100	14.39	13.62	12.99	12.47	12.03	11.66	11.34	11.06
1200	15.70	14.86	14.17	13.60	13.12	12.72	12.37	12.07
1300	17.01	16.10	15.35	14.74	14.22	13.78	13.40	13.07
1400	18.31	17.34	16.53	15.87	15.31	14.84	14.43	14.08
1500	19.62	18.57	17.72	17.00	16.40	15.90	15.46	15.09
1600	20.93	19.81	18.90	18.14	17.50	16.95	16.49	16.09
1700	22.24	21.05	20.08	19.27	18.59	18.01	17.52	17.10
1800	23.54	22.29	21.26	20.41	19.68	19.07	18.55	18.10
1900	24.85	23.52	22.44	21.54	20.78	20.13	19.58	19.11
2000	26.16	24.76	23.62	22.67	21.87	21.19	20.61	20.11
2100	27.47	26.00	24.80	23.80	22.96	22.25	21.64	21.12
2200	28.77	27.24	25.98	24.93	24.06	23.31	22.67	22.12
2300	30.08	28.48	27.16	26.07	25.15	24.37	23.70	23.13
2400	31.39	29.71	28.34	27.20	26.24	25.43	24.73	24.14
2500	32.70	30.95	29.52	28.33	27.34	26.49	25.76	25.14
2600	34.01	32.19	30.70	29.47	28.43	27.55	26.80	26.15
2700	35.31	33.43	31.88	30.60	29.52	28.61	27.83	27.15
2800	36.62	34.67	33.06	31.73	30.62	29.67	28.86	28.16
2900	37.93	35.90	34.24	32.87	31.71	30.73	29.89	29.16
3000	39.24	37.14	35.42	34.00	32.80	31.79	30.92	30.17
3100	40.54	38.38	36.61	35.13	33.90	32.85	31.95	31.17
3200	41.85	39.62	37.79	36.27	34.99	33.90	32.98	32.18
3300	43.16	40.86	38.97	37.40	36.08	34.96	34.01	33.18
3400	44.47	42.09	40.15	38.53	37.17	36.02	35.04	34.19
3500	45.77	43.33	41.33	39.67	38.27	37.08	36.07	35.20
3600	47.08	44.57	42.51	40.80	39.36	38.14	37.10	36.20
3700	48.39	45.81	43.69	41.93	40.45	39.20	38.13	37.21
3800	49.70	47.04	44.87	43.07	41.55	40.26	39.16	38.21
3900	51.01	48.28	46.05	44.20	42.64	41.32	40.19	39.22
4000	52.31	49.52	47.23	45.33	43.73	42.38	41.22	40.22
4100	53.62	50.76	48.41	46.46	44.83	43.44	42.25	41.23
4200	54.93	52.00	49.59	47.60	45.92	44.50	43.28	42.23
4300	56.24	53.23	50.77	48.73	47.01	45.56	44.31	43.24
4400	57.54	54.47	51.95	49.86	48.11	46.62	45.34	44.24
4500	58.85	55.71	53.14	51.00	49.20	47.68	46.37	45.25
4600	60.16	56.95	54.32	52.13	50.29	48.74	47.40	46.26
4700	61.47	58.19	55.50	53.26	51.39	49.80	48.43	47.26
4800	62.77	59.42	56.68	54.40	52.48	50.85	49.46	48.27
4900	64.08	60.66	57.86	55.53	53.57	51.91	50.49	49.27
5000	65.39	61.90	59.04	56.66	54.67	52.97	51.52	50.28
5100	66.70	63.14	60.22	57.80	55.76	54.03	52.55	51.28
5200	68.01	64.37	61.40	58.93	56.86	55.09	53.58	52.29
5300	69.31	65.61	62.58	60.06	57.95	56.15	54.62	53.29
5400	70.62	66.85	63.76	61.20	59.04	57.21	55.65	54.30
5500	71.93	68.09	64.94	62.33	60.13	58.27	56.68	55.30

9¾% MONTHLY PAYMENT NECESSARY TO AMORTIZE A LOAN

TERM AMOUNT	10 YEARS	11 YEARS	12 YEARS	13 YEARS	14 YEARS	15 YEARS	16 YEARS	17 YEARS
$ 5600	73.24	69.33	66.12	63.46	61.23	59.33	57.71	56.31
5700	74.54	70.56	67.30	64.60	62.32	60.39	58.74	57.32
5800	75.85	71.80	68.48	65.73	63.41	61.45	59.77	58.32
5900	77.16	73.04	69.67	66.86	64.51	62.51	60.80	59.33
6000	78.47	74.28	70.85	67.99	65.60	63.57	61.83	60.33
6100	79.77	75.52	72.03	69.13	66.69	64.63	62.86	61.34
6200	81.08	76.75	73.21	70.26	67.79	65.69	63.89	62.34
6300	82.39	77.99	74.39	71.39	68.88	66.74	64.92	63.35
6400	83.70	79.23	75.57	72.53	69.97	67.80	65.95	64.35
6500	85.01	80.47	76.75	73.66	71.07	68.86	66.98	65.36
6600	86.31	81.71	77.93	74.79	72.16	69.92	68.01	66.36
6700	87.62	82.94	79.11	75.93	73.25	70.98	69.04	67.37
6800	88.93	84.18	80.29	77.06	74.34	72.04	70.07	68.37
6900	90.24	85.42	81.47	78.19	75.44	73.10	71.10	69.38
7000	91.54	86.66	82.65	79.33	76.53	74.16	72.13	70.39
7100	92.85	87.89	83.83	80.46	77.62	75.22	73.16	71.39
7200	94.16	89.13	85.01	81.59	78.72	76.28	74.19	72.40
7300	95.47	90.37	86.19	82.73	79.81	77.34	75.22	73.40
7400	96.77	91.61	87.38	83.86	80.90	78.40	76.25	74.41
7500	98.08	92.85	88.56	84.99	82.00	79.46	77.28	75.41
7600	99.39	94.08	89.74	86.13	83.09	80.52	78.31	76.42
7700	100.70	95.32	90.92	87.26	84.18	81.58	79.35	77.42
7800	102.01	96.56	92.10	88.39	85.28	82.64	80.38	78.43
7900	103.31	97.80	93.28	89.52	86.37	83.69	81.41	79.43
8000	104.62	99.04	94.46	90.66	87.46	84.75	82.44	80.44
8100	105.93	100.27	95.64	91.79	88.56	85.81	83.47	81.45
8200	107.24	101.51	96.82	92.92	89.65	86.87	84.50	82.45
8300	108.54	102.75	98.00	94.06	90.74	87.93	85.53	83.46
8400	109.85	103.99	99.18	95.19	91.84	88.99	86.56	84.46
8500	111.16	105.23	100.36	96.32	92.93	90.05	87.59	85.47
8600	112.47	106.47	101.54	97.46	94.02	91.11	88.62	86.47
8700	113.78	107.70	102.72	98.59	95.12	92.17	89.65	87.48
8800	115.08	108.94	103.90	99.72	96.21	93.23	90.68	88.48
8900	116.39	110.18	105.09	100.86	97.30	94.29	91.71	89.49
9000	117.70	111.41	106.27	101.99	98.40	95.35	92.74	90.49
9100	119.01	112.65	107.45	103.12	99.49	96.41	93.77	91.50
9200	120.31	113.89	108.63	104.26	100.58	97.47	94.80	92.51
9300	121.62	115.13	109.81	105.39	101.68	98.53	95.83	93.51
9400	122.93	116.37	110.99	106.52	102.77	99.59	96.86	94.52
9500	124.24	117.60	112.17	107.66	103.86	100.64	97.89	95.52
9600	125.54	118.84	113.35	108.79	104.96	101.70	98.92	96.53
9700	126.85	120.08	114.53	109.92	106.05	102.76	99.95	97.53
9800	128.16	121.32	115.71	111.05	107.15	103.82	100.98	98.54
9900	129.47	122.56	116.89	112.19	108.24	104.88	102.01	99.54
10000	130.78	123.79	118.07	113.32	109.33	105.94	103.04	100.55
11000	143.85	136.17	129.88	124.65	120.26	116.53	113.35	110.60
12000	156.93	148.55	141.69	135.98	131.19	127.13	123.65	120.66
13000	170.01	160.93	153.49	147.32	142.13	137.72	133.96	130.71
14000	183.08	173.31	165.30	158.65	153.06	148.32	144.26	140.77
15000	196.16	185.69	177.11	169.98	163.99	158.91	154.56	150.82
16000	209.24	198.07	188.91	181.31	174.92	169.50	164.87	160.88
17000	222.31	210.45	200.72	192.64	185.85	180.10	175.17	170.93
18000	235.39	222.82	212.53	203.97	196.79	190.69	185.48	180.98
19000	248.47	235.20	224.33	215.31	207.72	201.28	195.78	191.04
20000	261.55	247.58	236.14	226.64	218.65	211.88	206.08	201.09

at a monthly payment of $60.33, it will take 15 years to amortize the note. Five years have passed, however, so there are 12 years left. Going to the "12 years" column, we find that the amount closest to $60 to $60.22. A move to the left of $60.22 to the left margin will reveal the sum of $5,100 now due.

Notice that in figuring the balance of the note now due we must take the monthly amount actually being paid ($60) and treat it as though it is an amortized payment. Actually, the loan was for a term of eight years. The monthly payment required to amortize a note of $6,000 at 9¾ percent interest for a term of eight years is $90.26. Since only $60 a month was actually being paid, this note is not amortized, and when the eight-year term is up, a balloon payment will be necessary.

AREA MEASUREMENT

The licensee often must determine the square footage contained in a parcel of land or in a building. Generally, these problems involve finding the area within rectangular or triangular shaped parcels. Certain irregular or circular shaped parcels are best left to a land measurement expert, such as a surveyor.

Example: The area of a rectangular shape is found by multiplying the width times the length.

Square feet in lot A:

$$50 \times 100 = 5,000 \text{ square feet}$$

Example: The area of a triangular shape, in which two of the sides form a right angle, is found by multiplying the length of these two sides and dividing by two.

Square feet in lot B:

$$50 \times 100 = 5,000$$
$$5,000 \div 2 = 2,500 \text{ square feet}$$

Examples:

1. What is the square footage of lot C? Solution:

$$50 \times 100 = 5,000 \text{ square feet}$$

2. What is the square footage of lot D? Solution: Lot D should be solved as though it were two parcels—a rectangle 50 feet by 75 feet and a triangle with the two sides forming the right angle, 50 feet and 25 feet.

$$50 \times 75 = 3,750$$
$$50 \times 25 = 1,250 \div 2 = 625$$
$$3,750 + 625 = 4,375 \text{ square feet in lot D}$$

3. To find the square footage in lot E, it is necessary to divide the lot into three parts.

$$50 \times 50 = 2,500$$
$$25 \times 50 = 1,250$$
$$25 \times 50 \div 2 = \underline{\quad 625}$$
$$4,375 \text{ square feet in lot E}$$

4. How many square yards in a room 15 feet by 21 feet? Solution: To find square yards, divide the number of square feet by nine, since there are nine square feet in a square yard.

$$15 \times 21 = 315 \text{ square feet} \div 9 = 35 \text{ square yards}$$

5. At $350 per front foot, what would lots C, D, and E together sell for? Solution: Each of the three lots has a 50-foot frontage. The three together consist of 150 front feet.

$$150 \times \$350 = \$52,500$$

6. Builder King owns a 50 by 100-foot lot. The lot zoning is such that he may erect a building

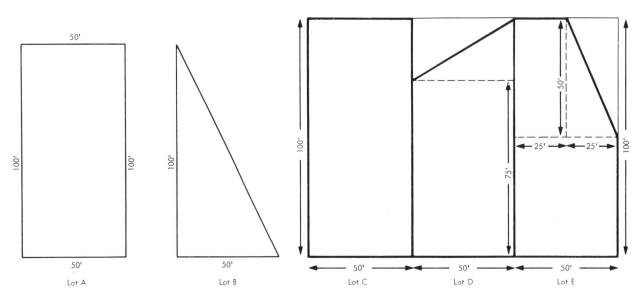

50'   50'   50'   50'   50'
Lot A   Lot B   Lot C   Lot D   Lot E

TABLE 11–8
Table of Monthly Payments to Amortize a $1,000 Loan

Term of years	10%	10½%	11%	11½%	12%	12½%	13%	13½%	14%	14½%	15%	15½%	16%	16½%	17%
1	87.92	88.15	88.38	88.62	88.85	89.08	89.32	89.55	89.79	90.02	90.26	90.49	90.73	90.97	91.20
2	46.14	46.38	46.61	46.84	47.07	47.31	47.54	47.78	48.01	48.25	48.49	48.72	48.96	49.20	49.44
3	32.27	32.50	32.74	32.98	33.21	33.45	33.69	33.94	34.18	34.42	34.67	34.91	35.16	35.40	35.65
4	25.36	25.60	25.85	26.09	26.33	26.58	26.83	27.08	27.33	27.58	27.83	28.08	28.34	28.60	28.86
5	21.25	21.50	21.75	22.00	22.25	22.50	22.76	23.01	23.27	23.53	23.79	24.06	24.32	24.59	24.86
6	18.53	18.78	19.04	19.30	19.56	19.82	20.08	20.34	20.61	20.87	21.15	21.42	21.69	21.97	22.25
7	16.61	16.87	17.13	17.39	17.66	17.93	18.20	18.47	18.75	19.03	19.31	19.58	19.86	20.15	20.44
8	15.18	15.45	15.71	15.98	16.26	16.53	16.81	17.09	17.38	17.66	17.95	18.24	18.53	18.82	19.12
9	14.08	14.36	14.63	14.91	15.19	15.47	15.76	16.05	16.34	16.64	16.93	17.22	17.53	17.83	18.15
10	13.22	13.50	13.78	14.06	14.35	14.64	14.94	15.23	15.53	15.83	16.13	16.44	16.75	17.06	17.38
11	12.52	12.81	13.10	13.39	13.68	13.98	14.28	14.58	14.89	15.20	15.51	15.82	16.14	16.46	16.79
12	11.96	12.25	12.54	12.84	13.14	13.44	13.75	14.06	14.38	14.70	15.02	15.34	15.67	15.99	16.32
13	11.48	11.78	12.08	12.38	12.69	13.00	13.32	13.63	13.96	14.28	14.60	14.93	15.27	15.60	15.94
14	11.09	11.39	11.70	12.01	12.32	12.64	12.96	13.28	13.61	13.94	14.27	14.61	14.95	15.29	15.64
15	10.75	11.06	11.37	11.69	12.01	12.33	12.66	12.99	13.32	13.66	14.00	14.34	14.69	15.04	15.39
16	10.46	10.78	11.10	11.42	11.74	12.07	12.40	12.74	13.08	13.42	13.77	14.12	14.47	14.83	15.19
17	10.22	10.54	10.86	11.19	11.52	11.85	12.19	12.53	12.88	13.22	13.58	13.93	14.29	14.65	15.02
18	10.00	10.33	10.66	10.99	11.32	11.67	12.01	12.36	12.71	13.06	13.42	13.78	14.14	14.51	14.88
19	9.82	10.15	10.48	10.82	11.16	11.50	11.85	12.21	12.56	12.92	13.28	13.65	14.02	14.39	14.76
20	9.66	9.99	10.33	10.67	11.02	11.37	11.72	12.08	12.44	12.80	13.17	13.54	13.91	14.29	14.67
21	9.51	9.85	10.19	10.54	10.89	11.24	11.60	11.96	12.33	12.70	13.07	13.45	13.82	14.20	14.59
22	9.38	9.73	10.07	10.42	10.78	11.14	11.50	11.87	12.24	12.61	12.99	13.37	13.75	14.13	14.52
23	9.27	9.62	9.97	10.33	10.69	11.05	11.42	11.79	12.16	12.54	12.92	13.30	13.69	14.07	14.46
24	9.17	9.52	9.88	10.24	10.60	10.97	11.34	11.72	12.10	12.48	12.86	13.25	13.63	14.02	14.42
25	9.09	9.45	9.81	10.17	10.54	10.91	11.28	11.66	12.04	12.42	12.81	13.20	13.59	13.98	14.38
26	9.01	9.37	9.73	10.10	10.47	10.84	11.22	11.60	11.99	12.38	12.76	13.16	13.55	13.95	14.34
27	8.94	9.30	9.67	10.04	10.41	10.79	11.17	11.56	11.95	12.34	12.73	13.12	13.52	13.92	14.32
28	8.88	9.25	9.61	9.99	10.37	10.75	11.13	11.52	11.91	12.30	12.70	13.09	13.49	13.89	14.29
29	8.82	9.19	9.57	9.94	10.32	10.71	11.09	11.48	11.88	12.27	12.67	13.07	13.47	13.87	14.27
30	8.78	9.15	9.53	9.91	10.29	10.68	11.07	11.46	11.85	12.25	12.64	13.05	13.45	13.85	14.25
35	8.60	8.99	9.37	9.77	10.16	10.56	10.96	11.36	11.76	12.16	12.57	12.98	13.38	13.79	14.21
40	8.49	8.89	9.28	9.68	10.08	10.49	10.90	11.30	11.71	12.12	12.53	12.94	13.36	13.77	14.18

142

on the entire area of the lot, subject only to a 10-foot setback requirement applicable to the front of the lot. If he erects a single-story building, what is the maximum number of square feet it may contain?

A setback requirement prohibits construction between the boundary line of a lot and the setback line. A lot in a higher priced residential district in the suburbs would probably be subject to setback requirements that result in the building being completely detached from those on adjacent lots.

Solution: King's lot is 50 by 100, or 5,000 square feet. A 10-foot setback requirement applicable to the front of the lot would mean an area of 50 by 10, or 500 square feet.

5,000 square feet − 500 square feet
$$= 4,500 \text{ square feet},$$

the maximum square footage a single-story building may contain.

Finding the square footage of a building

The square footage of a building is generally found by using the outside measurements. Thus, everything inside the building—rooms, closets, hallways, and stairways—is included. If the building is more than a single story, one must be careful to note whether the second story has the same outside dimensions as the first story. Such measurements are used in connection with the reproduction cost method in appraising where the building square footage is found and multiplied by the construction cost per square foot.

QUESTIONS FOR DISCUSSION

1. A total of $20,000 is deposited in a savings account that pays 8½ percent annual interest compounded quarterly. How much interest will be credited to the account for the first quarter?
2. What is the interest on a loan of $50,000 at 12 percent annual interest for 150 days?
3. What rate of interest is being charged if the amount of a loan is $16,000, the time is five years, and the amount of interest paid is $8,800.
4. If the amount of interest is $12,600, the rate is 10½ percent, and the time is six years, determine the principal amount of the loan.
5. Using the 60-day, 6 percent method, determine the interest on $5,800 at 9 percent for 120 days.
6. Brown purchases an apartment building on which owner Smith has already collected rents amounting to $2,980. Escrow is to be closed on the 16th day of a 30-day month. How is the rent apportioned between Brown and Smith?
7. Barbaix receives $2,932.50 representing a 12¾ percent return on an investment. What amount did Barbaix invest?
8. Marks' contract with broker Ohman states that, if Marks lists and sells property, she is to receive 70 percent of the commission with 10 percent deducted for advertising expense. What does Marks receive if she sells a building for $229,000 and the commission rate is 5 percent?
9. Brussell purchases a 20-acre vinyard at $3,500 per acre and wants to make a 20 percent profit on invested funds. For how much will Brussell have to sell the vinyard?
10. Williams purchases a building for $380,000. If it shows a net yearly income of $35,150, what is the rate of return to Williams?
11. Buoncristiani wishes to purchase a property offered at $525,000. He can assume a present loan of $320,000, and the seller will carry back a second loan of $58,000. What will Buoncristiani need for a downpayment?
12. If Grant's building is assessed for tax purposes at 25 percent of its market value of $532,000 and the tax rate is $4.30 per $100, what is the amount of the first tax installment payment?
13. What is the original amount of a note which has been discounted 35 percent if the amount of discount is $9,800?
14. At $5.50 per square foot, what must Clift pay for a commercial lot 52 feet wide and 221 feet deep?
15. If Fineman purchases a lot for $20,000 and later sells it for $34,400, what is his percent of profit based on original cost?

MULTIPLE CHOICE QUESTIONS

11–1. What is the number of square yards in an area that measures 75 by 150 feet? (a) 11,250, (b) 3,750, (c) 1,250, (d) 225.
11–2. How much must Armour invest at 8 percent in order to receive a $375 monthly income payment? (a) $56,250, (b) $56,000, (c) $4,687, (d) $46,875.
11–3. If rent from a building containing 18 apartments is $11,070 per month, what is the average monthly rental per apartment? (a) $750, (b) $600, (c) $615, (d) $915.
11–4. $20,000 capitalized at 8 percent is (a) $25,000, (b) $160,000, (c) $250,000, (d) $180,000.
11–5. What commission does broker Calvin make if she sells a $325,000 building and the commission rate is 6 percent of the first $100,000, 5 percent of the second $100,000, and 4 percent of anything exceeding $200,000? (a) $11,000, (b) $19,000, (c) $16,000, (d) $24,000.
11–6. If Clark borrows $21,000 with a three-year term and a 9 percent yearly interest rate, how much interest must Clark pay? (a) $1,890, (b) $5,670, (c) $3,780, (d) $5,220.

11–7. Arthur receives a real property tax bill of $1,102.50 based on an assessment ratio of 25 percent of market value and a tax rate of $4.90 per $100. The assessors estimate of market value is (a) $22,500, (b) $225,000, (c) $90,000, (d) $49,250.

11–8. With a loan fee set at 3 percent plus $250, Chinn borrows $162,000 and must pay a loan fee amounting to (a) $4,610, (b) $8,910, (c) $550, (d) $5,110.

Very few persons who purchase real estate are capable of paying, or would want to pay, all cash for the property. In virtually all real estate transactions, some form of financing is necessary to enable the buyer to borrow the money he needs to effect the purchase. Usually, a purchaser has a certain amount of money for a down payment and borrows the remainder needed to meet the purchase price. The purchaser will execute a note for the money borrowed and secure this note by executing a deed of trust in favor of the lender.

Persons entering into a discussion of real estate finance will use the term *mortgage* many times. Actually, a true mortgage contract is very seldom used in California. The device used instead is the deed of trust. Thus, when an individual in California refers to a mortgage on his property, he is really referring to a loan, which is actually in the form of a note secured by a deed of trust. California title insurance companies reported that in 1982, the trust deed was used in approximately 98 percent of all property transactions recorded. A discussion of the reasons behind the widespread use of the deed of trust as against the mortgage will follow discussion of the promissory note.

THE PROMISSORY NOTE

The promissory note is the principal instrument used to evidence the obligation or debt and is a negotiable instrument. California Civil Code contains the Uniform Commercial Code, which defines the rules governing promissory notes.

There are basically three kinds of promissory notes.

The *straight note* calls for payment of interest only during the term of the note and the full amount of the principal when the note falls due.

The *installment note* calls for periodic payments on the principal, such payments being separate from the interest payments.

The *fully amortized installment note* has been traditionally the most commonly used in California. This note requires certain periodic payments (usually monthly) of fixed amounts. The amount includes payment on both the principal and interest and is calculated so as to render the note fully paid at the end of the term. The periodic payments are usually referred to as installments, and thus, many persons refer to this type of note as an installment note. However, the correct definition is a fully amortized installment note.

The *adjustable rate note* is becoming most common due to fluctuating interest rates. With an adjustable rate note, the interest rate varies upward or downward during the term of the loan depending on money market conditions and an agreed on index or other specific indicator.

The promissory note is a negotiable instrument freely transferrable in commerce. In order to be negotiable, the Uniform Commercial Code requires that the following be incorporated into the note: *(a)* The note must contain an unconditional promise, *(b)* in writing, *(c)* made by one person to another, *(d)* signed by the maker, *(e)* promising to pay on demand or at a fixed or determinable future time, *(f)* a certain sum of money, *(g)* payable to order or to the bearer.

The negotiability of a note is not affected by inclusion of a clause adding court costs and reasonable attorney's fees if litigation becomes necessary in order to collect; neither does inclusion of an acceleration clause, which provides that default in one or more of the payments makes the entire

144

principal amount immediately due. In fact, these and similar provisions actually make the note more attractive to lenders and thus may be said to enhance negotiability.

It should be remembered with regard to real estate loans that the lender usually reserves the right to approve any person or persons to whom the loan may be subsequently transferred by the original borrower.

Figure 12–1 is an illustration of a fully amortized installment note. Reference to an amortization table will disclose that $135,000 at 14½ percent, with payments of $1,653.16 monthly, will mean a term of 30 years. The date of the last payment due is not shown on the note, since the note states that the borrowers are to pay $1,653.16 "or more" on the first day of each month. This allows the borrowers, should they so desire, to increase their monthly payment and pay the loan

off in a shorter time. The provision under which such prepayment may take place is only one of a number of subjects that will be covered in a separate agreement between the borrower and lender. All lending institutions have a rather lengthy set of conditions and regulations under which the loan is being made, and the borrowers must accept these prior to obtaining the loan.

Holder in due course

If any of the previously listed essential requirements for negotiability is missing in the document, it is still valuable and transferrable in much the same manner as an ordinary contract. As such, the transferee or assignee will receive no more than the transferor had, and defenses that were good against the assigner are good against the as-

---

TO 417.1 C

DO NOT DESTROY THIS NOTE: When paid, this note, with Deed of Trust securing same, must be surrendered to Trustee for cancellation before reconveyance will be made.

NOTE SECURED BY DEED OF TRUST

(INSTALLMENT—INTEREST INCLUDED)

$ 135,000.00 _____ Sacramento , California, _____ October 8, 19--

In installments as herein stated, for value received, I promise to pay to __ ABC Savings and Loan __ Association, __ 300 States Avenue, Sacramento, California __ , or order,

at __ 300 States Avenue, Sacramento, California __

the sum of _ One hundred thirty-five thousand dollars........(135,000.00) _ DOLLARS,

with interest from _ October 8, 19-- _ on unpaid principal at the

rate of __ 14 ½ __ per cent per annum; principal and interest payable in installments of

__ One thousand six hundred fifty-three Dollars and 16/ 100 .... Dollars

or more on the __ 1 st __ day of each _____ month, beginning

on the __ 1 st __ day of _ November, 19-- _

_____

_____ and continuing until said principal and interest have been paid.

Each payment shall be credited first on interest then due and the remainder on principal; and interest shall thereupon cease upon the principal so credited. Should default be made in payment of any installment when due the whole sum of principal and interest shall become immediately due at the option of the holder of this note. Principal and interest payable in lawful money of the United States. If action be instituted on this note I promise to pay such sum as the Court may fix as attorney's fees. This note is secured by a DEED OF TRUST to TITLE INSURANCE AND TRUST COMPANY, a California corporation, as trustee.

(s) John Purchaser

(s) Mary Purchaser

THIS FORM FURNISHED BY TITLE INSURANCE AND TRUST COMPANY

DO NOT DESTROY THIS NOTE

FIGURE 12–1

signee. However, it is possible with regard to a valid negotiable instrument that the transferee may receive more than the transferor had. If the holder of the instrument transfers it to a third party, who takes the notes as a holder in due course, then the one who takes the note may enjoy a favored position.

A holder in due course is one who has taken a negotiable instrument with the following conditions present:

1. The instrument, when taken, was complete and regular in appearance and form.
2. The instrument, when negotiated, was not overdue and was without notice of previous dishonor.
3. The instrument was taken in good faith and for a valuable consideration.
4. At the time it was negotiated to him, the person receiving the note had no knowledge of any infirmity in the instrument or any defect in the title of the negotiator.

If one who takes a note and qualifies as a holder in due course brings an action to collect on the note, the maker of the note cannot use any of the following defenses to refuse payment.

1. A lack or failure of consideration. The maker of the note cannot refuse payment by claiming that he has not received what the payee promised to give him for the note.
2. A claim of prior payment or cancellation. If the maker of the note actually pays the amount due to the payee but fails to receive proof that he has paid, and the payee meanwhile transfers the note to a holder in due course, the original maker may be still held responsible. This is one of the reasons why one who pays off a note should be sure he receives proof of payment. Such proof will usually be the note itself marked paid.
3. A claim of fraud in the inducement.
4. A setoff. A claim that the note was a setoff might be made when, for instance, the maker owes the payee $20,000 on the note, but the payee owes the maker $30,000 on another obligation.

The previous defenses, then, are good against the original payee but are not good against a subsequent holder in due course. However, certain real defenses are good against any person, a payee or holder in due course included. These defenses are:

1. Forgery, where the alleged maker did not really sign the note.
2. Material alteration, when an important change is made in the obligation without the knowledge of the parties involved.
3. Incapacity, where the maker is a minor or an incompetent.
4. Illegality of the instrument. If the instrument is executed in connection with an illegal act or if the rate of interest is usurious, then illegality of the instrument results.

Interest charge, usury, and Proposition 2

Section 1915 of the California Civil Code defines interests as "the compensation allowed by law or fixed by the parties for the use, forbearance, or detention of money." Any charge connected with a loan, whether it be called interest, service charge, placement charge, or points, may be considered by the courts as interest in determining if a usurious charge is being made. Thus, it may well be that when these additional charges are considered, along with the stated rate of interest on the note, the actual payment for the use of money may exceed the allowed maximum. No illegal interest can be collected in California on a note that is found to exceed the legal maximum, and in certain circumstances, the borrower can collect damages from the lender. A note that provides for a prepayment penalty is not considered usurious, nor does acceleration of maturity result in usury. It is interesting to note that California law exempts the following from restrictions of the usury law: banks, savings and loan associations, credit unions, industrial loan companies, and nonprofit cooperation associations.

Proposition 2, enacted in 1979, now defines the usury rate of interest as 10%, or the prevailing San Francisco Federal Reserve Bank discount rate plus 5%, whichever is higher.

Exempt from the usury law is any loan made or arranged by a California licensed real estate broker and secured wholly or in part by a lien on real property; or, a purchase money trust deed carried back by an owner who sells his real property.

TRUST DEEDS AND MORTGAGES

Mortgages and deeds of trust differ in many respects, and a comparison of these differences will make clear to the reader the reasons why the deed of trust is preferred by lenders and is the instrument generally used in California today. The mortgage and deed of trust differ with respect to *(a)* parties, *(b)* title, *(c)* statute of limitations, *(d)* remedy, and *(e)* redemption.

With respect to parties

In a mortgage, there are two parties—the mortgagor and the mortgagee. The mortgagor borrows the money to purchase the property, and the mortgagee is the lender.

In a deed of trust, there are three parties—the trustor, the trustee, and the beneficiary. The trustor borrows the money to purchase, and the beneficiary is the lender. The trustee is the third party to whom the borrower conveys the title to the property as security for the obligation owed to the lender. A deed of trust is shown in Figure 12–2.

Mortgage		Deed of Trust	
Mortgagor	Borrower	Trustor	Borrower
Mortgagee	Lender	Beneficiary	Lender
		Trustee	Holds title for the benefit of the lender

With respect to title

A mortgage does not convey any degree of title; it merely creates a lien. The mortgagor executes a note and a mortgage in favor of the mortgagee, who then has a lien on the property, which he may enforce if the mortgagor defaults on his obligation.

The deed of trust also may be considered a lien against property, but it has the additional important element of the passage of title to a third party for the benefit of the lender. It may seem that with a deed of trust, the borrower does not have title in the property any longer because he has given it to the trustee; this is not entirely correct. California law provides that the trustee has legal title only to the extent that it may become necessary for him to effect a sale of the property for the benefit of the beneficiary should the trustor default in his obligation. Otherwise, the trustor holds true title to the property, referred to as *equitable title,* and may sell, lease, or further encumber it so long as he does nothing adverse or inconsistent with the right of the beneficiary.

When the beneficiary notifies the trustee that the note has been paid in full, the rights and interests given the trustee in the deed of trust are reconveyed to the trustor. A request for full reconveyance is part of the trust deed, as shown in Figure 12–2 (continued).

With respect to statute of limitations

In a mortgage, an action to foreclose is barred when the statute of limitations has run out on the principal obligation. Thus, the rights of the mortgagee must be enforced during the term of the note.

With a deed of trust, the rights of the beneficiary are not ended when the statute of limitations has run on the note, for the trustee has title with power of sale for the benefit of the beneficiary and can sell the property to pay off the debt.

With respect to remedy

In a mortgage agreement, the only remedy of the mortgagee is foreclosure by court action. The deed of trust, however, allows the beneficiary the option of either foreclosing by court action or proceeding with a trustee's sale of the property. Obviously, the trustee's sale procedure is the method used with the deed of trust. This is one of the main reasons for the existence and lenders' use of the deed of trust. Some lenders employ a form mortgage document that includes a power of sale, which will be discussed later in this chapter. The actual procedures and steps used in foreclosing under a mortgage and in exercising the power of sale under a deed of trust (trustee's sale) are discussed in Chapter 16, dealing with public sales of real property.

With respect to redemption

Under a mortgage that has been foreclosed by court action, the right of the mortgagor to redeem exists for one year after the sale. It is not uncommon for legal proceedings to run for as long as two years after a sale before the rights of the mortgagor are finally eliminated.

Under a deed of trust, sale of the property by the trustee is an irrevocable, final, and absolute sale, and the trustor has no right of redemption. Approximately four months elapses from the time the trustor defaults on his obligation and a notice of default is filed to the actual sale of the property by the trustee. During this time, the trustor may save the property from being sold, but once the trustee's sale takes place, it is final.

Our preceding comparison of the mortgage and the deed of trust should help the reader to under-

————— SPACE ABOVE THIS LINE FOR RECORDER'S USE —————

TO 498 C (-OPEN END)

SHORT FORM DEED OF TRUST AND ASSIGNMENT OF RENTS

This Deed of Trust, made this 8 th day of October, 19-- , between

John Purchaser and Mary Purchaser, husband and wife , herein called TRUSTOR,
whose address is 200 Kennedy Drive, Sacramento, 95811, California ,
(number and street) (city) (zone) (state)

TITLE INSURANCE AND TRUST COMPANY, a California corporation, herein called TRUSTEE, and

ABC Savings and Loan Association, Sacramento, California , herein called BENEFICIARY,

Witnesseth: That Trustor IRREVOCABLY GRANTS, TRANSFERS AND ASSIGNS to TRUSTEE IN TRUST, WITH POWER OF SALE,
that property in City of Sacramento, Sacramento County, California, described as:

Lot 19, Block B, Parklake Addition (as recorded July 12, 1929, Book 3,

Page 59 of maps), City of Sacramento, County of Sacramento, State of

California. Commonly known as: 200 Kennedy Drive, Sacramento, California.

TOGETHER WITH the rents, issues and profits thereof, SUBJECT, HOWEVER, to the right, power and authority given to and conferred upon Beneficiary by paragraph (10) of the provisions incorporated herein by reference to collect and apply such rents, issues and profits.
For the Purpose of Securing: 1. Performance of each agreement of Trustor incorporated by reference or contained herein. 2. Payment of the indebtedness evidenced by one promissory note of even date herewith, and any extension or renewal thereof, in the principal sum of $ 135,000.00 executed by Trustor in favor of Beneficiary or order. 3. Payment of such further sums as the then record owner of said property hereafter may borrow from Beneficiary, when evidenced by another note (or notes) reciting it is so secured.
To Protect the Security of This Deed of Trust, Trustor Agrees: By the execution and delivery of this Deed of Trust and the note secured hereby, that provisions (1) to (14), inclusive, of the fictitious deed of trust recorded in Santa Barbara County and Sonoma County October 18, 1961, and in all other counties October 23, 1961, in the book and at the page of Official Records in the office of the county recorder of the county where said property is located, noted below opposite the name of such county, viz.:

COUNTY	BOOK	PAGE	COUNTY	BOOK	PAGE	COUNTY	BOOK	PAGE	COUNTY	BOOK	PAGE
Alameda	435	684	Kings	792	833	Placer	895	301	Sierra	29	335
Alpine	1	250	Lake	362	39	Plumas	151	5	Siskiyou	468	181
Amador	104	348	Lassen	171	471	Riverside	3005	523	Solano	1105	182
Butte	1145	1	Los Angeles	T2055	899	Sacramento	4331	62	Sonoma	1851	689
Calaveras	145	152	Madera	810	170	San Benito	271	383	Stanislaus	1715	456
Colusa	296	617	Marin	1508	339	San Bernardino	5567	61	Sutter	572	297
Contra Costa	3978	47	Mariposa	77	292	San Francisco	A332	905	Tehama	401	289
Del Norte	78	414	Mendocino	579	530	San Joaquin	2470	311	Trinity	93	366
El Dorado	568	456	Merced	1547	538	San Luis Obispo	1151	12	Tulare	2294	275
Fresno	4626	572	Modoc	184	851	San Mateo	4078	420	Tuolumne	135	47
Glenn	422	184	Mono	52	429	Santa Barbara	1878	860	Ventura	2062	386
Humboldt	657	527	Monterey	2194	538	Santa Clara	5336	341	Yolo	653	245
Imperial	1091	501	Napa	639	86	Santa Cruz	1431	494	Yuba	334	486
Inyo	147	598	Nevada	305	320	Shasta	684	528			
Kern	3427	60	Orange	5889	611	San Diego	Series 2 Book 1961, Page 183887				

(which provisions, identical in all counties, are printed on the reverse hereof) hereby are adopted and incorporated herein and made a part hereof as fully as though set forth herein at length; that he will observe and perform said provisions; and that the references to property, obligations, and parties in said provisions shall be construed to refer to the property, obligations, and parties set forth in this Deed of Trust.
The undersigned Trustor requests that a copy of any Notice of Default and of any Notice of Sale hereunder be mailed to him at his address hereinbefore set forth.

STATE OF CALIFORNIA City and
COUNTY OF Sacramento } ss.
On October 8, 19-- before me, the under-
signed, a Notary Public in and for said State, personally appeared
John Purchaser and Mary Purchaser

_____, known to me
to be the person s whose name s are subscribed to the within
instrument and acknowledged that they executed the same.
WITNESS my hand and official seal.

Signature_____ (s) Nathan Notary
Nathan Notary
Name (Typed or Printed)

Signature of Trustor

(s) John Purchaser

(s) Mary Purchaser

Title Order No. _____

Escrow or Loan No. _____

(This area for official notarial seal)

FIGURE 12–2

The following is a copy of provisions (1) to (14), inclusive, of the fictitious deed of trust, recorded in each county in California, as stated in the foregoing Deed of Trust and incorporated by reference in said Deed of Trust as being a part thereof as if set forth at length therein.

To Protect the Security of This Deed of Trust, Trustor Agrees:

(1) To keep said property in good condition and repair; not to remove or demolish any building thereon; to complete or restore promptly and in good and workmanlike manner any building which may be constructed, damaged or destroyed thereon and to pay when due all claims for labor performed and materials furnished therefor; to comply with all laws affecting said property or requiring any alterations or improvements to be made thereon; not to commit or permit waste thereof; not to commit, suffer or permit any act upon said property in violation of law; to cultivate, irrigate, fertilize, fumigate, prune and do all other acts which from the character or use of said property may be reasonably necessary, the specific enumerations herein not excluding the general.

(2) To provide, maintain and deliver to Beneficiary fire insurance satisfactory to and with loss payable to Beneficiary. The amount collected under any fire or other insurance policy may be applied by Beneficiary upon any indebtedness secured hereby and in such order as Beneficiary may determine, or at option of Beneficiary the entire amount so collected or any part thereof may be released to Trustor. Such application or release shall not cure or waive any default or notice of default hereunder or invalidate any act done pursuant to such notice.

(3) To appear in and defend any action or proceeding purporting to affect the security hereof or the rights or powers of Beneficiary or Trustee; and to pay all costs and expenses, including cost of evidence of title and attorney's fees in a reasonable sum, in any such action or proceeding in which Beneficiary or Trustee may appear, and in any suit brought by Beneficiary to foreclose this Deed.

(4) To pay: at least ten days before delinquency all taxes and assessments affecting said property, including assessments on appurtenant water stock; when due, all incumbrances, charges and liens, with interest, on said property or any part thereof, which appear to be prior or superior hereto; all costs, fees and expenses of this Trust.

Should Trustor fail to make any payment or to do any act as herein provided, then Beneficiary or Trustee, but without obligation so to do and without notice to or demand upon Trustor and without releasing Trustor from any obligation hereof, may: make or do the same in such manner and to such extent as either may deem necessary to protect the security hereof, Beneficiary or Trustee being authorized to enter upon said property for such purposes; appear in and defend any action or proceeding purporting to affect the security hereof or the rights or powers of Beneficiary or Trustee; pay, purchase, contest or compromise any incumbrance, charge or lien which in the judgment of either appears to be prior or superior hereto; and, in exercising any such powers, pay necessary expenses, employ counsel and pay his reasonable fees.

(5) To pay immediately and without demand all sums so expended by Beneficiary or Trustee, with interest from date of expenditure at the amount allowed by law in effect at the date hereof, and to pay for any statement provided for by law in effect at the date hereof regarding the obligation secured hereby any amount demanded by the Beneficiary not to exceed the maximum allowed by law at the time when said statement is demanded.

(6) That any award of damages in connection with any condemnation for public use of or injury to said property or any part thereof is hereby assigned and shall be paid to Beneficiary who may apply or release such moneys received by him in the same manner and with the same effect as above provided for disposition of proceeds of fire or other insurance.

(7) That by accepting payment of any sum secured hereby after its due date, Beneficiary does not waive his right either to require prompt payment when due of all other sums so secured or to declare default for failure so to pay.

(8) That at any time or from time to time, without liability therefor and without notice, upon written request of Beneficiary and presentation of this Deed and said note for endorsement, and without affecting the personal liability of any person for payment of the indebtedness secured hereby, Trustee may: reconvey any part of said property; consent to the making of any map or plat thereof; join in granting any easement thereon; or join in any extension agreement or any agreement subordinating the lien or charge hereof.

(9) That upon written request of Beneficiary stating that all sums secured hereby have been paid, and upon surrender of this Deed and said note to Trustee for cancellation and retention and upon payment of its fees, Trustee shall reconvey, without warranty, the property then held hereunder. The recitals in such reconveyance of any matters or facts shall be conclusive proof of the truthfulness thereof. The grantee in such reconveyance may be described as "the person or persons legally entitled thereto." Five years after issuance of such full reconveyance, Trustee may destroy said note and this Deed (unless directed in such request to retain them)

(10) That as additional security, Trustor hereby gives to and confers upon Beneficiary the right, power and authority, during the continuance of these Trusts, to collect the rents, issues and profits of said property, reserving unto Trustor the right, prior to any default by Trustor in payment of any indebtedness secured hereby or in performance of any agreement hereunder, to collect and retain such rents, issues and profits as they become due and payable. Upon any such default, Beneficiary may at any time without notice, either in person, by agent, or by a receiver to be appointed by a court, and without regard to the adequacy of any security for the indebtedness hereby secured, enter upon and take possession of said property or any part thereof, in his own name sue for or otherwise collect such rents, issues and profits, including those past due and unpaid, and apply the same, less costs and expenses of operation and collection, including reasonable attorney's fees, upon any indebtedness secured hereby, and in such order as Beneficiary may determine. The entering upon and taking possession of said property, the collection of such rents, issues and profits and the application thereof as aforesaid, shall not cure or waive any default or notice of default hereunder or invalidate any act done pursuant to such notice.

(11) That upon default by Trustor in payment of any indebtedness secured hereby or in performance of any agreement hereunder, Beneficiary may declare all sums secured hereby immediately due and payable by delivery to Trustee of written declaration of default and demand for sale and of written notice of default and of election to cause to be sold said property, which notice Trustee shall cause to be filed for record. Beneficiary also shall deposit with Trustee this Deed, said note and all documents evidencing expenditures secured hereby.

After the lapse of such time as may then be required by law following the recordation of said notice of default, and notice of sale having been given as then required by law, Trustee, without demand on Trustor, shall sell said property at the time and place fixed by it in said notice of sale, either as a whole or in separate parcels, and in such order as it may determine, at public auction to the highest bidder for cash in lawful money of the United States, payable at time of sale. Trustee may postpone sale of all or any portion of said property by public announcement at such time and place of sale, and from time to time thereafter may postpone such sale by public announcement at the time fixed by the preceding postponement. Trustee shall deliver to such purchaser its deed conveying the property so sold, but without any covenant or warranty, express or implied. The recitals in such deed of any matters or facts shall be conclusive proof of the truthfulness thereof. Any person, including Trustor, Trustee, or Beneficiary as hereinafter defined, may purchase at such sale.

After deducting all costs, fees and expenses of Trustee and of this Trust, including cost of evidence of title in connection with sale, Trustee shall apply the proceeds of sale to payment of: all sums expended under the terms hereof, not then repaid, with accrued interest at the amount allowed by law in effect at the date hereof; all other sums then secured hereby; and the remainder, if any, to the person or persons legally entitled thereto.

(12) That Beneficiary, or any successor in ownership of any indebtedness secured hereby, may from time to time, by instrument in writing, substitute a successor or successors to any Trustee named herein or acting hereunder, which instrument, executed by the Beneficiary and duly acknowledged and recorded in the office of the recorder of the county or counties where said property is situated, shall be conclusive proof of proper substitution of such successor Trustee or Trustees, who shall, without conveyance from the Trustee predecessor, succeed to all its title, estate, rights, powers and duties. Said instrument must contain the name of the original Trustor, Trustee and Beneficiary hereunder, the book and page where this Deed is recorded and the name and address of the new Trustee.

(13) That this Deed applies to, inures to the benefit of, and binds all parties hereto, their heirs, legatees, devisees, administrators, executors, successors and assigns. The term Beneficiary shall mean the owner and holder, including pledgees, of the note secured hereby, whether or not named as Beneficiary herein. In this Deed, whenever the context so requires, the masculine gender includes the feminine and/or neuter, and the singular number includes the plural.

(14) That Trustee accepts this Trust when this Deed, duly executed and acknowledged, is made a public record as provided by law. Trustee is not obligated to notify any party hereto of pending sale under any other Deed of Trust or of any action or proceeding in which Trustor, Beneficiary or Trustee shall be a party unless brought by Trustee.

REQUEST FOR FULL RECONVEYANCE
To be used only when note has been paid.

To TITLE INSURANCE AND TRUST COMPANY, Trustee: Dated_____

The undersigned is the legal owner and holder of all indebtedness secured by the within Deed of Trust. All sums secured by said Deed of Trust have been fully paid and satisfied; and you are hereby requested and directed, on payment to you of any sums owing to you under the terms of said Deed of Trust, to cancel all evidences of indebtedness, secured by said Deed of Trust, delivered to you herewith together with said Deed of Trust, and to reconvey, without warranty, to the parties designated by the terms of said Deed of Trust, the estate now held by you under the same.

MAIL RECONVEYANCE TO:

_____

_____

_____

By_____

By_____

Do not lose or destroy this Deed of Trust OR THE NOTE which it secures. Both must be delivered to the Trustee for cancellation before reconveyance will be made.

DEED OF TRUST
WITH POWER OF SALE
(SHORT FORM)

Title Insurance
and
Trust Company
AS TRUSTEE

TI

Title Insurance
and
Trust Company

COMPLETE STATEWIDE TITLE SERVICE
WITH ONE LOCAL CALL

FIGURE 12–2 *(concluded)*

stand the main reasons for the almost total use of the deed of trust by lenders in California. The two most important reasons are: (1) the ease and facility, without having to resort to court action, with which the property may be sold to satisfy the debt if the borrower defaults; and (2) the short period of redemption prior to the sale and the fact that the sale, once made, is absolute.

Mortgage with power of sale

Some lenders occasionally use a conventional mortgage form that has written into it a power-of-sale clause. This allows the mortgagee, on default by the mortgagor, to sell the property without the necessity of court proceedings. The mortgagor is usually bound to execute a deed to the purchaser after the mortgagee sells the property.

The main difference between the mortgage with the power of sale and the deed of trust is with regard to the statute of limitations. The mortgage with power of sale is in the same position as the conventional mortgage; a sale is barred when the statute of limitations has run on the principal obligation (the note). The opposite is true when using the deed of trust, and even though judicial enforcement of the debt may not be possible, the trustee can still sell the property because the trust deed gives him the power of sale in order to satisfy the debt.

TRUSTEE'S SALE

When a borrower defaults on his obligations under a note and deed of trust by virtue of his failure to make the necessary payments, the beneficiary notifies the trustee named in the deed of trust, and we have the beginning of what may eventually be a trustee's sale of the real property involved.

Statement of condition

On being notified by the beneficiary of the trustor's default, the trustee obtains from the beneficiary a statement showing the condition of the debt. The statement will show:

1. The amount of the unpaid balance on the obligation.
2. The amounts of periodic payments, if any.
3. The date on which the obligation is due in whole or part.

4. The date to which real estate taxes and special assessments have been paid.
5. The amount of insurance in effect, its terms and premium.
6. The amount in an account, if any, maintained to accumulate funds with which to pay taxes and insurance premiums.

On receipt of the above information, the trustee also obtains the deed of trust and note, together with receipts that may show any advances paid by the beneficiary for the protection of his security. Such advances may be in the form of taxes or insurance paid by the beneficiary because of the trustor's inability to do so.

The notice of default

Section 2924 of the Civil Code states that in order for the power of sale under a deed of trust to be carried out, the trustee must record a notice of default in the county where the property is located. This must be done at least three months before notice of sale is given. Some trust deeds require that the beneficiary execute the notice of default and then deliver it to the trustee with instructions to exercise the power of sale. At any rate, the requirements as set forth in the deed of trust must be fully met.

The notice of default illustrated in Figure 12–3 will contain the following:

1. Identification of the deed of trust, usually by means of the legal description of the property involved.
2. The name of the trustor.
3. A statement that a breach of the obligation has occurred.
4. A statement that the trustee has elected to proceed under his power of sale.
5. The names of the trustee and the beneficiary.

Within 10 days after the notice of default has been recorded in the county recorder's office, all persons who under Section 2924b of the Civil Code have so requested must be notified by mail that the notice has been filed. If no request for notice is contained in the deed of trust or if no request has been filed, then the notice of default must be published in a newspaper of general circulation once a week for four weeks.

Recent legislation makes it unlawful to take advantage of a property owner in default or foreclosure. The law provides for possible recision of such transactions and provides for strict notice and

NOTICE OF DEFAULT

TO 613 C

as ① _____ under that certain deed of or transfer in trust executed

by _____ , as trustor to

_____ , as trustee and

as beneficiary, dated _____ 19___ , and recorded _____ 19___ ,

in Book _____ , page _____ of Official Records, in the office of the County Recorder of

the _____ County of _____ State of California,

hereby gives notice that a breach of the obligations for which such transfer in trust is security has occurred, the nature of such breach being the failure to ②

_____

and that the beneficiary has declared and does declare that all sums secured by said deed of trust are immediately due and payable and elects to cause the trust property to be sold to satisfy said obligations. In this instrument, whenever the context so requires, the singular number includes the plural.

Dated: _____ _____

   ① "Trustee" or "Beneficiary."

   ② State each item of default such as failure to pay principal, or _____
      installments thereof, interest, taxes, insurance premiums, etc.

_____

_____

_____

(CORPORATION)

STATE OF CALIFORNIA
COUNTY OF _____ } SS.
On _____ before me, the under-
signed, a Notary Public in and for said County and State, personally
appeared _____
known to me to be the _____ President, and _____
_____ , known to me to be
_____ Secretary of the corporation that executed the
within Instrument, known to me to be the persons who executed the
within Instrument on behalf of the corporation therein named, and
acknowledged to me that such corporation executed the within instrument pursuant to its by-laws or a resolution of its board of directors.
WITNESS my hand and official seal.

(Seal)

Signature _____

Name (Typed or Printed)
Notary Public in and for said County and State

(INDIVIDUAL)

STATE OF CALIFORNIA
COUNTY OF _____ } SS.
On _____ before me, the under-
signed, a Notary Public in and for said County and State, personally
appeared _____
_____
_____
_____ , known to me
to be the person___ whose name _____ subscribed to the within
instrument and acknowledged that _____ executed the same.
WITNESS my hand and official seal.

(Seal)

Signature _____

Name (Typed or Printed)
Notary Public in and for said County and State

Application No. _____

FIGURE 12–3

publication requirements with respect to foreclosure resulting from contracts for the sale of goods or home improvements. Such contracts create what is termed an *Unruh* lien, and conveyance of title within 45 days after notice of default is voidable.

A notice of default is illustrated in Chapter 7.

Trustor's right of reinstatement

At any time during the three-month period following recordation of the notice of default, the trustor may reinstate the obligation by paying to the beneficiary:

1. All sums of money due up to that point.
2. Any additional costs incurred by the beneficiary.
3. A small fee to the trustee, usually consisting of .5 percent of the entire unpaid balance of the loan.

If the above is done during the three-month period, the default is cured, and the proceedings are discontinued. The obligation is restored, and the trustor goes back to making his regular periodic payments.

Payment in full

After the three-month period has passed, the right to reinstate is gone, and the trustor must then pay the entire amount of the obligation. If the entire obligation plus necessary costs and expenses are not paid, the property may then be sold by the trustee.

This is not to say that the beneficiary may not allow the trustor to reinstate, but only that beyond the three-month period, the beneficiary does not have to allow reinstatement if he does not wish to.

Notice of sale

Assuming that the beneficiary has decided to proceed with the sale of the property, he must now execute a notice of sale, stating:

1. Time of the sale.
2. Place of the sale.
3. Description of the property and occasion for the sale.

The notice of sale must be published in a newspaper of general circulation either in the city in which the property is located or, if there is no newspaper in the city, then in the judicial district or county. The notice must be published once a week for 20 days—that is, three publications not more than 7 days apart.

The notice of sale must also be posted in a conspicuous place on the property and in a public place. Every city hall has a bulletin board on which such notices are regularly posted. In most areas, when a title insurance company is acting as trustee, a copy of the notice of sale is posted on the premises of the title company.

The sale must be held within the county in which the property is located and may be postponed once or several times if the trustee has good reason to believe that this will best serve the interests of the concerned parties. Often, a sale may be temporarily postponed if it is thought that the trustor may be able to come up with the necessary funds to reinstate the obligation. In most cases, however, the sale is not postponed but is held as scheduled.

The sale

At the time and place specified in the published notice of sale, the trustee or his representative announces the purpose of the sale and identifies the property to be sold. The sale is then officially open to bidding, since the idea is to get the best price possible for the property.

All bids must be on the basis of cash or the equivalent, and only the holder of the debt under foreclosure can offset the amount owing to him without having to put up cash. Thus, the beneficiary can and usually does bid in the amount due him, and if there are no other bidders, the beneficiary obtains the property. If there are other interested purchasers at the sale, the beneficiary begins by bidding in the amount due him, and then bidding by all in attendance continues. Eventually, a high bid is declared and accepted by the trustee or his representative, and a trustee's deed is issued to the purchaser.

The trustee's deed gives to the buyer the title held by the maker of the deed of trust on the date the deed of trust was executed and also any title that may have been acquired afterward. There is, of course, no right of redemption by the former owner, who has now lost the property, and the purchaser is entitled to immediate possession.

Holder of a second loan

Brokers many times have considerable difficulty in convincing a seller to carry back a small second loan. The property owner usually likes to have all cash, since he thinks that in carrying back a second loan he will face a very difficult and complicated situation should the purchaser fail to make the necessary payments on the note.

Actually, the holder of a junior lien has the same rights as the holder of the first loan. Should a purchaser fail to make payments on a second loan, the holder of the second may record a notice of default, go through all the procedures outlined above, and finally effect a sale of the property.

Practically speaking, when a borrower is unable to make a payment on one loan against his property, he generally cannot make the payment on any other loan, so that he is actually in default with regard to both the first and second loans. To protect his interest, the holder of the second loan must bring action to effect the sale of the property and, in the meantime, must make the payments on the first loan but only for the few months required to effect the trustee's sale.

If the holder of the second note allows the holder of the first note to force the sale, the second loan holder may lose all that he has coming to him. If the beneficiary under the first deed of trust becomes the purchaser or if the sale of the property brings only enough to pay off the first loan, then the holder of the second note cannot sue the trustor, since there cannot be any deficiency judgment on a purchase money loan.

Effect of sale on liens

Although most junior liens are eliminated by a trustee's sale, a few are not. Federal tax liens are eliminated by following the procedures stipulated in the Federal Tax Lien Act of 1966. Mechanic's liens are not eliminated if the work of improvement commenced before the date on which the deed of trust was recorded. Also not affected are taxes and assessments against the property, which may be in the form of state, county, or city taxes.

Additional comments on trustee's sales

Since a trustee's sale is the result of a borrower's failure to make the necessary payments, the beneficiary may want to save the expense and time involved in forcing a sale and may enter into an agreement with the buyer-borrower to take back the property and obtain a deed in lieu of foreclosure.

Since the lender is in a very strong position in this type of situation, the courts are always quite concerned that the lender not take any unfair advantage of the borrower. Generally, however, the debt usually approximates the reasonable value of the property, and no additional consideration may be necessary. The borrower may be very pleased to get out from under and will accept a small amount from the beneficiary and execute a deed in his favor. Many brokers follow the recordation of notices of default and approach the borrower and try to effect a sale of the property before it is sold through a trustee's sale.

Title insurance companies are very careful about insuring this type of transaction and usually require special recitals in a deed in lieu of foreclosure.

Possession after sale

One of the most common problems with regard to properties sold at trustee's sales is that of possession by the purchaser. The former owner, by virtue of having failed to make his payments, has lost his property. He will certainly be in a less than cooperative mood as far as his leaving the premises is concerned. If the purchaser is the former beneficiary under the deed of trust, the best type of arrangement is one wherein the beneficiary and trustor have worked out an agreement that will result in some form of orderly procedure for vacating the premises after the trustee's sale. Many times, the purchaser must pay the former owner a sum of money and/or help him to move from the property.

If the purchaser at the trustee's sale is not the former beneficiary, he may purchase the building and then find that the former owner refuses to leave the premises. Since the new owner has not been able to make any prior arrangements with the former owner, a very difficult situation may result. The new owner may have to go through the complicated and time-consuming procedure of having the sheriff forceably evict the former owner. It is very important that anyone contemplating purchase of a property at a trustee's sale give some thought and prior attention, if possible, to the matter of possession.

MORTGAGE FORECLOSURE

California law states that the form of action that may be brought for the recovery of an obligation secured by a mortgage is foreclosure by court action. The object of the foreclosure is to sell the right, title, and interest held in the property by the mortgagor at the time of execution of the mortgage.

Foreclosure sale

The foreclosure sale is made by a commissioner appointed by the court in accordance with the code of civil procedure. The sale must be made in the same manner as sales by a sheriff on execution, and must be made to the highest bidder. A notice of the time and place of the sale must be given in writing, and must describe the property and be posted in a public place in the city where the property is sold. The notice is usually posted at the city hall for the required 20 days. In addition, the notice must be published once a week for 20 days in a newspaper of general circulation, published in the city where the property is located. If no newspaper is published there, then notice must be in a newspaper published in the county, preferably the one closest to the location of the property.

Persons who make bids at the foreclosure sale must bid cash, with the exception of the beneficiary, who can bid in the amount due him without the necessity of putting up cash in this amount. The title is given to the successful bidder and is deemed to relate to the title of the mortgagor as of the date of execution of the security. Except for certain tax liens, intervening liens are eliminated by the foreclosure purchase.

Redemption rights

The mortgagor, or anyone claiming under him, or certain creditors, have a statutory right of redemption. This may be done at any time within 12 months after the sale by paying the purchaser:

1. The price paid by the purchaser at the foreclosure sale.
2. In addition, 1 percent per month.
3. Any taxes or assessments paid by the purchaser.
4. Any reasonable sum for fire insurance, maintenance, upkeep, or repair.
5. Interest on these sums.

It should also be noted that after the foreclosure of a mortgage the mortgagor may remain in possession for the one-year redemption period. The purchaser is entitled to rent and any profits during this period, but cannot generally obtain possession. The restrictive character of mortgage foreclosures as regards the lender and subsequent purchaser is the main reason why the mortgage is seldom used in California and has been replaced by the deed of trust. There is no redemption right after a sale under a deed of trust, and the purchaser gets the right to possession as soon as he receives the trustee's deed.

SECOND TRUST DEEDS AND MORTGAGES

Quite often in the purchase of property, the down payment and proceeds of a first loan are not sufficient to equal the purchase price, and thus, secondary financing in the form of a second trust deed or second mortgage is necessary.

This second loan is generally for a short term and usually carries a higher rate of interest of the related promissory note because of the higher risk factor involved and the junior lien status of the loan. Most second loans are usually written for from three to seven years but can be for any length of time the parties desire.

A second loan is in appearance much the same as the first, but the basic difference is that the second loan is a junior lien and is thus subordinate to the first loan in all respects. A second loan is wiped out by foreclosure of the first if the sale of the property brings only enough to pay off the first loan. Thus, the law gives the holder of the second loan the right of reinstatement. Should the borrower default on his payments, the holder of the second may reinstate the first loan (by assuming the payments) and may bring an action to foreclose or elect to use the power of sale, depending on whether the second loan is in the form of a mortgage or a deed of trust.

EFFECTS AND INCIDENTS OF SECURITY ARRANGEMENTS

Some of the more common incidents of security arrangements will be defined and discussed, as well as certain special rules of law with which all real estate licensees should be familiar. The topics are presented alphabetically rather than in any particular order of importance.

Acceleration clause

A deed of trust or mortgage clause that on the happening of a certain event gives the lender the right to immediately demand payment of all sums owed to him is called an acceleration or alienation clause. Examples of an acceleration clause are *(a)* a statement in a mortgage or deed of trust that should the borrower default on payments for a certain period of time the entire obligation shall become immediately due and payable, or *(b)* a statement in a second trust deed, called a "due-on-sale clause," which makes the note immediately due and payable if the borrower should sell the property prior to the end of the note term.

A 1978 California Supreme Court decision (*Wellenkamp* v. *Bank of America*) now prohibits California chartered lending institutions from accelerating an existing loan upon sale of a property without showing impairment of their security. If the buyer is qualified to make the payments, such loans can now be assumed. In 1982, the California Supreme Court further stated that the Wellenkamp decision rules apply equally to private as well as institutional lenders, and to commercial as well as residential property.

The United States Supreme Court, in a 1982 decision (*De La Cuesta* v. *Fidelity Savings and Loan*) has ruled that federally chartered lending institutions are exempt from the Wellenkamp ruling and can, if they wish, call any loan containing a due-on-sale clause when the property is sold.

Agreement of sale (land contract)

The agreement-of-sale form is more commonly known as a land contract and may also be referred to as an installment and contract, contract of sale, or installment sale contract. This form is basically a type of contract wherein the buyer makes payments to the seller over a certain period of time. The deed is given by the seller either on the final payment of the purchase price or when a specified amount has been paid, at which time the seller agrees to execute and deliver a deed to the property. Further, the buyer does not receive a policy of title insurance until he receives the deed.

Often, this agreement-of-sale form is used when the seller is, in effect, financing the transaction himself and the buyer is not providing the financing by borrowing from a lending institution. Builders may use this form, or it may be used by sellers for buyers who have little or no down payment. The buyer frequently is actually paying off the down payment, since he receives no deed for some time.

While this type of agreement, essentially an installment contract for the purchase of real estate, may have certain advantages to the seller, it has many distinct disadvantages to the buyer. In the usual real estate transaction, the buyer receives a deed from the seller and a policy of title insurance when he buys the property, but here he does not.

During the past few years, there have been numerous California court decisions concerning this form and the equitable interest in the property obtained by the buyer. These decisions frequently have so modified the intent of the form that the seller has lost many of the advantages he apparently had over the buyer, and he would have been better off to use the ordinary trust deed arrangement. Of particular importance is the recent decision of the California Supreme Court in the *Tucker* v. *Lassen Savings and Loan Association* case. The court held that an acceleration clause or "due on sale" clause with respect to an existing loan cannot automatically be exercised when the borrower sells the property using a contract of sale payable in installments.

In distinguishing between an "outright sale" with transfer of title and a land sale contract, the Supreme Court observed that in the normal case, the seller having received a small down payment and retaining legal title, has a considerable interest in maintaining the property until having been paid in full, thus preserving the first lender's security without impairment.

The court held that in the land contract situation, a "due-on-sale" clause can only validly be enforced when the lender can demonstrate a threat to one of his legitimate interests: the preserving of the security from waste or depreciation or the guarding against having to resort to the security upon default.

The Supreme Court thus has created restrictions upon enforcement of a "due-on-sale" clause in land sales contract situations, but one should not assume that a "sale" which would otherwise trigger the right to accelerate can be avoided by the device of a land sale contract. Each transaction must stand the test of the buyer's qualifications, the absence of impairment of the lender's security, and the seller's retention of legal title pending payment in full.

Proper use of the land contract, however, will permit transactions which, prior to the decision of the court, may have been precluded. A real estate licensee may negotiate such transactions but should refrain from preparing a land sale contract and refer this function to the attorneys of the parties.

All-inclusive trust deed

An all-inclusive trust deed, commonly referred to as an overlapping or wraparound deed of trust, is an instrument that includes, and yet is subordinate to, existing trust deeds. It is in some respects similar to a contract of sale, except that the title to the property is transferred and may be insured by a title insurance company.

When a note secured by an all-inclusive deed of trust is used, the buyer is the trustor and the seller is the beneficiary. Since the seller is the trustor on prior existing liens, the all-inclusive deed of trust cannot be used if such liens have a due-on-sale clause and provision in an existing note and deed of trust.

Because of the complexities involved, competent legal counsel should be consulted in connection with the use and preparation of the all-inclusive deed of trust.

Assignment of debt

When a note secured by a mortgage or deed of trust is assigned by the creditor to another, it carries with it the security. An assignment of the mortgage or deed of trust without the note transfers nothing to the assignee. When a note is transferred, the transferee is entitled to the security.

An assignment of a mortgage or deed of trust may be recorded, and this recordation gives constructive notice to all persons. When the assignment of the mortgage has been recorded and the note transferred, the debtor is not protected if he pays the original creditor.

"Assumption of" versus "subject to"

When a property is sold or exchanged and the existing mortgage or trust deed is to be transferred to the purchaser, he may either "assume" the existing obligation or take the property "subject to" the existing obligation.

When a purchaser assumes an existing loan, he accepts full responsibility for repayment with the consent of the existing lender who must approve the assumption.

If the buyer takes subject to the existing obligation, he is responsible for making the necessary payments if he wants to eventually receive clear title to the property, but the seller remains legally liable for the promissory note. If the buyer fails to make the necessary payments, then the seller (former owner) will be held responsible for the obligation. Further, if one assumes an obligation, he may be liable for a deficiency judgment if conditions will allow one; but if he purchases subject to the obligation, he cannot be held liable for a deficiency judgment.

Chattel mortgage

A chattel mortgage is a contract whereby certain personal property is made security for a debt. It must be in writing, executed and acknowledged, and must be recorded in the office of the county recorder. It is but one of a number of personal property security devices.

In 1965, the Uniform Commercial Code (UCC) became law in California. The UCC regulates personal property security devices and recommends the use of an instrument called a security agreement. Since enactment of the UCC, the security agreement rather than a chattel mortgage has generally been used in connection with the sale of business opportunities when a lien is to be given on the personal property of a business. In addition, the UCC requires that a financing statement be filed in connection with a personal property security transaction.

Although the security agreement device seems to be replacing the chattel mortgage with regard to business opportunities, the broker should still be aware of the different classifications of personal property and the fact that, in certain cases, the chattel mortgage is still occasionally used, as well as a conditional sales agreement or a bill of sale accompanied by a note. A further discussion of the UCC and an illustration of a security agreement, will be found in Chapter 21.

Deficiency judgment

Aaron defaults on a $150,000 note and deed of trust held by Baker. At a subsequent sale, the property is sold for $143,000, leaving Baker with a deficiency of $7,000. Baker may wish to go into court seeking to obtain a deficiency judgment against Aaron for $7,000. If the property in question is a house, and the money was borrowed by Aaron for the purchase of this house, Baker will not be able to obtain a deficiency judgment. No deficiency judgment is allowed if *(a)* the security is a purchase money mortgage or trust deed, and *(b)* the remedy of foreclosure is accomplished by a trustee's sale.

Hypothecation

To hypothecate a piece of property means to give it as security without the necessity of giving up possession of it. Thus, when a purchaser executes a note and deed of trust for the money to purchase the property, he is said to have hypothecated his property in compliance with the terms of the deed of trust.

Impound or trust account

Impounds are moneys accumulated in a special account called an impound or trust account. These moneys are used to pay certain expenses on the property when they become due, usually taxes and insurance. Many conventional lenders require the establishment of such a special account in connection with the making of a loan for the purchase of real property, and a portion of the payment made each month by the borrower is set aside in the impound account. FHA and VA loans require such an account. The rationale given by lenders for the establishment of such impounds is that the monthly accumulation of these funds will allow for payment of taxes and insurance without the necessity of the borrower's having to come up suddenly with the required amounts at one particular time.

The California Civil Code states that with respect to single-family, owner-occupied dwellings, lenders cannot require impound accounts as a condition of the loan unless such impounds are required by state or federal regulations, such as a loan guaranteed by the VA or insured by the FHA; a loan exceeding 90 percent of the appraised value of the property; or where the borrower fails to pay two consecutive tax installments on the property prior to their delinquency dates.

Lender and borrower can mutually agree to an impound account if, prior to execution of the loan, the lender has furnished the borrower a statement in writing that the account is not required as a condition of the loan and that interest will not be paid on impounded funds.

Lien priorities

Section 2897 of the Civil Code states that different liens on the same piece of property generally have priority according to their time of creation and subject to the operation of the recording laws. Certain liens, such as tax liens and mechanic's liens, are given preferential treatment. Notice is an important element in the determination of priority; it may be actual or constructive through recordation. The lien created by a purchase money mortgage or purchase money trust deed has priority over all other liens created by or against the purchaser, subject to the operation of the recording laws.

Offset statement

When a purchaser buys a property and assumes or takes subject to existing obligation, he should receive an offset statement from the property owner or owner of the lien against the property (the lender). This statement should set forth the current status, terms, and conditions of the existing liens against the property.

Open-end loan

An open-end mortgage or trust deed is one that allows for future advances on the original loan using the same instruments as security. An example is that of a buyer who purchases a home in need of renovation and modernization and enters into an agreement with the lender that, upon completion of certain pre-agreed-upon work, the lender will increase the amount of the original loan. If a loan is not an open-end loan, then in order to borrow additional funds at a later date, an owner may be put in a position of having to negotiate a new loan, pay additional fees and perhaps a higher rate of interest.

Partial release clause

Generally speaking, an obligation must be paid in full before the mortgagee or trustee can be compelled to release any part of his security. It is possible, however, for a provision to be made in the mortgage or deed of trust for the release of certain portions of the security when a certain amount of the obligation has been paid.

This device is often used by subdividers who are developing residential property and want to release certain lots when the purchaser's total payments have reached a predetermined amount.

Points

Discounts, or points, as they are usually called, are paid to lenders and are, in effect, prepaid interest. This method is used by many lenders in order to adjust the effective rate of interest so that it is equal to or nearly equal to the prevailing rate charged on conventional loans. The discounts (points) are absorbed mostly by the sellers, since under FHA-insured or VA-guaranteed loans, buyers may only be charged 1 percent. This 1 percent is called a loan origination fee and is used to cover the expense of obtaining FHA or VA approval.

In a tight money market, when conventional

loan interest rates are high, the seller will usually have to pay a number of points to the lender in order to obtain the necessary loan for the buyer. A point is equivalent to 1 percent; thus, if the lender were to require that the seller pay three points for advancing an $80,000 loan to a prospective buyer under an FHA-insured loan, the seller will have to pay $2,400. Each point charged adds approximately ⅛ percent to the yield on the loan, and thus, a lender who makes a loan at an annual interest rate of 14¾ percent and charges the borrower a 2 point loan fee is, in effect, increasing the yield of the loan to 15 percent.

With regard to conventional financing, there is no restriction on the number of points that may be charged the borrower. This charge for making a loan at most institutions is called a *loan fee, service charge, commitment fee,* or merely *points to the buyer.* This loan fee will be a part of the buyer's closing costs and will vary depending on the type of property involved and the particular lending institution. Although the buyer and seller may agree that each will pay a portion of the loan fee, the general practice is for the borrower (buyer) to pay all of the fee for the loan.

Prepayment penalties and lock-in provisions

A prepayment penalty is a charge made by a lender for paying all or part of the outstanding principal amount of a loan before the due date. This situation generally arises in connection with the sale of property on which the seller still owes a sum of money to a lender. Prepayment penalty charges differ among various lenders. Many savings and loan associations, for instance, charge a penalty of three to six months' interest on 80 percent of the outstanding balance of the loan.

With respect to residential property of four units or less and a single family, owner-occupied residence, the law allows prepayment of 20 percent of the loan in any year without penalty. If the loan is fully paid within five years of inception, a penalty not to exceed six months' interest on 80 percent of the loan balance is allowed, but no prepayment penalty is allowed after five years.

A lock-in period is a period from inception of a loan during which the lender will not allow prepayment. Customarily, savings and loan associations and banks have not imposed a lock-in period in connection with loans made by them, while such lock-in periods have been imposed by life insurance companies, pension funds, and certain savings banks. Since procedures among lenders vary, the borrower should investigate and make himself aware of any such provision which may be present in connection with a contemplated loan.

Section 2954.9 of the Civil Code states that any loan secured by residential property of four units or less can be prepaid at any time and the beneficiary can charge a prepayment penalty. With respect to an installment sale, a seller may restrict prepayment within the calendar year of the sale.

Purchase money trust deed or mortgage

When a borrower gives a mortgage or deed of trust to a lender for money used to purchase property, the mortgage or deed of trust is called a "purchase money" mortgage or "purchase money" deed of trust. Also, if a seller carries back all or a portion of the purchase price and receives a note secured by a mortgage or deed of trust, these become a purchase money mortgage or purchase money deed of trust. Whether money borrowed is or is not purchase money is so clearly defined because under California law, a lender cannot obtain a deficiency judgment if the sale of the property does not bring enough to pay off the note. There is an exception to this rule, however: a third-party lender may secure a deficiency judgment when the purchase money loan was made on a building of four or more units or designed for housing more than four families.

Request for notice

Any lender or other individual interested in a particular deed of trust or mortgage with power of sale can make sure of being informed if a notice of default or a notice of sale is recorded. The holder of the second loan should record a request for notice with the county recorder. Some forms of mortgages and deeds of trust have such a request incorporated into the form, so that after recordation, a separate request for notice is not necessary.

The request for notice shown in Figure 12–4 must contain the recording data applying to the deed of trust or mortgage and the name and address of the person who wants the information. The recorder will enter this on the record of the deed of trust or mortgage, and if subsequently any notice of default or sale is recorded, the person named in the request will have to be notified.

RECORDING REQUESTED BY

AND WHEN RECORDED MAIL TO

Name

Street
Address

City &
State

———————————— SPACE ABOVE THIS LINE FOR RECORDER'S USE ————————

Request for Notice
UNDER SECTION 2924b CIVIL CODE

TO 422 C (9-67)

In accordance with Section 2924b, Civil Code, request is hereby made that a copy of any Notice of Default and a copy of any Notice of Sale under the Deed of Trust recorded as Instrument No._____ on_____ _____, in book_____, page_____, Official Records of_____ County, California, and describing land therein as

Executed by_____, as Trustor, in which_____is named as Beneficiary, and_____, as Trustee, be mailed to_____ at_____
     Number and Street

_____
     City and State

Dated_____   _____

STATE OF CALIFORNIA,
COUNTY OF_____ }SS.   _____
On_____before me, the under-   _____
signed, a Notary Public in and for said State, personally appeared
_____   _____
_____   _____
_____, known to me
to be the person____ whose name_____subscribed to the within
instrument and acknowledged that_____executed the same.
WITNESS my hand and official seal.

Signature_____
          Name (Typed or Printed)
*If executed by a Corporation the Corporation Form of
Acknowledgment must be used.*   (This area for official notarial seal)

Title Order No._____   Escrow or Loan No._____

FIGURE 12–4

Request for reconveyance

When a purchaser borrows money to buy property and signs a note secured by a deed of trust, the note is for the money borrowed, and the deed of trust puts the property up as security for the note. When the note has been paid, the lender-beneficiary requests the trustee to record a full reconveyance.

The deed of trust illustrated in Figure 12–2 contains the form of such a request. Figure 12–5 shows a full reconveyance which is prepared by the trustee and recorded. This gives evidence that the note has been paid, and the lien against the property is removed. Whatever interest the lender had in the property is thus reconveyed to the borrower-trustor.

Subordination clause

A subordination clause is an agreement written into a mortgage or deed of trust that provides that said obligation may be subordinated in priority to an anticipated future lien. The subordination agreement may be a separate instrument relating only to such subordination or it may be incorporated into the instrument, such as a trust deed, which is to become subordinate.

A subordination may be specific, giving priority to one or more specified encumbrances. Or it may be an automatic future subordination, which automatically provides priority—without further action of the holder of the encumbrance to be subordinated—for one or more encumbrances, the terms and conditions of which are specified in the subordination agreement, to be created in the future. An automatic subordination agreement, if any, is ordinarily contained in the trust deed that is to be subordinated.

The use of a subordination agreement is usually associated with the development of unimproved land as follows. Builder Brown wants to purchase from Farmer Franklin a 10-acre unimproved parcel of land on which to build a number of houses for sale to the public. Brown does not want to tie up a large amount of capital in purchase of the land, so he arranges with Franklin to give him a modest down payment and then execute a note and deed of trust in favor of Franklin for the balance of the purchase price. Having obtained title to the land, Brown now proceeds to Banker Baldwin for a construction loan. Baldwin will refuse to make the loan, since most lending institutions are prohibited by law from making any real estate loans not secured by first liens. In this case, the first lien is held by Farmer Franklin. Thus, when he originally negotiated with Franklin for the purchase of the land, Brown should have had incorporated into the agreement a subordination clause that would allow him later to obtain the construction loan and have it take priority as a first lien.

Most sellers in such a situation will agree to this condition, since the purchase price they receive depends in large measure on the future development and improvement contemplated by the purchaser.

CREATIVE FINANCING

The recent high interest, tight money market, has brought into renewed use the term, *creative or alternative financing*. It refers to other than traditional methods and forms of finance, some of which are still in a discussion stage, while others are being used in various parts of the state. A few of the more common are as follows:

FLIP or graduated payment loan

The Flexible Loan Insurance Program (FLIP) or graduated payment loan, already introduced in parts of California, allows smaller than usual loan payments to initially be made, with small increases in later years. After approximately five years, a payment level is reached which remains fixed for the loan term. It allows a buyer to have smaller payments at the beginning of the purchase and larger payments in later years when he can better afford to make such payments. With such an arrangement, more new buyers can qualify for financing and attain the ability to purchase a property.

Portable loan

As the name implies, such a loan is written to be portable and can be transferred from an old to a new property without any additional charges or increase of interest rate. Existing loans can often be assumed by a purchaser, but with a portable loan, a seller gains the same type of advantage by being able to take the loan with him and transfer it to a newly acquired property.

Reverse loan

A reverse loan enables older homeowners to borrow against their home equity and receive

RECORDING REQUESTED BY

AND WHEN RECORDED MAIL TO

Name

Street
Address

City &
State

——————————— SPACE ABOVE THIS LINE FOR RECORDER'S USE ———————————

TITLE ORDER NO.   TITLE OFFICER

TO 430—1 C

FULL RECONVEYANCE

TITLE INSURANCE AND TRUST COMPANY, a California corporation, as duly appointed Trustee under Deed of Trust hereinafter referred to, having received from holder of the obligations thereunder a written request to reconvey, reciting that all sums secured by said Deed of Trust have been fully paid, and said Deed of Trust and the note or notes secured thereby having been surrendered to said Trustee for cancellation, does hereby RECONVEY, without warranty, to the person or persons legally entitled thereto, the estate now held by it thereunder. Said Deed of Trust was executed by

Trustor,

and recorded in the official records of   County, California, as follows:

REC.   AS INSTR. NO.   IN BOOK   PAGE

DESC.

In Witness Whereof, Title Insurance and Trust Company, as such Trustee, has caused its corporate name and seal to be hereto affixed by its Assistant Secretary, thereunto duly authorized on the date shown in the acknowledgement certificate shown below.

TITLE INSURANCE AND TRUST COMPANY, as such Trustee

By_____
Assistant Secretary

STATE OF CALIFORNIA, }
COUNTY OF_____ } SS.

On_____, before me, the undersigned, a Notary Public in and for said State, personally appeared_____, known to me to be an Assistant Secretary of TITLE INSURANCE AND TRUST COMPANY, the corporation that executed the foregoing instrument as such Trustee, and known to me to be the person who executed said instrument on behalf of the corporation therein named, and acknowledged to me that such corporation executed the same as such Trustee. WITNESS my hand and official seal.

Signature_____

(This area for official notarial seal)   Name (Typed or Printed)

FIGURE 12–5

monthly payments needed to meet living costs and expenses. It can provide a monthly income for the homeowner without the necessity of having to sell the property. The amount advanced to the borrower plus interest charged is cumulatively totaled, and the lender is eventually repaid at such time as the property is sold or when the borrower expires.

Rollover loan

A rollover or renegotiated rate loan permits a lender to renegotiate the rate of interest with the borrower every three to five years. For practical purposes, it results in a 5-year loan with monthly payments figured on a 25- or 30-year basis. The Federal Home Loan Bank has approved such a loan limiting the rate of interest increase or decrease and specifying certain regulations with respect to late payment and prohibition of renewal fees. On a rollover loan with a 30-year term, the rate of interest increase or decrease is limited to 5 percent during the term of the loan, and the rate cannot fluctuate any more than ½ percent a year.

Shared appreciation loan

A shared appreciation loan is designed to offer a fixed-rate, long-term fully amortized loan with below-market interest rates and lender participation in property value appreciation. The lender's percentage share in appreciation is dependent on the amount of interest rate relief, expected appreciation of the property and projected future rates of inflation.

For receiving lower interest rates, certain purchasers of property may choose to accept the resultant lower monthly payment and share part of the future appreciation on their property with the bank or savings and loan association making the loan.

Swing loan

A swing loan is a short-term loan on a borrowers principal residence to enable him to have a down payment and closing costs to buy another residence. After the purchase, the homeowner can sell the old residence and pay off the loan. Savings and loan associations can make such an unamortized interim loan to enable a borrower to make the down payment on a home purchase which

they are financing. The loan can be in any amount which, together with the amount of any existing loan, does not exceed 80 percent of the fair market value of the property. In addition, the term of the swing loan is limited to 12 months with no prepayment penalty allowed. The borrower must use the loan proceeds to purchase a residence to be occupied as his principal residence, and the swing loan must be secured by a trust deed on a borrowers principal residence at the time the loan is made.

Variable interest rate loan

A variable or adjustable interest rate loan (VIR) is a loan in which the interest rate is not fixed and can increase or decrease according to a standard index. California banks and savings and loan associations offering a variable rate loan adjust the rate of interest based on the average cost of money to the lenders from the Federal Home Loan Bank (FHLB). The cost index is issued twice a year by the FHLB in San Francisco.

The law limits rate changes to once during any six-month period with a ¼ percent increase limit and an overall limit during the loan term of 2½ percent of the original loan rate. On notification of an increase, a borrower may prepay all or part of the loan with no prepayment penalty allowed. If the cost index falls, the lender must reduce the rate of interest. Such loans are considered by lenders to be a more equitable method of financing home purchases because the borrower does not have to pay a higher rate of interest to subsidize others who purchased years ago at lower interest rates.

Recent Federal Home Loan Bank rules now allow lenders to adjust to changes of interest rate and inflation by removal of yearly and term interest rate ceilings and instead substituting various indexes. The rules also require strict consumer disclosure procedures.

TRUTH-IN-LENDING LAW

On July 1, 1969, the Truth-in-Lending Law went into effect. The act is intended to enable consumers to know, through standardized language, exactly what they are paying in credit charges. Federal Reserve Regulation Z was issued under this law for the purpose of its implementation. The law does not set limits on interest or regulate trade practices. These are governed by individual state laws and may differ among the various states. Regulation Z merely requires that the consumer be fully advised of all of the details of his credit purchase. This requirement also applies to any advertising, in whatever form, that the seller engages in.

While the Truth-in-Lending Law regulates consumer credit of every form, we will, in our discussion, be concerned only with its effect upon real estate transactions. An extensive treatment of the law and Regulation Z, including sample forms, charts, and illustrations, may be obtained free by writing to the Federal Trade Commission, P.O.B. 36005, San Francisco 94102, and asking for the publication "What You Ought to Know about Truth-in-Lending." Supplementary material in connection with Regulation Z may also be obtained by writing to the Federal Reserve Bank, San Francisco, California.

Real estate transactions

All real estate credit in any amount is covered under Regulation Z when it is to an individual consumer. Any credit transaction that involves any type of security interest in real estate of a consumer is covered. Credit extended to corporations, partnerships, trusts, and governmental agencies is not covered by this act, nor does it apply to credit extended for business or commercial purposes, that is, nonconsumer purposes.

The act does require that any persons who, in the ordinary course of business regularly extend, or offer to extend, or arrange, or offer to arrange, for the extension of consumer credit, must make certain disclosures to the consumer.

Disclosure

The "finance charge" and the "annual percentage rate" are the two most important disclosures required. They tell the borrower how much he is paying for his credit and its cost in percentage terms. An exception is made in the sale of dwellings; the total finance charge in terms of dollars paid by both buyer and seller need not be stated. The annual percentage rate, however, must be stated clearly.

The finance charge. In general, the finance charge is the total of all costs imposed by a creditor and paid either directly or indirectly by the borrower or another party, such as points the seller may be required to pay in an FHA transaction as an incident to the extension of credit. It includes, in addition to interest, such costs as points or discounts, loan fees, finder's fees, inspection fees, timepiece differential, FHA mortgage insurance premiums, or even premiums on life insurance that a lender might require. The finance charge, however, does not include for purposes of real property transactions such charges as premiums or charges for title reports or title insurance, registration fees imposed by law, surveys, appraisal or inspection fees, transfer taxes, credit reports, legal fees for preparation of documents pursuant to a settlement, escrow, notary fees, utility costs, or payments to cover taxes not yet due and payable, but if any of these charges are included in the amount to be financed and are paid out of loan proceeds, they must be itemized and set forth separately in the disclosure statement.

The annual percentage rate. The annual percentage rate not only includes "interest" but also represents the relationship of the total finance charge to the total amount to be financed. Where points and other fees are involved, the rate shown will be higher than merely interest. A buyer who is told that the interest rate on his loan is to be 9 percent may wonder why it is shown as 9¼ percent on the disclosure statement. His broker will have to explain that the loan will carry an interest rate of 9 percent but that the annual percentage rate shown on the disclosure statement includes the total cost imposed by the lender for making the loan, which includes not only the interest on the sum borrowed but also the capitalized value of charges which must be paid by the borrower or anyone else at the inception of the loan.

The disclosure statement. A disclosure statement used by many savings and loan associations is shown in Figure 12–6, and a CAR form for brokers use is shown in Figure 12–7, and the law says that such disclosure shall be made before the credit transaction is consummated. Consummation may be generally defined here as the offer of credit to the borrower and his acceptance of the terms. In the normal real estate transaction, the disclosure of credit information would accompany the loan commitment. It would thus be after the purchase contract had been entered into but before close of escrow and consummation of the transaction. Certain problems arise in connection with second loans where, under the law, the lender may or may not be required to comply with the law. This will be discussed later in connection with the real estate licensee's role under Regulation Z of the Truth-in-Lending Law.

ABC SAVINGS AND LOAN ASSOCIATION
ADDRESS
NOTICE TO CUSTOMER REQUIRED BY FEDERAL LAW AND
FEDERAL RESERVE REGULATION Z
(To Be Executed in Duplicate)

CS&LL FORM Z-1
PURCHASE LOAN ON DWELLING

NAME OF BORROWER(S) _____ LOAN NO. _____

MAILING ADDRESS _____ LOAN AMOUNT $_____

A. Payments for principal and interest @_____% per annum on this transaction shall be in _____ monthly installments of $_____ each, beginning on the _____ day of _____, 19___, and due on the _____ day of each month thereafter.

B. The FINANCE CHARGE on this transaction will begin to accrue on _____
_____

C. CHARGES NOT PART OF FINANCE COSTS

	Pd. by Cash	Pd. from Loan
1. Title ins. premium	$_____	$_____
2. Recording fees	_____	_____
3. Appraisal fees	_____	_____
4. Credit report	_____	_____
5. Notary	_____	_____
6. To impounds	_____	_____
7. Prepare documents	_____	_____
8. _____	_____	_____
9. _____	_____	_____
Total Charges	$	$
Net proceeds to borrower		$

E. AMOUNT FINANCED $

D. PREPAID FINANCE CHARGE
(Paid from any source)

1. Origination fee	$_____
2. Loan fee pd. by buyer	_____
3. Int. prepaid (days)	_____
4. Mtge. ins. ( )	_____
5. _____	_____
6. _____	_____
7. _____	_____
8. _____	_____
9. _____	_____
PREPAID FINANCE CHARGE	$

NOTE: Any figures in Sections C & D above with asterisks are estimated

F. **ANNUAL PERCENTAGE RATE** _____%

G. LATE CHARGE — In the event a monthly payment is not paid by due date, the association will make the following charge:
_____

H. PREPAYMENT PRIVILEGE — Borrower may prepay the loan in whole or in part in the following manner and under the following conditions: _____
_____

I. SECURITY INTEREST — The association's security interest in this transaction is a trust deed covering real property and improvements located _____ and certain other rights and property relating thereto, all as described in the trust deed, a copy of which will be provided. The trust deed secures approved future advances and other indebtedness, the terms of which are described therein. The trust deed also covers after-acquired property located on or attached to the described real property. A security agreement _____ be taken on furniture, fixtures, and equipment situated therein.

J. INSURANCE — Fire and other hazard insurance protecting the property, if written in connection with this loan, may be obtained by borrower through any person of his choice, provided, however, the association may, for reasonable cause, refuse to accept an insurer on any such insurance which is required. If borrower desires property insurance to be obtained through the association's designated agency, the cost will be set forth in a separate insurance statement furnished by the association.

I(We) hereby acknowledge receiving and reading a completed copy of this disclosure along with copies of the documents provided. Notwithstanding any existing agreement with the association to the contrary, the association and each borrower understand that this is not an offer or commitment of the association to lend.

_____   _____
Association   Borrower

By _____
                                                     _____
                        Title   Borrower

Date _____   Date _____

FIGURE 12–6

REAL ESTATE LOAN DISCLOSURE STATEMENT
CALIFORNIA ASSOCIATION OF REALTORS® STANDARD FORM

BROKER/ARRANGER OF CREDIT: CREDITOR:

_____   _____
(NAME)   (NAME)

_____   _____
(ADDRESS)   (ADDRESS)

Purpose of Loan: _____

I.   Loan in the amount of $ _____ is to be secured by a note and Deed of Trust in favor of Creditor on property
      located at _____,
      which is □ is not □ expected to be the location of the Borrower's principal residence. (NOTE: If it is, a Notice of Right to
      Cancel must be provided unless this transaction involves a first lien for the purchase or initial construction of a dwelling.)
          The Deed of Trust may secure additional advances and may cover after-acquired property. The loan may also be secured
      by an assignment of proceeds from any required insurance protecting the property.

II.   Charges included which are not part of the Finance Charge:
                      1. Appraisal . . . . $ _____
                      2. Credit report . . . . $ _____
                      3. Notary . . . . $ _____
                      4. Recording . . . . $ _____
                      5. Title insurance . . . . $ _____
                      6. Document preparation . . . . $ _____
                      7. Property insurance . . . . $ _____
                      8. Termite inspection . . . . $ _____
                      9. Other_____ $ _____
                                       (DESCRIBE)
                          Total Charges . . . . . $ _____

      Property insurance may be obtained by Borrower through any person of his choice. If it is to be purchased through
      Broker or Creditor, the cost appears at Item II. 7 above.
      Credit life and disability insurance are not required to obtain this loan.

III. FINANCE CHARGE:
      A. Prepaid **FINANCE CHARGE**
                          Loan Broker's commission . . . . $ _____
                          Loan escrow fee . . . . $ _____
                          Other _____ $ _____
                          _____ $ _____
                                       (DESCRIBE)   (Total of A) $ _____
      B. Interest for period of loan . . . . $ _____
                                               FINANCE CHARGE   (A + B) $ _____
      Finance Charge accrues from _____ , 19_____ .

IV.   AMOUNT FINANCED:
      Amount of loan from Item I (includes all charges in Item II which are not paid in cash) . . . $ _____
      Less Prepaid **Finance Charge** (Item III. A) . . . . $ _____
                                                              AMOUNT FINANCED $ _____

V.   **ANNUAL PERCENTAGE RATE:**_____ %

VI.   PAYMENT TERMS:
      Payable in _____ payments of principal and interest as follows: _____
      monthly installments of $ _____ each, beginning _____ , 19_____ , and a
      final/balloon payment of $ _____ due on _____ , 19 _____ .
                                      TOTAL OF PAYMENTS (Item I + Item III. B) $ _____
      There are no arrangements for refinancing balloon payments.
          If any payment is not made within _____days after it is due, a late charge must be paid by Borrower,
      as follows: _____ .
      In addition, Creditor has the option to accelerate the indebtedness and to declare all payments immediately due
      and payable.
          In the event of acceleration or other prepayment in full, unaccrued interest is cancelled and a default or prepayment
      charge will be computed as follows: _____

                                          **I HAVE READ AND RECEIVED A COMPLETED COPY
                                          OF THIS STATEMENT.**

Date _____ , 19_____ .   _____
*IMPORTANT NOTE: (Borrower)
Asterisk denotes an estimate.   _____
                                             (Borrower)
                                             FORM LD-11

FIGURE 12–7

The following disclosures must be made:

1. The date on which the finance charges begin to accrue if it is different from the date of transaction.
2. Annual percentage rate of the finance charge.
3. Number, amount, and due dates or periods of payments scheduled to repay the indebtedness and,"except in the case of a loan secured by a first lien (or equivalent) on a dwelling to finance the purchase of that dwelling, or, in the case of credit sale of a dwelling," the sum of all these payments, using the term *total of payments*.
4. The method of computing the amount of any default or delinquency charge.
5. A description of any penalty charge that may be imposed by the creditor for prepayment of the principal sum.
6. Total amount of the finance charge, individually itemized, except in the case of a first mortgage lien given to finance the purchase of a dwelling.
7. Total amount of credit, including all charges, individually itemized, which are included in the amount of credit extended but which are not part of the finance charge, using the term *amount financed*.
8. Any finance charges, such as points and the like, including those paid out of loan proceeds, such as a discount, and any deposit balance or investment which the creditor required the borrower to make and which must either be paid by the borrower or another at settlement or before proceeds are disbursed, using the terms *prepaid finance charge* and *required deposit balance* as applicable.
9. The total finance charge,"except in the case of a loan secured by a first lien, or equivalent security interest, on a dwelling made to finance the purchase of that dwelling."
10. A description of any security interest retained by the creditor.
11. For a credit sale, land contract, or any others in which the credit is extended or arranged by the seller, the cash price, total down payment itemized to show cash and trade-in, and the unpaid balance of the cash price must be disclosed.

It should be noted that an important exception exists under the law. If circumstances require the issuance of a disclosure statement, the total amount of all monthly payments and the total finance charge need not be disclosed in connection with a purchase money first mortgage, or equivalent, to finance the construction or acquisition of a dwelling. Disclosure is required with regard to loans, secured or otherwise; to finance acquisition of raw acreage or building lots; refinancings; assumptions where the lender approves the new purchaser in writing; and certain second loans even though the first loan in the same transaction may be exempt from the requirement.

Right to rescind

The law gives the buyer the right to call off and cancel a credit transaction involving a security interest in any real property used or expected to be used as his principle residence. He has three business days after the credit contract is consummated or the disclosure statement is given, whichever is later, to rescind.

Excepted from this provision are purchase money first mortgages used to finance the acquisition or construction of a dwelling or the assumption of such an obligation. Thus, the purchaser has a right to cancel any credit transaction in which the lender takes back some security interest unless it is a first mortgage or assumption of a first mortgage given to finance the purchase or construction of a dwelling in which the buyer lives or expects to live. A contract of sale (also called a land contract or agreement of sale) is considered the equivalent of a first lien and is therefore not rescindable.

The right of recision requirement will not have any effect on second mortgages taken back by sellers who do not, in the regular course of business, extend credit. A person who does not regularly extend consumer credit in the course of his business is not considered a "creditor" and is exempt from compliance with the Truth-in-Lending Law, and therefore does not have to provide a disclosure statement or right to rescind.

If a second loan is taken by one who is deemed to be a "creditor" under the law, such as a builder, real estate licensee, institutional investor, or a private investor who invests in such loans primarily for income, the Truth-in-Lending Law will fully apply to the transaction and the right to rescind will exist.

Recision form. Whenever a borrower has the right to rescind a transaction, the creditor must give notice of the fact to the customer by furnishing him with two copies of a formal notice such as that shown in Figure 12–8. A customer may rescind a transaction by signing and dating the notice to cancel which he receives from the creditor and either *(a)* mailing the notice to the creditor at the address shown on the notice or *(b)* delivering the notice to the creditor at the address shown on the notice either personally, by messenger, or by other agents. A customer may also rescind by sending a telegram to the creditor at the address shown on the notice and stating that he has decided to cancel and also identifying in brief the transaction involved.

A customer who cancels a transaction will not be held liable for any finance charge or other type of charge, and any security interest acquired becomes void. The creditor, within 10 days after receiving notice that the purchaser has decided to rescind, must return any deposit money received and terminate any security interest created.

A creditor should allow a sufficient time after the required three-day period for receipt of a letter or telegram which the customer may have sent. During the three-day period, the creditor must not take any action to perform under the contract since such action may be wasteful of time and effort should the customer decide to cancel. The law provides that the use of printed forms for the purpose of allowing a waiver of right of recision is prohibited. Waiver of right of recision is allowed in certain cases, but this can only be accomplished by the customer's submitting to the creditor a dated and signed personal statement modifying or waiving his right of recision.

Joint owners. Where joint ownership is involved and the right of recision exists, the right may be exercised by any one of the joint owners and applies to all of them. Where a modification or waiver of the right of recision exists, all joint owners must sign the statement required.

Where there are joint owners, the right to receive disclosures and notice of the right of recision, the right to rescind, and the need to sign a modification of waiver of such right, apply only to those joint owners who are parties to the transaction.

Advertising. Regulation Z of Truth-in-Lending affects the use of credit terms in advertising the sale of residential real property. It is permissible to advertise in general terms, such as "low downpayment," "liberal terms available," or "FHA–VA financing available." Any finance charge, if mentioned, must be stated as "annual percentage rate," using that term.

The advertisement may state the annual percentage rate alone, but if the advertiser mentions any other credit terms, such as down payment, lack of down payment, monthly payment, amount of any finance charge, or the term of the loan, he must also mention the cash price, the required down payment, the annual percentage rate, and also the number, amount, and due dates of all payments.

Advertising includes newspapers, radio, TV, direct mail, giveaway literature, billboards, and posters.

Enforcement and penalties

A number of governmental agencies are involved in enforcement of the law. Penalties for violating the act can be both criminal and civil. For willful and knowing failure to comply, criminal punishment may result in a fine or imprisonment. A creditor who fails to disclose any required information may be civilly liable to the borrower for twice the finance charge but in no case less than $100 or more than $1,000. A creditor will have 15 days after discovering an error, before a civil action is begun or written notice of the error received from the customer, to correct the situation. Further, the creditor could avoid liability by showing through a preponderance of evidence that the violation was not intentional and resulted from a bona fide error. Civil liability could also extend to the assignee of the original creditor provided the assignee was in a continuing business relationship with the original creditor at the time the credit was extended or at the time of the assignment.

Effect upon the real estate licensee

The Truth-in-Lending Law defines a creditor as one who regularly extends or arranges for the extension of credit or offers to arrange for the extension of credit. According to the law, to arrange for the extension of credit means to provide or offer to provide consumer credit which is or will be extended by another person and where the person arranging such credit receives or will receive a fee or some other consideration for such service or has knowledge of the credit terms and participates in the preparation of the contract documents required in connection with the extension of credit.

The real estate licensee in general is not an

_____
(Creditor)

_____
(Office)

_____
(City)

NOTICE OF RIGHT TO CANCEL

Name(s) of Customer(s) _____

Type of Loan _____

Amount of Loan _____ $ _____

Notice to Customer Required By Federal Law:

    You have entered into a transaction on _____ , 19_____ which may result in a lien, mortgage, or other security interest on your home. You have a legal right under federal law to cancel this transaction, if you desire to do so, without any penalty or obligation within three business days from the above date or any later date on which all material disclosures required under the Truth in Lending Act have been given to you. If you so cancel the transaction, any lien, mortgage, or other security interest on your home arising from this transaction is automatically void. You are also entitled to receive a refund of any downpayment or other consideration if you cancel.

    If you decide to cancel this transaction you may do so by notifying:

_____
(Name of Creditor)

at _____
(Address of Creditor's Place of Business)

by mail or telegram sent not later than midnight of _____ , 19_____ .
(Date 3 business days after date
of receipt of this notice.)

    You may also use any other form of written notice identifying the transaction if it is delivered to the above address not later than that time. This notice may be used for that purpose by dating and signing below.

I hereby cancel this transaction.

_____ , 19 _____   _____
(Date)   (Customer's Signature)

_____

ACKNOWLEDGEMENT OF RECEIPT

I hereby acknowledge receipt of TWO copies of the foregoing Notice of Right to Cancel.

_____ , 19 _____   _____
(Date)   (Customer's Signature)

_____
(All joint owners must sign)

_____
| See reverse side for important information about your right of rescission. |

FIGURE 12–8

EFFECT OF RESCISSION

When a customer exercises his right to rescind, he is not liable for any finance or other charge, and any security interest becomes void upon such a rescission. Within 10 days after receipt of a notice of rescission, the creditor shall return to the customer any money or property given as earnest money, downpayment, or otherwise, and shall take any action necessary or appropriate to reflect the termination of any security interest created under the transaction. If the creditor has delivered any property to the customer, the customer may retain possession of it. Upon the performance of the creditor's obligations under this section, the customer shall tender the property to the creditor, except that if return of the property in kind would be impracticable or inequitable, the customer shall tender its reasonable value. Tender shall be made at the location of the property or at the residence of the customer, at the option of the customer. If the creditor does not take possession of the property within 10 days after tender by the customer, ownership of the property vests in the customer without obligation on his part to pay for it.

NOTICE OF INTENT TO PROCEED

I hereby certify that I have elected not to cancel or rescind the transaction referred to on the reverse side and that I have not delivered, mailed or filed for transmission by telegram to the Creditor any notice of cancellation or rescission of that transaction.

_____ , 19 _____   _____
(Date and mail or deliver no sooner than   (Customer's Signature)
3 business days after date of receipt)

                                               _____
                                                        (All joint owners must sign)

FIGURE 12–8 (*concluded*)

arranger of credit under the Truth-in-Lending Law and is therefore not personally responsible for any of its requirements. Licensees do not ordinarily receive fees either from the mortgage broker or the mortgage lender for referring housing purchasers to them. The commission is paid by the seller of the property out of the proceeds of the sale, and while the licensee may direct the purchaser to a savings and loan company, bank, or other source of credit, the licensee is not paid separately for doing so. The regulations of the Truth-in-Lending Law, Regulation Z, in no way suggest that the licensee should refrain from making direct contacts with lenders in behalf of real property purchasers or that they should cease supplying preliminary credit information. The important point is that the lender or lender's agent should be the one to make the judgment on the acceptability of the purchaser as a credit risk.

The licensee should be careful not to prepare or assist in the preparation of any of the credit instruments, such as the loan application, note, deed of trust, mortgage, or installment sales contract. Thus, the real estate licensee is not a creditor or an arranger of credit if he does not receive any independent fee for helping to place the loan or assist in any way in the preparation of the credit instruments.

The licensee who lends his own money or who operates an independent separate mortgage banking or lending facility will be personally responsible for complying with the Truth-in-Lending Law. Land contracts, also referred to as an agreement of sale, conditional sale contract, or an installment sale contract, are discussed elsewhere in this chapter, and the same principles discussed above apply to the land contract. If the licensee does not receive a separate fee for selling the land contract independent of the sale of the real property itself and does not prepare or assist in the preparation of the land contract, he is not an arranger under the law and is not responsible for any disclosures.

Secondary financing. A seller who takes back a second loan as an accommodation to the purchaser and for the purpose of effecting the sale of his property is not a creditor under the law and does not have to comply with the disclosure provisions. Thus, the typical seller who is not in the business of selling or dealing in real estate is exempt from the law if he takes back a second trust deed. However, an individual who with some regularity extends funds for second loans may well be considered as being in the business of regularly

extending credit and will have to comply with the law.

Even though an individual homeowner who takes back a second loan is usually exempt from compliance with the Truth-in-Lending Law, he must be the real lender to maintain his exemption. This may not be the case when he prearranges with a real estate licensee or second mortgage investor to discount and sell the instrument immediately. Thus, in cases where credit instruments are discounted by prearrangement, the real estate licensee should not rely on the seller's exemption and should comply fully with the disclosure provisions of the law. The licensee should make full disclosure of the terms of the second trust deed or contract of sale, and notification of the right to rescind must also be furnished to the purchaser. The seller's exemption from compliance with the law will not be lost because he may decide subsequently to sell his interest in the second loan or contract of sale. The exemption would be lost only in cases where it was clear from the outset that the seller had no intention of holding the instrument for any time at all but intended to sell it immediately.

REAL ESTATE SETTLEMENT PROCEDURES ACT

The Real Estate Settlement Procedures Act (RESPA) was enacted in 1974 and amended in 1976. The regulations of the act have been adopted by the Department of Housing and Urban Development (HUD) with respect to the sale or transfer of one- to four-family homes, co-ops, and condominiums financed through FHA, VA, or financial institutions with federally insured deposits. Current regulations require the following:

A uniform settlement statement must be made available to the borrower not later than the date of closing, unless waived by the borrower. HUD exempts such areas where settlement statements are usually provided as in the typical transaction using an escrow agent. If the borrower requests it, the borrower must be given the opportunity prior to close of escrow to inspect and review the settlements costs in connection with the transaction.

The lender is required to provide HUD's special information booklet to the borrower at the time the written loan application is received or within three days and also to furnish an estimate of the likely closing costs in connection with the transaction to be made by the lender. If the lender requires use of a particular attorney, title examiner, title insurer, or individual to conduct the settlement, the lender must state if any business relationship exists and give an estimate of that individual's charges.

Kickbacks or payment of unearned fees cannot be made in connection with the transaction. The sharing of commissions and referral fees between cooperating real estate brokers and agreements between real estate brokers and agents are not in violation of the law. RESPA regulations further state that a seller may not condition the sale of property on the buyer's purchase of title insurance from a particular title insurance company.

The purpose of the RESPA regulations is to provide full disclosure with respect to costs and charges in connection with real estate transactions and further benefits both the public and the real estate industry.

QUESTIONS FOR DISCUSSION

1. Discuss the differences among the basic types of promissory notes.
2. What is an offset statement, and when is it generally used?
3. Give some examples of real defenses that are good against anyone, including a holder in due course.
4. With respect to the statute of limitations, what is the main difference between a mortgage and a trust deed?
5. What two remedies are available to a beneficiary in a deed of trust?
6. What is the main difference in redemption privileges between a mortgage and a deed of trust?
7. Can a deficiency judgment be obtained when there is a purchase money mortgage or purchase money trust deed?
8. What is the difference in the sale of a property between a buyer's taking subject to an existing obligation or assuming the existing obligation?
9. Give some examples of an acceleration clause.

10. How may the holder of a second loan protect his investment if the borrower defaults on the first loan?
11. Discuss the particular function of a chattel mortgage and of a security agreement.
12. Which of the different types of creative and alternative financing seem most attractive to you and why?
13. Discuss the use of points and acceleration clauses by lenders.
14. Discuss the disclosure and right to cancel provisions of the Truth-in-Lending Law.
15. What is the effect of a lock-in provision in connection with a loan?

MULTIPLE CHOICE QUESTIONS

12–1. The type of note that calls for periodic payments is *(a)* straight, *(b)* trust, *(c)* installment, *(d)* none of these.

12–2. A term that refers to a borrower is *(a)* seller, *(b)* trustee, *(c)* trustor, *(d)* purchaser.

12–3. A charge in excess of the interest rate allowed by law is *(a)* trust account, *(b)* usury, *(c)* subordination, *(d)* acceleration.

12–4. A purchaser takes liability with respect to an existing loan by *(a)* purchasing subject to the existing loan, *(b)* signing a subordination agreement, *(c)* assuming the existing loan, *(d)* none of these.

12–5. Property is sold by a trustee as the result of *(a)* lien priority, *(b)* loan that allows future advances, *(c)* default, *(d)* deficiency judgment.

12–6. A trust account provides funds to *(a)* broker, *(b)* lender, *(c)* pay insurance and taxes, *(d)* establish a lien priority.

12–7. A disclosure statement provides buyer with *(a)* specific credit charges, *(b)* property appraisal, *(c)* amount of commission to broker, *(d)* amount of money seller owes to lender.

12–8. A term that refers to a lender is *(a)* trustor, *(b)* seller, *(c)* beneficiary, *(d)* purchaser.

13 Real estate finance—sources of funds

This chapter will deal with the various sources of funds, institutional and noninstitutional lenders, and governmental participation in real estate financing. In addition, we shall discuss the real estate broker acting as a loan agent and a real estate broker acting as a real property securities dealer. A number of the various forms used in connection with lending transactions will be illustrated, as well as the real estate broker's loan statement.

A WORD OF CAUTION

Throughout this chapter we shall, in connection with sources of funds, discuss such items as interest rates, amount of loan obtainable, down payments required as a percent of appraisal or sales price, loan fees, and the like. The reader should remember that rates, requirements, and other such conditions have been subject to constant change over the past few years. Interest rates on conventional loans, for example, have fluctuated from a low of 11 percent to a high of 17 percent during the three-year period from 1980 to 1983.

While the data presented in this chapter is correct as of date of publication, the reader is cautioned that the constant changes in real estate finance make it necessary to keep continually informed and up to date about prevailing conditions in his particular locality or special area of interest.

SOURCES OF FUNDS

There are many sources for obtaining funds necessary in real estate transactions. The entire real estate loan picture today is quite different from conditions that existed at the beginning of this century. Rates of interest have been appreci-

ably reduced from those that used to be charged by mortgage lenders, and instead of paying off the total amount of the principal at maturity of the loan, today's methods call for amortizing loans by monthly payments that include principal, interest, taxes, and insurance. The term of the loan has also been extended from the former periods of under 10 years to present terms of 15, 20, 25, and 30 years. Although the total interest payment will be higher, the monthly payment necessary will be lower, so that more persons are able to borrow money for the purchase of real estate. During 1981 and 1982, due to high interest rates, the long-term, fixed-rate loan declined in availability and was replaced by varying types of loans with shorter terms and fluctuating interest rates.

The emergence of FHA insured and VA guaranteed home loans has had a great influence on the pattern of home purchases and on prescribed standards for lending practices as well as for building construction. Generally, they have offered the borrower the lowest rate of interest, a fairly high loan ratio to appraised value, and a long term. The same is true of programs initiated by various states, such as the Cal-Vet program in California. With the exception of new tract sales, however, considerable time and red tape are involved in obtaining and processing these types of loans. In periods of tight money, they may be difficult to obtain, and the seller may have to pay a considerable amount of points in order for the borrower to be able to obtain the loan.

In connection with the sale of older properties and when the buyer has a substantial down payment, conventional loans assume tremendous importance. These loans offer faster processing, have more flexible terms, and may offer the borrower a higher loan ratio. A substantial amount of conventional financing is also used in connection with newer properties in the higher price categories.

AVAILABILITY OF FUNDS

Eight times since World War II mortgage money has been in short supply relative to the demand for this money, as evidenced by rapidly increasing mortgage interest rates during these periods. In recent years these mortgage credit shortages with their accompanying high mortgage rates have come to be called credit "crunches." Occurring in 1949, 1951–52, 1956–57, 1960, 1966, 1969–70, 1974–75, and most recently since 1979, these mortgage credit crunches were caused by several factors including relatively higher interest rates in nonmortgage markets, which attracted mortgage lenders away from mortgages to other types of investments, and the outflow of deposits from financial institutions that make or originate most mortgage loans. Depositors withdraw their funds from commercial banks, and savings and loan associations and invest in other markets, whether financial or nonfinancial, which offer a higher return. As a result financial institutions have fewer funds with which to make mortgage loans and mortgage credit becomes less available. Real estate borrowers must always compete with the needs of government, business, and other consumers for available funds. Figure 13–1 illustrates the share of available funds borrowed by the federal government from 1955 to 1983.

Higher interest returns in other markets occur

because of the pressing demand for funds in these markets, combined with a reduced supply of loanable funds caused by the Federal Reserve's tighter monetary policies. In recent years the constant demand for funds in nonmortgage markets has been due to, among other causes, (1) federal government borrowing to finance its deficits and to refinance its existing debts, (2) state and local government borrowing to build public projects, etc., (3) consumer borrowing to purchase automobiles, appliances, and furniture, (4) business borrowing for the purposes of constructing plants, modernizing equipment, and purchasing inventories, and (5) speculator borrowing for the purpose of purchasing goods whose prices were expected to rise more rapidly than general price levels inflate. The Federal Reserve can cause a reduced supply of loanable funds by using three policy instruments in the appropriate manner, namely raising the discount rate (and discouraging borrowing at the discount window), and/or increasing reserve requirements for member banks, and/or open-market sales of U.S. government securities.

The state of California has historically been a ready customer for mortgage funds. The following characteristics make California unique with respect to the national mortgage market and generally very attractive to suppliers of mortgage funds:

Generally high demand for mortgage funds.

Wide diversification of industry and generally high employment rate.

Large banks and savings and loan associations with numerous branches.

Common usage of title insurance and escrows.

Historically a large population with a steady growth rate.

Predominant use of trust deeds instead of mortgages as a legal basis to secure real estate loans.

Presence of experienced and highly efficient mortgage loan correspondent companies.

The existence of financial institutions that will package a number of loans for sale at a guaranteed rate of return and provide efficient and fast servicing for buyers.

In our discussion of various lenders, we shall deal with:

Institutional Lenders
a. Savings and Loan Associations
b. Commercial Banks
c. Insurance Companies

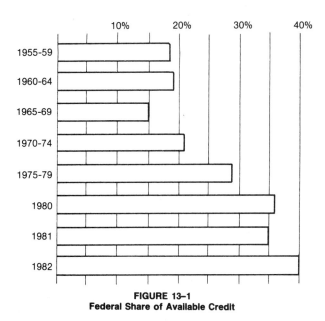

FIGURE 13–1
Federal Share of Available Credit

Noninstitutional Lenders
a. Private Individuals
b. Mortgage Companies
c. Investment Trusts
d. Pension Funds
e. Additional Sources

Government Insured and Guaranteed Mortgages
a. FHA
b. VA
c. Cal-Vet

INSTITUTIONAL LENDERS

Savings and loan associations

Among institutional lenders, savings and loan associations account for the greatest share of the home loan market. Loans made by institutional lenders without government insurance or guarantees are generally referred to as conventional loans.

The main function of the savings and loan association is to gather the savings of as many depositors as possible and to lend these savings safely to individuals for the purpose of buying, building, making improvements on, and refinancing real properties, and also for the purchase of mobile homes. Loans are usually restricted to first and second loans secured by a mortgage or deed of trust. Figure 13–2 illustrates a profile of the U.S. savings and loan industry and Figure 13–3 illustrates a savings and loan association loan application form.

In California, associations are either federally chartered or state chartered. All federally chartered associations and most state chartered associations are members of the Federal Home Loan Bank System and are subject to its supervision. In addition, most savings and loan associations have joined the Federal Savings and Loan Insurance Corporation (FSLIC). Individual accounts are currently insured up to $100,000, and much larger amounts can be insured by use of multiple account ownerships.

Each year conventional loans account for an even greater proportion of the mortgage portfolio of California's savings and loan associations. Of the loans currently on their books, 95 percent are conventional loans, 3 percent are VA loans, and FHA accounted for 2 percent.

Lending policies. Factors that will be considered are *(a)* interest rate, *(b)* term, *(c)* loan fee, *(d)* prepayment penalty, and *(e)* loan ratio.

Interest rate. California savings and loan asso-

ciations set their rates of interest in conformance with prevailing market conditions. During 1980, 1981, and 1982, savings and loan associations had to contend with increasing interest rates and a flight of depositors to money market mutual funds and other investments that were able to buy short-term, high-paying securities. The savings and loan associations had most of their funds in long-term

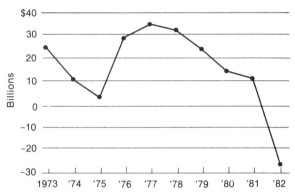

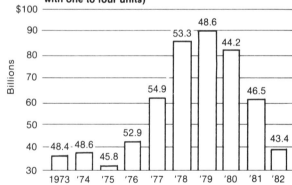

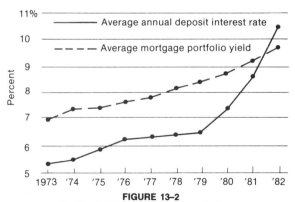

FIGURE 13–2
Profile of U.S. Savings and Loan Industry

RESIDENTIAL LOAN APPLICATION

MORTGAGE APPLIED FOR	☐ Conventional ☐ FHA ☐ VA ☐	Amount $	Interest Rate %	No. of Months	Monthly Payment Principal & Interest $	Escrow/Impounds (to be collected monthly) ☐ Taxes ☐ Hazard Ins. ☐ Mtg. Ins. ☐

Prepayment Option

SUBJECT PROPERTY

Property Street Address		City	County	State	Zip	No. Units

Legal Description (Attach description if necessary) | Year Built

Purpose of Loan: ☐ Purchase ☐ Construction-Permanent ☐ Construction ☐ Refinance ☐ Other (Explain)

Complete this line if Construction-Permanent or Construction Loan ☞	Lot Value Data	Original Cost	Present Value (a)	Cost of Imps. (b)	Total (a + b)	ENTER TOTAL AS PURCHASE PRICE IN DETAILS OF PURCHASE
Year Acquired	$	$	$	$		

Complete this line if a Refinance Loan

Year Acquired	Original Cost	Amt. Existing Liens	Purpose of Refinance	Describe Improvements [ ] made [ ] to be made
	$	$		Cost: $

Title Will Be Held In What Name(s)	Manner In Which Title Will Be Held

Source of Down Payment and Settlement Charges

This application is designed to be completed by the borrower(s) with the lender's assistance. The Co-Borrower Section and all other Co-Borrower questions must be completed and the appropriate box(es) checked if ☐ another person will be jointly obligated with the Borrower on the loan, or ☐ the Borrower is relying on income from alimony, child support or separate maintenance or on the income or assets of another person as a basis for repayment of the loan, or ☐ the Borrower is married and resides, or the property is located, in a community property state.

BORROWER				CO-BORROWER			
Name		Age	School Yrs	Name		Age	School Yrs
Present Address No. Years ___ ☐ Own ☐ Rent				Present Address No. Years ___ ☐ Own ☐ Rent			
Street				Street			
City/State/Zip				City/State/Zip			
Former address if less than 2 years at present address				Former address if less than 2 years at present address			
Street				Street			
City/State/Zip				City/State/Zip			
Years at former address		☐ Own ☐ Rent		Years at former address		☐ Own ☐ Rent	

Marital Status	☐ Married ☐ Separated ☐ Unmarried (incl. single, divorced, widowed)	DEPENDENTS OTHER THAN LISTED BY CO BORROWER NO. AGES	Marital Status	☐ Married ☐ Separated ☐ Unmarried (incl. single, divorced, widowed)	DEPENDENTS OTHER THAN LISTED BY BORROWER NO. AGES

Name and Address of Employer	Years employed in this line of work or profession? ___ years Years on this job ___ ☐ Self Employed*	Name and Address of Employer	Years employed in this line of work or profession? ___ years Years on this job ___ ☐ Self Employed*
Position/Title	Type of Business	Position/Title	Type of Business
Social Security Number***	Home Phone Business Phone	Social Security Number***	Home Phone Business Phone

GROSS MONTHLY INCOME				MONTHLY HOUSING EXPENSE**			DETAILS OF PURCHASE	
Item	Borrower	Co-Borrower	Total		PRESENT	PROPOSED		
Base Empl. Income	$	$	$	Rent	$	$	a. Purchase Price	$
Overtime				First Mortgage (P&I)		$	b. Total Closing Costs (Est.)	
Bonuses				Other Financing (P&I)			c. Prepaid Escrows (Est.)	
Commissions				Hazard Insurance			d. Total (a + b + c)	$
Dividends/Interest				Real Estate Taxes			e. Amount This Mortgage	( )
Net Rental Income				Mortgage Insurance			f. Other Financing	( )
Other† (Before completing, see notice under Describe Other Income below.)				Homeowner Assn. Dues			g. Present Equity in Lot	( )
				Other			h. Amount of Cash Deposit	( )
				Total Monthly Pmt.	$	$	i. Closing Costs Paid by Seller	( )
				Utilities			j. Cash Reqd. For Closing (Est.)	$
Total	$	$	$	Total	$	$		

DESCRIBE OTHER INCOME

☞ B—Borrower C—Co-Borrower	NOTICE: † Alimony, child support, or separate maintenance income need not be revealed if the Borrower or Co-Borrower does not choose to have it considered as a basis for repaying this loan.	Monthly Amount
		$

IF EMPLOYED IN CURRENT POSITION FOR LESS THAN TWO YEARS COMPLETE THE FOLLOWING

B/C	Previous Employer/School	City/State	Type of Business	Position/Title	Dates From/To	Monthly Income
						$

THESE QUESTIONS APPLY TO BOTH BORROWER AND CO BORROWER

If a "yes" answer is given to a question in this column, explain on an attached sheet.	Borrower Yes or No	Co-Borrower Yes or No		Borrower Yes or No	Co-Borrower Yes or No
Have you any outstanding judgments? In the last 14 years, have you been declared bankrupt?					
Have you had property foreclosed upon or given title or deed in lieu thereof?			Do you have health and accident insurance?		
Are you a co-maker or endorser on a note?			Do you have major medical coverage?		
Are you a party in a law suit?			Do you intend to occupy this property?		
Are you obligated to pay alimony, child support, or separate maintenance?			Will this property be your primary residence?		
			Have you previously owned a home?		
Is any part of the down payment borrowed?			Sales Price of previously owned home? $	$	$

*FHLMC requires self employed to furnish signed copies of one or more most recent Federal Tax Returns or audited Profit and Loss Statements. FNMA requires business credit report, signed Federal Income Tax returns for last two years, and, if available, audited P/L plus balance sheet for same period.
**All Present Monthly Housing Expenses of Borrower and Co-Borrower should be listed on a combined basis.
***Neither FHLMC nor FNMA requires this information.

FHLMC 65 Rev. 3/77   FNMA 1003 Rev. 3/77

FIGURE 13–3

This Statement and any applicable supporting schedules may be completed jointly by both married and unmarried co-borrowers if their assets and liabilities are sufficiently joined so that the Statement can be meaningfully and fairly presented on a combined basis; otherwise separate Statements and Schedules are required (FHLMC 65A/FNMA 1003A). If the co-borrower section was completed about a spouse, this statement and supporting schedules must be completed about that spouse also. ☐ Completed Jointly ☐ Not Completed Jointly

ASSETS		LIABILITIES AND PLEDGED ASSETS			

Indicate by (*) those liabilities or pledged assets which will be satisfied upon sale of real estate owned or upon refinancing of subject property

Description	Cash or Market Value	Creditors' Name, Address and Account Number	Acct. Name If Not Borrower's	Mo. Pmt. and Mos. left to pay	Unpaid Balance
Cash Deposit Toward Purchase Held By	$	Installment Debts (include "revolving" charge accts)		$ Pmt./Mos. /	$
Checking and Savings Accounts (Show Names of Institutions/Acct. Nos.)				/	
				/	
Stocks and Bonds (No./Description)				/	
				/	
Life Insurance Net Cash Value Face Amount ($)		Automobile Loans		/	
SUBTOTAL LIQUID ASSETS	$				
Real Estate Owned (Enter Market Value from Schedule of Real Estate Owned)		Real Estate Loans			
Vested Interest in Retirement Fund					
Net Worth of Business Owned (ATTACH FINANCIAL STATEMENT)					
Automobiles (Make and Year)		Other Debts Including Stock Pledges			
Furniture and Personal Property		Alimony, Child Support and Separate Maintenance Payments Owed To			
Other Assets (Itemize)					
		TOTAL MONTHLY PAYMENTS		$	
TOTAL ASSETS	A $	NET WORTH (A minus B) $		TOTAL LIABILITIES	B $

SCHEDULE OF REAL ESTATE OWNED (If Additional Properties Owned Attach Separate Schedule)

Address of Property (Indicate S if Sold, PS if Pending Sale or R if Rental being held for income)	◇	Type of Property	Present Market Value	Amount of Mortgages & Liens	Gross Rental Income	Mortgage Payments	Taxes, Ins. Maintenance and Misc.	Net Rental Income
			$	$	$	$	$	$
		TOTALS →	$	$	$	$	$	$

LIST PREVIOUS CREDIT REFERENCES

◇ B—Borrower C—Co-Borrower	Creditor's Name and Address	Account Number	Purpose	Highest Balance	Date Paid
				$	

List any additional names under which credit has previously been received _____

AGREEMENT: The undersigned applies for the loan indicated in this application to be secured by a first mortgage or deed of trust on the property described herein, and represents that the property will not be used for any illegal or restricted purpose, and that all statements made in this application are true and are made for the purpose of obtaining the loan. Verification may be obtained from any source named in this application. The original or a copy of this application will be retained by the lender, even if the loan is not granted. APPLICANT, IF MARRIED, MAY APPLY FOR A SEPARATE LOAN ACCOUNT.
I/we fully understand that it is a federal crime punishable by fine or imprisonment, or both, to knowingly make any false statements concerning any of the above facts as applicable under the provisions of Title 18, United States Code, Section 1014.

_____ Date _____   _____ Date _____
Borrower's Signature   Co-Borrower's Signature

VOLUNTARY INFORMATION FOR GOVERNMENT MONITORING PURPOSES

If this loan is for purchase or construction of a home, the following information is requested by the Federal Government to monitor this lender's compliance with Equal Credit Opportunity and Fair Housing Laws. The law provides that a lender may neither discriminate on the basis of this information nor on whether or not it is furnished. Furnishing this information is optional. If you do not wish to furnish the following information, please initial below.

BORROWER: I do not wish to furnish this information (initials)_____

| RACE/ NATIONAL ORIGIN | ☐American Indian, Alaskan Native ☐Asian, Pacific Islander ☐Black ☐Hispanic ☐White ☐Other (specify)_____ | SEX ☐Female ☐Male |

CO-BORROWER: I do not wish to furnish this information (initials)_____

| RACE/ NATIONAL ORIGIN | ☐American Indian, Alaskan Native ☐Asian, Pacific Islander ☐Black ☐Hispanic ☐White ☐Other (specify)_____ | SEX ☐Female ☐Male |

FOR LENDER'S USE ONLY

(FNMA REQUIREMENT ONLY) This application was taken by _____ (Interviewer), a full time employee of California Federal Savings and Loan Association, in a face to face interview with the prospective buyer.

Existing Cal Fed Loan No. _____ Name of Seller _____ Escrow No. _____ Name of Escrow _____

Address of Escrow _____ Escrow Officer _____ Phone _____

Loan Amount $	Mo. P & I Pmt.	Int. Rate %	Term Yrs.	Min. Ins. Reqd. $	Water Stock ☐Yes ☐No	Pmt. Date 1 10 20	Guarantor—Name & Relationship

2nd T.D.—If yes show amt. ☐Yes ☐No	Termite Clrnce. ☐Yes ☐No	Impound Acct. ☐Yes ☐No	Cal Fed Ln. Fee $	Commission—Amt. and To Whom Paid $			Total Ln. Fee $

Vesting/Legal Ckd. By	Credit Ckd. By	Loan Cert. By (Br. Ln. Off/Rep.)	Loan Committee Approval By Vice Pres.	Date	Loan No.

CF 3284B (3/77)   REVERSE

FIGURE 13–3 (concluded)

real estate loans which had been made years ago and were paying low, fixed-rate yields. At the same time, new deposits had to be attracted by paying higher and higher rates, and in 1980 the cost of funds became greater than the yield being received from loan portfolios. In addition, the savings and loan associations found it difficult to replenish their loan portfolios with higher interest paying loans because at the higher interest rates being charged to borrowers, real estate sales and loan demand decreased.

Term. The term means the number of years given to repay the loan. A loan for a period of 30 years will require a lower monthly payment than the same loan for a 20-year term, since the sooner the borrower must repay the amount borrowed, the larger his monthly payment must be.

The term allowed on older properties will generally be between 15 and 20 years, while post-World War II buildings will get 20- to 30-year repayment terms. However, purchasers of select properties in large urban areas are often given 30-year repayment terms.

Many borrowers want a shorter term since they do not want to take forever to repay the loan, while other borrowers want a term as long as possible so that the monthly payment will be lower. A recent tendency by numerous savings and loan associations has been to shorten loan terms or provide for a means of renegotiation after perhaps 5, 7, or 10 years.

Loan fee. Savings and loan associations usually charge a loan fee of from 1 to 3 percent of the amount of the loan. The loan fee is one of these items that make up the closing costs paid by the buyer-borrower and charged in escrow. For instance, a buyer who borrows $120,000 and is charged a loan fee of 2½ percent will have to pay $3,000.

Prepayment penalty. Savings and loan associations generally charge a penalty of some sort if a loan is paid off before maturity. Since very few borrowers stay in the same location long enough to actually pay off a 20- to 30-year loan, the associations receive a considerable amount of revenue in this way.

Generally, the prepayment penalty charged will be three to six months of interest on 80% of the remaining balance of the loan. The charge is paid by the original borrower. The law presently provides that with respect to one- to four-family buildings, no prepayment penalty can be charged if the loan has been in effect for more than five years.

Many associations waive this penalty if the new purchaser finances through them. For this reason, the broker often will tell a purchaser to seek financing from the same savings and loan association that holds the seller's note, which may save the seller from paying a prepayment penalty. The price the seller will accept should then reflect such saving.

Loan ratio. Maximum loan ratios and terms allowed are set by law for savings and loan associations. Different regulations apply to different property classifications, such as single-family dwellings, two- to four-family buildings, five or more units, business property, and commercial property. Federally chartered savings and loan associations are allowed maximums slightly higher than those for state chartered associations.

The law prescribes the maximum limits and allows up to 95 percent of appraised value, but as a practical matter, all the savings and loan associations have set for themselves limits that are well below the maximum allowed. Since policies vary among the separate associations, the licensee must keep constantly abreast of the current practices of associations in his own locality.

In addition to their own loan, some associations will allow a second loan to be recorded against the property, while others will slightly lower the amount they will loan if they know that a second loan is to be recorded.

Most savings and loan associations will appraise the property at the same amount as the selling price if they believe the selling price reflects the current market value. This practice differs from that of banks, which often appraise a property at slightly below what it may bring on the open market. For this reason, in actual dollars loaned, a conventional loan from a savings and loan company usually will be more than one that may be obtained from a bank.

Commercial banks

Banks in California are either nationally chartered or state chartered. Federal laws regulate the national banks, while state laws regulate the state chartered institutions. In regard to activity in the real estate market, banks are traditionally known for their conversative appraisal and lending practices. Banks tend to favor short-term lending, so real estate loans, especially conventional ones, have never been a significant part of their lending program. They tend to favor business and short-term credit loans and automobile financing and recently have devoted much of their effort to the credit card area.

The distribution of all real estate loans held by California banks is approximately 60 percent conventional loans, 35 percent FHA insured loans, and 5 percent VA guaranteed loans. A large proportion of the conventional real estate loans were devoted to nonresidential properties in the business, commercial, and industrial areas. In making mortgage investments, liquidity and marketability are of prime importance. For banks, government underwritten loans have the important advantage of not having to be counted as part of their mortgage total, which is restricted by law to approximately 65 percent of their time deposits or the bank's combined capital and surplus, whichever is greater.

Policies and practices of various banks differ according to the particular banking firm and local area.

Interest rate. Interest rates fluctuate, depending on conditions in the money market at any given time. Rates charged by banks have traditionally been slightly below those in effect at savings and loan associations; however, while some banks still follow this pattern, others charge the same interest rate as their local savings and loan associations.

Blended rate. Some banks and savings and loan associations recently have offered a blended rate with respect to purchase or refinancing of properties on which they hold the current loan. Table 13–1 shows an example of such blending offered by Bank of America in mid-1982.

Term. Bank terms vary from a high of 25 to 30 years for prime property, to 20 years for good property, and approximately 15 years for acceptable property.

Loan fee. One of the advantages of a bank loan has traditionally been the low loan fee charged to the borrower. During the past few years, however, most banks have begun to charge a percentage fee based on the amount borrowed. Those banks doing so are charging 1 to 3 percent of the loan amount.

Prepayment penalty Some banks do not charge the borrower any prepayment penalty, and the borrower may, at any time, pay off the entire obligation without having a prepayment penalty assessed. Others charge a penalty of from 1 to 3 percent of the outstanding balance of the loan.

Loan ratio. Fully amortized conventional real estate loans made by all national and state chartered banks are generally limited to 80 percent of the bank's appraised value of the property or the selling price, whichever is lower.

A most important fact to remember, however, is that with the exception of new construction, the traditionally conservative banking approach to value results in the bank appraisal being 5 to 15 percent below the actual selling price of the

TABLE 13–1

Rate on Present Loan	Remaining Term on Present Loan	Blended Rate If New Money Rate of 17%			
		If 50% of Loan Is New Money		If 75% of Loan Is New Money	
		Blended Rate	Estimated APR	Blended Rate	Estimated Rate
8%	18 yrs.	13.30%	13.62%	15.20%	15.66%
8%	22 yrs.	13.00%	13.31%	15.00%	15.45%
9%	18 yrs.	13.70%	14.03%	15.40%	15.86%
9%	22 yrs.	13.40%	13.72%	15.20%	15.66%
9%	25 yrs.	13.30%	13.62%	15.20%	15.66%
10%	22 yrs.	13.90%	14.23%	15.40%	15.86%
10%	27 yrs.	13.70%	14.03%	15.30%	15.76%
11%	27 yrs.	14.10%	14.44%	15.60%	16.07%
12%	28 yrs.	14.60%	14.95%	15.80%	16.28%
13%	28 yrs.	15.00%	15.37%	16.00%	16.48%
14%	28 yrs.	15.50%	15.88%	16.30%	16.79%

property. The licensee must remember not to apply the bank's loan ratio to the selling price of the property as in savings and loan associations but rather to the bank's appraised value of the property.

Loans on prime residential properties will be made at between 70 and 80 percent of appraised value. Middle-aged and older properties regarded as acceptable will receive a loan of 60 to 70 percent of appraised value. Loans on economically sound farm properties will be made at approximately 65 percent of appraised value, and commercial and industrial properties will receive a 60 to 65 percent loan ratio.

Insurance companies

Life insurance companies generally make conventional loans on all types of properties, but they favor loans on properties that require large amounts, such as shopping centers, developments, large commercial properties, industrial properties, and hotels. They invest heavily in mortgages insured by the FHA and in those guaranteed by the VA. Many loans are purchased from mortgage companies, who make loans in their respective communities and deliver them when completed to the insurance company. For a fee, the mortgage company usually serves as the agent for the insurance company in making such loans.

Of the loans held by insurance companies, approximately 50 percent are FHA and VA loans, 30 percent commercial income development properties, and 20 percent are on higher priced, new or rather recently built individual houses. The licensee who deals in resales of existing houses, duplexes, and smaller income units will seldom seek financing from an insurance company.

Life insurance companies incorporated in California or doing business in California are restricted to conventional mortgage loans of 75 percent of market value for single-family residences and 65 percent of market value for other types of property. There is no state restriction on term, but most insurance companies use 20 to 25 years. Interest rates are generally the same as those charged by commercial banks.

Since their investment objectives are long-term in nature, insurance companies generally do not have due-on-sale clauses in their loans. They generally have a lock-in provision during the initial portion of the term and charge a high prepayment penalty. Assumption of a loan is usually allowed if borrowers meet requirements.

Insurance companies at times have tended to favor those who are policyholders of the company or, when granting the loan, will require that the borrower take out an insurance policy with the company.

NONINSTITUTIONAL LENDERS

Private individuals

Private individual lenders make more loans from month to month than do any other class of lenders. Although at the present time they account for a little less than a quarter of the total mortgage debt, they rank number one as the source of junior mortgage (second) loans. Most of such loans are made on one- to four-family dwelling unit properties.

Aside from being sellers who carry back either first or second loans, individuals obtain loans through title companies, mortgage companies, and real estate brokers, by advertising, or through others who deal in real estate transactions. Many individuals have money to lend where real estate is to be the security. Many loan brokers deal with such private individuals, who are more than willing to pay the broker a fee for bringing them into transactions where they may make loans secured by real estate.

Individuals follow no uniform lending practices, and in general they are not subject to national or state licensing laws or the requirements of other regulatory agencies. Thus, they can take greater risks in their investments, such as acceptance of high loan-to-value ratios. They usually do not use the technical credit-analysis procedures that have been developed by institutional lenders, and many of the loans made by individuals would not be acceptable to institutional lenders.

Most loans made by private individuals are second loans and usually in connection with residential resales. The loan term is usually from 3 to 10 years, with the average being approximately x years. The interest rate charged will depend on the security risk involved and market conditions but are generally less than the rate charged by institutional lenders.

Balloon payments. Most second loans are carried back by the seller of a property. Such second loans generally contain a due-on-sale clause, which means that the entire amount is due the lender should the property be sold during the loan term. The monthly payment is usually 1 percent of the amount of the loan. This, of course, does not fully amortize the loan, and the borrower will have to make a substantial payment at the end of the term; such payment is generally called a balloon payment.

In recent years a number of loans containing balloon payments were made as illustrated in Figure 13–4, and a large number of these borrowers will be seeking means of refinancing during the 1980s.

Mortgage companies and investment trusts

Mortgage companies operate primarily as mortgage loan correspondents of life insurance companies, mutual savings banks, pension funds, and other financial institutions. They may furnish mortgage loans to these institutions from only one

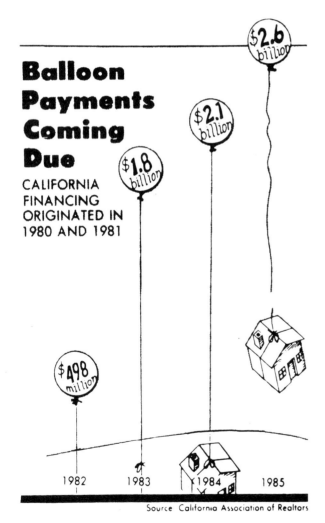

Balloon Payments Coming Due

CALIFORNIA FINANCING ORIGINATED IN 1980 AND 1981

$2.6 billion

$2.1 billion

$1.8 billion

$498 million

1982   1983   1984   1985

Source California Association of Realtors

FIGURE 13–4

metropolitan area, or one state, or sometimes several states. The mortgage companies, with their loan brokerage functions, are one of the many sources for mortgage loans. They make loans on houses, on income property, and also under FHA and VA.

Many mortgage companies have sizable funds of their own and are consistent lending sources in the mortgage market. Many also engage in additional business operations, such as property rentals, leases, management of properties, and insurance. A few even operate as real estate brokerage firms.

The companies are usually free of many of the lending limitations placed on other institutional leaders, and except for inspections by an examiner in conformity with state laws, they assume entire responsibility and make all decisions about their mortgage lending operations and their loan servicing. Some companies serve only as intermediaries and resell the loans as soon as they are made.

Mortgage companies are also active in construction lending. Such loans are made with their own funds or with the funds of the companies they represent. When the buildings are completed and sold, these funds are converted to long-term mortgage loans.

Probably the most dominant policy of these mortgage companies is to deal in mortgages that are most readily salable in the secondary market. As a result, these lenders prefer government insured or government guaranteed mortgages as well as conventional or uninsured mortgages for which they have advance purchase commitments. Generally, mortgage companies restrict their conventional loans to selected residential and business risks and to loans in price ranges suitable to the needs of investment firms that comprise the secondary mortgage market.

Investment trust formation is governed by tax laws enacted in 1960. The trust is taxed on retained earnings, and if it distributes all its earnings to stockholders, it goes completely untaxed. With respect to taxation, the investors are treated the same as direct investors in real estate mortgages or in real estate.

The real estate investment trust differs from the stock investment company in that it invests primarily in real estate and real estate loans, while the stock company concerns itself with investment in stock and securities. A real estate investment trust, therefore, is an unincorporated trust or association of investors which is managed by one or more trustees and, because of the tax exemption provided by the law, is not taxed as a corporation.

Further information on investment trusts may be obtained from the nearest office of the State Division of Corporations.

Pension funds

The assets of California pension funds totaled approximately $65 billion in 1982. A number of pension funds are becoming involved in real estate loans as part of their investment portfolio. Federal law now requires these funds to diversify investments and obtain the best yield for their participants commensurate with safe practices.

The California Carpenters Pension Fund of Northern California, for example, has approximately $150 million invested in California real estate loans, representing 35 percent of its total assets. In 1982, the fund earned 10 percent on its total investments compared to a reported 7½ percent earned by both the California Public Employees Retirement System and State Teachers Retirement System, both of which have the bulk of their funds in stock and bond investments.

Additional sources

Credit union funds are expected to provide more real estate loan money as the result of recent legislation allowing such funds to make real estate loans secured by trust deeds. A credit union is an organization of individuals having a common bond of association or occupation. The members purchase shares or deposit various amounts of money, and the fund provides them with credit and different types of loans for both small and large purchases.

The state of California and various cities such as San Francisco and Los Angeles have enacted legislation which permits the issuance of bonds to provide funds for individuals who wish to purchase real property. The available programs vary, but generally provide a method of reducing interest rates and monthly payments during the early years of a loan. A purchaser is thus able to defer part of the usual payment to later years, which reduces initial monthly payments and the amount of annual income needed to qualify them for a loan.

GOVERNMENT INSURED AND GUARANTEED LOANS

The more important features of FHA, VA, and Cal-Vet loans are summarized in Table 13–2. Each is discussed separately in the text that follows, and detailed information with respect to the programs of any of these agencies can easily be obtained by any interested individual by merely requesting same from the nearest office of the FHA, VA, or Cal-Vet.

FHA (Federal Housing Administration)

The FHA program has been in operation since its establishment in 1934. Since that time, the FHA has written mortgage and loan insurance in the aggregate amount of approximately $135 billion and has helped more than 39 million families improve their housing standards and conditions.

The FHA does not build houses or lend money. It acts only as an insurer of privately made loans from approved lenders. In California, the FHA will insure a loan secured by either a mortgage or a deed of trust. The soundness of the FHA concept has been shown by the fact that mortgage and property improvement loans insured by the FHA have been made by banks, savings and loan associations, mortgage companies, and other FHA approved lending institutions. By protecting these lenders against loss, FHA insurance has enabled them to advance loans to moderate-income families who would otherwise have found it impossible to acquire the necessary funds for purchasing real estate. The FHA has helped to make the low down payment, long-term, fully amortized loan the standard throughout the nation.

In addition to its original programs of insuring loans made for the purposes of home purchase, home improvement, and multifamily rental housing, the FHA now insures loans for land development, low-income family housing, urban renewal housing, housing for the elderly, nursing homes, cooperative housing, condominiums, housing at military installations, housing for servicemen and their families when on active duty, and long-term loans for major home improvements.

Since this program is detailed and quite complex, all real estate licensees must keep their knowledge of FHA operations current by obtaining a copy of *The Digest of Insurable Loans*, published by the Federal Housing Administration, Washington 25, D.C., and usually available through all FHA regional offices.

When the Federal Housing Administration Act was originally passed by Congress, it contained two sections—Title I and Title II. Title I contains the provisions for modernization of existing

TABLE 13–2
Government Loan Information

	FHA Title II (203b)	VA (GI Loan)	Cal-Vet
Loan eligibility	Anyone	W. W. II, Korean War, or post Korean	California Veteran, W. W. II, Korean War, or Vietnam
Source of funds	Approved lending institutions	Approved lending institutions	State bond issues
Loan security	Deed of trust or mortgage	Deed of trust or mortgage	Conditional sales contract
Interest rate	As set by government, plus 0.5% mortgage insurance	As set by VA	As set by state of California
Term	Maximum allowed 35 years Average 20 to 30 years	30-years, real estate 20 years, mobile homes	25-year maximum
Maximum purchase price allowed	No maximum	No limit, but loan cannot exceed VA appraisal (CRV, or certified reasonable value)	No limit
Maximum amount of loan	1 unit, 90,000; 2–3 units, 101,300–122,600; 4 units, 142,600	No maximum, but guarantee only 60% of loan to set maximum	$55,000 house $180,000 farm
Down payment	3% of 1st $25,000 of appraisal 5% of balance of appraisal 100% of excess of selling price over the appraisal	None required by VA, lender may require a down payment	5% of sales price, house 5%, farms
Prepayment penalty	None	None	2% during 1st 2 years
Assignable to	Anyone	Anyone	Cal-Vet at same interest Other Vets higher interest
Secondary financing	Not allowed concurrently with first (can add later)	Not allowed concurrently with first (can add later)	Allowed with limits
Monthly cost in addition to principal and interest	1/12 annual taxes 1/36 of 3-year fire insurance policy 1/12 of 0.5% mortgage insurance	1/12 annual taxes 1/36 of 3-year fire insurance policy	1/12 annual taxes, plus fee for life insurance
Government agency	Federal Housing Administration	Veterans Administration	State of California
Monthly salary required after federal taxes	3½ to 4 times monthly payment, including principal, interest, taxes, and insurance	3½ to 4 times monthly payment including principal, interest, taxes, and insurance	4 times monthly payment, plus 1/12 of taxes
Purpose of loan	Residence, to 4 units	Residence, to 4 units, condominiums or mobilehomes,	Residence, farm, mobilehome, condominium

houses and also provides for the conversion, repair, and alteration of existing structures. All these are generally referred to as home improvement loans. Title II provides for the purchase of new or existing properties. Title III was later established as a means of providing a secondary market for FHA insured mortgages. The most important and most used section of the FHA Act over the years has been Title II, which governs loans for the purchase of real estate.

Title I, home improvement and mobile home loans. Title I allows the FHA to insure lending institutions against loss on loans made to finance alterations, repairs, and improvements to existing structures.

The individual lending institutions require the borrower to meet certain satisfactory income and credit requirements, and in addition, the borrower must own the property or have a lease that

expires not less than six months beyond the maturity of the loan, or he must be purchasing the property on contract.

Title I, Section 2 also allows insurance of the purchase of a mobile home and lot which is to be the principal residence of the buyer. FHA standards of construction must be met, and the maximum term and insured loan amount is 12 years and $10,000 for single-module mobile homes and $15,000 and 15 years for double-module mobile homes.

Title II, home purchase loans. Title II of the FHA Act contains a number of sections. Selected sections are briefly outlined below and will be followed by a more detailed discussion of Section 203b, which deals with loans for construction or purchase of one- to four-family dwellings.

Section 203. To finance the construction or purchae of one- to four-family dwellings, single-family dwellings for disaster-area residents, and low-cost single-family homes in suburban and outlying areas.

Section 207. To finance the construction of large-scale rental housing projects, seasonal homes, loans to certain veterans, and for trailer or mobile-home parks.

Section 213. To finance the construction of nonprofit cooperatives of the management or sales type and the purchase of individual mortgages released from a sales-type project mortgage.

Section 220. To finance the rehabilitation of existing dwellings and the construction of new dwellings in designated urban renewal areas.

Section 221. To finance low-cost new or rehabilitated housing for the relocation of families displaced by slum clearance projects or other governmental action.

Section 222. To finance the purchase or construction of dwellings by servicemen on active duty with the Armed Forces, including the Coast Guard.

Section 223. To finance purchase or refinancing of existing multifamily dwellings.

Section 225. To finance additional advances under an open-end mortgage for repairs or improvements to one- to four-family dwellings.

Section 231. To finance the construction or rehabilitation of rental housing projects designed specifically for elderly persons.

Section 232. To finance the construction of facilities for skilled nursing care, convalescents, and others who do not need hospital treatment.

Section 233. To finance single and multifamily units where the design and/or material used is of a nature to be considered experimental.

Section 234. To finance the purchase or construction of multifamily structures where the individual purchases the unit and is given deed to same along with undivided interest in common areas and facilities. This section is commonly known as the Condominium Housing Program.

Section 235. To provide home ownership assistance in the form of periodic payments by the FHA to mortgagees, which would reduce interest costs to the purchaser on market rate home mortgages and on the share of a cooperative association mortgage.

Section 236. To provide assistance to tenants and cooperators in the form of periodic interest reduction payments by FHA to the mortgagee for rental and cooperative housing projects serving low-income families.

Section 237. To finance home ownership for certain lower-income families who cannot qualify under normal standards because of their poor credit records but who can meet mortgage payments with appropriate budget and financial counseling.

There are, in addition to the above, many other programs for land development, group facilities, nonprofit hospitals, armed services housing and rentals, and programs in connection with the Department of Housing and Urban Development (HUD).

Whenever the terms *mortgage* and *mortgagee* are used in our discussion, the reader should remember that in California they include the terms *deed of trust* and *beneficiary.*

Title II, Section 203b. Title II has several subsections, but the one we shall be concerned with is Section 203b, which covers insured loans for the purchase of one- to four-family dwellings.

Secondary financing (second loans) to provide the purchaser with additional funds exceeding the FHA-insured loan is prohibited.

Owner-occupied dwellings and condominiums are insurable as follows:

a. Up to $90,000 for a one-family dwelling.
b. Up to $101,300 and $122,600 for a two- or three-family dwelling.
c. Up to $142,600 for a four-family dwelling.

These figures represent the maximum permissible amount of loan that will be insured by FHA. Such loans are calculated as follows:

1. On proposed construction approved for FHA insurance prior to the beginning of construction or for existing dwellings more than one year old, the limit is: 97 percent of the first $25,000 of FHA appraised value plus 95 percent of remainder of appraised value.

2. For construction completed less than one year and not approved for FHA insurance prior to its beginning, the limit is: 90 percent of appraised value.

3. A nonoccupant owner is limited to 85 percent of the amount an occupant owner could obtain. The maximum amounts are: $76,500 for a single-family dwelling, $86,150 and $104,250 for a two- or three-family dwelling, $121,250 for a four-family dwelling.

4. Special terms are offered to a veteran who has not already received any direct, guaranteed, or insured loan from the Veterans Administration home loan program, known as the "GI bill": 100

percent of the first $25,000 of appraised value, plus 95 percent of the remainder of appraisal.

Most FHA-insured loans are made on property in classification 1, which is FHA-approved prior to construction or more than one year old.

Term allowed. The term of repayment cannot be more than 35 years, but in practice, lending institutions limit FHA loans to a maximum of 30 years. The FHA itself recommends the 30-year maximum, and although this is generally used, loans are made for 25- and 20-year terms also.

Interest rate. To the prevailing rate of interest at any given time, an additional ½ percent must be added for mortgage insurance required by FHA. This charge is included in the borrower's monthly payment.

Table 13–3 illustrates the maximum loan and monthly payment necessary for regular FHA house purchases with an interest rate of 13 percent plus ½ percent for a total of 13½ percent.

FHA forms required. A variety of forms must be completed and processed when the sale of a property involves an FHA-insured loan. Most commercial banks, savings and loan associations, and other lenders who accept applications for FHA-insured loans will have available all the necessary forms.

A considerable amount of time can be saved if the property seller applies for a conditional commitment before placing the property on the market or at the time the property is listed by the broker. Where tract homes are offered with FHA-insured loans available, much of this preliminary work has already been done by the developer. When an individual owner lists his property for sale, it will be quite helpful if at the time the broker shows the property to a prospective purchaser, he already knows the FHA appraisal on the property and the amount of loan FHA will insure. Such action by the owner is optimal, however, and many times an FHA-insured loan will not be sought unless a prospective purchaser makes this a condition of the purchase contract.

Veterans Administration (GI loan)

The Veterans' Readjustment Benefits Act of 1966 and subsequent Veterans' Housing Act provide a program of loans for veterans of the U.S. Armed Forces. Eligible veterans and servicemen may obtain GI loans from private lenders for houses, mobile homes, condominiums, and buildings of up to four residential units.

Eligibility for loans. Veterans who served on active duty for 181 days or more, any part of it after January 31, 1955, and who were not dishonorably discharged, are eligible as post-Korean veterans. However, persons whose military service after January 31, 1955, consisted of "active duty for training" are not eligible. Members of the U.S. Armed Forces who have served at least two years in active duty status, even though not discharged, are eligible while they continue serving. The Veterans' Benefit Act of 1978 now provides eligibility for Vietnam-conflict veterans who served on active duty for 90 days or more, any part of it between August 5, 1964 and May 7, 1975.

Loan provisions. The VA will guarantee a home loan made by a private lender up to $25,000 or 60 percent of the loan, whichever is less. A lending institution will receive the government's guaranty, which is intended to be in lieu of a down payment or to reduce the down payment the lender normally requires.

The difference between a guaranteed and an insured loan is in the amount that will be paid to the lender in the event of a default. If there is a default on a guaranteed loan, the government pays the lender a specified maximum amount. This amount is reduced proportionately as the loan is paid off by the borrower. In the case of an insured loan, the VA will pay the net loss of the lender up to the amount of the lender's insurance account. The maximum amount of the loan the VA will guarantee is $25,000.

VA direct home loans are available for the purchase of residences in areas where such loans have been authorized, usually where private lenders are scarce and funds difficult to obtain. California is not such an area and is not eligible for any direct loans from the VA.

There is no maximum on the amount of a guaranteed loan itself, and most California lenders will make a guaranteed loan to a qualified veteran of up to $100,000.

TABLE 13–3
Typical FHA Loans

FHA Appraisal	Maximum FHA Loan	Down Payment	Monthly Payment 30-Year Term
90,000	86,000	4,000	1,020.94
100,000	95,500	4,500	1,133.72
110,000	105,000	5,000	1,246.50
120,000	114,500	5,500	1,353.34
130,000	124,000	6,000	1,472.05
140,000	133,500	6,500	1,584.83
$150,000	$143,000	$7,000	$1,697.61

Interest rate and term. The VA sets and periodically adjusts its interest rate, and the maximum term of a VA loan is 30 years.

Additional VA provisions. The loan amount is determined by a CRV, certificate of reasonable value. The CRV is ordered from the VA, and they assign an independent fee appraiser to determine the value of the property being purchased. Veterans must be informed of the reasonable value established by the VA before signing an offer or contract to pay a price greater than the CRV, although the veteran may pay more if he has the cash resources necessary.

No down payment is required by the VA. However, individual lenders may require a down payment. The VA loan is generally amortized on the standard plan of equal monthly payments, but the lender has flexibility in determining this procedure.

A lender is allowed to charge reasonable costs in connection with the loan. These costs usually include the VA appraisal, tax service, credit report, title policy, and recording fees. However, the purchaser is not allowed to pay any escrow charges.

In those parts of the state where termites may present a problem, the VA will generally require a termite inspection on the property.

Mobile home loans. Loans made to veterans for the purchase of mobile homes are guaranteed by the VA. The mobile home must conform to certain VA specifications, and the maximum loan for the purchase of a double-module mobile home is $20,000 for a term of 20 years. If the purchase includes an undeveloped lot and site preparation or a developed lot, the VA will guarantee a mobile home site loan up to $27,500 with a term of 20 years.

California-Veterans loans (Cal-Vet)

The California Veterans Farm and Home Purchase Program, created by the legislature in 1921, permits the state Department of Veterans Affairs to assist qualified veterans in acquiring farm or home properties. The state of California actually lends the funds, which are obtained through state bond issues.

Eligibility requirements. A veteran's eligibility is established by filing a loan application and discharge papers with the Department of Veterans Affairs, P.O. Box 1599, Sacramento, California.

A veteran must be a native Californian or have been a bona fide resident of the state at the time he entered the service. He must have served in time of war or participated in a military campaign or expedition for which a medal is authorized by the U.S. government. He must have served 90 days on active duty, a portion of which must have been in one of the following:

World War I: April 6, 1917 to November 11, 1918 (90-day requirement waived for World War I veterans only).

World War II: December 7, 1941 to December 1, 1946.

Korea: June 27, 1950 to January 31, 1955.

Vietnam: July 1, 1958 to end of U.S. military involvement.

Lebanon: July 1, 1958 to November 1, 1958.

Quemoy and Matsu: August 23, 1958 to June 1, 1963.

Taiwan Straits: August 23, 1958 to January 1, 1959.

Congo: July 14, 1960 to September 1, 1962.

Laos: April 19, 1961 to October 7, 1962.

Berlin: August 14, 1961 to June 1, 1963.

Cuba: October 24, 1962 to June 1, 1963.

Dominican Republic: April 27, 1965 to September 20, 1966.

Korea: October 1, 1966 to present.

Vietnam Medal: July 4, 1965 to present.

California veterans discharged with less than 90 days of service because of a war service-connected disability are eligible. To be eligible, all veterans must have been honorably discharged or currently on active duty.

Terms and conditions of loan (home purchase). The current amounts that may be loaned are up to $55,000 for the purchase of a house or condominium and up to $180,000 for the purchase of a farm. The rate of interest is subject to periodic redetermination and is set by the California legislature.

The house to be purchased must be a single-family dwelling and must meet certain standards set by the veterans department. The amount to be loaned may not exceed 95 percent of the department's appraisal of the house itself; the value of the land is not included in this appraisal. The veteran must pay in cash the difference between the department's loan and the sales price of the property, and no secondary financing is permitted in connection with the purchase of a house.

The current term of the loan is 25 years. However, the department may extend this term in special cases, but this is an exception rather than the rule. The veteran must agree to reside on the property, or agree that a member of his family will do so, within 60 days from date of purchase. He may not transfer, encumber, assign, or rent the property without the written consent of the veterans department.

Title to the property is held by the state of California and is transferred to the veteran on completion of his purchase contract. The Department of Veterans Affairs offers low-cost insurance coverage to a veteran making a loan. The premiums are added to the veteran's monthly payment and include life insurance, mortgage protection insurance, fire insurance, and other protective coverages.

The department will advance funds in a series of payments to a licensed and bondable contractor to pay for construction of a house when:

1. The veteran owns the lot.
2. The lot is inspected by the department and found acceptable.
3. The veteran furnishes plans and specifications approved by the department.
4. The veteran deposits in escrow any cash difference between loan and building cost.
5. The veteran pays a processing fee.
6. A formal building agreement is entered into by the veteran and the department.

On lot approval, the department will issue a conditional commitment. This may allow the veteran to obtain necessary temporary financing needed for construction.

The same general terms and conditions discussed previously apply to a veteran's purchase of a farm. The department will loan up to $180,000 for a term of 25 years. Loan payment with regard to a farm may be annual or monthly, whereas for the purchase of a house the payments must be monthly. The farm loan may be used to: (1) purchase a farm, (2) refinance a farm loan, (3) add new land to a farm, and (4) improve a farm.

The farm must be appraised by the Department of Veterans Affairs and found able to produce a reasonable net income for the operator. The veteran must plan to live on the farm.

California-Veterans Loans can be made for the purchase of a mobile home which is designed for single-family occupancy. The loan may include purchase of an approved site.

Secondary financing may be permitted if certain conditions are met, and improvement loans are also available.

FNMA and GNMA

The Federal National Mortgage Association (FNMA), popularly known as Fannie Mae, was originally established in connection with Title III of the National Housing Act and is engaged in the business of expanding the amount of capital available to finance home building and home buying. Its primary function is to buy FHA-insured and VA-guaranteed mortgages made by private lenders. These are purchased at a discount and then sold to other private lenders or investors.

The Housing and Urban Development Act of 1968 partitioned FNMA into two separate corporations resulting in the formation of the Government National Mortgage Association, called Ginnie Mae. The FNMA is authorized to issue and sell securities backed by a portion of its mortgage portfolio, with GNMA guaranteeing payment on such securities. GNMA also guarantees similar securities issued by other private issuers where they are backed by FHA, VA, and some Farm Home Administration mortgages or loans.

In 1982, the FNMA established two new programs to help facilitate home purchases. The Home Seller Loan Plan allows the seller of a property who provides the purchaser with either a first or second loan, to sell the loan to the FNMA for cash. An additional plan allows reduction of prevailing interest rates by using buydown mortgages. With a tight real estate market prevailing, such plans should promote additional property sales.

The home seller loan plan. The credit rating of the borrower and condition of the property offered as security must conform to FNMA's general requirements at the time the loan is sold to Fanny Mae. The loan must be a real estate loan secured by a trust deed and can be either a first or second loan. Loan limits are $107,000 for a single-family home, $136,800 for a two-family dwelling, $165,000 for a three-family dwelling, and $205,300 for a four-family dwelling. If the loan carries a prevailing market interest rate acceptable to FNMA, the seller will receive the full principal balance of the loan at time of sale subject to deduction of certain fees established by FNMA. If the interest rate of the loan is less than a prevailing market rate acceptable to FNMA, an adjustment will be made and the seller will receive slightly less than the full loan balance at the time it is sold to FNMA.

Interest buydown plans. The main advantage of a buydown loan is that when the interest rate is reduced, the monthly payment is reduced and a borrower can qualify for a loan with a lower annual income. The terms of buydowns which meet FNMA guidelines are quite flexible and most lenders who sell loans to Fanny Mae can help work out plans that meet the needs of individual clients.

At close of escrow, the amount needed for buydown, whether supplied by a builder, seller, or the purchaser, is deposited in escrow. For a specified period, the purchaser makes reduced monthly payments and the balance of the payment comes from the funds in escrow.

To illustrate the advantages of buydowns, we will look at an example of a straight buydown and then at a graduated buydown. Assume that the purchasers need a loan of $67,500 and the fixed-rate is 16½ percent for 30 years, with a monthly payment of $935.

The sellers of the property agree to a buydown which will reduce the interest rate 2 percent a year for the first five years of the loan. At 14½ percent interest, the monthly payment is reduced to $827 for 60 months. The $108 monthly reduction multiplied by 60 equals approximately $5,688 which is the amount needed from the sellers. If we assume that the lender requires a 28 percent payment to income ratio, the purchasers can qualify for the loan with an annual income of $39,711 rather than the $44,356 needed without a buydown.

With a graduated buydown, a loan at 16½ percent is reduced to 12½ percent for the first year, 13½ percent the second year, 14½ percent the third year, and 15½ percent the fourth year. The purchaser's monthly payments are $720 the first year, $773 the second year, $827 the third year, and $881 the fourth year. Beginning with the fifth year, the monthly payment will be $935. The total amount needed for buydown in this example is approximately $5974. Because the purchasers are qualified on the basis of the payments made during the first year, they will qualify for the loan with an income of $35,160. Lower annual income requirements allow more purchasers to qualify for a loan and facilitate more purchases of real property.

PROHIBITION AGAINST REDLINING

New legislation prohibiting financial institutions from engaging in the practice known as redlining became effective January 1, 1978. Known as the Housing Financial Discrimination Act of 1977, the law provides a unique opportunity for real estate licensees to aid in stamping out redlining, a practice which is discriminatory and which,

by restricting the free flow of mortgage capital, makes it more difficult for real estate licensees to put bona fide transactions together.

The Act prohibits financial institutions such as federal or state licensed savings and loans, state or national banks or credit unions, and thrift companies from engaging in discriminatory loan practices due, in whole or in part, to the consideration of conditions, characteristics, or trends in the neighborhood or geographic area surrounding the housing accommodations. Certain exceptions may be allowed if the financial institution can demonstrate that such consideration in the particular case is required to avoid an unsafe and unsound business practice. Consideration of race, color, religion, sex, marital status, national origin, or ancestry is also prohibited in regard to the composition of the neighborhood, the geographic area surrounding a housing accommodation, trends in the area, or in appraising a housing accommodation.

The Real Estate Commissioner will take disciplinary action against any real estate licensees found to be engaged in or connected with such activities.

BROKER ACTING AS LOAN AGENT

In the normal course of business, not only may a broker aid a prospective purchaser in making application for a loan from a financial institution, but quite often, the broker may himself become a representative or agent for a mortgage lending institution. The broker may also represent private interests who have funds to lend on notes secured by real property. Many real estate firms have set up a special loan division within the office or have established a subsidiary mortgage company.

It is required by law that anyone acting for compensation in negotiating a new loan or selling an existing loan secured by real estate must be a real estate licensee. Because of a number of complaints the Commissioner received over the years concerning exorbitant charges of some licensees in connection with the above activities, the Real Property Loan Brokerage Law was passed by the legislature. In 1961, the legislature revised and added to the existing law and passed Assembly Bill 1344, which is regarded as the most comprehensive mortgage loan legislation ever enacted up to that time. Further provisions have been added to the law by the legislature, including the Mortgage Loan Brokers Reform Act of 1973. The complete provisions of the law are contained in Article 7, Sections 10240 to 10249.2, Division

Four, Real Estate Law, Business and Professions Code.

Broker's loan disclosure statement

The provisions of the law do not apply when the real estate licensee negotiates a loan in connection with a property sale or exchange or when he sells or exchanges a note in connection with such a transaction. The provisions of the law do apply when the licensee solicits or advertises for borrowers or lenders, or performs services for them in connection with loans secured by real property, or when the licensee either offers to or actually does sell, buy, or exchange a real property sales contract or a promissory note secured by real property.

When a licensee negotiates a loan to be secured directly or collaterally by a lien or real property, he must deliver to the borrower a statement containing certain information before the borrower becomes obligated to complete the loan. The California Real Estate Association form, Mortgage Loan Disclosure Statement, illustrated in Figure 13–5, is approved by the real estate commissioner for meeting the provisions of the law.

Commissions and charges

Besides being required to provide the borrower with a statement, the licensee is also restricted in the amount of commissions and other charges he may make. Section 10242 of the Real Estate Law details all of the charges which may be made for a loan in addition to the commission. Each of these charges must be supported by adequate records and cannot exceed the actual costs and expenses incurred by the licensee. If a loan is negotiated in violation of any provision of the mortgage loan broker law, the licensee is obliged to return any bonus, brokerage, or commission on demand to the borrower. Costs and expenses of making the loan, such as appraisal fees, escrow fees, title charges and notary, recording, and credit investigation fees charged to the borrower cannot exceed 5 percent of the principal of the loan.

For mortgage loan brokers making 400 or more loans per year or whose advertising costs connected with mortgage loan brokerage activities amount to more than 5 percent of gross revenue and at least $10,000 per year, the law requires submission of advertising by such brokers to the Department of Real Estate and requires an annual report to be submitted to the Commissioner.

REAL PROPERTY SECURITIES DEALER

Sections 10237 through 10239.35 of the Business and Professions Code relate to real property securities and real property securities dealers, spell out registration and regulatory requirements for such dealers, and are intended to control bulk transactions in trust deeds and real property sales contracts and investment plans dealing with them.

To secure endorsement as a real property securities dealer, an individual must have a real estate broker's license. An application for endorsement is sent to the commissioner together with a required fee and a corporate surety bond in the amount of $5,000. In lieu of the bond, the applicant may submit evidence of having filed with the state treasurer a cash bond in the amount of $5,000 or United States or state securities in the amount of $6,000.

A real property securities dealer is defined as any person acting as principal or agent who engages in the business of:

1. Selling real property securities, that is, promissory notes or sales contracts, as defined by subdivision (a) Section 10237.1 to the public.

2. Offering to accept or accepting funds for continual reinvestment in real property securities or for placement in an account, plan, or program whereby the dealer implies that a return will be derived from a specific real property sales contract or promissory note secured directly or collaterally by a lien on real property which is not specifically stated to be based upon the contractual payments thereon.

Sale to the public, however, is interpreted as excluding sales to corporations; pension, retirement, or similar trust funds; institutional lending agencies; or real estate brokers, attorneys, or licensed general building contractors.

A generalized definition of real property securities as set forth in Section 10237.1 holds them to be deeds of trust sold under an investment contract where the dealer guarantees the deed of trust in any one of several ways or makes advances to or on behalf of the investor. Also included in the definition is the sale of one of a series of promotional notes or sales contracts. Promotional refers to a note secured by a trust deed on unimproved real property; or a note executed after construction of an improvement on the property, but be-

MORTGAGE LOAN DISCLOSURE STATEMENT

CALIFORNIA ASSOCIATION OF REALTORS® STANDARD FORM

(APPROVED BY STATE DEPARTMENT OF REAL ESTATE)

_____

(Name of Broker/Arranger of Credit)

_____

(Business Address of Broker)

I. SUMMARY OF LOAN TERMS

A. PRINCIPAL AMOUNT OF LOAN . . . . $ _____

B. ESTIMATED DEDUCTIONS FROM PRINCIPAL AMOUNT

1. Costs and Expenses (See Paragraph III-A) . . . . $ _____

2. Brokerage Commission (See Paragraph III-B) . . . . $ _____

3. Liens and Other Amounts to be Paid on Authorization of Borrower
(See Paragraph III-C) . . . . $ _____

C. ESTIMATED CASH PAYABLE TO BORROWER (A Less B) . . . . $ _____

II. GENERAL INFORMATION CONCERNING LOAN

A. If this loan is made, you will be required to pay the principal and interest at _____ % per year, payable

as follows: _____ _____ payments of $ _____
         (number of payments)   (monthly/quarterly/annual)

and a FINAL/BALLOON payment of *S _____ to pay off the loan in full.

> *CAUTION TO BORROWER: If you do not have the funds to pay the balloon payment
> when due, it may be necessary for you to obtain a new loan against your property for this
> purpose, in which case, you may be required to again pay commission and expenses for
> arranging the loan. Keep this in mind in deciding upon the amount and terms of the loan
> that you obtain at this time.

B. This loan will be evidenced by a promissory note and secured by a deed of trust in favor of lender/creditor on
property located at (street address or legal description): _____

_____

_____

C. Liens against this property and the approximate amounts are:

Nature of Lien	Amount Owing
_____	_____
_____	_____
_____	_____

D. If you wish to pay more than the scheduled payment at any time before it is due, you may have to pay a PREPAY-
MENT PENALTY computed as follows:

_____

_____

_____

_____

E. The purchase of credit life or credit disability insurance is not required of the borrower as a condition of making
this loan.

F. The real property which will secure the requested loan is an "owner-occupied dwelling"*   YES _____ NO _____
                                                            (Borrower initial opposite
                                                                    YES or NO)
*An "owner-occupied dwelling" means a single dwelling unit in a condominium or cooperative or a residential
building of less than three separate dwelling units, one of which will be owned and occupied by a signatory to the
mortgage or deed of trust for this loan within 90 days of the signing of the mortgage or deed of trust.

FIGURE 13–5

III. DEDUCTIONS FROM LOAN PROCEEDS

    A.   ESTIMATED COSTS AND EXPENSES to be paid by borrower out of the principal amount of the loan are:

PAYABLE TO

	Broker	Others
1. Appraisal fee	_____	_____
2. Escrow fee	_____	_____
3. Fees for policy of title insurance	_____	_____
4. Notary fees	_____	_____
5. Recording fees	_____	_____
6. Credit investigation fees	_____	_____
7. Other Costs and Expenses:		
_____	_____	_____
_____	_____	_____

TOTAL COSTS AND EXPENSES . . . . $ _____

    B.   LOAN BROKERAGE COMMISSION . . . . $ _____

    C.   LIENS AND OTHER AMOUNTS to be paid out of the principal amount of the loan on authorization of the borrower are estimated to be as follows:

PAYABLE TO

	Broker	Others
1. Fire or other property insurance premiums	_____	_____
2. Credit life or disability insurance premiums (see paragraph II-E)	_____	_____
3. Beneficiary statement fees	_____	_____
4. Reconveyance and similar fees	_____	_____
5. Liens against property securing loan:		
_____	_____	_____
_____	_____	_____
6. Other:		
_____	_____	_____

TOTAL TO BE PAID ON AUTHORIZATION OF BORROWER $ _____

The undersigned certifies that the lender for this loan will not be the broker or designated representative, either directly or indirectly, and that the loan will be made in compliance with the provisions of the California Real Estate Law.

_____   OR   _____
(Broker)   (Designated Representative)

_____   _____
(License Number)   (License Number)

NOTICE TO BORROWER

DO NOT SIGN this statement until you have read and understand all of the information in it. All parts of the form must be completed before you sign.

The broker will rely on the INFORMATION ON LIENS in Paragraph II-C which was supplied by you. Be sure that you have stated all liens accurately. If you contract with the broker to arrange this loan and if the loan cannot be made because you did not state these liens correctly, you may be liable for payment of commission, fees and expenses.

The commission to be paid by you to the broker as shown in Paragraph III-B is customarily a percentage of the principal amount of the loan. The percentage that may be charged as a commission increases with the length of the loan. Keep this in mind in deciding upon the term for repayment of the loan.

Borrower hereby acknowledges the receipt of a copy of this statement.

DATED: _____   _____
                                           (Borrower)

                                               _____
                                               (Borrower)

FIGURE 13–5 (concluded)

fore the first sale; or executed as a means of financing the first purchase of property as so improved, and subordinated to another trust deed. A standard purchase money second trust deed on a new subdivision house is an example of this latter type of promotional note.

Real property securities permit

Before selling real property securities to the public, a permit must be obtained from the Real Estate Commissioner. This permit may be obtained to sell existing securities or may authorize the applicant to acquire and sell securities under any proposed plan or program. In the latter case, the permit would be obtained prior to acquisition of the securities. Before issuing a permit, the Commissioner will inquire into the subject matter of the application to determine whether the proposed plan and proposed sale would be fair, just, and equitable. The fee for the application for a permit is the same as that required for a permit to issue stock in a California corporation, and fee schedules are available at any office of the Department of Real Estate.

An annual audit report listing total number of sales, dollar volume, and other pertinent data must be filed with the Real Estate Commissioner by every real property securities dealer. All advertising material must be filed with the Commissioner 10 days prior to its use, and no dealer shall use any such material in any way after receiving notice in writing that such material contains any statement that is false or misleading or omits to state material information necessary to make the statement therein complete and accurate.

Securities dealer's statement. A disclosure statement called a *real property security statement,* must be furnished to the purchaser of the real property security. The form of the statement is shown in Section 2977 of the Commissioner's rules and regulations and provides the necessary information as required by law.

QUESTIONS FOR DISCUSSION

1. Discuss the various institutional lenders in your particular area and their policies with regard to real estate loans.

2. Discuss the loans and terms available through non-institutional lenders in your area.

3. What types of loans may banks make that savings and loan associations may not?

4. Discuss the basic differences between the Cal-Vet, FHA, and VA programs.

5. Discuss the specific conditions which require a broker to conform with the Real Property Loan Brokerage Law.

6. Define real property securities and special requirements imposed upon a dealer in such securities.

7. Why might a seller of property prefer a buyer to obtain conventional rather than FHA-insured financing?

8. In addition to FHA-insured loans for home purchase, what other types of loans does FHA insure?

9. From what source are funds for the Cal-Vet program obtained?

10. In what basic way do the FHA and VA programs differ?

MULTIPLE CHOICE QUESTIONS

13-1. The greatest amount of loan funds in the real estate market is provided by: *(a)* FHA, *(b)* commercial banks, *(c)* savings and loan associations, *(d)* VA.

13-2. The best loan term is generally obtainable with respect to: *(a)* commercial properties, *(b)* industrial developments *(c)* newer properties, *(d)* purchasers having a large down payment.

13-3. A dealer in real property securities must hold a license as: *(a)* real estate broker, *(b)* stockbroker, *(c)* securities analyst, *(d)* none of these.

13-4. Secondary financing is most often provided by: *(a)* banks, *(b)* federal savings and loan associations, *(c)* private parties, *(d)* state of California.

13-5. The Federal Housing Administration: *(a)* guarantees loan funds, *(b)* builds tract developments, *(c)* provides money to federal banks, *(d)* acts as insurer.

13-6. Title to property purchased with a California-Veterans loan is held by: *(a)* purchaser, *(b)* title company, *(c)* state of California, *(d)* none of these.

13-7. Bank appraisal policies are generally: *(a)* very liberal with respect to commercial properties, *(b)* conservative, *(c)* set by FHA, *(d)* very favorable to speculative properties.

13-8. The Veterans Administration guarantee provides protection to: *(a)* veteran, *(b)* seller, *(c)* bank, *(d)* title company.

14   Appraisal and valuation of real property

Since property valuation is the basis of all real estate transactions, real estate licensees should be familiar with the theoretical aspects and concepts of value, the forces that influence values, and the methods by which such values may best be estimated. Each day clients will question the licensee about such things as the worth, fair price, fair rental, fair basis for trade, or proper amount of insurance coverage for a particular piece of property. The licensee must be able to answer such questions correctly and in detail. The broker must remember that when he accepts a listing he obligates himself to put forth his best efforts to find a buyer for the property, and he can only do so if he and the owner have set a fair price that will attract potential purchasers.

FACTORS INFLUENCING VALUE

Directional growth

In any estimate of value, attention should be paid to the directional growth of the area. This growth refers to the manner and direction in which the city or town tends to grow. Properties in the direction of growth tend to increase in value, especially if the growth is steady and rapid.

Location

The value of all types of properties is greatly affected by location, and quite often, all other factors being equal, the location is the greatest determinant of the market value of a particular property.

Utility

This factor involves judgment about the best use to which a property may be put and includes the capacity of the property to produce income. Local ordinances such as building codes and restrictions and zoning ordinances affect the utility of a property.

Land composition

The type of soil and its size, shape, and slope all affect the value of the property. It is easier to build on a level lot than on a sloping one, and shopping centers must always be on level land. View lots, however, which tend to be quite valuable, usually have quite a bit of slope, as do hillside properties. Additional problems of slides and drainage play an important part in the determination of value.

Character of the neighborhood

The socioeconomic level of the neighborhood is a very important factor regulating value. The general age of the properties, the number and quality of the schools, transportation facilities, shopping centers, and recreational facilities are all quite important.

Economic trends

These include business trends, wage levels, available money and credit, interest rates, tax loads, and population growth.

Political and governmental regulations

Included here are such items as building codes, health codes and regulations, zoning laws, fire regulations, credit controls, and government guaranteed and insured loans.

Different types of value

Although most individuals think of value as monetary value, it is interesting to note that there are many types of value, such as:

1. Economic value
2. Appraised value
3. Potential value
4. Book value
5. Depreciated value
6. Face value
7. Cash value
8. Exchange value
9. Market value
10. Salvage value
11. Tax value
12. Assessed value
13. Replacement value
14. Rental value
15. Liquidation value
16. Mortgage loan value
17. Insurance value
18. Leasehold value
19. Nuisance value
20. Equity value

MARKET VALUE

When people refer to the value of property, they most generally mean the market value. The market value is the price for which a property will sell in the open market if the seller is not under any extreme pressure to sell and the buyer is not under any extreme pressure to buy, with a reasonable time allowed the broker to effect the sale. It is also assumed that both the seller and prospective buyer are fully informed of all uses to which the property is adapted and for which it is capable of being used.

APPRAISAL

To appraise means to arrive at an estimate and opinion of the value of a property. An appraisal is usually a statement of the market value and/or value for loan purposes of a particular piece of property as of a specific date. It is generally accepted that there are three ways to approach a value estimate: (1) market-comparison approach, (2) cost approach, and (3) income-capitalization approach.

The market-comparison approach

This is the most commonly used of all approaches to value. Quite simply, the broker finds comparables, that is, he finds properties very similar to the one he is appraising. These comparables must be properties that have sold recently. By comparing the selling prices of these properties, the broker can arrive at a valid estimate of value for the property he is appraising. Comparable properties that have been placed on the market but have not sold are excellent indicators of the uppermost limit of value.

The market-comparison approach is the one most generally used by real estate brokers and salesmen. It lends itself well to the appraisal of land, buildings, and other properties that exhibit a high degree of similarity and for which a ready market exists. This method is also particularly applicable as a check against the other two methods of appraising, when the end result is to obtain a market value.

The mechanics of the process involve the use of market data of all kinds in order to compare closely the property being appraised with other similar properties. The sources used for determining a market value are:

1. The practical everyday experience the broker has obtained from dealing in properties in a given locale for a reasonable period of time.
2. The past listings in the brokers' own office and records of the local real estate board and multiple listing service.
3. Real estate advertisements in the local newspapers, to learn asking prices for properties in the area.
4. Regular contact with other brokers, salesmen, loan officers, escrow officers, and others who are continually in touch with the local real estate market.
5. A knowledge of the influence of such factors as location, size of lot, condition, number, and size of units in a building, rental market, and operating expenses in connection with the piece of property to be appraised.

Asking prices. One must remember that the asking price of a piece of property may not be its ultimate selling price. The price at which a property is listed may often indicate the probable top market value rather than the average actual selling price. Actual selling price are what purchasers are willing to pay and are the truest indication of the market value of a property.

A piece of real estate correctly listed is said to be half sold. Brokers who take a listing at any price, no matter how ridiculous, do a disservice both to their clients and to themselves, in addition to wasting a great deal of effort.

Proper comparison. Proper comparison is most important. For nearly comparable properties, the value will decrease for such conditions as poor repair, poor design, and existing nuisances, while the price will increase for cleanliness, good design, special features, view, landscaping, and the like. Unless the sales being compared are of recent date, consideration must also be given to adjusting the values in keeping with the general economic conditions.

Some of the advantages of the market-comparison approach are:

1. It is the easiest of the various methods to learn and to use.
2. It is particularly applicable to single family residences, which make up the bulk of real estate transactions.
3. It is the method most easily understood by the nonlicensee.

It is important to remember that comparisons must be suitable, adequate in number, and reliable in source if they are to justify conclusions drawn from them. A CAR competitive market analysis form is illustrated in Figure 14–1, and a CAR standard residential appraisal data sheet in Figure 14–2.

The cost approach

The cost approach to value, also called reproduction-cost approach or replacement-cost approach, is relatively simple in principle. The cost approach is an estimate of the amount of money that would be necessary to duplicate the property under appraisal. Since people ordinarily will not pay more for a property than it would cost to replace the property or to obtain an equally satisfactory substitute property, the cost approach tends to set the upper limit of value.

The key to the correct use of the cost approach is the amount of depreciation the appraiser must allow for property that is not new. The subject of depreciation will be discussed in detail later in this chapter.

Steps in the cost approach. The first step is to make an independent estimate of the value of the land. This is always the current market value of the land, considered as vacant and available for improvement to its highest and best use.

The second step is to make an estimate of the replacement cost, new, of all improvements on the land. Accuracy requires the application of principles of building-cost estimating.

Replacement cost to the appraiser means how much it would cost today to construct a building identical to the one being appraised. This implies taking an inventory of the materials and manufactured equipment that make up the property and then applying to this inventory the current prices of similar materials, equipment, labor costs, and all overhead costs necessary to construct a suitable replacement of the property as of the appraisal date. The methods in such estimates vary from the very technical and detailed procedures used by contractors and mortgage loan companies to the simpler shortcut methods, such as the square-foot and cubic-foot methods, used by most appraisers.

To use the simpler methods, an estimate of the total cost is made by comparison with other similar buildings whose costs are known and have been reduced to units per square foot of floor area of living space, or per cubic foot of the building content. Applying these costs to the actual area of the property under appraisal will give an approximate valuation, provided the data about costs are accurate and the buildings and improvements are similar in quality and design. Corrections must be made for such differences, as well as for changes in cost levels that may have taken place between the date of the basic costs and the date of the new estimate.

Cost figures may be obtained from local contractors or from numerous services that publish building costs. Actually, building costs will vary greatly, based on the efficiency of the builder and the amount of design and quality of construction, so that unless the appraiser is experienced in such matters his estimates of value in this approach may be inaccurate. In appraising older buildings, it is also possible for an appraiser to use a depreciation rate that may cause his estimate under the cost approach to come out the way he wants it to, and thus market comparison and capitalization-of-income approaches.

The third step in the cost-approach method is

COMPETITIVE MARKET ANALYSIS
CALIFORNIA REAL ESTATE ASSOCIATION STANDARD FORM

PROPERTY ADDRESS __165 BALBOA AVENUE,   SAN BERNARDINO, CALIFORNIA__   DATE __July 25, 19--__

FOR SALE NOW:	BED-RMS	BATHS	DEN	SQ. FT.	1ST LOAN	LIST PRICE	DAYS ON MARKET	TERMS
127 Carter Avenue	3	2	No	1350	63,000	109,950	42	CTL or CTNL
801 Thomas Road	3	2	Yes	1450	19,000	114,500	17	35% Dn., 1st to Seller
73 Anza Avenue	3	2	No	1290	71,200	105,950	71	CTNL, 2nd to Seller
83 Center Street	3	2	No	1320	42,700	107,500	43	CTNL
980 Balboa Avenue	4	2	Yes	1400	26,000	114,950	22	35% Dn., 1st to Seller

SOLD PAST 12 MOS.	BED-RMS	BATHS	DEN	SQ. FT.	1ST LOAN	LIST PRICE	DAYS ON MARKET	DATE SOLD	SALE PRICE	TERMS
1153 Savannah Avenue	3	2½	Yes	1380	83,400	109,500	34	7/8	106,500	CTL
23 Thomas Road	3	2	No	1300	48,600	103,950	27	6/21	101,000	20% CTNL
129 Connor Street	3	2	No	1270	24,800	102,500	32	5/18	100,950	CTL
1521 Moraga Street	4	2	Yes	1430	51,300	112,500	73	7/21	109,950	25% CTNL
173 Cervantes Street	3	2	Yes	1400	15,700	109,450	20	6/5	107,000	15% CTL + 2nd

EXPIRED PAST 12 MOS.	BED-RMS	BATHS	DEN	SQ. FT.	1ST LOAN	LIST PRICE	DAYS ON MARKET	TERMS
328 Anza Avenue	3	2½	Yes	1425	47,200	116,950	90	CTNL
1920 Casper Street	3	2	No	1250	31,500	107,500	120	CTNL
1677 Balboa Avenue	4	2	Yes	1360	22,400	113,950	120	CTNL / Submit Terms

F.H.A. ---- V.A. APPRAISALS

ADDRESS	APPRAISAL	ADDRESS	APPRAISAL
1204 Stern Circle	108,500		
1910 Balboa Avenue	105,000		

BUYER APPEAL
(GRADE EACH ITEM 0 TO 20% ON THE BASIS OF DESIRABILITY OR URGENCY)

1. FINE LOCATION __Close to schools/shopping__   20 %
2. EXCITING EXTRAS __Beautiful garden and patio__   20 %
3. EXTRA SPECIAL FINANCING __Seller 1st or 2nd__   20 %
4. EXCEPTIONAL APPEAL __Good condition__   20 %
5. UNDER MARKET PRICE _____ YES _____ NO __0__ %

RATING TOTAL _____ 80 %

MARKETING POSITION

1. WHY ARE THEY SELLING __Business Transfer__   20 %
2. HOW SOON MUST THEY SELL __60 days__   20 %
3. WILL THEY HELP FINANCE . . . . YES __20__ NO _____ %
4. WILL THEY LIST AT COMPETITIVE MARKET VALUE . . YES __20__ NO _____ %
5. WILL THEY PAY FOR APPRAISAL . . . . YES __5__ NO _____ %

RATING TOTAL _____ 85 %

ASSETS __Centrally located. Nearby to public transportation + employment centers__
DRAWBACKS __Older-type gravity hot-air furnace located in basement area.__
AREA MARKET CONDITIONS __Steady demand for this neighborhood. Competitively priced properties are selling.__
RECOMMENDED TERMS __Conventional financing with 20-25% Dn., Seller will carry 2nd loan at 12% for 5 years or may carry 1st at same terms with substantial down payment.__

TOP COMPETITIVE MARKET VALUE . . . . $__107,500__

PROBABLE FINAL SALES PRICE . . . . $__105,000__

SELLING COSTS

BROKERAGE	$	6,300
LOAN PAYOFF	$	32,000
PREPAYMENT PRIVILEGE	$	835
FHA --- VA POINTS	$	
TITLE AND ESCROW FEES: IRS STAMPS RECONS RECORDING	$	890
TERMITE CLEARANCE	$	75
MISC. PAYOFFS: 2ND T.D., POOL, PATIO, WTR. SFTNR., FENCE, IMPROVEMENT BOND.	$	200
	$	
	$	
TOTAL	$	40,300

TOTAL . . . . $ 40,300

NET PROCEEDS $ 64,700   PLUS OR 300 MINUS $

FIGURE 14-1

Standard Residential Appraisal Data Sheet

1. Location		City			Parcel	

2. Legal

3. Owner		Address			Phone	
4. Tenant		Rent Paid $	Mo. to Mo.	☐ Leased to		Fair Mo. Rental $

LAND DESCRIPTION

5. Location	On	side of			St.		Feet from				St.

6. Lot	x	ft.	sf	Typical ☐	Alley ☐	Level ☐	Hilly ☐	Filled ☐

	At Grade ☐	Above ft.	Below ft.	Drainage		Retaining Wall

7. Street	Paved ☐	Oiled ☐	Dirt ☐	Walks ☐	Curbs ☐	Gutters ☐	St. Lights ☐
8. Utilities	Water ☐	Gas ☐	Light ☐	Phone ☐	Sewer ☐	Cesspool ☐	Sep. Tank ☐

9. Zoning

10. Deed Restrictns.	Use		Archt.	Cost $	Race ☐	Liquor ☐	Expire Yr.
11. Taxes	County Taxes:	Land $	Impts. $	City:	Land $	Impts. $	Total $

DESCRIPTION OF IMPROVEMENTS

12. Building	Age yrs.	Useful Life yrs.	No. Rooms	No. B. Rms.	No. Baths	No. Porches	No. Stories
13. Style	Spanish ☐	Colonial ☐	English ☐	Monterey ☐	Farm House ☐	Plain ☐	Calif. ☐
14. Livability	Plan	Housework	Socially	Homey	Built-ins	Closets	Yard
15. Garage— x	Attached ☐ Detached ☐	Floor	Roof	Walls	Type Door		Work Bench ☐
16. Special							

YARD DESCRIPTION

17. Lawn	Front ☐	Side ☐	Rear ☐	Flowers ☐	Vines ☐	Hedge ☐	
18. Sprinkling Sys.	Front ☐	Side ☐	Rear ☐	Fountain ☐	Fish Pond ☐	No. Faucets ☐	
19. Shrubs—Trees	Front	Side	Rear	Shade ☐	Fruit ☐	Ornamental ☐	
20. Wall—Fence	Height ft.	Lineal ft.	Concrete ☐ Tile ☐	Wood ☐	Stucco ☐	Brick ☐	
21. Special	Rock Garden ☐	Barbecue ☐	Plunge ☐	Dressing Rooms ☐	Sun Deck ☐ Sun Patio ☐	Tennis ☐ Badminton ☐	
22. Driveway	Width ft	Area sf	Cement ☐	Asphalt ☐	Ribbon ☐	Dirt ☐	
23. Walks	Front ☐	Area sf	Side ☐	Area sf	Back ☐	Area sf	Total

DESCRIPTION OF DISTRICT

24. District	Years old		Built up %	Growing ☐	Static ☐	Receding ☐	
25. Property Adj.	To left		To right		Opposite		
26. Setting	Typical ☐	Fits District ☐	Over-Improved	Under-Improved			
27. Distances to	Gr. School blks	Hi. School blks	Bus/car blks	Stores blks	Park blks	Theatre blks	
28. Nuisances	Noises ☐	Odors ☐	Smoke ☐	Dust ☐	Encroachments		
29. Owner occupied	Pride in ☐						

PLAT OF BUILDING

STREET LOCATION

COMPARABLE SALES IN DISTRICT

Location	No. Rooms	Price	Date Sold
1.		$	
2		$	
3.		$	

FIGURE 14–2

BUILDING DESCRIPTION

REMARKS

30.	Building type	Single ☐	Double ☐	Duplex ☐	Flat ☐	Court ☐	Apt. ☐				
31.	Class of Bldg.	1 story ☐	1½ story ☐	2 story ☐	Frame ☐	Stucco ☐	Brick ☐				
32.	Exterior	Siding ☐	B.B. ☐	Stucco ☐	Tile ☐	Brick ☐	Adobe ☐				
33.	Foundation	Concrete ☐	Stone ☐	Brick ☐	Mudsill ☐	Piers ☐	Posts ☐				
34.	Under-pinning	Joists x in.	Set in. o.c.	Clearance in.	Vents ☐	Bracing					
35.	Floors	Hdw. ☐	Pine ☐	Cement ☐	Sub-floor ☐	Diagonal ☐	Horizontal ☐				
36.	Basement	x ft.	Height ft.	Conc. floor ☐	Conc. wall ☐	Dirt ☐	Furnace ☐				
37.	Roof	Shingle ☐	Tile ☐	Slate ☐	Comp. ☐	Flat ☐	Pitch ☐				
38.	Porches	Front ☐	Side ☐	Back ☐	Conc. floor ☐	Wood floor ☐	Tile Floor ☐				
39.	Heating	Unit heat ☐	Floor heater ☐	Wall heater ☐	Gas jets ☐	Fireplace ☐	Elect. ☐				
40.	Elec. wiring	Conduits ☐	B.X. ☐	Tube ☐	Ceiling ☐	Wall ☐	Floor Plugs ☐				

ROOM DESCRIPTION

CONDITION

						Poor	Fair	Good
41.	Living Room	Floor	Walls	Ceiling	Trim			
42.	Dining Room	Floor	Walls	Ceiling	Trim			
		Built-Ins						
43.	Breakfast Room	Floor	Walls	Ceiling	Trim			
44.	Bed Rooms. No.	Floor	Walls	Ceiling	Sleeping Porch ☐			
45.	Bath Rooms. No.	Floor	Walls	Ceiling	Gas Heat ☐ / Electric ☐			
		Toilet ☐	Basin ☐	Tub (shower) ☐	Stall shower ☐			
46.	Kitchen	Floor	Walls	Ceiling	Trim			
		Sink	Built-Ins					
47.	Service Porch	Floor	Walls	Ceiling	Laundry tray ☐			
		Basin ☐	Toilet ☐	Water heater ☐	Ironing Board ☐			
48.	Servants Quarters	Maids room ☐	Chauffeur ☐	Bath ☐	Area sf			
	Guests House	No. rooms	Built on Separate Bldg. ☐	Bath ☐	Area sf			
49.	Other	Den ☐	Powder Room ☐	Sun Room ☐	Wash room ☐			

CONSTRUCTION AND CONDITION

50.	Construction	Poor ☐	Fair ☐	Good ☐	Best ☐
51.	Sq. Ft. Area	House sf	Porches sf	Basement sf	Garage sf
52.	General	Termites	Dampness	Dry Rot	Settling
53.	Repairs Needed				

REPLACEMENT COST

54.	House (Porches ½)	sf @ $.	$
55.	Basement	sf @ $.	$
56.	Other	sf @ $.	$
	Garage	sf @ $.	$
57.	Walks–Drive	sf @ $.	$
58.	Fence–Walls–Special		$
59.	Landscaping–Sprinkling		$
60.	Replacement Cost New		$
61.	Less Depreciation Yrs.	$	$
62.	Less Needed Repairs	$	$
63.	Depreciated Cost Improvements		$
64.	Value Land as Improved		$
65.	Replacement Cost Depreciated		$
66.	Value Indicated by Comparable Sales		$
67.	Estimated Fair Market Value		$

SUMMARY ITEMS

Taxes	$
Insurance	$
Street Bonds	$
Yearly Rental	$
Present Loan	$
Loan Recommended	$
Mortgagee?	
Lessee?	
Remarks	

Date   Signed   Address   Phone

FIGURE 14–2 (*concluded*)

to determine the existing depreciation of the property. This amount must be deducted from the replacement cost new to determine the value of the building. The difficulty of correctly estimating depreciation tends to increase with the age of the property, and requires skill, experience, and good judgement on the part of the appraiser. A value determined by using the cost approach on any building more than a few years old is no more reliable than is the estimate of depreciation the appraiser used in his calculations.

There is no justification in always assuming that improvements depreciate at a rate corresponding to their age, although too often this is done by the inexperienced appraiser. It is common knowledge to the experienced broker that older property in a good location will sell for more than a similar newer property elsewhere. It is not uncommon for property to actually appreciate rather than depreciate in value as it gets older.

The fourth step in the cost-approach method is to add the value of the land to the amount the appraiser has decided to apply to the value of the building, which he has determined by calculating the replacement cost new, less depreciation.

The cost-approach method is frequently used to get a ceiling on the value established by the other two approaches to value. It is particularly appropriate for appraising newly built properties, where there is virtually no depreciation. It is also a good method for public-service properties, which have no active market and thus lack market data that can be used for a market-comparison approach, and which also produce no income on which to base an income-capitalization approach. Examples of this type of property are (a) government buildings, (b) churches, (c) recreational structures, and (d) buildings that are unique and specialized, so that few comparables exist in the community.

The capitalization-of-income approach

The income approach is concerned with the present worth of future income of property. This method is particularly important in the valuation of income-producing properties. It is measured by the net income one assumes the property will produce during its remaining economic life. The following is a simple example.

Paul Fisher wants to purchase an income property that shows a present annual net income of $23,000. Fisher thinks that he should receive a return of 10 percent on his investment. Thus, Fisher would capitalize the $23,000 income at a rate of 10 percent and would arrive at a value of $230,000 for the building. This means that if Fisher pays $230,000 for the building, the $23,000 net income he receives each year equals a 10 percent return on his investment, since 10 percent of $230,000 is $23,000.

Steps in the income-capitalization approach. Three main steps are involved in the income-capitalization approach. First, a net annual income is derived by deducting total expenses from the gross income of the property. Unless such figures have remained fairly constant, it is important that current trends in income and expenses be taken into account in figuring the net income.

Second, a selection is made of an appropriate capitalization rate, or, as it is sometimes called, the present worth factor. This is the most important step in using the income approach to value. The rate selected depends on the return investors actually demand before they will be attracted by a particular investment. The greater the risk of recapturing the investment price, the higher the accompanying rate as determined in the market for such properties.

By analyzing and knowing market prices on various types of income properties and checking against the net income produced, a broker can determine the going capitalization rate for various types of properties in his area of operation. The rate of return will generally be higher on older properties and lower on new buildings, although there may be exceptions to the rule.

It is important to note that a slight variation in the rate used makes a substantial difference in the capitalized value of the income. Using a net income of $28,000 capitalized at 9 percent, the property value is approximately $311,000. Using a 10 percent capitalization rate, the property value is $280,000.

The third step after having determined the net income, then, is to apply the capitalization rate selected against the net income and arrive at a figure that represents the appraised value of the property.

Establishing net income. As important as the selection of a realistic rate is the proper determination of the net income of the property under appraisal. The net income figure is determined by deducting from the total gross income of the building the following items: taxes, utilities (gas, electric, water), refuse collection costs, insurance, license, management, vacancy factor, repairs, janitor, gardener, replacement reserve, and furniture depreciation.

Not all buildings will have all the above expenses. A large office building or hotel would have a very complicated and detailed operating expense statement, whereas the typical smaller income property would have only the more common expenses, such as taxes, water, gas and electric, garbage, insurance, and miscellaneous expenses.

Once the net income has been established, the capitalization rate is applied and a valuation figure is determined. The net income at present is considered to be perpetuity, and on this net income the appraisal is determined. Actually, a purchaser may improve a piece of income property after he buys it, and within a short time he may have increased the net income and realized an even greater percentage return on his investment than he had anticipated at the time of purchase. The net income divided by the capitalization rate desired equals the appraised value by the income capitalization method.

Determination of the capitalization rate. A look at some of the commonly recognized textbooks on appraisal will reveal various methods, many of them mathematically complex and detailed, for determining an appropriate capitalization rate to be used in the income-capitalization method. Those who are not expert appraisers must, of course, have some fairly simple and basic rules for determining the rate. The following rules will allow an individual to arrive at a capitalization rate that, for all practical purposes, is as valid as one arrived at by the use of complicated mathematical formulas.

1. While one tries to make an investment that will bring the best rate of return possible, the lower limit should never be very much less than the current rate of interest for long-term loans on the particular type of property under appraisal.

2. Rates at any particular time tend to be uniform for comparable types of properties in any particular geographical area. The real estate licensee who deals with these properties day after day will certainly be aware of the general rates of return investors may expect to receive. One way that many licensees arrive at a quick estimate of the capitalization rate for a building being offered for sale is to divide the net income by the price being asked. Assuming a building offered for $640,000 showing a net income of $48,000, the capitalization rate can be determined as follows:

$$\frac{\$48,000}{\$640,000} = 0.075 = 7\frac{1}{2}\%$$

The rate arrived at in the above example assumes that the purchaser will pay the full asking price. Since the selling price will usually be less than the asking price, the actual rate of return will be slightly higher. Assuming that the building finally sells for $600,000, instead of the asking price, we divide the $600,000 into the $48,000 net income and the result will be a rate of 8 percent.

3. Rates of return on investments other than real estate have an effect here. What the investor might realize on his investment in something other than real estate is an important consideration. If the rate of return will be little more than what might be received from good stocks or bonds, the investor may not want to purchase a piece of property with all the inherent problems of management.

4. An extremely important consideration, and perhaps the most important to many investors, is the effect of the investment on the purchaser's tax setup. Income property may be depreciated for tax purposes and the depreciation used as an offset against income from the property. This may give the owner a considerable amount of tax-free income in connection with this investment.

5. The rate the investor is willing to accept also is determined by such factors as: special features of the property, which the purchaser wants and which cannot be measured purely in terms of income; the amount of appreciation the property will experience in the future; and plans for modernizing and upgrading that will increase the net income. All these are important in the final decision the buyer makes about the rate of return he feels he should receive from a particular piece of property.

6. Buildings may contain illegal dwelling units, and often brokers look at properties where original large units have been divided into smaller ones. In some cases, additional units have been added. In many cases the broker often finds that these units were not inspected and passed at the time of their construction, and are thus in violation of local building and health codes. Many older properties are found in disrepair and contain numerous code violations. It is evident that on such properties the investor will demand a different rate of return, since he assumes a much higher risk factor as far as the stability of the property and its income are concerned. He may also have to expend a large amount for upkeep and repairs.

Since the capitalization rate measures the risk

involved in the investment, it is generally true that the higher the risk, the higher the rate; the lower the risk, the lower the rate. Rates of return on income properties may vary greatly depending on the general age and condition of the property and degree of risk involved.

Building- and land-residual methods

In our previous discussion of the capitalization-of-income approach, land and improvements were not considered separately, but rather as a whole, and a single rate was applied to the net income to determine the value. Often, however, appraisers do not consider the property as a whole but instead separate the process of finding the value attributable to the land from that attributable to the building. This involves the use of a residual process of capitalization in which a portion of the net income is first capitalized to find the value of the land or the improvements separately, with the residual, that is the remaining portion of the net income, capitalized to determine the value of the other portion of the real estate. The two are then added together to arrive at the value of the property as a whole.

Where the improvements are new or fairly new and their value is easy to ascertain, the land assumes the residual role, and the process used by the appraiser is known as the land-residual method. Under the land-residual method the value of the improvements is first determined apart from the land and then the value of the land is found.

The position of improvements and land are reversed under the building-residual method, which is when the land value is more clearly known, as might be the case with an extremely valuable commercial site improved with an old residential structure. Where neither the land nor building value can easily be determined, appraisers use what is termed the *property-residual method*, in which the land and improvements are considered together and the net income is applied to the whole.

The income of real property may in some cases be considered as continuing indefinitely into perpetuity, or it may be expected to last only for certain periods of time, in which case it is termed nonperpetuity income. The appraiser has a choice of various methods of capitalization, such as straight line, sinking fund, and annuity. These three methods may also be used to determine an-

ticipated future depreciation, which is discussed later in this chapter.

Gross multipliers

A gross-multiplier or gross-monthly-multiplier method is used by many real estate licensees to assist in making an estimate of the value of real property. This method is based upon the market relationship between rental value and the sale price of such properties. For instance, a certain type of property might often be sold as a price that is approximately 100 times the monthly gross income. Thus a property with a gross monthly income of $6000 will show an indicated value of $600,000. A gross multiplier, then, is applied to an income amount to arrive at an approximate market value figure.

Prices determined by gross multipliers are usually considered only as general indications of value and not as a substitute for actual appraisal. Assuming that care has been taken to use comparable properties and that multipliers have been developed from adequate factual evidence, estimates made on such a basis can be quite useful for a quick approximation of market value.

Appraisal organizations

Many organizations work to standardize and upgrade techniques of appraising. Among these are The American Institute of Real Estate Appraisers, The American Society of Appraisers, and The Society of Real Estate Appraisers.

To obtain the designation MAI (member of the American Institute), the candidate must meet the age, experience, and study requirements, and must pass extensive examinations covering the entire field of appraising. Similarly, the Society of Real Estate Appraisers awards the SREA designation, and the American Society of Appraisers the ASA designation.

Depreciation

Since depreciation is so important to the appraisal of real property, we shall, at this point, define it in more detail. Depreciation in its real sense means a loss in value from any cause. A simple example is an automobile. Each year it depreciates and is worth less money. The reasons are (1) age and (2) wear. Depreciation in the real sense of the word is sometimes hard to relate to real estate. It is quite common to find aging buildings that are selling for higher prices than in years past. Instead of depreciating in value, real property over the years has tended to appreciate in value.

In addition to depreciation in the sense of a loss in value, another common type of depreciation that affects property is depreciation for tax purposes. It is actually a method of returning to the investor in business or income property, over a certain number of years, an amount equal to the purchase price of the building.

Before discussing depreciation for tax purposes, let us return to the traditional depreciation we first defined above, a loss in value from any source. This depreciation includes all the influences that reduce the value of the property below its replacement cost new. The principal influences are physical deterioration, functional obsolescence, and economic and social obsolescence.

Physical deterioration is wear and tear from use and from the elements. It may also result from negligent care, damage by termites, and damage from dry-rot or from wood-destroying organisms.

Functional obsolescence means poor architectural design and style—the lack of modern facilities and out-of-date equipment and/or poorly planned interiors and lack of adequate space.

Economic and social obsolescence means misplacement of improvement. An area that 50 years ago was completely residential has changed over the years, so that now it is a mixture of residential, commercial, and perhaps light manufacturing. What few residences remain are now economically and socially obsolete. They are wrong for the location as far as their use is concerned. Detrimental influence of supply and demand and zoning or legislative restrictions also cause this type of obsolescence.

While the first and second groups above are considered to be inherent in the property itself, the third group of influences consists of factors that are extraneous to the property itself. Physical and functional depreciation may be corrected by modernization and improvement of the existing structure. New wiring may be installed, plumbing modernized, kitchens and bathrooms brought up to date, and modern heating systems installed. Economic and social obsolescence is much more difficult to correct, and usually necessitates an urban renewal and redevelopment project on a large scale.

Determining depreciation. In using the reproduction cost approach, the appraiser must determine the amount of depreciation that has occurred. Several methods are in current use.

Observed-condition method. This is the most widely used in actual practice today and is also referred to as the cost-to-cure method. The appraiser must correctly determine the total cost of making all the necessary repairs in order to correct any curable physical deterioration and functional obsolescence, and, in addition, he must estimate the actual loss in value as a result of all types of depreciation in connection with the building.

The steps in utilizing the observed-condition or cost-to-cure method are as follows:

1. The deficiencies of the building, both inside and outside, are observed, and their costs to cure are calculated. This cost to cure is the amount of accrued depreciation which has taken place.

2. An amount for physical deterioration or deferred maintenance for needed repairs and replacements is computed.

3. Functional obsolescence due to outmoded plumbing fixtures, lighting fixtures, and kitchen equipment is determined and assigned a dollar value.

4. Functional obsolescence which cannot economically be cured, such as poor room arrangements, improved construction materials, and the like, is measured by calculating the estimated loss in rental value due to this condition.

5. Economic obsolescence is caused by conditions outside the property and is measured by determining the estimated loss of rental value of the property as compared with a similar property in an economically stable neighborhood. The capitalized rental loss is distributed between the building value and land value.

Age-life method. This method is based on depreciation tables that have been developed to reflect age-life experience in the depreciation of structures of various types and uses, assuming average care and maintenance. Such tables may be obtained from the Bureau of Internal Revenue, by requesting Publication 534 which deals with depreciation.

Additional methods. Appraisal textbooks generally explain methods other than those referred to above, and these methods are mainly mathematical ones that capitalize an income. One of the more popular is the building-residual method mentioned previously. In this method, the land is valued independently of the building, and the fair annual net return of the land is deducted from the estimated net annual income of the prop-

202

erty. The residual amount is said to be attributable to the depreciated building and is capitalized to indicate the building value. The depreciation figure is the building value. The depreciation figure is the difference between the residual value of the building, as shown above, and that of a new structure of a similar type.

It is in the use of the cost approach to appraisal that methods of determining depreciation are most important. This method is widely used in the field of appraisal and yet its validity rests mainly on a correct determination of depreciation, which is both difficult and confusing at times. It is this weakness that causes the reproduction-cost method to be most valid only if it is used to determine the value of new or nearly new property for which reproduction costs can be accurately determined without having to determine a complicated depreciation figure.

Providing for future depreciation. With respect to the income approach to value, various methods have been developed to provide for anticipated future depreciation and they involve the use of certain types of interest tables. The three commonly used methods are the straight-line depreciation method, the sinking-fund method, and the annuity method.

With the straight-line method, a fixed amount is set for depreciation and applied each year over the estimated life of the improvements. For example, if a building valued at $800,000 is estimated to have a 20-year life, then the value divided by the number of years would, in this case, result in an annual depreciation amount of $40,000.

The sinking-fund method employs an annual amount of depreciation, which if invested each year at compound interest will recapture the amount attributable to the building at the end of the number of years assigned to it as its estimated life. The annuity method is similar to the sinking-fund method, but with the annuity method a part of the invested capital is periodically recaptured and is paid to the investor, together with a return on the invested capital in the same payment.

Depreciation for tax purposes. The depreciation we have been discussing in this chapter on appraisal and valuation is generally referred to as traditional depreciation. However, what most licensees, accountants, and others in real estate dealings mean when they refer to depreciation is not traditional depreciation but depreciation as it relates to income tax and the Internal Revenue Service.

It is this depreciation for tax purposes that is of vital importance to real estate investors. The Internal Revenue Code states that depreciation (as used for tax purposes) is a reasonable allowance for the exhaustion, wear and tear, and normal obsolescence of property that is (1) used in a trade or business, and (2) held for the production of income. This depreciation allowance may be deducted from the gross income received from such property in arriving at the net income. This type of depreciation is discussed in detail in Chapter 17, Income Tax and Real Estate.

Summary of appraisal and valuation methods

The *market-comparison method* is by far the most logical and simple technique for establishing the value of property, and it is the method commonly used by brokers and salesmen in the field.

The value most sought by those dealing in real estate is the market value, that is, the price the property will sell for in the open market. Comparables exist for virtually all existent types and kinds of properties. The actual selling prices in the marketplace are much more valid for computation than are many of the complex mathematical processes that many appraisers use. Indeed, it is interesting to note that in many appraisal reports the appraiser may purposefully use mathematics in such a way that the figures obtained by the income capitalization and reproduction cost methods will agree with the amount obtained by the market comparison approach.

The *income-capitalization method* has merit to a limited extent, since some of the assumptions the appraiser must make in using this approach are certainly matters of personal judgment alone, and may or may not be entirely correct. It is very easy to misjudge in attempting either to arrive at a net income or to select the appropriate capitalization rate for use in the appraisal. Assuming that both the net income and rate selected are proper for the particular location and market in which the property is located, the valuation arrived at by the use of this method is merely a check against the others.

The *replacement-cost method* is correctly used only in appraising new or nearly new buildings. For other types of structures this method merely sets an upper limit of value. The depreciation factor is the main problem in this approach. When replacement cost is employed in the appraisal of older properties, it is too easy for the appraiser to manipulate the depreciation allowance so that

VETERANS ADMINISTRATION
RESIDENTIAL APPRAISAL REPORT

	CASE NUMBER
	LH 37298

1. MAJOR STRUCTURES	A. TYPICAL COND.	B. BUILT-UP	C. AGE	TYPE BLDG.	D. OWN OCCUP	E. VACANCY	F. ZONING	G. LAND USE CHGS.	2. PROPERTY IS	3. BLDG. WARRANTY IN FORCE?
NEIGHBORHOOD	Good	100-	10		95 -	0 -	R-1	None	[X] OCCUPIED	[ ] YES [X] NO
BLOCK	Good	100-	10		95 -	0 -	R-1	None	[ ] VACANT	[ ] UNKNOWN

4. STATUS OF PROPERTY
[ ] A. PROPOSED   [ ] B. EXISTING, NOT PREVIOUSLY OCCUPIED   [X] C. EXISTING, PREVIOUSLY OCCUPIED   [ ] D. ALTERATIONS IMPROVEMTS. OR REPAIRS   [ ] E. REFINANCING - VETERAN APPLICANT OWNS AND OCCUPIES RESIDENCE AS HOME

5. CONSTRUCTION COMPLETED BEFORE DATE HEREOF
[ ] A. WITHIN 12 CALENDAR MOS.   [X] B. MORE THAN 12 CALENDAR MOS.

6. NAME AND ADDRESS OF FIRM OR PERSON MAKING REQUEST (Complete mailing address. Include ZIP Code)

Aladdin Mortgage Company
123 Rainbow Parkway
Berkeley, California 94704

7. PROPERTY ADDRESS (Include ZIP Code)

456 Pioneer Way
Concord, California 94519

8. TYPE OF PROPERTY	9. MANDATORY HOME ASSOCIATION MEMBERSHIP?	10A. NO. BLDGS.
[X] HOME		1
[ ] MOBILE HOME LOT	[ ] YES [X] NO	10B. NO. LIVING UNITS 1

11. LOT DIMENSIONS   60' X 120'

12. DESCRIPTION

	WOOD SIDING	CINDER BLOCK	SPLIT LEVEL	6 NO. ROOMS	1 DINING ROOM	2 CAR GARAGE X	GAS X	CEN AIR COND
[X] DETACHED	WOOD SHINGLE	STONE	% BASEMENT	3 BEDROOMS	1 KITCHEN	CAR CARPORT	UNDERGRD. WIRE	TYPE HEAT. & FUEL
SEMI-DET.	ALUM. SIDING	BRICK & BLOCK	SLAB	2 BATHS	FAMILY RM. X	WATER (Public) X	SEWER (Public) X	FA Gas
ROW	ASB. SHINGLE X	STUCCO X	CRAWL SPACE	1/2 BATHS	UTILITY RM.	WATER (Comm.)	SEWER (Comm.)	ROOFING DESCRIP.
CONDOMINIUM	BRICK VENEER X 1	STORIES 10	YRS. EST. AGE 1	LIVING RM. 1	FIREPLACE 1	WATER (Ind.)	SEPTIC TANK	Asph. Shgl.

13. LEGAL DESCRIPTION

Lot 3, Block 24
Tract 1259
Contra Costa County,
California

14. TITLE LIMITATIONS, INCLUDING EASEMENTS, RESTRICTIONS, ENCROACHMENTS, HOMEOWNERS ASSOCIATION AND SPECIAL ASSESSMENTS, ETC.

PUE across rear 5 feet of lot.

15. OFFSITE IMPROVEMENTS

A. STREET SURFACE	Asphalt	
B. STREET ACCESS	D. ADD'L. IMPROVEMENTS	
[ ] PRIV. [X] PUB.	[X] STORM SEWER	
C. STREET MAINT.	[X] SIDEWALK	
[ ] PRIV. [X] PUB.	[X] CURB/GUTTER	

16. REPAIRS NECESSARY TO MAKE PROPERTY CONFORM TO APPLIC. MPR'S

17. REMARKS (Complete A through F. Use supplemental sheet or reverse, if necessary.)

A. DETRIMENTAL INFLUENCES	None
B. REAL ESTATE MARKET IN COMMUNITY	Moderate Demand
C. HIGHEST AND BEST USE	Single-Family Residential
D. FEDERAL FLOOD HAZARD MAP ISSUED?	[X] YES [ ] NO (If "Yes," complete Item 17E)
E. PROP. IN SPECIAL FLOOD HAZARD AREA?	[ ] YES [X] NO
F. EXPLAIN DEPRECIATION	Normal physical deterioration

TOTAL ESTIMATED COST OF REPAIRS $ - 0 -

18. MARKET DATA

ITEM	SUBJECT PROPERTY	COMPARABLE NO. 1	COMPARABLE NO. 2		COMPARABLE NO. 3	
ADDRESS		20 Ranch Avenue	49 Miner Way		273 Golden Road	
SALE PRICE		$ 118,000	$ 108,000		$ 109,500	
TYPE OF FINANCING		Conv.	Conv.			
	DESCRIPTION	DESCRIPTION ADJ.	DESCRIPTION	ADJ.	DESCRIPTION	ADJ.
DATE OF SALE	6/3/--	4/12/-- + $2,000	3/6/-- +	$3,000	2/9/-- +	$
LOCATION	Good	Good	Good		Good $ 4,000	
SITE IMPROVEMENT	Average	Good - 500	Average		Average	
AGE/CONDITION	10/Good	12/Good	10/Average +	3,000	10/Good	
GARAGE/CARPORT	2/Garage	2/Garage	2/Garage		2/Garage	
CONSTRUCTION	Frame	Frame	Frame		Frame	
PORCHES, POOL, ETC.						

ROOM COUNT, SIZE	ROOMS	BDRMS.	BATH	S.F. AREA	ROOMS	BDRMS	BATH	S.F. AREA	ROOMS	BDRMS	BATH	S.F. AREA	ROOMS	BDRMS	BATH	S.F. AREA
	6	3	2	1,500	6	3	2	1,600 -2,500	6	3	2	1,500 -0-	6	3	2	1,400 +2500

NET ADJUSTMENT (Show (+) or (-) adjustment)		$ -1,000	$ + 6,500	$ + 6,500
INDICATED VALUE OF SUBJECT PROPERTY		117,000	114,000	116,000

19. PROPERTY SHOWS EVIDENCE OF (Check)
[ ] TERMITE [ ] DRY ROT [ ] DAMPNESS [ ] SETTLEMENT [X] NO EVIDENCE

20. ESTATE (Check)
[X] A. FEE SIMPLE [ ] B. LEASEHOLD

21. REMAINING ECONOMIC LIFE (Years)
MAIN 50 OTHER 50

22. COST APPROACH LA

	MAIN	1,500	CU [X] SQ.	OTHER 500
	$ 55.00	RATE PER FT.		$15.00

23. DATA

	DESCRIPTION	CONDITION
ROOF	Asp.Sh.	Good
FOUND.	Conc.	Good
BSMT.	No	
FLOORS	Carpet	Good
INT. WALLS	Gypsum	Good
BATH FINISH	Gypsum	Good
GUTTERS	Galv.	Good

24. EQUIP.

DESCRIPTION	DEPR. VALUE
GFWA Furnace	$ Bs.
Water Heater	100
Built Ins:	
Fan-Hood	150
Rng.Oven	300
Dshwash.	200
Disposal	50

25. OTHER IMPROVEMENTS

DESCRIPTION	DEPR. VALUE
Fireplace	$ 1,500
Conc. Flatwork	800
Fence	800
W/W Carpeting	1,500
Landscaping	1,000

	$ 82,500	REPLMT. COST	$ 6,000
	$ 8,250	PHYSICAL DEP.	$ 600
	$	FUNCTIONAL	$
	$	ECONOMIC	$
	$ 8,250	TOTAL DEP.	$ 600
	$ 74,250	DEPR. COST	$ 5,400
	TOTAL DEPR. COST OF IMPR	$ 79,650
	OTHER IMPR. AND EQUIP.	$ 5,680
	LAND VALUE	$ 30,000

26. ANNUAL TAXES

GENERAL	SPECIAL	OTHER
$ 1,300	$	

TOTAL (24) $ 800   TOTAL (25) $ 5,600

TOTAL DEPR. COST OF PROP $115,330

27. DOES PROPERTY CONFORM TO APPLICABLE MINIMUM PROPERTY REQUIREMENTS?
[X] YES [ ] NO (If "No" explain on reverse)

28. ESTIMATE FAIR MONTHLY RENT TIMES RENT MULTIPLIER (If applicable)
$ 600 × 190 = $ 114,000

29. RECONCILIATION

A. MARKET APPROACH	B. COST APPROACH	C. INCOME APPROACH (If applicable)
$ 115,000	$ 115,500	$ 114,000

NOTE: No determination of reasonable value may be made unless a completed appraisal report is received (38 U.S.C. 1810). I HEREBY CERTIFY that (a) I have carefully viewed the property described in this report, INSIDE AND OUTSIDE, so far as it has been completed; that (b) it is the same property that is identified by description in my appraisal assignment; that (c) I HAVE NOT RECEIVED, HAVE NO AGREEMENT TO RECEIVE, NOR WILL I ACCEPT FROM ANY PARTY ANY GRATUITY OR EMOLUMENT OTHER THAN MY APPRAISAL FEE FOR MAKING THIS APPRAISAL; that (d) I have no interest, present or prospective, in the applicant, seller, property, or mortgage; that (e) in arriving at the estimated reasonable value I have not been influenced in any manner whatsoever by the race, color, religion, national origin, or sex of any person residing in the property or in the neighborhood wherein it is located. I understand that violation of this certification can result in removal from the fee appraiser's roster.

30. I ESTIMATE "REASONABLE VALUE"	31. ESTIMATED REASONABLE VALUE	32. SIGNATURE OF APPRAISER	33. DATE SIGNED
[X] "AS IS" [ ] "AS REPAIRED" [ ] "AS COMPLETED"	$ 115,000	(s) A. B. SMITH	7/1/--

FIGURE 14-3

the result obtained will agree with the actual market price of the property.

Finally, for the real estate licensee who deals in properties in a given area, appraisal is not too difficult. He knows the prices being asked and the prices being obtained. He knows the property, the rental market, typical expenses, and incomes. He knows other licensees, bankers, title men, loan officers, appraisers, and others engaged in the real estate business. He usually belongs to a local real estate board and multiple listing service that gives him access to records of past sales in the area. Thus, he is able to adequately appraise the majority of buildings he comes in contact with. He relies on the most used method, a combination of market comparison and experience.

Form of the appraisal report

An appraisal report is a written statement of the value of property prepared by a real estate broker, a professional appraiser, or any other person who may be qualified by virtue of training and experience to appraise real property properly. Although most reports are prepared by professional appraisers or real estate brokers, there is no law in California for specifically licensing individuals to act as real property appraisers.

The actual form, length, and contents of an appraisal report vary considerably depending on the client for whom the report is being prepared, the type of property being appraised, and the purpose for which the appraisal is being made. Some reports are only a single page or two, while others are quite formal and lengthy. A Veterans Administration Appraisal Report is illustrated in Figure 14–3. All reports, however, should contain basically the following information:

1. The date on which the value is estimated and the report prepared.
2. The estimate of value.
3. The purpose of the appraisal and its scope.
4. A description of the property.
5. A description of the general location and neighborhood.
6. The factual data necessary, together with their analysis and interpretation by the use of one or more of the three common approaches.
7. Additional supporting material, such as maps, photographs, or plans.
8. The name, address, and qualifications of the person preparing the appraisal and his signature.

QUESTIONS FOR DISCUSSION

1. What common errors might be made in connection with the income approach to value?
2. Which of the factors influencing value would be most applicable to a single-family residence in a housing tract?
3. What factors are most important in the use of the market-comparison approach to valuation?
4. Discuss the types of properties in which the asking price and actual selling price would be close, and those properties in which there might be a considerable difference.
5. How many of the various appraisal methods could be used in determining the value of an apartment house?
6. What are some of the difficulties that might arise in trying to determine the net income of a large property?
7. Will the same capitalization rate be applied by investors to all income properties at any given time?
8. Discuss the types of depreciation considered to be inherent within the property itself.
9. Discuss the methods by which the appraiser seeks to determine the amount of depreciation that has occurred with respect to a given building.
10. What professional organizations and publications are available to the property appraiser?

MULTIPLE CHOICE QUESTIONS

14–1. An appraisal is most commonly used to set: (a) utility standards, (b) cost estimates, (c) market value, (d) tax rates.

14–2. A broker listing properties in a large residential tract most often uses: (a) competitive-market analysis, (b) tax assessor's estimate of value, (c) original square-footage costs, (d) opinion of property owner.

14–3. All other factors being equal, the greatest determinant of property value is its: (a) tax assessment, (b) location, (c) age, (d) utility.

14–4. The cost approach is most properly used with respect to: (a) commercial properties, (b) industrial properties, (c) newer properties, (d) none of these.

14–5. The income approach uses application of a capitalization rate to: (a) purchase price, (b) gross income, (c) net income, (d) none of these.

14–6. A real property appraiser may determine value by applying a gross multiplier to: (a) purchase price, (b) gross income which property produces, (c) functional design, (d) taxes.

14–7. Functional obsolescence is generally corrected by: (a) increasing taxes, (b) building modernization, (c) rezoning the area, (d) none of these.

14–8. A real estate appraisal license may be obtained by applying to: (a) real estate commissioner, (b) state building inspector, (c) State of California, (d) none of these.

15 Escrow and title insurance

When a broker has obtained a signed offer from a prospective buyer and an acceptance of the offer from the seller, he is then ready to go into escrow and close the transaction. A slight division of opinion is found in real estate textbooks regarding the difference between closing the deal and the escrow procedure. Some authors state that closing pertains to getting an offer in writing from the buyer and then obtaining the seller's acceptance and signature on the Purchase Contract and Receipt for Deposit. Other authorities believe that closing involves all the work and procedures necessary after the offer and acceptance have been obtained by the broker.

This textbook follows the position that closing the transaction includes not only obtaining the offer and acceptance but all of the work which follows. This means obtainment of a title insurance policy and initiation of the escrow procedure, which is successfully concluded when certain documents are officially recorded and funds involved are disbursed to those persons entitled to them.

ESCROW DEFINED

The California Financial Code, Section 17003, defines escrow as follows:

Escrow means any transaction wherein one person for the purpose of affecting the sale, transfer, encumbering, or leasing of real or personal property to another person, delivers any written instrument, money, evidence of title to real or personal property or any other thing of value to a third person to be held by such third person until the happening of a specified event or the performance of a prescribed condition, when it is then to be delivered by such third person to a grantee, grantor, promisee, promissor, obligee, obligor, bailee, bailor, or any agent or employee of any of the latter.

The California Civil Code defines escrow as follows:

A grant may be deposited by the grantor with a third person to be delivered on the performance of the condition, and, on delivery by the depository, will take effect. While in the possession of the third person, and subject to the condition, it is called an escrow.

ESSENTIALS OF A VALID ESCROW

To have a valid escrow, there must be a binding contract between buyer and seller, and the conditional delivery of transfer instruments to a third party. The binding contract may appear in any legal form; the most common are a deposit receipt, agreement of sale, exchange agreement, option, or mutual instructions of buyer and seller.

Escrow instructions supplement the original binding contract, above, and both the escrow instructions and the contract are interpreted together, if possible. If the supplemental escrow instructions should contain any terms in conflict with the original contract, the instructions, constituting the later contract usually control. It is thus important that all conditions, whether in the original contract or in subsequent instructions, be clear and concise and that they be fully understood by all parties to the agreement.

In addition to a binding contract, there must be a conditional delivery of transfer instruments to a third party (usually called the escrow agent or escrow officer), together with instructions to deliver the instruments on fulfillment or performance of certain conditions.

The actual procedures followed by an escrow officer may vary, depending on the particular locale within the state. The licensee should understand that the procedures we shall discuss are general in nature, and he should, in addition, familiarize himself with certain special practices that may exist in his particular area.

COMPLETE ESCROW

A complete escrow contains all the necessary instructions that reflect an understanding by the parties in all the essential requirements of the transaction. If properly drawn and executed, it becomes an enforceable contract binding on all the parties. An escrow is termed *complete* when all the terms of the instructions have been met.

Generally, to have a correct escrow, a valid and binding contract must be entered into between the grantor and the grantee, and an irrevocable deposit must be made with the escrow holder. If a contract did not exist, the grantor could recover his deed from the escrow holder at any time before the conditions were performed. Where the contract does exist, the escrow officer exceeds his authority if he attempts to deliver any instruments to the grantee before the performance of any conditions specified, and in actual practice, the escrow officer will refuse such delivery prior to satisfactory performance of conditions.

THE ESCROW AGENT

All escrow agencies must be licensed by the California Corporation Commissioner. The regulations under which these escrow agents must operate will be found in Sections 17000 to 17614 of the California Financial Code.

Section 17004 of the Financial Code defines an escrow agent as "Any person engaged in the business of receiving escrows for deposit or delivery, for a compensation." Any corporation, partnership, firm, or individual who wants to engage in business as an escrow agent in California must be licensed.

Certain exceptions are made with regard to banks, savings and loan companies, insurance companies, title insurance companies, real estate brokers, and attorneys. An attorney may escrow a transaction only if it is incidental to the duty he is performing for his client or a client's estate as an attorney at law. A real estate broker may escrow only a transaction in which he acts as the broker.

Duties and responsibilities of the escrow holder

For a detailed description of the duties and responsibilities of the escrow holder, the licensee is referred to the sections mentioned above in the Financial Code. A few of the more important are as follows.

1. An escrow is confidential, and no information concerning the escrow may be given to any persons not a party to the escrow.
2. If disputes arise between the parties in an escrow, it is not the duty of the escrow agent to act as mediator. The escrow agent accepts and follows instructions from the parties and must be very careful not to give either party any advice that is not within the generally accepted scope of his duties as the escrow holder. For instance, one of the parties to the escrow may ask the escrow agent for some legal advice about alternative methods of taking title to real property. The escrow officer must give the party the same answer the real estate broker is so often cautioned to give; he must suggest that the party consult with his attorney.
3. An escrow holder may not deliver documents or funds unless there has been a strict compliance with the conditions of the escrow. If an instrument is delivered by the escrow holder before all the conditions of the escrow have been met, the delivery is not valid and title does not pass.
4. An escrow agent is prohibited by law from paying referral fees to anyone except a regular employee of the escrow company. Usually, this also prohibits payment of commissions to real estate licensees and to outsiders for sending business to a particular escrow company. Such fees include gifts of merchandise or other items of value.
5. An escrow agent may not permit any person to make an addition to, deletion from, or alteration of an escrow instruction or amended or supplemental escrow instruction unless it is signed or initialed by all persons who had signed or initialed the instructions or amendments thereto. An escrow holder must at the time of execution deliver any escrow instruction or amended or supplemental instruction to all persons executing it.

Termite reports. The question of ordering a termite report should never be raised by the escrow holder. This is strictly a matter for the parties to the escrow to decide on, and unless the subject of a termite report is made a condition to the escrow by one of the parties involved, the escrow holder should refrain from making any statement regarding the subject. Actually, the practice in California is for the parties to the contract to reach some agreement about a termite report before going into escrow. The agreement is usually stated on the deposit receipt. In Chapter 5, where deposit receipts are discussed, the subject of the termite report in connection with a sale of real property is dealt with more fully.

Escrow holder as an agent

The escrow holder in a sale of property through an escrow is at first the agent of both parties. When the conditions are performed, the escrow holder becomes the agent of each party—that is, of the grantor to deliver the deed and of the grantee to pay over the purchase money. This agency relationship is considered a limited one, and the only obligations to be fulfilled by the escrow holder are those set forth in the instructions and those that impart no general duties but are composed of facts connected with the transaction only.

TERMINATION OF ESCROW

An escrow is usually terminated when any one of the following occurs:

1. Full performance of the conditions of the escrow by the parties involved is the most common method by which an escrow is completed.
2. Cancellation by mutual consent of the parties involved usually occurs when the buyer and seller mutually agree to end negotiations and so instruct the escrow holder.
3. Revocation by one of the parties to the escrow occurs when one of the parties to the escrow decides not to meet conditions previously agreed on. The result may be the termination of the escrow; however, such action by some of the parties will usually result in litigation, and the escrow holder will do nothing pending a decision by the court.
4. An intervening condition or event may make it impossible for one of the parties to perform, a result if one of the escrow parties expires or becomes incapacitated prior to close of escrow.

DIFFERING ESCROW PRACTICES

Every real estate transaction involving the transfer of an equitable or legal title will involve a final closing statement or settlement sheet. Both the buyer and seller must be shown, in writing, the cash requirement, the proceeds, the expense or charge allotments, and the prorations in the transaction.

Customs in closing vary in different parts of California, particularly between the northern and southern parts of the state. In southern California, most transactions are closed in escrows performed by the escrow departments of banks, specialized escrow companies, or title insurance companies. The escrow function is an independent transaction, as is the issuance of a policy of title insurance. A separate fee is charged for each separate function. Although the title insurance company always issues the policy of title insurance, it may or may not perform the escrow function. Escrow instructions are generally more formalized, especially when a bank or specialized escrow company performs the escrow function.

In northern California, the prevailing practice is for the title insurance company to issue the policy of title insurance and also perform the escrow function. The title company charges one fee—for the policy of title insurance—and this takes care of the escrow function also; one fee covers both.

Practices also vary among firms. Many large real estate firms throughout the state perform the escrow function within their own offices and use the title company only to obtain the title insurance policy and see that the necessary instruments are publicly recorded.

In northern California, the form showing the financial aspects of the transaction is called the Buyer's Statement and the Seller's Statement. In southern California, this same type of form is referred to as the Settlement Sheet.

DIVISION OF ESCROW CHARGES

Division of the various charges in escrow also differs, depending on the particular locale involved. The customary divisions of charges is shown below, but the licensee should remember that this is customary and not mandatory. Occasionally, the parties to the escrow may decide to divide certain charges in other than the customary way, and there is nothing to prevent them from doing so.

The seller is generally responsible for:

1. Drawing instruments in favor of the purchaser.
2. Real estate transfer tax.
3. Any notarial fee on instruments in favor of purchaser.
4. Broker's commission.

The purchaser is generally responsible for:

1. Drawing instruments in favor of the seller or lender.
2. Recording fee for deed.
3. Recording fee for trust deed in favor of the lender.
4. Notarial fee on instruments in favor of seller or lender.

The title insurance policy fee is an important part of the closing costs. In the majority of counties, the buyer pays for the title insurance policy, while in some, the seller pays; in still others, the cost is divided equally between the buyer and the seller.

Such items as taxes, insurance, and rents are prorated between the buyer and seller as of the date of close of escrow. In southern California where the escrow fee may be separate from the title insurance fee, the escrow fee is generally split 50–50 between the buyer and seller, or two thirds to the seller and one third to the buyer.

Any variation from what is customary in the division of fees should be agreed on by the parties in advance of close of escrow. Often, through sheer bargaining power, one party can be relieved of all or some of the customary charges that might otherwise be assigned against him.

CHECKLIST FOR REAL ESTATE TRANSACTIONS

The *Reference Book,* published by the California Division of Real Estate, contains an extensive checklist of items that may be part of a real estate transaction. Often, only certain of these items will apply in any one particular transaction. After looking over the list, the reader will appreciate the reason most brokers prefer to let an expert handle the escrow function in a transaction. For instance, when a title company performs the escrow function in connection with the issuance of a title insurance policy, many of the items shown on the checklist below become the responsibility of the title company rather than of the broker. An example is the preparation and examination of most of the documents and forms necessary to the transaction.

Factors to be considered and preparations to be made prior to and during the preparation of the purchase contract are:

1. The date of the contract.
2. The name and address of the seller.
3. Is the seller a citizen of full age and competence?
4. The legal status of the seller.
5. The full name of the seller's wife.
6. The name and legal status of the purchaser.
7. The full name of the purchaser's wife.
8. The address and telephone number of the purchasers.
9. The purchase price and the terms of the contract.
10. The kind of deed to be delivered.
11. What special agreement will have to be made regarding any personal property?
12. Is the mortgage to be assumed, or is the buyer purchasing subject to the mortgage?
13. What type of note will be involved?
14. Will a deed of trust be involved, and will there be any special conditions or provisions?
15. Do mortgages or trust deeds contain acceleration or restrictive conditions?
16. Are there to be any special reservations or exceptions in the deed?
17. Special conditions or provisions to be inserted into the contract.
18. Rights of tenants or lessees.
19. Items to be adjusted at close of escrow.
20. Division of charges in escrow.
21. Any special arrangements concerning liens, easements, assessments, taxes, covenants, or restrictions?
22. Place and date on which escrow is to be closed.
23. How will the buyer take title to the property?
24. Name and address of escrow holder and of broker making the sale.
25. How will the problems of termite inspection and possession be taken care of?

After acceptance of an offer and during escrow, the seller may need to furnish the following:

1. Copy of contract.
2. Latest tax, water, and receipted assessment bills.

3. Latest water meter readings.
4. Latest gas meter readings.
5. Information regarding last payment of interest on mortgages or trust deeds.
6. Insurance policies on the property.
7. Certificate or offset statement from any holder of a mortgage or deed of trust.
8. Any subordination agreements that may be called for in the contract.
9. Certificate showing satisfaction of mechanic's liens, chattel mortgages, judgments, or mortgages to be paid at or prior to close of escrow.
10. A rental statement listing tenants, amount of rents paid or due, and moneys being held as advance rents or deposits.
11. Assignment of leases affecting the property.
12. Notification to tenants regarding subsequent rent payments.
13. Bill of sale for any personal property involved in the sale.
14. Seller's last deed and deed he is to prepare for buyer.
15. Any instruments the seller is to prepare or deliver at close of escrow.
16. Any unrecorded instruments that may affect the title.

The purchaser should have and/or check on the following:

1. Purchaser's copy of the contract and certificate of title or policy of insurance showing title vested in the grantor.
2. Examination of the deed to see that it conforms to the contract.
3. Examination of property description on deed to see that it is correct.
4. Examination of the deed to see that it is properly executed.
5. Disposition of all liens that must be removed.
6. Sufficient cash to make necessary payment required at close of escrow.
7. Names and information concerning tenants, leases, and rent.
8. Bill of sale if any personal property involved.
9. Examination of preliminary title search or survey.
10. Any matters that may affect title or use of the property.
11. Bills for any unpaid taxes, water, or assessments.
12. Any unrecorded instruments that may affect title.

13. Copies of any loan papers signed in connection with the sale.
14. Examination of purchase money mortgages.
15. Examination of note and deed of trust.
16. Adjustments completed if called for in the contract.

CHRONOLOGICAL STEPS IN THE ESCROW

Although the sequence of steps in any type of escrow may vary slightly, there is a general order in which they occur. Figure 15–1 illustrates basic escrow procedures. We shall briefly look at the steps in a southern California escrow where the escrow function and issuance of a title insurance policy are performed separately. Then, we shall examine a northern California escrow where the title insurance company performs the escrow function and issues the policy of title insurance.

Southern California escrow steps

1. After obtaining a completed deposit receipt signed by all parties to the transaction, the broker will open an escrow and prepare escrow instructions. He will generally use a standard printed form prepared by the escrow holder for drafting instructions.
2. The escrow instructions are signed by all parties to the contract, and the escrow holder orders a title search from a title company. A report is subsequently made to the escrow officer by the title company.
3. The escrow officer requests a Beneficiary's Statement from the beneficiary shown on the recorded deed of trust. The statement will show the condition of the indebtedness and the unpaid balance of the loan.
4. Matters disclosed by the preliminary title report that are not approved by the escrow instructions are reported to the seller for clearance or to the buyer for approval.
5. When the escrow officer receives all the documents and funds necessary to close the escrow, he makes the necessary adjustments and prorations between the parties on what is called a settlement sheet.
6. The necessary instruments are then forwarded to the title insurance company with instructions to record them.
7. The title search is run to date as of the close of business on the date set for close of escrow, and if no change of title is found, the deed and other instruments are recorded on the

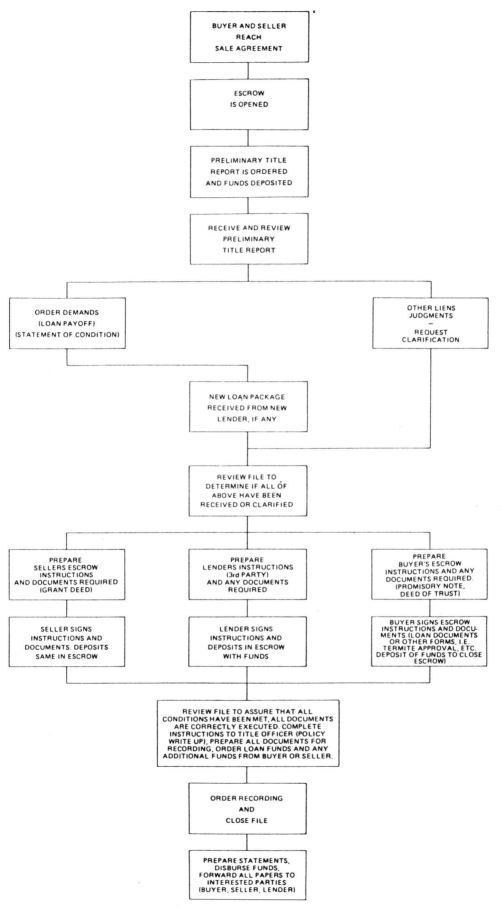

FIGURE 15–1

following morning at 8 A.M. By filing the moment the recorder's office opens at 8 A.M., the title company can issue a title policy with the assurance that there are no intervening matters of record against the property.

8. On the day that recordation has taken place, the escrow officer will disburse funds to the parties entitled to them, cause any fire insurance policies to be transferred or amended, and present closing statements to the parties entitled to them. The title insurance company generally tries to issue the policy of title insurance to the purchaser on the same day or as soon after recordation as possible. Within a few weeks, the recorder's office will return the recorded deed to the escrow officer, who will forward it to the purchaser.

Northern California escrow steps

In many respects, the outline of steps below resembles the one for southern California. The main difference here is that the title company does both jobs; that is, it issues the policy of title insurance and takes care of recordation, and also performs the escrow function. The general sequence of steps is as follows:

1. After obtaining a completed deposit receipt signed by all parties to the transaction, the broker will open an escrow at the title company. If the broker does not maintain a trust account at a bank, he will at this point deposit with the title officer (who is also the escrow officer) any money received from the purchaser as deposit.
2. A preliminary title search is prepared, and sufficient copies are sent to the broker so that he may give one to the purchaser and one to the seller.
3. Matters disclosed by the preliminary title search are considered and are taken care of with the approval, if necessary, of buyer and/or seller. The title officer will receive any instructions that may be necessary in addition to those agreed on in the deposit receipt.
4. The title officer requests, from any beneficiary under an existing deed of trust, a statement of the condition of indebtedness and balance of the loan.
5. When the title officer receives all the documents necessary in order to close the escrow, he will make the necessary prorations in financial adjustments and prepare a seller's state-

ment and a buyer's statement. These forms are also called buyer's and seller's instructions.
6. The instructions are presented to the respective parties to the transaction, and the parties sign their respective instructions and any other documents, such as a grant deed, note, and deed of trust, that may be necessary.
7. The title officer requests and obtains all funds necessary to close. The title search is run to date as of the close of business on the date set for close of escrow; and if no change of title is found, the deed and other pertinent instruments are recorded on the following morning at 8 A.M.
8. Following recordation, the title policy is issued and funds are disbursed to the parties entitled to them. Necessary insurance endorsements are obtained or may have been obtained just before recordation, and the policy and copies are sent to those entitled to them. When the title officer receives the recorded documents from the recorder's office, he will forward them to the necessary parties.

ESCROW PROBLEM AND STATEMENTS

An understanding of some common escrow procedures and the preparation of escrow statements for the seller and buyer are best explained by the use of an example involving a real estate transaction.

The basic facts concerning the transaction are given, followed by an explanation and the computations necessary in preparing the escrow statements for the parties involved. Prorations in connection with escrow are also discussed in the chapter dealing with real estate mathematics. Following the explanation, Figures 15–2 and 15–3 illustrate the actual escrow statement to be prepared for the sellers and buyers. These statements are also often referred to as settlement sheets.

Transaction facts and agreements

Taylor-Brown sale. The sale is of a residence at 390 Royal Court Road, San Tomas, California, belonging to John A. Taylor and Mary L. Taylor, husband and wife. Buyers are Thomas P. Brown and Carol V. Brown, husband and wife. The Realtor® is Ann Craig of ABC Realty Company.

1. Purchase price is $160,000 with buyers to obtain a loan of $128,000 with interest at 13½ percent per annum, term of 30 years, and payments of $1,466.14 per month.

2. Closing date is May 25, 19—.
3. Buyers deposit 10 percent of purchase price with escrow and balance due at close of escrow.
4. Buyers' loan charges to XYZ Savings and Loan include loan fee of 2 points plus $200.00; credit report, $30.00; tax service, $22.50; and interest at $48.00 per day from May 25 to June 1.
5. Buyers to pay $110.55 ALTA title policy premium for $128,000 loan amount.
6. Sellers' existing note and trust deed payable to XYZ Savings and Loan with principal balance of $59,594.00 and interest from April 1 at $15.10 per day; plus reconveyance fee $50.00; statement fee, $15.00; and late charge, $47.50.
7. Sellers' second note and trust deed payable to J. Smith with principal balance $8,887.50 and interest from April 1 at $2.47 per day and $50.00 reconveyance fee.
8. Both installments of property tax have been paid by seller at $523.75 per installment.
9. Buyers to pay $90.00 for termite inspection, sellers to pay $825.00 for termite work.
10. Buyers to pay insurance premium of $447.00 to L. Brown Insurance Company.
11. Buyers to pay $4.00 notary and $12.00 recording fees.
12. Sellers to pay 6 percent commission to ABC Realty Company.
13. Sellers to pay $588.00 premium for $160,000 title insurance policy.
14. Sellers to pay $4.00 notary and $8.00 recording fees.
15. Sellers to pay transfer tax of $176.00.
16. Escrow fee is $258.00. Sellers pay $129.00 and buyers pay $129.00.

Escrow statements

Forms of escrow statements vary from place to place, but it makes no difference what form is used—the principles remain the same. There are two general types:

1. The *ledger account* form, which represents a reproduction of the ledger accounts of the purchaser and seller. This is also called the débit-and-credit approach.
2. The *report* or accumulated deduction form, which is like an income statement if one is familiar with accounting. However, it requires no knowledge of accounting, and many claim it is more easily understood by the layman.

The *ledger account* form applying the facts presented in the Taylor-Brown sale is presented in Figures 15–2 and 15–3. The two statements to seller and buyer may be combined on a single sheet, or separate sheets may be made for each party.

Explanation of procedures

Following is an explanation of the procedures used in arriving at the figures shown on the escrow statements to the sellers and the buyers. The numbers in the escrow statements' right margins correspond to explanation numbers.

Seller's statement. The credit column shows amounts credited to the seller.

1. $160,000 purchase price.
2. Tax proration, $104.75. The seller has paid the second installment of property tax, $523.75, which is for January 1 to June 30. For this escrow calculation, every month is presumed to be 30 days. Mr. and Mrs. Brown become the owners on May 25 and must pay Mr. and Mrs. Taylor for 6 days in May and 30 days in June. The calculation is: $523.75 ÷ 180 × 36 = $104.75.

The debit column shows amounts to be paid by seller.

3. The premium for a standard CLTA owners title insurance policy for $160,000 is $588. Although the payment for title insurance is by agreement between the parties, the general custom in southern California is for the seller to pay, while the buyer pays in northern California.
4. Total escrow fee is $258, and by custom in southern California, the seller pays half, $129, and the buyer pays half, $129. In northern California, the buyer pays the full escrow fee.
5. Reconveyance fee, $50 in connection with second loan to J. Smith.
6. Notary fee, $4.
7. Transfer tax, $176.00. Based on $1.10 per $1,000 of sales price. Calculation is: $1.10 × 146.5 = $128.70.
8. Recording fee, $8.
9. Termite work, $825. This amount will be held by the escrow pending completion of work and issuance of certificate of completion by termite company.
10. Real estate commission, $9,600. Calculation is $160,000 × .06 = $9,600.

11. Amount necessary to pay off second loan, $9,023.35.
12. Amount necessary to pay off existing seller's loan to XYZ Savings. $60,537 for principal, interest, reconveyance fee, statement fee, and late charge. Because sellers did not make a May 1 loan payment, interest is charged for 30 days in April and 25 days in May. Calculation is: 55 × $15.10 = $830.50.
13. The total amount of expenses (debits) against the seller, 3 through 12, is $80,940.35. The amount credited to the seller, 1 and 2, is $160,104.75. The amount of money the sellers will receive at close of escrow is $79,160.40. Calculation is: $160,104.75 − $80,940.35 = $79,164.40.

Buyer's statement. The debit column shows amounts to be paid by buyers.

1. $160,000 purchase price is shown.
4. Prorata property taxes. Buyer owes seller $104.75 as explained in seller's statement, 2.
5. Buyer pays $110.55 premium for $128,000 ALTA title policy insuring lender's interest.
6. Buyer's half of $258 escrow fee is $129.
7. Notary fee, $4.
8. Recording fee, $12.
9. Buyer pays for termite report, $90.
10. Property insurance policy, $447.
11. Buyer's loan charges to XYZ Savings, $2,760. Loan fee is 2 points plus $200. ($2,560 + $200 = $2,760). Additional charges required by lender are for credit report, tax service, tax reserve, insurance reserve, and interest at $48.00 per day from close of escrow on 5/25 to 6/1, a total of seven days. Since regular loan payments represent interest charged for a preceding month, the regular loan payment of $1,466.14 will begin July 1.
13. The purchase price of $160,000 and closing costs of $4,045.80 equal $164,045.80.

The buyer is credited with the following amounts.

2. $16,000 representing 10 percent of purchase price deposited in escrow.
3. $128,000 loan from XYZ Savings.
12. Purchase price, $160,000, and closing costs, $4,045.80, equal $164,045.80. The buyer has been credited with a 10 percent deposit of $16,000 and loan proceeds of $128,000, which equals $144,000. To close escrow, the buyer must deposit the additional down payment, of $16,000 and $4,045.80 closing costs, totaling $16,000. Calculation is: $164,045.80 − $144,000.00 = $20,045.80.

TITLE INSURANCE

A transfer of the ownership of real property involves not only the preparation of necessary documents but also an examination and interpretation of public records for matters affecting that property in order to ascertain rights, interest, and liens of others. A policy of title insurance is an insured statement of the condition of the title of a particular piece of property. The policy shows who owns the land according to the public records and also what is recorded against the property in the way of taxes, mortgages, and deeds of trust, and any other liens and encumbrances of record.

It is thus very difficult to find a buyer who does not make use of a title report when buying a piece of property or a lender who will advance funds for the purchase of property without receipt of a title insurance policy. The title policy is a policy of indemnity since the title insurance company is insuring against loss in the event that its interpretation of the condition of title is incorrect. The beneficiary of the insurance is either the buyer of the property or the lender who has loaned money with the property as security for the loan.

A title insurance company, before issuing a policy, will perform an extensive search of the relevant public records to determine if any individual, other than the seller and including a government entity, has any right, lien, claim, or encumbrance which must be taken into account. This search can be very complex because in certain cases records may be located in various federal, state, county and municipal facilities.

Claims against title, even when they are without merit, frequently involve lengthy and expensive litigation, and part of the protection offered by a title insurance company is payment for any defense necessary against such claims.

TYPES OF POLICIES

Standard coverage policy

The basic form of coverage used in California, and illustrated in Figure 15–4, is known as the "California Land Title Association Standard Coverage Policy Form." This form has been established and standardized by the California Land Title Association (CLTA), the trade organization

214

ES 293 (12-73)

ESCROW STATEMENT
SELLER

John A. and Mary L. Taylor   ORDER NO.

SELLER ☑   BUYER ☐   BORROWER ☐

DESCRIPTION		DEBIT	CREDIT	
SALE/PURCHASE PRICE			160,000.00	1
DEPOSITS				
DEPOSIT RETAINED				
EXISTING LOAN ASSUMED				
NEW LOAN(S)				
PRO RATA TAXES 5/25/-- to 7/1/--			104.75	2
PRO RATA INSURANCE				
PRO RATA RENTS				
PRO RATA				
TITLE INSURANCE	☐ LOAN ☐ JOINT			
PREMIUM FOR $ 160,000.00	☑ OWNERS POLICY	588.00		3
$	☐ **ALTA** POLICY			
ESCROW FEE 1/2		129.00		4
RECONVEYANCE FEE		50.00		5
PREPARING DOCUMENTS				
NOTARY FEES		4.00		6
TRANSFER TAX		176.00		7
RECORDING		8.00		8
TAXES				
TERMITE WORK		825.00		9
COMMISSION ABC Realty Company		9,600.00		10
INSURANCE PREMIUM				
LOAN ~~CHARGES~~ PAYOFF: J. Smith		9,023.35		11
Principal	8,887.50			
Interest at $ 2.47 per day from 4/1 to 5/25	135.85			
LOAN PAY OFFS XYZ Savings		60,537.00		12
Principal	59,594.00			
Interest at $ 15.10 per day from 4/1 to 5/25	830.50			
Reconveyance Fee	50.00			
Statement Fee	15.00			
Late Charge	47.50			
BALANCE/BALANCE DUE TO SELLER		79,164.40		13
TOTALS		160,104.75	160,104.75	14

APPROVED: ADDRESS:

(s)   John A. Taylor   390 Royal Court Road, San Tomas

(s)   Mary L. Taylor   564-1919

DATE: TELEPHONE:

May 25, 19--

FIGURE 15-2
Seller's Escrow Statement

ES 293 (12-73)

 **TITLE INSURANCE AND TRUST**

ESCROW STATEMENT
BUYER

Thomas P. and Carol V. Brown

ORDER NO.

SELLER ☐   BUYER ☑   BORROWER ☐

DESCRIPTION	DEBIT	CREDIT	
SALE/PURCHASE PRICE	160,000.00		1
DEPOSITS		16,000.00	2
DEPOSIT RETAINED			
EXISTING LOAN ASSUMED			
NEW LOAN(S) XYZ Savings		128,000.00	3
PRO RATA TAXES 5/25/-- to 7/1/--	104.75		4
PRO RATA INSURANCE			
PRO RATA RENTS			
PRO RATA			
TITLE INSURANCE ☐ LOAN ☐ JOINT			
PREMIUM FOR $ ☐ OWNERS POLICY			
$ 128,000.00 ☑ ALTA POLICY	110.55		5
ESCROW FEE 1/2	129.00		6
RECONVEYANCE FEE			
PREPARING DOCUMENTS			
NOTARY FEES	4.00		7
TRANSFER TAX			
RECORDING	12.00		8
TAXES			
TERMITE REPORT	90.00		9
COMMISSION			
INSURANCE PREMIUM L. Brown Insurance Company	447.00		10
LOAN CHARGES XYZ Savings	3,148.50		11
Loan Fee $ 1,750.00 Interest at $ 48.00			
Credit Report 30.00 per day from 5/25 to			
Tax Service 22.50 6/1 $ 336.00			
LOAN PAY OFFS			
BALANCE/BALANCE DUE		20,045.80	12
TOTALS	164,045.80	164,045.80	13

APPROVED:

(s) Thomas P. Brown

(s) Carol V. Brown

DATE:

May 25, 19--

ADDRESS:

299 Lincoln Way, San Tomas

564-8090

TELEPHONE:

FIGURE 15–3
Buyer's Escrow Statement

for the title companies in California, to comply with the form and coverage approved and recommended by the American Title Association for use throughout the United States. It may be issued to insure an owner only, or a lender only, or it may insure both the owner and lender and thus be a joint-protection standard coverage policy. A leasehold policy can be issued to insure a lessee or sublessee, and an easement policy is available to insure the owner of an easement.

The standard policy insures the ownership of the estate or interest in the described land and the priority and lien, upon said estate or interest, of the insured mortgage or deed of trust. Its coverage is not limited to matters revealed by public records and includes protection against such defects as forged instruments in the chain of title; acts of minors and incompetents whose disability is undisclosed; instruments which may be void; and undisclosed rights of husband and wife when recorded instruments contain false recitals that an individual in question is unmarried.

The standard policy generally excludes claims not shown by the public record, mining claims, reservations in patents, and water rights. These exemptions result from the fact that the title insurance company does not ordinarily make a physical inspection or survey of the land or premises involved in a standard coverage policy. Where the buyer or lender is familiar with or has inspected the property in question, this type of coverage is sufficient.

Extended coverage policy

Extended coverage policies are available to both owners and lenders and, of course, cost more than the standard policy. The general exceptions contained in the standard policy are eliminated in the extended coverage policy.

The most commonly used extended coverage form policy is called the "American Land Title Association Policy—Additional Coverage," commonly known as an ALTA policy. In this policy, insurance is given that the lender has a valid and enforceable lien, subject only to the exclusions from coverage, if any, and such defects, liens, and encumbrances on the title as are shown on the policy. The policy expressly includes priority insurance to cover mechanic's liens and assessments for street improvements.

This type of extended coverage can also be issued for an owner, lender, or both together. The insurance is generally written by using the standard coverage form and deleting therefrom the printed general exceptions shown on the policy.

There are, in addition to the two policies and coverages already discussed, many other types of special coverages for specific situations.

Payment of title insurance fees

The title insurance policy fee forms a part of the "closing costs" in the purchase of real estate. In the following counties it is customary for the buyer to pay for the title insurance: Alameda, Calaveras, Colusa, Contra Costa, Lake, Marin, Mendocino, Napa, San Francisco, San Mateo, Solano, and Sonoma.

In the following cities, it is customary for the seller to pay: Del Norte, El Dorado, Fresno, Glenn, Humboldt, Imperial, Inyo, Kern, Kings, Lassen, Los Angeles, Madera, Modoc, Monterey, Mono, Nevada, Orange, Placer, Riverside, Sacramento, San Benito, San Bernardino, San Diego, San Luis Obispo, Santa Barbara, Santa Clara, Santa Cruz, Shasta, Siskiyou, Stanislaus, Sutter, Tehama, Tulare, Ventura, Yolo, and Yuba.

The buyer and seller generally split the title fee equally in Amador, Merced, Plumas, San Joaquin, and Tuolumne, while in Butte County, the fee is generally split on the basis of 75 percent to the seller and 25 percent to the buyer. There is no legal requirement, however, that the cost of title insurance be assigned or split in any particular way; and if the buyer and seller agree, either party may pay the entire cost regardless of the county in which the transaction takes place.

Various risks

Proper protection for a property owner is necessary because of the numerous risks and hazards which can be found in connection with title to real property. The following are examples of such risks:

1. Any instruments which have been forged or improperly executed.
2. Instruments executed by individuals with a legal disability, such as a minor or an incompetent.
3. Illegal acts of trustees or attorneys-in-fact.
4. Taxes which are now liens against a property.
5. Assessments or bonds which are liens against a property.
6. Fraud, duress, or coercion in securing essential signatures.

SUBJECT TO SCHEDULE B AND THE CONDITIONS AND STIPULATIONS HEREOF, TITLE INSURANCE AND TRUST COMPANY, a California corporation, herein called the Company, insures the insured, as of Date of Policy shown in Schedule A, against loss or damage, not exceeding the amount of insurance stated in Schedule A, and costs, attorneys' fees and expenses which the Company may become obligated to pay hereunder, sustained or incurred by said insured by reason of:

1. Title to the estate or interest described in Schedule A being vested other than as stated therein;

2. Any defect in or lien or encumbrance on such title;

3. Unmarketability of such title; or

4. Any lack of the ordinary right of an abutting owner for access to at least one physically open street or highway if the land, in fact, abuts upon one or more such streets or highways;

and in addition, as to an insured lender only;

5. Invalidity of the lien of the insured mortgage upon said estate or interest except to the extent that such invalidity, or claim thereof, arises out of the transaction evidenced by the insured mortgage and is based upon.

    a. usury, or
    b. any consumer credit protection or truth in lending law;

6. Priority of any lien or encumbrance over the lien of the insured mortgage, said mortgage being shown in Schedule B in the order of its priority; or

7. Invalidity of any assignment of the insured mortgage, provided such assignment is shown in Schedule B.

Title Insurance and Trust Company

by _John E. Flood, Jr._
                            President

Attest

                            Secretary

FIGURE 15–4

Conditions and Stipulations

1. Definition of Terms

The following terms when used in this policy mean:

(a.) "insured": the insured named in Schedule A, and, subject to any rights or defenses the Company may have had against the named insured, those who succeed to the interest of such insured by operation of law as distinguished from purchase including, but not limited to, heirs, distributees, devisees, survivors, personal representatives, next of kin, or corporate or fiduciary successors. The term "insured" also includes (i) the owner of the indebtedness secured by the insured mortgage and each successor in ownership of such indebtedness (reserving, however, all rights and defenses as to any such successor who acquires the indebtedness by operation of law as described in the first sentence of this subparagraph (a) that the Company would have had against the successor's transferor), and further includes (ii) any governmental agency or instrumentality which is an insurer or guarantor under an insurance contract or guaranty insuring or guaranteeing said indebtedness, or any part thereof, whether named as an insured herein or not, and (iii) the parties designated in paragraph 2(a) of these Conditions and Stipulations.

(b.) "insured claimant": an insured claiming loss or damage hereunder.

(c.) "insured lender": the owner of an insured mortgage.

(d.) "insured mortgage": a mortgage shown in Schedule B, the owner of which is named as an insured in Schedule A.

(e.) "knowledge": actual knowledge, not constructive knowledge or notice which may be imputed to an insured by reason of any public records.

(f.) "land": the land described specifically or by reference in Schedule C, and improvements affixed thereto which by law constitute real property; provided, however, the term "land" does not include any area excluded by Paragraph No. 6 of Part I of Schedule B of this Policy.

(g.) "mortgage": mortgage, deed of trust, trust deed, or other security instrument.

(h.) "public records": those records which by law impart constructive notice of matters relating to the land.

2. (a.) Continuation of Insurance after Acquisition of Title by Insured Lender

If this policy insures the owner of the indebtedness secured by the insured mortgage, this policy shall continue in force as of Date of Policy in favor of such insured who acquires all or any part of said estate or interest in the land described in Schedule C by foreclosure, trustee's sale, conveyance in lieu of foreclosure, or other legal manner which discharges the lien of the insured mortgage, and if such insured is a corporation, its transferee of the estate or interest so acquired, provided the transferee is the parent or wholly owned subsidiary of such insured; and in favor of any governmental agency or instrumentality which acquires all or any part of the estate or interest pursuant to a contract of insurance or guaranty insuring or guaranteeing the indebtedness secured by the insured mortgage. After any such acquisition the amount of insurance hereunder, exclusive of costs, attorneys' fees and expenses which the Company may be obligated to pay, shall not exceed the least of:

(i) the amount of insurance stated in Schedule A;

(ii) the amount of the unpaid principal of the indebtedness plus interest thereon, as determined under paragraph 6(a) (iii) hereof, expenses of foreclosure and amounts advanced to protect the lien of the insured mortgage and secured by said insured mortgage at the time of acquisition of such estate or interest in the land; or

(iii) the amount paid by any governmental agency or instrumentality, if such agency or instrumentality is the insured claimant, in acquisition of such estate or interest in satisfaction of its insurance contract or guaranty.

(b.) Continuation of Insurance After Conveyance of Title

The coverage of this policy shall continue in force as of Date of Policy, in favor of an insured so long as such insured retains an estate or interest in the land, or owns an indebtedness secured by a purchase money mortgage given by a purchaser from such insured, or so long as such insured shall have liability by reason of covenants of warranty made by such insured in any transfer or conveyance of such estate or interest; provided, however, this policy shall not continue in force in favor of any purchaser from such insured of either said estate or interest or the indebtedness secured by a purchase money mortgage given to such insured.

3. Defense and Prosecution of Actions — Notice of Claim to be Given by an Insured Claimant

(a.) The Company, at its own cost and without undue delay, shall provide for the defense of an insured in litigation to the extent that such litigation involves an alleged defect, lien, encumbrance or other matter insured against by this policy.

(b.) The insured shall notify the Company promptly in writing (i) in case of any litigation as set forth in (a) above, (ii) in case knowledge shall come to an insured hereunder of any claim of title or interest which is adverse to the title to the estate or interest or the lien of the insured mortgage, as insured, and which might cause loss or damage for which the Company may be liable by virtue of this policy, or (iii) if title to the estate or interest or the lien of the insured mortgage, as insured, is rejected as unmarketable. If such prompt notice shall not be given to the Company, then as to such insured all liability of the Company shall cease and terminate in regard to the matter or matters for which such prompt notice is required; provided, however, that failure to notify shall in no case prejudice the rights of any such insured under this policy unless the Company shall be prejudiced by such failure and then only to the extent of such prejudice.

(c.) The Company shall have the right at its own cost to institute and without undue delay prosecute any action or proceeding or to do any other act which in its opinion may be necessary or desirable to establish the title to the estate or interest or the lien of the insured mortgage, as insured; and the Company may take any appropriate action, whether or not it shall be liable under the terms of this policy, and shall not thereby concede liability or waive any provision of this policy.

(d.) Whenever the Company shall have brought any action or interposed a defense as required or permitted by the provisions of this policy, the Company may pursue any such litigation to final determination by a court of competent jurisdiction and expressly reserves the right, in its sole discretion, to appeal from any adverse judgment or order.

(e.) In all cases where this policy permits or requires the Company to prosecute or provide for the defense of any action or proceeding, the insured hereunder shall secure to the Company the right to so prosecute or provide defense in such action or proceeding, and all appeals therein, and permit the Company to use, at its option, the name of such insured for such purpose. Whenever requested by the Company, such insured shall give the Company, at the Company's expense, all reasonable aid (1) in any such action or proceeding in effecting settlement, securing evidence, obtaining witnesses, or prosecuting or defending such action or proceeding, and (2) in any other act which in the opinion of the Company may be necessary or desirable to establish the title to the estate or interest or the lien of the insured mortgage, as insured, including but not limited to executing corrective or other documents.

4. Proof of Loss or Damage — Limitation of Action

In addition to the notices required under Paragraph 3(b) of these Conditions and Stipulations, a proof of loss or damage, signed and sworn to by the insured claimant shall be furnished to the Company within 90 days after the insured claimant shall ascertain or determine the facts giving rise to such loss or damage. Such proof of loss or damage shall describe the defect in, or lien or encumbrance on the title, or other matter insured against by this policy which constitutes the basis of loss or damage, and, when appropriate, state the basis of calculating the amount of such loss or damage.

Should such proof of loss or damage fail to state facts sufficient to enable the Company to determine its liability hereunder, insured claimant, at the written request of the Company, shall furnish such additional information as may reasonably be necessary to make such determination.

No right of action shall accrue to insured claimant until 30 days after such proof of loss or damage shall have been furnished.

Failure to furnish such proof of loss or damage shall terminate any liability of the Company under this policy as to such loss or damage.

5. Options to Pay or Otherwise Settle Claims and Options to Purchase Indebtedness

The Company shall have the option to pay or otherwise settle for or in the name of an insured claimant any claim insured against, or to terminate all liability and obligations of the Company hereunder by paying or tendering payment of the amount of insurance under this policy together with any costs, attorneys' fees and expenses incurred up to the time of such payment or tender of payment by the insured claimant and authorized by the Company. In case loss or damage is claimed under this policy by the owner of the indebtedness secured by the insured mortgage, the Company shall have the further option to purchase such indebtedness for the amount owing thereon together with all costs, attorneys' fees and expenses which the Company is obligated hereunder to pay. If the Company offers to purchase said indebtedness as herein provided, the owner of such indebtedness shall transfer and assign said indebtedness and the mortgage and any collateral securing the same to the Company upon payment therefor as herein provided. Upon such offer being made by the Company, all liability and obligations of the Company hereunder to the owner of the indebtedness secured by said insured mortgage, other than the obligation to purchase said indebtedness pursuant to this paragraph, are terminated.

6. Determination and Payment of Loss

(a.) The liability of the Company under this policy shall in no case exceed the least of:

(i) the actual loss of the insured claimant; or

(ii) the amount of insurance stated in Schedule A, or, if applicable, the amount of insurance as defined in paragraph 2(a) hereof; or

(iii) if this policy insures the owner of the indebtedness secured by the insured mortgage, and provided said owner is the insured claimant, the amount of the unpaid principal of said indebtedness, plus interest thereon, provided such amount shall not include any additional principal indebtedness created subsequent to Date of Policy, except as to amounts advanced to protect the lien of the insured mortgage and secured thereby.

(b.) The Company will pay, in addition to any loss insured against by this policy, all costs imposed upon an insured in litigation carried on by the Company for such insured, and all costs, attorneys' fees and expenses in litigation carried on by such insured with the written authorization of the Company.

(c.) When the amount of loss or damage has been definitely fixed in accordance with the conditions of this policy, the loss or damage shall be payable within 30 days thereafter.

7. Limitation of Liability

No claim shall arise or be maintainable under this policy (a) if the Company, after having received notice of an alleged defect, lien or encumbrance insured against hereunder, by litigation or otherwise, removes such defect, lien or encumbrance or establishes the title, or the lien of the insured mortgage, as insured, within a reasonable time after receipt of such notice; (b) in the event of litigation until there has been a final determination by a court of competent jurisdiction, and disposition of all appeals therefrom, adverse to the title or to the lien of the insured mortgage, as insured, as provided in paragraph 3 hereof; or (c) for liability voluntarily admitted or assumed by an insured without prior written consent of the Company.

FIGURE 15–4 ***(continued)***

8. Reduction of Insurance; Termination of Liability

All payments under this policy, except payment made for costs, attorneys' fees and expenses, shall reduce the amount of the insurance pro tanto; provided, however, if the owner of the indebtedness secured by the insured mortgage is an insured hereunder, then such payments, prior to the acquisition of title to said estate or interest as provided in paragraph 2(a) of these Conditions and Stipulations, shall not reduce pro tanto the amount of the insurance afforded hereunder as to any such insured, except to the extent that such payments reduce the amount of the indebtedness secured by such mortgage.

Payment in full by any person or voluntary satisfaction or release of the insured mortgage shall terminate all liability of the Company to an insured owner of the indebtedness secured by the insured mortgage, except as provided in paragraph 2(a) hereof.

9. Liability Noncumulative

It is expressly understood that the amount of insurance under this policy as to the insured owner of the estate or interest covered by this policy, shall be reduced by any amount the Company may pay under any policy insuring (a) a mortgage shown or referred to in Schedule B hereof which is a lien on the estate or interest covered by this policy, or (b) a mortgage hereafter executed by an insured which is a charge or lien on the estate or interest described or referred to in Schedule A, and the amount so paid shall be deemed a payment under this policy. The Company shall have the option to apply to the payment of any such mortgage any amount that otherwise would be payable hereunder to the insured owner of the estate or interest covered by this policy and the amount so paid shall be deemed a payment under this policy to said insured owner.

The provisions of this paragraph 9 shall not apply to an owner of the indebtedness secured by the insured mortgage, unless such insured acquires title to said estate or interest in satisfaction of said indebtedness or any part thereof.

10. Subrogation Upon Payment or Settlement

Whenever the Company shall have paid or settled a claim under this policy, all right of subrogation shall vest in the Company unaffected by any act of the insured claimant, except that the owner of the indebtedness secured by the insured mortgage may release or substitute the personal liability of any debtor or guarantor, or extend or otherwise modify the terms of payment, or release a portion of the estate or interest from the lien of the insured mortgage, or release any collateral security for the indebtedness, provided such act occurs prior to receipt by such insured of notice of any claim of title or interest adverse to the title to the estate or interest or the priority of the lien of the insured mortgage and does not result in any loss of priority of the lien of the insured mortgage. The Company shall be subrogated to and be entitled to all rights and remedies which such insured claimant would have had against any person or property in respect to such claim had this policy not been issued and the Company is hereby authorized and empowered to sue, compromise or settle in its name or in the name of the insured to the full extent of the loss sustained by the Company. If requested by the Company, the insured shall execute any and all documents to evidence the within subrogation. If the payment does not cover the loss of such insured claimant, the Company shall be subrogated to such rights and remedies in the proportion which said payment bears to the amount of said loss, but such subrogation shall be in subordination to an insured mortgage. If loss should result from any act of such insured claimant, such act shall not void this policy, but the Company, in that event, shall as to such insured claimant be required to pay only that part of any losses insured against hereunder which shall exceed the amount, if any, lost to the Company by reason of the impairment of the right of subrogation.

11. Liability Limited to this Policy

This instrument together with all endorsements and other instruments, if any, attached hereto by the Company is the entire policy and contract between the insured and the Company. Any claim of loss or damage, whether or not based on negligence, and which arises out of the status of the lien of the insured mortgage or of the title to the estate or interest covered hereby, or any action asserting such claim, shall be restricted to the provisions and Conditions and Stipulations of this policy.

No amendment of or endorsement to this policy can be made except by writing endorsed hereon or attached hereto signed by either the President, a Vice President, the Secretary, an Assistant Secretary, or validating officer or authorized signatory of the Company.

No payment shall be made without producing this policy for endorsement of such payment unless the policy be lost or destroyed, in which case proof of such loss or destruction shall be furnished to the satisfaction of the Company.

12. Notices, Where Sent

All notices required to be given the Company and any statement in writing required to be furnished the Company shall be addressed to it at the office which issued this policy or to its Home Office, 6300 Wilshire Boulevard, P.O. Box 92792, Los Angeles, California 90009.

13. THE PREMIUM SPECIFIED IN SCHEDULE A IS THE ENTIRE CHARGE FOR TITLE SEARCH, TITLE EXAMINATION AND TITLE INSURANCE.

FIGURE 15–4 (*continued*)

SCHEDULE A

Amount $160,000.00   Premium $588.00

Effective Date   May 25, 19—   Policy Number   C-228

1. Name of Insured: XYZ SAVINGS AND LOAN ASSOCIATION, a corporation,
                                    and
            THOMAS P. BROWN and CAROL V. BROWN, husband and wife

2. The estate or interest referred to herein is at Date of Policy vested in:

     THOMAS P. BROWN and CAROL V. BROWN, husband and wife, as joint tenants

3. The estate or interest in the land described in Schedule C is a fee.

SCHEDULE B

Part I

This policy does not insure against loss or damage by reason of the following:

1. Taxes or assessments which are not shown as existing liens by the records of any taxing authority that levies taxes or assessments on real property or by the public records.
Proceedings by a public agency which may result in taxes or assessments, or notices of such proceedings, whether or not shown by the records of such agency or by the public records.

2. Any facts, rights, interests or claims which are not shown by the public records but which could be ascertained by an inspection of the land or by making inquiry of persons in possession thereof.

3. Easements, liens or encumbrances, or claims thereof, which are not shown by the public records.

4. Discrepancies, conflicts in boundary lines, shortage in areas, encroachments, or any other facts which a correct survey would disclose, and which are not shown by the public records.

5. (a) Unpatented mining claims; (b) reservations or exceptions in patents or in Acts authorizing the issuance thereof; (c) water rights, claims or title to water.

6. Any right, title interest, estate or easement in land beyond the lines of the area specifically described or referred to in Schedule C, or in abutting streets, roads, avenues, alleys, lanes, ways or waterways, but nothing in this paragraph shall modify or limit the extent to which the ordinary right of an abutting owner for access to a physically open street or highway is insured by this policy.

7. Any law, ordinance or governmental regulation (including but not limited to building and zoning ordinances) restricting or regulating or prohibiting the occupancy, use or enjoyment of the land, or regulating the character, dimensions or location of any improvement now or hereafter erected on the land, or prohibiting a separation in ownership or a reduction in the dimensions or area of the land, or the effect of any violation of any such law, ordinance or governmental regulation.

8. Rights of eminent domain or governmental rights of police power unless notice of the exercise of such rights appears in the public records.

9. Defects, liens, encumbrances, adverse claims, or other matters (a) created, suffered, assumed or agreed to by the insured claimant; (b) not shown by the public records and not otherwise excluded from coverage but known to the insured claimant either at Date of Policy or at the date such claimant to the Company prior to the date such insured claimant became an insured hereunder; (c) resulting in no loss or damage to the insured claimant; (d) attaching or created subsequent to Date of Policy; or (e) resulting in loss or damage which would not have been sustained if the insured claimant had been a purchaser or encumbrancer for value without knowledge.

10. Any facts, rights, interests or claims which are not shown by the public records but which could be ascertained by making inquiry of the lessors in the lease or leases described or referred to in Schedule A.

11. The effect of any failure to comply with the terms, covenants and conditions of the lease or leases described or referred to in Schedule A.

FIGURE 15-4 (continued)

Part II

1. City and County Taxes for 19---19--, a lien, not yet payable. Assessor's lot 56, Block 619.

2. Public service easements appearing on map and granted to the Pacific Telephone and Telegraph Company and Pacific Gas and Electric Company in 222 O.R. 896. (Affects rear five feet.)

3. Declaration of restrictions by South Coast Insurance Company, a corporation, dated March 20, 1933, recorded April 10, 1933 in 8337 O.R. 821. No express words of forfeiture.

4. Trust Deed to secure the payment of $128,000.00 as follows:
   Trustor   : Thomas P. Brown and Carol V. Brown, husband and wife
   Trustee   : Columbia Reconveyance Company, a California corporation
   Beneficiary : XYZ Savings and Loan Association, a corporation
   Dated   : May 23, 19--
   Recorded   : May 23, 19-- Series Number A-89011.

SCHEDULE C

The specific land referred to in this policy is described as follows:

Being all that certain real property situated in the City of San Tomas, County of Los Angeles, State of California, described as follows, to wit:

Portion of Lot 56, Block 619, according to the map of Adams Terrace, filed July 18, 1931, in Book "P" of Maps, pages 21 and 22, in office of the Recorder of the City of San Tomas, County of Los Angeles, State of California, described as follows:

BEGINNING at a point on the northwest corner of the intersection of Royal Court Road and 20th Avenue; thence 200 feet northerly along the westerly line of Royal Court Road to point of beginning. Thence at a right angle 200 feet west; thence at a right angle 150 feet north; thence at a right angle 200 feet east; thence at a right angle 150 feet south to the point of beginning.

FIGURE 15-4 (continued)

ADDITIONAL PROTECTION INDORSEMENT
FOR HOME OWNERS

ATTACHED TO POLICY NO. C-228

ISSUED BY

Title Insurance and Trust Company

1. This Indorsement shall be effective only if at Date of Policy there is located on the land described in said Policy a one-to-four family residential structure, in which the Insured Owner resides or intends to reside. For the purpose of this Indorsement the term "residential structure" is defined as including the principal dwelling structure located on said land and all improvements thereon related to residential use of the property, except plantings of any nature and except perimeter fences and perimeter walls.

2. The Company hereby insures the Insured Owner of the estate or interest described in Schedule A against loss or damage which the Insured Owner shall sustain by reason of:

   a. the existence at Date of Policy of any of the following matters:

      (1) lack of a right of access from said land to a public street;

      (2) any taxes or assessments levied by a public authority against the estate or interest insured which constitute liens thereon and are not shown as exceptions in Schedule B of said Policy;

      (3) any unrecorded statutory liens for labor or material attaching to said estate or interest arising out of any work of improvement on said land in progress or completed at Date of Policy, except a work of improvement for which said Insured Owner has agreed to be responsible;

   b. the enforced removal of said residential structure or interference with the use thereof for ordinary residential purposes based upon the existence at Date of Policy of:

      (1) any encroachment of said residential structure or any part thereof onto adjoining lands, or onto any easement shown as an exception in Part II of Schedule B of said Policy, or onto any unrecorded subsurface easement;

      (2) any violation of any enforceable covenants, conditions or restrictions affecting said land and shown in Part II of Schedule B;

      (3) any violation of applicable zoning ordinances, but this Indorsement does not insure compliance with, nor is it in any way concerned with, building codes or other exercise of governmental police power;

   c. damage to said residential structure resulting from the exercise of any right to use the surface of said land for the extraction or development of minerals, if minerals are excepted from the description of said land or shown as an exception or reservation in Schedule B.

The total liability of the Company under said Policy and all indorsements attached thereto shall not exceed, in the aggregate, the amount of said Policy and costs which the Company is obligated under the conditions and stipulations thereof to pay; and nothing contained herein shall be construed as extending or changing the effective date of said Policy.

This indorsement is made a part of said Policy and is subject to the schedules, conditions and stipulations therein, except as modified by the provisions hereof.

Title Insurance and Trust Company

By *John J Eagan*   *Secretary*

FIGURE 15–4 (*concluded*)

7. Unfiled mechanic's liens or undisclosed restrictions.
8. False representation with respect to appointment of guardians or administrators.
9. Claims of undiscovered or unknown individuals who may be heirs or a decedent whose property has been distributed.
10. Joint tenancy deed or other instruments which are held to be invalid.
11. Defective court actions resulting from failure to include all necessary parties or failure to give proper notice.
12. Mistakes with respect to recording or indexing documents.
13. Mistakes due to individuals with similar or identical names.
14. Instruments executed by individuals supposedly single but actually married.
15. Liens in favor of the United States or California and not disclosed in the records.

ADDITIONAL TITLE COMPANY PROTECTIONS

Various specific reports, guarantees, and protections are available to serve particular needs. A few of these are as follows:

Leasehold policy. Insurance for an owner of a leasehold or subleasehold.

Vendee policy. Insurance of the title to the interest of a vendee (purchaser) or successor or assignee of a vendee where a contract of sale or purchase has been recorded. The insured is the vendee, and title is shown vested in the vendee as to the equitable title created by the specific contract of sale and purchase, and in the vendor (seller) as to the legal title.

Open-end advances. Insurance is available to lenders making advances where an open-end loan is used. The protection is to insure the lender against loss as the result of ownership changes, impairment of the security device, or mechanic's liens.

Mechanic's liens. Protects against mechanic's liens in connection with completed or in-progress structures which might gain priority over an insured mortgage or deed of trust.

Construction protection. Insures a lender that the foundations of a building being constructed are within specific boundaries and do not violate existing covenants, conditions, and restrictions and do not encroach on specific easements.

Litigation guarantee. This type of report is generally issued for the benefit of attorneys to furnish them with information pertinent to the commencement of a judicial proceeding. It discloses condition of record title, names and addresses of property owners, encumbrances, present deed on record, and any legal incapacities of the present owners.

Trustee's sale guarantee. Provides specific information to a trustee who must proceed with a trustee's sale. Gives information about title, ownership, and liens together with possible bankruptcy data about the owner and any information regarding federal tax liens.

Chain of title guarantee. Lists all recorded instruments in the chain of title of a specific real property parcel together with data concerning parties, dates, and recordings.

Property search guarantee. A property search is made for the purpose of determining what specific property is recorded in the name of a specific individual or corporation.

Restriction and easement guarantee. Provides copies of building and tract restrictions together with copies of easements which affect a particular property.

QUESTIONS FOR DISCUSSION

1. Why may the escrow not act as mediator in disputes between the parties to the escrow?
2. What are the various methods by which an escrow can be terminated?
3. For which of the parties in an escrow is the escrow holder an agent?
4. How do escrow practices differ between northern and southern California?
5. How is the division of charges between buyer and seller made in your locality?
6. What escrow practices are used in your own locality?
7. What is the purpose of the seller's and buyer's statements?
8. What is the purpose of a proration?
9. Of what particular importance is the preliminary title search?
10. What particular circumstances allow a real estate broker to perform an escrow?

MULTIPLE CHOICE QUESTIONS

15–1. The title policy fee: *(a)* is paid by seller, *(b)* is paid by lender, *(c)* payment varies according to county, *(d)* none of these.
15–2. The following statement that best describes the escrow holder: *(a)* is paid by broker, *(b)* neutral party, *(c)* gives legal advice to parties in the escrow, *(d)* guarantees validity of purchase contract.
15–3. A broker may escrow a transaction if: *(a)* broker

is acting as agent with respect to the transaction, *(b)* parties to the agreement request it, *(c)* title company pays broker a commission, *(d)* none of these.

15–4. Charges to the parties in connection with the escrow are shown in: *(a)* purchase contract, *(b)* title search, *(c)* escrow statements, *(d)* tax statements.

15–5. The escrow holder: *(a)* arranges financing, *(b)* must request a termite inspection, *(c)* generally pays a referral fee to broker, *(d)* none of these.

15–6. The payment of various escrow charges between the parties is set by: *(a)* real estate law, *(b)* escrow company, *(c)* agreement by parties and customary practices in area, *(d)* broker.

15–7. Escrow agencies must be licensed by: *(a)* real estate commissioner, *(b)* superior court, *(c)* corporation commissioner, *(d)* none of these.

15–8. The basic purpose of a title insurance policy is to: *(a)* prepare financial statements, *(b)* provide property inspection, *(c)* insure clear title to property, *(d)* pay taxes and judgments.

16 Taxation of real property

The general field of taxation and its relationship to dealings in real property has become quite detailed and complex. Tax laws have a great effect on most of the decisions made in real estate transactions, especially the larger ones. A knowledge of taxation and tax laws regarding property has become a necessity for the successful real estate licensee and investor alike.

It is important for those engaged in the real estate business to know the variety of taxes, their bases, and their effect on property transfers so that they may be able to counsel their clients correctly in this area. All persons, licensed or not, who take part in a real estate transaction will, to a certain degree, be made aware of the effect of taxation and tax laws upon real property. Brokers and their clients will often have to work along with accountants, attorneys, and others who specialize in the field of taxation. This chapter, as well as the following one, will deal with the more important aspects of taxation and its effect upon real property.

PROPOSITION 13—JARVIS-GANN

Officially passed by the voters June 6, 1978, and legally effective July 1, 1978, Proposition 13, commonly known as the Jarvis-Gann Amendment, is now law in California. This law, which adds Article XIII A to the State Constitution, is officially titled, "Tax Limitation—Initiative Constitutional Amendment" and its sections state as follows:

1. *(a)* The maximum amount of any ad valorem tax on real property shall not exceed one percent (1%) of the full cash value of such property. The one percent (1%) tax to be collected by the coun-

ties and apportioned according to law to the districts within the counties.

(b) The limitation provided for in subdivision (a) shall not apply to ad valorem taxes or special assessments to pay the interest and redemption charges on any indebtedness approved by the voters prior to the time this section becomes effective.

2. *(a)* The full cash value means the County Assessor's valuation of real property as shown on the 1975–76 tax bill under "full cash value," or thereafter, the appraised value of real property when purchased, newly constructed, or a change in ownership has occurred after the 1975 assessment. All real property not already assessed up to the 1975–76 tax levels may be reassessed to reflect that valuation.

(b) The fair market value base may reflect from year to year the inflationary rate not to exceed two percent (2%) for any given year or reduction as shown in the consumer price index or comparable data for the area under taxing jurisdiction.

3. From and after the effective date of this article, any changes in State taxes enacted for the purpose of increasing revenues collected pursuant thereto whether by increased rates or changes in methods of computation must be imposed by an Act passed by not less than two thirds of all members elected to each of the two houses of the Legislature, except that no new ad valorem taxes on real property, or sales or transaction taxes on the sales of real property may be imposed.

4. Cities, Counties, and special districts, by a two-thirds vote of the qualified electors of such district, may impose special taxes on such district, except ad valorem taxes on real property within such City, County or special district.

5. This article shall take effect for the tax year beginning on July 1st following the passage of this Amendment, except Section 3 which shall become effective upon the passage of this article.

6. If any section, part, clause, or phrase hereof is held to be invalid or unconstitutional, the remaining sections shall not be affected but will remain in full force and effect.

Basic intention of Proposition 13

The basic effect of Proposition 13 is to place a limit on the amount of property taxes that can be collected by local governments, restrict the growth in the assessed value of property subject to taxation, require a two-thirds vote of the Legislature to increase state tax revenues, and authorize local governments to impose certain non-property taxes if two thirds of the voters give their approval in a local election.

In addition to implementation by the California Legislature and the California Board of Equalization, the California Supreme Court has found this new tax reduction amendment to the state constitution to be constitutional. Its intention is to reduce state income from property taxes necessitating a state reduction in expenditures.

ASSESSMENT OF REAL PROPERTY

The tax year is not based on the January 1 to December 31 calendar, but rather on the fiscal year of July 1 to June 30. Every tax due on personal property is a lien on the real property of the owner. This is true of both city and county personal property taxes. Taxes due on real property are liens against the property assessed. Property taxes become a lien on property on the first day in March preceding the tax year.

As of this lien date, the assessment period begins. During this period the office of the county assessor sets a valuation on the property for tax purposes. The Petris-Knox Bill, passed by the legislature in 1966, now makes it mandatory that all property on the tax rolls be assessed at 25 percent of actual cash value.

Assessors have a legal directive on how to determine values for tax purposes. The California constitution requires that all property shall be taxed in proportion to its value. "Value" is based on full cash value or market value, terms that the state supreme court holds are synonymous. The court further defines such value as the highest price that a property will bring if exposed for sale in the open market allowing a reasonable time to find a purchaser who buys with knowledge of all the uses to which it is adapted and for which it is capable of being used. Assessors divide the property value between land and improvements, and both amounts are shown in the tax bill and added together to arrive at full value.

When the valuation of property is completed, assessment rolls are prepared by the assessor and are then turned in to the county board of supervisors, who give them to the county auditor. The auditor lists the total number of acres of land, value of all real estate, personal property, improvements, and moneys. He thus arrives at the entire value of county property.

The same general procedure is followed by cities. Some make their own independent assessed valuations. The city board of supervisors performs the same function as the county board of supervisors. Some cities, such as Oakland in Alameda County, arrange with the county to handle all city tax assessments and collections. The city of San Francisco is unique in that it is a city and a county combined, and its supervisors are both city and county supervisors. The assessor is, likewise, city and county assessor.

THE TAX RATE

Previous to Proposition 13, at the same time that the assessor's office was preparing the assessment rolls, the various executive and administrative agencies of the county were preparing their yearly budgets to submit to the board of supervisors. Then, simply by knowing the amount of money necessary and by knowing the assessed value of county property, it was possible to arrive at the tax rate per $100 of assessed value to bring in the required amount of money.

Previously, tax rates varied among different localities, but now, with a 1 percent of market value tax limit, property owners will pay the same basic rate of approximately $4 per $100 assessed valuation. This is because assessments are 25 percent of market value.

Assessors divide the property value between the land and improvements, and so an owner's tax bill might show the full cash value of the land as $35,000 and improvements as $105,000, for a total full cash value of $140,000. The assessed value for tax purposes would then be $8,750 for the land and $26,250 for the improvements for a total assessed value of $35,000, or 25 percent of the full cash or market value as required by law.

TAX COLLECTION CALENDAR

The tax rate, then, is approved by the board of supervisors by September 1, and the tax collector is required on or before November 1st of each year to mail a tax bill or copy of it to each fee owner of the property. See Figure 16–1.

The real property owner may pay his taxes in one payment, or he may pay in two installments. On the first day of November, the first installment is due and covers the period of July through December. The first installment (first half) becomes delinquent if not paid by 5 P.M. December 10, at which time a penalty of 6 percent is added to the first installment. The second installment (second half) of the real property tax, which covers the period of January through June, is due on February 1 and becomes delinquent if not paid by 5 P.M. April 10.

To review:

1. Fiscal year basis—July 1 to June 30.
2. First Monday in March—taxes become a lien on real property.
3. First installment—due November 1 and delinquent on December 10 at 5 P.M.

BOARD OF EQUALIZATION

The board of supervisors of each county is the county board of equalization, before whom an owner appeals if he feels that his property has been overassessed. The state board is an elective body whose function is to check on the various

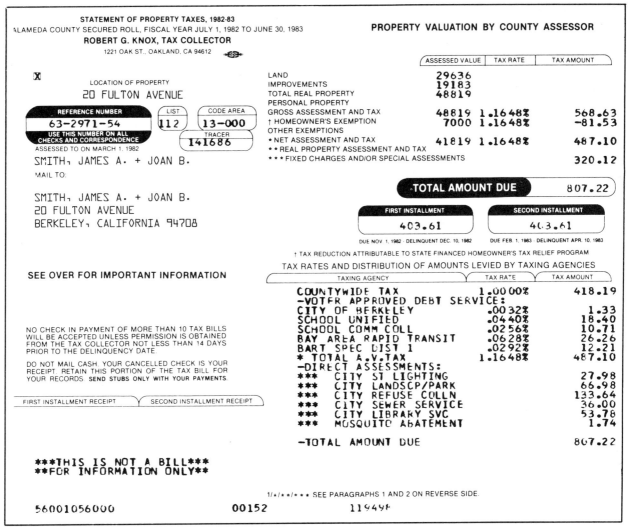

FIGURE 16–1

county assessors and assure that the taxation process is properly conducted throughout the counties of the state. In some areas the board of supervisors establishes a separate appeals board that hears appeals.

REPORTING OWNERSHIP CHANGE

Revenue and Taxation Code, Section 480, requires any individual acquiring an interest in real property to file a change of ownership statement with the county recorder or assessor of the county in which the property is located. The change of ownership statement must be filed within 45 days of the recording date or, if the ownership change is not recorded, within 45 days of the date of ownership change.

Local assessors and recorders will, on recordation of any ownership change, send a change of ownership form to the new owners of record, and such form must be completed and returned. It asks for specific information regarding the transfer, name of parties, how acquired, type of property, form of ownership, and details of financing.

PROPERTY REASSESSMENT

Real estate licensees must be aware of ownership changes which will result in a reassessment of property and tax increase as such information will be requested by prospective purchasers. The California state board of equalization has prepared a detailed and complex set of rules for county assessors with respect to which transfers will result in and which will not result in reassessment. A few of the more common reassessment transfers discussed in these rules are as follows:

The following will generally result in a reassessment of the property.

a. Traditional sale of real property from present to new owner.
b. Creation or transfer of a leasehold with a term of 35 years or more.
c. Transfer of lessors interest in real property subject to a lease with a remaining term of less than 35 years.

The following will generally not result in a reassessment of the property.

a. Creation of joint tenancy with original owner remaining on title.
b. Creation of a life estate.
c. Owners of tenancy in common create a joint tenancy.

d. Transfer of property between spouses.
e. Partnership owners add a partner.
f. Transfer of property to a revocable trust.
g. Transfer of separate property to a spouse.
h. Transfer to trustee for beneficial use of a spouse.
i. Property settlement or dissolution decree transfeers.
j. Transfer due to expiration of a spouse.

HOMEOWNERS' PROPERTY TAX EXEMPTION

State Proposition 1–A, enacted in 1968, and subsequent additions provide that:

1. All household furnishings and personal effects of a householder are exempt from taxation.
2. A dwelling occupied by an owner as his principal place of residence will receive an exemption of $1,750 in assessed value.

A form upon which to make claim for the assessed value exemption is made available by the assessor and must be filed by the claimant prior to April 15. Only a person who both owns and occupies the property as his principal place of residence may file the claim for homeowner's property tax exemption. The form must be dated and signed by the claimant, under penalty of perjury, and contains statements that say in effect that:

a. The claimant holds title to the property or is buying under a contract of sale, and is occupying the property as his principal place of residence.
b. The dwelling is a single living unit, either in a separate structure or a multiple-unit structure.
c. During the current fiscal year neither the claimant nor anyone with whom the claimant shares ownership received or expects to receive from the state, county, or city any assistance (other than senior citizen's property tax assistance) containing an allowance for property tax on the described dwelling.
d. The claimant has not filed a claim for home owner's exemption on any other property in California, and no other person whose principal residence is the dwelling identified in the claim has filed or will file a claim for the same dwelling.

The homeowner's property tax exemption excuses $1,750 of assessed value, which equals $7,000 of cash value. This results in tax savings to the homeowner of $70.

TAX CREDIT FOR RENTERS

California allows a renter's credit on the California income tax return to those individuals who meet certain requirements. The allowance varies depending on the adjusted gross income of the individual.

SENIOR CITIZENS PROPERTY TAX ASSISTANCE

The Gonsalves-Deukmejian-Petris Property Tax Assistance Law provides direct cash reimbursement for part of the property taxes on the residence of qualified individuals with total household incomes of $12,000 or less who are either: (1) 62 or older; (2) blind, or; (3) disabled.

This assistance to California residents is not automatic and will not be granted at the time that property taxes are paid. To claim assistance for property taxes paid, the taxpayer must file a claim form between May 16 and August 31 in order for the cash reimbursement to be received. Forms may be obtained from the office of the Franchise Tax Board in your area.

Taxpayers filing a claim for property tax assistance will not reduce the amount of property taxes owed to the County Tax Collector nor will the filing of such claim result in a lien being placed on their property.

SENIOR CITIZENS PROPERTY TAX POSTPONEMENT

The Senior Citizens Property Tax Postponement Law gives qualified individuals who are 62 or older with household income of $30,200 or less the option of having the state pay all or part of the taxes on their homes. In return, a lien is placed on their property for the amount of taxes the state pays. The lien is payable when the homeowner sells the property, moves, or expires. A claim form must be filed for each year that a postponement of taxes is desired. Individuals who qualify for postponement may also qualify for property tax assistance. Claim forms or information regarding either the Property Tax Assistance or Postponement Programs may be obtained from the Franchise Tax Board Office in your area or by calling the Franchise Tax Board toll-free at 800–852–7050.

SOLAR TAX CREDITS

The state and federal governments allow a tax credit for solar installations. California provides a credit of 55 percent, not to exceed $3,000, for all installations (residential and nonresidential) which cost less than $12,000. If a solar system is installed in a building other than a single-family residence and the cost is more than $12,000, the tax credit is 25 percent or $3,000, whichever is greater.

The solar tax credit is subtracted from the buyer's state income taxes. It is not just a deduction used to compute the total amount of income tax. If, for instance, the buyer's tax credit is greater than his total state tax bill, the unused credit is carried over to the next year or until the buyer has received the full credit due.

For example, if the buyer installs a solar water heating system that costs $3,000, he will be entitled to a tax credit of $1,650. If his state income tax is $900 for the year, he will get all of his withholding tax back and still have the remaining credit of $750 to apply the following year.

The federal government allows a 30 percent tax credit on the first $2,000 of the cost of installation and 20 percent of the next $8,000 for a total credit of $2,200 on the buyer's income tax.

The most common uses of solar systems are for swimming pool heating, household water heating, and space heating. Wind is generally considered a solar product and can be used to generate mechanical or electrical power.

There are two types of systems, active and passive. Active solar systems use air or water to store and circulate heat. In active systems, radiant solar energy becomes heat when it strikes a blackened surface. Active systems employ specialized hardware powered by mechanical or electrical energy to gather and carry heat; example—rooftop collectors made of glass and black-coated copper pipe. Liquids in the pipe absorb the sun's heat and then are circulated to a storage tank that feeds heat to household living areas and the water supply.

Passive solar systems collect heat without hardware; they make use of a structure itself to capture and store heat; example—large south-facing windows admit solar heat; if the walls of a building are made of brick, concrete, or adobe, they absorb heat and gradually release it. Temperature is modified throughout the day.

VETERAN'S EXEMPTION

A California veteran who has served in the military in time of war is entitled to an exemption of $1,000 on the assessed value of his property. The same advantage is given to the widow, widowed mother, or pensioned parent of a deceased veteran.

The property may not have an assessed valuation of over $5,000 or, if community property, $10,000. Claim for the exemption must be filed each year by the veteran or his spouse, or other person entitled to do so, with the assessor between noon on the first Monday in March and 5 P.M. on the first Monday in May. This exemption applies only to real and personal property taxes, and not to taxes levied by special assessment districts.

A veteran may not receive the $1,000 veteran's exemption and the $1,750 homeowner's exemption on the same property. If a veteran owns property other than his principal place of residence, the veteran may take the $1,750 homeowner's exemption on his residence and the $1,000 veteran's exemption on his other property if such other property qualifies.

California law allows a greater exemption for disabled California veterans.

SPECIAL ASSESSMENTS

While annual property taxes are levied for the support of general governmental functions, special assessments are levied for the cost of such specific local improvements as streets, sewers, irrigation, drainage, flood control, special lighting, and other public conveniences.

Special assessment districts are regulated by state law. Assessment districts issue bonds to finance the necessary improvements. Proposition 13 authorizes cities, counties, special districts, and school districts to impose such special taxes if two thirds of the voters approve. Such taxes cannot be based on the value or sale of real property.

Sometimes, if an improvement will be located completely within a particular city or county, the city or county merely establishes an improvement area and need not establish a separate assessment district for the particular improvement.

Often, a city issues improvement bonds that are sold to the general public to finance improvements. Special assessments are usually of three general types:

a. Assessments at rates fixed annually and collected at the same time as the local taxes.
b. Separately collected assessments for the maintenance of special districts, such as irrigation districts.
c. Nonrecurring assessments levied for the cost of a particular local improvement.

The state of California has enacted various laws relating to special assessment districts in the state.

Those interested may investigate the applicable legislation. Mutual water companies and irrigation districts are discussed in Chapter 18.

PROPERTY EXEMPT FROM TAXATION

Properties owned by local, state, or federal governments are not subject to taxation. Obviously, this accounts for the large percentage of property excluded from the tax rolls. In California, almost three-quarters of all the land is exempt from taxation. Properties owned by religious, charitable, and educational institutions are also exempt from taxation. It is said that these properties should be excluded because the institutions are nonprofit in nature and contribute to the religious, cultural, and charitable needs of the community.

TAX SALE OF REAL PROPERTY

Property sold at tax sale is quite simply property on which the taxes have not been paid for a certain period of time and that is finally being sold by the state, county, or city tax collector in order to satisfy the tax delinquency.

First sale

On June 8 of each year a delinquent tax list is published, showing all properties for which one or both real property tax installments are delinquent. On June 30, such property is said to be first sold to the state. Although the property is not actually sold at this time, the important point is that at this time the statutory five-year period of redemption begins. At any time during the five years, the owner of the property may redeem it and save it from ultimately being sold by paying all delinquent taxes and any attendant penalties.

Second sale

After five years have passed from the date of the so-called first sale, the state of California now actually acquires an absolute title in the tax-delinquent property. The property must be sold for at least the full amount that was due for the year in which the property was first sold to the state, plus the unpaid taxes for each of the five subsequent years. In addition, there must be included in the sale price all statutory penalties, interest, and costs that may have accrued.

Actual sale to the public

If real property to be sold is outside an incorporated area, it is sold under the authority of the state controller. If the property is in an incorporated area, the city or county tax collector is in charge of the sale. Because tax may be due to local, state, and federal agencies at the same time, the official in charge of the sale, whoever he may be, must confer with these agencies and reach an agreement on the disposition of the purchase price received for the property.

After publishing the required notice, giving details of the sale, description of the property, and other particulars, the property involved is sold at public auction. A minimum bid is established, and any interested party may bid and purchase the property.

Tax deed and title insurance

On completion of the sale, the tax collector in charge issues to the purchaser a deed commonly referred to as a tax deed. This deed should be recorded by the purchaser in the office of the county recorder. After the sale the former owner loses any claim he may have had and cannot redeem the property.

Most title insurance companies insure tax titles if one year has passed since issuance of the tax deed, if the former owner is not in possession, if current taxes have been paid and if no serious defects are shown by examination of the events leading up to the sale. If the title insurance company refuses to insure the tax title after an investigation of the case, the new owner must proceed with a quiet title action against the former owner.

DOCUMENTARY TRANSFER TAX

California law allows a county to adopt a documentary transfer tax to apply on all transfers of real property located in the county. Notice of payment is entered on the face of the deed or on a separate paper filed with the deed at time of recordation. A city within a county that has adopted the transfer tax may also adopt its own transfer tax ordinance with the tax fixed at half the rate charged by the county. In effect this merely means that the county collects the total tax and turns half the amount over to the city.

In most counties tax is computed at the rate of $1.10 per $1,000 or $0.55 per $500 or any lesser amount. If a property is sold with a trust deed or mortgage against it and the existing encumbrance is assumed by the buyer, the tax is payable only on the seller's equity. If the trust deed or mortgage is newly executed in connection with the sale, the tax is payable on the entire purchase price of the property.

As part of closing costs in escrow, the documentary transfer tax is a charge against the seller. An example of the calculation of this charge appears in the chapter dealing with escrows.

CALIFORNIA GIFT AND INHERITANCE TAX

California Gift and Inheritance Taxes have effectively been abolished as of June 9, 1982.

Previously, California had levied a tax on inheritances since 1893 and a tax on gifts since 1939. The California gift tax was a tax levied on gifts of real or personal property made to individuals and based on the value of the gift. The California inheritance tax was a tax on the right to receive or inherit real or personal property and was based on the value of inheritance received by individual heirs and beneficiaries.

A major revision was made with respect to gift and inheritance taxes in 1980. The California legislature enacted provisions which exempted from gift and inheritance taxes all property transfers between spouses and increased amounts exempt from taxation for all other classes of beneficiaries. The law further allowed qualified farms and closely held businesses to be valued on the basis of their current use, rather than fair market value, and additionally allowed an estate to be distributed to the heirs or beneficiaries before the full amount of inheritances taxes were paid to the state.

State Propositions 5 and 6 were approved by California voters on June 8, 1982 becoming effective as of June 9, 1982. The law now prevents the state or any local government from levying any gift or inheritance tax except for a *pickup* tax which is discussed later. The law prohibits the California Legislature, without approval of a majority of the electors voting in a statewide election, from changing any provisions of the law, except to provide for the collection and administration of the California estate "pickup" tax.

California estate "pickup" tax

The Federal Estate Tax Law allows a taxpayer to reduce his or her tax liability, up to certain

232

limits, by the amount of the taxpayers state liability for inheritance taxes. The California law now requires the state of California to levy a California estate tax (called "pickup" tax) equal to the maximum federal credit allowable. The effect of this provision is give the state of California a portion of the tax due to the federal government. A taxpayer's total combined state and federal tax will not in any way be increased because the California estate tax will now be an offset against the federal tax.

Inheritance and probate proceedings

Property is usually held jointly by husband and wife or other joint tenants in order to escape the time and expense of going through probate proceedings. If the property is held in joint tenancy vesting title in the surviving spouse or joint tenants is a comparatively simple and inexpensive process compared with the commissions and fees payable to administrators, executors, and attorneys in a probate proceeding. In addition to the statutory fees, which are percentage amounts applied against the total value of the estate, there are additional fees allowed the executor, administrator, or attorney, as the case may be, in the event that they are required to perform any extraordinary service or incur other than regular expenses in connection with the probating of the estate. In order to avoid these fees and save the considerable time involved in the probate of an estate, most married couples hold title as joint tenants, thus eliminating probate proceedings.

State law provides that if a spouse expires without a will, or by will confers his or her interest in community property to the surviving spouse, such property after 40 days from date of expiration may be sold or otherwise dealt with by the surviving spouse without the necessity of probate with respect to the property. This law will eliminate the necessity for probate sale procedures in a great number of estates.

Cost basis

Married couples are often advised against holding property as joint tenants because of the problem of the tax basis, or cost basis, as it is often called. In addition to our discussion here, the method of determining the basis is covered in Chapter 17, Income Tax and Real Estate. The

method of determining the basis for a residential property differs slightly from that of determining the basis for income or business properties where a depreciation deduction comes into the picture.

For our discussion, we will assume the property to be a single-family residential dwelling. The cost basis of this residence is the purchase price originally paid plus the costs at the time of purchase, such as title insurance, escrow fees, and loan fees. In addition, improvements added, such as a new bathroom, are included. Some years later, when the property is sold, the profit for tax purposes is the difference between the cost basis and the selling price, less costs of the sale, such as the broker's commission and other fees. This profit is known as the capital gain.

Example: Jack and Jill purchased a house some years ago at a cost of $54,000. They have added $22,000 worth of improvements and now sell the property for $192,000. The cost basis of $76,000 subtracted from a selling price of $192,000 equals a gain of $116,000. Assuming that Jack and Jill incurred $18,000 worth of expenses in connection with the sale, they will show a net gain of $98,000 and will be taxed on the basis of this $98,000 gain. As discussed in Chapter 17, the amount of tax will vary, depending on a number of factors.

Stepped-up tax basis

In California, a surviving spouse will inherit community property with what is called a stepped-up basis; that is, the value of the property at the time of inheritance becomes the new cost basis. Assuming Jill to be a surviving spouse, she will inherit the residence and receive a stepped-up basis. Instead of the old basis of $76,000, the residence will have a new basis of $192,000 (market value of property at time of inheritance), and if Jill now sells the property for $192,000, there is mathematically no gain and no tax to pay.

It is important to remember that only community property is treated in this way. If the property is held as joint tenancy property, Jill only gets a stepped-up basis on half of the property and half retains the old basis. If Jack and Jill held the property as joint tenants and Jill cannot prove that the property is community property, she will inherit the house with a new cost basis of $134,000. Half of the old base ($76,000 divided by 2) equals $38,000 plus $96,000, which equals $134,000. Now if Jill sells the property for $192,000, she will have a gain of $58,000. After deducting

$18,000 of selling expenses, Jill has a taxable gain of $40,000.

If Jack and Jill had owned a large apartment building or income property that had greatly increased in value, we can see the importance to a surviving spouse with respect to a stepped-up basis on all or just half of a property. In California, if a surviving spouse can prove that a property held as joint tenants was, in fact, community property and had as its source community funds, the state will treat the property as community property and the surviving spouse will receive a stepped-up basis for the entire property. Additionally, joint tenancy property will avoid probate proceedings.

It is usually not difficult for a surviving spouse to show that real property, although held as joint tenants, was actually acquired during marriage with community funds. If a husband and wife wish to, they can prepare and sign a statement declaring specific property they own to be community property although they hold title as joint tenants in order to avoid probate proceedings.

Cost basis and federal gift tax

With respect to the sale of property acquired by gift, both California and federal laws hold that the cost basis to the donee now selling is the basis of the original donor. However, the value of property for purposes of determining the amount of federal gift tax that may be payable is the market value of the property at the time of the gift.

Professional advice

The subjects of taxation and methods of holding titles are quite complex, and most individuals and real estate licensees should seek the advice of either a certified public accountant, attorney, or bank officer with respect to taxation, title, or estate planning matters.

FEDERAL GIFT AND ESTATE TAXES

The Tax Reform Act of 1976 brought about a major overhaul of estate and gift tax laws and was generally structured to favor small- and medium-sized estates. The Economic Recovery Tax Act of 1981 has added significant changes to the law, including a substantial increase in the amount of inheritance or gifts that are now exempt from any payment of taxes.

The gross estate of a decedent includes all real and personal property owned by a decedent at date of expiration, such as stocks, bonds, checking and savings accounts, and real property. When the property that makes up the gross estate has been determined, it is given a value. The fair market value of the property is generally its value for estate tax purposes.

From the gross estate are deducted certain expenses, claims against the estate, expenses of administration, expenses of last illness and burial, transfers to exempt charitable and religious institutions, accrued taxes, unpaid mortgages, and executors' commissions and attorneys' fees.

What remains after deductions is called the net estate, and previously, any amount of net estate in excess of $60,000 was taxed. The Economic Recovery Tax Act of 1981 increases the amount of exemption, which will reach $600,000 in 1987. This means that only net estates in excess of $600,000 will be subject to any taxation. The law also provides a special benefit for spouses. A gift to a spouse, or any amount inherited from a deceased spouse, is now free of any gift or inheritance taxes no matter what the amount.

Unified credit and tax rates

With respect to the gift tax, previous law allowed a donor an annual exclusion of $3,000 per gift to each donee with no limitation as to the number of donees, plus a $30,000 lifetime amount which could be either taken in any single year, or cumulatively in smaller amounts until the $30,000 was used up. A husband and wife had a $60,000 exemption, plus an annual exemption per donee of $6,000. With respect to estate taxes, a $60,000 exemption was provided.

The Tax Reform Act of 1976 retained the annual exclusion of $3,000 per gift to each donee but replaced the $30,000 gift tax exemption and the $60,000 estate tax exemption with a unified credit of $47,000 (equivalent to an exemption of $175,625) for both estate and gift taxes and also provided a unified tax rate schedule applicable to both gift and estate taxes in those cases where gift or estate taxes have to be paid.

The Economic Recovery tax Act of 1981 increased the annual gift tax exclusion per donee from $3,000 to $10,000 which allows a husband and wife to give gifts of $20,000 per donee, and continues to 1987. The estate and gift tax credit is as follows:

Year	Estate and Gift Tax Credit	Estate or Gift Exemption Equivalent
1977	$ 30,000	$120,700
1978	34,000	134,000
1979	38,000	147,300
1980	42,500	161,600
1981	47,000	175,600
1982	62,800	225,000
1983	79,300	275,000
1984	96,300	325,000
1985	121,800	400,000
1986	155,800	500,000
1987	192,800	600,000

The Federal Gift and Estate Tax Rates are illustrated in Table 16–1. The tax due applies to the sum of (a) the amount of taxable estate and/or (b) the amount of taxable gifts after taking into account any allowable exclusions. The 1981 law reduces the maximum 70 percent tax rate to 50 percent by 1985.

The marital deduction

A deduction known as the marital deduction was intended to equalize taxes between residents of states that were not community property states and residents of states that were community property states. It did this by accepting the concept of ownership prevailing between husband and

TABLE 16–1
Federal Gift and Estate Tax Rates

From	To	Tax is	Plus Percent	Of Excess Over
—	$ 10,000	18% of such amount		
$ 10,000	20,000	$ 1,800	20%	$ 10,000
20,000	40,000	3,800	22	20,000
40,000	60,000	8,200	24	40,000
60,000	80,000	13,000	26	60,000
80,000	100,000	18,200	28	80,000
100,000	150,000	23,800	30	100,000
150,000	250,000	38,800	32	150,000
250,000	500,000	70,800	34	250,000
500,000	750,000	155,800	37	500,000
750,000	1,000,000	284,300	39	750,000
1,000,000	1,250,000	345,800	41	1,000,000
1,250,000	1,500,000	448,300	43	1,250,000
1,500,000	2,000,000	555,800	45	1,500,000
2,000,000	2,500,000	780,800	49	2,000,000
2,500,000	3,000,000	1,025,800	53	2,500,000
3,000,000	3,500,000	1,290,800	57	3,000,000
3,500,000	4,000,000	1,575,800	61	3,500,000
1984 Over	3,000,000	1,290,800	55	3,000,000
1985 Over	2,500,000	1,025,800	50	2,500,000

wife in community property states, namely, that each owns half of the property.

With respect to gifts, the law provided up to $100,000 of gifts to a spouse tax-free. The amount between $100,000 and $200,000 was fully taxable, and 50 percent of any amount over $200,000 was taxable. With respect to estate taxes, the law allowed a deduction for property passing to a surviving spouse which was limited to $250,000 or half of the adjusted gross estate, whichever was greater.

The Economic Recovery Tax Act of 1981 established an unlimited marital deduction. There is no longer any dollar limit on the estate and gift tax marital deduction, and either spouse can transfer to the other, by gift or at expiration, any amount of property free of taxes.

Transfers within three years of death

Previously, a transfer of interest in property made by a decedent within three years of death was presumed to have been made in contemplation of death, and the full value of the property was included in the gross estate and taxed. However, the amount of gifts was not included in the estate if the executors were able to prove that the decedent was healthy and mentally competent and that the gifts were not made with the intent of avoiding estate taxes.

The areas in dispute were most often with respect to gifts of property in place of a testamentary disposition or the giving of a gift deed with instructions that it be recorded after expiration of the donor.

The Economic Recovery Tax Act of 1981 now eliminates fully the three-year rule and provides that any such gifts made are now excluded from the taxable estate.

Family farm or business property

The 1981 tax act provides an exception to the general rule that all property of a decedent is taxed at its fair market value if such property is either a family farm or real property used in a family business. This type of property may now be valued on the basis of its present use, termed a special use valuation, rather than at its highest and best use. This will result in a valuation that can be substantially less than a fair market value amount.

The purpose of the special-use valuation for family farms and businesses is to allow continuation of family ownership of farms and businesses which might otherwise have to be sold in order to pay estate taxes. The law further provides that within certain provisions, any estate taxes due with respect to a family farm or business may be paid on an installment basis during a 10-year period.

Although this chapter may seem to be quite detailed in its presentation of the material covered, it actually presents only the basic essentials in an area that is extremely difficult and complex. The real estate licensee will have to work closely with accountants, attorneys, and other experts in order to achieve a high degree of professional success. The validity of the preceding statement will be all the more apparent as the reader proceeds to Chapter 17, which deals with income taxes.

QUESTIONS FOR DISCUSSION

1. Discuss how the tax base in your community affects the taxes and burden of taxation on those who must pay.
2. What are your feelings regarding the taxing of the personal property of a homeowner, business, or industry?
3. How many different kinds and types of property in your community can you list that are tax-exempt?
4. Discuss the types of tax-assistance available to senior citizens.
5. How has the Economic Recovery Tax Act of 1981 affected the marital deduction with respect to the federal estate tax?
6. What types of ownership changes will affect a reassessment of property values for tax purposes?
7. Why is it easier to avoid gift taxes when giving money than when giving real property?
8. What is the effect of a married couple's holding a piece of community property as joint tenants?
9. Do you feel it is proper for the state and federal government to collect gift or estate taxes?
10. What are special assessments, and how do they affect property in your community?

MULTIPLE CHOICE QUESTIONS

16-1. The following property that is subject to taxation is: (a) municipal court building, (b) apartment building, (c) city and county budgets, (d) state property.
16-2. The tax act which has most affected federal gift and estate taxes is: (a) Sales Tax Act, (b) Revenue Act of 1978, (c) Economic Recovery Tax Act of 1981, (d) Special Assessment Laws.
16-3. Real property tax assessment rolls are prepared by: (a) county supervisors, (b) tax collector, (c) county assessor, (d) none of these.
16-4. The tax year with respect to collection of real property taxes is: (a) calendar year, (b) same as federal income tax, (c) fiscal year, (d) set by county supervisors.
16-5. Real property taxes must be paid: (a) at the time such taxes become a lien, (b) in two installments, (c) by the individual who resides on the property, (d) none of these.
16-6. State law requires a residential building with a $200,000 full cash value to be assessed at: (a) $200,000 (b) $75,000 (c) varies according to tax rate, (d) none of these.
16-7. The individual making a taxable gift is: (a) a trustor, (b) a donee, (c) a donor, (d) none of these.
16-8. The sale of real property will result in its assessed value changing to reflect: (a) sales prices, (b) loan amounts, (c) 1975 assessments, (d) special tax rates and assessments.

17 Income tax and real estate

All real estate transactions are influenced in varying degrees by our income tax laws. It is the effect of these laws on the individual that often defines the course of action he will take and the type of real estate transaction in which he will become involved.

An understanding of the basic principles in this area is essential for the real estate licensee. This chapter will consider capital gains and losses, sale of a residence, depreciation, installment and deferred payment sales, the Economic Recovery Tax Act of 1981, and Schedule E, which accompanies IRS Form 1040 of the U.S. Treasury Department.

The California taxpayer has two partners who share profits and losses, the U.S. government and the state of California. Tax laws affect real estate dealings either before acquisition, during ownership, or in connection with disposition. These laws can become quite complex, and both the licensee and his clients should realize that they will often need to seek the counsel of a CPA, a tax attorney, or other experts.

CAPITAL GAINS AND LOSSES

When an asset is sold or exchanged, the resultant gain or loss may be classified as either an ordinary gain or loss, or a capital gain or loss. While the tax on capital gains does not generally exceed a maximum of 20 percent, the tax on an ordinary gain may be as high as 50 percent. Obviously, it is extremely advantageous for an individual to be able to qualify for the capital gains treatment and the correspondingly lower tax rate, and much of the time spent in tax planning is directed toward achieving this benefit.

Capital assets

In order to be eligible for capital gains benefits, the asset sold or exchanged must be a capital asset or it must be an asset afforded the same treatment as a capital asset. The Treasury Department defines a capital asset by saying what it is not. Everything a person owns is a capital asset except:

1. Stock in trade.
2. Real or personal property includable in inventory.
3. Real or personal property held for sale to customers.
4. Accounts or notes receivable acquired in the ordinary course of a trade or business for services rendered, or from the sale of any of the properties described above, or for services rendered as an employee.
5. Depreciable property used in a trade or business.
6. Real property used in a trade or business.
7. A copyright, or a literary, musical, or artistic composition, or similar property created by one's personal efforts or acquired from the creator in a manner entitling the recipient to the creator's basis.
8. Certain federal, state, or municipal short-term obligations.

Since 1 through 8, above, are not capital assets, it appears that a substantial amount of real property is excluded from capital gains treatment. However, there always seem to be exceptions to the general rule, and although the definition of capital assets excludes business real property or any depreciable business property, the tax law contains a special provision for such property under Code Section 1231.

Section 1231 property. While the property defined under this section includes, in addition to certain real property, such items as livestock, timber, crops, domestic iron ore, and coal, we will be concerned only with the real property under this section, as follows:

1. Property used in a trade or business subject to depreciation and held for more than six months.
2. Real property used in a trade or business and held for more than six months.
3. Leases for an indefinite period, such as certain oil and gas leases, which are considered as real property.
4. Trade or business property involuntarily converted or other capital assets involuntarily converted and held for more than six months. Involuntary conversion occurs when money or other property is received for property that was destroyed, stolen, or condemned for public use.

Thus, with respect to Section 1231 property, when there is a sale or exchange and the gains exceed the losses, each gain and loss is treated as though it were derived from the sale of a capital asset and is given capital gains treatment. If the losses exceed the gains, ordinary loss benefits will apply.

Were it not for the capital gains provisions in the tax law, the income derived from the sale or exchange of a large amount of real property would be classified as ordinary income and taxed in the same manner as are salaries, commissions, and the like. The income from the sale or exchange of real property is the difference between the amount realized on the sale or exchange and the seller's cost basis of the property. This point will be discussed later in the chapter.

Classification of real property

The preceding discussion of what constitutes a capital asset and how a capital gains treatment may be allowed brings us to the problem of how to classify real property in order to determine what treatment it will receive.

Real property held by the taxpayer for investment or production of income and not used in his trade or business or held primarily for sale to customers is a capital asset that will receive capital gains treatment. The real estate holdings of most individuals fall into this classification. Their primary means of livelihood have nothing to do with the purchase and sale of real estate. The property itself—income producing, a house, or unimproved land—is held basically as a long-term investment.

Real estate used by the taxpayer in a trade or business but not held for sale to customers is not a capital asset but is, instead, Section 1231 property, and if certain conditions are met, it will be given a capital gains treatment. Although a property may receive the capital gains treatment either because it is a capital asset or because it is Section 1231 property, determination of the type of property it is may be very important to the taxpayer. For instance, if a taxpayer sustains a loss from one sale and a gain from another, the tax consequences will be different if both sales involved capital assets or if one sale was of a capital asset and the other was of a Section 1231 property.

Finally, property held for sale to customers will not be given any capital gains benefits. Any gain or loss from the sale or exchange of such property will result in an ordinary gain or loss.

Dealer or investor

One of the greatest areas of argument and litigation between individuals and the Internal Revenue Service is concerned with whether the taxpayer is classified as an investor or as a dealer. An investor receives the capital gains treatment, while a person deemed to be a dealer cannot. The real estate licensee often finds himself in a most difficult position in this regard and must plan his personal real estate transactions very carefully if he is to receive any capital gains benefits. The courts have held that it is possible for a person to be both a dealer and an investor at the same time. The dealer classification is not reserved for licensees alone; it will be applied to any person deemed to be in the real estate business to a certain degree, regardless of whether he deals openly on his own or through third persons in the acquisition and sale of real estate.

In attempting to determine whether an individual shall be classified as an investor or as a dealer with respect to a sale or exchange of real property, the Internal Revenue Service uses the following general guidelines.

Factors leading to classification as a dealer:

1. A real estate licensee who maintains an office or who is actively engaged in the real estate business.
2. The number of real estate transactions within a given period. A frequent number of pur-

chases and sales or exchanges, continuously during any given year or years, by oneself or through third persons.

3. One who is primarily engaged in the business of subdividing, developing, or building.

4. The sale of property immediately after purchase or shortly thereafter; regular speculation and quick turnover.

Factors leading to classification as an investor:

1. Primary occupation or business is not in real estate.

2. Property being sold or exchanged has been held for an extensive period of time. Rental property held for investment.

3. Few purchases, sales, or exchanges over an extended period of time.

4. If the taxpayer can show that the sale or exchange is merely the liquidation of an investment, he will probably be allowed capital gains treatment.

Obviously, there may arise many instances in which it is difficult to decide whether the taxpayer is an investor or a dealer. Each case may have to be decided individually by the Internal Revenue Service. An individual may be deemed to be an investor in one transaction and a dealer in another.

Short- and long-term capital gains

After determining that the asset sold or exchanged is a capital asset, the taxpayer must determine whether the gain or loss is a short-term capital gain or loss or a long-term capital gain or loss. If the taxpayer holds the asset for less than 12 months, its sale or exchange results in a short-term capital gain or loss, but if the real estate is held for more than 12 months, its sale or exchange results in a long-term capital gain or loss. To determine the 12-month period, one should begin counting on the day following the day title was acquired. The same day of each succeeding month is the beginning of a new month, regardless of the number of days in the preceding month. The day the property is disposed of is included in the computation.

Short-term capital gains and losses are merged with each other by adding the gains and losses separately and subtracting one total from the other to obtain the net short-term capital gain or loss. Long-term gains and losses are merged in the same manner to determine the net long-term capital gain or loss, and the law limits the

amount of ordinary income against which capital losses may be offset to $3,000.

The total net gain or loss is then determined by merging the net short-term capital gain or loss with the net long-term capital gain or loss. The taxpayer who is able to show a net long-term capital gain on the sale or exchange of his property, and who qualifies for the capital gains treatment, can deduct 60 percent of the capital gain from gross income and save a considerable amount of tax; such are the benefits of the capital gains treatment. While the federal tax law allows 60 percent of the capital gain to be exempt from taxation, the California tax law subjects capital gains to full taxation if property is held less than a year; 65 percent between one and five years; and 50 percent if held five years or longer.

Cost basis and adjusted basis

The basis of property is a key figure in computing the gain or loss when the property is sold or exchanged. The basis is also used in order to compute depreciation, which will be discussed later in this chapter. The original basis, also called the cost basis, is the original purchase price or cost to the taxpayer. In most cases, it is the original purchase price; however, the property may have been acquired by gift or inheritance, or in some other manner that requires use of a basis other than cost. There are many ways of acquiring property, and each will require a specific method of determining the cost basis. If the property was purchased, then the purchase price will be the basis, but the taxpayer will probably have to consult a tax expert if the property was:

1. Received for services rendered.
2. Received in a trade.
3. Converted to business or rental use.
4. Acquired in a nontaxable exchange.
5. Acquired by gift.
6. Acquired from a decedent.
7. Property to replace seized or destroyed property.

Adjusted basis of property is the original basis or cost increased or reduced as follows:

1. The original basis or cost of property should be increased by adding the cost of improvements that have a life of more than one year, purchase commissions, legal fees, title fees, certain capital expenditures the taxpayer is entitled to add to the original basis.

2. Settlement fee, the cost of purchase commis-

sions, and legal and recording fees are also added to the original basis or cost of property.

3. Real estate taxes assessed on property at the time of purchase are added to the property if it was purchased prior to 1954.

The original basis or cost is decreased as follows:

1. Depreciation deductions taken are considered to be a return of capital and must be deducted from the original basis or cost.
2. Deductible losses that have been taken or are allowable are included.
3. If an easement was granted on the property, the amount of consideration received for the easement must be deducted.

When the adjusted basis amount is finally determined, it is the difference between the adjusted basis and the selling price of the property that the seller must report as gain. In addition, any selling costs, such as the broker's commission, may be deducted from the amount of the gain.

Example: William and Mary Fulton purchased a property for $120,000 in 1979. They sold the building in 1982 for $190,000. Improvements made totaled $16,200; the cost of the sale, including the broker's commission, totaled $12,500; and depreciation deductions amounted to $18,500. As the result of this sale, what is the amount of gain?

Purchase price	$120,000	Original basis
Improvements	16,200	
	$136,200	
Depreciation deducted	18,500	
	$117,700	Adjusted basis
Sale price	190,000	
Less: Expenses of the sale	12,500	
	$177,500	Amount realized
Amount realized from sale	$177,500	
Less: Adjusted basis	117,700	
	$ 59,800	Gain

William and Mary must report a capital gain of $59,800 on their income tax return and may be allowed to deduct 60 percent of this amount because of the capital gains treatment, leaving the sum of $23,920 to be taxed. The gain on this sale is, of course, a long-term capital gain, since William and Mary held the property primarily for investment and for a period of longer than 12 months from the date of purchase.

SALE OF RESIDENCE

If a residence is sold or exchanged at a gain, the gain is taxable. Two special benefits are available to the taxpayer.

1. If within 24 months preceeding or after sale of the old residence, the seller buys and occupies another residence, the gain is not taxed at the time of the sale if the cost of the new residence equals or exceeds the adjusted sale price of the old residence. The seller is allowed additional time after selling the old residence if he is *(a)* constructing a new residence or *(b) on active duty in the U.S. Armed Forces.*
2. If the taxpayer is 55 years of age or older and can meet certain qualifications, special provisions, discussed later in the chapter, will apply to the sale.

If the seller purchases another residence within the time allowed, the tax may be postponed. Any gain not taxed in the year the old residence is sold is subtracted from the cost of the residence acquired to replace it, providing a lower basis to be used when the second residence is eventually sold. The tax may continue to be deferred as long as the taxpayer purchases another residence each time he sells his present one and meets certain qualifications.

Example: Art Taylor sells his residence and realizes a $35,000 gain on the sale. Immediately afterward, he purchases another residence for $152,000, which is more than the price he received for his old house. Taylor will not be taxed on the gain; instead, the $35,000 will be deducted from the $152,000 purchase price of the new residence, giving it a basis of $117,000.

The example indicates that the purchase price of the new residence is more than the adjusted sale price of the old residence, and this generally is the case. However, where the adjusted sale price of the old residence is more than the purchase price of a new residence, the gain taxed in the year of the sale is limited to the lesser of *(a)* the gain realized on the sale of the old residence or *(b)* the excess of the adjusted sale price of the old residence over the cost of the new one.

Where there is a loss on the sale or exchange of a residence, this loss may not be deducted and has no effect on the basis of a new residence.

Principal residence

The house that is sold and the house that is acquired to replace it must be principal residences of the taxpayer. Ordinarily, the house one lives in is his principal residence. Besides a single-family residence in the principal residence classification, the following also may be the principal resi-

240

dence of a taxpayer: a trailer, a houseboat, a cooperative apartment, or a condominium apartment. A taxpayer is limited to one principal residence.

Example: Philip Andrews owns and lives in a house in Los Angeles during most of the year, but he occupies a house at Lake Tahoe during the summer. Internal Revenue Service will hold that the home in Los Angeles is his principal residence, while the Lake Tahoe house is not. Let us assume that Andrews is transferred by his firm to San Francisco. He does not sell his Los Angeles or Lake Tahoe properties but merely moves to San Francisco where he rents a house. The Internal Revenue Service will now hold that Andrews rented house in San Francisco is his principal residence. It does not matter that Andrews owns property elsewhere; it is the property one lives in that is considered the principal residence.

How to determine gain or loss

Although we have previously touched on this subject, it may be well to review the methods for determining gain or loss on the sale of property. Gain is the excess of the amount realized from a sale or exchange over the adjusted basis of the property sold or exchanged. Loss is the excess of the adjusted basis of the property over the amount realized from the sale or exchange.

The adjusted basis is the original cost or other basis adjusted for such things as casualty losses, improvements, and depreciation when appropriate. The amount realized from a sale or exchange of property is everything received for the property disposed of reduced by any cost incurred in effecting the transfer, such as commissions, advertising, and costs of legal fees.

Property, other than money, that may be received is included at fair market value. In the case of notes or other evidences of indebtedness received as a part of the sale price, the fair market value is usually the best amount that can be obtained from the sale to, or discount with, a bank or other purchaser of such notes or paper.

Indebtedness against the property. An indebtedness against the owner of the property or against the property, which is paid off as a part of the transaction or is assumed by the purchaser, must be included at its face value in the amount realized. If an indebtedness is attached to the property transferred, such indebtedness must be

included at face value in the amount realized, even though neither the seller nor purchaser is personally liable for the debt.

Payment of boot. If a person trades a piece of property for another and in addition to giving the property must also pay some money, the amount of money paid is known as "boot." Thus, if an individual trades one property for another and pays cash to boot, the amount he realizes is the fair market value of the property received minus cash paid.

An example of computing gain or loss is the following. Bob Martinez sells a property with an existing $89,200 mortgage. He receives $65,000 in cash, and the buyer is able to assume the existing mortgage. The property has a cost basis to Martinez of $27,900, and his selling costs total $12,600. What is the amount of gain realized by Martinez?

Cash received	$ 65,000	
Mortgage assumed by buyer	89,200	
	$154,200	Selling price
Less: Martinez's cost basis	27,900	
	$126,300	
Less: Selling costs	12,600	
	$113,700	Gain

Special problems regarding residences

Many special problems arise with regard to the sale or exchange of a residence; some require quite complex calculations which should be attempted only by a tax expert. Examples of such situations are the following.

1. The property in question is only partially a residence as far as the owner is concerned. A person who owns a six-unit apartment house and lives in one of the apartments decides to sell the units and purchase a house. Only the portion of the selling price allocable to the residential unit of the former owner need be reinvested in the new residence in order to postpone the tax on that part of the gain. Quite often, the sale of a multiple-unit building in which the former owner was a resident must be treated as though it were a sale of two properties.

2. A building that was used as a residence and is subsequently converted to rental property takes on an entirely new dimension, for it now becomes business property or property held for the production of income.

3. A property owner may not sell but may trade in his house to a builder for a new one. In such

a case, the transaction is generally treated as a sale and purchase.

Age 55 or older

Persons who sell or exchange their principal residence during the year may generally elect to exclude from their gross income part or all of the gain on the sale or exchange if *(a)* they were age 55 or older before the date of the sale or exchange and *(b)* they owned and used the property as their principal residence for a period of time, continuous or interrupted, totaling at least three years within the five-year period ending on the date of sale or exchange.

Taxpayers who meet these requirements can elect to exclude up to $125,000 of gain free of any taxes. The exclusion can only apply to a specific sale and no portion of the $125,000 can be carried over to a subsequent sale. If the taxpayer uses the exclusion and subsequently purchases and sells another residence, the exclusion cannot be used again, and tax will have to be paid if there is a gain.

Example: Paul Fisher sold his principal residence for $135,000 in 1983, when he was 57 years old. He is eligible to and does elect to exclude from his gross income for the current year the resulting gain. His selling price and selling expenses are shown below:

1.	Sale Price		$135,000
2.	Less:		
	Real estate commission	$ 8,100	
	Escrow costs and fees	800	
	Termite repairs	3,700	
		$12,600	12,600
3.	Amount Realized		$122,400
4.	Less Basis of Residence Sold:		
	Original purchase price	$42,500	
	Purchase escrow fees	500	
	Add copper pipes	900	
	Install 220 wiring	650	
	Terazzo front steps	350	
		$44,900	$ 44,900
5.	Gain Realized on Sale		$ 77,500

The exclusion of up to $125,000 of capital gain allows Paul to receive a $77,500 tax-free gain.

Any individual who meets the ownership, use, and age requirements will be allowed to claim the special exclusion. Also, when the sale is being made by a husband and wife who otherwise meet the ownership and use requirements, if only one is over 55, they may elect the special exclusion.

DEPRECIATION—CALIFORNIA TAX RETURNS

In Chapter 14, concerned with appraisal and valuation, we discussed depreciation in terms of physical deterioration and functional, social, and economic obsolescence. Here, we discuss depreciation as brokers and investors generally do—as an offset against income in connection with properties held for investment or property used in a trade or business.

The Economic Recovery Tax Act of 1981 brought about a major change in depreciation rules for real and personal property acquired on or after January 1, 1981. It is called the Accelerated Cost Recovery System (ACRS) and allows for a more rapid depreciation of capital assets and reduces the amount of tax to be paid by real property investors. The state of California has not changed its depreciation tax rules to conform with those of the federal government. This means that for property acquired on or after January 1, 1981, the taxpayer will have to maintain two separate depreciation schedules, the old method for the California tax return and the new ACRS method for the federal tax return. For the owner who acquired a property prior to 1981, the old method must continue to be used for both his state and federal returns. To avoid a loss of revenues, California will probably continue to use the old depreciation rules.

First, we will discuss the old depreciation methods which continue to be used with the California income tax return and then look at the new Accelerated Cost Recovery System (ACRS) depreciation methods used with the federal tax return for depreciable property acquired on or after January 1, 1981.

The Internal Revenue Code allows a deduction of depreciation as a reasonable allowance for the exhaustion, wear and tear, and normal obsolescence of property (1) used in a trade or business or (2) held for the production of income, and said depreciation may be deducted from gross income.

Depreciation taken on business or income property, then, will be subtracted from any rent or other income received from the property, thereby providing a partially tax-free income. At times, the depreciation allowance may exceed the income for a particular year, and the taxpayer may deduct this excess depreciation from any other income he may receive from other sources.

The Internal Revenue Service will not allow the taxpayer to take depreciation on a house, its furnishings, an automobile, or other items used only for personal or pleasure purposes. If, however, a personal item such as an automobile is used partially for business, the taxpayer will be allowed to depreciate that portion used for business.

Estimated useful life

One of the most important factors in the calculation of depreciation is to determine the useful life of the asset being depreciated. The useful life of an asset depends on how long one expects to use it, its age when acquired, policies concerning repairs, upkeep, and replacement, and other conditions. Useful lives prescribed by the Internal Revenue Service for depreciation purposes are applicable to all assets used in a particular industry or business rather than to individual assets. Longer or shorter useful lives than those given by the Internal Revenue Service may be used, but the taxpayer should consult his accountant to be sure that they are consistent with general practices in common use.

The Treasury Department guideline lives, with regard to real property, are as follows:

Type of Building	Years
Apartments	40
Banks	50
Dwellings	45
Factories	45
Farm buildings	25
Garages	45
Grain elevators	60
Hotels	40
Loft buildings	50
Machine shops	45
Office buildings	45
Stores	50
Theaters	40
Warehouses	60

Land not depreciable

Both the old tax rules and new ACRS rules provide that land may not be depreciated; only the improvements thereon may be depreciated. Therefore, when an investor purchases a building, he must allocate the purchase price between the land and the building. It is difficult to state any exact mathematic formula to use in making this allocation, since values may vary widely depending on the particular property. In one case, the building may represent most of the value, while in another, the land itself is the main factor in arriving at the purchase price. Generally, the relative assessed valuations of the tax assessor are used in determining the allocation to be made.

Example: Eugene Brussell purchases a building for $300,000. The records of the tax assessor show that he has assessed the value of the land at $18,000 and the improvements at $14,000. The $42,000 value set on the improvements represents 70 percent of the total assessed value of $60,000. Brussell may now allocate 70 percent of the purchase price to the building and the remaining 30 percent to the land. The $300,000 purchase price is thus divided $210,000 to the depreciable building and $90,000 to the nondepreciable land.

Basis for determining depreciation

The basis for determining depreciation is the same as the basis used to determine gain if the property is sold. Usually, the cost of the property is its basis for depreciation after division is made in the amount to be allocated to building and the amount to land. In the previous example, Mr. Brussell's basis for depreciation is $210,000. If at any time during the term of ownership the owner improves the property, the additional cost is added to the basis and may be depreciated.

Salvage value

An asset may not be depreciated below its salvage value at the time it is disposed of or at the end of the guideline life assigned to it for depreciation purposes. The estimated salvage value must be deducted from the basis of the asset in determining the annual depreciation if either the straight-line or sum-of-the-years'-digits method is used. Not all assets will have depreciated in value over the years; for instance, a truck purchased new and used for 5 years will obviously be worth much less when it is replaced than when it was purchased, but a piece of real estate may be held for 10 years and be worth much more when sold than when it was purchased.

The matter of salvage value in setting up a depreciation schedule for real property is something for the taxpayer and his accountant to decide. Interpretations vary, but since the value of a property at the end of its depreciable life is many times the salvage value of the building, most accountants merely use the allocated portion of the purchase price to the property when setting up the depreciation schedule and make no calculation whatsoever for salvage value, regardless of the depreciation method to be used. In line with this approach, in the following section, no arbitrary amount will be assigned as salvage value in any of the examples, since all the examples will deal with real property. The ACRS rules for federal returns eliminate any consideration of salvage value for real property.

Methods of depreciation

The three methods most commonly used in the computation of depreciation are (1) straight-line, (2) declining balance, and (3) sum-of-the-years'-digits. The second and third are accounting methods for applying accelerated depreciation in the early years.

Straight-line method. This is the most-used method of computing depreciation and may be used for any depreciable property. It gives the investor an equal amount of depreciation each year over the life assigned to the asset. The amount of yearly depreciation is determined by dividing the amount allocated to the building by the years of useful life.

Example: Dr. Kenneth Washington purchases a piece of investment property consisting of rental units at a purchase price of $280,000. The purchase price is to be allocated 75 percent to the building and 25 percent to the land. A useful life of 30 years is to be assigned to the building for depreciation purposes. Seventy-five percent of the purchase price of $280,000 equals $210,000. The basis of $210,000 is divided by 30, equaling the sum of $7,000 which represents the yearly depreciation amount.

The straight-line method of depreciation causes a fixed percentage of depreciation to be taken each year during the assigned useful life of the depreciable asset. Shown below are the corresponding yearly depreciation percentage rates for selected terms of useful life using straight-line and declining balance methods of depreciation.

Declining balance method. In this method, the amount of depreciation taken each year is subtracted from the cost or other basis of the property before computing the following year's depreciation, so that the same depreciation rate applies to a smaller or declining balance each year. Thus, the largest amount of depreciation is taken in the first year, with continually decreasing amounts of depreciation in successive years.

Within certain limits, a depreciation rate may be used that is greater than the rate used in the straight-line method. In some circumstances, a rate twice the straight-line rate may be used; this is known as 200 percent depreciation. In other circumstances, the taxpayer is limited to a rate one and a quarter times the straight-line rate. This is known as 125 percent depreciation.

Rules governing the selection of the depreciation method vary. Generally, straight-line depreciation can be used on any real property, new or used. The 125 percent declining balance method can be applied to used residential property with 20 years or more of useful life. The 150 percent declining balance method is for new nonresidential real estate, and the 200 percent declining balance method and sum-of-the-years'-digits methods are for new residential rental properties.

Example: Sarah Pepper purchases for investment a building from the Ace Building Construction Company. The building is new, and Pepper is the first user. The basis for depreciation is $160,000, and the depreciable life is 40 years. What is the depreciation deduction for the first three years using the straight-line method, and what is the amount of depreciation possible using the declining balance method for these years?

To determine the straight-line depreciation, we merely take the $160,000 basis and divide by 40, or we can multiply by the depreciation rate for 40 years, which is 2.5 percent.

$$\$160,000 \div 40 \text{ equals } \$4,000$$

$$\$160,000 \times .025 \text{ equals } \$4,000.$$

The straight-line depreciation for the first year is $4,000, and the same amount for each succeeding year, since $4,000 each year over 40 years will return the $160,000 cost basis. Pepper's depreciation for the first three years will amount to $12,000.

Years	Depreciation Percent per Year Using Straight-Line	125 Percent Declining Balance	150 Percent Declining Balance	200 Percent Declining Balance
5	20	25	30	40
10	10	12.5	15	20
15	6.6	8.3	10	13.3
20	5	6.25	7.5	10
25	4	5	6	8
30	3.3	4.17	5	6.67
35	2.86	3.58	4.29	5.72
40	2.5	3.125	3.75	5
45	2.22	2.78	3.33	4.44
50		2.5	3	4

Since Pepper is the first user of a new building, she may elect to use 200 percent depreciation—that is, twice the straight-line rate. Using this method, the depreciation for the first year will be $8,000. This is calculated by taking twice the straight-line rate of 2.5 percent, which is 5 percent.

.05 × $160,000 equals $8,000
for the first year's depreciation.

Since this is a declining balance method, the depreciation taken for the first year must be subtracted from the cost basis of $160,000 before calculating the depreciation for the second year.

$160,000 − $8,000 equals $152,000.
.05 × $152,000 equals $7,600
depreciation for the second year.

The second year's depreciation is now deducted from the cost basis in order to arrive at the third year's depreciation.

$152,000 − $7,600 equals $144,400.
.05 × $144,400 equals $7,200
depreciation for the third year.

Thus, at the end of three years, Pepper will have taken $12,000 in depreciation using the straight-line method of $4,000 annually. The 200 percent declining balance method will have resulted at the end of the third year in a total depreciation of $22,820.

Let us now assume that Pepper had purchased the building from its original owner when it was eight years old. We will use the same cost basis and depreciable life so that the straight-line rate will remain at $4,000 yearly. Since Pepper has now purchased a used building and is considered a second or subsequent owner, she will be limited to 125 percent depreciation if she elects to use the declining balance method. The first three years of depreciation is calculated as follows.

First year:
$160,000 × 0.3125 = $5,000
[1¼ times the straight-line rate of 2.5% is 3.125% which is expressed decimally as .03125].
Second Year:
$160,000 − $5,000 = $155,000.
$155,000 × .03125 = $4,843.75.
Third year:
$155,000 − $4,843.75 = $150,156.25.
$150,156.25 × .03125 = $4,692.38.

Total depreciation taken after three years and using 125 percent depreciation is $14,536.13 as against $12,000 by the straight-line method.

Sum-of-the-years'-digits method. The sum-of-the-years'-digits method may be used only for property that qualifies for 200 percent depreciation—that is, first users of new residential property. In this method, the taxpayer applies a different fraction to the basis of the property. The denominator (bottom of the fraction) is the total of the numbers representing the depreciable life of the property. Thus, if the depreciable life is five years, the denominator is 15 (1 + 2 + 3 + 4 + 5 = 15). The numerator (top of the fraction) is the number of years of depreciable life remaining at the beginning of the year for which the computation is made. Thus, if the depreciable life is five years, the fraction to be applied to the basis of the property for the first year is $\frac{5}{15}$. The fraction for the second year is $\frac{4}{15}$, for the third year, $\frac{3}{15}$, and so on. In actual practice, this method is little used for real property; virtually all accountants prefer the 200 percent depreciation method.

Change of method

In certain circumstances, the taxpayer is allowed to switch from a declining balance method to the straight-line method for the remaining depreciable life of the property. This has the effect of allowing accelerated depreciation in the early years with the balance of the allowable depreciation being taken in equal yearly amounts over the later years of depreciable life.

Comparison of methods of depreciation

Table 17–1 shows a comparison of the methods of depreciation that have been discussed. For purposes of illustration, we shall assume a basis of $10,000 and a depreciable life of 10 years.

TABLE 17–1
Comparison of Methods of Depreciation

Year	Straight-Line	200 Percent Declining Balance	125 Percent Declining Balance	Sum-of-the-Years'-Digits
1	$ 1,000	$2,000	$1,250	$ 1,818
2	1,000	1,600	1,094	1,636
3	1,000	1,280	957	1,455
4	1,000	1,024	837	1,273
5	1,000	819	733	1,091
6	1,000	655	641	909
7	1,000	524	561	727
8	1,000	420	491	545
9	1,000	336	430	364
10	1,000	268	376	182
Total	$10,000	$8,926	$7,370	$10,000

It is obvious that the accelerated methods of depreciation allow larger depreciation deductions in the earlier years than those allowed in the straight-line method. This depreciation is an offset against current income; however, the cost basis is reduced by this depreciation and will result in a greater gain when the property is later sold or exchanged. The advantage of each dollar of depreciation is that it offsets a dollar of income that would be taxed at ordinary income rates in the year received; the gain realized at the time of a later sale will usually be afforded capital gains treatment and, consequently, a much lower tax will be paid.

The length of time the investor plans to keep a property also has an important bearing on the method of depreciation selected. If he plans to retain the property for a long time, then the straight-line method will give him a more even offset against income. Since the income from a good piece of property increases over the years, an even depreciation offset is better than a method that continually decreases the offset.

The selection of a depreciation method should be made only after the investor has thoroughly examined the effect it will have on his overall business, investment, and tax picture.

Recapture of depreciation

Another important area of consideration for the investor is the recapture of depreciation rules and regulations. The recapture rules are designed to limit to a certain extent the capital gains treatment advantage.

When a building is sold, and within certain limits, the amount of depreciation that has been taken in excess of straight-line depreciation is recaptured, which means it is taxed as ordinary income.

DEPRECIATION—FEDERAL TAX RETURNS

Enacted into law in an attempt to improve the economy and stimulate personal and real property investment, the Economic Recovery Tax Act of 1981 brought about significant changes in depreciation rules by allowing for a more rapid depreciation of capital assets.

Estimated useful life

The problems formerly encountered with respect to selection of a useful life for depreciable property has been greatly simplified. Real property, new or used, may be currently depreciated over 15, 35, or 45 years. Personal property, new or used, may be currently depreciated over 5, 12, or 25 years. Taxpayers who desire to maximize their depreciation deductions will generally select 15 years for real property and 5 years for personal property used in connection with the real property.

Basis for depreciation

The basis for determining depreciation is the same as previously discussed, and salvage value is no longer taken into consideration. If an individual holds property for a personal use, such as a residence, and later converts it into business or rental property, the basis for depreciation will generally equal the original cost plus the cost of any permanent improvements or additions.

Methods of depreciation

The new law allows the taxpayer only two depreciation methods for buildings acquired on or after January 1, 1981; these are the straight-line method and the 175 percent accelerated depreciation method. As explained previously, the straight-line method gives the taxpayer an equal amount of depreciation each year during the useful life assigned to the asset and eliminates any problems with respect to a possible later recapture of any accelerated depreciation.

With respect to the 175 percent accelerated depreciation method, the 1981 tax act provides a table which the taxpayer must use to calculate the yearly amount of depreciation deduction. The table uses a 15-year life and is illustrated as Table 17–2.

Example: Smith purchases a rental property in April of 1983 for $400,000. He allocates $300,000 to building cost and $100,000 to land cost and decides to use a 15-year life and straight-line depreciation. What will be his first and second year deduction for depreciation?

$300,000 divided by 15 years equals a yearly deduction of $20,000. In 1983 the property was owned for nine months and Smith can deduct $\frac{9}{12}$ of $20,000 or $15,000 for the first year. The second year's deduction is a full $20,000.

If Smith decides to use 175 percent accelerated depreciation, Table 17–2 will allow Smith a deduction of 9 percent for the first year. $300,000 × .09 equals a first year deduction of $27,000. For

TABLE 17–2
ACRS Cost Recovery Table for Real Estate, All Real Estate
(except low-income housing):
The Applicable Percentage Is:
(use the column for the month in the first year the
property is placed in service)

Year	Month Placed in Service											
	1	2	3	4	5	6	7	8	9	10	11	12
1st	12%	11%	10%	9%	8%	7%	6%	5%	4%	3%	2%	1%
2nd	10%	10%	11%	11%	11%	11%	11%	11%	11%	11%	11%	12%
3rd	9%	9%	9%	9%	10%	10%	10%	10%	10%	10%	10%	10%
4th	8%	8%	8%	8%	8%	8%	9%	9%	9%	9%	9%	9%
5th	7%	7%	7%	7%	7%	7%	8%	8%	8%	8%	8%	8%
6th	6%	6%	6%	6%	7%	7%	7%	7%	7%	7%	7%	7%
7th	6%	6%	6%	6%	6%	6%	6%	6%	6%	6%	6%	6%
8th	6%	6%	6%	6%	6%	6%	6%	6%	6%	6%	6%	6%
9th	6%	6%	6%	6%	5%	6%	5%	5%	5%	6%	6%	6%
10th	5%	6%	5%	6%	5%	5%	5%	5%	5%	5%	6%	5%
11th	5%	5%	5%	5%	5%	5%	5%	5%	5%	5%	5%	5%
12th	5%	5%	5%	5%	5%	5%	5%	5%	5%	5%	5%	5%
13th	5%	5%	5%	5%	5%	5%	5%	5%	5%	5%	5%	5%
14th	5%	5%	5%	5%	5%	5%	5%	5%	5%	5%	5%	5%
15th	5%	5%	5%	5%	5%	5%	5%	5%	5%	5%	5%	5%
16th	—	—	1%	1%	2%	2%	3%	3%	4%	4%	4%	5%

the second year, the table allows a deduction of 11 percent, which equals $33,000.

For taxpayers wishing to maximize their depreciation deduction, the 175 percent accelerated depreciation calculation is the best. A comparison, using both methods of depreciation with respect to Smith's property is as follows:

Year	SL	175%
1	$ 20,000	$ 36,000
2	20,000	30,000
3	20,000	27,000
4	20,000	24,000
5	20,000	21,000
6	20,000	18,000
7	20,000	18,000
8	20,000	18,000
9	20,000	18,000
10	20,000	15,000
11	20,000	15,000
12	20,000	15,000
13	20,000	15,000
14	20,000	15,000
15	20,000	15,000
Total	$300,000	$300,000

Recapture of depreciation

The 1981 tax law provides for recapture of accelerated depreciation deductions at the time a property is sold. At the time of sale, the amount recaptured will be taxed as ordinary income.

If a property is used as a residential rental, the amount recaptured at time of sale will be the difference between the 175 percent accelerated depreciation which has been deducted and the allowable 15 year straight-line depreciation.

If the property is used for offices, stores, or any purpose other than residential rentals, all of the 175 percent accelerated depreciation deducted will be recaptured and taxed as ordinary income. The 1981 tax law is obviously intended to discourage commercial property investors from using other than the straight-line method of depreciation.

In order to avoid recapture of accelerated depreciation deductions, most investors, rather than sell their properties, will enter into a tax-deferred exchange. Such exchanges are discussed in Chapter 21.

ADDITIONAL EFFECTS OF THE 1981 AND PRIOR TAX LAWS

The following discussion will consider some of the effects relating to real property as a result of the Economic Recovery Tax Act of 1981 and prior tax acts of 1976 and 1978. Any newly enacted legislation, especially in a complex area such as taxation, will be subject to changes. In addition, certain rules and procedures may differ between federal and state of California legislation. The real estate licensee must keep informed and work with tax experts, such as a tax account or tax attorney, when necessary.

Prepaid interest and loan points

Prepaid interest or points paid on a loan must be deducted during the term of the loan to the extent the interest represents the cost of using the borrowed funds during each taxable year in the term. An exception is made with respect to a loan in connection with the purchase or improvement of, and secured by, the taxpayer's principal residence. Points which are paid in connection with such a loan are considered prepaid interest, and the full amount of such points or any other prepaid interest may be deducted in full during the year in which paid.

Business use of homes

The law now provides definitive rules relating to deductions for expenses attributable to the business use of homes. A taxpayer is not permitted to deduct any expenses attributable to the use of his home for business purposes except to the extent attributable to the portion of the home used exclusively on a regular basis: *(a)* as the taxpayer's principal place of business, *(b)* as a place of business which is used for patients, clients, or customers in meeting or dealing with the taxpayer in the normal course of business, or *(c)* in the case of a separate structure which is not attached to a dwelling, in connection with the taxpayer's trade or business.

Further, in the case of an employee, the business use of the home must be for the convenience of his employer. An exception to the exclusive use test is provided where the dwelling unit is the sole fixed location of a trade or business which consists of selling products at retail or wholesale and the taxpayer regularly uses a separate identifiable portion of the residence for inventory storage. An overall limitation is provided which limits the amount of the deductions to the gross income generated by the taxpayer's home business activity.

Rental of vacation homes

Previously, there was no definitive ruling relating to how much personal use of vacation property might result in the disallowance of deductions because the rental activities are not engaged in for profit. The law now provides a limitation on deductions for expenses attributable to the rental of a vacation home if the home is used by a taxpayer for personal purposes in excess of the greater of two weeks or 10 percent of the actual business use (rental time) during a year. In this case, the deductions allowed in connection with a vacation home cannot exceed the gross income from the business use of the vacation home, less expenses which are allowable in any event (such as interest and taxes).

In addition, if a vacation home is actually rented for less than 15 days during the year, no business deductions or income derived from the use of the vacation home are to be taken into account in the taxpayer's return for the taxable year.

Personal property for business use

The law previously allowed a taxpayer purchasing personal property for business to deduct 20 percent of the cost of such property in the year of purchase. The 1981 tax law allows an owner to immediately deduct up to $5,000 for business personal property purchased in 1983, and up to $7,500 per year starting in 1984.

This ruling will provide a substantial deduction for property owners who purchase either new or used stoves, refrigerators, furniture, or other such items for rental properties or other properties used in their trade or business.

Sale and purchase of principal residence

The law previously allowed a taxpayer to defer any gain as the result of selling a principal residence if the taxpayer purchased and moved into a replacement residence during a period beginning 18 months before, and ending 18 months after, sale of the old residence.

The 1981 tax act increases the time to 24 months before, and ending 24 months after, sale of the old residence.

Investment tax credit for rehabilitation

Prior law provided for a 10 percent tax credit for certain rehabilitation expenditures for nonresidential building at least 20 years old. The tax credit has been increased but is now limited to rehabilitation expenditures on buildings at least 30 years old.

The tax credit is now 15 percent of qualified rehabilitation expenditures for nonresidential buildings between 30 and 39 years old, 20 percent for nonresidential buildings at least 40 years old, and 25 percent for certified historic structures.

INSTALLMENT AND DEFERRED PAYMENT SALES

The sale of real property using a plan by which a part or all of the sale price is to be paid by the purchaser to the seller after the close of the tax year in which the sale is made is known as an installment or deferred payment sale. When this type of sale is made, the seller generally elects to use the installment sale method or, occasionally, the deferred payment method. If the seller meets certain requirements he will be able to report his taxable gain over a number of years and thus spread out his tax payments. Depending on the particular circumstances of the seller, it may be very advantageous to be able to spread out tax payments rather than having to pay all the tax in the year of the sale. The installment method of reporting income will relieve the seller of the burden of paying tax on income that has not been collected, and it permits him to include in his gross income only that portion of each collection which constitutes profit.

General requirements

The taxpayer must be the payee or mortgagee if a note or a first or second deed of trust or mortgage is given by the buyer for the unpaid balance of the selling price. If the buyer gives his note, mortgage, or deed of trust to another party in order to finance his purchase, and he pays the seller the proceeds he receives, the seller may not use the installment or deferred payment method of reporting taxable gain. With most ordinary purchases of real estate, the buyer borrows the necessary money from a bank or savings and loan company, so the outstanding debt is not owed to the seller. It is when the seller himself carries back the major portion of the financing that the installment method comes into use.

The former requirement that the sale is considered to be on the installment plan only if there is no payment to the seller in the year of the sale or that such payments do not exceed 30 percent of the selling price is eliminated and a seller can now accept any desired amount.

Payments received in the year of the sale include not only the down payment but also all other cash payments and property received in that year. Liabilities of the seller that are paid by the buyer in the year of the sale, such as liens and accrued interest and taxes, are included. Any deposit money or option payments that were received in any preceding year in accordance with the con-

tract became part of the down payment and must be included.

Notes given to the seller or other evidences of indebtedness of the buyer are not included in payments in the year of the sale. Where property is sold subject to an existing loan and the buyer assumes the loan, the loan is not included in the collections received in the year of the sale unless such loan exceeds the seller's basis of the property.

Where the loan assumed by the buyer exceeds the seller's basis of the property, the excess of the loan over the adjusted basis of the property will be included in the payments received in the year of the sale. If the buyer pays off the seller's loan at the time of the sale instead of assuming it, he has, in effect, paid the seller an additional amount to the extent of the loan payment, and the seller must include this amount in the payments received in the year of the sale.

Calculation of gain

Deferred payment sales are now automatically reported as installment sales. The income from installment collections must be reported each year and is determined by the use of a gross profit percentage. The gross profit percentage for any sale is the percent that the gross profit to be realized is of the total contract price.

Example: Warren White sells a property at a contract price of $200,000, and there is a gross profit of $50,000. The gross profit percentage is 25 percent ($50,000 divided by $200,000). Thus, 25 percent of each payment collected on the sale, including the down payment, is gain and must be included in gross income for the tax year in which collected. This percentage amount remains the same for all installment payments received on the sale.

Let us now consider an example of a sale that involves the assumption of an existing loan, a second loan, and a cash down payment, and let us determine what mathematical computations will be necessary if this is to be reported as an installment sale.

Assume that in 1976 Lindsey bought a lot for $16,000 and in 1977 he borrowed money to erect a house, which he occupied. The house cost $48,000, making Lindsey's total cost $64,000. In 1983, Lindsey sold the house to Kerr for a total of $110,000 and paid commission and other expenses amounting to $8,500 on the sale. Kerr paid $30,000 in cash and assumed Lindsey's existing loan in the amount of $38,000. Lindsey carried back a second loan of $32,000 for a term of five years at 12 percent annual interest with payments of $338. per month beginning January 1984.

The transaction qualifies as an installment sale. The existing first loan assumed by the buyer and the second loan both represent debts of the purchaser and are not considered in determining the amount of the payments received in the year of the sale. The percentage of each installment payment to be reported as profit is computed as follows:

Sale price of house	$110,000
Less: Commission and expenses	8,500
Net sale price	101,500
Cost basis of property to Smith	64,000
Gross profit to be realized on sale	$ 37,500
Contract price:	
Sale price	$110,000
Less: Loan assumed by Jordan	38,000
Contract price	$ 72,000

Gross profit percentage:

$$\frac{\text{Gross profit to be realized, \$37,500}}{\text{Contract price, \$72,000}} = 52\%$$

Accordingly, the profit realized on the 1983 receipts of $30,000 is 52 percent thereof, or $15,600. The monthly payments of $338. on the second loan will amount to $4,056 per year, and in 1984, the profit to be realized will be 52 percent of $4,056 or $2,109.12.

Since the property was a capital asset held by Lindsey for more than 12 months, the realized profit is a long-term capital gain. Thus, in determining his net long-term capital gains and losses on his income tax return, Lindsey will include for 1983 the $15,600 profit realized in that year, and on his 1984 return Lindsey will include the $2,109.12 realized in 1981. Since the annual amount received will be the same over the term of the second loan, Lindsey will have the same $2,109.12 of gain to enter on his annual tax return until the second loan is paid off in five years.

Disposition of installment obligations

Gain or loss will usually result when an installment obligation, such as a note or mortgage, is disposed of by the seller. Such gains or losses are considered to result from the sale or exchange of the property for which the installment obligations were received. Thus, if the sale of the property resulted in a capital gain, the disposition of the obligation will result in a capital gain or loss;

if the sale of the property produced income subject to ordinary tax, the disposition of the obligation will result in ordinary income or loss.

If the obligations are sold or exchanged, the gain or loss is measured by the difference between the basis of the obligations and the amount realized. If the obligations are disposed of by other than sale or exchange (for instance, by gift), the gain or loss is measured by the difference between the basis of the obligations and their fair market value at the time of such disposition.

SCHEDULE E

Schedule E (Form 1040) is called the Supplemental Income Schedule and includes income from pensions and annuities, rents and royalties, partnerships, and estates or trusts. Figure 17–1 shows a Schedule E prepared by Silas Kirkham, 2000 Quintara Street, Daly City. In it, the only supplemental income shown is received from a duplex that Mr. Kirkham purchased for investment and has rented to tenants.

Mr. Kirkham purchased this duplex from a friend who retired and moved to Palm Springs. The building is 35 years old and is in generally good condition. It is located in a good rental area, and Kirkham believes that the $92,000 he paid is approximately $10,000 below market value. He put $25,000 cash down and received a loan from the seller in the amount of $67,000 with interest at 13½ percent and payments of $781.22 per month based on a 25-year term but with a due date of 10 years.

Kirkham took title to the building on January 9, with both units having been vacated prior to close of escrow. He had some painting and minor repair work done and at the beginning of February Kirkham had rented the units for $500 each per month. He feels this is a good investment since the property in the area is appreciating and the rent he is receiving will approximately equal his monthly payments.

We will now look at Mr. Kirkham's Schedule E form for the tax year.

The location and description of the property is entered in Part V. It is located at 809–811 Fifth Avenue, Daly City, California, and consists of two five-room units.

The total amount of rents, depreciation, expenses, and profit or loss is shown in Part I. Each of the units was rented for $500 per month effective February. Thus, Kirkham received rent for 11 months for a total of $11,000.

Supplemental Income Schedule

(From rents and royalties, partnerships, estates and trusts, etc.)
► Attach to Form 1040. ► See Instructions for Schedule E (Form 1040).

OMB No. 1545–0074

19

Name(s) as shown on Form 1040	Your social security number
SILAS KIRKHAM 2000 QUINTARA STREET, DALY CITY, CALIFORNIA 94112	123 45 6789

Part I Rent and Royalty Income or Loss.

1 Are any of the expenses listed below for a vacation home or similar dwelling rented to others (see Instructions)? . ☐ Yes ☑ No

2 If you checked "Yes" to question 1, did you or a member of your family occupy the vacation home or similar dwelling for more than 14 days during the tax year? . . . . ☐ Yes ☐ No

Rental and Royalty Income (describe property in Part V)		Properties A		B	C		Totals	
3 a Rents received		11,000.	00			3	11,000.	00
b Royalties received								
Rental and Royalty Expenses								
4 Advertising	4							
5 Auto and travel	5							
6 Cleaning and maintenance	6							
7 Commissions	7							
8 Insurance	8	385.	00					
9 Interest	9	9,022.	00					
10 Legal and other professional fees . .	10							
11 Repairs	11							
12 Supplies	12							
13 Taxes (do NOT include Windfall Profit Tax, see Part III, line 35)	13	950.	00					
14 Utilities	14	180.	00					
15 Wages and salaries	15							
16 Other (list) ►								
Painting		250.	00					
Plumbing repair		185.	00					
Roof repair		170.	00					
17 Total deductions (add lines 4 through 16)	17	11,142.	00			17	11,142.	00
18 Depreciation expense (see Instructions), or Depletion (attach computation)	18	7,084.	00			18	7,084.	00
19 Total (add lines 17 and 18)	19	18,226.	00					**E**
20 Income or (loss) from rental or royalty properties (subtract line 19 from line 3a (rents) or 3b (royalties))	20	(7,226.	00)					

21 Add properties with profits on line 20, and enter total profits here	21		
22 Add properties with losses on line 20, and enter total (losses) here	22	(7,226.	00)
23 Combine amounts on lines 21 and 22, and enter net profit or (loss) here	23	(7,226.	00)
24 Net farm rental profit or (loss) from Form 4835, line 50	24		
25 Total rental or royalty income or (loss). Combine amounts on lines 23 and 24. Enter here and include in line 37 on page 2	25	(7,226.	00)

For Paperwork Reduction Act Notice, see Form 1040 Instructions.

FIGURE 17–1

The amount claimed for depreciation is $7,084. The purchase price was $92,000; and since Kirkham's tax bill shows that his assessment is divided on the basis of just over 70 percent to the improvements and the remainder to the land, he will allocate the sum of $64,400 to the building as the basis for depreciation. Kirkham decides to use a 15 year life and 175 percent accelerated depreciation. Table 17–2 shows that an 11 percent depreciation deduction is allowable for the year. Thus, 11 percent of $64,000 equals $7,084.

Expenses of $11,142 are shown and are itemized in Part I. Adding up to the total amount is $950 taxes, $385 insurance, $180 water, $9,022 loan interest, $250 painting, $185 plumbing repairs, and $170 for repair of the roof gutter.

The $7,084 depreciation and $11,142 expenses total $18,226 which exceeds the $11,000 rental income by $7,226 which Kirkham may show as a loss. It is interesting to note that not only does Kirkham receive $11,000 in rental income free from taxes, but in addition he will enter the $7,226 loss on another part of his Form 1040 and will offset $7,226 of his ordinary taxable income.

Information used in connection with the calculation of depreciation is shown in Part V, and the amount of depreciation taken for the tax year is shown as 175 percent accelerated depreciation of $7,084.

This example, involving a rather inexpensive and simple piece of income property, points up the advantages available to investors in real estate. In addition to the tax-free income feature, we must remember that the property in question is actually appreciating in value each year, and the monthly payments made by the tenants are used to pay off a loan, which results in an equity buildup for the owner.

QUESTIONS FOR DISCUSSION

1. How can the taxpayer benefit by being able to classify a gain as capital rather than as ordinary?
2. Discuss the types of real property which qualify as Section 1231 property and the significance of this classification.
3. What are the factors leading to classification as a dealer rather than an investor?
4. What is the difference between a cost basis and an adjusted basis?
5. What is the difference between long-term and short-term capital gains?
6. Discuss the conditions which allow an owner to sell a principal residence and exclude payment of taxes on any gain.
7. What has the determination of estimated useful life to do with the subject of depreciation?
8. Discuss allowance of tax deductions with respect to business or vacation uses of residences.
9. What is meant by accelerated depreciation?
10. Discuss the various benefits of the ACRS method of calculating depreciation.
11. What may be the advantage of selling property using an installment plan?
12. With respect to installment sales, what is meant by a 30 percent rule, and what is its present status?

MULTIPLE CHOICE QUESTIONS

17–1. With respect to capital gains, real estate licensees are generally classified as: (a) agent, (b) principal, (c) dealer, (d) investor.
17–2. The cost basis of property is its: (a) purchase cost, (b) appraisal set by tax collector, (c) net proceeds to seller, (d) none of these.
17–3. Appreciation generally refers to: (a) tax computation, (b) property value increases, (c) special sales methods to provide tax benefits, (d) none of these.
17–4. A seller will generally elect to use an installment sale in order to: (a) provide FHA financing, (b) meet capital-gain requirements, (c) spread tax payments, (d) none of these.
17–5. Salvage value is most often considered with respect to: (a) tract sales, (b) cost basis calculation, (c) property acquired by gift, (d) none of these.
17–6. Proper interpretation of complex tax laws is best accomplished by: (a) real estate broker, (b) attorney, (c) CPA, (d) none of these.
17–7. Proper calculation of depreciation helps provide the property investor with: (a) better interest rates, (b) greater appreciation, (c) tax shelter, (d) VA financing.
17–8. A possible tax advantage to investors in real property as against common stock investors is: (a) capital gains, (b) appreciation, (c) depreciation, (d) none of these.

Governmental controls

18

This chapter will concern itself with various governmental controls of special importance to the real estate industry and real estate licensee, and will contain separate sections devoted to zoning, city planning, environmental laws, eminent domain, geologic hazard zones, redevelopment and urban renewal, housing and construction, water conservation and use, and fair housing laws.

ZONING

Zoning ordinances regulate the use of land and buildings, and are enacted under the police power of the state, which gives it the authority to enact laws within constitutional limits to promote the order, safety, health, morals, and general welfare of the people. The California constitution provides authorization for zoning laws and ordinances, and such regulations are also authorized by the government code which provides that the legislative unit of a city or county may pass ordinances that:

a. Regulate the use of buildings and land for such purposes as residential, business and commercial, industrial and manufacturing, agricultural, and other uses such as park and recreational.

b. Regulate location, size, and height of buildings, and structures.

c. Regulate the size of open areas, yards, and percent of lot that may be covered by a building or other type of structure.

d. Create such areas as civic centers, public parks, and planned development areas, and review the plans for all buildings to be erected in such areas.

e. Establish building setback lines along streets, highways, freeways, or any other type of thoroughfare or roadway.

Most cities and towns have enacted their own zoning ordinances to meet the particular needs of their community and surrounding areas. All counties are required by law to have a planning commission, and cities and towns are permitted to have one if they wish. Most municipalities have a designated zoning board or zoning commission that administers the local zoning laws. As long as a particular zoning ordinance meets the needs of promoting order, safety, health, general welfare, and the like, the courts will uphold the validity of the ordinance. A zoning ordinance may, however, be held to be invalid if it is obviously discriminatory against a particular piece of property, creates a monopoly or acts against established uses that are not nuisances, or creates an obviously unfair and inequitable situation.

Zoning changes and variances

A property owner may feel that the zoning ordinance covering his property is incorrect or unreasonable. In such a case, he has several means of bringing his objections to the attention of the local government. If the matter involves a number of parcels, the owner or owners may file a petition for rezoning with the local governmental agency. The petition may be referred to the local planning commission, which will hold public hearings in addition to having its technical staff investigate the situation and make recommendations. An adverse decision may be appealed to the local city council or board of supervisors.

If only a single parcel of land is involved, the owner may file a petition for exception to use, also referred to as a variance. The owner attempts to show that exceptional circumstances are applicable to his property and that an exception will not be detrimental to the public.

Nonconforming use

It often occurs that when an area is zoned or rezoned certain uses are existent at the time that do not conform to the new ordinance. These are known as nonconforming uses. In most cases, the tendency is for the application legislation to allow the nonconforming use to remain for a specified period of years, after which the use must be terminated. Another method is to provide that the use may continue until alterations or changes are made in the building, at which time there must be conformance with the existing zoning ordinance.

General types of zoning

A zoning plan that is the result of a master plan for the development and regulation of an entire community or area is known as a comprehensive type of zoning. Often, a deteriorated area may be designated for urban renewal, and this redevelopment area will be rezoned as it is redeveloped; this is often referred to as urban renewal zoning. Partial or limited zoning is often found with reference to certain types of uses, businesses, or industries within a certain municipality or area. Spot zoning has to do with a small number of parcels zoned differently from a larger surrounding area, for instance a small business section located in the center of a large residentially zoned area.

An example of a comprehensive zoning plan is shown in Figure 18–1, prepared by the city planning department of the city of Los Angeles. In addition to the various zone classifications and uses, the regulations set forth requirements for such items as maximum heights, required yards, minimum area per lot and dwelling unit, parking requirements, and loading space.

A recently enacted piece of legislation authorizes cities, if they wish, to enact an ordinance that requires the seller of a residence to obtain a report prepared by a city department to show the authorized use, occupancy, and zoning classification of the building and property. This report would have to be given to the prospective purchaser prior to close of escrow. Such ordinances have already been enacted in some areas; in other areas a report of this type must be given to the prospective purchaser of any type of real property, and the purchaser must by signature evidence receipt of the report prior to close of escrow.

CITY PLANNING

One of the very essences of government itself is planning directed toward the common need of the people. A comprehensive plan of physical development is requisite to community efficiency and progress. The public health, safety, order, and prosperity are dependent upon the proper regulation of municipal life. The free flow of traffic with a minimum of hazard depends upon the number, location, and width of streets, their relation to one another, and the location of building lines; these considerations likewise enter into the growth of trade, commerce, and industry. Housing, always a problem in congested areas, affects the moral and material life of the people and is necessarily involved in both municipal planning and zoning. It is essential to plan adequately, not only for present community needs, but also to make provision for future community needs that may be reasonably anticipated.

There are too many examples all about us of planless growth and haphazard development. The evils caused by absence of proper planning affect the health, safety, and moral climate of the individuals who must live in such an environment, and eventual correction of such conditions necessitates the expenditure of extremely large sums of money for urban renewal, redevelopment, and other such programs. It is obvious that proper planning is a virtual necessity in connection with the community growth being experienced in California today.

California planning

The California state legislature passed its first city planning enabling act in 1915, and it was assumed that with the opening of the Panama Canal there would be a surge of immigration from Europe through the canal to California. This did not materialize due to the advent of World War I. During the 1920s the major effort in city planning was confined to the development of private land-use controls such as zoning ordinances. During the 1930s, urban land development began to spread out beyond the existent confines of estab-

SUMMARY OF ZONING REGULATIONS
CITY OF LOS ANGELES

CLASSIFICATION	ZONE	USE	MAXIMUM HEIGHT STORIES	MAXIMUM HEIGHT FEET	REQUIRED YARDS FRONT	REQUIRED YARDS SIDE	REQUIRED YARDS REAR	MINIMUM AREA PER LOT	MINIMUM AREA PER DWELLING UNIT	MINIMUM LOT WIDTH	PARKING SPACE	EAGLE PRISMACOLOR PENCIL CHART
AGRICULTURAL	A1	AGRICULTURAL — ONE-FAMILY DWELLINGS - PARKS - PLAYGROUNDS - COMMUNITY CENTERS GOLF COURSES - TRUCK GARDENING - EXTENSIVE AGRICULTURAL USES	3	45 FT.	25 FT.	25 FT. MAXIMUM 10% LOT WIDTH 3 FT MINIMUM	25 FT.	5 ACRES	2½ ACRES	300 FT	TWO SPACES PER DWELLING UNIT	909 GRASS GREEN
	A2	AGRICULTURAL — A1 USES	3	45 FT.	25 FT.	25 FT. MAXIMUM 10% LOT WIDTH 3 FT. MINIMUM	25 FT.	2 ACRES	1 ACRE	150 FT	TWO SPACES PER DWELLING UNIT	912 APPLE GREEN
	RA	SUBURBAN — LIMITED AGRICULTURAL USES	3	45 FT.	25 FT.	10'-1 & 2 STORIES 11'-3 STORIES	25 FT.	17,500 SQ. FT. ✱	17,500 SQ. FT. ✱	70 FT ✱	TWO GARAGE SPACES PER DWELLING UNIT	910 TRUE GREEN
ONE FAMILY RESIDENTIAL	RE40	RESIDENTIAL ESTATE — ONE-FAMILY DWELLINGS PARKS PLAYGROUNDS COMMUNITY CENTERS TRUCK GARDENING	3	45 FT.	25 FT.	10 FT.	25 FT	40,000 SQ. FT. ✱	40,000 SQ. FT. ✱	80 FT. ✱	TWO GARAGE SPACES PER DWELLING UNIT	950 GOLD
	RE20				25 FT.	10 FT.	25 FT	20,000 SQ. FT. ✱	20,000 SQ. FT. ✱	80 FT. ✱		
	RE15				25 FT.	10 FT. MAXIMUM 10% LOT WIDTH 5 FT. MINIMUM	25 FT.	15,000 SQ. FT. ✱	15,000 SQ. FT. ✱	80 FT. ✱		
	RE11				25 FT.	5'-1 & 2 STORIES 6'-3 STORIES	25 FT.	11,000 SQ FT ✱	11,000 SQ. FT ✱	70 FT ✱		
	RE9				25 FT.	5 FT. MAXIMUM 10% LOT WIDTH 3 FT. MINIMUM	25 FT.	9,000 SQ. FT. ✱	9,000 SQ. FT. ✱	65 FT ✱		
	RS	SUBURBAN — ONE-FAMILY DWELLINGS - PARKS PLAYGROUNDS - TRUCK GARDENING	3	45 FT.	25 FT.	5'-1 & 2 STORIES 6'-3 STORIES	20 FT	7,500 SQ. FT.	7,500 SQ. FT.	60 FT.	TWO GARAGE SPACES PER DWELLING UNIT	911 OLIVE GREEN
	R1	ONE-FAMILY DWELLING — RS USES	3	45 FT.	20 FT.	5'-1 & 2 STORIES 6'-3 STORIES	15 FT.	5,000 SQ. FT.	5,000 SQ. FT.	50 FT	TWO GARAGE SPACES PER DWELLING UNIT	916 CANARY YELLOW
	RW1	ONE-FAMILY RESIDENTIAL WATERWAYS ZONE	2	30 FT.	10 FT.	4' PLUS 1' EACH STORY ABOVE 2ND ● 10% LOT WIDTH	15 FT.	2,300 SQ FT	2,300 SQ FT	28 FT	TWO GARAGE SPACES PER DWELLING UNIT	914 CREAM
MULTIPLE RESIDENTIAL	RW2	TWO-FAMILY RESIDENTIAL WATERWAYS ZONE	3	45 FT.					1,150 SQ. FT.			
	R2	TWO-FAMILY DWELLING — R1 USES TWO-FAMILY DWELLINGS			20 FT.	5'-1 & 2 STORIES 6'-3 STORIES	15 FT.	5,000 SQ. FT.	2,500 SQ. FT.	50 FT.	TWO SPACES ONE IN A GARAGE	917 YELLOW ORANGE
	RD1.5	RESTRICTED DENSITY MULTIPLE DWELLING ZONE — TWO-FAMILY DWELLING APARTMENT HOUSES MULTIPLE DWELLINGS	HEIGHT DISTRICT NO. 1 3 STORIES 45 FT. — HEIGHT DISTRICT NOS. 2,3 OR 4 6 STORIES 75 FT.		20 FT.	6 FT.	20 FT.	6,000 SQ. FT.	1,500 SQ. FT.	60 FT	ONE SPACE EACH DWELLING UNIT OF LESS THAN THREE ROOMS / ONE AND ONE HALF SPACES EACH DWELLING UNIT OF THREE ROOMS / TWO SPACES EACH DWELLING UNIT OF MORE THEN THREE ROOMS / ONE SPACE EACH GUEST ROOM (FIRST THIRTY)	940 SAND
	RD2				20 FT.	10 FT.	25 FT.	12,000 SQ. FT.	2,000 SQ. FT.	70 FT		
	RD3								3,000 SQ. FT.			
	RD4								4,000 SQ. FT.			
	RD5								5,000 SQ. FT.			
	RD6								6,000 SQ. FT.			
	R3	MULTIPLE DWELLING — R2 USES APARTMENT HOUSES MULTIPLE DWELLINGS			15 FT.	5'-1 & 2 STORIE 6'-3 STORIES	15 FT.	5,000 SQ. FT.	800 TO 1,200 SQ. FT.	50 FT.		918 ORANGE
	R4	MULTIPLE DWELLING — R3 USES CHURCHES HOTELS - SCHOOLS	UNLIMITED ✱		15 FT.	5' PLUS 1' EACH STORY ABOVE 2ND 16 FT. MAX.	15' PLUS 1' EACH STORY ABOVE 3ND 20 FT. MAX.	5,000 SQ. FT.	400 TO 800 SQ. FT.	50 FT.		943 BURNT OCHRE
	R5	MULTIPLE DWELLING — R4 USES CLUBS - HOSPITALS LODGES - SANITARIUMS	UNLIMITED ✱		15 FT.	5' PLUS 1' EACH STORY ABOVE 2ND 16 FT. MAX.	15' PLUS 1' EACH STORY ABOVE 3ND 20 FT. MAX.	5,000 SQ. FT.	200 TO 400 SQ. FT.	50 FT.		946 DARK BROWN

✱ SEE HEIGHT DISTRICTS AT THE BOTTOM OF PAGE 2

● FOR TWO OR MORE LOTS THE INTERIOR SIDE YARDS MAY BE ELIMINATED, BUT 4 FT IS REQUIRED ON EACH SIDE OF THE GROUPED LOTS.

✱ "H" HILLSIDE OR MOUNTAINOUS AREA DESIGNATION MAY ALTER THESE REQUIREMENTS IN THE RA-H OR RE-H ZONES, SUBDIVISIONS MAY BE APPROVED WITH SMALLER LOTS, PROVIDING LARGER LOTS ARE ALSO INCLUDED. EACH LOT MAY BE USED FOR ONLY ONE SINGLE-FAMILY DWELLING SEE MINIMUM WIDTH & AREA REQUIREMENTS BELOW.

ZONE COMBINATION	MINIMUM TO WHICH NET AREA MAY BE REDUCED	MINIMUM TO WHICH LOT WIDTH MAY BE REDUCED
RA-H	14,000 SQ. FT	63 FT
RE 9 -H	7,200 SQ. FT	60 FT
RE11 -H,	8,800 SQ. FT	63 FT
RE15 -H	12,000 SQ. FT	72 FT.
RE 20 -H	16,000 SQ. FT	72 FT.
RE 40 -H	32,000 SQ. FT	NO REDUCTION

SHEET 1 OF 2

PREPARED BY CITY PLANNING DEPARTMENT

FIGURE 18–1

SUMMARY OF ZONING REGULATIONS
CITY OF LOS ANGELES

CLASSIFICATION	ZONE	USE	MAXIMUM HEIGHT		REQUIRED YARDS			MINIMUM AREA PER LOT AND UNIT	MINIMUM LOT WIDTH	LOADING SPACE	PARKING SPACE	
			STORIES	FEET	FRONT	SIDE	REAR					
COMMERCIAL	CR	LIMITED COMMERCIAL — BANKS, CLUBS, HOTELS, CHURCHES, SCHOOLS, BUSINESS & PROFESSIONAL OFFICES, PARKING AREAS	6	75 FT.	10 FEET	5'-10' CORNER LOT, RESIDENTIAL USE OR ADJOINING AN "A" OR "R" ZONE SAME AS R4 ZONE	15' PLUS 1' EACH STORY ABOVE 3rd NONE	SAME AS R4 FOR DWELLINGS OTHERWISE NONE		HOSPITALS, HOTELS INSTITUTIONS, AND WITH EVERY BUILDING WHERE LOT ABUTS ALLEY	ONE SPACE FOR EACH 500 SQ. FT. OF FLOOR AREA	939 FLESH
	C1	LIMITED COMMERCIAL — LOCAL RETAIL STORES, OFFICES OR BUSINESSES, HOTELS, LIMITED HOSPITALS AND/OR CLINICS, PARKING AREAS				3'-5' CORNER LOT OR ADJOINING AN "A" OR "R" ZONE RESIDENTIAL USE OR ABUTTING AN "A" OR "R" ZONE SAME AS R4 ZONE	15' PLUS 1' EACH STORY ABOVE 3rd RESIDENTIAL USE OR ABUTTING AN "A" OR "R" ZONE OTHERWISE NONE	SAME AS R3 FOR DWELLINGS EXCEPT 5000 SQ FT PER UNIT IN C1-H ZONES — OTHERWISE NONE	50 FEET FOR RESIDENCE USE OTHERWISE NONE	MINIMUM LOADING SPACE 400 SQUARE FEET ADDITIONAL SPACE REQUIRED FOR BUILDINGS CONTAINING MORE THAN 50,000 SQUARE FEET OF FLOOR AREA	ONE SPACE FOR EACH 500 SQUARE FEET OF FLOOR AREA IN ALL BUILDINGS ON ANY LOT MUST BE LOCATED WITHIN 750 FEET OF BUILDING	929 PINK
	C1.5	LIMITED COMMERCIAL — C1 USES — DEPARTMENT STORES, THEATRES, BROADCASTING STUDIOS, PARKING BUILDINGS, PARKS & PLAYGROUNDS	UNLIMITED ✻		NONE							928 BLUSH
	C2	COMMERCIAL — C1.5 USES — RETAIL BUSINESSES WITH LIMITED MANUFACTURING, AUTO SERVICE STATION & GARAGE, RETAIL CONTRACTORS BUSINESSES, CHURCHES, SCHOOLS						SAME AS R4 FOR DWELLINGS OTHERWISE NONE				922 SCARLET RED
	C4	COMMERCIAL — C2 USES — (WITH EXCEPTIONS, SUCH AS AUTO SERVICE STATIONS, AMUSEMENT ENTERPRISES, CONTRACTORS BUSINESSES, SECOND-HAND BUSINESSES)				NONE FOR COMMERCIAL BUILDINGS RESIDENTIAL USES — SAME AS IN R4 ZONE	NONE FOR COMMERCIAL BUILDINGS RESIDENTIAL USES — SAME AS IN R4 ZONE			NONE REQUIRED FOR APARTMENT BUILDINGS 20 UNITS OR LESS	SEE CODE FOR ASSEMBLY AREAS, HOSPITALS AND CLINICS	924 CRIMSON RED
	C5	COMMERCIAL — C2 USES — LIMITED FLOOR AREAS FOR LIGHT MANUFACTURING OF THE CM-ZONE TYPE										925 CRIMSON LAKE
	CM	COMM'L MANUFACTURING — WHOLESALE BUSINESSES, STORAGE BUILDINGS, CLINICS, LIMITED MANUFACTURING, C2 USES — EXCEPT HOSPITALS, SCHOOLS, CHURCHES						SAME AS R3 FOR DWELLINGS OTHERWISE NONE				905 AQUA-MARINE
INDUSTRIAL (RESIDENTIAL USES PROHIBITED IN ALL INDUSTRIAL ZONES)	MR1	RESTRICTED INDUSTRIAL — CM USES — LIMITED COMMERCIAL & MANUFACTURING USES, HOSPITALS, CLINICS, SANITARIUMS, LIMITED MACHINE SHOPS		15 FT.	NONE FOR INDUSTRIAL OR COMMERCIAL BUILDINGS RESIDENTIAL USES — SAME AS IN R4 ZONE	NONE FOR INDUSTRIAL OR COMMERCIAL BUILDINGS RESIDENTIAL USES — SAME AS IN R4 ZONE				HOSPITALS, HOTELS INSTITUTIONS, AND WITH EVERY BUILDING WHERE LOT ABUTS ALLEY	ONE SPACE FOR EACH 500 SQUARE FEET OF FLOOR AREA IN ALL BUILDINGS ON ANY LOT	901 INDIGO BLUE
	MR2	RESTRICTED LIGHT INDUSTRIAL — MR1 USES — ADDITION INDUSTRIAL USES, MORTUARIES, AGRICULTURE						NONE EXCEPT FOR DWELLINGS	50 FEET FOR RESIDENCE USE OTHERWISE NONE	MINIMUM LOADING SPACE 400 SQUARE FEET ADDITIONAL SPACE REQUIRED FOR BUILDINGS CONTAINING MORE THAN 50,000 SQUARE FEET OF FLOOR AREA	MUST BE LOCATED WITHIN 750 FEET OF BUILDING	906 COPEN-HAGEN BLUE
	M1	LIMITED INDUSTRIAL — CM USES — LIMITED INDUSTRIAL & MANUFACTURING USES — NO "R" ZONE USES, NO HOSPITALS, SCHOOLS OR CHURCHES	UNLIMITED ✻									904 LIGHT BLUE
	M2	LIGHT INDUSTRIAL — M1 USES — ADDITIONAL INDUSTRIAL USES, STORAGE YARDS OF ALL KINDS, ANIMAL KEEPING — NO "R" ZONE USES		NONE							SEE CODE FOR ASSEMBLY AREAS, HOSPITALS AND CLINICS	902 ULTRA-MARINE
	M3	HEAVY INDUSTRIAL — M2 USES — ANY INDUSTRIAL USES — NUISANCE TYPE - 500 FT. FROM ANY OTHER ZONE — NO "R" ZONE USES			NONE	NONE		NONE —NOTE— "R" ZONE USES PROHIBITED	NONE	NONE REQUIRED FOR APARTMENT BUILDINGS 20 UNITS OR LESS		931 PURPLE
PARKING	P	AUTOMOBILE PARKING — SURFACE & UNDERGROUND — PROPERTY IN A "P" ZONE MAY ALSO BE IN AN "A" OR "R" ZONE PARKING PERMITTED IN LIEU OF AGRICULTURAL OR RESIDENTIAL USES						NONE UNLESS ALSO IN AN "A" OR "R" ZONE	NONE UNLESS ALSO IN AN "A" OR "R" ZONE	—	—	967 COLD GREY LIGHT
	PB	PARKING BUILDING — AUTOMOBILE PARKING WITHIN OR WITHOUT A BUILDING	✻✻	—	0', 5', OR 10' DEPENDING ON ZONING IN BLOCK AND ACROSS STREET	5' PLUS 1' EACH STORY ABOVE 2nd IF ABUTTING OR ACROSS STREET FROM "A" OR "R" ZONE	5' PLUS 1' EACH STORY ABOVE 2nd IF ABUTTING AN "A" OR "R" ZONE, TO A 16' MAXIMUM	NONE	NONE	—	—	936 SLATE GREY
SPECIAL	SL	SUBMERGED LAND ZONE — COMMERCIAL SHIPPING, NAVIGATION, FISHING, RECREATION										919 SKY BLUE
	(T)	TENTATIVE CLASSIFICATION — USED IN COMBINATION WITH ZONE CHANGE ONLY - DELAYS ISSUANCE OF BUILDING PERMIT UNTIL SUBDIVISION OR PARCEL MAP RECORDED										
	(F)	FUNDED IMPROVEMENT CLASSIFICATION — AN ALTERNATE MEANS OF EFFECTING ZONE CHANGES AND SECURING IMPROVEMENTS (WHEN NO SUBDIVISION OR DEDICATIONS ARE INVOLVED)										
	(Q)	QUALIFIED CLASSIFICATION — USED IN COMBINATION WITH ZONE CHANGES ONLY EXCEPT WITH RA, RE, RS OR R1 ZONES - RESTRICTS USES OF PROPERTY AND ASSURES DEVELOPMENT COMPATIBLE WITH THE SURROUNDING PROPERTY										

SUPPLEMENTAL USE DISTRICTS: G ROCK AND GRAVEL • O OIL DRILLING • S ANIMAL SLAUGHTERING • RPD RESIDENTIAL PLANNED DEVELOPMENT   K HORSE-KEEPING • CA COMMERCIAL AND ARTCRAFT
(ESTABLISHED IN CONJUNCTION WITH ZONES)

✻ HEIGHT DISTRICT				✻✻ MAXIMUM PB ZONE HEIGHTS		
	Nº 1	FLOOR AREA OF MAIN BUILDING MAY NOT EXCEED THREE TIMES THE BUILDING AREA OF THE LOT			Nº 1	2 STORIES AND ROOF
	Nº 1L	SAME AS Nº 1 AND MAXIMUM HEIGHT - 6 STORIES OR 75 FT			Nº 2	6 STORIES
	Nº 1-VL	SAME AS Nº 1 AND MAXIMUM HEIGHT - 3 STORIES OR 45 FT			Nº 3	10 STORIES
	Nº 1-XL	SAME AS Nº 1 AND MAXIMUM HEIGHT - 2 STORIES OR 30 FT			Nº 4	13 STORIES
	Nº 2	FLOOR AREA OF MAIN BUILDING MAY NOT EXCEED SIX TIMES THE BUILDABLE AREA OF THE LOT				
	Nº 3	FLOOR AREA OF MAIN BUILDING MAY NOT EXCEED TEN TIMES THE BUILDABLE AREA OF THE LOT				
	Nº 4	FLOOR AREA OF MAIN BUILDING MAY NOT EXCEED THIRTEEN TIMES THE BUILDABLE AREA OF THE LOT				

NOTE: ALL INFORMATION GENERAL - FOR SPECIFIC DETAILS CHECK WITH DEPARTMENT OF BUILDING AND SAFETY

SHEET 2 OF 2

PREPARED BY CITY PLANNING DEPARTMENT

FIGURE 18-1 *(concluded)*

lished cities and into unincorporated areas. As a result, county planning programs were introduced. As a result of World War II, the population of California began to increase substantially and has not slowed down since. At present, well over 200 cities in California have city planning commissions, many of them with permanent professional staffs.

Basic elements of a city planning program

There are various elements in connection with a city planning program. The first and most important is the development of a general or master plan for the orderly development of the community involved. This should include such features as a clear statement of goals and a general physical design with relation to land use, community facilities, transportation, such districts as residential, commercial, and industrial, and the like.

Another element to be considered is the passage of specific laws that will enable the general plan to be carried out, and an example of such laws would be those relating to zoning and subdivision control. The council must also set up the machinery for meeting regularly with the city planning department or commission in order to keep informed and supervise the work involved.

In addition to the above, the council must plan for the preparation of an annual capital improvement program with the usual problems of priorities and available funds. Developmental studies must be carried out and presented for the council's consideration with regard to the various improvement projects, and the council should also be aware of their duties and responsibilities in educating the public concerning the continuing program and various issues that will arise as a result of the physical projects and developments involved.

City planning commission

The members of the planning commission are generally appointed by the city council, mayor, or city manager. In some cases the mayor or members of the city council sit as ex-officio members of the commission. The planning commission may usually appoint consulting experts from time to time or, depending upon the size of the city or community, may hire specialists and other necessary personnel permanently with civil service ratings.

The duties and responsibilities of the planning commission personnel include the preparation of policies, plans, and programs for local development; the preparation of special projects for specific neighborhoods and districts in the community; and continuing responsibilities of the planning department such as capital improvements and zoning.

Professional city planners

The present-day planning profession has emerged in response to the rapid growth, changing character, and problems of twentieth-century urban development. Planning has become an accepted function of government, both in overall terms and in connection with particular programs, while planning techniques are likewise employed by large-scale private developers. City and regional planning is a rapidly expanding field, with some 3,500 professionals in the United States, most of them members of the American Institute of Planners.

In addition to working within a local city planning department, city planners are also relied upon in other types of public agencies including local, state, and federal agencies dealing with highways, transportation, housing, urban renewal, public works, economic development, human and natural resources development, education, and health. A significant portion of the profession engages in consulting to city planning and other governmental agencies and to private firms of various sorts. The University of California offers a two-year graduate program in its City and Regional Planning Department leading to the Master of City Planning (M.C.P.) Degree.

ENVIRONMENTAL LAWS

The increased attention given to various problems connected with the environment in recent years has been reflected in the actions of legislative bodies at the federal, state, and local levels. Included are problems with respect to the energy crisis, population growth, smog control, endangered species of certain wildlife, disposal of garbage and refuse, conversion of prime agricultural lands to other uses, and the quality of life in general.

Environmental impact reports. State legislators have advanced numerous proposals to solve these problems such as prohibitions on certain land uses, acquisition of land for use by the public, and attempts to control land development by changes in tax laws and assessment practices. The Environmental Quality Act was enacted into law by the California state legislature in 1970, and with subsequent amendments, provides for the preparation and evaluation of environmental impact reports (EIR) by public agencies, developers, and other entities who propose projects that will have a significant impact on the environment.

California Coastal Act. In 1972 Proposition 20 was approved by the voters and resulted in the establishment of the Coastal Zone Conservation Commission with its various regional commissions. The Commission is charged with conducting studies to determine the ecological planning principles needed to ensure conservation of the resources of the coastal zone of the state. Any individual or governmental unit proposing a development within the coastal zone must obtain a permit from the appropriate regional commission.

The coastal zone generally runs the length of the state from the ocean inland about 1,000 yards, with wider spots in coastal estuary, habitat, and recreational areas. It includes about 1,800 square miles.

EMINENT DOMAIN

The right of eminent domain is the supreme power inherent in the state to take land by due process of the law from the owner, when necessary for its use for the public welfare. The two basic requirements that must be met are *(a)* the use must be public, and *(b)* a just compensation must be paid to the owner.

The power of eminent domain is different from the "police power" of the state, which is the regulation of the use of private property without a "taking." The power of eminent domain involves a taking and the payment of compensation to the property owner. In contrast, any loss in value suffered by the property owner by an exercise of police power is usually not compensable.

The federal government, states, cities, counties, improvements districts, public utilities, public education institutions, and similar public and semipublic units may all exercise the power of eminent domain. Examples of public uses, so declared by the state legislature, include streets, irrigation, electric power, public housing, off-street parking, farmers' market, extension of hospital or school facilities, and the like.

The use of the power of eminent domain is often referred to as *condemnation*. The main issue

in condemnation or eminent domain cases is the amount of just compensation required to be paid to the owner of the property. The law has fixed a general standard of fair market value that must be followed by all appraisers in reaching their conclusions. Fair market value is here defined as the highest price the property would bring if exposed for sale in the open market with reasonable time allowed to find a purchaser with knowledge of all uses and purposes to which the land is adapted, the seller not being required to sell or the purchaser required to purchase.

The law further specifically excludes certain items from consideration in arriving at fair market value. These noncompensable items include damages to business in the form of loss of profits and good will, expenses of moving, personal inconveniences, rerouting of traffic, value of options, and value of equitable servitudes.

Formal condemnation action by a public political unit is usually preceded by negotiations with the property owner through the public unit's right-of-way agent or other representative. If negotiations are successful, the property is usually purchased rather than condemned. If negotiations are unsuccessful, a formal proceeding in eminent domain is filed in court against the property owner.

In certain cases the taking of land by eminent domain becomes quite complex, and it must be clearly shown that the taking is for a public use. The Civil Code even makes provision in certain cases for a private individual to maintain an eminent domain action. There are also instances in which the taking of property under eminent domain has been allowed to a private nonprofit institution such as a university where the court has found that the taking constituted a public use.

Generally, when land is acquired through condemnation proceedings for a public use, a fee simple estate is acquired, since the resultant use may be the construction of a public housing, airport, or railway station, or a public housing project. One of the general rules covering the exercise of eminent domain, however, is that no greater estate should be taken than that which the intended public use will require. Thus, where the taking is for public improvements such as power lines, drainage and sewer systems, or construction of a road, the right acquired will be an easement or right of way rather than a fee simple estate.

Sometimes public works are started and damage to property results but no condemnation action is filed by the public unit. In such a case the property owner may initiate the suit himself as an inverse condemnation action. If a condemnation action is filed and the public unit decides eventually not to take the land, the owner may take action to recover costs and expenses he may have incurred as a result.

In an attempt to stop population growth and limit residential development, ordinances have been passed in the California cities of Livermore and Petaluma. But these ordinances were overthrown by the courts, which ruled that prohibiting housing construction violates the civil rights of individuals to move about freely within California.

Another method of limiting the use of land are proposals in law to add fees or charges to compensate for public expenditures. A decision by the California legislature that required a subdivider to dedicate land for park purposes, or to pay fees in lieu of such dedication, has been upheld as constitutional by the U.S. Supreme Court. Current state law allows a property owner to contract with a county to maintain his property in agricultural or other open-space use for a minimum period of ten years and in exchange receive a tax assessment reflecting such present use rather than a higher assessment based on the possibility of future residential or commercial development. We can expect a continuing increase in proposed new legislation with respect to land control and the environment.

GEOLOGIC HAZARD ZONES

California laws now require that any application for new real estate development or structure for occupancy by individuals must be accompanied by a geologic report prepared by a registered geologist, unless such report is waived by a city or by a county in the case of unincorporated areas. In order to waive a report the city or county must find that no earthquake hazard exists and must have the approval of the State geologist.

Potentially and recently active traces of earthquake faults that may constitute a hazard have been mapped by the California Division of Mines and Geology. Special study zones are designated that generally extend one-eighth mile or 660 feet on either side of a trace or fault, although many faults are so wide that some special study zones, as projected in State maps, are actually more than one mile in width.

Individuals purchasing property within such zones should be informed by the seller or real estate licensee representing the seller of these var-

ious regulations and requirements, especially when the purchaser is contemplating development and construction. The State has prepared maps of special study zones in 173 different California counties, and further information with respect to these maps and the Alquist-Priolo Geologic Hazard Act may be obtained from the California Division of Mines and Geology, Sacramento, California.

REDEVELOPMENT AND URBAN RENEWAL

In our discussion of traditional depreciation in Chapter 14, we noted that economic and social obsolescence occurs when a neighborhood ages and certain detrimental influences of supply and demand, zoning, and legislative restrictions begin to take their effect upon the area. It was noted that economic and social obsolescence is difficult to correct and usually necessitates an urban renewal and redevelopment project on a large scale.

Early efforts at redevelopment were made by private groups, some sponsored by syndicate groups, realty boards, and large insurance companies. The ability, however, to assemble the necessary plottage by private negotiation alone resulted in very little progress. What was needed was the authority of a governmental unit to exercise its right of eminent domain to bring to process of law the court condemnation orders. In 1949, federal legislation brought forth the Housing Act, which recognized slums as a national menace. Title I of this act provides federal loans and grants to clear the following:

a. Residential slums and blight areas for the purpose of redeveloping the land for any locally approved residential, commercial, industrial, or combination of such uses.

b. Nonresidential blighted areas, provided such areas are to be redeveloped predominantly for residential purposes; provided further that, if the area is not predominantly residential, the proposed use need not be predominantly residential.

c. Predominantly open areas which, because of obsolete plotting or faulty site improvement, are impeding sound city growth. Redevelopment of such areas too must be principally for residential purposes.

Through this plan a city establishes a local public agency under state law to begin the project of redevelopment. This agency may apply for a temporary loan to finance the cost of planning, clearing, and assembling the various plots and to prepare the land for subsequent sale or lease. Also included is the cost of relocation of former occupants of cleared areas. When the area is cleared parcels may be sold or leased to private or public investors who will improve the land in keeping with the master plan originally projected. From the total cost of redevelopment is subtracted the proceeds realized by the sale of the cleared lands. Any deficit, should one occur, is shared two thirds by the federal government and one third by the local city government.

Sacramento, the capital city of California, was one of the first cities in the state to take advantage of this program, and was also one of the first in the United States to finance its local one-third share of the net project costs by the sale of tax allocation bonds. These bonds are to be retired out of the increased tax revenue produced by new construction in the project area. Over 75 blocks located west of the capitol towards the Sacramento River will ultimately be redeveloped to produce a capital mall, residential apartments, commercial areas with only pedestrian access, state and other office buildings, hotels, parkways, a new Chinese center, and a light industrial complex. In addition to the work being done in Sacramento, many other projects are underway throughout the state, especially in the San Francisco and Los Angeles areas.

The Community Redevelopment Law, a part of the Health and Safety Code, provides for creation of Community Redevelopment Agencies (CRA) to implement programs at the local level. CRA's, at a minimum, must develop on a one-to-one basis, replacement housing for any units removed from the moderate or low-income housing market as a part of a redevelopment project.

Urban renewal

The term *urban renewal* came into widespread use as a result of Congressional passage of the Housing Act of 1954. The main goal behind this act is not only to clear existing slum areas, but also to rehabilitate and save areas that can be restored before they become slums. Private enterprise plays a large part in such restoration, and federal assistance is provided for these urban renewal projects.

The Act provides that a local municipality, through its department of public works or housing authority, may designate certain neighborhoods as conservation areas. Each individual parcel of property in the conservation areas is inspected by the local bureau of building inspection, and a report of the condition of improvements on the land is given to the owner of the property. Violations of local building codes are detailed and steps required to comply with the local codes are outlined. The owner is then required to bring his building up to code, and under the federally assisted code enforcement program he may obtain a low-interest loan to effect the necessary improvements if he is in a low-income classification. Thus, many property owners who could not otherwise afford to do so are able to bring their property up to the local code requirements and the entire neighborhood designated as a conservation area is ultimately rehabilitated.

There are many forms of special assistance and aid that have been provided by the federal government in connection with redevelopment and urban renewal. The FHA may insure certain loans with extremely liberal terms for the construction of new, or the rehabilitation of existing, low-cost public and private housing; certain loans and subsidies are provided for low-rent public housing; relocation payments are provided for those displaced from an area that is being redeveloped; rent supplement programs have been made available; and provision is made in certain cases for a five-year write-off (depreciation deductions) for capital improvements made on residential buildings for low and moderate income families as defined by the secretary of Housing and Urban Development, and Internal Revenue Service Publication 534 dealing with depreciation.

HOUSING AND CONSTRUCTION

The housing construction industry has made great strides during the past 35 years. Before that time it was the practice of an individual who wished to have a home built to consult an architect who would detail drawings and a list of specifications of materials and construction methods. These would be changed back and forth between the parties until the owner and architect finally agreed on an acceptable plan. The job of erecting the house was then usually put out for competitive bid among several general contractors, with the low bidder usually granted the contract.

Payments were made to the contractor at periodic intervals based upon certain stages of completion. The architect supervised and inspected the materials and their installation to be sure that the owner was getting what he had bargained for in the contract. The owner either had to have the total cash needed or he had to secure it on some form of general credit, or else the builder would have to wait until completion when a permanent loan could be placed. Gradually, it became common for institutional lenders to enter into what was called a construction loan by placing a mortgage or trust deed for the full amount of the loan.

The lender doled out the money to the contractor, always protecting the advances by the prerecorded lien and carefully watching to see that the contractor paid his labor and material suppliers so there could be no mechanic's liens placed upon the property to jeopardize title. The general contractor sublet phases of the work to subcontractors, who ranged up to 10 to 15 in number. Home building was thus strictly custom building and, in effect, was based upon the old feudal system of craftsmen, each specializing in a particular material and job.

There is at the present time still a demand for fine custom-built homes, but in recent years the tract builder has been responsible for the largest volume of new residential construction. Concerted efforts have been made to lower the cost of homes with such methods as the following:

a. Eliminate or combine certain functions and specialties.
b. Use precut or prefabricated materials in modular units or standard measurements.
c. Use more labor-saving devices and mechanize tools and equipment.
d. Make more use of multiple or flexible rooms and areas.
e. Use assembly line and mass production methods on the job site.
f. Attempt to eliminate the need for highly skilled and specialized tasks by standardization.
g. A shift in some areas to prefabrication.
h. Adaptation to use of new types of construction materials.

Even though use of the above methods have brought a greater degree of efficiency to production, total cost of home construction and construction in general has risen sharply with inflation and the demands of the customer for more refinements and installed or built-in equipment. If modern residential building operations have a trend, it is in combining the function of the architect and builder in construction of attractive homes of semistandard designs in multiples, thus gaining savings simultaneously in mass production, selling, and financing.

The basic regulation of the housing and construction industries in California is accomplished by the State Housing Law, Factory-Built Housing Law, local building, health, and safety codes and ordinances, and the State Contractors' License Law.

State Housing Law

The State Housing Law, administered by the Division of Building and Housing Standards, Department of Housing and Community Development, is designed to provide minimum construction and occupancy requirements for all hotels, apartment houses, and dwellings throughout the state. These are the basic requirements, and any city or county may impose additional and more stringent requirements if it wishes. In certain locales particular perils such as the possibility of flooding or earthquake damage may result in special requirements being imposed in addition to those of the state. Construction regulations are enforced by local building inspectors, while occupancy and sanitation regulations are generally enforced by local health officers.

Factory-Built Housing Law

In November 1969 the Factory-Built Housing Law became effective. This law authorized the California Commission of Housing and Community Development to adopt administrative regulations for factory-built housing. Subsequently, such regulations were presented and approved by the Commission and also by the State Building Standards Commission.

The new regulations constitute a code for factory-built housing and preempt local government building codes with regard to housing manufactured off the building site. Under the regulations, the State Department of Housing and Community Development will approve plans, inspect construction at the factory level, and issue a state seal of approval that the construction meets state building code requirements.

Inspection of on-site installation will remain the responsibility of local building officials. Such matters as zoning and site development standards will also remain the responsibility of local governments and local building and planning officials. The new regulations adopt by reference the provisions of the nationwide Uniform Building Code, Uniform Plumbing Code, and the National Electrical Code.

Provision is made for use of new concepts and alternate and equivalent equipment and systems, provided the Department of Housing and Community Development finds that they meet performance standards. Many individuals feel that this new code will open the door to large-scale factory-produced housing in California, since such housing will no longer be subjected to a maze of conflicting local building regulations. The terms *mobile home* and *prefabricated housing* seem to have given way to *factory-built housing*, and its supporters feel that the use of modern factory methods can well be applied to the production of housing and may substantially reduce the cost of housing construction.

Building, health, and safety codes

The basic purpose of building, health, and safety codes is to guard public health and safety by the regulation of the construction and occupancy of buildings. Such regulatory ordinances may be enacted by a municipality as an exercise of its police powers. Most communities have departments of health, safety, and building inspection. These departments carry on the enforcement of existing codes, and permits are issued for the construction of new structures and for work to be performed on existing buildings.

The typical procedure for new construction or building alterations requires an initial application to the local bureau of building inspection for a building permit. The application must be accompanied by plans, specifications, and plot plan. After examination of the application and accompanying exhibits, and revision where necessary, the corrected application is approved and a building permit is issued. No construction or alteration can usually be legally commenced prior to issuance of a building permit. During the work, and at the time of completion, it is inspected again for compliance with applicable codes by building, plumbing, electrical, or health and safety inspectors, as may be necessary.

If all of the requirements have been complied with, a certificate attesting to this fact is issued. Such a certificate may be termed a certificate of completion, certificate of compliance, or certificate of occupancy. Whether one purchases a new building or an older one, the existence of such permits and certificates will evidence the fact that

any work performed was up to code and met the necessary requirements.

Contractors' state license law

The state law pertaining to the licensing of contractors provides for a contractor's state license board. The board concerns itself with the solvency of the applicant for a contractor's license and those who may apply for reinstatement of a license. The purpose is to protect the public against incompetent building contractors and subcontractors. This protection is achieved by requiring construction to be done by licensed persons. This includes subcontract work as well as general and engineering contract work.

An additional indirect regulation of housing and construction is in effect by virtue of various governmental financing devices in the FHA, VA, or California Veterans programs. These programs require, as a prerequisite to participation, that the improvements involved meet certain minimum property requirements, referred to as MPR's, which in certain details are more demanding than either the State Housing Law or local building codes.

Building materials and diagram

The details of home construction methods, materials used, special installations, and the like are too encompassing to be discussed in detail here. The real estate licensee, however, should acquire a basic understanding of standard construction practices in his particular locale, and this should include some knowledge of efficient planning, suitable building materials, and elements of sound construction.

In order to test the real estate license applicant on his knowledge of construction, questions on housing terms for the different wood members in the framework of a house are included in the real estate examinations. These various construction members are enumerated in Figure 18–2. Definitions of housing terms are also incorporated into Appendix A of this text entitled "Definition of Real Estate and Building Construction Words and Phrases."

The real estate licensee will find that he will continually be asked questions by prospective clients with regard to building construction, alterations, modernization, and repair. In many cases, especially with respect to older properties, one of the important considerations in the purchaser's

262

DETAILS OF CONSTRUCTION - The State Department of Real Estate believes that licensees should have a knowledge of construction details. The following diagram and definitions should be mastered for possible State Examination questions.

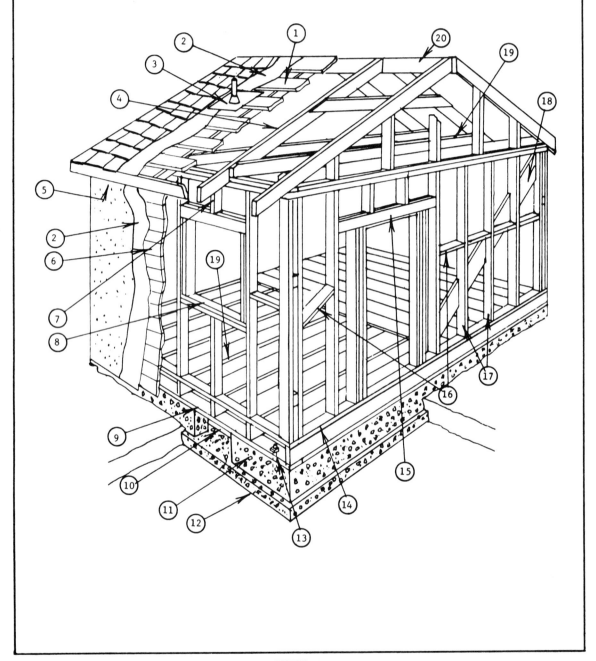

FIGURE 18-2
Building Diagram

EXPLANATION OF DIAGRAM DETAILS

1. OPEN SHEATHING — Boards nailed to rafters as foundation for the roof covering. Open sheathing is used with wood shingles.

2. BUILDING PAPER — Heavy water proofed paper used between sheathing and roof covering or siding.

3. FLASHING — Sheet metal used to protect against water seepage.

4. RAFTERS — Sloping members of a roof used to support the roof boards and shingles. (Maximum 24" apart)

5. EAVE — Protruding underpart of roof overhanging exterior walls.

6. CLOSED SHEATHING — Boards nailed to studding as foundation for exterior siding. Closed means butted together.

7. CRIPPLE — Stud above or below a window opening or above a doorway.

8. SILL — Bottom portion lining doorway or window fits here.

9. MUD SILL — Treated member (or redwood) bolted to the foundation.

10. CRAWL SPACE — Unexcavated area under the house. Min. 18".

11. FOUNDATION — Concrete base of house.

12. FOOTING — Expanded portion of concrete foundation.

13. ANCHOR BOLT — Large bolt used for fastening mud sill to foundation. Bolt is anchored into concrete foundation.

14. SOLE PLATE — Support on which the studs rest.

15. HEADER (LINTEL) — The beam over a doorway or window.

16. FIRE STOP — Blocking used to restrict flames from spreading to attic. May be placed horizontally or diagonally.

17. STUDS — Vertical 2" x 4" framework of the walls spaced 16" on center.

18. BRACING — Board running diagonally across the wall framing to prevent sway.

19. JOISTS — Structural parts supporting floor or ceiling loads.

20. RIDGE BOARD — Highest point of construction in a frame building.

FIGURE 18-2 *(concluded)*

decision to buy will involve the amount that must later be spent to effect certain changes and improvements in the property.

The following are only a few of the areas with which the real estate licensee should be conversant with regard to properties in his particular locale: materials used in building construction; electrical, plumbing, and heating installations and systems; approximate costs for various types of alterations and modernizations; prevention of termite and dry-rot and other fungus conditions; insulation materials; standard requirements for height of ceilings; advantages of various types of building foundations; types of venting required; local requirements for septic tank installations; types of building design and architectural styles; types of finishing materials for roofs, flooring, and interior and exterior surfaces; and various types of installations and improvements that may be made beneath or upon the surface of the land apart from the building itself.

WATER CONSERVATION AND USE

The conservation of natural resources has become an increasingly important topic for discussion lately, especially in connection with the subject of ecology and the environment. The California law recognized the principle of conservation long ago, and with respect to water rights the policy has been established that such rights are limited to taking only such amount of water as is reasonably required for beneficial use. The courts are authorized to refer all water litigation to the state Department of Water Resources for either investigation and report, or hearing and preliminary determination, subject to final court decision.

Mutual water company

A mutual water company is one organized by water users in a given district with the object of securing an ample water supply at a reasonable rate. The Civil Code sets forth the requirements for the establishment of a mutual water company. Articles of incorporation are filed with the secretary of state, and a permit to distribute stock must be obtained from the state Department of Corporations. The stock is usually made appurtenant to the land; that is, each share of stock is attached to a particular portion of land and cannot be sold separately. The advantages of this method are that

it enables the company to plan its distribution more easily and prevents speculation in shares that are primarily to permit uniform development of the district.

Irrigation districts

An irrigation district is a district created for the purpose of conservation and production of water to be used for agricultural purposes. It is a quasi-public corporation created in and by virtue of a general act of the state legislature. An irrigation district is not a municipal corporation but rather a public corporation for a municipal purpose. In creating an irrigation district a petition must be signed by 50 or a majority of the freeholders of a proposed district. The petition sets forth the purpose of the formation of the irrigation district, together with a metes and bounds description thereof. This application is filed with the board of supervisors, time is set for hearing of the application, and notice is duly given and published of the date of the hearing. In addition, a bond of faithful performance must also be filed by the applicants and submitted with the application.

The board of supervisors, at the time of the hearing of the application, hears claims for the inclusion or exclusion of the various lands in the proposed district. After the hearing, the board of supervisors includes or excludes such lands as it deems proper, and certifies to the creation of the irrigation district. An election is then held for the purpose of approving the issuance of bonds for the construction of the irrigation system and the election of directors of the irrigation district. After the election is held and the bond issue is authorized, the matter is then presented by the directors of the irrigation district to the superior court for the validation of the bonds authorized to be issued. The court makes findings and issues a decree of confirmation and validation.

The only power given to the board of directors is to acquire, by purchase or condemnation, a system of canals and water works in conjunction with dams or wells, as the case may be, of that district. An apportionment is made of the water and charges for the use of the water are made. The district may be divided into several classes of users, and each class of users may be charged a different toll or charge for the use of the water; their water rights and the amount of water allotted to the various classes of users may be limited and regulated.

FAIR HOUSING LAWS

The California Fair Housing Act, also known as the Rumford Act, became law on September 20, 1963. It is enforced by the Fair Employment Practice Commission through its offices in San Diego, Los Angeles, Fresno, and San Francisco. An amendment to the state constitution to repeal the act was approved by the electorate (Proposition 14), but that amendment was declared unconstitutional, and the act remains in effect. The Unruh Act, enacted in 1959, precludes real estate brokers from discriminatory practices based on race, color, religion, national origin, or ancestry because the broker operates a "business establishment."

The California Fair Housing Act declares that discrimination because of race, color, religion, national origin, or ancestry in housing accommodations is against public policy in California.

The act covers the following types of housing: public and redevelopment housing; publicly assisted, owner-occupied, single-unit homes; apartments in structures of three or more units; all activities of real estate brokers and salesmen; and, generally, activities of persons or firms engaged in the business of housing or mortgage lending. The act does not cover privately financed, single family homes and duplexes and housing operated by religious, fraternal, or charitable organizations not for profit. These exceptions, however, have now been eliminated by federal law.

California Senate Bill 610, effective January 1978, expands the application of the Rumford Act in the prohibition of discrimination in housing in making it apply to all housing accommodations, including single family houses, except it will not apply to renting or leasing to a roomer or boarder in a single family house provided that no more than one roomer or boarder is to live within the household.

The term *discrimination* includes refusal to sell, rent, or lease housing accommodations, including misrepresentation as to availability, inferior terms and cancellations, and prohibits for-sale or rent advertisements containing discriminatory information.

The federal rules and California

There is now a whole new all-encompassing set of rules prohibiting discrimination on the part of owners of property and their agents. The CAR general counsel, in the June 1969 issue of the CAR magazine, stated that there are no longer any exceptions and that all discrimination is against the law. The basis for this opinion derives from the U.S. Supreme Court case (1968) *Jones* v. *Meyer*, and from Title VIII of the Civil Rights Act of 1968.

The sum of the matter is that every prohibition of the Unruh and Rumford Acts remains in effect, and what discrimination they did not prohibit federal law now does. There are now no exceptions, and all discrimination is against the law. Thus, no one may refuse to sell, lease, or rent to another because of race or color, and no real estate licensee may do so, regardless of his principal's directions. Should a principal seek to restrict a listing according to race or color, the licensee must refuse to accept the listing. Real estate licensees must not discriminate, and to that end should not accept restrictive listings or make, print, or publish any notice, statement, or advertisement with respect to a sale or rental of a dwelling that suggests discrimination because of race, color, religion, or national origin.

The Unruh Civil Rights Act (Section 51, California Civil Code) states that all persons within the jurisdiction of this state are free and equal, and no matter what their race, color, religion, ancestry, or national origin are entitled to the full and equal accommodations, advantages, facilities, privileges, or services in all business establishments of every kind whatsoever. The operation of a real estate broker has been declared by the courts to be a business, and thus the provisions of the Unruh Civil Rights Act apply to all real estate licensees.

For the denial of the rights provided for in the Unruh Act, a real estate licensee would be liable for each such offense for the actual damages, and $250 in addition thereto, suffered by any person denied the rights provided by the act. The Code of Practices of the California Association of Realtors® is a reflection of current law relating to a Realtor's® responsibilities in transacting business with a member of a minority group. In addition to the penalties described above, a violation by a real estate licensee may subject him to penalties under Title VIII of the federal Fair Housing Act as well as the possibility of losing his license under the provisions of Section 10177 (m) of the Business and Profession Code, which is discussed in Chapter 20.

If any Realtor, his associates, or employees were to call attention to the cooperating office or to the owner that an interested party wishing to rent, lease, or buy real property is of any race, religion,

EQUAL HOUSING OPPORTUNITY

We Do Business in Accordance With the Federal Fair Housing Law

(Title VIII of the Civil Rights Act of 1968)

IT IS ILLEGAL TO DISCRIMINATE AGAINST ANY PERSON BECAUSE OF RACE, COLOR, RELIGION, OR NATIONAL ORIGIN

- In the sale or rental of housing or residential lots
- In advertising the sale or rental of housing
- In the financing of housing
- In the provision of real estate brokerage services

Blockbusting is also illegal

Anyone who feels he has been discriminated against should send a complaint to:

U.S. Department of Housing and Urban Development
Assistant Regional Administrator for Equal Opportunity
Region IX
450 Golden Gate Avenue P.O. Box 36003
San Francisco, California 94102
or
U.S. Department of Housing and Urban Development
Assistant Secretary for Equal Opportunity Washington, D.C. 20410

FIGURE 18–3

or ethnic group, he would be in violation of the Code and the law and subject to discipline or prosecution. Any objector to a Realtor's® following that policy would also be subjecting himself to discipline under the Code or prosecution under the law. Material regarding fair housing is available from any office of the Fair Employment Practice Commission. In most of the printed matter available from the FEPC, the point is stressed that the purpose of these laws is not to force any landlord, manager, owner, or agent to lower the standards he applies consistently with regard to the property under his control, but merely to prevent discrimination based solely on race, color, religion, national origin, or ancestry.

Included in the Regulations of the Real Estate Commissioner are sections 2780 and 2781 which deal with discrimination and panic selling. In July 1977 the commissioner added additional personnel to the antidiscrimination enforcement program and urged full compliance with the law by all real estate licensees.

Figure 18–3 illustrates a poster that by law is required to be displayed by any bank, savings and loan association, or other mortgage lender and in all real estate brokerage offices, and subdivision model homes.

QUESTIONS FOR DISCUSSION

1. Discuss the implications of zoning ordinances in your own community.
2. What is meant by a nonconforming use in connection with zoning?
3. Discuss the basic advantages of a good city planning program.
4. How many examples can you give of condemnation of private property for public use in your own community?
5. How may a local community engage in urban renewal in compliance with the Housing Act passed by Congress?
6. In what way is the Factory-Built Housing Law intended to help provide more housing in California?
7. Discuss the possible advantages and disadvantages of uniform codes for housing construction.
8. Are there any specialized materials or methods of construction that can be said to be peculiar to your local area?
9. How should the real estate licensee conduct himself with respect to problems that may arise in connection with fair housing laws?
10. In what areas of housing do you feel government controls have been too excessive, and where might the need for an increase in such controls exist?

MULTIPLE CHOICE QUESTIONS

18–1. An owner who wishes to begin construction or alteration work must obtain: *(a)* a building permit, *(b)* a property appraisal, *(c)* an occupancy certificate, *(d)* none of these.

18–2. The basic intent in designating a neighborhood as a conservation area is to: *(a)* require existing buildings to comply with building codes, *(b)* conserve water, *(c)* clear slum areas, *(d)* none of these.

18–3. California counties are required by law to establish: *(a)* real estate licensing laws, *(b)* a planning commission, *(c)* an irrigation district, *(d)* none of these.

18–4. The various uses to which real property may be put is regulated by: *(a)* California planning laws, *(b)* urban construction laws, *(c)* zoning ordinances, *(d)* none of these.

18–5. Laws with respect to racial discrimination: *(a)* vary between counties, *(b)* affect certain types of properties, *(c)* permit discrimination if owner acts as principal, *(d)* none of these.

18–6. Factory housing construction is regulated by the: *(a)* State Housing Act, *(b)* City Planning Commission, *(c)* State Department of Housing and Community Development, *(d)* none of these.

18–7. Basic construction and occupancy requirements pertaining to residential construction in California are specified by: *(a)* contractor license law, *(b)* State Planning Commission, *(c)* the State Housing Law, *(d)* none of these.

18–8. An irrigation district: *(a)* provides water stock to county agricultural districts, *(b)* sets agricultural building requirements, *(c)* regulates water conservation and production, *(d)* none of these.

19 Land development and subdivisions

California is one of the fastest-growing states in the United States, with a population of nearly 25 million and accounting for approximately 10 percent of the nation's population. With the continued growth of population and the movement of people into the cities and suburban areas, new problems arise that only concerted public effort through governmental action can solve. These problems include the prevention of fraud, misrepresentation, and deceit in the sale of subdivided property; the regulation of lot design and physical improvements for the orderly and proper development of the community; the construction of streets and highways and parking facilities adequate for motorized society; the provision of an adequate supply of water; the protection of life and property by police and firemen; the regulation of pollution and purification of the air we breathe; the abatement of noise; the disposal of sewage and waste; and the provision of essential utility services.

BASIC SUBDIVISION LAWS

The two basic laws under which subdivisions are regulated in California are the Subdivision Map Act, which is contained in the Government Code, as well as the Subdivided Lands Act (California Real Estate Law).

The Subdivided Lands Act (California Real Estate Law), which the Real Estate Commissioner administers, is designed primarily to protect the purchasing public from misrepresentation, deceit, and fraud in the sale of new subdivisions by disclosing to the prospective purchaser the pertinent facts concerning the project. The law requires that the results of the Commissioner's investigation of the subdivision be submitted to each prospective purchaser in the form of a public report covering the condition of the subdivision and its sales plan. It also gives the Commissioner the responsibility of ensuring that the seller of subdivision parcels can deliver them as represented to the purchasing public. The property may be located in California or any other state or country, but if sales are proposed to be made in California, the Real Estate Commissioner has jurisdiction.

The State Subdivision Map Act regulates the filing of subdivision maps with the recorder in the county in which the land is located and provides a definition of terms and an outline of methods of subdivision filing procedure applicable on a statewide basis. This is primarily an overall statewide enabling act permitting the enactment of subdivision ordinances by local governmental authorities having direct jurisdiction over subdivisions in the communities affected, within the limitations and scope set forth in the act.

This act has two major objectives: *(a)* to coordinate the subdivision plans and planning, including lot design, street patterns, and rights of way for drainage and sewers with the community pattern and plan as laid out by the local planning authorities, and *(b)* to ensure that the areas dedicated for public purposes by the filing of the subdivision maps, including public streets and other public areas, will be properly improved initially by the subdivider so that they will not become an undue burden in the future upon the general taxpayers of the community. Most new California subdivisions are additionally subject to the requirements of recently enacted environmental laws discussed in Chapter 18.

TYPES OF SUBDIVISIONS

A subdivision is essentially defined as improved or unimproved land divided for the purpose of sale, lease, or financing, whether immediate or future, into five or more parcels. This includes not only residential land but also the sale or lease of lands used for any purpose, including business, industry, recreation, or agriculture. Excepted from the definition is the leasing of apartments, offices, or stores or space in an apartment, industrial, or commercial building. Certain exceptions which may be found in the Subdivision Map Act do not extend to the subdivision provisions of the real estate law administered by the commissioner.

With respect to ownership interest, subdivisions may be classified as follows:

Standard. A land division with no common or mutual rights of either ownership or use among the various owners of the individual parcels created by the division.

Common interest. Individuals own or lease a separate lot or unit, or an interest therein, together with an undivided interest in the common areas of the entire project, which common areas are usually governed by a homeowners association. These subdivisions vary both in physical design and statutory form. Condominiums, planned developments, stock cooperatives, and community apartment projects are examples, as are time-sharing projects.

Undivided interests. The purchaser receives an undivided interest in a parcel of land as a tenant in common with all the other owners. All owners have the nonexclusive right to the use and occupancy of the property. A recreational vehicle park, with campground and other recreational amenities is an example.

Land project. Briefly, it is a remote area subdivision of 50 or more parcels without onsite improvements, with less than 1,500 registered voters residing within certain distances from the subdivision.

Standard subdivision

The standard subdivision consisting of five or more parcels is the most common type. Usually, unimproved lots in the subdivision have been developed with the necessary utilities installed. The market for lots in a standard subdivision generally consists of people interested in building their own homes and building contractors who purchase one or more lots for building and sale. Many develop-

ers construct the dwellings themselves and offer a completed package with the financing arranged for the purchasers. While the majority of subdivisions might be classified as lot and residential subdivisions, there are the resort and recreational land subdivisions where lots are usually offered to persons who propose to build a retirement home or a second vacation home. Another type of subdivision occurs when the subdivider has the intention of creating an industrial or commercial complex.

Planned development project

A planned development is similar to a standard subdivision, having in addition, however, lots or areas owned in common and reserved for the use of some or all of the owners of the separately owned lots. Townhouses are often found in planned development projects. Townhouses have common or party walls and are often grouped in cluster patterns. Generally, an owners' association with powers to enforce any obligation in connection with membership is set up as a vehicle to provide management, maintenance, and control of the common areas. A planned development contains five or more lots.

Community apartment project

Community apartment projects, or cooperative apartment houses as they are sometimes called, are subdivisions. Operation, maintenance, and control are usually exercised by a governing board elected by the owners of the fractional interests. In a community apartment project an undivided interest in the property is conveyed, coupled with the right to occupy a certain unit or apartment. Community apartment projects having two or more apartments are within the definition of a subdivision.

Condominium project

Prior to 1963, the word *condominium* did not appear anywhere in the California statutes. Condominiums were treated as subdivisions under the Business and Professions Code, but no special legislation had been passed to provide answers to the several legal problems presented to title companies, tax authorities, insurance companies, and others by this variant from conventional development. The 1963 legislature moved to close this gap by enacting statutes that defined *condomin-*

ium and added provisions to the Civil Code, Business and Professions Code, and Revenue and Taxation Code dealing specifically with this particular type of ownership.

The Civil Code in Section 783 defines a condominium as "an estate in real property consisting of an undivided interest in common in a portion of a parcel of real property together with a separate interest in space in a residential, industrial or commercial building on such real property, such as an apartment, office or store." A condominium, it continues, "may include, in addition, a separate interest in other portions of such property." In effect, this provides that a purchaser of a condominium owns in fee simple the air space in which his particular unit is situated, has a deed thereto, gets a separate tax assessment, may apply for and acquire a title insurance policy on his property, may indeed deal with it as he would with any real property. In addition to this, he has an undivided interest in common in certain other defined sectors of the whole property involved. Here again, an elected governing board performs the management function. Condominium projects having two or more condominiums or units are within the definition of a subdivision.

Stock cooperative project

A stock cooperative is a corporation that is formed or availed of primarily for the purpose of holding title to improved real property, either in fee simple or for a term of years. An essential element is that all or substantially all of the shareholders of such a corporation receive a right of exclusive occupancy of a portion of the real property, title to which is held by the corporation. This right of occupancy is transferable only concurrently with the transfer of the share or shares of stock in the corporation held by the person having such right of occupancy.

Prior to September 1965, jurisdiction over stock cooperative projects was exercised by the Commissioner of Corporations. Then a subdivider was required to obtain a permit to sell securities. Jurisdiction at the state level is now vested solely in the Real Estate Commissioner, and sales agents are now only required to have a real estate salesperson or real estate broker license in order to list and sell such holdings for compensation. Most stock cooperative projects are of the apartment house type, operating with a board of directors. A number of these projects provide community recreation facilities for the benefit of the members. Stock cooperative projects having two or more shareholders are within the definition of a subdivision.

A different kind of cooperative project is a sales type project. In this plan each individual purchaser becomes a stockholder in a cooperative housing corporation that is organized for the purpose of financing and constructing the entire project of dwellings on individual lots. The buyer is an investor, and does not receive title to an individual lot until after completion of the entire project. Individual loans are made on each improved lot. Following delivery of deeds to all the lots, the cooperative housing corporation is dissolved.

Mobile and manufactured homes

California has been called the most mobile state in the nation. This generally has been with regard to the great amount of automobile and truck travel, but now it also has come to refer to mobile homes. Such homes offer permanent housing and have become a significant factor in the housing industry. Federal legislation now generally uses the term manufactured home rather than mobile home. The sale or lease of five or more lots in a mobile home park is within the jurisdiction of the Real Estate Commissioner and the provisions of the Subdivided Lands Act apply.

Section 18214 of the Mobile Home Parks Act defines a mobile home park as any area or tract of land where one or more mobile home lots are rented or leased. The rental of individual lots in a mobile home park is within the jurisdiction of the State Department of Housing and Community Development.

The Real Estate Law allows real estate brokers to list, sell, or exchange certain mobile homes and manufactured or factory-built housing.

Although the terms mobile, manufactured, factory-built, prefabricated, and modular housing each refers to certain technical differences with respect to construction and detail, these terms are often used interchangeably, and any such housing which is placed on a permanent foundation and site is considered to be real property and is taxed as such.

Mineral, oil, and gas subdivisions

No public report on a mineral, oil, or gas subdivision has been issued in California for a number of years. The Commissioner has adopted special regulations applying to such subdivisions, and certain reports and disclosures are required of the subdivider. See Figure 19–1 p. 274.

Time-share projects

The Business and Professions Code defines a time-share project as a project in which a purchaser receives the right in perpetuity, for life, or for a term of years, to the recurrent, exclusive use or occupancy of a lot, parcel, unit, or segment of real property, annually or on some other periodic basis, for a period of time that has been or will be allotted for the use or occupancy periods into which the project has been divided.

Such projects have become popular in recent years, especially with respect to vacation and recreational areas. A time-sharing program involves long-term rights to use and occupy real property for short-term periods into which the property has been divided; for example, the right to use a dwelling unit for two weeks of each year for the next 10 years. In some cases, a time-share purchaser acquires an undivided interest in the real property as well as the periodic use right, and this is termed a time-share estate. In other cases, the purchaser acquires only a right to use, and this is termed a time-share use. In either case, the right to use may be specified, for example, the first two full weeks in July of each year or it may be on a first reserved, first served basis.

Time-share projects are considered to be subdivisions if they consist of 12 or more time-share estates or time-share uses having terms of five years or more, or having terms of less than five years which also include options to renew. Time-share offerings in apartments and hotel or motel rooms are included as are time-share estate offerings in real property that is not a structural dwelling place such as campgrounds and recreational vehicle parks. A public report must be obtained before sales of 12 or more time-share interests in real property can be made within the state of California.

Land projects

The California legislature has found that sales of lots in some subdivisions located in sparsely populated areas of the state have occurred as the result of intensive promotional efforts which tend to obscure the highly speculative nature of the offerings. Such subdivisions are referred to as land projects and contain 50 or more parcels.

To protect the public, laws have been enacted which grant authority to the Real Estate Commissioner to require that reasonable arrangements be made to assure completion and maintenance of improvements in such types of subdivision offerings and to determine that the probable continuing financial burden with respect to the financing of completion and maintenance of such improvements bears a reasonable relationship to the value of lots within such subdivisions.

There is further public protection by provisions requiring advance delivery of the public report to lot purchasers, affording purchasers a right to rescind any purchase agreement within a limited time period.

Out-of-state subdivisions

The Business and Professions Code provides that the offering, sale, or lease within California of lots or parcels in a subdivision situated outside the state of California shall be governed by the real property securities sections of the Real Estate Law, as well as by the regular subdivision law. An out-of-state subdivision requires a real property securities permit as well as the usual Commissioner's public report before it can be offered for sale in California. Before the permit and public report on an out-of-state subdivision are issued, the commissioner applies a "fair, just, and equitable" test to the property proposed for sale just as he would in the case of any real property security.

PROCEDURES PRESCRIBED BY SUBDIVISION MAP ACT

The Subdivision Map Act requires the developer of a proposed subdivision to file a subdivision map with the proper authorities, and it must contain certain specified information. The subjects of concern to local governing authorities include physical features and boundaries, accessibility, neighboring properties, drainage, flood hazards, geologic hazards, disposal of sewage, water supply and utilities. Although the term *map* is used in the singular, it actually refers to a number of maps, each of which provides certain information.

Property line or boundary survey map

This is the primary map of the property and should show the following information:

272

a. Bearings and distances of all boundaries.
b. Location and dimensions of connecting and adjacent streets and tracts.
c. Any encroachments on the property as well as easements within and contiguous to the property.
d. Names of record owners or reference to recorded subdivisions of adjacent property.
e. All monuments found or set that determine the boundary or boundary references.
f. Computed areas and other special data pertinent to the parcel.

The property line or boundary survey map may be prepared from record data for preliminary purposes without including all of the suggested modifications above, but will have to be made precise and include the above information at the time the final map is prepared.

Topographic map

The topographic map should show the physical features of the property as follows:

a. Elevations or contours to show adequately the topography of the property.
b. Location and elevations of all structures such as buildings, bridges, wall, culverts, and the like.
c. Location and elevations of all physical features such as roads, watercourses, marsh or pond areas, and rock outcrops.
d. Location and size of wooded areas and trees.
e. Location of test pits or borings if required.

Public utilities map

The availability of water, sanitary and storm sewers, telephones, electricity, gas, and public transportation are important factors in site selection. This information can be compiled on a utilities map, but is more commonly combined with the topographic map. The following data should be shown:

a. All utility easements and rights of way.
b. Location, size, and invert elevations of all parts of the storm and sanitary sewer systems.
c. Location and size of all underground conduits for water, gas, steam, and electricity.
d. Location of public transportation, police and fire alarms, and similar facilities.

Site location map

It is advisable for the subdivider to have a site location map that will show the following:

a. Highway and street pattern.
b. Size and extent of commercial establishments.
c. Character of neighboring area and employment potentials.
d. Location of churches, schools, and recreational facilities.
e. Zoning and areas of jurisdiction.
f. Aerial photographs of the general area and any other special features that pertain to the site location.

TENTATIVE MAP FILING

After tentative maps of a proposed subdivision have been prepared and the subdivider has met all prefiling requirements of the local planning commission, he is ready to file the number of copies specified by local ordinance with the planning agency, or the clerk of the city council or of the board of supervisors, as the case may be. Most large jurisdictions within the state of California have established planning agencies whose duty it is to make investigations and reports on the design and improvements of the proposed tract. The agency transmits a copy of the map to other departments and agencies having an interest in land subdivision, such as the road department, health department, flood control district, parks and recreation department, or the local school department.

A copy is also sent to the Real Estate Commissioner and the city or county surveyor, depending upon the jurisdiction in which the tract is located. A city or county adjacent to the area in which the proposed tract is located may desire to make recommendations regarding its approval although the subdivision is outside its jurisdiction. If the tract is bounded or traversed by a state highway, the district engineer of the Division of Highways or the state Department of Public Works is also sent a copy of the map.

Recommendations

The notified officials study the map with regard to special departmental concerns and report their findings to the planning agency. The reports may recommend approval, conditional approval if certain conditions are met, or disapproval. An opportunity may be provided for the subdivider to meet with representatives of all interested departments as a group or individually to discuss his proposed tract and the conditions recommended for approval.

Decision on map

It is customary for the governing board to authorize an advisory agency, usually the planning commission, to report its action on a map direct to the subdivider. If no planning agency exists, the governing board must decide upon the map after it has been received from the clerk of the governing board. The recommendation in each case will be either approval, conditional approval, or disapproval. Conditional approval means that the subdivider must meet the conditions recommended.

Appeal

If the subdivider is dissatisfied with the decision reached by the planning commission, he may appeal to the city council or the board of supervisors, or an appeal board if such has been established.

FINAL MAP PREPARATION

In the event of approval or conditional approval by the agency or governing board, the subdivider is allowed a period of 12 months for the preparation and recordation of a final map, which may be prepared in units or as a whole. In cases where difficult problems arise in meeting the conditions of approval, the subdivider may be granted an extension of time not to exceed an additional 18 months. If the tract is not recorded within this time, it must be resubmitted as a tentative map.

Following approval or conditional approval of the tentative map, the subdivider is ready to begin preparation of the final map. This is an accurate and detailed map prepared by a registered civil engineer or licensed surveyor and based upon his accurate survey of the land. The map should conform to all specifications of the Subdivision Map Act, the local ordinances on subdivisions, and the conditions imposed with the approval. All streets within the tract must be named and all lots designated in detail. In addition, the local ordinance usually requires the preparation of detailed road, sanitary sewer, and other utility and drainage plans.

Certificates

The Subdivision Map Act requires that several certificates appear on the final map. One certificate is the owners' certificate consenting to the preparation and recordation of the final map. This certificate also offers certain parcels of land for dedication for specified public uses. This is signed and acknowledged by all parties having any recorded title interest in the land subdivided, with the exception that the signatures of parties owning certain types of interests such as easements, rights of way, or mineral rights may be omitted if their names and the nature of their respective interests are endorsed on the map.

In addition, there must be a certificate for execution by the clerk of each governing political unit that considers the tract, stating that this board approved the map and accepted or rejected any parcels offered for dedication. A certificate by the engineer or surveyor who made the survey and prepared the final map is also required.

Taxes and assessments

Before filing the final map a subdivider must file with the clerk of the governing political unit in which the subdivision is located a certificate showing that no liens against the tract exist for unpaid state, county, municipal, or local taxes, or special assessments collected as taxes.

Improvements

Prior to approval of the final map the subdivider will be required to improve or agree to improve portions of land to be used for public or private streets, highways, ways, and easements necessary for the use of lot owners in the subdivision and for local traffic and drainage needs.

Final map filing and recordation

After all conditions and requirements have been met and all certificates that appear on the final map have been signed, it may be filed with the appropriate jurisdiction in which the subdivision is located for approval by the governing political unit.

After the map is approved, it is accepted for recordation. A copy is transmitted to the clerk and recorder of the jurisdiction. At the time of recordation the subdivider must furnish a certifi-

Preliminary Planning

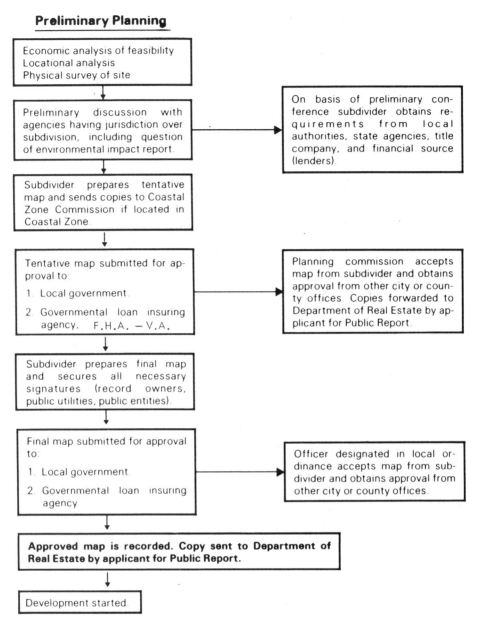

FIGURE 19–1
Basic Outline of Subdivision Map Preparation and Approval

cate of title guaranteeing that the parties consenting to recordation actually include all those having any record title interest in the land to be subdivided.

Parcel maps

Article 6 of the Map Act provides for the use of the parcel map and requirement for its preparation and recordation. Local ordinances may provide certain conditions for maps when land is so divided that it does not fall into the subdivision definition. Parcel maps may be required when any piece of land is divided into two or more parcels, and the maps must be prepared by a registered civil engineer or a licensed land surveyor. A parcel map must usually be submitted to the county surveyor or city engineer for examination prior to filing for record.

PROCEDURES PRESCRIBED BY CALIFORNIA SUBDIVIDED LANDS ACT

The California Subdivided Lands Act is the subdivision law that the Real Estate Commissioner enforces and, as was explained at the beginning of this chapter, is designed to protect the public from misrepresentation, deceit, and fraud. This is done by the issuance of a Commissioner's public report that must be provided to any prospective purchaser by the owner, subdivider, or his agent.

Subdivision questionnaire requirements

Before subdivided land can be sold or leased, a notice of intention must be filed with the Commissioner. Usually, the notice of intention is incorporated into the subdivision questionnaire form that has been prepared by the Department of Real Estate. When anyone proposes to issue promissory notes secured by individual lots in an unrecorded subdivision, a notice of intention must also be filed with the commissioner.

With regard to the subdivision questionnaire, the law says a filing may be by the owner, subdivider, or their agent. Usually, however, the owner assumes this responsibility. In most cases the owner and subdivider are the same, but sometimes the owner will turn over the development of the land to someone else and will give necessary authority to offer it for sale. The second party is then known as the subdivider, and if he does the filing for the owner he must have the written authorization of the owner to do so.

In some cases, the subdivider does not handle the selling program and an agent comes into the picture. The agent must be a licensed real estate broker, and anyone, except the owner himself, who sells the properties must be licensed as a broker or salesman. Even salaried employees of the owner or subdivider must be licensed to do such selling legally.

Questionnaire information and form

The subdivider need not wait until he has complied with all the local requirements before he files his questionnaire. He may start with an incomplete filing at any time after he has decided how he plans to lay out the subdivision. When an incomplete filing is made, the subdivider can furnish additional information and documents as the arrangements progress. Filing early may have the advantage of allowing the investigatory work to proceed as the development is completed, and

thus allow issuance of the final report at approximately the same time that the subdivision is ready for sale to the public. Subdivision questionnaires are filed at the Department of Real Estate district office responsible for the territory where the subdivision is located, and out-of-state subdivision questionnaires should be filed at the principal office in Sacramento. Various fees and charges are made depending upon the type of subdivision and number of lots.

Different questionnaires are supplied by the Department of Real Estate for standard subdivisions, condominiums, community apartments, planned developments, stock cooperative projects, mineral, oil, and gas subdivisions, and out-of-state subdivisions. Many requirements apply to all subdivision filings, but the varying nature of the types of subdivisions calls for special information and documentation that may differ depending upon the type of subdivision. The general information that the Commissioner requires of all subdivision filings is concerned with:

a. On-site or off-site conditions that may affect the intended use of the land.
b. Provisions for essential utilities, such as water supply and sewage disposal.
c. The nature of the on-site improvements, existing or proposed.
d. The condition of title, including any restrictions or reservations affecting building, use, or occupancy.
e. The financing of community, recreational, or other common facilities, if any.
f. The terms and conditions of sales or leases.
g. The ability of the subdivider to deliver the interest contracted for.
h. The method of conveyance.
i. Any representations of guarantees or warranties made as part of a sales program.

COMMISSIONER'S FINAL SUBDIVISION PUBLIC REPORT

The Commissioner's Final Subdivision Public Report must be obtained before offering the property for sale or lease and must be delivered to the prospective purchaser, and a receipt on an approved form must be obtained. An example of such a report is shown in Figure 19–2. The approved form of a receipt for public report is shown in Figure 19–3. Receipts must be kept on file for the commissioner's inspection for at least three years.

DEPARTMENT OF REAL ESTATE
OF THE
STATE OF CALIFORNIA

In the matter of the application of

CADILLAC FAIRVIEW HOMES WEST -
CALIFORNIA, a Partnership

for a Final Subdivision Public Report on

CROWN COLONY

SAN MATEO COUNTY, CALIFORNIA

CONDOMINIUM
FINAL SUBDIVISION
PUBLIC REPORT

FILE NO. 17,706 SF

ISSUED: APRIL 25, 1982

EXPIRES: APRIL 24, 1987

This Report Is Not a Recommendation or Endorsement of the Subdivision
But Is Informative Only.

Buyer or Lessee Must Sign That He Has Received and Read This Report.

This Report Expires on Date Shown Above. If There Has Been a Material Change in the Offering, an Amended Public Report Must Be Obtained and Used in Lieu of This Report.

Section 35700 of the California Health and Safety Code provides that the practice of discrimination because of race, color, religion, sex, marital status, national origin or ancestry in housing accommodations is against public policy.

Under Section 125.6 of the California Business and Professions Code, California real estate licensees are subject to disciplinary action by the Real Estate Commissioner if they make any discrimination, distinction or restriction in negotiating a sale or lease of real property because of the race, color, sex, religion, ancestry or national origin of the prospective buyer. If any prospective buyer or lessee believes that a licensee is guilty of such conduct, he or she should contact the Department of Real Estate.

Information Regarding Schools can be found on **Page 6**.

READ THE ENTIRE REPORT on the following pages before contracting to purchase a lot in this SUBDIVISION.

R/E Form 618
10/76

Page 1 of 6 Pages

3000-003 11-77 25M 08P

FIGURE 19–2

COMMON INTEREST SUBDIVISION GENERAL INFORMATION

The project described in the attached Subdivision Public Report is known as a common-interest subdivision. **Read the Public Report carefully** for more information about the type of subdivision. The subdivision includes common areas and facilities which will be owned and/or operated by an owners' association. **Purchase of a lot or unit automatically entitles and obligates you as a member of the association and, in most cases, includes a beneficial interest in the areas and facilities.** Since membership in the association is mandatory, **you should be aware of the following information before you purchase:**

Your ownership in this development and your rights and remedies as a member of its association will be controlled by governing instruments which generally include a Declaration of Restrictions (also known as CC&R's), Articles of Incorporation (or association) and Bylaws. The provisions of these documents are intended to be, and in most cases are, enforceable in a court of law. Study these documents carefully before entering into a contract to purchase a subdivision interest.

In order to provide funds for operation and maintenance of the common facilities, **the association will levy assessments against your lot/unit. If you are delinquent in the payment of assessments, the association may enforce payment through court proceedings or your lot/unit may be liened and sold through the exercise of a power of sale.** The anticipated income and expenses of the association, including the amount that you may expect to pay through assessments, are outlined in the proposed budget. Ask to see a copy of the budget if the subdivider has not already made it available for your examination.

A homeowner association provides a vehicle for the ownership and use of recreational and other common facilities which were designed to attract you to buy in this subdivision. The association also provides a means to accomplish architectural control and to provide a base for homeowner interaction on a variety of issues. **The purchaser of an interest in a common-interest subdivision should contemplate active participation in the affairs of the association.** He or she should be willing to serve on the board of directors or on committees created by the board. In short, "they" in a common-interest subdivision is "you". Unless you serve as a member of the governing board or on a committee appointed by the board, your control of the operation of the common areas and facilities is limited to your vote as a member of the association. There are actions that can be taken by the governing body without a vote of the members of the association which can have a **significant impact upon the quality of life for association members.**

Until there is a sufficient number of purchasers of lots or units in a common-interest subdivision to elect a majority of the governing body, it is likely that the subdivider will effectively control the affairs of the association. It is frequently necessary and equitable that the subdivider do so during the early stages of development. **It is vitally important to the owners of individual subdivision interests that the transition from subdivider to resident-owner control be accomplished in an orderly manner and in a spirit of cooperation.

When contemplating the purchase of a dwelling in a common-interest subdivision, you should consider factors beyond the attractiveness of the dwelling units themselves. Study the governing instruments and give careful thought to whether you will be able to exist happily in an atmosphere of cooperative living where the interests of the group must be taken into account as well as the interests of the individual. Remember that managing a common-interest subdivision is very much like governing a small community . . . the management can serve you well, but you will have to work for its success.** DRE

File No. 17,706 SF   Page 2 of 6 Pages

FIGURE 19–2 *(continued)*

278

SPECIAL NOTES

THIS PROJECT IS A COMMON-INTEREST SUBDIVISION OF THE TYPE REFERRED TO
AS A CONDOMINIUM. IT WILL BE OPERATED BY AN INCORPORATED OWNERS
ASSOCIATION.

SINCE THE COMMON PROPERTY AND FACILITIES WILL BE MAINTAINED BY AN
ASSOCIATION OF HOMEOWNERS, AND IT'S ESSENTIAL THAT THIS ASSOCIATION BE
FORMED EARLY AND PROPERLY, THE DEVELOPER MUST:

1. PAY ALL THE MONTHLY ASSESSMENTS WHICH HE OWES TO THE HOMEOWNERS
    ASSOCIATION FOR UNSOLD UNITS -- THE PAYMENTS MUST COMMENCE IMME-
    DIATELY AFTER SUBDIVIDER CLOSES FIRST SALE (Regulations 2792.9 and
    2792.16).

THE HOMEOWNER ASSOCIATION MUST:

2. CAUSE THE FIRST ELECTION OF THE ASSOCIATION'S GOVERNING BODY TO BE
    HELD WITHIN 45 DAYS AFTER 51% SELL-OUT, OR IN ANY EVENT, NO LATER
    THAN SIX MONTHS AFTER CLOSING THE FIRST SALE. (Regulations
    2792.17 and 2792.19); AND

3. PREPARE AND DISTRIBUTE TO ALL HOMEOWNERS A BALANCE SHEET AND
    INCOME STATEMENT. (Regulation 2792.22).

THE SUBDIVIDER STATED THAT HE WILL PROVIDE YOU WITH A COPY OF THE
ARTICLES OF INCORPORATION, RESTRICTIONS AND BYLAWS, BY POSTING THEM IN
A PROMINENT LOCATION IN THE SALES OFFICE AND/OR FURNISHING YOU COPIES
PRIOR TO CLOSE OF ESCROW. THESE DOCUMENTS CONTAIN NUMEROUS MATERIAL
PROVISIONS THAT SUBSTANTIALLY AFFECT AND CONTROL YOUR RIGHTS, PRIVI-
LEGES, USE OBLIGATIONS, AND COSTS OF MAINTENANCE AND OPERATION. YOU
SHOULD READ AND UNDERSTAND THESE DOCUMENTS BEFORE YOU OBLIGATE YOUR-
SELF TO PURCHASE A UNIT.

THE SUBDIVIDER STATED HE WILL FURNISH THE CURRENT BOARD OF OFFICERS OF
THE HOMEOWNERS ASSOCIATION THE BUILDING PLANS TO INCLUDE DIAGRAMS OF
LOCATION OF MAJOR COMPONENTS, UTILITIES AND RELATED DATA.

THESE ITEMS WILL BE IMPORTANT TO THE BOARD OF OFFICERS OR THOSE WHO
WILL MANAGE OR REPAIR COMMON FACILITIES IN THIS SUBDIVISION.

File No. 17,706 SF   Page 3 of 6 Pages

FIGURE 19–2 *(continued)*

IF YOU PURCHASE TWO OR MORE UNITS YOU MAY BE REQUIRED TO OBTAIN
AMENDED PUBLIC REPORT BEFORE OFFERING TWO OR MORE OF THE UNITS FOR
SALE TO OTHERS. IF YOU INTEND TO SELL TWO OR MORE UNITS OR LEASE THEM
FOR MORE THAN ONE YEAR, YOU ARE REQUIRED TO OBTAIN AN AMENDED SUBDI-
VISION PUBLIC REPORT BEFORE YOU CAN OFFER THE UNITS FOR SALE OR
LEASE.

WARNING: WHEN YOU SELL YOUR CONDOMINIUM UNIT TO SOMEONE ELSE, YOU
MUST GIVE THAT PERSON A COPY OF THE DECLARATION OF RESTRICTIONS, THE
ARTICLES OF INCORPORATION, AND OF THE BYLAWS. IF YOU FORGET TO DO
THIS, IT MAY COST YOU A PENALTY OF $500.00 -- PLUS ATTORNEY'S FEES
PLUS DAMAGES. (SEE CIVIL CODE SECTION 1360).

INTERESTS TO BE CONVEYED: You will receive title to a specified unit,
together with undivided fractional interest as tenant in common in the
common area together with a membership in the Crown Colony Homeowners
Association and rights to use the common area.

LOCATION AND SIZE: This subdivision is located at Junipero Sierra Blvd.
and Hickey Blvd. within the city limits of Daly City and is serviced by
the usual city amenities.

This is a condominium which consists of approximately 23.685 acres on
which twenty seven buildings containing 920 units and 1362 parking
spaces have been constructed, together with common facilities consisting
of private streets, a recreation center, 2 swimming pools, tennis
courts, landscaping which have been constructed.

The subdivider has posted a bond into escrow to assure completion of
renovation work.

MANAGEMENT AND OPERATION: The Crown Colony Homeowners Association,
which you must join, will manage and operate the common area(s) in
accordance with the Restrictions, Articles of Incorporation, and
the Bylaws.

MAINTENANCE AND OPERATIONAL EXPENSES: The subdivider has submitted a
budget for the maintenance and operation of the common areas and for
long-term reserves. This proposed budget was reviewed by the Department
of Real Estate, in March, 1980, but you should obtain a copy of this
proposed budget from the subdivider. Under this proposed budget, the
average monthly assessment against each subdivision unit is estimated at
$88.05 of which $9.53 is to be a monthly contribution to long-term
reserves and is not to be used to pay for current operating expenses.
Actual expenses vary from $76.62 to $147.47 per unit per month.

File No. 17,706 SF   Page 4 of 6 Pages

FIGURE 19–2 *(continued)*

IF THE FINAL, APPROVED BUDGET FURNISHED TO YOU BY THE DEVELOPER SHOWS
A MONTHLY ASSESSMENT FIGURE WHICH VARIES 10% OR MORE FROM THE AS-
SESSMENT AMOUNT SHOWN IN THIS PUBLIC REPORT, YOU SHOULD CONTACT THE
DEPARTMENT OF REAL ESTATE BEFORE ENTERING INTO AN AGREEMENT TO PURCHASE.

The association may increase or decrease assessments at any time in
accordance with the procedure prescribed in the proposed CC&R's or
Bylaws. In considering the advisability of a decrease (or a smaller
increase) in assessments, care should be taken not to eliminate
amounts attributable to reserves for replacement or major maintenance.

   THE BUDGET INFORMATION INCLUDED IN THIS PUBLIC REPORT IS APPLICABLE
   AS OF THE DATE OF BUDGET REVIEW AS SHOWN ABOVE. EXPENSES OF
   OPERATION ARE DIFFICULT TO PREDICT ACCURATELY AND EVEN IF ACCUR-
   ATELY ESTIMATED INITIALLY, MOST EXPENSES INCREASE WITH THE AGE OF
   FACILITIES AND WITH INCREASES IN COST OF LIVING.

Monthly assessments will commence on all units during the month
following the closing of the first sale of a unit. From that time,
the subdivider is required to pay the association a monthly assessment
for each unit which he owns.

The remedies available to the association against owners who are
delinquent in the payment of assessments are set forth in the CC&R's.
These remedies are available against the subdivider as well as against
other owners.

The subdivider has posted a bond as partial security for his obligation
to pay these assessments. The governing body of the association
should assure itself that the subdivider has satisfied his obligations
to the association with respect to the payment of assessments before
agreeing to a release or exoneration of the security.

This development is a conversion of an existing apartment to condominium use. The structure is 6 years old.

EASEMENTS: Easements for utilities and other purposes are shown on the
title report and subdivision map recorded in the Office of the
San Mateo County Recorder, in Book 83 of Maps, Pages 21-24.

RESTRICTIONS: This subdivision is subject to restrictions to be
recorded in the Office of the San Mateo County Recorder, in Reel 7952 at
Image 1582, Official Records, and is subject to Condominium Plan recorded in Reel 7952, at Image 1675, Official Records.

File No. 17,706 SF   Page 5 of 6 Pages

FIGURE 19-2 *(continued)*

FOR INFORMATION AS TO YOUR OBLIGATIONS AND RIGHTS, YOU SHOULD READ THE RESTRICTIONS. THE SUBDIVIDER SHOULD MAKE THEM AVAILABLE TO YOU.

TAXES: The maximum amount of any tax on real property that can be collected annually by counties is 1% of the full cash value of the property. With the addition of interest and redemption charges on any indebtedness, approved by voters prior to July 1, 1978, the total property tax rate in most counties is approximately 1.25% of the full cash value.

For the purchaser of a lot or unit in this subdivision, the "full cash value" of the lot or unit will be the valuation, as reflected on the tax roll, determined by the county assessor as of the date of purchase of the lot or unit or as of the date of completion of an improvement on the lot if that occurs after the date of purchase.

PURCHASE MONEY HANDLING: The subdivider must impound all funds received from you in escrow depository until legal title is delivered to you. (Ref. Section 11013.2(a) of the Business and Professions Code). If the escrow has not closed on your lot within six (6) months of the date of your deposit receipt, you may request return of your deposit.

GEOLOGIC CONDITIONS: THE UNIFORM BUILDING CODE, CHAPTER 70, PROVIDES FOR LOCAL BUILDING OFFICIALS TO EXERCISE PREVENTIVE MEASURES DURING GRADING TO ELIMINATE OR MINIMIZE DAMAGE FROM GEOLOGIC HAZARDS SUCH AS LANDSLIDES, FAULT MOVEMENTS, EARTHQUAKE SHAKING, RAPID EROSION OR SUBSIDENCE. THIS SUBDIVISION IS LOCATED IN AN AREA WHERE SOME OF THESE HAZARDS MAY EXIST. SOME CALIFORNIA COUNTIES AND CITIES HAVE ADOPTED ORDINANCES THAT MAY OR MAY NOT BE AS EFFECTIVE IN THE CONTROL OF GRADING AND SITE PREPARATION.

PURCHASERS MAY DISCUSS WITH THE DEVELOPER, THE DEVELOPER'S ENGINEER, THE ENGINEERING GEOLOGIST, AND THE LOCAL BUILDING OFFICIALS TO DETER-MINE IF THE ABOVE-MENTIONED HAZARDS HAVE BEEN CONSIDERED AND IF THERE HAS BEEN ADEQUATE COMPLIANCE WITH CHAPTER 70 OR AN EQUIVALENT OR MORE STRINGENT GRADING ORDINANCE DURING THE CONSTRUCTION OF THIS SUBDIVISION.

PUBLIC TRANSPORTATION: There is a Sam Trans Bus stop at Gellert and Hickey, approximately 1/4 mile from the subdivision.

For further information in regard to this subdivision, you may call (415) 557-0486, or examine the documents at the Department of Real Estate 185 Berry Street, Room 5816, San Francisco, CA 94107.

CWK:vld

File No. 17,706 SF   Page 6 of 6 Pages

FIGURE 19–2 *(concluded)*

FIGURE 19–3

Preliminary public report

A preliminary public report may be issued by the commissioner upon receipt of the filing fee and subdivision questionnaire filing that is complete except for some particular requirement or requirements that is or are at the time not fulfilled, but that it is reasonable to assume will be completed. Preliminary reports and permits are not issued on out-of-state subdivision.

In the event a preliminary public report is issued, the owner, subdivider, or agent may accept a reservation to purchase or lease a lot or parcel in the subdivision under the following conditions:

a. A copy of the preliminary public report has been given to the prospective purchaser, and he has been given an opportunity to read it and his receipt has been taken therefore.

b. A copy of the reservation agreement is signed by the prospective purchaser and by the subdivider or his agent and placed in a neutral escrow depository acceptable to the Commissioner, together with any valuable consideration involved.

c. The reservation to purchase or lease contains a clause allowing the proposed purchaser the option to cancel his reservation at any time and immediately have returned to him without deduction any valuable consideration deposited with the reservation.

d. Any preliminary report issued shall expire when a final report on the same land is published or one year from date of issuance, whichever is sooner.

Material changes

Any material changes in the subdivision or its procedures after the filing is made or the public report is issued must be reported to the Commissioner.

The owner of a standard type subdivision or a planned development must report to the commissioner the sale of five or more parcels to an individual. The sale to a single purchaser of two or more units in a community apartment, condominium, or stock cooperative project must likewise be reported. Failure to report material changes not only violates the law, but may also furnish a basis for recision of purchases through court action.

Grounds for denial of public report

After investigation of a subdivision is completed, the commissioner issues a public report in which findings are incorporated, unless there are grounds for denial. In that case the report is denied and no offerings or sales of the subdivided property can be made until the subdivider has remedied the unsatisfactory conditions. The subdivider has recourse to administrative hearing and the courts if he chooses.

While there are a number of reasons for the denial of a report, the more common grounds for denial are:

a. Failure to comply with any of the provisions of the subdivision law and regulations of the commissioner pertaining thereto.

b. The sale or lease could constitute misrepresentation to or deceit or fraud of the purchasers or lessees.

c. Inability to deliver title or other interest contracted for.

d. Inability to demonstrate that adequate financial arrangements have been made for all off-site improvements included in the offering.

e. Inability to demonstrate that adequate financial arrangements have been made for any community, recreational, or other facilities included in the offering.

f. Failure to make a showing that the parcels can be used for the purpose for which they are offered.

g. Failure to provide in the contract or other writing the use or uses for which the parcels are offered, together with any covenants or conditions relative thereto.

h. Agreements or bylaws to provide for management or other services pertaining to common facilities in the offering that fail to comply with the Commissioner's regulations.

i. Failure to demonstrate that adequate financial arrangements have been made for any guaranty or warranty included in the offering.

j. Inability by the subdivider to demonstrate that the soil within the subdivision has been, or will be, prepared in accordance with the recommendations of a registered civil engineer in such a manner that structural damage is not likely to result.

Desist and refrain orders

Should the commissioner find that any owner, subdivider, or other person is violating any of the subdivision provisions of real estate law or of the regulations pertaining to these provisions, or should investigation reveal evidence that the further sale or lease of lots in a given subdivision would constitute grounds for a denial of the issuance of a public report, then the commissioner may effect the immediate cessation of such violations or the immediate termination of selling or leasing of the property by issuance of an order to desist and refrain from such activity.

CRITERIA FOR ADVERTISING OF SUBDIVISIONS

Since the public is primarily made aware of the offering for sale of lots or units in a subdivision by the use of various forms of advertising, it is important at this point to discuss what the Commissioner considers to be misleading advertising of the type that would lead to the office of the commissioner's issuing an order to cease, desist, and refrain. The items listed below would serve as an excellent checklist for any prospective purchaser of lots or units in a subdivision since they provide an excellent listing of conditions that the purchaser should guard against and fully investigate if he feels that any exist.

The Commissioner may hold to be misleading any advertisement, radio broadcast, or telecast that contains any of the following:

a. The use of a name or trade style which implies that the subdivider or his agent is a bona fide research organization, public bureau, nonprofit group, or other establishment when such is not the case.

b. Reference to any improvements or facilities in the subdivision that do not actually exist or are not yet completed, unless completion is provided for by bonding or other means approved by the Real Estate Commissioner.

c. Reference to streets, roads, sewers, drainage, or other utilities that have not been accepted for maintenance by a public entity, unless such fact is fully disclosed.

d. Reference to the availability of financing for on-site construction, unless written evidence thereof is in the possession of the subdivider.

e. Reference to unimproved subdivided lands as "developments" or "homesites" or other similar expressions, without adequate qualifying phrases.

f. Failure to disclose the true nature of the roads.

g. Reference to roads as improved unless they conform to applicable city and county specifications and have an all-weather surface.

h. Failure to disclose the fact that no road exists as direct access to the parcels being offered for sale or lease, if such is the case.

i. Reference to the property being offered by illustrations that do not substantially portray its present state, without adequate qualifying phrases.

j. Reference by illustrations to points of interest some distance removed from the subdivision, unless the distance in miles from the subdivision to the points of interest is mentioned.

k. The use of "artists' conceptions" or renderings of the property or of the facilities, or both, unless they are described as such.

l. The use of maps to show proximity to other communities or points of interest, unless such maps are drawn to scale and the scale appears on the map, or the distance in miles is shown.

m. Reference to distances to any facilities or features located more than one mile from the nearest point in the subdivision, unless said distances are disclosed in road mile.

n. Reference to the distance to nearest cities, towns, or villages, unless said distances are disclosed in road miles measured from the locations being advertised.

o. In referring to water supply, the use of superlatives or phrases such as *abundant water,* *plenty of water,* and the like, unless such phrases are fully supported by the facts.

p. Unqualified reference to any utility services as "available" unless such utility services are installed and ready for use, or adequate financial arrangements have been made for their installation.

REGULATION OF PURCHASER'S DEPOSIT MONEY

The requirements for the disposition of the purchaser's deposit money is provided for in the Business and Professions Code and is common to all types of subdivisions.

Blanket encumbrance

Where all of the parcels contained in the subdivision are made security for the payment of a trust deed note or other lien, the land is said to be developed subject to a blanket encumbrance. Under the law, the owner or subdivider cannot sell or lease lots or units in the subdivision unless they can be released to the purchaser free and clear of the blanket encumbrance. A condition is usually provided for in the encumbrance that will allow for a partial release of individual lots or units from the encumbrance upon the payment of certain sums of money to the lien holder. Such a condition is known as a partial release clause.

Lacking a release provision, the owner or subdivider may select one of the following methods:

1. Monies obtained from a prospective purchaser must be placed in a neutral escrow depository acceptable to the Commissioner until *(a)* a proper release is obtained from the blanket encumbrance, *(b)* there is a default by one of the parties with determination as to the disposition of impounded monies, or *(c)* the owner or subdivider orders the return of such monies to the purchaser or lessee.
2. Title to the subdivision property is held and placed in trust, under an agreement of trust acceptable to the Commissioner, until a proper release is obtained from the blanket encumbrance.
3. The owner or subdivider may furnish a bond to the state of California, the bond to be in an amount and subject to such terms as may be approved by the Commissioner. The bond would provide for the return of moneys paid or advanced by purchasers or lessees if proper release from the blanket encumbrance is not obtained.

Realizing that numerous plans are used to finance home-building projects, and understanding the many complications that may arise, the legislature has provided that the Commissioner may approve other alternative requirements or methods. Any plans will be acceptable that follow the intent of the law, which is to protect purchasers' and lessees' deposits and payments made prior to receipt of title or other interest for which the party contracted.

No blanket encumbrance

Even though the subdivision is not subject to a blanket encumbrance, the disposition of deposit monies is still regulated by the Commissioner. Requirements are basically the same as those outlined above; the money must either be placed in escrow, or the owner or subdivider can choose from a few alternative methods.

Contract of sale

A contract of sale, for this purpose, is defined in the California Civil Code as an agreement wherein one party agrees to convey title to real property to another party upon the satisfaction of specified conditions set forth in the contract and that does not require conveyance of title within one year from the date of formation of the contract. The use of the contract of sale, or agreement of sale as it is also called, is not confined to newly subdivided properties. This form is discussed in Chapter 9, Real Estate Contracts.

When lots, parcels, or units in a subdivision that is not subject to a blanket encumbrance are sold or are to be sold using contracts of sale, the disposition of deposit money and installment payments are closely regulated by the Business and Professions Code. When selling a parcel of land under a sales contract that is not recorded, the seller is prohibited from otherwise encumbering the parcel to an aggregate amount exceeding the amount due under the contract without the written consent of the purchasing parties. When selling improved or unimproved real property under a contract of sale, the seller must apply installment payments from the buyer first to payments that might be due on obligations secured by an encumbrance or encumbrances on the property. The law further requires that each contract of sale relating to purchase of real property in a subdivision shall clearly set forth the legal description of the property, all the existing encumbrances at the date of the contract, and the terms of the contract.

In all contracts of sale involving parcels that have been subdivided for residential purposes and that contain dwellings for not more than four families, there can be no "lock-ins." This means that the buyer can prepay all or any part of the balance due at any time, and any waiver by the buyer of this privilege is unenforceable and void should the buyer decide at any time to prepay.

BASIC CONSIDERATIONS IN CREATING A SUBDIVISION

A good many economic factors must be studied and analyzed in determining whether or not to create a subdivision in any particular geographic area. This is usually done by preparing a market analysis that will study the general economic conditions and the supply and demand forces operative in the area under consideration. Satisfactory market analysis is not only a prerequisite of a successful tract development, but is also a frame of reference for the lending agencies, the federal government as guarantor or insuror in FHA and VA loans, the California Veterans home purchase plan, and the interested public agencies such as city and county governments, planning commissions, and utility companies.

The decisions regarding land costs, subdivision improvements, type and style of improvements that may be provided, price range, financing, merchandising, overhead, and profit are all correlated in the process of subdivision market and cost analysis. The economic problems that are involved in the development of a subdivision are complex when one realizes the speculative nature of subdivision ventures. Market and financing conditions have to be anticipated a year in advance, and the success of any type of development is governed by local supply and demand conditions and how well the subdivider succeeds in formulating his plans to fit the existing market within the limits of local community requirements for subdivision improvements.

Residential subdivision market analysis

The basic steps in residential subdivision market research involve the collection, recording, classification, and summarizing of factual information about the housing market. This information is then measured and evaluated in order to develop some conclusions regarding the economic trends in the area, the size and condition of the existing housing market, and its trends and characteristics.

Measure of demand. Demand is the basis of all market analysis, but particularly so for residential subdivisions. The smaller the community or the farther away from the major sources of employment, the more important a careful analysis becomes. Before purchasing land the subdivider should carefully examine market conditions in the area in order to determine whether or not an active demand is likely to exist. If it is an area where other tracts are on the market, the prevailing rate of sale will generally provide a good indicator of current demand.

Site analysis. Since a subdivision is an entity created out of unimproved land for habitation by people, it must of necessity be located where both of these elements can be satisfactorily combined. Normally, this has been adjacent to or in the area of an established community or urban area. The proximity of the site to the major sources of employment will have a definite bearing on the marketability of the subdivision. In considering a location, consideration must be given to shopping centers, service facilities, schools, churches, highways and other access routes, and transportation in general.

A physical survey of the proposed site should include data on topography, water table, soil, drainage and sewage conditions, accessibility, neighboring property, and utilities. A subdivider must provide a soil report and is required to provide the Commissioner with information as to the maximum of depth of fill used, or proposed to be used, on each lot, and a true statement on soil conditions supported by engineering reports showing that the soil has been, or will be, prepared in accordance with recommendations of a registered civil engineer.

Development cost. In many instances the actual cost of developing the land into individual building sites is a greater factor in total costs than the price of the raw land. The availability of services such as water, electricity, gas, drainage, and sewage disposal are of prime importance in development costs. If utilities are adjacent to the site or will be provided by the public utility company or municipality, the problem is minor. If, however, as is frequently the case, the subdivider has to bear the responsibility of connecting lines for water or sewage, or perform extensive drainage work, development costs will be greatly increased.

Establishing a price. In determining the price range of houses, lots, or other types of units being offered, the subdivider should be guided by the nature of surrounding improvements in the area. The purchase price of the land plus its cost of development roughly establishes a minimum figure from which to start, and the financing terms available may also create a tentative ceiling. If the subdivider is offering finished houses for sale he must be aware of the latitude in which he can operate economically and attempt to adapt his plans and construction costs to the price range most in demand.

Interstate Land Sales Full Disclosure Act

A part of the Housing and Urban Development Act, is the Interstate Land Sales Full Disclosure Act. It is administered by the Office of Interstate Land Sales Registration (OILSR) in the Department of Housing and Urban Development.

The act makes it unlawful for any developer to sell or lease lots in a subdivision as a common promotional plan in interstate commerce or by utilization of the mails unless a statement of record is in effect and a copy of the property report is furnished to the purchaser or lessee. In order to comply, the California developer is required to file with OILSR a copy of the subdivision questionnaire filed with the Department of Real Estate, together with all supporting documents and appropriate filing fee. An abbreviated statement of record is also required. The filing is completed when a copy of the California final public report (which substitutes for the federal property report) is received.

Contracts or agreements for the purchase or lease of a lot in a subdivision where the property report has not been given to the purchaser in advance or at the time of signing the contract are voidable at the option of the purchaser.

Condominiums are included in the Interstate Land Sales Full Disclosure Act, and the Department of Housing and Urban Development has ruled that a condominium is equivalent to a subdivision, each unit being regarded as a lot. In California, any contract or agreement to purchase a lot or parcel within a land project may be rescinded by the purchaser, without cause, up to 14 days following the day the contract was executed. Any money or other consideration received as a down payment must be returned to the purchaser.

QUESTIONS FOR DISCUSSION

1. What are the various types of subdivisions found in California?
2. Discuss the various protections both the Subdivided Lands Act and Subdivision Map Act provide the public.
3. How may the Commissioner prevent issuance of a subdivision public report?
4. How is a prospective purchaser protected by the Commissioner's issuance of a public report in connection with a subdivision?
5. Give examples of what might constitute misleading advertising.
6. What are the basic considerations that must be taken into account by those wishing to subdivide and offer land for sale?
7. Discuss the regulation of a purchaser's deposit money.
8. What material must be included in the subdivision questionnaire required by the Department of Real Estate?
9. Discuss the investment potential for a small individual purchaser in California land today.
10. If you were interested in the purchase of land for recreational use, what kind of information would you seek?

MULTIPLE CHOICE QUESTIONS

19–1. Stock cooperative projects are generally found in connection with: *(a)* commercial properties, *(b)* resort properties, *(c)* residential apartment buildings, *(d)* none of these.

19–2. A fee ownership and tenancy in common combination is most often found with respect to: *(a)* community apartments, *(b)* condominium ownership, *(c)* mineral rights, *(d)* none of these.

19–3. The commissioner prepares a public report in order to: *(a)* protect the public, *(b)* provide financing statements, *(c)* regulate prices, *(d)* set building standards.

19–4. A prospective purchaser who receives a copy of the Commissioner's Public Report must: *(a)* sign a purchase contract, *(b)* deposit funds in escrow, *(c)* sign a receipt, *(d)* none of these.

19–5. Which of the following is not regulated by the Subdivision Map Act: *(a)* filing procedures, *(b)* obtaining certificates, *(c)* proper recordation, *(d)* none of these.

19–6. The questionnaire that a subdivider must prepare is obtained from: *(a)* county recorder, *(b)* planning commission, *(c)* Real Estate Commissioner, *(d)* state engineer.

19–7. The most common subdivision is: *(a)* stock cooperative project, *(b)* community apartment, *(c)* standard subdivison, *(d)* commercial development.

19–8. A subdivider studies general economic factors by preparing: *(a)* financing statements, *(b)* building plans, *(c)* market analysis, *(d)* public reports.

Department of Real Estate, laws, licensing, education, and trade and professional associations

This chapter will discuss the California Department of Real Estate and the duties and responsibilities of the Real Estate Commissioner, state real estate commission, and real estate broker and real estate salesperson. The various types of licenses issued and requirements for obtaining them are listed. The California Real Estate Law and its enforcement by the Commissioner are considered, along with common real estate law violations, the rules and regulations of the Commissioner, the Commissioners Code of Ethics and Professional Conduct, and the Administrative Procedure Act. Education and research are discussed, along with trade and professional associations such as local real estate boards, the California Association of Realtors®, the National Association of Realtors®, the Code of Ethics, and a discussion of the use of the term *Realtor*®.

CALIFORNIA DEPARTMENT OF REAL ESTATE

The California Department of Real Estate was created by legislative act in 1917. It provided for the licensing and regulation of real estate agents and was the first legislation of its kind in the United States. Certain parts of the legislation were subsequently found unconstitutional. In 1919 legislation that deleted the unconstitutional provisions of the 1917 act was passed, and it, with subsequent amendments, has remained in effect since then. In 1943 the original law, the Real Estate Act, was codified and became a part of the Business and Professions Code. It may be properly referred to as the Real Estate Law, and comprises Division 4 of the Business and Professions Code beginning at Section 10000.

Among the strongest supporters of the real estate licensing law was the organized real estate industry itself. The law is designed primarily for the protection of the public in real estate transactions when the services of an agent are employed. By requiring qualifications for a license and by the establishment and enforcement of definite standards and practices, the law has also played an important part in the professionalization of the industry and of those engaged in real estate and related activities.

CALIFORNIA REAL ESTATE COMMISSIONER

The California Real Estate Commissioner is appointed by the governor for a four-year term and is the chief executive of the department. It is his duty to determine administrative policy and to enforce the provisions of the law. Among the duties involved in administering the provisions of the law are investigation of complaints against licensees, regulation of the sale of subdivisions, screening and qualifying of applicants for licenses, and investigation of nonlicensees alleged to be performing acts for which a license is required by law.

The Commissioner has all the powers granted by the Administrative Procedure Act to hold formal hearings for determination of issues involving a license, license applicant, or subdivider. After a hearing the Commissioner may suspend or revoke or deny the license, or issue an order halting sales in a subdivision.

STATE REAL ESTATE ADVISORY COMMISSION

In 1937, a state real estate board was established by legislative act and in 1957 became the state real estate commission. In 1977 it officially became the Real Estate Advisory Commission, comprised of six real estate brokers and four public members, appointed by the Real Estate Commissioner to serve at the Commissioner's pleasure. Except for the Commissioner, they serve without pay and are reimbursed only for actual and necessary travel expenses while on official business.

The Real Estate Law authorizes the advisory commission to:

1. Inquire into the needs of the real estate licensees of California, the functions of the department, and the matter of the business policy thereof.
2. Confer and advise with the Commissioner and other state officers as to how the department may best serve the state and the real estate licensees of the department.
3. Make such recommendations and suggestions of policy to the Commissioner as the commission deems beneficial and proper for the welfare and progress of the real estate licensees and of the public, and of the real estate business of California.

TYPES OF REAL ESTATE LICENSES

The definition of a real estate broker and a real estate salesperson, and a discussion of who is required to secure a real estate license is contained in Chapter 7, Agency and the Real Estate Licensee.

Various types of licenses are issued by the Real Estate Commissioner, and application for all licenses issued must be made on forms that the Department of Real Estate provides and that may be obtained at any of the department offices. The Real Estate Law permits the Commissioner to suspend or revoke the license of a real estate licensee who has procured a license for himself through fraud, misrepresentation, or deceit, or has made any material misstatement of fact in his application. The various types of licenses issued are:

(a) Individual broker. This is the most common type of broker's license, and it licenses the individual to act for his own personal account in conducting a brokerage business using his own name or using a fictitious business name.

Although practically all broker's licenses issued are real estate broker's licenses, the Department of Real Estate also issues a "mineral, oil, and gas broker license" for individuals who are solely concerned with the brokerage of mineral, oil, and gas properties. It is known as an MOG broker's license, and no MOG salesman's license is issued.

The Commissioner used to issue a business opportunity broker and business opportunity salesman license, but they have been discontinued and now the holder of a real estate broker or real estate salesperson license may engage in the sale of business opportunities. Business opportunity brokerage is defined and discussed in Chapter 21.

(b) Corporations as licensed brokers. In certain cases brokers will set up a corporation. The corporation can be licensed as a real estate broker, but only if at least one officer of the corporation is a duly qualified real estate broker.

The corporation must file articles of incorporation with the secretary of state before the Real Estate Commissioner will issue a real estate broker's license to it. A corporation licensed as a real estate broker may include among its officers any of the licensed real estate salespersons employed by it, providing its chief executive officer who is primarily responsible for its management and operations has a real estate broker's license to act on behalf of the corporation. The use of the individual proprietorship, partnership, and corporate form for the real estate office is further discussed in Chapter 21 in the section dealing with the real estate office.

(c) Partnerships. The department of real estate no longer issues formal partnership licenses. Real estate business partnerships are quite common among real estate licensees and may be formed in compliance with laws regarding creation of business partnerships.

(d) Salesperson. This license is issued to individuals who will be employed as salespersons, and whose activities will be controlled and supervised by a licensed real estate broker. The salesperson license permits activity in the real estate business in the employ of a broker only and never as an independent agent. The salesperson can only receive compensation for work as an agent from the employing broker.

(e) Branch office. This is the license required for each additional location if a broker maintains more than one office or place of business in the state.

(f) Using a fictitious business name. A licensed broker, partnership, or corporation can operate using a fictitious business name. Before issuing a license with a fictitious business name to an individual broker or corporation, the commissioner must receive a certified copy of the *fictitious business name statement* filed with the county clerk in the county where the principal

place of business is maintained. The broker license, when issued, will show the name of the broker and the fictitious business name selected.

(g) Restricted license. There are certain types of restricted licenses issued by the Commissioner in some cases where a license has been suspended, revoked, or denied after a hearing. In effect, they are probationary licenses and contain specific restrictions.

Real estate broker's license

The applicant for the real estate broker license must:

1. Be at least 18 years of age.
2. Have had previous experience or education as required by law.
3. Be honest and truthful.
4. Submit proof of having completed six statutory collegiate courses as required by law.
5. Pass the examination.

Experience and education. The real estate law requires two years' active experience as a licensed real estate salesperson within the past five years or equivalent experience. This experience must be in the general field of real estate or may be in the form of graduation from a collegiate institution.

Most candidates for the broker license base their claims for qualification upon two years of experience as a real estate salesperson. However, the Commissioner does not allow any person who has been merely licensed as a salesperson for two years to qualify. The applicant must submit proof of having been actively employed as a full-time 40-hour-per-week salesperson or part time for the equivalent of two years' full time. A form is provided the applicant so that he may obtain the signature of his employing broker or brokers, who must certify as to the required employment.

The requirement may be met by a combination of full-time experience as a licensed salesperson and certain equivalent qualifying real estate experience. All claims of equivalent qualifying real estate experience must be supported by valid evidence in the form of letters or statements from responsible parties who have been in a position to note the applicant's duties or activities as they have related to the general field of real estate. Examples of such equivalent experience are:

1. Employment in the real estate department of a savings and loan association or bank.

2. Experience as a subdivider or contractor.
3. Experience and employment in the field of real estate appraisal.
4. Employment as a public employee in such departments as that of the tax assessor or city planning department.
5. Employment in a title insurance or escrow company.

Equivalent experience may also include formal collegiate education. Some examples are:

1. An individual who holds a baccalaureate degree from any accredited college or university qualifies without any real estate salesman employment.
2. An applicant may qualify with one year's full-time employment as a licensed salesperson and graduation from a California Community College with a major in real estate.

Statutory courses. In addition to the salesperson experience or equivalent requirement, all applicants for the California Real Estate Broker License must submit proof of having completed six college-level courses as follows:

I. Legal Aspects of Real Estate Real Estate Practice Real Estate Finance Real Estate Appraisal
II. Real Estate Economics, or Accounting
III. A course selected from one of the following: real estate principles, business law, property management, real estate office administration, escrows, or an advanced course in legal aspects of real estate, real estate finance, or real estate appraisal.

The four courses listed in Group I must be completed by the broker applicant. The additional two courses required may be satisfied by completing both of the courses listed in Group II or by completing one of the courses from Group II and one of the courses listed in Group III.

The required courses must be college-level courses with a value of three semester-units or four quarter-units each. Three semester- or four quarter-units means 45 hours of classroom work, so that the six courses will require a total of 270 hours.

An attorney who is a member of the California or other state bar association will generally qualify for the real estate broker examination on the basis of education and experience and is exempt from the statutory courses requirement.

Broker license examination. The makeup and

content of the license examination is discussed later in the chapter. The examination fee, which must accompany the application for the broker license, is $50. If the applicant does not pass the examination, his fee is not refundable but will be held to his credit for a period of two years. If the applicant passes the examination, he is so notified and may then apply for the broker license, which is valid for four years. The fee for the license is $165. At the end of the four years, and every four years thereafter, the license may be renewed without an examination merely by making application, meeting the continuing education requirement, and paying the required $165 fee.

The examination is scheduled for one day, and the applicant is allowed a maximum of two and one-half hours in the morning session and two and one-half hours in the afternoon session to complete the test, which consists of 200 multiple choice questions. To pass, an applicant must answer a minimum of 150 questions correctly.

Individuals taking the broker or salesman license examination may use slide rules and pocket size, silent, battery-operated electronic calculators without a printout or program storage capacity.

Real estate salesperson's license

The applicant for the real estate salesperson license must:

1. Be at least 18 years of age.
2. Be honest and truthful.
3. Pass the examination.

Salesperson license examination. There is no specific experience, education, or course requirement that must be met prior to taking the salesperson examination. The initial step for the applicant for a real estate salesperson license is to fill out and forward, with the $25 examination fee, an application that can be obtained at any Department of Real Estate office and at many local board of Realtors® offices.

The applicant is scheduled for examination, and if the applicants pass the test they are entitled to file the application for license which must contain the signature of the broker who intends to employ them. This application for a four-year license is filed with a $120 fee.

The examination for the salesperson license is similar in content to that of the broker license, but is not so thorough and searching in nature. It has been devised with emphasis on testing whether the candidate has sufficient practical and everyday working knowledge. It is, in form, a totally objective three-and-one-quarter-hour test having a total of 150 multiple choice questions. To pass, an applicant must answer at least 105 questions correctly.

Effective January 1978, Assembly Bill 960 declares in the general provisions part of the Real Estate License Law that whenever the term *salesman* is used in the said license law, the Subdivided Lands Act, or in the rules and regulations of the Commissioner, it means *salesperson.* A licensee, however, may elect to refer to the licensed status as *real estate salesman, real estate saleswoman* or *real estate salesperson.*

LICENSE EXAMINATION CONTENT

In 1973 California real estate salesman and broker examinations were revised to separate questions that are universal and multistate in their application from those that deal with subject matter peculiar to real estate law and practice in California.

The purpose was to institute a certain element of reciprocity between states that agree with California to administer the same multi-state portion as part of their own salesperson and broker license examination.

However, effective July 1980, California no longer participates in any multi-state reciprocal testing program.

The ratio of questions with respect to specific areas in the California salesperson and broker examinations are given in the Department of Real Estate Reference Book as follows:

1. *In law*—a reasonable understanding of general real estate law and the license law and its application to real estate transactions. This includes the analysis of listings and deposit receipts. Total weight: 50 percent.

2. *In matters of public control*—a general understanding of the impact of federal, state, and local authority in zoning, subdividing, in exercising the power of eminent domain and in general real estate transactions. Total weight: 10 percent.

3. *In valuation*—a sufficient knowledge of valuation methods to enable the licensee to serve his clients and the general public in a useful and dependable manner in carrying out his function in the real estate market. Total weight: 15 percent.

4. *In finance*—a general knowledge of available financial sources, procedures, practices and government participation sufficient to assist clients in obtaining and utilizing credit in real estate transactions. Total weight: 10 percent.

5. In special areas pertaining to real estate with which the licensee should be sufficiently familiar to perform his duties and live up to his responsibilities adequately, including:
   a. *Income taxation*—applied to sale of residences, types of installment sales, capital gains, corporations, real estate investment trusts.
   b. *Land development*—water supply, sewage, drainage, streets, community facilities.
   c. *Canons of business ethics*—including familiarity with the Code of Ethics promulgated by the National Association of Realtors.
   d. *Rentals*—property management.
   e. *Escrows*—nature and purposes, requisites, obligations of parties.
   f. *Arithmetical calculations*—as required for computation in real estate transactions.
   g. *Title insurance.*
   h. *Residential building, design and construction.*
   Total weight: 15 percent.

Applications, forms, and fingerprinting

Applications and forms for all examinations, and licenses issued by the Real Estate Commissioner, must be made on forms furnished by the Department of Real Estate. Forms, as well as a booklet entitled, "Instructions to License Applicants," can be obtained by calling at any one of the department's offices throughout the state or writing to the principal office in Sacramento.

Principal Office

Sacramento 95816
1719–24th Street
916–445–6776

Branch Offices
Fresno 93721
State Office Bldg., Rm. 3070
2550 Mariposa St.
209–488–5009

Los Angeles 90012
State Office Bldg., Rm. 8107
107 S. Broadway
213–620–5903

Sacramento 95823
4433 Florin Rd., Suite 250
916–445–6776

San Diego 92101
State Bldg., Rm. 5008
1350 Front Street
714–237–7345

San Francisco 94107
185 Berry Street, Rm. 5816
415–557–2136

Santa Ana 92701
28 Civic Center Plaza, Rm. 324
714–558–4491

Duplicate sets of fingerprints are also required of all applicants who have not filed prints with the department during the immediately preceding five-year period.

There are a number of required procedures that must be followed if a broker or salesperson wishes to inactivate a license, change a name or address, or change to a different office, and certain procedures must also be followed when a salesperson is discharged by a broker.

CONTINUING EDUCATION REQUIREMENT

All real estate broker and salesperson licensees, effective January 1983, as a condition for license renewal every four years, are required to evidence completion of 45 clock hours of instruction in educational courses, seminars, or conferences in current real estate related areas. License renewals must be accompanied by certificates of attendance, official transcripts, or certified copies of attendance showing a total of no less than 45 clock hours of approved continuing education during the immediately preceeding four years. A 3-hour course in ethics, professional conduct, and legal aspects of real estate must be included as a part of the requirement of 45 clock hours.

The new law is consistent with the availability of real estate courses, educational seminars, and programs presently offered throughout the State. Courses required for licensure, general training or education to obtain a license, or examination preparation offerings will not be acceptable toward meeting the continuing education requirement. Acceptable offerings must qualify for continuing education credit purposes through application to and approval by the Real Estate Commissioner and approved offering entities are required to issue a uniform certificate of attendance to each student successfully completing approved offerings.

THE REAL ESTATE LAW AND REGULATIONS OF THE COMMISSIONER

The Business and Professions Code of the state of California contains, as a portion of the Code, Division 4, Real Estate, and this is cited and recognized as the California Real Estate Law. The Business and Professions Code allows the Commissioner to adopt regulations for the administration and enforcement of the Real Estate Law and the Subdivided Lands Act. Duly adopted regulations become part of the California Administrative Code and, in effect, have the force and authority of the law itself.

All prospective licensees and subdividers should be thoroughly familiar with the Real Estate Commissioner's regulations. They should be considered in conjunction with the law, as they specifically outline procedure directed and authorized by the statutes. These rules and regulations are contained in Title 10, California Administrative Code and may be obtained from the Department of Real Estate.

Enforcement of the law by the Commissioner

The Real Estate Commissioner, as the chief officer of the Department of Real Estate, is duty bound to enforce the provisions of the Real Estate Law. The Commissioner may upon his own motion—and he shall on any verified complaint in writing—investigate the actions of any person engaged in the business or acting in the capacity of a licensee within this state, and he has the power to suspend the license or to revoke it permanently. He also has the authority to deny a license to an applicant if the applicant does not meet the full requirements of the law. If, through the screening process and fingerprint record of an application for license, it is ascertained that he has a criminal record or some other record that may reflect on his character, an investigation is made by the Commissioner's staff. A formal hearing may be ordered to determine whether or not to issue a real estate license to the applicant.

Formal hearings. A formal hearing procedure in connection with a complaint against a licensee may be conducted in accordance with the Administrative Procedures Act. A record is made of the proceedings, and the hearing is conducted very largely according to rules of evidence in civil matters. Testimony is taken under oath. A hearing officer from the administrative procedure panel hears the case and the Commissioner's case is presented by his counsel. The hearing officer makes a proposed decision based upon his findings. The Commissioner may reject or accept the proposed decision or reduce the proposed penalty and then make his official decision. The respondent has the right of appeal to the courts.

If the charges are not sustained at the hearing they are dismissed. If, however, the testimony substantiates the charges and they appear to be suffi-ciently serious, the license of the respondent is suspended or revoked. After a license is revoked, the person affected may not apply for reinstatement until a year has passed. Deputies in the department also investigate persons or firms who appear to be operating improperly or without benefit of a license, or who subdivide land without complying with the subdivision laws enforced by the commissioner.

COMMON REAL ESTATE LAW VIOLATIONS

Sections 10176 and 10177 of the Real Estate Law should be thoroughly understood by all real estate licensees. Violations with regard to these sections constitute the foundation for most license suspensions or revocations.

Section 10176 is concerned with the actions of a licensee while engaged in the practice and performance of any of the acts within the scope of the Real Estate Law. Section 10177 applies to situations in which the individual involved was not necessarily acting as an agent or as a licensee. The reader will recall the detailed discussion in Chapter 7 regarding the duties and responsibilities of the real estate licensee as an agent.

In discussing violations, we should realize that the vast majority of those engaged in the real estate business are honest individuals who conduct business in an honorable and ethical way. Many mistakes and violations are made, not intentionally, but because the licensee was unaware that a violation was being committed. It is important that the real estate licensee know what he may not do as well as what he may do.

Section 10176(a), misrepresentation. The licensee must disclose to his principal material facts that his principal should know. Failure to do this is cause for disciplinary action. A large percentage of the complaints the Commissioner receives allege misrepresentation on the part of the real estate salesman and/or real estate broker.

California courts have consistently said that real estate purchasers are relieved from any responsibility to independently investigate facts represented as true by an owner or broker unless a purchaser knows that the statements are false.

Section 10176(b), false promise. Although it may seem that a false promise and a misrepresentation are the same thing, they are not. A misrepresentation is a false statement of fact, while a false promise is a false statement about what the promisor is going to do in the future. The false promise is usually proved by showing that the promise was impossible of performance and that the person making the promise knew it was impossible.

Section 10176(c), misrepresentation through agents. This section gives the Commissioner the right to discipline a licensee who misrepresents or makes false promises through other real estate agents, or who pursues a continued and flagrant course of misrepresentation.

Section 10176(d), divided agency. A licensee must inform all his principals if he is acting as an agent for, or receiving a commission from, more than one party in a transaction. This prevents a licensee from receiving a selling commission from the owner of the property, and at the same time receiving a fee from the buyer without both parties to the transaction being aware and approving of it.

Section 10176(e), commingling. Commingling is the mixing together of the funds of a licensee and those of his principals. To avoid this, the licensee is cautioned to maintain a trust account and to keep all moneys entrusted to him separate from his own personal funds. If we go a step beyond the mere mixing together of funds, we come to an even more serious offense—conversion. Conversion is the misappropriation and use of the funds of another. If a licensee takes a deposit and then spends it immediately, he has converted these funds.

Section 10176(f), definite termination date. This section requires a definite termination date for all exclusive listings relating to transactions for which a real estate license is required. Generally, if the termination date is specified in the agreement, or if a definite period of time is indicated, the requirement is satisfied.

Section 10176(g), secret profit. A licensee is prohibited from making a secret profit in a real estate transaction. An example of a secret profit is the action of a broker who makes a low offer for a property, usually through a dummy purchaser, when the broker already has a higher offer from a legitimate buyer. When the dummy buyer, who is really acting for the broker, acquires the property, it is then sold to the real buyer whom the broker has waiting. The profit to the broker is generally much more than receipt of a normal commission.

Section 10176(h), listing option. This section requires a licensee, when he has used a form that is both an option and a listing, to inform his principal of the amount of profit he will make and to obtain the written consent of his principal approv-

ing the amount of such profit before he may exercise the option. This section does not apply when a licensee is using an option only. This section of the Real Estate Law has had the effect of greatly minimizing the use of combination option listing forms. A situation similar to a listing option, however, is found in connection with home trade-in plans discussed in Chapter 21.

Section 10176(i), dishonest dealing. This is a catchall section covering acts which require a real estate license.

Section 10176(j), signatures of prospective purchasers. This section makes it a violation for brokers engaged in the sale of business opportunities to use what is known as a "send-out list." Brokers who have no written or oral listings to sell the businesses give the list to a prospective purchaser. The purchaser signs the list of businesses for sale, and in so doing promises that he will pay a commission to the broker who furnished him the list should he eventually buy one of the listed businesses, even though he may not deal with the broker who furnished him the list.

Section 10177

We shall now briefly review Section 10177, which covers acts performed while the individual involved may or may not have been acting as a real estate agent or as a licensee.

Section 10177(a), obtaining license by fraud. If it is found that a licensee obtained his license by fraud, misrepresentation, or deceit, the commissioner may revoke the license. This section is commonly used when it is found that the licensee failed to mention a previous criminal record on his license application.

Section 10177(b), convictions. This section permits the commissioner to proceed against a licensee who has been convicted of either a felony or a misdemeanor that involves moral turpitude.

Section 10177(c), false advertising. This section makes licensees who are parties to false advertising subject to disciplinary action. The ban extends to subdivision sales as well as general property sales. A similar section in the subdivision law permits the department of real estate to proceed against a person for criminal prosecution when he is not a licensee, and to discipline him when he is a licensee.

Section 10177(d), violations of other sections. This section gives the Commissioner the authority to proceed against a licensee for violation of any of the other sections of the Real Estate

Law, the Rules and Regulations of the Commissioner, and the Subdivision Laws.

Section 10177(e), misuse of trade name. This section refers to the misuse of any terms or insignia of any real estate organization. Only active members of the national association or local associations of real estate boards are permitted to use the term *Realtor®*. This is a term belonging exclusively to such members, and no licensee may advertise or hold himself out to be a Realtor® without proper entitlement.

Section 10177(f), conduct warranting denial. This is a general section of the Real Estate Law, and almost any act involving crime or dishonesty will fall within the purview of this section.

Section 10177(g), negligence or incompetence. Demonstrated negligence or incompetence while acting as a licensee is cause for disciplinary action. The department proceeds in those cases where the licensee is so careless or unqualified that to allow him to conduct a transaction would endanger the interests of his clients or customers.

Section 10177(h), supervision of salesmen. A broker is subject to disciplinary action if he fails to exercise reasonable supervision over the activities of his salesmen.

Section 10177(i), violating government trust. This section provides disciplinary liability for using government employment to violate the confidential nature of records made available by such employment.

Section 10177(j), other dishonest conduct. This section specifies that any other conduct, not necessarily connected with real estate, that constitutes dishonest dealing or fraud may subject the individual so involved to license suspension or revocation.

Section 10177(k), restricted license violation. Violation of the terms, conditions, restrictions, and limitations contained in any order granting a restricted license is grounds for disciplinary action.

Section 10177(l), inducement of panic selling. A cause for disciplinary action is the soliciting or inducing of the sale, lease, or the listing for sale or lease of residential property on the ground, wholly or in part, of loss of value, increase in crime, or decline of the quality of the schools due to the present or prospective entry into the neighborhood of a person or persons of another race, color, religion, ancestry, or national origin. A common term used to indicate the above practices is *blockbusting*, and any such practices by a real estate licensee will result in disciplinary action.

Section 10177(m), Franchise Investment Law. Violation of any provisions of the Franchise In-

vestment Law or Commissioner's regulations pertaining to this law.

Section 10177(n), securities. Violation of Corporations code sections and Commissioners regulations pertaining to securities.

Additional penalty sections

There are additional sections in the California Real Estate Law that provide for the revocation or suspension of licenses for acts other than those contained in the general disciplinary action sections just described, and these violations might be included in Section 10177(d) previously discussed. Some of these additional sections are as follows:

Section 10137. Provides that the license of any real estate broker may be revoked or suspended if he employs or compensates any unlicensed person to perform acts requiring a license.

Section 10141. Provides that a broker must cause notice of sales price to be given both to buyers and sellers within 30 days after sale is completed.

Section 10142. Provides that a licensee must give a copy of any contract to the party signing it at the time it is signed.

Section 10143. Provides that rental agents collecting advance fees shall use approved contracts and make refunds under certain circumstances.

Section 10178. Makes it a violation if a broker discharges a salesman for cause and then fails to notify the Commissioner.

Section 10136. States that no person engaged in the business or acting in the capacity of a real estate broker or a real estate salesman within this state shall bring or maintain any action in the courts of this state for the collection of compensation for the performance of any of the acts defined as within the scope of a broker or salesman without alleging and proving that he was a duly licensed real estate broker or a real estate salesman at the time the alleged cause of action arose.

Section 10148. Makes it a requirement that a real estate broker retain for three years copies of all listings, deposit receipts, canceled checks, trust records, and other documents executed by him or obtained by him in connection with any transactions for which a real estate broker's license is required.

RULES AND REGULATIONS OF THE COMMISSIONER

The rules and regulations of the Commissioner have been mentioned previously and are adopted by the Commissioner to aid him in enforcing the law. Each licensee should be familiar with these rules and regulations, as well as with the real estate law itself. These rules and regulations have the force and authority of the law itself since they are a part of the California Administrative Code. The following are a few examples.

Regulation 2725, review of instruments

Every instrument prepared or signed by a real estate salesperson in connection with any transaction for which a real estate license is required, which may have a material effect upon the rights or obligations of a party to the transaction shall be reviewed, initialed, and dated by the salesperson's broker within five working days after preparation or signing by the salesperson or before the close of escrow, whichever first occurs.

A broker may delegate his responsibility and authority described above in the ways listed below so long as the broker does not relinquish his overall responsibility for supervision of the acts of salespersons licensed to him:

1. To any licensed real estate broker who has entered into a written agreement relating thereto with the broker;
2. To a real estate salesperson licensed to the broker if the salesperson has accumulated at least two years' full-time experience as a salesperson licensee during the immediately preceding five-year period and has entered into a written agreement with the broker with respect to the delegation of responsibility.

Regulation 2726, broker-salesperson agreements

A real estate broker is required to have a written agreement with each of his salespersons as to whether such individual is licensed as a salesperson or as a broker. An individual with a broker license may, by agreement, work for another broker as a salesperson. The agreement must be dated and signed by the parties and must cover material aspects of the relationship between the parties, including supervision of licensed activities, compensation, and duties. An example of such an agreement is contained in Chapter 21.

Regulation 2903, structural defects, disclosure

A licensee shall disclose to any and all purchasers or prospective purchasers, and to any and all sellers or prospective sellers or parties to an exchange any and all knowledge he may have, as soon as it is practical for him to do so, of any infestation of wood-destroying organisms in any improvement or premises, the sale, purchase, or exchange of which said licensee negotiates.

Regulation 2785, code of ethics and professional conduct

In order to enhance the professionalism of the California real estate industry and maximize protection for members of the public dealing with real estate licensees, the following standards of professional conduct and business practices are adopted:

a. Unlawful conduct. Licensees shall not engage in "fraud" or "dishonest dealing" or "conduct which would have warranted the denial of an application for a real estate license" within the meaning of Business and Professions Code Sections 10176 and 10177 including, but not limited to, the following acts and omissions:

1. Knowingly making a substantial misrepresentation of the likely market value of real property to its owner (1) for the purpose of securing a listing or (2) for the purpose of acquiring an interest in the property for the licensee's own account.

2. The statement or implication by a licensee to an owner of real property during listing negotiations that the licensee is precluded by law, regulation or by the rules of any organization, other than the broker firm seeking the listing, from charging less than the commission or fee quoted to the owner by the licensee.

3. The failure by a licensee acting in the capacity of an agent in a transaction for the sale, lease or exchange of real property to disclose to a prospective purchaser or lessee facts known to the licensee materially affecting the value or desirability of the property, when the licensee has reason to believe that such facts are not known to, nor readily observable by, a prospective purchaser or lessee.

4. When seeking a listing, representation to an owner of the real property that the soliciting licensee has obtained a bona fide written offer to purchase the property, unless at the time of the representation the licensee has possession of a bona fide written offer to purchase.

5. The willful failure by a listing broker to present or cause to be presented to the owner of the property any offer to purchase received prior to the closing of a sale, unless expressly instructed

by the owner not to present such an offer, or unless the offer is patently frivolous.

6. Presenting competing offers to purchase real property to the owner by the listing broker in such a manner as to induce the owner to accept the offer which will provide the greater compensation to the listing broker, without regard to the benefits, advantages, and/or disadvantages to the owner.

7. Knowingly underestimating the probable closing costs in a transaction in a communication to the prospective buyer or seller of real property in order to induce that person to make or to accept an offer to purchase the property.

8. Failing to explain to the parties or prospective parties to a real estate transaction the meaning and probable significance of a contingency in an offer or contract that the licensee knows or reasonably believes may affect the closing date of the transaction, or the timing of the vacating of the property by the seller or its occupancy by the buyer.

9. Knowingly making a false or misleading representation to the seller of real property as to the form, amount and/or treatment of a deposit toward purchase of the property made by an offeror.

10. The refunding by a licensee, when acting as an agent or subagent for seller, of all or part of an offeror's purchase money deposit in a real estate sales transaction after the seller has accepted the offer to purchase, unless the licensee has the express permission of the seller to make the refund.

11. Failing to disclose to the seller of real property in a transaction in which the licensee is acting in the capacity of an agent, the nature and extent of any direct or indirect interest that the licensee expects to acquire as a result of the sale. The prospective purchase of the property by a person related to the licensee by blood or marriage, purchase by an entity in which the licensee has an ownership interest, or purchase by any other person with whom the licensee occupies a special relationship where there is a reasonable probability that the licensee could be indirectly acquiring an interest in the property, shall be disclosed.

b. Unethical conduct. In order to maintain a high level of ethics in business practice, real estate licensees should avoid engaging in any of the following activities:

1. Representing, without a reasonable basis, the nature and/or condition of the interior or exterior features of a property when soliciting an offer.

2. Failing to respond to reasonable inquiries of a principal as to the status or extent of efforts to market property listed exclusively with the licensee.

3. Representing as an agent that any specific service is free when, in fact, it is covered by a fee to be charged as part of the transaction.

4. Failing to disclose to a person when first discussing the purchase of real property, the existence of any direct or indirect ownership interest of the licensee in the property.

5. Recommending by a salesperson to a party to a real estate transaction that a particular lender or escrow service be used when the salesperson believes his or her broker has a significant beneficial interest in such entity without disclosing this information at the time the recommendation is made.

6. Claiming to be an expert in an area of specialization in real estate brokerage, e.g., appraisal, property management, industrial siting, etc., if, in fact, the licensee has had no special training, preparation, or experience in such area.

7. Using the term *appraisal* in any advertising of offering for promoting real estate brokerage business to describe a real property evaluation service to be provided by the licensee unless the evaluation process will involve a written estimate of value based upon the assembling, analyzing and reconciling of facts and value indicators for the real property in question.

8. Failing to disclose to the appropriate regulatory agency any conduct on the part of a financial institution which reasonably could be construed as a violation of The Housing Financial Discrimination Act of 1977 (anti-redlining)—Part 6 (commencing with Section 35800) of Division 24 of the Health and Safety Code.

9. Representing to a customer or prospective customer that because the licensee of his or her broker is a member of, or affiliated with, a franchised real estate brokerage entity, that such entity shares substantial responsibility, with the licensee, or his or her broker, for the proper handling of transactions if such is not the case.

10. Participating in the organized disclosure to a representative, agent, or employee of a public or private school, firm, association, organization, or corporation conducting a real estate preparatory course the language of any question used in a state real estate license examination, at the request of such person or entity.

11. Demanding a commission or discount by a licensee purchasing real property for one's own account after an agreement in principle has been

reached with the owner as to the terms and conditions of purchase without any reference to price reduction because of the agent's licensed status.

c. Beneficial conduct. In the best interests of all licensees and the public they serve, brokers and salespersons are encouraged to pursue the following beneficial business practices:

1. Measuring success by the quality and benefits rendered to the buyers and sellers in real estate transactions rather than by the amount of compensation realized as a broker or salesperson.

2. Treating all parties to a transaction honestly.

3. Promptly reporting to the California Department of Real Estate any apparent violations of the Real Estate Law.

4. Using care in the preparation of any advertisement to present an accurate picture or message to the reader, viewer, or listener.

5. Submitting all written offers as a matter of top priority.

6. Maintaining adequate and complete records of all one's real estate dealings.

7. Keeping oneself current on factors affecting the real estate market in which the licensee operates as an agent.

8. Making a full, open, and sincere effort to cooperate with other licensees, unless the principal has instructed the licensee to the contrary.

9. Attempting to settle disputes with other licensees through mediation or arbitration.

10. Complying with these standards of professional conduct and the Code of Ethics of any organized real estate industry group of which the licensee is a member.

Nothing in this regulation is intended to limit, add to, or supersede any provision of law relating to the duties and obligations of real estate licensees or the consequences of violations of law. Subdivision *a* lists specific acts and omissions which do violate existing law and are grounds for disciplinary action against a real estate licensee. The conduct guidelines set forth in subdivisions *b* and *c* are not intended as statements of duties imposed by law nor as grounds for disciplinary action by the Department of Real Estate but as guidelines for elevating the professionalism of real estate licensees.

THE ADMINISTRATIVE PROCEDURE ACT

Throughout the real estate law, reference is made to the holding of hearings on the rights of persons to licenses. All hearings must be conducted in accordance with certain legal regulations that are set forth in the Administrative Procedure Act. The Department of Real Estate and other licensing agencies must conduct hearings with strict regard for the rules set forth in the act. The rights of the individual are thus protected, and the individual's course of conduct and procedure, when his license or claim to a license is threatened, are also outlined in this act.

EDUCATION AND RESEARCH

California, the first state to enact a real estate license law, also pioneered by providing, through legislation, a system whereby funds contributed by licensees can be used to stimulate real estate education and research. As far back as 1949 the state legislature, acting upon the recommendation of the Real Estate Commissioner and the organized industry, appropriated moneys from the real estate fund to the University of California to aid in developing a professional real estate education and research program.

As a result, graduate and undergraduate students at the University of California can now qualify for a degree with a field of emphasis in real estate. The University of California also offers real estate courses through its University Extension Program and correspondence courses offered by the Department of Independent Study. The University of California also conducts continuing real estate research programs in its Graduate Schools of Business Administration at Berkeley and Los Angeles, studying and reporting on the characteristics of the real estate industry, real estate marketing problems, the growing problems of urbanization, growth trends, and other aspects of real estate development in the state.

In 1956 the legislature created the Real Estate Education and Research Fund, separate from the Real Estate Fund, which supports the general operation of the Department of Real Estate. The new fund, sustained by a fixed portion of license fees, is used for the advancement of education and research not only at the University of California but at the California state colleges and California community colleges as well. The Commissioner may also contract with private universities in the state for specific research projects in the real estate field.

Commissioner's real estate education and research committee

To assist the Commissioner in allocating to the public institutions of higher learning monies appropriated by the legislature for this purpose, the Commissioner in 1958 appointed the Commissioner's Real Estate Education and Research Committee, now known familiarly as the CREERAC. On the committee are representatives of the real estate industry, the Real Estate Commissioner, the universities, the state colleges, and the community colleges of California. Areas of responsibility and emphasis are defined for each of the participants in the program.

In the 1970s Real Estate Education and Research Fund monies were transferred to the University of California, the California State University and Colleges, the California Student Aid Commission, and the California Community Colleges as follows:

In May 1973, $500,000 was provided to UC. The earnings from this endowment are to be used by the University to establish a professorship or chair in Real Estate and Land Economics at both the Berkeley and Los Angeles Campuses of UC.

In April 1974, one million dollars was transferred to the Trustees of the California State University and Colleges system. The earnings from this endowment are to be used for the maintenance, development, and improvement of real estate degree specializations or certification programs in the CSUC system designed to accommodate credit for California Community Colleges real estate courses.

In January 1975, $200,000 was transferred to the California Student Aid Commission. The earnings from this amount are to be used for scholarship awards for worthy and disadvantaged students enrolled in a real estate career-oriented program in institutions in the California State University and Colleges.

In January 1975, $1,900,000 was transferred to the Board of Governors of the California Community Colleges. The earnings from $1,500,000 of this amount are to be used for the maintenance, development, and improvement of real estate courses, degree specializations and certification programs in the California Community Colleges. The income from the remaining $400,000 is to be used for the maintenance and support of a scholarship program for worthy and disadvantaged students enrolled in a real estate career-oriented program in institutions in the California Community Colleges.

Real estate programs

In addition to offerings at the University of California, various California Community Colleges presently offer professional-level courses in real estate subjects including broker preparation courses, continuing education courses and an eight-course program leading to the issuance of the California Real Estate Certificate. In addition, most of these community colleges offer the A.A. degree with a major in real estate.

Each community and state college is expected to have a local real estate advisory committee whose members the college selects from the local real estate industry and allied vocations. In the case of community colleges, the committees help evaluate programs, assist in recruitment of instructors, publicize local offerings, and suggest special complementary features. A state college advisory committee is expected to present regional industry feeling as to needs in education and research to the college, and to evaluate research projects advanced for consideration by members of the college faculty. Private vocational schools that have obtained formal approval from the Real Estate Commissioner by meeting certain prescribed requirements, may offer statutory courses required of the broker applicant. Some of these schools offer both classroom and correspondence study. Private school courses usually are not transferable for credit to public institutions of higher learning.

Real estate recovery fund

In 1963 the California legislature established a real estate recovery fund which is supported by a portion of the license fees collected by the Real Estate Department.

The recovery fund provides payment of otherwise uncollectable court judgments obtained against a real estate license on the basis of fraud, misrepresentation, or deceit in a transaction in which the judgment debtor participated as a real estate licensee. It is thus possible for an innocent party who obtains a judgment against a licensee to collect payment even though the licensee does not have sufficient assets to meet the amount of the judgment.

Commissioner's plan for professionalism

In 1966 the Real Estate Commissioner's office drafted and distributed a "Blueprint for Professionalization of the Real Estate Business in California." In the text of the paper, it was explained that the intention was to provide a frame of reference and general plan of procedure for raising the standards of real estate practitioners in California. The plan was subsequently revised and updated several times.

For many years, both nationally and in the state of California, articulate real estate practitioners have been urging the cause of professionalism. Through the years the California Association of Realtors® not only supported legislation raising licensing standards, thus providing increased protection for the public dealing through licensees, but it steadily enlarged opportunities for its members to increase their knowledge and improve their skills.

Two of the principal ingredients for achievement of professional status are *(a)* specialized education in depth and *(b)* recognition by the public that a professional type of service is indeed involved.

TRADE AND PROFESSIONAL ASSOCIATIONS

This section will deal with the local, state, and national associations that strive to educate, inform, and promote ethical standards among real estate practitioners not only in California, but throughout the United States. We will discuss local boards, the California Association of Realtors® (CAR), the National Association of Realtors® (NAR), use of the term *Realtor®*, and the Code of Ethics of CAR and NAR.

Local real estate boards

A local real estate board or board of Realtors® is a voluntary organization of persons in the real estate business in a particular locality. Full membership is restricted to those individuals who hold a real estate broker's license, while real estate salesperson licensees may obtain associate membership. In addition, most boards maintain an affiliate classification of membership that is open to banks, trust companies, title companies, escrow companies, and others whose duties or interests are related to the real estate business.

Local boards provide various types of services to their members, such as a multiple listing service, area maps, sales records and listing information, legal and other publications pertaining to local property, a library, real estate forms, educational materials, business and educational meetings, insurance protection, and other such benefits.

The California Association of Realtors®

The California Association of Realtors® was formed at Los Angeles in 1905. It is the largest such organization in the United States, and is composed of the members of about 180 local real estate boards in California and also individual members. At the present time there are approximately 115,000 licensees on the CAR roster.

The following objects and purposes of the California Association of Realtors® are set forth in its constitution:

a. To unite its members and to promote high standards.
b. To safeguard the land-buying public.
c. To foster legislation for the benefit and protection of real estate and to cooperate in the economic growth and development of California.

A few of the CAR's standing committees concern themselves with education, ethics and professional standards, exchanges, insurance, real property taxation, legislation, political affairs, and finance. There are numerous divisions within CAR, which deal with such areas as property management, investment, syndication, and industrial-commercial brokerage.

CAR now provides legal advice to members who may call a toll-free number, (213) 739–9292, and ask a CAR attorney questions ranging from landlord-tenant relations to real estate contract problems. Additional facts about the CAR may be obtained by writing to California Association of Realtors®, 505 Shatto Place, Los Angeles, California 90020.

National Association of Realtors®

The National Association of Realtors®, 155 East Superior Street, Chicago, Illinois 60611, was organized in 1908. The national association unites the organized real estate interests throughout the United States and presents a common cause and program in behalf of national legislation affecting real property and the real estate industry. It is composed of approximately 1,500 local real estate boards throughout the nation and at present there are approximately 600,000 NAR members. The Code of Ethics of the NAR is subscribed to by the CAR and local boards and is shown in Figure 20–1. It is only through membership in the NAR that the right to use the term *Realtor®* may be had by licensees. Many specialized interest groups have been founded within the framework of the National Association of Realtors such as The American Institute of Real Estate Appraisers, The Institute of Farm Brokers, Society of Industrial Realtors, American Society of Real Estate Counselors,

CODE OF ETHICS

National Association of Realtors

California Association of Realtors

REALTOR ®

Preamble

Under all is the land. Upon its wise utilization and widely allocated ownership depend the survival and growth of free institutions and of our civilization. The interests of the nation and its citizens require the highest and best use of the land and the widest distribution of land ownership. They require the creation of adequate housing, the building of functioning cities, the development of productive industries and farms and the preservation of a healthful environment.

Such interests impose obligations beyond those of ordinary commerce. They impose grave social responsibility and a patriotic duty to which the REALTOR" should dedicate himself, and for which he should be diligent in preparing himself. The REALTOR", therefore, is zealous to maintain and improve the standards of his calling and shares with his fellow-REALTORS" a common responsibility for its integrity and honor. The term REALTOR" has come to connote competency, fairness and high integrity resulting from adherence to a lofty ideal of moral conduct in business relations. No inducement of profit and no instruction from clients ever can justify departure from this ideal.

In the interpretation of his obligation, a REALTOR" can take no safer guide than that which has been handed down through the centuries, embodied in the Golden Rule, "Whatsoever ye would that men should do to you, do ye even so to them."

Accepting this standard as his own, every REALTOR" pledges himself to observe its spirit in all of his activities and to conduct his business in accordance with the tenets set forth below.

Where the word REALTOR" is used in this Code and Preamble, it shall be deemed to include REALTOR"-Associate. Pronouns shall be considered to include REALTORS" and REALTOR"-Associates of both genders.

ARTICLE 1

The REALTOR" should keep himself informed on matters affecting real estate in his community, the state, and nation so that he may be able to contribute responsibly to public thinking on such matters.

ARTICLE 2

In justice to those who place their interests in his care, the REALTOR" should endeavor always to be informed regarding laws, proposed legislation, governmental regulations, public policies, and current market conditions in order to be in a position to advise his clients properly.

ARTICLE 3

It is the duty of the REALTOR" to protect the public against fraud, misrepresentation, and unethical practices in real estate transactions. He should endeavor to eliminate in his community any practices which could be damaging to the public or bring discredit to the real estate profession. The REALTOR" should assist the governmental agency charged with regulating the practices of brokers and salesmen in his state.

ARTICLE 4

The REALTOR" should seek no unfair advantage over other REALTORS" and should conduct his business so as to avoid controversies with other REALTORS".

ARTICLE 5

In the best interests of society, of his associates, and his own business, the REALTOR" should willingly share with other REALTORS" the lessons of his experience and study for the benefit of the public, and should be loyal to the Board of REALTORS" of his community and active in its work.

ARTICLE 6

To prevent dissension and misunderstanding and to assure better service to the owner, the REALTOR" should urge the exclusive listing of property unless contrary to the best interest of the owner.

ARTICLE 7

In accepting employment as an agent, the REALTOR® pledges himself to protect and promote the interests of the client. This obligation of absolute fidelity to the client's interests is primary, but it does not relieve the REALTOR® of the obligation to treat fairly all parties to the transaction.

ARTICLE 8

The REALTOR® shall not accept compensation from more than one party, even if permitted by law, without the full knowledge of all parties to the transaction.

ARTICLE 9

The REALTOR® shall avoid exaggeration, misrepresentation, or concealment of pertinent facts. He has an affirmative obligation to discover adverse factors that a reasonably competent and diligent investigation would disclose.

ARTICLE 10

The REALTOR® shall provide equal professional services to all persons regardless of race, creed, sex, or country of national origin. The REALTOR® shall not be a party to any plan or agreement to discriminate against a person or persons on the basis of race, creed, sex, or country of national origin.

FIGURE 20–1

ARTICLE 11

A REALTOR® is expected to provide a level of competent service in keeping with the Standards of Practice in those fields in which the REALTOR® customarily engages.

The REALTOR® shall not undertake to provide specialized professional services concerning a type of property or service that is outside his field of competence unless he engages the assistance of one who is competent on such types of property or service, or unless the facts are fully disclosed to the client. Any person engaged to provide such assistance shall be so identified to the client and his contribution to the assignment should be set forth.

The REALTOR® shall refer to the Standards of Practice of the National Association as to the degree of competence that a client has a right to expect the REALTOR® to possess, taking into consideration the complexity of the problem, the availability of expert assistance, and the opportunities for experience available to the REALTOR®.

ARTICLE 12

The REALTOR® shall not undertake to provide professional services concerning a property or its value where he has a present or contemplated interest unless such interest is specifically disclosed to all affected parties.

ARTICLE 13

The REALTOR® shall not acquire an interest in or buy for himself, any member of his immediate family, his firm or any member thereof, or any entity in which he has a substantial ownership interest, property listed with him, without making the true position known to the listing owner. In selling property owned by himself, or in which he has any interest, the REALTOR® shall reveal the facts of his ownership or interest to the purchaser.

ARTICLE 14

In the event of a controversy between REALTORS® associated with different firms, arising out of their relationship as REALTORS® or as cooperating brokers, the REALTORS® shall submit the dispute to arbitration in accordance with the regulations of their board or boards rather than litigate the matter.

ARTICLE 15

If a REALTOR® is charged with unethical practice or is asked to present evidence in any disciplinary proceeding or investigation, he shall place all pertinent facts before the proper tribunal of the member board or affiliated institute, society, or council of which he is a member.

ARTICLE 16

When acting as agent, the REALTOR® shall not accept any commission, rebate or profit on expenditures made for his principal-owner, without the principal's knowledge and consent.

ARTICLE 17

The REALTOR® shall not engage in activities that constitute the unauthorized practice of law and shall recommend that legal counsel be obtained when the interest of any party to the transaction requires it.

ARTICLE 18

The REALTOR® shall keep in a special account in an appropriate financial institution, separated from his own funds, monies coming into his possession in trust for other persons, such as escrows, trust funds, clients' moneys and other like items.

ARTICLE 19

The REALTOR® shall be careful at all times to present a true picture in his advertising and representations to the public. He shall neither advertise without disclosing his name nor permit any person associated with him to use individual names or telephone numbers, unless such person's connection with the REALTOR® is obvious in the advertisement.

ARTICLE 20

The REALTOR®, for the protection of all parties, shall see that financial obligations and commitments regarding real estate transactions are in writing, expressing the exact agreement of the parties. A copy of each agreement shall be furnished to each party upon his signing such agreement.

ARTICLE 21

The REALTOR® shall not engage in any practice or take any action inconsistent with the agency of another REALTOR®.

ARTICLE 22

In the sale of property which is exclusively listed with a REALTOR®, the REALTOR® shall utilize the services of other brokers upon mutually agreed upon terms when it is in the best interests of the client.

Negotiations concerning property which is listed exclusively shall be carried on with the listing broker, not with the owner, except with the consent of the listing broker.

ARTICLE 23

The REALTOR® shall not publicly disparage the business practice of a competitor nor volunteer an opinion of a competitor's transaction. If his opinion is sought and if the REALTOR® deems it appropriate to respond, such opinion shall be rendered with strict professional integrity and courtesy.

ARTICLE 24

The REALTOR® shall not directly or indirectly solicit the services or affiliation of an employee or independent contractor in the organization of another REALTOR® without prior notice to said REALTOR®.

FIGURE 20–1 *(concluded)*

Womens Council, Institute of Real Estate Management, National Marketing Institute, Securities and Syndication Institute, and others. In addition, there are independent organizations such as the Society of Real Estate Appraisers, American Society of Appraisers, National Association of Home Builders, American Bankers Association, U.S. Savings and Loan League, and numerous trade and professional organizations which are closely related to the real estate business.

USE OF THE TERM *REALTOR®* AND *REALTOR®-ASSOCIATE*

In California the term *Realtor®* may be used only by a licensed real estate broker who is either an individual member of the National Association of Realtors® or a full member of a local real estate board that is affiliated with the NAR. An individual who is licensed in California as a real estate salesman and is employed by a Realtor® or affiliated with a Realtor® as an independent contractor, may apply for Realtor®-Associate membership in the NAR and use the Realtor-Associate designation.

In California the unauthorized use of the term *Realtor®* is a violation of the California Real Estate Law. To every member authorized to use the term *Realtor®* the national association issues a certificate signed by the officers of the national association designating the member as a Realtor®.

Realtists

In 1947, a national organization of black real estate brokers known as the National Association of Real Estate Brokers was formed in Miami, Florida, and in turn, adopted the name, Realtist. The address of the National Association of Real Estate Brokers, Inc., is 1025 Vermont Avenue, N.W., Washington, D.C. 20005.

A Realtist must be a member of a local board as well as a member of the national organization. The California Association of Real Estate Brokers, affiliated with the National Association of Real Estate Brokers, was organized in 1955 and now has four board affiliates: Associated Real Property Brokers, Oakland; Consolidated Real Estate Brokers, Sacramento; Consolidated Realty Board, Los Angeles; and Logan Heights Realty Board, San Diego.

Independent boards

Virtually all local boards in California are affiliated with state and national associations. There are, however, a few independent boards in the state, some of which are strong in membership and influential in their communities. Many of the members of such boards are also members of boards affiliated with the state and national associations.

Affiliation not mandatory

There are many real estate licensees in California who are not members of any trade or professional association. A broker who is licensed by the State Department of Real Estate is not, of course, under any compulsion to join any group. He is at liberty to join local boards affiliated with the CAR and the NAR, independent boards, or remain entirely unaffiliated and merely use the designation *licensed real estate broker*.

QUESTIONS FOR DISCUSSION

1. What are the basic duties of the California Real Estate Commissioner?
2. How does the state real estate commission aid the Commissioner?
3. What types of real estate licenses are issued in California?
4. May a licensed real estate salesman be a partner in a real estate brokerage firm?
5. What procedures are necessary when a salesman wishes to transfer from the employment of one broker to that of another?
6. How may the commissioner investigate an applicant for a real estate license?
7. Discuss the common real estate law violations that may result in the suspension or revocation of a real estate license.
8. What is the basic purpose of the Rules and Regulations of the Commissioner?
9. Discuss the educational programs in real estate that are available through colleges in your particular locality.
10. How do you feel the continuing education requirements will affect the real estate licensee and the public?
11. Discuss the benefits a licensee may obtain from membership in his local real estate board, the California Association of Realtors®, and other professional organizations in the industry.
12. Discuss the proper use of the terms Realtor-Associate and Realtor.
13. Does the Department of Real Estate require membership in a trade or professional association as a necessary condition for being a real estate licensee?
14. Discuss the similarities and differences of activities performed by advanced fee rental agents and real property securities dealers.

15. How must a real estate licensee treat knowledge he may have of any structural defects in connection with the sale or purchase of real property?

MULTIPLE CHOICE QUESTIONS

20–1. In addition to the Real Estate Commissioner, the number of members of the Real Estate Advisory Commission is: *(a)* 3 *(b)* 7 *(c)* 10 *(d)* none of these.

20–2. The Real Estate Law authorizes which of the following to suspend real estate licenses: *(a)* state licensing commission, *(b)* Real Estate Commissioner, *(c)* state legislature, *(d)* state real estate commission.

20–3. Which of the following is not required of a real estate license applicant? *(a)* state examination, *(b)* 18 years of age or older, *(c)* U.S. citizenship, *(d)* submit set of fingerprints.

20–4. Broker A can receive a commission from both the buyer and seller in a transaction if: *(a)* Broker A receives approval of the commissioner, *(b)* both parties pay an equal amount of commis-

sion, *(c)* the fact is disclosed to both parties, *(d)* none of these.

20–5. A California corporation desiring to obtain a real estate broker license must: *(a)* maintain branch offices, *(b)* offer real property securities to California residents, *(c)* obtain a restricted real estate license or special permit, *(d)* none of these.

20–6. Which of the following may properly use the Realtor® designation: *(a)* any individual acting as a real estate agent who expects to receive a commission, *(b)* a real estate licensee who belongs to any professional organization, *(c)* a real estate broker who belongs to the National Association of Realtors®, *(d)* an attorney specializing in real estate law.

20–7. The basic purpose in establishing state licensing procedures is to: *(a)* protect the public, *(b)* collect license fees, *(c)* conform with federal regulations that require licensing agents, *(d)* comply with statute of frauds.

20–8. The funds to support real estate education and research are provided by: *(a)* state grants, *(b)* real estate license fees, *(c)* community colleges, *(d)* none of these.

21 Real estate brokerage

We shall begin this chapter with a discussion of brokerage in general and then proceed to individual sections as follows: *(a)* the real estate office and personnel, *(b)* property management, *(c)* real estate exchanges, *(d)* trade-in programs, and *(e)* business opportunity brokerage.

REAL ESTATE BROKERAGE

The term *brokerage* signifies an activity that involves the selling of a commodity through an intermediary who acts as agent for the seller and/or buyer, receiving a previously agreed-upon compensation based on a percentage of the gross selling price. Real estate brokerage varies little from this definition except for the greater need of specific written authorization or agency employment agreements from the seller. In the real estate business these are called listing contracts, and have been discussed in Chapter 9. It is the fiduciary and trust relationship implicit in the agency relationship that permeates real estate brokerage practice.

Although a certain amount of real estate sales are made directly between buyer and seller, the licensee performs a much needed function in our economic and social system, and the large proportion of real estate transactions negotiated through a broker is sufficient proof of this statement. The brokerage operation may be divided into the phases of: securing listings; prospecting for and finding buyers; bringing together buyers and sellers and negotiating a contract for the purchase and sale, exchange or lease of the real property; and the escrow procedure that involves the legal transfer of the property with the required instru-

ments and, invariably, arrangements for the financing and disbursement of funds.

While selling is the chief purpose in real estate brokerage, there is considerable administrative and paperwork involved. In the small office these duties will usually be performed by the broker, perhaps with some secretarial assistance, while in the larger office the function may be detached and delegated to a specialized department.

Selling real estate differs from selling many other products:

1. The product being sold is quite complex and very individualized.
2. The sales period is longer and more time-consuming.
3. The transfer of property involves many legal requirements and restrictions, which must be understood by the salesman.
4. The licensee quite often is acting as an intermediary between two parties, and must sell each party in order to make the sale and earn his commission.
5. Each product to be sold has its own special features and problems, such as location, value, financing, and many others that the licensee must be aware of.

The real estate licensee must have much more than a mere layman's knowledge of the city and district in which he resides or in which he seeks to operate. He must constantly circulate throughout the community, as he cannot expect to sell much real estate from behind a counter or in a sitting position. It is important that the licensee know his product generally, and specifically with regard to those particular pieces of property he has listed at any given time so far as value, construction, the neighborhood, and the type of purchaser who will be attracted.

General brokerage and specialization

A beginning real estate salesperson generally goes through what may be termed an apprenticeship period, working for a real estate broker on a commission basis. Salaried personnel are seldom found except in the very large real estate firm, where certain office personnel may be employed on a salary basis.

A salesperson may receive excellent, indifferent, or no training on the job, depending upon the brokerage firm with which he affiliates. Firms that are more selective of their personnel usually offer a higher degree of training. A beginner in the real estate business, however, in addition to the practical experience he receives, would do well to acquaint himself with the real estate offerings of the collegiate institutions in his community and get into the habit of taking at least one course each semester or quarter. If the licensed salesperson is serious about continuing in the real estate business and desirous of eventually obtaining a real estate broker's license, he will have to present evidence of at least having completed certain prescribed courses as discussed in Chapter 20.

While residential selling probably accounts for the bulk of sales made by a typical real estate office, an apprentice may, after a basic grounding in general home sales, wish to specialize and become an expert in a particular area of real estate brokerage. General brokerage, then, is the base upon which to stand, and can become a stepping stone to advanced specialties. The ambitious person entering real estate as a profession should examine carefully his interests, aptitudes, and limitations and plan his career accordingly.

THE REAL ESTATE OFFICE AND PERSONNEL

Most real estate offices in California are single-office operations, as opposed to firms that have a main office plus branch office locations. In addition, the most common form of operation is the individual proprietorship—that is, a single broker who runs and operates his own firm. The main factor common to most successful offices is that they operate under clearly outlined procedures for all activities, and all personnel are expected to adhere to them. A study of unsuccessful offices will show that they operate with a general lack of adequate internal organization and, further, that they have a large turnover in sales personnel.

BASIC COMPANY FORMS

Three basic forms of company formation are found in the real estate business. These are (a) individual proprietorship, (b) partnership, and (c) corporation.

Individual proprietorship

A real estate office set up as an individual proprietorship is run and operated by a single broker-owner who makes and is responsible for all business decisions. A recent California survey showed that the majority of licensees in the state were employed in offices staffed by no more than six salespersons and run by a single broker. Some brokers, of course, do not choose to employ any salespersons at all, and in many cases this type of office is a husband-wife combination, with the husband devoting his time to the outside duties while the wife performs the office duties.

Some of the advantages of the individual proprietorship form of operation may be (a) absolute control of business, (b) decisions made quickly, (c) independence of action, (d) ownership of all profits, and (e) psychological and intangible rewards.

Some of the disadvantages may be (a) limited availability of capital, (b) unlimited legal liability, (c) difficulty of adequately taking care of all specialized phases of a real estate brokerage operation, (d) need for continuous personal attention, (e) success completely dependent on the ability of a single individual, and (f) difficulty of budgeting one's time to service all clients adequately.

The partnership

A partnership is an agreement between two or more persons to carry on, as co-owners, a business for profit. In the real estate partnership all partners generally hold a real estate broker's license. A real estate salesperson licensee may hold an interest in and perform acts on behalf of a partnership formed by a written agreement if his employing broker is a member of the partnership.

Partnerships fall into two broad categories—a general partnership, created to conduct a general

306

continuing type of business, and a limited partnership, formed for a specific and limited purpose such as a building or subdivision project. The limited partnership or joint venture is dissolved when the project is completed. The continuing real estate partnership is a general partnership.

A mutual agency relationship exists among partners; each partner is empowered to bind the firm, himself, and his partners to third persons on transactions within the scope of the partnership business. Most successful partnerships are made up of persons who are able to work well with each other, who have a good general background in real estate, and, in addition, possess knowledge and experience in a specialized area of real estate. One partner may be expert in income properties, another partner in residential real estate, while another partner may specialize in commercial and industrial offerings. Other areas in which individual partners may excel are taxation, exchanges, office management, listing, selling, or property management.

The corporate form

Less than one sixth of all California real estate firms are incorporated. An individual broker, as well as two or more brokers, may form a corporation. One must have the services of an attorney in order to incorporate, since certain statutory legal requirements must be met.

The decision to incorporate usually results because a firm grows to a size so large that the corporate form offers distinct tax advantages. Generally, large-scale operations lend themselves best to use of the corporate form, and because such operations carry with them the risk of tremendous liability the limited liability feature of the corporation is very important. Individuals are liable only to the extent of their investment in the corporation, and their personal assets are thus protected.

The opportunity for raising capital through the sale of stock is another reason for incorporation. Some real estate offices incorporate and offer shares of stock to certain key personnel as inducements to remain with the firm.

The three forms of real estate organization discussed thus far—the individual broker-owner, the partnership, and the corporation—generally concern the permanent operation of a business of a continuing nature. In many instances parties join forces for a single project or transaction. Where this is the intent of the parties involved, we often find a joint venture or syndicate form used. These forms lend themselves best to the single-purpose, one-time-only real estate project or transaction.

REAL ESTATE OFFICE PERSONNEL

Personnel in the typical office consists of the broker or brokers who own and run the operation, the licensees employed as salesmen, and persons employed as secretaries and bookkeepers and for other office activities that do not require a real estate license.

A recent California Association of Realtors membership survey shows that while there is no single set of characteristics which fits all licensees, there are certain factors applicable to a majority of those surveyed.

The distribution of salespersons as to men and women is just about 50–50 with women slightly ahead. With respect to brokers, men substantially outnumbered women. The average age for brokers is 50 and for salespersons, 43, although 25 percent of salespersons are in the 18–35 age bracket.

Experience levels are diverse, with about 50 percent of salespersons having less than five years in real estate while 60 percent of brokers have more than nine years experience. The broker typically spends 50 hours a week engaged in real estate activities while salespersons spend 44. About 30 percent of all licensees reported working in excess of 60 hours per week. Ninety percent of brokers and 80 percent of salespersons reported that they are engaged in real estate as a full-time activity.

Average business income is most difficult to state with the ranges between high and low amounts varying widely. However, for full-time licensees the median income for a broker can be stated as approximately $39,000 and for a salesperson $23,000.

The typical brokerage office employs between 7 and 15 salespersons and 25 percent have a staff of 3 or less while 20 percent employ over 25 salespersons. Approximately 25 percent of real estate offices have a franchise affiliation and are generally larger offices. Approximately 85 percent of salespersons are employed as independent contractors.

Most licensees specialize in residential sales. Residential income properties come next followed by commercial and industrial real estate and building development. Specialization seems related to experience with more experienced licensees specializing in areas such as business opportunities, farms, appraising, property management, and building and condominium developments.

Ninety percent of real estate licensees report owning their own residence, with 80 percent having additional real estate holdings.

Sales manager

In the smaller office the broker will assume the responsibility for management of the operation and supervision of the salespersons, if any. A sales manager is generally not required unless the sales force numbers 8 to 10 or more persons. At this point the volume of activity justifies the appointment of a sales manager who will devote his time to salesperson's problems with regard to typical transactions, training programs, advertising preparation, public relations, participation in local board and service club activities, and relations with such persons as escrow officers, loan officers, pest control inspectors, and others with whom the office constantly deals.

The compensation of the sales manager is usually based upon the sales production of the office, with a fixed minimum generally provided. The income of the sales manager generally reflects the size of the firm, the number of salespersons employed and supervised by him, and whether or not he is permitted to list and sell in addition to acting as sales manager.

The salespersons

The sales staff should consist of individuals interested in real estate as a career and willing to put in time and effort necessary to be successful. When interviewing an applicant for a sales position the experienced broker will certainly be interested in the applicant's previous work experience, manner and appearance, education and/or special training, present family status, and personality.

In past years too many persons unqualified in one way or another to be successful real estate salespersons have nonetheless been readily acceptable to many real estate firms. This has led to a traditionally large turnover of real estate salespersons and a resultant poor opinion of the real estate licensee on the part of much of the public.

A movement has begun during the last few years to make the real estate licensee truly a professional person. Standards for licensees have gradually risen as a result of pressures from the public and the real estate industry. The Department of Real Estate and the California Association of Realtors® have done a particularly effective job of sponsoring legislation to raise licensing standards, and of encouraging the development of educational offerings throughout the state.

TRAINING PROGRAM

Almost without exception, one finds that the most successful real estate firms also have the best training programs for their personnel. One of the chief reasons for the failure of beginning salespersons is the lack of guidance and training given to them by their employing broker. The well-rounded, complete training program should encompass three general areas: *(a)* individual on-the-job training, *(b)* staff meetings, and *(c)* outside academic instruction.

On-the-job training

Before newly employed salespersons are put on the floor of the office, where they will be expected to meet clients, answer the telephone, and conduct the business of the office in general, they will need a certain amount of intensive individual training. The initial training must give the salespersons a complete understanding of the company's policies and procedures, its commission schedule, and in general what is expected of them and what they may expect from the office.

A complete set of all forms used should be made available to the licensee for referral and study. Such information as well as an outline of the basic policies and procedures of the office is usually compiled in the form of a loose-leaf binder or mimeographed booklet and termed a "Policy and Procedure Manual."

Staff meetings

Staff meetings, or sales meetings, as they are sometimes called, provide an excellent opportunity for both formal and informal personnel training. Discussion at such meetings may include: *(a)* a topic of general interest, such as current market conditions, present state of financing, new legislation affecting real estate, successful sales techniques, or methods of listing; *(b)* a recently completed transaction, with the salesperson involved explaining the steps as they took place; *(c)* a review of the firm's current listings with up-to-date information relevant to any particular listing; *(d)* a new film relating to real estate or a taped talk by an expert; *(e)* persons from the outside invited to speak to the staff, in addition to a presentation by a member of the firm.

Broker-salesperson contract

Section 2726 of the Commissioner's Regulations requires a broker-salesperson contract.

The interests of both the broker and salesperson are better served, and the terms of employment better understood by both if everything is reduced to writing. While employment contracts may vary slightly in form, depending upon the emphasis the broker may wish to place on certain parts of the contract, a form that may be used is shown in Figure 21–1 and may be obtained from the California Association of Realtors®.

COSTS OF OPERATING A REAL ESTATE OFFICE

Figure 21–2 shows the results of a survey conducted by the California Association of Realtors® of real estate firms throughout the state to determine a breakdown of the average expenses involved in running an office. The shaded portion represents all commissions paid. The unshaded portion is defined as the "company dollar" and is then projected as a 100 percent dollar. It includes the amount left to the broker-owner after payment of all commissions, including salesmen, multiple, and co-op commission splits. The percentages shown are, of course, only averages, and will vary from office to office, depending on the size of the operation, high or low periods of business activity, type of specialization, and efficiency of operation.

Each real estate firm, regardless of size or type of operation, has a fairly basic cost of operation that must be returned each month before a profit is earned. The basic cost varies, but the expenses that contribute to it are the same type for all offices. The common expenses are:

a. Fixed salaries (if any) of management, salespersons, and other employees.
b. Rent, maintenance, and utilities.
c. Stationery, supplies, and office materials.
d. Equipment, office machines, and depreciation on these items.
e. Telephones and answering services or systems.
f. Specific and promotional advertising.
g. Automobile and travel expenses.
h. Professional associations, local board and multiple listing expenses.
i. Insurance and possible health plan costs.
j. Legal, accounting, and other specialized service fees.

MAINTAINING TRUST FUND RECORDS

The maintenance of adequate trust funds records is essential because of the nature of the real estate broker's fiduciary responsibility. The size of the office and the number of transactions involved will to some extent determine the type and complexity of the records kept, but regardless of size or volume of business all brokers must keep an accurate and officially acceptable record of all trust funds passing through the office.

Section 10148 of the Business and Professions Code states that "all listings, deposit receipts, cancelled checks, trust records, and other documents" executed or obtained by a licensed real estate broker in connection with any transaction for which a real estate license is required shall be retained for a period of three years. Further sections of the code make it mandatory that certain types of records be kept available for inspection for a period of four years from the date of the transaction.

Even though a broker does not maintain a trust account in a bank because he places trust funds directly into escrow, he is still responsible for keeping records of all trust funds received by him, including uncashed checks held pending receipt of instructions from his principal. Section 2830 of the California State Real Estate Commissioner's Regulations makes this necessary, and Section 2831 states that the record kept shall set forth in columnar form:

a. Date funds received.
b. From whom funds received.
c. Amount of funds received.
d. With respect to funds deposited to bank trust account, date of said deposit.
e. With respect to funds previously deposited to bank trust account, check number or date of related disbursement.
f. With respect to funds not deposited in bank trust account, nature of other depository and date funds were deposited.
g. Daily balance of bank trust account if one is maintained.

BROKER - SALESPERSON CONTRACT

(INDEPENDENT CONTRACTOR)

CALIFORNIA ASSOCIATION OF REALTORS® STANDARD FORM

THIS AGREEMENT, made this _____ day of _____ , 19____ , by and between

_____ hereinafter referred to as Broker and_____

_____ hereinafter referred to as Salesperson,

WITNESSETH:

WHEREAS, Broker is duly licensed as a real estate broker by the State of California, and

WHEREAS, Broker maintains an office, properly equipped with furnishings and other equipment necessary and incidental to the proper operation of business, and staffed suitably to serving the public as a real estate broker, and

WHEREAS, Salesperson is now engaged in business as a real estate licensee, duly licensed by the State of California.

NOW, THEREFORE, in consideration of the premises and the mutual agreements herein contained, it is understood and agreed as follows:

1. Broker agrees, at Salesperson's request, to make available to Salesperson all current listings in the office, except such as Broker may choose to place in the exclusive possession of some other Salesperson. In addition, at Salesperson's discretion and at Salesperson's request Broker may, from time to time, supply Salesperson with prospective listings; Salesperson shall have absolute discretion in deciding upon whether to handle and the method of handling any such leads suggested by Broker. Nothing herein shall be construed to require that Salesperson accept or service any particular listing or prospective listing offered by Broker; nor shall Broker have any right or authority to direct that Salesperson see or service particular parties, or restrict Salesperson's activities to particular areas. Broker shall have no right, except to the extent required by law, to direct or limit Salesperson's activities as to hours, leads, open houses, opportunity or floor time, production, prospects, reports, sales, sales meeting, schedule, services, inventory, time off, training, vacation, or other similar activities.

At Salesperson's request and at Salesperson's sole discretion Broker agrees to furnish such advice, information and full cooperation as Salesperson shall desire. Broker agrees that thereby Broker obtains no authority or right to direct or control Salesperson's actions except as specifically required by law (including Business and Professions Code Section 10177 (h)) and that Salesperson assumes and retains discretion for methods, techniques and procedures in soliciting and obtaining listings and sales, rentals, or leases of listed property.

2. Broker agrees to provide Salesperson with use, equally with other Salespersons, of all of the facilities of the office now operated by Broker in connection with the subject matter of this contract, which office is now maintained at_____

_____ .

3. Until termination hereof, Salesperson agrees to work diligently and with Salesperson's best efforts to sell, lease or rent any and all real estate listed with Broker, to solicit additional listings and customers, and otherwise promote the business of serving the public in real estate transactions to the end that each of the parties hereto may derive the greatest profit possible, provided that nothing herein shall be construed to require that Salesperson handle or solicit particular listings, or to authorize Broker to direct or require that Salesperson to do so. Salesperson assumes and agrees to perform no other activities in association with Broker, except to solicit and obtain listings and sales, rentals, or leases of property for the parties' mutual benefit, and to do so in accordance with law and with the ethical and professional standards as required in paragraph 4 below.

4. Salesperson agrees to commit no act of a type for which the Real Estate Commissioner of the State of California is authorized by Section 10176 of the California Business & Professions Code to suspend or to revoke license.

5. Broker's usual and customary commissions from time to time in effect, shall be charged to the parties for whom services are performed except that Broker may agree in writing to other rates with such parties.

Broker will advise all Salespersons associated with Broker of any special commission rates made with respect to listings as provided in this paragraph.

When Salesperson shall have performed any work hereunder whereby any commission shall be earned and when such commission shall have been collected, Salesperson shall be entitled to a share of such commission as determined by the current commission schedule set forth in Broker's written policy, except as may otherwise be agreed in writing by Broker and Salesperson before completion of any particular transaction.

6. In the event that two or more Salespeople participate in such work, Salesperson's share of the commission shall be divided between the participating Salespersons according to agreement between them or by arbitration.

7. In compliance with Section 10138 of the California Business and Professions Code, all commissions will be received by Broker; Salesperson's share of such commissions, however, shall be payable to Salesperson immediately upon collection or as soon thereafter as practicable.

8. In no event shall Broker be personally liable to Salesperson for Salesperson's share of commissions not collected, nor shall Salesperson be entitled to any advance or payment from Broker upon future commissions, Salesperson's only remuneration being Salesperson's share of the commission paid by the party or parties for whom the service was performed. Nor shall Salesperson be personally liable to Broker for any commission not collected.

9. Broker shall not be liable to Salesperson for any expenses incurred by Salesperson or for any of his acts except as specifically required by law, nor shall Salesperson be liable to Broker for office help or expense. Salesperson shall have no authority to bind Broker by any promise or representation unless specifically authorized in writing in a particular transaction. Expenses which must by reason of some necessity be paid from the commissions, or are incurred in the collection of, or in the attempt to collect the commission, shall be paid by the parties in the same proportion as provided for herein in the division of commissions.

FIGURE 21-1

Salesperson agrees to provide and pay for all necessary professional licenses and dues. Broker shall not be liable to reimburse Salesperson therefor.

In the event Broker elects to advance sums with which to pay for the account of Salesperson professional fees or other items, Salesperson will repay the same to Broker on demand and Broker may deduct such advances from commissions otherwise payable to Salesperson.

10. This agreement does not constitute a hiring by either party. It is the parties' intention that so far as shall be in conformity with law the Salesperson be an independent contractor and not Broker's employee, and in conformity therewith that Salesperson retain sole and absolute discretion and judgment in the manner and means of carrying out Salesperson's selling and soliciting activities. Therefore, the parties hereto are and shall remain independent contractors bound by the provisions hereof. Salesperson is under the control of Broker as to the result of Salesperson's work only and not as to the means by which such result is accomplished. This agreement shall not be construed as a partnership and Broker shall not be liable for any obligation incurred by Salesperson.

11. In accordance with law, Salesperson agrees that any and all listings of property, and all employment in connection with the real estate business shall be taken in the name of Broker. Such listings shall be filed with Broker within twenty-four hours after receipt of same by Salesperson.

Salesperson shall receive a commission in accordance with the current commission schedule set forth in the Broker's written policy based upon commissions actually collected from each firm listing solicited and obtained by Salesperson. In consideration therefore Salesperson agrees to and does hereby contribute all right and title to such listings to the Broker for the benefit and use of Broker. Salesperson and all other Salespeople associated with Broker to whom Broker may give the listing. Salesperson shall have the rights provided in paragraph 13 hereof with respect to listings procured by Salesperson prior to termination.

12. On completion of work in process, this agreement may be terminated by Salesperson at any time. Except for cause, this agreement may not be terminated by Broker except on 30 days' prior written notice to Salesperson. On the occurrence of any of the following causes, Broker may terminate this agreement:

   (a) Election of Broker to sell its entire business, or to cease doing business at the office specified in paragraph 2;
   (b) Any breach of this agreement by Salesperson;
   (c) Cessation of Salesperson to be licensed;
   (d) Failure of Salesperson to comply with any applicable law, or regulation of the Real Estate Commissioner;
   (e) The filing by or against Salesperson of any petition under any law for the relief of debtors; and
   (f) Conviction of Salesperson of any crime, other than minor traffic offenses.

13. When this agreement has been terminated, Salesperson's regular proportionate share of commission on any sales Salesperson has made that are not closed, shall, upon the closing of such sales, be paid to Salesperson, if collected by Broker, and except in cases of termination for cause Salesperson shall also be entitled to receive the portion of the commissions, received by Broker after termination, allocable to the listing (but not the sale) as set forth in Broker's current commissions schedule, on any listings procured by Salesperson during Salesperson's association with Broker, subject, however, to deductions as provided in paragraph 14.

14. In the event Salesperson leaves and has transactions pending that require further work normally rendered by Salesperson, Broker shall make arrangements with another Salesperson in the organization to perform the required work, and the Salesperson assigned shall be compensated for completing the details of pending transactions and such compensation shall be deducted from the terminated Salesperson's share of the commission.

15. Arbitration—In the event of disagreement or dispute between Salesperson in the office or between Broker and Salesperson arising out of or connected with this agreement which cannot be adjusted by and between the parties involved, the disputed disagreement shall be submitted to the Real Estate Board of which Broker is a member for arbitration pursuant to the provisions of its Bylaws, said provisions being hereby incorporated by reference, and if the Bylaws of such Board include no provision for arbitration, then arbitration shall be pursuant to the rules of the American Arbitration Association, which rules are by this reference incorporated herein.

16. Salesperson shall not after the termination of this contract use to Salesperson's own advantage, or the advantage of any other person or corporation, any information gained for or from the files or business of Broker.

17. Salesperson agrees to indemnify Broker and hold Broker harmless from all claims, demands and liabilities, including costs and attorney's fees. to which Broker is subjected by reason of any action by Salesperson taken or omitted pursuant to this agreement.

18. All notices hereunder shall be in writing. Notices may be delivered personally, or by mail, postage prepaid, to the respective addresses noted below. Either party may designate a new address for purposes of this agreement by notice to the other party. Notices mailed shall be deemed received as of 5:00 P.M. of the second business day following the date of mailing.

WITNESS the signatures of the parties hereto the day and year first above written. In duplicate.

_____   _____
WITNESS   BROKER

                                                _____
                                                ADDRESS

_____   _____
WITNESS   SALESPERSON as INDEPENDENT CONTRACTOR

                                                _____
                                                ADDRESS

For these forms address California Association of Realtors®
505 Shatto Place, Los Angeles 90020. All rights reserved.

FIGURE 21-1 *(concluded)*

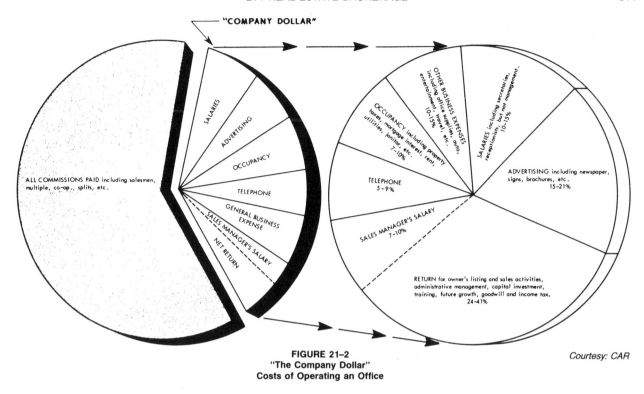

FIGURE 21–2
"The Company Dollar"
Costs of Operating an Office

Courtesy: CAR

Each broker who maintains a formal trust cash receipts journal and a formal cash disbursement journal, or other similar records, in accordance with standard recognized accounting procedures, will have complied with the above requirements. All records and funds shall be open to inspection by the commissioner or his deputies. An excellent publication is available from the California Association of Realtors entitled "Real Estate Trust Fund Records and Requirements." Approved by the Department of Real Estate, it provides a starter set of necessary forms and complete record keeping system.

LOCATION AND PHYSICAL FEATURES OF THE REAL ESTATE OFFICE

The broker should locate his office in the area he intends to serve best. Most of the business transacted by the typical real estate office will be in the neighborhood where the office is located. The location will quite often depend on whether the broker wants to engage in general real estate sales or to specialize in a particular type of property.

An office dealing mainly in the sales, management, or leasing of commercial and industrial properties would locate in the central business district, while an office dealing mostly in residential properties would locate in a suburban area

or in the residential area it intends to serve best.

The physical appearance of the real estate office will quite often influence the opinion of prospective clients with regard to the efficiency and businesslike attitude of the firm. The exterior and interior appearance should blend together to give a professional, businesslike picture to the passerby and entering clients. A real estate office should not look like a hot dog stand or a drive in.

The office interior should be well planned to provide adequate space and working area. The area immediately inside the front entrance is the reception area. It should contain a large counter, receptionist's or secretary's desk, and adequate seating facilities for customers who may be waiting for a particular broker or salesman.

Behind the counter is the salesperson's working area. The broker's desk may be in this area also, but usually he has a private office or an enclosed area that offers a certain degree of privacy.

A conference or closing room is a necessity. It is difficult for a salesperson to talk to customers in the main part of the office while others are moving about and talking on the telephone. In an office not large enough to have a separate conference room or closing room, the broker's office is generally used.

Each office should have a separate area to be used as a work room. Such items as typewriters, mimeograph machines, photocopy machine, files, forms, signs, adding machine, dictating machine, and the like are located here. Finally, each office should provide clean and sanitary rest room facilities for the use of the staff as well as for clients.

PROPERTY MANAGEMENT

Since most real estate brokerages offices usually participate to a certain degree in the function of property management, all licensees should have at least an elementary knowledge of the general responsibilities and principles relating to this field. Property management is a specialized area of operation for the licensee. Many licensees devote a substantial portion, if not all, of their time to managing properties, and many of these individuals have obtained the CPM designation.

Certified property manager (CPM)

The Institute of Real Estate Management of the National Association of Realtors® currently confers on those persons who meet their requirements the title of Certified Property Manager (CPM). To obtain this designation, a candidate must:

1. Be a member of a local real estate board or a member of the National Association of Realtors®.
2. Have been actively engaged in the real estate management business in a responsible position for a minimum of three years.
3. Demonstrate his ability to manage real estate.
4. Pass certain minimum educational requirements.
5. Subscribe to the institute bylaws and pledge.
6. Give evidence of honesty and integrity.

In addition to the above requirements, the candidate for the CPM designation must:

1. Pass two written examinations prepared by the institute; or
2. Pass the examinations in the institute's Lecture Courses I and II, thereby eliminating part or all of the examinations in 1 above; or
3. Present proof of 15 years of active management experience in order to be allowed to take a special examination.

Types of properties managed

Licensees who engage in the management of real property, whether they have received the CPM designation or not, will find themselves managing many different types of property for others. Among the more common are: office buildings, apartment buildings, commercial structures, residences, shopping centers, public buildings, hotels, motels, recreational centers, specialized factories, restaurants, and theaters. A few other types of special properties that have been gaining in importance in recent years are parking lots, garages, harbors and their installations, and airports.

Goals of management

Quite simply, the owner of a building wants to rent or lease space at a rate that will bring sufficient return to enable him to pay the operating expenses, taxes, insurance, capital retirement, and other fixed charges, and still show a certain return on the capital invested. The tenant wants to lease space at a rate that is within his income and will allow him to utilize the space at a profit to him.

To satisfy their requirements and those of their tenants, owners have found that the best method is to employ trained and experienced managers. The return far offsets the expense involved, and it is usually greater than the cost because a trained property manager is involved in the operation of the property.

Types of property managers

There are generally three types of property managers—real estate licensee, individual property manager, and resident manager.

Real estate licensee. This property manager is a real estate licensee in a real estate office that manages a number of properties for various owners. Most real estate firms, regardless of size, generally perform some degree of property management. Many individuals who invest in residential properties do not wish to be burdened with the responsibility of renting, rent collection, and general maintenance required, and will be glad to turn these responsibilities over to the broker from whom they have purchased the property. In fact, the availability of the management function is often an important selling point to be used by the broker. Additionally, the managing broker will usually be the one to receive a listing on the property should the owner decide later to sell, exchange, or trade.

Individual property manager. This individual manages an individual building for the owner, and he may or may not be a real estate licensee. He is generally employed by the owner on a salary basis and is usually found in charge of a large office building or large residential complex.

The resident manager. The resident manager, or building superintendent, as he is sometimes called, not only manages a building but also lives on the premises as well. He is generally employed by the real estate firm that manages the building but is not himself a real estate licensee. There are local ordinances in many areas that require buildings with units over a certain number to have a resident manager on the premises. The California Department of Real Estate does not require a resident manager to hold a real estate license.

Functions and duties of the property manager

The professional property manager should:

a. **Be a specialist in merchandising.** Whether he is showing an apartment or negotiating for the lease of commercial space, he must be able to sell the prospective tenant on the merits of his particular building.

b. **Be a leasing expert.** Leases can become quite complex and involved, and the manager must be well versed in the different types and kinds of leases applicable or beneficial to particular types of clients.

c. **Have maintenance know-how.** The manager is often required to take full charge of the maintenance problems inherent in the building. He must survey the building and know the probable current maintenance and deferred maintenance.

d. **Understand accounting procedures.** Specialized records must be kept for any type of property. The manager must make monthly reports to the owner, as well as submit a detailed annual statement that is a necessity for income tax purposes.

e. **Understand taxation aspects.** The effects of taxation are everywhere, and the property manager must understand property taxes and their effect on the property he manages. He must understand the problems of depreciation that apply to the building owner, and the relation of depreciation to the income and profit of the specific operation.

f. **Understand insurance.** Different forms of insurance must be carried on the property, and there is a good deal of specialized information in this area which must be understood by the property manager.

g. **Be a credit expert.** The credit rating of a prospective tenant is of vital importance to the manager, since he must be sure the tenant will be able to meet the terms of his lease or rental agreement and is financially able to meet his obligations.

h. **Establish the rental schedule.** The manager must establish a proper rental schedule. He should make a thorough neighborhood analysis of competing properties in the area, and the results will enable him to set up a realistic rent schedule to bring the maximum income to the owner.

i. **Supervise purchasing.** The manager must know the prices for various items and what is available on the market. He must keep up with technological advances in building materials and be able to get the best value for the money spent. In many cases a worn out item may be replaced with a new one of the same type, but quite often the manager has the opportunity to modernize and update the property by replacing an obsolete installation with a modern and more efficient one.

j. **Develop employee policies.** Many management operations succeed or fail in direct proportion to the ability of the manager to choose, train, and direct personnel. He must, therefore, know each job to be done so that he can properly direct those who do the job.

Earnings

The property management function is usually performed on a commission basis—that is, a percentage of the gross rent collected. The charge varies for different types of properties and in different areas, and may be as low as 1 percent on a very large building and as high as 10 percent for a small residential building.

In addition to the commission an additional fee is usually charged for the negotiation of new leases and for the supervision of major repairs or alterations to the building. Salaries for resident managers and office building managers depend largely on the local conditions and vary with the locale and size of the property involved.

Management contract

A management contract is a written contract that clearly sets forth the responsibilities of the broker and of the owner. It should indicate the terms and period of the contract, the policies pertaining to management of the building, management fees, and the authority and powers given by the owner to the broker who will manage the property. In his capacity as an agent the manager is subject to all the legal restrictions imposed on an agent, as well as to those specifically included in the contract.

Standard management agreement forms are available from local real estate boards. An excellent form is available from the National Association of Realtors®, 155 E. Superior St., Chicago, Illinois 60011. This form is shown in Figure 21–3.

REAL ESTATE EXCHANGES

The real estate licensee will often be involved in an exchange of real properties, since there are often certain advantages to a property owner in exchanging his property rather than disposing of it in an outright sale. Of particular advantage to the real estate licensee is the fact that in an exchange of properties a commission is generally paid with respect to each of the individual properties, and thus the licensee may earn two commissions in the single transaction. An example of an exchange agreement involving a simple exchange transaction is contained in Chapter 9, Real Estate Contracts.

Reasons for an exchange

Individuals may enter into a real estate exchange situation for various reasons.

1. The most common reason is for tax advantages. The tax-free exchange and trading-up in real estate allow the property owner certain immediate tax advantages. We shall touch upon these later in this discussion.

2. Many persons who want a change of location or climate seek to exchange their properties.

3. An owner who wants no disruption of income may be able to exchange his units for others without losing income during negotiations.

4. An owner who has no cash may want to use his equity in his present property in order to acquire another.

5. During a tight money market an owner may benefit by exchanging his property instead of selling outright and having to carry back a large mortgage.

6. A person may want another property but may not want to go through the process of a sale and new purchase, with all the pressures and time factors involved.

The tax-free exchange

The Internal Revenue Code, Section 1031, deals with tax-free exchanges. Such exchanges are generally of most benefit to persons who want to exchange their property for one that is worth substantially more than theirs. This is commonly referred to as *trading up*. Many individuals think that the term *tax-free exchange* means that the Internal Revenue Service will completely forgive a certain amount of gain on the exchange as far as tax payment is concerned. Actually, the tax is merely deferred until a time in the future when the owner disposes of the property in a taxable transaction. While the term *tax-free exchange* is generally used, it is more proper to refer to such an exchange as a *tax-deferred exchange*.

Many owners have exchanged their properties a number of times over the years and have traded up each time. Years later, if the owner sells the final piece of property in a normal sale, he may find that 80 or 90 percent of the sale price will be a taxable gain. This is because he has been deferring the payment of tax over the years during which he exchanged his property. The gain, however, is a capital gain and subject to a maximum tax of approximately 20 percent. If an owner trades up for a number of years and instead of eventually selling his property wills it to his heirs, there is no longer any California inheritance tax but the heirs may be subject to payment of Federal estate taxes.

Like kind defined

The Internal Revenue Code states that no gain or loss shall be recognized if property held for investment or for productive use in a trade or business is exchanged solely for property of like kind also to be held for investment or for use in a trade or business. Thus any real property being held for investment or for productive use in a trade or business may be exchanged for any other business or investment property. The size or worth of the properties exchanged does not defeat the like kind requirement, so that an individual may exchange an apartment house with 6 units valued at $295,000 for an apartment house with 16 units valued at $595,000.

PROPERTY MANAGEMENT AGREEMENT

THIS IS INTENDED TO BE A LEGALLY BINDING AGREEMENT — READ IT CAREFULLY

CALIFORNIA ASSOCIATION OF REALTORS® STANDARD FORM

_____ (hereinafter "Owner"), and

_____ (hereinafter "Agent"),

agree as follows:

1. The owner hereby employs and grants Agent the exclusive right to rent, lease, operate and manage the property known as _____

_____

_____

upon the terms hereinafter set forth, for the period of_____ beginning on the date hereof and terminating the_____ day of _____, 19____; provided, however, that either party hereto may terminate this contract as of the _____ day of_____ during any year of the term hereof, by giving to the other party not less than 30 days prior written notice on an intention to so terminate.

2. Agent shall:
   (a) Use due diligence in the performance of this contract:
   (b) Render_____ statements of receipts, expenses and charges and to remit to Owner receipts less disbursements. In the
       monthly/other
       event the disbursements shall be in excess of the rents collected by the Agent, the Owner hereby agrees to pay such excess promptly upon demand of the Agent.

   (c) Accumulate as a reserve in the Owner's account each month approximately one-twelfth of the previous year's taxes, and bond payments or assessments, if any, and to pay same when due.
   (d) Deposit all receipts collected for Owner (less any sums properly deducted or otherwise provided herein) in a Trust account in a national or state institution qualified to engage in the banking or trust business, separate from Agent's personal account. However, Agent will not be held liable in event of bankruptcy or failure of a depository.
   (e) Bond by a fidelity bond in adequate amount any employee who handles or is responsible for Owner's monies.

3. The Owner grants Agent the following authority and powers and Owner shall pay the expenses in connection herewith:
   (a) To advertise the availability for rental of the herein described premises or any part thereof, and to display "for rent" signs thereof; to sign, renew or cancel leases for the premises or any part thereof; to collect rents or other charges and expenses due or to become due and give receipts therefor; to terminate tenancies and to sign and serve in the name of the Owner such notices as are appropriate; to institute and prosecute actions to evict tenants and to recover possession of said premises in the name of the Owner and recover rents and other sums due; and when expedient, to settle, compromise, and release such actions or suits or reinstate such tenancies. Any lease executed for the Owner by the Agent shall not exceed _____ years.
   (b) To make or cause to be made and supervise repairs and alterations, and to do decorating on said premises; to purchase supplies and pay all bills therefor. The Agent agrees to secure the prior approval of the Owner on all expenditures in excess of $ _____ for any one item, except monthly or recurring operating charges and emergency repairs in excess of the maximum, if in the opinion of the Agent such repairs are necessary to protect the property from damage or prevent damage to life or to the property of others or to avoid suspension of necessary services or to avoid penalties or fines or to maintain services to the tenants as called for in their leases.
   (c) To hire, discharge and supervise all labor and employees required for the operation and maintenance of the premises. Agent may perform any of its duties through Owner's attorneys, agents or employees and shall not be responsible for their acts, defaults or negligence if reasonable care has been exercised in their appointment and retention.
   (d) To make contracts for electricity, gas, fuel, water, telephone, window cleaning, ash or rubbish hauling and other services or such of them as the Agent shall deem advisable; the Owner to assume the obligation of any contract so entered into at the termination of this agreement.
   (e) To pay loan indebtedness, property and employees taxes, special assessments and insurance as designated by Owner.

4. The Owner shall:
   (a) Indemnify and save the Agent harmless from any and all costs, expenses, attorney's fees, suits, liabilities, damages or claim for damages, including but not limited to those arising out of any injury or death to any person or persons or damage to any property of any kind whatsoever and to whomsoever belonging, including Owner, in any way relating to the management of the premises by the Agent or the performance or exercise of any of the duties, obligations, powers or authorities herein or hereafter granted to the agent; to carry, at Owner's sole cost and expense, such public liability, property damage and worker's compensation insurance as shall be adequate to protect the interests of the Agent and Owner, the policies for which shall name the Agent as well as the Owner as the party insured.

FIGURE 21-3

(b) To pay the Agent:

(1) For Management _____

(2) For Leasing _____

(3) In the event that the Owners shall request the Agent to undertake work exceeding that usual to normal management, then a fee shall be agreed upon for such services before the work begins. Normal management does not include modernization, refinancing, fire restoration, major rehabilitations, obtaining income tax advice, presenting petitions to planning or zoning committees, advising on proposed new construction or other counseling.

(4) For assignment: The Owner hereby agrees that Agent may be compensated by the party or parties requesting an assignment of lease for services rendered in negotiating the consent of assignment.

(5) Other _____

_____

_____

5. If it shall become necessary for Agent or Owner to give notice of any kind, the same shall be written, and served, by sending such notice by certified mail to the address shown under their signature.

6. This Agreement shall be binding upon the successors of the Agent, and the heirs, administrators, executors, successors and assigns of the Owner.

Parties acknowledge having read the foregoing prior to execution and receipt of a duplicate original dated this _____

day of _____ 19 _____.

WITNESS:

_____

_____   _____
                                                                                OWNER

                                                          _____
                                                                               ADDRESS

                                                          _____
                                                                                AGENT

                                                          _____
                                                                               ADDRESS

NO REPRESENTATION IS MADE AS TO THE LEGAL VALIDITY OF ANY PROVISION OR THE ADEQUACY OF ANY PROVISION IN ANY SPECIFIC TRANSACTION. A REAL ESTATE BROKER IS THE PERSON QUALIFIED TO ADVISE ON REAL ESTATE. IF YOU DESIRE LEGAL ADVICE CONSULT YOUR ATTORNEY.

FIGURE 21–3 *(concluded)*

Boot received or given

Boot is cash or any other property given or received in addition to the property that may be exchanged tax free. When boot is involved in an exchange, it is important to identify the person giving boot and the person receiving it. For the person giving boot, the new basis of the property he receives is the basis of the property he gave in exchange plus the amount of boot given.

Example: A owns an income property with a market value of $250,000 and a cost basis of $100,000. A exchanges this building for B's income property, which has a market value of $300,000. A gives B his building plus $50,000 in cash. The cost basis to A of his newly acquired building is (1) the $100,000 cost basis of the building traded in and (2) the $50,000 cash boot given. Thus, A now has a building with a cost basis of $150,000. This has been a tax-free exchange so far as A is concerned.

For the person receiving boot, the exchange may become partly taxable. The taxable portion, however is limited to the amount of boot received.

Example: The market value of the building exchanged by B is $300,000, and we will assume that his cost basis is $175,000.

Cost basis of building exchanged by B	$175,000
Received by B:	
Fair market value of A's building	250,000
Boot in the form of cash	50,000
Total received	$300,000

The potential gain to B is $125,000 ($300,000 minus $175,000).

Taxable gain when boot is received is limited to the amount of boot received, so B will be taxed on only $50,000 of the $125,000 gain. Thus, for B, who received the boot, the exchange of property between himself and A has resulted in a partially taxable exchange.

Depreciation considered

The importance of depreciation has been discussed previously, especially in Chapter 17, Income Tax and Real Estate. The necessity for increased depreciation is one of the main reasons for entering into an exchange. It is quite common to find many persons who have owned a property for so many years that there is virtually no depreciation left to deduct against the building, especially if an accelerated method of depreciation has been used. In the meantime, the income from the property has greatly increased, and since the owner has very little offset, he finds himself paying a considerable amount of tax. Further, many times the mortgage has been greatly reduced or paid off, so that there is very little if any deduction for interest paid.

An owner in such a position would probably want to acquire another building so that he will have substantial depreciation to offset income. However, in a tax-free exchange the basis for a newly acquired property is merely what the basis for the old property was. This problem is solved if the owner exchanges his property for one that is worth much more and has a large mortgage against it. The basis for the new property is the basis for the old building, plus the difference between the old mortgage, if any, and the new one.

Example: A has a building worth $300,000 with a cost basis of $30,000. He trades his building for another worth $900,000 and subject to a mortgage of $600,000. A has no mortgage on his old property; it is clear. The basis of the new building to A would be his old basis of $30,000 plus the new mortgage of $600,000, which means he now has on the new building a basis of $630,000. Not only is A building up an equity in a building much more valuable than the one he had previously, but he also now has a substantial depreciation and interest deduction to offset the building's income.

Basis for newly acquired property

Determination of the basis for property acquired in an exchange is one area that can become quite complex, since so many different factors need to be considered. Often the broker and his client will need the advice of a tax accountant in order to make this determination. The problem of boot, whether given or received; the exchange of existing mortgages; an exchange involving many pieces of property; an exchange involving more than two parties; an exchange resulting in a partial loss for one party and a gain for the other; and many other possible combinations—each results in a detailed and complex set of calculations. Many brokers have thus studied and earned the Certified Property Exchanger (CPE) designation.

The following outline shows the basic framework within which calculations are made in order to arrive at the basis for property acquired in an exchange. *Old property* refers to property traded off, and *new property* refers to the property received as a result of the exchange. The basis of newly acquired property is determined as follows:

1. Start with the basis of the old property.
2. To the basis of the old property, add:
    a. Any cash paid.
    b. Any other boot paid.
    c. Any loans on the new property (an existing loan assumed or taken subject to, or a new loan).

    Any recognized gain. (total of 1 and 2)
3. From the total of 1 and 2 above, subtract any of the following:
    a. Any loans on the old property assumed or taken subject to by the other party.
    b. Any cash received.
    c. Any boot received.

Thus, the basis of the newly acquired property will be the total of 1 and 2, minus the total of 3.

Three-way exchange

In certain cases a licensee may find himself involved in a three-way exchange. A three-way exchange, or multiple exchange as it is sometimes called, results when there are more than two parties to an exchange. This is also covered in Section 1031 of the Internal Revenue Code. If certain requirements are met, all parties in a multiple exchange may enjoy the benefits of a tax-free exchange. The Internal Revenue Service is extremely strict in its interpretation of certain rules and regulations regarding exchanges involving three or more owners, and the brokers and clients involved in such an exchange must exercise extreme caution in properly documenting all steps and meeting all requirements. If not, the Internal Revenue Service may declare that a taxable sale, and not a tax-free exchange, has taken place.

If two owners, each of whom wants to exchange his property, can get together and agree on terms and conditions, it is a fairly simple exchange situation that should take place without any undue difficulty. Quite often, however, we find a situation in which one party wants to exchange his property for the property of another party, but the other party wants to sell rather than exchange. In such a case, a third party must be brought into the picture.

Example: A wants to exchange his property for property B owns. However, B wants to sell his property rather than exchange it. Thus, a third party C, who wants to purchase A's property must be found. A and B can then exchange properties, and C purchases the property B has received in the exchange (A's former property). An alternative method might be for the broker to find someone who will purchase B's property and then enter into an exchange agreement with A.

Time-delay exchange—Starker case

California investors who previously avoided an exchange because of the difficulty in locating a necessary property (up-leg) for which to exchange can now take advantage of a recent decision of the Ninth Circuit Court of Appeals.

In *Starker v. Internal Revenue Service*, the court ruled that a time-delay exchange with an "open leg" will qualify for tax-deferred treatment if there is a contractual agreement giving the selling party the right to receive like-kind property in exchange at some future time.

If the parties place funds to acquire property in an escrow or impound account, the taxpayer should not have any control over such funds or be able to cancel any agreement and receive the money. Otherwise, the IRS can claim that the taxpayer has constructively received any funds placed into escrow and attempt to refuse allowance of exchange benefits. The exchange party should acquire title to the exchange property and transfer it to the taxpayer.

Involuntary conversion

In the area of tax-free exchanges, one often hears the term *involuntary conversion*. Involuntary conversion occurs when a person receives money or other property for his property, which was destroyed, stolen, or condemned for public use.

The person whose property is involuntarily converted may receive a substantial amount of cash by an insurance award or condemnation award. If the money received amounts to more than the adjusted basis of the property destroyed or condemned, the owner will have realized a gain. However, Section 1033 of the Internal Revenue Code, holds that there is no taxable gain under involuntary conversion if, within a prescribed period of time, the money received is used to purchase property similar to, or similar in use or service to, that property that was involuntarily converted.

TRADE-IN PROGRAMS

There is a sharp and distinct difference between exchanging a property and trading in a property. Exchanging is basically the transferring of one property for another. The broker acts as a negotiator only, and is customarily not a principal in the transaction. In a trade-in, however, the broker is active as one who provides time, knowledge, and capital as a principal in the transaction.

Trade-in programs are generally limited to the residential sales field, since the basis of this program as it operates in the real estate industry is to make it easier for a prospective client to purchase a house. Persons who want to exchange larger properties usually tend to favor the benefits inherent in the tax-free exchange method.

In the discussion that follows we shall refer to the house the purchaser presently owns as the old house, and to the property the purchaser wants to buy as the new house.

The basic problem

One of the main problems confronting persons who already own a house but want to purchase another is what to do with the old house. Some of the common courses of action are the following:

1. Buy a new house and keep the old one. If the old house is in good condition and in a neighborhood where values are stable and will tend to appreciate over the years, it may be argued that to keep the house and rent it out would be a good investment and should be considered. However, the owner must also consider such problems as future maintenance and repair, dealings with tenants, distance between the old house and the new one he wants to buy, and equity he has in the old house.

2. Sell the old house first and then buy a new one. While this may seem the logical thing to do, most owners quickly realize that when they enter into an agreement with a prospective purchaser to buy their old house, the buyers will want occupancy on close of escrow. This means that the seller must find a new house within a relatively short period of time, and will be under a certain amount of pressure in doing so. Very few persons want to be put in such a position, especially if they are going to buy the new house in the same general locality and are not under any particular pressure to sell.

3. Buy a new home first and then sell the old one. Here is another course of action available to the owner, but it too has certain drawbacks. The owner must have enough money to be able to purchase a new house without the funds he has tied up in the old one; he would not be able

immediately to move a great distance away; and, most of all, he would generally be making two mortgage payments at the same time—one on the old house and one on the new.

4. Purchase a new house from a real estate firm that offers the owner a trade-in plan. This action will enable him to buy the new house and dispose of the old one at the same time.

Common trade-in programs

The benefits of the various trade-in programs discussed below are available to all types of purchasers and sellers, and developers of large tracts of new houses as well as real estate brokerage firms have long understood the benefits and increased sales that result from offering to the general public some plan to trade in the old house and buy a new one. The FHA also provides special assistance to brokers or builders in financing property taken in trade on the sale of another.

The conditional trade-in plan. Under this plan, the prospective purchaser agrees to buy a particular house, provided that he can sell his old house within a certain period of time. This is often referred to as a contingent sale—that is, the sale of one house is contingent on the sale of another. The prospective purchaser is committed by a written agreement to buy the new house if he sells his old one during the agreed-on time period. This type of trade-in plan relies to a great extent on the willingness of the seller to wait for the buyer to sell his old house.

Most sellers may agree to an offer contingent on the sale of another property, but will usually reserve the right to accept another offer during the time period agreed on. It is for this reason that the most used trade-in plan is not the conditional trade-in plan but rather the guaranteed trade-in plan.

The guaranteed trade-in plan. Under this plan, the real estate firm guarantees the buyer that it will either sell his old house within a certain period of time or buy it from him for a certain specified price. With such a guarantee, the buyer will be able to negotiate and enter into a contract for the purchase of a new property.

If the broker can sell the client's property within the agreed-on time, generally 90 days, he will usually earn a standard commission on the sale. While many persons feel that they may lose money if they trade in a house, this is not often the case for the following reasons:

1. Since the client is a prospective purchaser

and is actively seeking to buy another property, he usually has a fair understanding of the prevailing market conditions and property prices.

2. Thus, the broker must guarantee a price that is fair to the client. In trying to agree with the client on what constitutes a fair price, the broker is also in the position of obtaining a listing on the property. He must carefully appraise the house and convince the owner of the validity of his final appraisal. Under the circumstances it would be very difficult for the broker to get the owner to agree to a guaranteed price that is very much below market value.

3. In most cases the guaranteed price is such that it is much more advantageous for the broker to sell the property and earn a commission on the sale than to have to buy the property himself.

4. The responsible broker makes every attempt to sell the trade-in property during the time allowed; he then makes two commissions—one on the old property and one on the new property—and avoids all the detail of actually having to purchase the old property himself and then resell it.

Different real estate offices have different procedures for their trade-in programs. However, a common procedure found in many offices is as follows:

1. The house to be traded in is appraised to determine fair market value.
2. An exclusive listing is obtained.
3. The guaranteed price is set at about 85 percent of the appraised price.
4. The firm advances the down payment to the buyer for the new property.
5. If the property is sold, the firm receives a standard commission.
6. If the property is not sold by the end of the listing term, the firm purchases it for the amount agreed on in 3 above.

An excellent example of the type of form used in a guaranteed trade situation is shown in Figure 21–4.

BUSINESS OPPORTUNITY BROKERAGE

The Real Estate Law defines *business opportunity* as meaning and including business, business opportunity, and good will of an existing business, or any one of a combination thereof. The term *good will* as applied to a business means the expectation of continued patronage. It includes the value added to the business because of the owner's

policies toward his clients and customers with regard to advertising, merchandise, and/or services, as well as the reputation the business has in the particular locale where it operates. The sale of a business opportunity involves the sale of personal property, and the rules governing transfer of chattels apply.

The usual transaction involves such businesses as grocery stores, bakeries, bars, and leases and fixtures of operating rooming houses and hotels. The sale of these general types of businesses almost always includes stock, fixtures, and goodwill. Certain permits, licenses, and the like must be transferred and/or obtained, and other legal requirements not commonly encountered in the sale of houses, multiple units, and other types of nonbusiness opportunity properties must be met. Any real estate licensee holding a broker's or salesperson's license may legally negotiate the sale of business opportunities.

FACTORS IN THE SALE AND PURCHASE OF A BUSINESS OPPORTUNITY

The sale of business opportunities is a specialized field, and licensees who deal in this area are specialists just as are those who deal in industrial properties, unimproved acreage, or recreational properties. Even within the broad area of business opportunities, many brokers specialize to the extent of dealing with one type of business opportunity, such as service stations or grocery stores.

The average real estate licensee seldom engages in the sale of a business opportunity as such. The closest many have ever come is having sold a building that happened to contain a shop or a few stores on the ground floor. In such cases, the merchant is merely thought of as a tenant or lessee in the same way as other persons who occupy dwelling units in the building. The real estate licensee, then, has merely sold a building and not a business opportunity.

The broker must remember that when he sells a business opportunity he is dealing with a buyer who may be investing life savings and therefore expects to be able to earn a livelihood from the business he is purchasing. While real property always retains some value, a bankrupt business is usually worthless. Thus, the licensee has a tremendous responsibility of correctly representing to the buyer the business for sale and of qualifying the buyer not only on his ability to buy, but also, to a certain degree, on his ability to succeed in the business after he purchases it.

Guaranteed Sales Plan Agreement

THIS AGREEMENT, made this_____day of_____19____ by and

between_____and_____

his wife, of_____

California, hereinafter called Seller, First Party, and_____

hereinafter called Buyer, second party.   (Broker)

WITNESSETH

A. Sellers warrant that they are the owners of that certain real property located at_____

_____

B. Sellers have purchased or are in the process of purchasing real property for which they are
committed or intend to be committed to pay purchase monies.

C. Sellers are unable to pay said purchase monies unless property now owned by them and
hereinabove first described is sold and escrow closed; and

D. Sellers are desirous of establishing a guaranteed sales price; and Buyers for a set fee are
willing to guarantee such price;

NOW, THEREFORE, it is understood and agreed by and between the parties hereto as
follows;

I. **General Provisions:**

a. Buyer herein guarantees to seller in consideration of the covenants and conditions herein
contained to buy Sellers said property on SELLERS WRITTEN REQUEST on or

before the _____day of_____19____ for the total purchase

price of $_____, subject to the terms and conditions herein contained.

b. Seller agrees to deliver subject property to Buyer free and clear of bonds, liens, attachments, judgments, or any other items affecting the title or Seller's equity in said prop-

erty excepting as follows:_____

_____

_____

c. Seller represents that the existing encumbrance(s) on the subject property may be paid
in full at any time prior to maturity of said note and trust deed.

d. Seller represents that he is not in default on any payments for subject property and
covenants to make all payments as they fall due until close of escrow. In connection
with said purchase agreement Seller agrees to correct any default within twenty-four
(24) hours after notification by Buyer.

e. Seller agrees not to sell, agree to sell, or execute any documents relating to a sale of the
subject property without the written consent of Buyer.

f. Seller represents that (s)he has free and clear title to any and all personal property included in this sale.

g. Seller agrees to maintain the subject premises in good condition and repair and to deliver the property in the same or better condition than now exists.

h. Possession of the subject property shall be delivered to Buyer upon close of escrow. In
the event Seller fails to surrender possession, Seller agrees to pay as rental two per cent

FIGURE 21-4

(2%) of the sales price per month on a prorata basis and shall be a month to month tenant. Seller agrees to hold Buyer harmless from any and all liabilities for injuries to persons or for property damage as a result of the use and occupation of the property until Seller surrenders possession of the property to Buyer.

i. As Buyer's fee for this guarantee, Seller agrees to pay Buyer $_____.

j. Seller agrees forthwith to list said property with _____
(Broker)
for a period of _____ days, under the terms found in the Standard Exclusive Listing Agreement used by that company.

II. Sale of Seller's Property by Broker

In the event of a sale of said property by _____, Seller
(Broker)
shall pay to Buyer from the proceeds in escrow the amount of Buyer's guarantee fee, and the parties hereto are released from any further obligation under this Agreement.

III. Sale of Seller's Property to Buyer Herein

In the event Buyer is required to purchase hereunder, escrow shall be opened immediately, and sale shall be completed as follows:

A. Buyer will assume the balance due as of the close of escrow upon aforedescribed loans, or at the option of the Buyer, may place new financing on the property.

B. Seller will deliver to Buyer a termite report from a licensed pest control company showing the above property to be free of any visible termites, dry rot and fungus.

C. Seller agrees, at his expense, to furnish Buyer a Standard Policy of Title Insurance.

D. Interest, taxes, insurance and rentals and any and all charges arising out of ownership of the property will be prorated as of the date of closing of escrow.

E. Buyer and Seller agree to pay customary escrow charges.

F. Sellers will execute such deeds and other documents, as may be necessary or desirable to carry out the purpose of this Agreement.

IV. Cancellation

Sellers shall have the right at any time prior to his giving written notice to Buyer to purchase hereunder, to cancel this Agreement upon the payment of guarantee fee to Buyers.

Seller_____   _____
(Broker)

Seller_____ by_____

FIGURE 21–4 *(concluded)*

Specific information to be disclosed

Business opportunity listings should only be taken when a broker feels that the value of the business is correctly represented by the owner. In the case of smaller businesses, where everything, including the stock, will be sold at a given price, the listing should include a guaranteed inventory to assure the buyer that he is getting a correct dollar value. Prior to completion of the sale a physical inventory should be taken to assure that the figure previously represented by the seller is correct. Should the inventory fall below or above the figure expected, an adjustment in the purchase price must be made.

The broker should inform the seller that his books and other business records will have to be opened for inspection to the potential purchaser after a deposit has been obtained.

Technical qualifications license

Real estate licensees engaged in the sale of business opportunities must be especially careful when selling a business in which the owner must be examined for technical qualifications and licensed by the state. If a license to engage in the sale of alcoholic beverages is involved, the purchaser will have to meet certain qualifications for such a license. In addition to this type of license there are others that require the purchaser to meet special requirements and/or pass a certain type of examination. Examples of such licenses are those required to operate a dry cleaning establishment, beauty shop, or barber shop.

SPECIFIC RULES AND REGULATIONS

Following preparation of the deposit receipt and prior to close of escrow, the broker must be sure that certain legal requirements are met. In addition, he must understand and be able to explain the bill of sale for personal property sold, the escrow agreement and instructions, and the various prorations involved. The licensee must be familiar with and understand the requirements of (1) the Uniform Commercial Code (UCC), (2) the Bulk Transfer Act of the UCC, (3) California sales and use tax provisions, and (4) the Alcoholic Beverage Control Act.

Uniform Commercial Code (UCC)

Division 9 of the UCC establishes a unified and comprehensive method for regulation of security transactions in personal property with regard to any transaction that is intended to create a security interest in goods, documents, installments, chattel paper, accounts, and contract rights.

The UCC provides for a simplified filing system by means of a financing statement to perfect security interest provided for under the code. Financing statements may have to be filed with the secretary of state or in the county recorder's office. In many business opportunity transactions it is important that the buyer obtain information or copies of financing statements that affect the seller. Division 9 is further designed to protect the purchasers and creditors from the rights of prior secured parties who have a security interest in the property. This is done by requiring the secured party to file a financing statement. The office of the secretary of state publishes a booklet, "Procedures and Forms for Filing under Divisions 9 and 10 of the Uniform Commercial Code." Copies of this booklet as well as the standard forms may be obtained by request.

Bulk sales and the UCC

Division 6 of the UCC pertains to bulk transfers of goods in California. The purpose of this UCC section is to protect the creditors of a person who sells a business. Recordation and publication are used to warn the transferor's (seller's) creditors of the impending transfer (due to the sale). This allows the creditors to protect their rights before the assets are disposed of or encumbered.

When a retail or wholesale merchant wants to transfer in bulk (and not in the ordinary course of his business) a substantial part of his material, supplies, merchandise, or other inventory. Division 6 requires that the transferee (buyer) give public notice to the transferor's (seller's) creditors. This requirement is fulfilled by: (1) recordation of a notice in the office of the recorder in the county where the property is located, at least 10 days before the bulk transfer is to be made, and (2) publication of the notice at least once in a newspaper of general circulation published in the judicial district where the property is located, or if there is none, then in a newspaper of general circulation in the county where the business is located. Notice must be published at least five days before the bulk transfer is to take place. Noncompliance may result in a fraudulent transfer.

California sales and use tax provisions

The Sales and Use Tax Law is of interest to licensees engaged in the sale of business opportu-

324

nities where sales of tangible personal property at retail are made. The following are of particular importance:

1. The necessity of acquiring a seller's permit when engaging in business.
2. The necessity of posting security for the collection of the required sales tax.
3. The obtainment of a clearance receipt in order to protect the purchaser against successor's liability.
4. The obtainment of releases or subordination agreements covering sales tax liens against real or personal property.
5. The matter of tax liability on the sale price of a business in proportion to the fair retail value of the tangible personal property involved.

Alcohol Beverage Control Act

The sale of many businesses involves, as part of the transaction, the sale and transfer of a license or permit to engage in the sale of alcoholic beverages. Thus, the licensee engaged in the sale of business opportunities should be familiar with the legal controls imposed on the sale and distribution of alcoholic beverages, and especially with the methods governing the issuance of licenses or permits to those persons engaged in such sale or distribution.

Department of Alcoholic Beverage Control. The Department of Alcoholic Control is charged with administration of the Alcoholic Beverage Control Act (Division 9 of the Business and Professions Code), and issues licenses. Local officials and the department are charged with the duty of enforcing the law.

Transfer of a license. A person who intends to engage in the sale of alcoholic beverages should not make any investment on the assumption that a license authorizing him to engage in such business will be issued or transferred. Before filing a transfer application with the department, the applicant and licensee must file a notice of intended transfer with the county recorder and establish an escrow, as required by law. No consideration may be paid out of the escrow before approval of the transfer, and the transfer of title to the licensed business must coincide with the transfer of the license.

Information for brokers and applicants. Brokers who negotiate a business opportunity involving the transfer of a license and persons who seek

such a license must be familiar with the statutes and regulations governing such activity. These are available on request through any office of the Department of Alcoholic Beverage Control (ABC). An on-sale license means that the alcoholic beverage will generally be consumed on the premises, as at a restaurant or bar, while an off-sale license means that the alcoholic beverage will be purchased on the premises but not consumed, as in a grocery store or supermarket. The Department of Alcoholic Beverage Control may file a complaint against any broker who participates in speculation on licenses or their transfer. The only person who may have an interest in an alcoholic beverage license is the person who is operating or intends to operate the licensed business.

GENERAL CHRONOLOGICAL SALE PROCEDURE

The steps involved in the sale of a business opportunity will vary, depending on the size and complexity of the business being sold. The following steps are merely intended to show the general sequence of events as they may occur in an ordinary sale.

1. The broker secures a listing for the sale of a business opportunity or has a client who wants to purchase a certain type of business.
2. When a prospective purchaser evidences interest in a particular business, the broker secures a deposit and prepares a deposit receipt that includes the terms of the sale and any contingencies that may be necessary. The broker obtains the signature of the buyer and gives him a copy of the deposit receipt. A licensee must always remember that a copy of a listing, deposit receipt, or other important form must always be given to the person who affixes his signature thereto.
3. The broker presents the offer to the seller, and on obtaining his acceptance has him sign the deposit receipt, and gives him a copy.
4. An escrow is opened, and instructions are prepared for the signatures of the buyer and seller. Business escrows are conducted by attorneys, a bank, an escrow company, or a title company.
5. In accordance with Division 6 of the Uniform Commercial Code, provision is made for notice to creditors of the intended sale and transfer of stock in trade by recording and publishing a notice of intended sale in bulk,

thus conforming with the requirements of the Bulk Sales Act.

6. In accordance with Division 9 of the Uniform Commercial Code, the necessary financing statement is filed with the secretary of state and/or the recorder's office, if necessary.
7. The appropriate forms for the transfer of any types of liquor licenses necessary are filed with the Department of Alcoholic Beverage Control.
8. The broker secures the lessor's consent on a lease assignment form so that the lease may be transferred, if necessary.
9. In accordance with the Sales and Use Tax Law, the seller's permit and the clearance receipt are obtained from the board of equalization, thereby protecting the buyer against successor's liability.
10. When the sale of a business involves some employees, adjustments pertaining to prepaid vacation periods or sick leave may have to be worked out and a clearance may have to be obtained from the Department of Employment with regard to unemployment insurance tax.
11. An inventory of stock in trade, fixtures, or other personal property is taken, and the seller executes a bill of sale for all personal property involved.
12. Prior to and on close of escrow, the broker delivers to the buyer and seller the closing statements and any other necessary documents pertaining to the sale of the business.

ADDITIONAL EMPLOYMENT OPPORTUNITIES

Numerous employment opportunities are available to individuals with real estate knowledge and training, in addition to those found in the various areas of real estate brokerage. Many jobs are constantly being offered by:

Appraisers
Banks
Builders and developers
Corporate real estate departments
Escrow companies
Finance companies
Governmental agencies
  Federal
  State
  County
  City
Insurance companies
Investments counselors
Investment trusts
Mortgage companies
Savings and loan companies
Title insurance companies

QUESTIONS FOR DISCUSSION

1. How would you define a profession, and how do you think professional status is attained?
2. If you were a salesman looking for an office to affiliate with, what things would you look for?
3. Discuss the advantages and disadvantages of working for an established real estate firm as against opening and operating your own firm.
4. Why do you think so much emphasis is placed on the subject of trust fund records?
5. How would you go about trying to determine the basic costs involved, prior to opening your own office?
6. If you were a broker looking for salesmen for your office, what standards would you set for prospective employees?
7. What is the general purpose and function of a property manager?
8. If you were planning, to go into the area of property management, what type of property would you want to manage, and why?
9. List the various specific duties for which you feel a property manager would be responsible.
10. For what reasons, other than tax advantages, might a property owner enter into an exchange?
11. What kind of tax picture might eventually result for a person who has been trading up for a number of years and deferring payment of tax?
12. In what type of situation might a three-way exchange occur?
13. What are some of the factors that must be considered in determining the basis for property acquired in an exchange?
14. What is the difference between a conditional and a guaranteed trade-in plan?
15. What steps are taken by the broker in a guaranteed trade-in situation?
16. In what way is the broker who sells business opportunities dealing with intangibles?
17. What special requirement must a beauty shop purchaser meet that a doughnut shop purchaser need not?
18. If a liquor license is involved in the sale, why should the sale be made contingent on transfer of the license?
19. What problems in connection with the sale of business opportunities are not generally found in connection with the sale of other types of properties?
20. What is meant by the "good will" of a business and how might its monetary value be determined?

21. Why is it important that a careful inventory of stock in trade be taken just before close of escrow?

22. What type of real estate license is required to act as an agent in the sale of a business opportunity?

23. In what ways does the sale of real estate differ from the sale of other types of products?

24. What type of on-the-job training do you feel should be given by a broker to a new salesman in the real estate business?

25. What is meant by involuntary conversion and how might it enter into an exchange of real property?

MULTIPLE CHOICE QUESTIONS

21-1. A real estate license is necessary in order to act as: *(a)* a rental agent, *(b)* an escrow agent, *(c)* a bookkeeper, *(d)* a secretary.

21-2. Real estate licensees in most offices are classified as: *(a)* a general agent, *(b)* a general partner, *(c)* an independent contractor, *(d)* none of these.

21-3. The basic requisite to a successful partnership is: *(a)* financial resources, *(b)* mutual agreement, *(c)* business location, *(d)* branch offices.

21-4. Most individuals enter into a property exchange to: *(a)* receive better property prices, *(b)* comply with trust account law, *(c)* gain tax advantages, *(d)* none of these.

21-5. Most real estate offices in California operate as: *(a)* a partnership, *(b)* a stock company, *(c)* a corporation, *(d)* none of these.

21-6. Which of the following is mostly associated with business opportunities: *(a)* purchase contract in writing, *(b)* escrow is necessary, *(c)* correct inventory, *(d)* none of these.

21-7. C.P.M. is a designation earned in connection with: *(a)* real estate sales, *(b)* commercial building construction, *(c)* property management, *(d)* real estate exchanges.

21-8. A broker must be familiar with standard accounting procedures to: *(a)* properly prepare a purchase contract, *(b)* appraise residential property, *(c)* keep adequate trust fund records, *(d)* none of these.

22 Property insurance

Although most insurance policies sold today are through insurance brokers and agents, a number of real estate brokers also sell insurance. The insurance department of a real estate firm may be likened to that of a loan or property management department. It is a natural adjunct to the main business, and since all lenders generally require at least fire insurance coverage before they will release any funds into escrow, the broker is in a good position to effect placement of insurance on the properties he sells. Quite often, a purchaser prefers to deal with his own insurance broker or agent, and the ethical real estate licensee will never attempt to place any undue influence on his client in order to obtain the insurance business.

The major areas in the insurance business are life insurance and property and casualty insurance. One who sells life insurance generally restricts himself to this area, as does the property and casualty agent. Basically, property insurance means fire insurance and extended coverages, while casualty insurance means liability coverage. In addition, there are coverages to protect against a consequential loss. Such a loss would result from the destruction of property leading to a business interruption or a loss of rental income.

In this chapter we will confine our emphasis to those forms of insurance that cover the risks of ownership of real property.

INSURANCE CONCEPT OF PROPERTY

The insurance concept of property is divided into two groups—real and personal property. There are two broad subdivisions within the personal property concept: (1) property used in connection with a residence or a business, such as furniture, fixtures, machinery, and equipment; and (2) property that is for sale or in the process of manufacturing, such as stocks or merchandise.

Insurance against loss to property is written primarily as fire and marine insurance. Ocean marine was the earliest form of insurance; from it developed inland marine coverages, and eventually fire insurance developed separately. Whereas the main emphasis of marine coverages was transportation, fire insurance concentrated on fixed locations—hence its application to real property. It can be said generally that fire insurance protects against loss to buildings and, with additional endorsements to the policy, covers against loss to furniture, fixtures, and stock. Other risks can be covered under a fire policy; these will be discussed later in this chapter. Inland marine insurance covers property in transit and property away from the insured premises.

THE PACKAGE POLICY

The American system of insurance divides insurance into special lines, such as fire, casualty, and marine. This is not true of European insurance, because in much of Europe any kind of insurance may be written by any company any place in the world. The system of line specialization was based on the theory that expertise could be developed for each line, thus offering better solutions to complex problems.

Line specialization gradually led to the development of the package policy. A package policy combines several traditional lines into one policy. For the policyholder, the advantages are in terms of cost, coverage, and convenience. One policy costs less than several. Duplicated coverages are eliminated, and at the same time certain gaps in coverage are reduced or eliminated. Before package policies the insured often neglected to purchase theft insurance when he bought fire insurance. A package takes care of such problems by including several automatic coverages. There also is only one agent, company, and renewal date. For the insurance company, the main advantage is the diversification of business and a greater spread of risk. When there are separate policies on risk and peril, usually only those who are most susceptible to loss will want insurance protection. A package policy has mandatory coverages that must be purchased by all the policyholders. This means that even if an insurance company has heavy losses on theft, the profits from the fire and liability portions of the policy may offset the losses.

A typical package policy generally has three sections. *(a)* General conditions that apply to the whole policy. Term and cancellation provisions and other conditions applicable to the entire policy are found in this part. *(b)* Provisions relating to property losses are called Section I. Combined with the general provisions, Section I is a complete insurance policy. It shows the perils covered, limits of liability, exclusions, and limitations. *(c)* Liability and medical payment coverages are found in Section II. Again, if combined with the general conditions, Section II could be a separate policy. In addition to these three sections, some package policies such as mercantile and industrial have a fourth section relating to crime and burglary coverages.

THE HOMEOWNER'S POLICY

The homeowner's policy is a single package that includes coverage formerly available only through separate contracts. Forms are available from basic coverages to what might be called the super deluxe form, which covers just about everything the homeowner has in his possession and protects against virtually all possible perils.

Section I of the homeowner's policy indemnifies the insured when either he or his property is injured or damaged. Section II covers liability imposed by law when others are injured or their property is damaged. Such damages can be the result of bodily injury or property damage while on the insured's premises or the result of the activities of the insured. Generally, the law of negligence determines the fact and event of liability. If a guest trips and accidently falls while coming up the front stairs of the policyholder's house, the degree of liability depends on whether the steps were or were not in good repair, clean, and free from obstruction. Medical payments coverage provides medical expenses for any person, other than trespassers, injured on the insured's premises.

Physical damage is also covered in Section II. If the insured party damages the property of others, he is covered under his homeowner's policy for damages he must pay to the injured party. In addition to the above, the policyholder may be covered for loss resulting from theft, larceny, burglary, and robbery. Farmers can purchase coverage similar to the homeowner's policy. The general policy layout is the same, and there are special conditions for farmers and farm property; this type of policy is called a farmowner's policy.

The homeowner's policy is a package designed to provide those coverages most likely to be needed by a property owner. Such package policies are flexible enough to suit the needs of the policyholders and offer reduced premiums when compared to separate policies.

RISKS AND COVERAGES

The various risks and coverages available with regard to or in connection with real property are outlined in Figure 22–1 and Figure 22–2.

California homeowner's insurance policy

The standard form homeowner's policy, to which may be added a broad form that covers contents and a comprehensive personal liability form, will not only cover all the perils listed for the standard fire insurance policy, but will also include coverage for bodily injury, property damage, defense, personal liability including medical payments, and voluntary property damage. A tenant may also be covered against the perils listed, excluding only those applicable to the building.

Commercial—multiperil policy

A special multiperil basic form policy is often used to cover a business. This policy has a purpose similar to the homeowner's policy in that it combines line coverages for commercial enterprises. It starts with certain fundamental concepts: (1) a basic fire policy, containing standard provisions; (2) special forms for special occupancies; and (3) a uniform set of rules. Special multiperil policies have been developed to cover special types and

BUSINESS RISKS

OUTLINE OF STANDARD COVERAGES AVAILABLE AND POLICY FORMS USED

California Standard Form Fire Insurance Policy

Building, Equipment, Stock, Merchandise, Loss of Earnings, Extra Expense, Rental Income, and Leasehold may be insured together or individually.

I. Standard Form Fire Insurance Policy plus Building, Equipment, and Stock (Merchandise) Form will insure against:

a) Fire   b) Lightning

II. To the above may be added an Extended Coverage Endorsement which will insure against:

a) Windstorm   f) Riot

b) Explosion   g) Vehicles

c) Hail   h) Riot attending a strike

d) Aircraft   i) Civil commotion

e) Smoke

III. To the above may be added a Vandalism and Malicious Mischief Endorsement which will insure against:

a) Vandalism   b) Malicious mischief

IV. To the above may be added the following endorsements which will cover the named perils or risks:

a) Earthquake Endorsement   d) Leasehold Interest Endorsement

b) Business Interruption Endorsement   e) Sprinkler Leakage Endorsement

c) Rental Income Endorsement   f) Special Extended Coverages Endorsements

FIGURE 22-1

PERSONAL RISKS

OUTLINE OF STANDARD COVERAGES AVAILABLE AND POLICY FORMS USED

California Standard Form Fire Insurance Policy

Dwelling Building, Private Structures, Personal Property, Rental Value, and Additional Living Expense may be insured together or individually.

I. Standard Form Fire Insurance Policy plus Dwelling and Contents Form will insure against:

a) Fire   b) Lightning

II. To the above may be added an Extended Coverage Endorsement which will insure against:

a) Windstorm and hail   e) Civil commotion

b) Explosion   f) Aircraft

c) Riot   g) Vehicles

d) Riot attending a strike   h) Smoke

III. To the above may be added a Vandalism and Malicious Mischief Endorsement which will insure against:

a) Vandalism   b) Malicious mischief

IV. To the above may be added an Earthquake Damage Endorsement which will insure against:

a) Earthquake

V. To the above may be added a Broad Form Endorsement which will insure against all of the above plus:

a) Collapse

b) Falling objects

c) Weight of ice, snow, or sleet

d) Breakage of glass

e) Freezing of plumbing, heating, and air conditioning systems and domestic appliances

f) Sudden and accidental tearing, cracking, burning, or bulging of appliance for heating water for domestic consumption (excluding any of the above as a result of wear and tear, deterioration or rust).

g) Electrical injury to appliances

VI. For a Dwelling Building Only, the Dwelling Special Form will insure against all of the perils described in I, II, III, IV, and V above.

FIGURE 22–2

kinds of businesses and commercial enterprises, such as motel-hotel, apartment house, mercantile, institutional offices, processing-service, and manufacturing.

Liability policy

The standard forms used to cover liability are the standard liability policy, owners-landlords-tenants form, and the manufacturers and contractors form. The following may be insured: any expenses when responsible for damage that may arise to others as the result of business activities, ownership or use of property, liability under a contract, professional services, expense for medical care of others, use of products, completed work, and activities of contractors. The perils covered are: bodily injury, property damage, and defense.

Workers' compensation insurance

Workers' compensation insurance provides protection to the employer against the liability, imposed on him by law, to pay benefits to any worker because of injury sustained by him in the course of and arising out of his employment, without regard to fault or negligence on his part or that of any other person.

In California, all employers of one or more employees must secure liability for workers' compensation. A standard workers' compensation policy form in general use covers the employer for any injury that may result to an employee during the course of or in connection with his work.

COINSURANCE

Most property owners do not carry fire insurance to cover the full value of their property, since very few fires result in a complete loss of the property insured. Most homeowners carry an amount of insurance equal to 70 or 80 percent of the full cash value of the property. Because of this partial coverage, the principle of coinsurance has been developed by insurance companies.

The policyholder is generally required to carry insurance to cover a stated percent, usually 80 percent, of the value of his property. The company's liability for any loss is limited to the proportion of the loss that the amount of its policy bears to the amount obtained by applying the specified percentage to the value of the property at the time of the loss. Thus, if the policyholder fails to carry an amount of insurance equal to the speci-

fied percentage of the value of the property he cannot recover his full loss.

In effect, to the extent of the deficit, the policyholder takes the place of another insurance company and contributes proportionately to any loss—in other words, becomes a coinsurer. Remember that when we speak of property value here, we mean only the value of the buildings and improvements. Land is not considered nor insured because it cannot be lost.

An example of the operation of a requirement that the insured carry a policy of at least 80 percent of the value of his property follows:

1. Value of the improvements .... $160,000.
2. Amount of insurance policyholder should carry is 80 percent of value.......... $128,000.
3. Amount of insurance policyholder is actually carrying .... $ 96,000.
4. A fire occurs, and the amount of actual loss is .... $ 40,000.
5. Amount of company's liability is:

$$\frac{\$96,000}{\$128,000} \times \$40,000 = \$30,000.$$

Insurance company pays to policyholder .... $ 30,000.
6. Policyholder (insured) must stand the difference of .... $ 10,000.
7. Since the policyholder only carried 75 percent of the insurance coverage required ($96,000 instead of $128,000) the company will only be liable for 75 percent of the actual loss.

For this reason, any person whose fire insurance policy contains an 80 percent clause should periodically check the amount of coverage he carries, so that if the value of his property appreciates over the years he will keep the amount of the insurance he should carry up to the proper level.

INSURANCE LICENSES AND LICENSING PROCEDURE

Under the insurance laws of the state of California, no person may transact insurance or act as an insurance agent, broker, or solicitor until he has obtained an appropriate license from the California state Insurance Commissioner. The three main licenses in the property and casualty field are agent's, broker's, and solicitor's license.

Agent

An insurance agent is a person authorized by and acting on behalf of an insurer (company) to transact insurance. With an application for license as an insurance agent, at least one notice of company appointment of agent must be filed. This notice is a document wherein a company appoints the applicant as an agent on his obtaining a license.

An agent can transact insurance only with the companies that have appointed him as their agent. The company itself must qualify as an admitted insurer. An admitted insurer is one who has received a certificate of authority from the Insurance Commissioner to transact specified classes of insurance business in California.

Generally, there is no limit to the number of companies for which a licensee may act as an agent. Most agents represent a number of companies in order to be able to offer a wider variety of insurance services to their clients.

Specific requirements. There are no specific requirements with regard to degree of education or prior experience. The applicant for an agent's license has only to pass the examination given by the Insurance Commissioner, which consists of a number of questions. The applicant must obtain a score of 70 percent or better in order to pass. In addition to passing the examination, the applicant must be appointed by a company as its agent, as mentioned above. Although the Commissioner imposes no special education or experience requirement, the applicant must realize that very few insurance companies will consent to appointing him as their agent unless they feel that he has the ability and potential for becoming a successful agent. It may thus be said that the industry itself sets certain standards for those who want to become insurance agents.

To obtain a license to act as a fire and casualty insurance agent, the applicant must:

1. Be a citizen or national of the United States, or an applicant for citizenship.
2. Be at least 18 years of age.
3. Before being licensed, file one or more notices of company appointment.
4. Pass an examination given by the insurance commissioner.

Broker

An insurance broker is a person who acts for compensation on behalf of another person and transacts insurance with, but not on behalf of, an insurance company. A broker may be thought of as an individual who may place insurance and do business with whatever insurance company he wants, as opposed to an agent, who may represent only those companies for whom he has been appointed an agent. One who has an insurance broker's license may also obtain an agent's license, without examination, by filing an application form with the Insurance Commissioner, together with a notice of company appointment.

Compensation for brokers and agents is generally a portion of the premium the client (insured) pays for the policy. The applicant for a broker's license must meet a more stringent set of requirements than the applicant for an agent's license.

Specific requirements. To obtain a license to act as a broker, the applicant must:

1. Be a citizen or national of the United States, or an applicant for citizenship.
2. Be at least 18 years of age.
3. File and maintain in effect a surety bond with the Insurance Commissioner. The contingency of the bond is that the broker will account to those dealing with him for insurance moneys and premiums received by him during the course of business.
4. Take the qualifying examination for a license to act as an insurance broker, after he has: (a) successfully completed within three years of the application date a course of instruction previously approved by the Insurance Commissioner, requiring at least 90 hours of classroom work or the equivalent in correspondence work and covering the principal branches of the insurance business; or (b) successfully completed, within three years of the application date, a United States Armed Forces Institute insurance course if it has been previously approved by the Insurance Commissioner; or (c) been regularly employed by an insurance company, insurance broker, or insurance agent, or been licensed as an insurance agent, broker, or solicitor for an aggregate of one year in the three years preceding the date of application. Such employment must have been in responsible insurance duties.
5. Pass an examination given by the Insurance Commissioner. The examination consists of a number of questions and requires a passing score of 75 percent or better.

Solicitor

A solicitor is employed by a licensed agent or broker to aid in transacting insurance business.

A solicitor cannot at the same time be licensed as an agent or a broker. The solicitor is an employee of the agent or broker, and is responsible to his employer. On filing with the Commissioner a notice of company appointment, he may obtain an agent's license without taking another examination.

Specific requirements. To obtain a license as a solicitor, the applicant must:

1. Be a natural person (individuals only will be issued a solicitor's license), and a citizen or national of the United States or an applicant for citizenship.
2. File a written statement signed by a fire and casualty agent or broker stating that such agent or broker will employ the applicant if he passes the examination and is licensed.
3. Pass an examination given by the Insurance Commissioner. This examination is the same as that given for an agent's license, and a score of 70 percent or better is required to pass.

Certificate of convenience

A certificate of convenience is a temporary license issued to a person who wants to transact insurance as an agent or solicitor but has not yet passed the appropriate examination. It allows the holder to gain experience while preparing for the examination, and it is issued for a term not to exceed six months.

GENERAL RULES GOVERNING INSURANCE LICENSEES

Insurance licensees must adhere to certain rules and regulations set by the insurance commissioner and the California Insurance Code in much the same way that the real estate licensee is regulated by the Real Estate Commissioner and the Real Estate Law. Publications regarding insurance laws in California and information about licensing may be obtained from the main office of the California Insurance Commissioner at 1407 Market Street, San Francisco, California.

HOME WARRANTY INSURANCE PROGRAMS

Brokers have long been aware that a common problem with respect to the sale of homes has to do with the inoperability or malfunction of certain items in the property after the purchaser moves in.

To alleviate this problem, a number of firms have recently been organized which provide insurance for the seller and buyer with respect to repairs which may be necessary to the plumbing, electrical and heating systems, and to common appliances such as a dishwasher, range, oven, garbage disposal, and exhaust fan.

Many brokers claim that the advertising and provision of such protection in connection with the listing, is an excellent selling tool. Costs, fees, and the degree of protection vary, but in general the arrangement for such warranty is made at the time the listing is obtained and the seller pays for the cost of the policy.

Commonly, such policies provide labor, parts, and materials to repair or replace, as necessary, the following:

Electrical Systems: Main service panels, all subpanels, all wall receptacles, light switches, and all outside receptacles attached to the main structure.

Built-In Appliances

Garbage Disposal: Disposal motor, motor shaft bearing, disposal blades, electrical connection, or complete disposal. The repair of disposal is for normal usage. Breakage by foreign object or extreme misuse is not covered under this warranty.

Dishwasher: Gasket leaks, timer, motor and pump, impeller and sprayer unit, dryer element, electrical connections, and safety limit switches. Excluded are door latches and hinges.

Surface Range (Gas Fired): Gas controls, burners, orifices, gas valves, gas cocks, flex line, pilot, and pilot lines.

Surface Range (Electric): Burner switches, burner elements, and burner wiring harness.

Oven (Gas): Burners, orifices, thermostat control unit, gas safety valve, pilot, pilot lines, and thermocouplings. Excluded are timers, glass oven doors, latches, and hinges.

Oven (Electric): Elements (bake and broil), wiring, thermostat control unit, and bake and broil selector switches. Excluded are timers, glass oven doors, latches, and hinges.

Bathroom and Kitchen Exhaust Fan: Motor, switches, and sockets.

Heating Systems

Electrical and Gas Fired: Wall furnaces—Electrical Perimeter Heating Systems (excluding baseboard casing). Floor Furnace—Forced Air Systems (heat only): Repair and replacement of the following: Gas valves, gas lines, control valves, pilot generators, thermocouplings, pilots, cleaning and regulating of burners, blower limit controls, blower motors, blower belts, variable speed pulleys, vents, vent pipes, thermostat (heat only), and thermostat wiring.

Hot Water and Steam Systems (Gas or Oil Fired): Repair or replacement of circular motors, expansion tanks, boilers, all control valves, pressure gauges, pressure switches, burners, thermostat, radiators, convertors, electrical heating units and wiring, fuel pumps, fuel lines, all ignition components necessary for the operation of the heating units. Excluded are all inaccessible radiant and steam lines in floors and interior walls.

Plumbing Systems

Plumbing: Repair leaks and breaks in water lines on the interior of the house, including riser lines on the interior of the house and riser lines to plumbing fixtures. Excluded are all water lines on the exterior, sewer line waste lines and main service lines.

Toilet Tanks: Repair or replacement of all interior components of the water closet, tank bolts and washers, flushing mechanism and overflow tube, flapper valve and chain, ball cock, float arm, supply valve and line. Excluded are tank, tank lids, toilet seat, and bowls.

Hot Water Heater (Gas Fired): Repair and replacement of the following: gas valve, line, thermocouple, pilot, cleaning and regulating of burners, thermostat heating control, pressure relief valve, vent pipes, and main water tank.

Hot Water Heater (Electrical): Repair and replacement of the following: electrical heating element, heating control, valves, and tanks as necessary.

There are, of course, certain limitations, exclusions, and minimal charges in connection with repair calls, but in general such policies seem to be excellent protection for the seller and the buyer. They are gaining in popularity in the real estate industry.

QUESTIONS FOR DISCUSSION

1. What is usually the minimum amount of insurance coverage required by lenders in your community when a home is sold?
2. What is meant by the statement that an insurance contract is basically one of indemnity?
3. How does a homeowner's policy offer a homeowner special advantages?
4. What common risks should a property owner insure against?
5. The owner of a business might want to insure against what special risks?
6. How does coinsurance affect the policyholder?
7. Discuss the advantages and/or disadvantages of selling both real estate and insurance, assuming a licensee who has just opened a new office.
8. In what way does the placing of insurance differ between an agent and a broker?
9. How do the requirements for an agent's license differ from those for a broker's license?
10. Discuss the similarity of the rules and regulations which regulate both insurance and real estate licensees.

Appendix A: Definitions of real estate and building construction words and phrases

ALTA title policy: A type of title insurance policy issued by title insurance companies that expands the risks normally insured against under the standard type policy to include unrecorded mechanics' liens, unrecorded physical easements, facts a physical survey would show, water and mineral rights, and rights of parties in possession, such as tenants and buyers under unrecorded instruments.

Abandonment: Giving up any further interest in a right or thing.

Abatement of nuisance: Extinction or termination of a nuisance.

Abstract of judgment: A condensation of the essential provisions of a court judgment.

Abstract of title: A summary or digest of the conveyances, transfers, and any other facts relied on as evidence of title, together with any other elements of record that may impair the title.

Abut: To be adjacent to, touch, or border on another property.

Accelerated depreciation: A method of taking a tax deduction for depreciation in which depreciation allowances are greater in earlier years of ownership than in subsequent years.

Acceleration clause: A clause in a trust deed or mortgage giving the lender the right to call all sums owed him to be immediately due and payable upon the happening of a certain event.

Acceptance: The act by which the seller or agent's principal agrees to the terms of the agreement of sale and approves the negotiation on the part of the agent and acknowledges receipt of the deposit in subscribing to the agreement of sale.

Access right: The right of an owner to have ingress and egress to and from his property.

Accession: An increase or addition to property by forces of nature or individuals.

Accretion: An addition to land from natural causes, such as from gradual action of ocean or river waters.

Accrued depreciation: The difference between the cost of replacement new as of the date of the appraisal and the present appraised value.

Acknowledgment: A formal declaration before a duly authorized officer by a person who has executed an instrument that such execution is his act and deed.

Acoustical tile: Blocks of fiber, mineral, or metal, with small holes or a rough-textured surface to absorb sound, used as covering for interior walls and ceilings.

Acquisition: The act or process by which a person procures property.

Acre: A measure of land equaling 160 square rods, or 4,850 square yards, or 43,560 square feet, or a square tract 208.71 feet on a side.

ACRS: Accelerated Cost Recovery System of depreciation for tax purposes.

Actual fraud: An act intended to deceive such as a false statement of fact.

Administrator: A person appointed by the probate court to administer the estate of a person deceased.

Ad valorem: According to valuation.

Adverse possession: The open and notorious possession and occupancy under an evident claim or right, in denial or opposition to the title of another claimant.

Affidavit: A statement or declaration reduced to writing sworn to or affirmed before some officer who has authority to administer an oath or affirmation.

Affirm: Confirm, aver, ratify, verify.

Agency: The relationship between principal and agent that arises out of a contract, either expressed or implied, written or oral, wherein the agent is employed by the principal to do certain acts dealing with a third party.

Agent: One who represents another from whom he has derived authority.

Agreement: An exchange of promises, a mutual arrangement, a contract.

Agreement of sale: A written agreement or contract between seller and purchaser in which they reach a meeting of minds on the terms and conditions of the sale.

Alienation: The transferring of property to another; the transfer of property and possession of lands, or other things, from one person to another.

Alluvion (Alluvium): Soil deposited by accretion. Increase of earth on a shore or bank of a river.

Amenities: Satisfaction of enjoyable living to be derived from a home; conditions of agreeable living or a beneficial influence arising from the location or improvements.

Amortization: The liquidation of a financial obligation on an installment basis; also recovery, over a period, of cost or value.

Annuity: An amount of money received at fixed intervals such as a series of payments received by a landlord or a lender.

Appraisal: An estimate and opinion of value; a conclusion resulting from the analysis of facts.

Appraiser: One qualified by education, training, and experience who is hired to estimate the value of real and personal property based on experience, judgment, facts, and use of formal appraisal processes.

Appreciation: An increase in value.

Appurtenance: Something annexed to another thing that may be transferred incident to it. That which belongs to another thing, as a barn, dwelling, garage, or orchard is incident to the land to which it is attached.

APR: Annual Percentage Rate. The cost of credit as determined in accordance with Regulation Z of the Federal Reserve System in order to implement the Federal Truth-in-Lending Act.

Articles of incorporation: An instrument setting forth basic rules and purposes for which a private corporation is formed.

A.S.A.: American Society of Appraisers.

Assessed value: Value placed on property as a basis for taxation.

Assessment: The valuation of property for the purpose of levying a tax, or the amount of the tax levied.

Assessor: The official who has the responsibility of determining assessed values.

Assignment: A transfer or making over to another of the whole of any property, real or personal, in possession or in action, or of any estate or right therein.

Assignor: One who assigns or transfers property.

Assigns; assignees: Those to whom property shall have been transferred.

Assumption agreement: An assumption or adoption of a debt or obligation primarily resting upon another individual.

Assumption fee: A lender's charge to a purchaser who is assuming an existing loan.

Assumption of mortgage: The taking of title to property by a grantee, wherein he assumes liability for payment of an existing note secured by a mortgage or deed of trust against the property; becoming a co-guarantor for the payment of a mortgage or deed of trust note.

Attachment: Seizure of property by court order, usually done to have it available in event a judgment is obtained in a pending suit.

Attest: To affirm to be true or genuine; an official act establishing authenticity.

Attorney-in-fact: One who is authorized to perform certain acts for another under a power of attorney; power of attorney may be limited to a specific act or acts, or be general.

Avulsion: The sudden tearing away or removal of land by action of water flowing over or through it.

Backfill: The replacement of excavated earth into a hole or against a structure.

Balance sheet: A statement of the financial condition of a business at a certain time, showing assets, liabilities, and capital.

Balloon payment: An installment payment on a note that is greater than the preceding installment payments and that pays the note in full.

Base and meridian: Imaginary lines used by surveyors to find and describe the location of private or public lands.

Baseboard: A board placed against the wall around a room next to the floor.

Base molding: Molding used at the top of a baseboard.

Base shoe: Molding used at the junction of baseboard and floor: commonly called a carpet strip.

Batten: Narrow strips of wood or metal used to cover joints, interiorly or exteriorly; also used for decorative effect.

Beam: A structural member transversely supporting a load.

Bearing wall or partition: A wall or partition supporting any vertical load in addition to its own weight such as a roof or floor.

Bench mark: A location indicated on a durable marker by surveyors.

Beneficiary: (1) One entitled to the benefit of a trust. (2) One who receives profit from an estate, the title of which is vested in a trustee. (3) The lender on the security of a note and deed of trust.

Bequeath: To give or hand down by will; to leave by will.

Bequest: That which is given by the terms of a will.

Betterment: An improvement upon property that increases the property value and is considered as a capital asset, as distinguished from repairs or replacements in which the original character or cost is unchanged.

Bill of sale: A written instrument given to pass title of personal property from vendor to vendee.

Blacktop: Asphalt paving used in streets and driveways.

Blanket mortgage: A single mortgage that covers more than one piece of real estate.

Blighted area: A declining area in which real property values are seriously affected by destructive economic forces, such as encroaching inharmonious property usages and/or rapidly depreciating buildings.

Blockbusting: The practice of inducing panic selling of property by using methods which exploit racial prejudices.

Board foot: A unit of measurement of lumber one foot wide, one foot long, and one inch thick; 144 cubic inches.

Board of Realtors: A local organization of real estate licensees who are additionally members of the National Association of Realtors.

Bona fide: In good faith, without fraud.

Bracing: Framing lumber nailed at an angle in order to provide rigidity.

Breach: The breaking of a law, or failure of duty, either by omission of commission.

Breezeway: A covered porch or passage, open on two sides, connecting house and garage or two parts of the house.

Bridging: Small wood or metal pieces used to brace floor joists.

BTU: British thermal unit. The quantity of heat required to raise the temperature of one pound of water one Fahrenheit degree.

Building codes: Federal, state, or local laws that set minimum construction standards.

Building line: A line set by law a certain distance from a street line in front of which an owner cannot build on his lot. (A setback line.)

Building paper: A heavy waterproofed paper used as sheathing in wall or roof construction as a protection against air passage and moisture.

Built in: Cabinets or similar features built as part of the house.

Bundle of rights: Beneficial interests or rights.

Capital assets: Assets of a permanent nature being held for investment or used in the production of an income, such as land, buildings, machinery, and equipment, etc. Under income tax law, it is usually distinguishable from *inventory*, which comprises assets held for sale to customers in the ordinary course of the taxpayer's trade or business.

Capital gain: Gain received from sale of capital assets and given preferential tax treatment.

Capitalization: In appraising, determining value of property by considering net income and percentage of reasonable return on the investment.

Capitalization rate: The rate of interest that is considered a reasonable return on the investment and used in the process of determining value based upon net income.

CAR: California Association of Realtors®.

Casement window: Frames of wood or metal that swing outward.

Caveat emptor: Let the buyer beware. The buyer must examine the goods or property and buy at his own risk.

Chain of title: A history of conveyances and encumbrances affecting the title from the time the original patent was granted, or as far back as records are available.

Chattel real: An estate related to real estate, such as a lease on real property.

Chattels: Goods or every species of property movable or immovable that are not real property.

Circuit breaker: An electrical device that automatically interrupts an electric circuit and can be reset.

Clapboard: Boards usually thicker at one edge used for siding.

Cloud on the title: Any conditions revealed by a title search that affect the title to property; usually relatively unimportant items, but ones which cannot be removed without a quitclaim deed or court action.

Collar beam: A beam that connects the pairs of opposite roof rafters above the attic floor.

Collateral: Property subject to the security interest. (See definition of security interest.)

Collateral security: A separate obligation attached to a contract to guarantee its performance; the transfer of property or of other contracts or valuables to insure the performance of a principal agreement.

Collusion: An agreement between two or more persons to defraud another of his rights by the forms of law, or to obtain an object forbidden by law.

Color of title: That which appears to be good title but that is not title in fact.

Combed plywood: A grooved building material used primarily for interior finish.

Commercial acre: The remainder of an acre of newly subdivided land after the area devoted to streets, sidewalks, and curbs, and so forth, has been deducted from the acre.

Commercial paper: Bills of exchange used in commercial trade.

Commingling: Mixing together the funds of an agent and principal without proper authorization.

Commission: An agent's compensation for performing the duties of his agency; in real estate practice, a percentage of the selling price of property, percentage of rentals, and so forth.

Commitment: A pledge or a promise or firm agreement.

Common law: The body of law that grew from customs and practices developed and used in England "since the memory of man runneth not to the contrary."

Community property: Property accumulated through joint efforts of husband and wife living together.

Compaction: Whenever extra soil is added to a lot to fill in low places or to raise the level of the lot, the added soil is often too loose and soft to sustain the weight of buildings. Therefore, it is necessary to compact the added soil so that it will carry the weight of buildings without the danger of their tilting, settling, or cracking.

Competent: Legally qualified.

Compound interest: Interest paid on original principal and also on the accrued and unpaid interest that has accumulated.

Condemnation: (1) The act of taking private property for public use by a political subdivision; (2) declaration that a structure is unfit for use.

Conditional commitment: A commitment of a definite loan amount for some future unknown purchaser with a satisfactory credit standing.

Conditional sale contract: A contract for the sale of property stating that delivery is to be made to the buyer, title to remain vested in the seller until the conditions of the contract have been fulfilled. (See definition of security interest.)

Condominium: A system of individual fee ownership of units in a multifamily structure, combined with joint ownership of common areas of the structure and the land. (Sometimes referred to as a vertical subdivision.)

Conduit: Usually a metal pipe in which electrical wiring is installed.

Confirmation of sale: A court approval of the sale of property by an executor, administrator, guardian, or conservator.

Consideration: Anything of value given to induce entering into a contract; it may be money, personal services, or even love and affection.

Constructive fraud: A breach of fiduciary duty without an actual fraudulent intent.

Constructive notice: Notice given by any public records.

Contiguous: Adjacent, touching upon, or adjoining.

Contingency: A condition upon which a valid contract is dependent.

Contour: The surface configuration of real property.

Contract: An agreement, either written or oral, to do or not to do certain things.

Consumer goods: Goods used or bought for use primarily for personal, family, or household purposes.

Conversion: Change from one character or use to another, as in the misappropriation of funds.

Conveyance: The transfer of the title of land from one to another. It denotes an instrument that carries from one person to another an interest in land.

Corporation: A group or body of persons established and treated by law as an individual or unit with rights and liabilities both distinct and apart from those of the persons composing it. A corporation is a creature of law having certain powers and duties of a natural person. Being created by law, it may continue for any length of time the law prescribes.

Counterflashing: Flashing used on chimneys at roofline to cover shingle flashing and to prevent moisture entry.

Covenant: Agreement written into a deed or other instrument promising performance or nonperformance of certain acts or stipulating certain uses or nonuses of the property.

CPM: Certified Property Manager; a member of the Institute of Real Property Management of the National Association of Realtors.

Crawl space: Exterior or interior opening permitting access underneath a building, as required by building codes.

Curtain schedule: A listing of the amounts by which the principal sum of an obligation is to be reduced by partial payments, and of the dates when each payment will become payable.

Courtesy: The right that a husband has in his wife's estate at her death.

Damages: The indemnity recoverable by a person who has sustained an injury, either in his person, property, or relative rights, through the act or default of another.

Debtor: The party who "owns" the property that is subject to the security interest. Previously he was known as the *mortgagor* or the *pledgor*, et cetera.

Deciduous trees: Trees that lose their leaves in the autumn and winter.

Deck: Usually an open porch on the roof of a ground or lower floor, porch, or wing.

Dedication: An appropriation of land by its owner for some public use accepted for such use by authorized public officials on behalf of the public.

Deed: A written instrument that, when properly executed and delivered, conveys title.

Default: Failure to fulfill a duty or promise or to discharge an obligation; omission or failure to perform any act.

Defeasance clause: The clause in a mortgage that gives the mortgagor the right to redeem his property upon the payment of his obligations to the mortgagee.

Deferred maintenance: Existing but unfulfilled requirements for repairs and rehabilitation.

Deficiency judgment: A judgment given when the security pledge for a loan does not satisfy the debt upon its default.

Depreciation: Loss of value in real property brought about by age, physical deterioration, or functional or economic obsolescence. Broadly, a loss in value from any cause.

Desist and refrain order: The Real Estate Commissioner is empowered by law to issue an order directing a person to desist and refrain from committing an act in violation of the real estate law.

Deterioration: Impairment of condition. One of the causes of depreciation, reflecting the loss in value brought about by wear and tear, disintegration, use in service, and the action of the elements.

Devisee: One who receives a bequest made by will.

Devisor: One who bequeaths by will.

Directional growth: The location or direction toward which the residential sections of a city are destined or determined to grow.

Disintermediation: The relatively sudden withdrawal by savers of substantial sums of money from lending institutions.

Documentary transfer tax: A method of taxing real property transfers by requiring a tax to be paid prior to deed recordation.

Donee: A person to whom a gift is made.

Donor: A person who makes a gift.

Dual agency: An agency relationship where the same agent acts for both principals in a transaction.

Duress: Unlawful constraint exercised upon a person whereby he is forced to do some act against his will.

Easement: The right, privilege, or interest created by grant or agreement for a specific purpose that one party has in the land of another. (Example: right-of-way.)

Eaves: The lower part of a roof projecting over a wall.

Economic life: The period over which a property will yield a return on the investment, over and above any economic or ground rent due to land.

Eminent domain: The right of the government to acquire property for necessary public or quasi-public use by condemnation; the owner must be fairly compensated.

Encroachment: Trespass; the building of a structure or construction of any improvements partly or wholly on the property of another.

Encumbrance: Anything that affects or limits the fee simple title to property, such as mortgages, easements, or restrictions of any kind. Liens are special encumbrances that make the property security for the payment of a debt or obligation, such as mortgages and taxes.

Endorsement: Signature on reverse side of check or promissory note for purpose of transfering ownership.

Equity: (1) The interest or value that an owner has in real estate over and above the liens against it; (2) branch of remedial justice by and through which relief is afforded to suitors in courts of equity.

Equity of redemption: The right to redeem property during the foreclosure period, such as a mortgagor's right to redeem within a year after a foreclosure sale.

Erosion: The wearing away of land by the action of water, wind, or glacial ice.

Escalator clause: A clause in a contract providing for the upward or downward adjustment of certain items to cover specified contingencies.

Escheat: The reverting of property to the state when heirs capable of inheriting are lacking.

Escrow: The deposit of instruments and funds with instruction to a neutral third party to carry out the provisions of an agreement or contract; when everything is deposited to enable carrying out the instructions, it is called a complete or perfect escrow.

Estate: The degree, quantity, nature, and extent of interest that a person has in real or personal property.

Estate of inheritance: An estate that may descend to heirs. All freehold estates are estates of inheritance, except estates for life.

Estate for life: A freehold estate, not of inheritance, but which is held by the tenant for his own life or the life or lives of one or more other persons, or for an indefinite period that may endure for the life or lives of persons in being and beyond the period of life.

Estate for years: An interest in lands by virtue of a contract for the possession of them for a definite and limited period of time. A lease may be said to be an estate for years.

Estate of will: The occupation of lands and tenements by a tenant for an indefinite period terminable by one or both parties.

Estoppel: A doctrine that bars one from asserting rights that are inconsistent with a previous position or representation.

Ethics: That branch of moral science, idealism, justness, and fairness that treats of the duties that a member of a profession or craft owes to the public, to his clients or patron, and to his professional colleagues or members.

Exclusive agency listing: A written instrument giving one agent the right to sell property for a specified time but reserving the right of the owner to sell the property himself without the payment of a commission.

Exclusive-right-to-sell listing: A written agreement between owner and agent giving the right to collect a commission if the property is sold by anyone during the term of the agreement.

Execute: Complete, make, perform, do, follow out; execute a deed, make a deed, including especially signing, sealing, and delivery; to execute a contract is to perform the contract, to follow out to the end, to complete.

Executor: A person named in a will to carry out its provisions as to the disposition of the estate of a decedent.

Executory contract: A contract in which something still remains to be completed by either or both of the parties.

Expansible house: Home designed for further expansion and additions in the future.

Expansion joint: A bituminous fiber strip used to separate units of concrete to prevent cracking due to expansion as a result of temperature changes.

Facade: Front of a building.

Fair market value: The amount of money that will be paid for a property offered for sale on the open market for a reasonable time with both buyer and seller knowing all uses to which the property can be put and neither party being pressured to buy or sell.

Federal Housing Administration: (FHA) An agency of the federal government which insures loans made by private lenders such as savings and loan associations and banks.

Fee: An estate of inheritance in real property.

Fee simple: In modern estates, the terms *fee* and *fee simple* are substantially synonymous. The term *fee* is of Old English derivation. *Fee simple absolute* is an estate in real property by which the owner has the greatest power over the title that it is possible to have, being an absolute estate. In modern use, it expressly establishes the title of real property in the owner, without limitation or end. He may dispose of it by sale, trade, or will, as he chooses.

Fiduciary: A person in a position of trust and confidence, as between principal and broker; a broker as fiduciary owes certain loyalty that cannot be breached under rules of agency.

Financing statement: This is the instrument that is filed in order to give public notice of the security interest and thereby protect the interest of the secured parties in the collateral. (See definitions of security interest and secured party.)

Finish floor: Finish floor strips are applied over wood joists, deadening felt, and diagonal subflooring before finish floor is installed; finish floor is the final covering on the floor: wood, linoleum, cork, tile, or carpet.

Fire stop: A solid, tight closure of a concealed space, placed to prevent the spread of fire and smoke through such a space.

Fiscal year: A business, accounting, or tax year which may differ from a calendar year.

Fixtures: Appurtenances attached to the land or improvements, which usually cannot be removed without agreement since they become real property. Examples: plumbing fixtures, store fixtures built into the property, and so forth.

Flashing: Sheet metal or other material used to protect a building from seepage of water.

Footing: The base or bottom of a foundation wall, pier, or column.

Foreclosure: Procedure whereby property pledged as security for a debt is sold to pay the debt in event of default in payments or terms.

Forfeiture: Loss of money or anything of value due to failure to perform.

Foundation: The supporting portion of a structure below the first floor construction or below grade, including the footings.

Franchise: A specific legal right or privilege to conduct a certain type of business or activity using a specified trademark or name.

Fraud: The intentional and successful employment of any cunning, deception, collusion, or artifice, used to circumvent, cheat, or deceive another person, whereby that person acts upon it to the loss of his property and to his legal injury.

Frontage: A term which describes that portion of real property which faces the street or sidewalk area.

Front foot: Property measurement for sale or valuation purposes; the property measures by the front foot on its street line, each front foot extending the depth of the lot.

Frostline: The depths of frost penetration in the soil. It varies in different parts of the country. Footings should be placed below this depth to prevent movement.

Furring: Strips of wood or metal applied to a wall or other surface to even it, to form an air space, or to give the wall an appearance of greater thickness.

Gable roof: A pitched roof with sloping sides.

Gambrel roof: A curb roof, having a steep lower slope with a flatter upper slope.

General lien: A lien which applies against all property of an individual rather than against a specific property.

Gift deed: A deed for which the consideration is love and affection and where there is no material consideration.

Girder: A large beam used to support beams, joists, and partitions.

Goodwill: An intangible but saleable asset of a business derived from the expectation of continued public patronage.

Grade: Ground level at the foundation.

Graduated lease: Lease that provides for a varying rental rate, often based upon future determination; sometimes rent is based upon result of periodical appraisals; used largely in long-term leases.

Grant: A technical term made use of in deeds of conveyance of lands to import a transfer.

Grantee: The purchaser; a person to whom a grant is made.

Grantor: Seller of property; one who signs a deed.

Grid: A chart used in rating the borrower risk, property, and the neighborhood.

Gross income: Total income from property before any expenses are deducted.

Gross Multiplier: A method of appraising income property based upon a multiple of the gross annual income of the property.

Ground lease: An agreement for the use of the land only, sometimes secured by improvements placed on the land by the user.

Ground rent: Earnings of improved property credited to earnings of the ground itself after allowance is made for earnings of improvements; often termed *economic rent*.

Header: A beam placed perpendicular to joists and to which joists are nailed in framing for chimney, stairway, or other opening.

Highest and best use: An appraisal phrase meaning that use which at the time of an appraisal is most likely to produce the greatest net return to the land and/or buildings over a given period of time; that use which will produce the greatest amount of amenities or profit. This is the starting point for appraisal.

Hip roof: A pitched roof with sloping sides and ends.

Holder in due course: One who has taken a note, check, or bill of exchange in due course: (1) before it was overdue; (2) in good faith for value: and (3) without knowledge that it has been previously dishonored and without notice of any defect at the time it was negotiated to him.

Homestead: A home upon which the owner or owners have recorded a declaration of homestead, as provided by California statutes. The declaration protects the home against judgments up to specified amounts.

Hundred percent location: A city retail business location that is considered the best available for attracting business.

Hypothecate: To give a thing as security without the necessity of giving up possession of it.

Incompetent: One who is mentally incompetent, incapable; any person who, though not insane, is, by reason of old age, disease, weakness of mind, or any other cause, unable, unassisted, to properly manage and by reason thereof would be likely to be deceived or imposed upon by artful or designing persons.

Increment: An increase. Most frequently used to refer to the increase of value of land that accompanies population growth and increasing wealth in the community. The term unearned increment is used in this connection since values are supposed to have increased without effort on the part of the owner.

Independent contractor: One who exercises independent judgment in doing a job and is responsible to employer only as to the results of the work.

Indirect lighting: The light is reflected from the ceiling or other object external to the fixture.

Indorsement: The act of signing one's name on the back of a check or a note, with or without further qualification.

Injunction: A writ or order issued under the seal of a court to restrain one or more parties to a suit or proceeding from doing an act that is deemed to be inequitable or unjust in regard to the rights of some other party or parties in the suit or proceeding.

Installment note: A note which provides that payments of a certain sum or amount be paid on the dates specified in the instrument.

Instrument: A written legal document created to effect the rights of the parties.

Interest rate: The percentage of a sum of money charged for its use.

Interim financing: A loan used to finance construction and due at its completion.

Intestate: A person who dies having made no will or having made one that is defective in form, in which case his estate descends to his heirs at law or next of kin.

Involuntary lien: A lien imposed against property without consent of an owner, for example taxes, special assessments, federal income tax liens, and so forth.

Irrevocable: Incapable of being recalled or revoked; unchangeable.

Irrigation districts: Quasi-political districts created under special laws to provide for water services to property owners in the district.

Jalousie: A slatted blind or shutter, like a venetian blind but used on the exterior to protect against rain as well as to control sunlight.

Jamb: The side post or lining of a doorway, window, or other opening.

Joint: The space between the adjacent surfaces of two components joined and held together by nails, glue, cement, mortar, et cetera.

Joint note: A note signed by two or more persons who have equal liability for payment.

Joint tenancy: Joint ownership by two or more persons with right of survivorship; all joint tenants own equal interest and have equal rights in the property.

Joist: One of a series of parallel beams to which the boards of a floor and ceiling lath are nailed, and supported in turn by larger beams, girders, or bearing walls.

Judgment: The final determination of a court of competent jurisdiction of a matter presented to it; money judgments provide for the payment of claims presented to the court, or are awarded as damages, and so forth.

Jurisdiction: The authority by which judicial officers take cognizance of and decide cause; the power to hear and determine a cause; the right and power that a judicial officer has to enter upon the inquiry.

Laches: Delay or negligence in asserting one's legal rights.

Land contract: A contract ordinarily used in connection with the sale of property in cases where the seller does not wish to convey title until all or a certain part of the purchase price is paid by the buyer; often used when property is sold on a small down payment.

Lateral support: The support that the soil of an adjoining owner gives to his neighbor's land.

Lath: A building material of wood, metal, gypsum, or insulating board fastened to the frame of a building to act as a plaster base.

Lease: A contract between owner and tenant, setting forth conditions upon which the tenant may occupy and use the property and the term of the tenant's occupancy.

Legal description: A description recognized by law; a description by which property can be definitely located by reference to government surveys or approved recorded maps.

Lessee: One who contracts to rent property under a lease contract.

Lessor: An owner who enters into a lease with a tenant.

Leverage: Use of borrowed funds to reduce any amount of cash down payment and increase the percent of return on actual cash invested.

Lien: A form of encumbrance that usually makes property security for the payment of a debt or discharge of an obligation. Example: judgments, taxes, mortgages, deeds of trust, et cetera.

Limited partnership: A partnership composed of some partners whose contribution and liability are limited.

Lintel: A horizontal board that supports the load over an opening such as a door or window.

Liquidated damages: An agreement in a contract providing for a definite sum of money to be paid in the event of a breach of the contract.

Lis pendens: Suit pending, usually recorded so as to give constructive notice of pending litigation.

Listing: An employment contract between principal and agent authorizing the agent to perform services for the principal involving the latter's property; listing contracts are entered into for the purpose of securing persons to buy, lease, or rent property. Employment of an agent by a prospective purchaser or lessee to locate property for purchase or lease may be considered a listing.

Loan commitment: A lender's contractual commitment to make a loan to a borrower.

Loan-value ratio: The percentage of a property's value that a lender can or may loan to a borrower.

Louver: An opening with a series of horizontal slats set at an angle to permit ventilation without admitting rain, sunlight, or vision.

MAI: Designates a person who is a member of the American Institute of Appraisers of the National Association of Realtors®.

Margin of security: The difference between the amount of the mortgage loan(s) and the appraised value of the property.

Marginal land: Land that barely pays the cost of working or using.

Market price: The price paid regardless of pressure, motives, or intelligence.

Market value: (1) The price at which a willing seller would sell and a willing buyer would buy, neither being under abnormal pressure. (2) As defined by the courts, the highest price estimated in terms of money that a property will bring if exposed for sale in the open market allowing a reasonable time to find a purchaser with knowledge of the property's use and capabilities for use.

Marketable title: Merchantable title; title free and clear of objectionable liens or encumbrances.

Material fact: A fact that the agent should realize would be likely to affect the judgment of the principal in giving his consent to the agent to enter into the particular transaction on the specified terms.

Mechanic's lien: May be recorded by any supplier of work, labor, or materials for the construction or improvement of real estate if payment is not received for such work, labor, or materials.

Meridians: Imaginary north-south lines that intersect east-west base lines to form a starting point for the measurement of land.

Metes and bounds: A term used in describing the boundary lines of land, setting forth all the boundary lines together with each of their terminal points and angles.

Minor: All persons under 18 years of age. Any person who is 18 or over is deemed an adult person for the purpose of entering into an engagement or transaction respecting property.

Misrepresentation: False and misleading statements and concealment of material facts.

Modular: A system for construction of buildings using component parts, termed modules, which are factory produced.

Molding: Usually patterned strips used to provide ornamental variation of outline or contour, such as cornices, bases, or window and door jambs.

Monument: A fixed object and point established by surveyors to establish land locations.

Moratorium: The temporary suspension, usually by statute, of the enforcement of liability for debt.

Mortgage: An instrument recognized by law by which property is hypothecated to secure the payment of an debt or obligation; procedure for foreclosure in event of default is established by statute.

Mortgage guaranty insurance: Insurance against financial loss available to mortgage lenders from Mortgage Guaranty Insurance Corporation.

Mortgagee: One to whom a mortgagor gives a mortgage to secure a loan or performance of an obligation; a lender. (See definition of secured party.)

Mortgagor: One who gives mortgage on his property to secure a loan or assure performance of an obligation; a borrower. (See definition of debtor.)

Multiple listing: A listing, usually an exclusive right to sell, taken by a member of an organization composed of real estate brokers, with the provisions that all members will have the opportunity to find an interested client; a cooperative listing.

Mutual water company: A water company organized by or for water users in a given district with the object of securing an ample water supply at a reasonable rate; stock is issued to users.

NAR: National Association of Realtors®.

Negotiable: Capable of being negotiated; that is, assignable or transferable in the ordinary course of business.

Net listing: A listing which provides that the agent may retain as compensation for his services all sums received over and above a net price to the owner.

Note: A signed written instrument acknowledging a debt and promising payment.

Notice of nonresponsibility: A notice provided by law designed to relieve a property owner from responsibility for the cost of work done on the property of materials furnished therefor; notice must be verified, recorded, and posted.

Notice to quit: A notice to a tenant to vacate rented property. If a tenant is delinquent in rental payments, a three-day notice to quit is required by law in connection with an unlawful detainer suit.

Obsolescence: Loss in value due to reduced desirability and usefulness of a structure because its design and construction become obsolete; loss because of becoming old-fashioned and not in keeping with modern needs, with consequent loss of income.

Offset statement: Statement by owner of property or owner of lien against property setting forth the present status of liens against said property.

Open-end mortgage: A mortgage containing a clause that permits the mortgagor to borrow additional money after the loan has been reduced, without rewriting the mortgage.

Open listing: An authorization given by a property owner to a real estate agent wherein said agent is given the nonexclusive right to secure a purchaser; open listings may be given to any number of agents without liability to compensate any except the one who first secures a buyer ready, willing, and able to meet the terms of the listing, or secures the acceptance by the seller of a satisfactory offer.

Option: A right given for a consideration to purchase or lease a property upon specified terms within a specified time.

Oral contract: A verbal agreement; one that is not reduced to writing.

Orientation: Placing a house on its lot with regard to its exposure to the rays of the sun, prevailing winds, privacy from the street, and protection from outside noises.

Overhang: The part of the roof extending over a wall in order to shade a building or cover walks.

Overimprovement: An improvement that is not the highest and best use for the site on which it is placed by reason of excess size or cost.

Par value: Market value; nominal value.

Parquet floor: Hardwood flooring laid in squares or patterns.

Partition action: Court proceedings by which co-owners seek to sever their joint ownership.

Partnership: According to the California Supreme Court, "A partnership as between partners themselves may be defined to be a contract of two or more persons to unite their property, labor or skill, or some of them, in prosecution of some joint or lawful business, and to share the profits in certain proportions."

Party wall: A wall erected on the line between two adjoining properties, which are under different ownership, for the use of both properties.

Patent: Conveyance of title to government land.

Percentage lease: Lease on property, the rental for which is determined by amount of business with provision for a minimum rental.

Perimeter heating: Baseboard heating, or any system in which the heat registers are located along the outside walls of a room, especially under the windows.

Periodic tenancy: Tenancy for successive time periods of the same length.

Personal property: Any property that is not real property.

Pier: A column of masonry, usually rectangular in horizontal cross section, used to support other structural members.

Pitch: The incline or rise of a roof.

Plate: A horizontal board placed on a wall or supported on posts or studs to carry the trusses of a roof or rafters directly; a shoe, or base member as of a partition or other frame; a small flat board placed on or in a wall to support girders, rafters, etc.

Pledge: The depositing of personal property by a debtor with a creditor as security for a debt or engagement.

Pledgee: One who is given a pledge or a security. (See definition of secured party.)

Pledgor: One who offers a pledge or gives security. (See definition of debtor.)

Plottage increment: The appreciation in value created by joining smaller ownerships into a large single ownership.

Plywood: Laminated wood made up in panels; several thicknesses of wood glued together with grain at different angles for strength.

Points: A fee charged by a lender for making a loan. For example, 1½ points represents a fee of 1½ percent of the loan amount.

Police power: The right of the state to enact laws and enforce them for the order, safety, health, morals, and general welfare of the public.

Power of attorney: An instrument authorizing a person to act as the agent of the person granting it, and a general power authorizing the agent to act generally in behalf of the principal. A special power limits the agent to a particular or specific act. For example, a landowner may grant an agent special power of attorney to convey a single and specific parcel of property. Under the provisions of a general power of attorney, the agent having the power may convey any or all property of the principal granting the general power of attorney.

Power of sale: The power of a trustee or mortgagee to sell a property if a borrower defaults in loan payments.

Prefabricated building: A building manufactured, and sometimes partly assembled, before delivery and erection on a particular lot.

Prepayment penalty: Penalty for the payment of a mortgage or trust deed note before it actually becomes due.

Present value: The value today of an amount of money or payment to be received at a future specified date.

Prescription: The securing of title to property by adverse possession; by occupying it for the period determined by law barring action for recovery.

Prima facie: Presumptive on its face.

Principal: The employer of an agent or the amount of money borrowed in a loan.

Privity: Mutual relationship to the same rights of property; contractual relationship.

Procuring cause: That cause originating from a series of events that, without break in continuity, results in an agent producing a ready, willing, and able buyer.

Promissory note: Written instrument used to evidence a basic obligation or debt.

Property: Anything of which there may be ownership rights.

Proration of taxes: To divide or prorate the taxes equally or proportionately to time of use.

Purchase money mortgage or trust deed: A trust deed or mortgage given as part or all of the purchase consideration for property.

Quarter round: A molding that presents a profile of a quarter circle.

Quiet enjoyment: Right of an owner to the use of property without interference of possession.

Quiet title: A court action brought to establish title; to remove a cloud on the title.

Quitclaim deed: A deed to relinquish any interest in property that the grantor may have.

Radiant heating: A method of heating usually consisting of coils or pipes in the floor, wall, or ceiling.

Rafter: One of a series of boards of a roof designed to support roof loads. The rafters of a flat roof are sometimes called *roof joists.*

Range: A strip of land six miles wide determined by a government survey, running in a north-south direction.

Ratification: The adoption or approval of an act performed on behalf of a person without previous authorization.

Real estate trust: A special arrangement under federal and state law whereby investors may pool funds for investments in real estate and mortgages and yet escape corporation taxes.

Real property: Land and anything permanently affixed to it, incidental or appurtenant to it, or immovable by law.

Realtor®: A real estate broker who is a member of the National Association of Realtors®.

Recapture: The rate of interest necessary to provide for the return of an investment. Not to be confused with interest rate, which is a rate of interest on an investment.

Reconveyance: The transfer of the title of land from one person to the immediately preceding owner. This particular instrument of transfer is commonly used in California when the performance or debt is satisfied under the terms of a deed of trust, when the trustee conveys the title he has held on condition back to the owner.

Recordation: To file a document for record in the office of the county recorder. Gives constructive notice of the contents to any party searching the records.

Redemption: The right of a former owner to repurchase a property after a judicial sale.

Redlining: A practice of certain lenders, now against California law, of refusing to make purchase loans to buyers of property in a certain area or neighborhood which generally has a large minority population.

Reformation: An action to correct a mistake in a deed or other document.

Release clause: A stipulation that upon the payment

of a specific sum of money to the holder of a trust deed or mortgage, the lien of the instrument as to a specific described lot or area shall be removed from the blanket lien on the whole area involved.

Remainder: An estate that vests after the termination of the prior estate, such as a life estate.

Recision of contract: The abrogation or annulling of contract; the revocation or repealing of contract by mutual consent by parties to the contract, or for cause by either party to the contract.

Reservation: A right retained by a grantor in conveying property.

Restriction: As used relating to real property, it means that the owner of real property is restricted or prohibited from doing certain things relating to the property or using the property for certain purposes—for instance, the requirement in a deed that a lot may be used for the construction of not more than a one-party dwelling, costing not less than ninety thousand dollars ($90,000), is termed to be restriction; also, a legislative ordinance affecting all properties in a given area, requiring that improvements on property shall not be constructed any closer than 25 feet to the street curb, is a restriction by operation of law.

Reversion: The right to future possession on enjoyment by the person, or his heirs, creating the preceding estate.

Reversionary interest: The interest that a person has in lands or other property upon the termination of the preceding estate.

Ridge: The horizontal line at the junction of the top edges of two sloping roof surfaces. The rafters at both slopes are nailed at the ridge.

Ridge board: The board placed on edge at the ridge of the roof to support the upper ends of the rafters; also called roof tree, ridge piece, ridge plate, or ridgepole.

Right of survivorship: Right to acquire the interest of a deceased joint owner; distinguishing feature of a joint tenancy.

Right-of-way: A privilege operating as an easement upon land whereby the owner does by grant or by agreement give to another the right to pass over his land, to construct a roadway or use as a roadway a specific part of his land, or the right to construct through and over his land telephone, telegraph, or electric power lines, or the right to place underground water mains, gas mains, or sewer mains.

Riparian rights: The right of a landowner to water on, under, or adjacent to his land.

Riser: The upright board at the back of each step of a stairway. In heating, a riser is a duct slanted upward to carry hot air from the furnace to the room above.

Roman brick: Thin brick of slimmer proportions than standard building brick.

Sales contract: A contract by which buyer and seller agree to terms of a sale.

Sale-leaseback: A situation where the owner of a piece of property wishes to sell the property and retain occupancy by leasing it from the buyer.

Sandwich lease: A leasehold interest that lies between the primary lease and the operating lease.

Sash: Wood or metal frames containing one or more window panes.

Satisfaction: Discharge of mortgage or trust deed lien from the records upon payment of the evidenced debt.

Scribing: Fitting woodwork to an irregular surface.

Seal: An impression made to attest the execution of an instrument.

Secondary financing: A loan secured by a second mortgage or trust deed on real property.

Section: An area of land established by government survey and containing 640 acres.

Secured party: The party having the security interest. Thus the mortgagee, the conditional seller, the pledgee, et cetera, are all now referred to as the secured party.

Security agreement: An agreement between the secured party and the debtor that creates the security interest.

Security interest: A term designating the interest of the creditor in the property of the debtor in all types of credit transactions. It thus replaces such terms as the following: chattel mortgage, pledge, trust receipt, chattel trust, equipment trust, conditional sale, inventory lien, et cetera.

Separate property: Property owned by a husband or wife that is not community property; acquired by either spouse prior to marriage or by gift or devise after marriage.

Septic tank: An underground tank in which sewage from the house is reduced to liquid by bacterial action and drained off.

Setback ordinance: An ordinance prohibiting the erection of a building or structure between the curb and the set back line.

Severalty ownership: Owned by one person only. Sole ownership.

Shake: A hand-split shingle, usually edge grained.

Sheathing: Structural covering, usually boards, plywood, or wallboards, placed over exterior studding or rafters of a house.

Sheriff's deed: Deed given by court order in connection with sale of property to satisfy a judgment.

Sill: The lowest part of the frame of a house, resting on the foundation and supporting the uprights of the frame. The board or metal forming the lower side of an opening, such as a door sill, window sill, etc.

Sinking fund: Fund set aside from the income from property that, with accrued interest, will eventually pay for replacement of the improvements.

Soil pipe: Pipe carrying waste out from the house to the main sewer line.

Sole or sole plate: A member, usually a 2-by-4, on which wall and partition studs rest.

Span: The distance between structural supports such as walls, columns, piers, beams, girders, and trusses.

Special assessment: A public authority created to pay the cost of public improvements such as street lights, sidewalks, and street improvements.

Specific performance: An action to compel performance of an agreement, as the sale of land.

SRA: Designates a person who is a member of the Society of Residential Appraisers.

Statute of frauds: State law which provides that certain contracts must be in writing in order to be enforceable at law. Examples: real property lease for more than one year; agent's authorization to sell real estate.

Straight-line depreciation: A definite sum set aside annually from income to pay the cost of replacing improvements, without reference to interest it earns.

String, stringer: A timer or other support for cross members. In stairs, the support on which the stair treads rest.

Studs or studding: Vertical supporting timbers in the walls and partitions.

Subject to mortgage: When a grantee takes a title to real property subject to mortgage, he is not responsible to the holder of the promissory note for the payment of any portion of the amount due. The most that he can lose in the event of a foreclosure is his equity in the property. See also *assumption of mortgage* in this section. In neither case is the original maker of the note released from his responsibility.

Sublease: A lease given by a lessee.

Subordinate: To make subject to, or junior to.

Subordination clause: Clause in a junior or a second lien permitting retention of priority for prior liens. A subordination clause may also be used in a first deed of trust, permitting it to be subordinate to subsequent liens such as, for example, the liens of construction loans.

Subpoena: A process to cause a witness to appear and give testimony.

Subrogation: The substitution of another person in place of the creditor, to whose rights he succeeds in relation to the debt. The doctrine is used very often when one person agrees to stand surety for the performance of a contract by another person.

Surety: One who guarantees the performance of another; guarantor.

Survey: The process by which a parcel of land is measured and its area ascertained.

Syndicate: A partnership organized for participation in a real estate venture.

Tax-free exchange: A method of deferring capital gains taxes by exchanging real property for other like property.

Tax sale: Sale of property after a period of nonpayment of taxes.

Tenancy in common: Ownership by two or more persons who hold undivided interest, without right of survivorship; interests need not be equal.

Tentative map: The Subdivision Map Act requires subdividers to submit initially a tentative map of their tract to the local planning commission for study. The approval or disapproval of the planning commission is noted on the map. Thereafter a final map of the tract embodying any changes requested by the planning commission is required to be filed with the planning commission.

Tenure in land: The mode or manner by which an estate in lands is held.

Termites: Ant-like insects that feed on wood.

Termite shield: A shield, usually of noncorrodible metal, placed on top of the foundation wall or around pipes to prevent passage of termites.

Testator: Any individual who makes a will.

Threshold: A strip of wood or metal beveled on each edge and used above the finished floor under outside doors.

Time is of the essence: One of the essential requirements to forming of a binding contract; contemplates a punctual performance.

Title: Evidence that the owner of land is in lawful possession thereof; an instrument evidencing such ownership.

Title insurance: Insurance written by a title company to protect the property owner against loss if the title is imperfect.

Topography: Nature of the surface of land; topography may be level, rolling, mountainous.

Torrens title: System of title records provided by state law (no longer used in California).

Tort: A wrongful act; wrong, injury; violation of a legal right.

Township: A territorial subdivision six miles long, six miles wide and containing 36 sections, each one mile square.

Trade fixtures: Articles of personal property annexed to real property, but which are necessary to the carrying on of a trade and are removable by the owner.

Trade-in: An increasingly popular method of guaranteeing an owner a minimum amount of cash on sale of his present property to permit him to purchase another. If the property is not sold within a specified time at the listed price, the broker agrees to arrange financing to purchase the property at an agreed-upon discount.

Treads: Horizontal boards of a stairway.

Trim: The finish materials in a building, such as moldings, applied around openings (window trim, door trim) or at the floor and ceiling (baseboard, cornice, picture molding).

Trust account: A special account set up by an agent into which monies of principals are deposited with such monies kept separate and not commingled with monies belonging to the agent.

Trust deed: A deed given by the borrower to a trustee to be held pending fulfillment of an obligation, which is ordinarily repayment of a loan to a beneficiary.

Trustee: One who holds property in trust for another to secure the performance of an obligation.

Trustor: One who deeds his property to a trustee to be held as security until he has performed his obligation to a lender under terms of a deed of trust.

Undue influence: Use of a fiduciary or confidential relationship to obtain any fraudulent or unfair advantage of another's weakness of mind, distress, or necessity.

Unearned increment: An increase in value of real estate due to no effort on the part of the owner, often due to increase in population.

346

Uniform commercial code: Effective January 1, 1965, it establishes a unified and comprehensive scheme for regulation of security transactions in personal property, superseding the existing statutes on chattel mortgages, conditional sales, trust receipts, assignment of accounts receivable, and others in this field.

Urban property: City property: closely settled property.

Usury: On a loan, claiming a rate of interest greater than that permitted by law.

Valid: Having force, or binding force; legally sufficient and authorized by law.

Valley: The internal angle formed by the junction of two sloping sides of a roof.

Valuation: Estimated worth or price. Estimation. The act of valuing by appraisal.

Vendee: A purchaser; buyer.

Vendor: A seller; one who disposes of a thing in consideration of money.

Veneer: Thin sheets of wood.

Vent: A pipe installed to provide a flow of air to or from a drainage system or to provide a circulation of air within such a system to protect trap seals from siphonage and back pressure.

Verification: Sworn statement before a duly qualified officer to the correctness of the contents of an instrument.

Vested: Bestowed upon someone; secured by someone, such as title to property.

Void: To have no force or effect; that which is unenforceable.

Voidable: That which is capable of being adjudged void, but is not void unless action is taken to make it so.

Voluntary lien: Any lien placed on property with consent of, or as a result of, the voluntary act of the owner.

Wainscotting: Wood lining of an interior wall; lower section of a wall when finished differently from the upper part.

Waive: To relinquish or abandon; to forego a right to enforce or require anything.

Warranty deed: A deed used to convey real property that contains warranties of title and quiet possession; the grantor thus agrees to defend the premises against the lawful claims of third persons. It is commonly used in other states, but not in California, where the grant deed has supplanted it. The modern practice of securing title insurance policies has reduced the importance of express and implied warranty in deeds.

Waste: The destruction, or material alteration of, or injury to, premises by a tenant for life or years.

Water table: Distance from the ground surface to a depth at which natural groundwater is found.

Zone: The area set off by the proper authorities for a specific use subject to certain restrictions or restraints.

Zoning: The act of city or county authorities specifying the type of use to which property may be put in specific areas.

Appendix B: Answers to multiple choice questions

Chapter 1
1–1. *(c)*
1–2. *(b)*
1–3. *(a)*
1–4. *(c)*
1–5. *(c)*
1–6. *(a)*
1–7. *(c)*
1–8. *(d)*

Chapter 2
2–1. *(c)*
2–2. *(c)*
2–3. *(c)*
2–4. *(d)*
2–5. *(d)*
2–6. *(c)*
2–7. *(b)*
2–8. *(a)*

Chapter 3
3–1. *(c)*
3–2. *(a)*
3–3. *(b)*
3–4. *(c)*
3–5. *(d)*
3–6. *(c)*
3–7. *(d)*
3–8. *(c)*

Chapter 4
4–1. *(c)*
4–2. *(c)*
4–3. *(c)*
4–4. *(d)*
4–5. *(d)*
4–6. *(d)*
4–7. *(b)*
4–8. *(a)*

Chapter 5
5–1. *(c)*
5–2. *(b)*
5–3. *(c)*
5–4. *(d)*
5–5. *(c)*
5–6. *(b)*
5–7. *(b)*
5–8. *(c)*

Chapter 6
6–1. *(c)*
6–2. *(b)*
6–3. *(c)*
6–4. *(c)*
6–5. *(d)*
6–6. *(c)*
6–7. *(a)*
6–8. *(c)*

Chapter 7
7–1. *(c)*
7–2. *(b)*
7–3. *(a)*
7–4. *(c)*
7–5. *(d)*
7–6. *(c)*
7–7. *(b)*
7–8. *(c)*

Chapter 8
8–1. *(c)*
8–2. *(a)*
8–3. *(b)*
8–4. *(c)*
8–5. *(d)*
8–6. *(c)*
8–7. *(d)*
8–8. *(d)*

Chapter 9
9–1. *(c)*
9–2. *(b)*
9–3. *(a)*
9–4. *(c)*
9–5. *(d)*
9–6. *(c)*
9–7. *(c)*
9–8. *(d)*

Chapter 10
10–1. *(c)*
10–2. *(c)*
10–3. *(b)*
10–4. *(c)*
10–5. *(d)*
10–6. *(c)*
10–7. *(c)*
10–8. *(a)*

Chapter 11
11–1. *(c)*
11–2. *(c)*
11–3. *(c)*
11–4. *(d)*
11–5. *(c)*
11–6. *(b)*
11–7. *(a)*
11–8. *(c)*

Chapter 12
12–1. *(c)*
12–2. *(c)*
12–3. *(b)*
12–4. *(c)*
12–5. *(c)*
12–6. *(c)*
12–7. *(a)*
12–8. *(c)*

Chapter 13
13–1. *(c)*
13–2. *(c)*
13–3. *(a)*
13–4. *(c)*
13–5. *(d)*
13–6. *(c)*
13–7. *(b)*
13–8. *(c)*

Chapter 14
14–1. *(c)*
14–2. *(a)*
14–3. *(b)*
14–4. *(c)*
14–5. *(c)*
14–6. *(b)*
14–7. *(b)*
14–8. *(d)*

Chapter 15
15–1. *(c)*
15–2. *(b)*
15–3. *(a)*
15–4. *(c)*
15–5. *(d)*
15–6. *(c)*
15–7. *(c)*
15–8. *(c)*

Chapter 16
16–1. *(b)*
16–2. *(c)*
16–3. *(c)*
16–4. *(c)*
16–5. *(d)*
16–6. *(d)*
16–7. *(c)*
16–8. *(a)*

Chapter 17
17–1. *(c)*
17–2. *(a)*
17–3. *(b)*
17–4. *(c)*
17–5. *(d)*
17–6. *(c)*
17–7. *(c)*
17–8. *(c)*

Chapter 18
18–1. *(a)*
18–2. *(a)*
18–3. *(b)*
18–4. *(c)*
18–5. *(d)*
18–6. *(c)*
18–7. *(c)*
18–8. *(c)*

Chapter 19
19–1. *(c)*
19–2. *(b)*
19–3. *(a)*
19–4. *(c)*
19–5. *(d)*
19–6. *(c)*
19–7. *(c)*
19–8. *(c)*

Chapter 20
20–1. *(c)*
20–2. *(b)*
20–3. *(c)*
20–4. *(c)*
20–5. *(d)*
20–6. *(c)*
20–7. *(a)*
20–8. *(b)*

Chapter 21
21–1. *(a)*
21–2. *(c)*
21–3. *(b)*
21–4. *(c)*
21–5. *(d)*
21–6. *(c)*
21–7. *(c)*
21–8. *(c)*

Appendix C: Sample real estate salesperson test

1. Jim and Mary are both licensees working for Broker Smith. Mary obtains an offer on an office listing and a few hours later Jim brings in an offer on the same property. Which of the following is correct: *(a)* Mary should present her offer to the sellers and if not accepted, Jim should present his offer, *(b)* the highest offer should be presented to the seller, *(c)* both offers must be presented to the seller, *(d)* whichever way Broker Smith decides is proper.

2. Which of the following best describes a simple contract: *(a)* must be written, *(b)* offer and acceptance, *(c)* an acknowledgment, *(d)* monetary consideration.

3. Which of the following statements is correct: *(a)* a real estate broker license allows the broker to sell a business opportunity, *(b)* net listings must state the broker's commission as a percent of the selling price, *(c)* a college graduate with a major in business can take the real estate broker examination without having to take any required real estate courses, *(d)* residential properties are most often appraised by the cost approach.

4. Severalty ownership means: *(a)* ownership by two or more individuals as joint tenants, *(b)* several pieces of property owned by the same individual, *(c)* sole ownership, *(d)* none of these.

5. The Code of Ethics followed by Realtors® is a product of: *(a)* California Real Estate Law, *(b)* California Civil Code, *(c)* National Association of Realtors®, *(d)* Real Estate Commissioner.

6. The rental value of industrial property is generally set by the: *(a)* square foot, *(b)* front foot, *(c)* income produced, *(d)* availability of public transportation.

7. Which of the following most closely defines an escrow officer: *(a)* fiduciary, *(b)* agent, *(c)* counsellor, *(d)* legal advisor on methods of taking title to real property.

8. Which of the following is least affected by the Statute of Frauds: *(a)* real property sales contract, *(b)* two-year lease, *(c)* monthly tenancy agreement, *(d)* grant deed.

9. Which of the following is not a way to create an easement: *(a)* written agreement, *(b)* prescription, *(c)* legal implication, *(d)* recording deed of trust.

10. Which of the following is not a method of determining whether or not an item is a fixture: *(a)* intent of parties, *(b)* agreement between parties, *(c)* monetary value, *(d)* method of annexation.

11. The funds used in a California Veterans loan are obtained from: *(a)* U.S. Treasury, *(b)* bond issues, *(c)* Federal Reserve Bank, *(d)* savings and loan associations and banks.

12. An acceleration clause in a promissory note usually does which of the following: *(a)* increases monthly payments, *(b)* requires full payment of the loan balance if certain events occur, *(c)* makes allowance for variable interest rates, *(d)* allows the loan to be repaid without any prepayment penalties.

13. A contract for the exchange of buildings containing 12 and 16 units respectively, must be: *(a)* signed by a Realtor® or C.P.A., *(b)* approved by the local Internal Revenue office, *(c)* written, *(d)* witnessed by a Notary Public or court clerk.

14. The prepayment penalty required by law on an F.H.A. insured loan is: *(a)* 3 percent of original amount of loan, *(b)* six months' interest on unpaid balance, *(c)* .05 percent of remaining balance, *(d)* none of these.

15. With respect to a V.A. loan, the purchase money is advanced by: *(a)* State of California Mutual Funds, *(b)* Veterans Administration, *(c)* Federal Housing Authority, *(d)* any approved lender.

16. If annual net income is $28,000 and a capitalization rate of 8 percent is used, what should be the selling price of the property: *(a)* $350,000 *(b)* $224,000 *(c)* $35,000 *(d)* none of these.

17. With respect to the sale of a business, the term *good will* is best defined as: *(a)* trade fixtures, *(b)* credit given with respect to transfer of business stock in trade, *(c)* expectation of continued public patronage, *(d)* renewal of current lease agreement.

18. Mary owns a piece of property worth $225,000 and her property tax bill for the current year is

348

$6,200. If she makes a 7 percent return on the property this year the monthly amount Mary makes is: *(a)* $1,575 *(b)* $1,312.50 *(c)* $1,312.50 *(d)* $1,276.33.

19. Which of the following methods of calculating depreciation allow the greatest amount of recapture in later years: *(a)* 175 percent *(b)* accrued depreciation percent *(c)* straight line, *(d)* none of these.

20. Which of the following is true with respect to a standard policy of title insurance: *(a)* it must insure both buyer and seller, *(b)* always insures against unrecorded documents and possible easements, *(c)* just insures lender, *(d)* none of these.

21. The most commonly used method of real property valuation is: *(a)* cost approach, *(b)* income approach, *(c)* competitive market analysis, *(d)* assessor's appraisal.

22. Which of the following is not necessary in order to acquire an easement by prescription: *(a)* hostile to title of true owner, *(b)* use is open and notorious for a five-year period, *(c)* pay property taxes, *(d)* none of these.

23. A grant deed can best be described as: *(a)* a document describing a particular property, *(b)* instrument conveying title, *(c)* an abstract, *(d)* an instrument affecting real property which can be recorded.

24. Buyer Smith and owner Brown sign a contract for the purchase of Brown's property. Twenty days later Smith decides not to purchase. A suit for specific performance may be brought by: *(a)* Brown, *(b)* Smith, *(c)* lender, *(d)* title company.

25. Alan earns $520 per month from an investment showing a 12 percent return per annum. The value of the investment is approximately: *(a)* $4,333 *(b)* $43,000 *(c)* $52,000 *(d)* $62,400.

26. Which of the following is a requirement for a real estate license: *(a)* at least 21 years old, *(b)* California resident for three years, *(c)* U.S. citizen, *(d)* none of these.

27. Which of the following contracts is voidable: *(a)* contract obtained by duress, *(b)* real estate purchase contract signed by minor, *(c)* a contract which has as its subject an unlawful object, *(d)* none of these.

28. Which of the following is incorrect with respect to the cost approach in appraisal: *(a)* generally used in connection with appraisal of public buildings, *(b)* most accurate with respect to newer buildings, *(c)* sets the lower limit of value, *(d)* requires knowledge of current building costs for various components of a building.

29. Phillips borrowed $16,000 on a straight note for 90 days and paid $640 interest. What was the rate of interest: *(a)* 9½ percent, *(b)* 16 percent, *(c)* 8 percent, *(d)* none of these.

30. The insurance which is provided in an F.H.A. loan insures the: *(a)* borrower, *(b)* title company, *(c)* lender, *(d)* federal government.

31. Which of the following is not a necessary element of a valid contract: *(a)* mutual consent, *(b)* sufficient consideration, *(c)* acknowledgement, *(d)* lawful object.

32. Which of the following statements is incorrect: *(a)* a broker may make a property appraisal for an owner without charging a fee, *(b)* a savings and loan association cannot charge interest in excess of 10 percent for a purchase money loan, *(c)* a Realtor® is a licensee who belongs to the National Association of Realtors®, *(d)* a multiple listing agreement can be given for a 180-day term.

33. A real estate licensee is prohibited from: *(a)* taking an option listing, *(b)* acting as a principal in a real estate transaction, *(c)* accepting payment for arranging a commercial lease of real property, *(d)* none of these.

34. Which of the following is considered to be constructive notice: *(a)* recordation, *(b)* registered letter, *(c)* telegram, *(d)* none of these.

35. Broker Dorothy sells a residence to a newly married couple who ask her how they should take title to the property. She should advise them to: *(a)* take title as joint tenants, *(b)* consult their attorney, *(c)* take title as community property, *(d)* take title as tenants in common since separate funds may be part of the cash down payment.

36. The party in a trust deed who borrowed money, is the: *(a)* trustor, *(b)* trustee, *(c)* beneficiary, *(d)* escrow agent.

37. Sylvia is interested in purchasing a property showing a net income of $32,600 per year. If she uses a capitalization rate of 11 percent, the purchase price should be approximately: *(a)* $300,000 *(b)* $322,000 *(c)* $296,000 *(d)* none of these.

38. Which of the following accounts for the greatest share of the real estate loan market: *(a)* savings and loan associations, *(b)* commercial banks, *(c)* F.H.A., *(d)* Veterans Administration.

39. Minimum standards for building construction are provided by: *(a)* local city or county supervisors, *(b)* State Contractors License Law, *(c)* State Housing Act, *(d)* none of these.

40. In which of the following instances may a real estate licensee properly restrict buyers with respect to ethnic classification: *(a)* following orders from property owner, *(b)* with respect to the sale of condominiums having a common recreational area, *(c)* if government guaranteed or insured financing is used, *(d)* none of these.

41. Laura is considering an investment which yields 9 percent per annum. In addition to her monthly salary of $1,600 she wishes to earn an additional $750. per month. What amount should Laura invest: *(a)* $90,000 *(b)* $83,000 *(c)* $100,000 *(d)* none of these.

42. Which of the following generally occurs in a tight money market: *(a)* interest rates increase, *(b)* loan fees decrease, *(c)* tax assessments are generally reduced by tax assessor, *(d)* none of these.

43. Marty owns a building containing 20 apartments located in Sacramento although he resides in San Francisco. Which of the following is correct: *(a)* collection of the rents must be made by a real estate licensee residing in Sacramento, *(b)* a resident manager must reside on the premises, *(c)*

350

a comprehensive liability insurance policy must be recorded at the Sacramento city hall, *(d)* none of these.

44. Which of the following is least likely to be regulated as part of a zoning law: *(a)* school and park locations, *(b)* building heights, *(c)* construction costs, *(d)* parking requirements.

45. The enforcement of local building codes is the responsibility of: *(a)* county sheriff, *(b)* Real Estate Commissioner, *(c)* State Planning Director, *(d)* none of these.

46. A condominium is often referred to as: *(a)* common easement, *(b)* severalty ownership, *(c)* vertical subdivision, *(d)* dividend interest ownership.

47. Which of the following designations does not pertain to property appraisal: *(a)* A.S.A., *(b)* M.A.I., *(c)* C.A.R., *(d)* S.R.A.

48. Although laws prohibiting racial discrimination have been in effect for some time, the courts have ruled that an owner may racially restrict prospective purchasers if the owner: *(a)* provides financing to the purchaser, *(b)* is selling a building in which the owner will continue to reside, *(c)* is selling a mobile home or condominium, *(d)* none of these.

49. The law which states the time limits within which legal action may be instituted in connection with breach of a contract to purchase real estate is known as: *(a)* Real Estate Law, *(b)* Uniform Commercial Code, *(c)* Statute of Limitations, *(d)* Statute of Frauds.

50. A real estate broker license is required for which of the following acts: *(a)* charging an owner for collection of rents, *(b)* a trustee selling property at a trustee's sale, *(c)* an administrator acting on order of a court, *(d)* none of these.

51. Although both a formal and holographic will are in writing, it is the formal will which is required to be: *(a)* properly recorded in the county in which the testator resides, *(b)* nuncupative, *(c)* witnessed, *(d)* submitted to a title company or trust department of a bank for proper verification.

52. Which of the following is not a California base line: *(a)* Mt. Tamalpais, *(b)* Humboldt, *(c)* San Bernardino, *(d)* Mt. Diablo.

53. The basis of California real property law derives from: *(a)* Spanish law, *(b)* English common law, *(c)* Statutes enacted by the California State Legislature, *(d)* None of these.

54. A loan containing a VA guarantee protects the: *(a)* borrower, *(b)* seller, *(c)* lender, *(d)* none of these.

55. With respect to a property description contained in a grant deed, if it is a metes and bounds description, it: *(a)* relates to easements, *(b)* shows block number, *(c)* describes boundary lines, *(d)* shows base and meridian lines.

56. Smith is shown a property by Broker Green. She makes an offer and signs a standard deposit receipt. The offer can be withdrawn by Smith: *(a)* if Broker Green agrees in writing, *(b)* before it is accepted by the seller, *(c)* by agreeing to forfeit any deposit given, *(d)* if fraud can be shown.

57. The most common type of interest charged on a loan for the purchase of residential property is: *(a)* simple, *(b)* compound, *(c)* bank discount, *(d)* cumulative interest as prescribed by the corporations commissioner.

58. Broker Laura Storm listed a condominium for $93,500 with a commission of 6 percent. If the owner accepted an offer of 10 percent less than the listed price, what is paid to Laura: *(a)* $5,610 *(b)* $6,171 *(c)* $5,049 *(d)* none of these.

59. Which of the following relates to time, title, interest, and possession: *(a)* tenants in common, *(b)* covenants, conditions, and restrictions, *(c)* right of survivorship, *(d)* none of these.

60. If Lansing owns a fee simple estate and leases it to Jordan for three years, the estates becomes: *(a)* a joint tenancy estate, *(b)* a leasehold estate, *(c)* a severalty estate, *(d)* none of these.

61. The lien created by recording a trust deed is generally removed from the public records by recording: *(a)* additional encumbrances affecting the property, *(b)* a security bond, *(c)* deed of reconveyance, *(d)* none of these.

62. Which of the following cannot become a lien against real property: *(a)* property taxes, *(b)* court judgement, *(c)* deed of trust, *(d)* listing contract.

63. The most likely place to obtain funds for an FHA loan is: *(a)* California Veterans Administration, *(b)* FHA office closest to the property, *(c)* bank or savings and loan association, *(d)* HUD.

64. After recording a notice of default, a trustee must wait three months before: *(a)* accepting an offer from a purchaser, *(b)* transferring title to beneficiary, *(c)* publishing notice of sale as required by law, *(d)* ordering an appraisal.

65. Broker Hall lists Cruz's property exclusively for 90 days. Hall advertises and shows the property but after 60 days has not received any offers. Cruz becomes upset and tells Hall to consider the listing cancelled. Which of the following is correct: *(a)* Cruz must pay Hall for any advertising expenses, *(b)* Hall can sue Cruz for the amount of commission shown in the listing contract, *(c)* the law requires Cruz to honor the listing contract and allow Hall to show the property to prospective purchasers, *(d)* none of these.

66. Adverse possession is: *(a)* continuous possession of a property contrary to the owner's interest, *(b)* property purchased at a tax sale by an adjoining property owner *(c)* property acquired by condemnation or eminent domain, *(d)* no longer allowed by California law.

67. A standard title insurance policy protects against: *(a)* a mining claim, *(b)* water rights, *(c)* unrecorded easements, *(d)* none of these.

68. With respect to a quitclaim deed, which of the following is correct: *(a)* it cannot be used in California, *(b)* it must be prepared by an attorney, *(c)* it guarantees nothing, *(d)* none of these.

69. *Potable* relates to: *(a)* natural gas, *(b)* easements, *(c)* water, *(d)* sewer pipes.

70. A real estate broker may act as an escrow agent in: *(a)* any sale of property in which he is the

agent, *(b)* any real estate sale, *(c)* any real estate sale with exception of a business opportunity which must have a bank or title company as escrow agent, *(d)* California law prohibits real estate brokers from acting as escrow agents.

71. Which of the following is properly classified as a lien: *(a)* common driveway easement, *(b)* attachment, *(c)* a fence which extends across adjoining property, *(d)* none of these.

72. A building is purchased for $196,500 subject to trust deeds of $125,000 and $12,000. The buyer's equity is: *(a)* $137,000 *(b)* $59,500 *(c)* $233,500 *(d)* $71,500.

73. A fiduciary relationship exists between: *(a)* broker and principal, *(b)* buyer and seller, *(c)* broker and escrow officer, *(d)* landlord and tenant.

74. The utility value of a property has most to do with its: *(a)* location, *(b)* market value, *(c)* use, *(d)* original cost.

75. Carroll purchases a property for $270,000. If he accepts an offer of $324,000 what is his percent of profit: *(a)* 20 percent, *(b)* 27 percent, *(c)* 17 percent *(d)* none of these.

76. Which of the following is least likely to influence the value of a 20-year-old apartment building: *(a)* location, *(b)* gross income, *(c)* original construction cost, *(d)* condition of building.

77. Which of the following is incorrect with respect to a listing agreement: *(a)* agreement to pay a commission to a real estate broker, *(b)* establishes agency relationship between broker and principal, *(c)* must show specific term, *(d)* none of these.

78. Brown has a loan which allows prepayment of up to 20 percent of the remaining balance in any year without a prepayment penalty. If he has $20,000 in cash, how much of this can be applied to the loan if the remaining loan balance is $62,320: *(a)* $12,320 *(b)* $23,320 *(c)* $12,464 *(d)* $6,232.

79. A gross multiplier is least likely to be used in appraising which of the following: *(a)* public buildings, *(b)* residential apartment complex, *(c)* commercial property, *(d)* office building.

80. Tax delinquent property is sold after taxes have been delinquent: *(a)* five years, *(b)* three years, *(c)* varies according to amount of tax lien, *(d)* none of these.

81. If the foundation of Arnold's garage is found to be partly on an adjacent property, this is an: *(a)* encroachment, *(b)* easement, *(c)* example of overlapping fixtures, *(d)* none of these.

82. Which of the following requires the owner to pay a commission even though the owner himself sells the property during the term of the listing: *(a)* open listing, *(b)* exclusive right, *(c)* open listing containing option to purchase, *(d)* none of these.

83. Which of the following goes with real property when it is sold and is not separated from it: *(a)* encroachment, *(b)* trade fixture, *(c)* appurtenance, *(d)* existing loan.

84. Where private property is taken by condemnation for a public use, the basis for compensation to the owner is: *(a)* market value, *(b)* assessed value, *(c)* original cost to owner, *(d)* none of these.

85. Which of the following is best classified as a voluntary lien: *(a)* tax lien, *(b)* judgement, *(c)* trust deed, *(d)* bankruptcy action.

86. A homestead is recorded in order to protect: *(a)* mineral rights, *(b)* mining claims, *(c)* commercial property against lease options, *(d)* none of these.

87. Which of the following best describes the most used form in connection with the purchase of residential properties: *(a)* residential option to purchase, *(b)* installment sale contract, *(c)* deposit receipt, *(d)* listing.

88. A mechanic's lien cannot be recorded to protect which of the following: *(a)* real estate broker's commission, *(b)* material supplier, *(c)* contractor, *(d)* architect.

89. Both buyers and sellers signed a deposit receipt containing a condition which stated that purchaser was to obtain a loan at 13½ percent. The contract is: *(a)* valid and enforceable, *(b)* merely an offer since it is conditional on obtaining a loan, *(c)* unilateral, *(d)* invalid because it is bilateral.

90. Smith lists his property with Broker Brown telling him that the plumbing is faulty and the water pressure is low. Brown produces buyer Catlin who purchases the property and subsequently discovers the problem with respect to the plumbing. Which of the following is correct: *(a)* Catlin can sue both Smith and Brown, *(b)* Catlin cannot sue Smith, but must sue Brown as the agent in the transaction, *(c)* Catlin must report the problem to the Real Estate Commissioner who will instigate the suit, *(d)* suit cannot be brought after close of escrow.

91. Wong signs a five-year lease for a commercial building belonging to Carr. Two years later Carr sells the building to York. Which of the following is correct: *(a)* the lease must be renegotiated by York and Wong, *(b)* commercial leases revert to monthly tenancies upon sale or transfer of the property, *(c)* the lease is valid and binding on York, *(d)* none of these.

92. The basis for rent in a supermarket percentage lease is generally: *(a)* gross sales, *(b)* real estate taxes, *(c)* a percent of the value of the building, *(d)* based on stock turnover.

93. The instrument used to secure a loan on business merchandise and stock is: *(a)* stock certificate, *(b)* bill of sale, *(c)* security agreement, *(d)* note and deed of trust.

94. Which of the following is not essential to a valid contract: *(a)* lawful object, *(b)* competent parties, *(c)* consideration, *(d)* recordation.

95. Martha's tenancy agreement terminated last week and she is remaining in possession. If the owner has not given her permission to stay, Martha has a: *(a)* fee estate, *(b)* life estate, *(c)* tenancy in common, *(d)* none of these.

96. Title to trade fixtures in connection with the sale of a business is transferred by: *(a)* escrow, *(b)* purchase contract, *(c)* a bill of sale listing the fixtures, *(d)* transfer of real property which always includes trade fixtures.

97. A cloud on a title is most often removed by: *(a)* public sale of the property, *(b)* quiet title action, *(c)* partition, *(d)* private sale of the property.

98. Which of the following is not classified as real property: *(a)* trade fixtures, *(b)* fences, *(c)* party wall, *(d)* storage buildings.

99. An example of chattels are: *(a)* leases, *(b)* buildings, *(c)* fixtures, *(d)* none of these.

100. Which of the following is a government limitation on private property ownership: *(a)* private easement, *(b)* taxation, *(c)* zoning, *(d)* recordation.

101. A bilateral contract is: *(a)* exchanging of promises between two parties, *(b)* purchase contract signed by husband and wife, *(c)* A offers to paint B's building for $2,000 and B agrees to respond within three days, *(d)* made with respect to a rental agreement.

102. Which of the following best describes a *time is of the essence* clause: *(a)* specific legal time which is given for performing a condition in a contract, *(b)* amount of time given a seller to reply to an offer, *(c)* term of a listing agreement, *(d)* number of days allowed to close escrow.

103. Which of the following is not a contract: *(a)* listing agreement for 120 days, *(b)* a monthly tenancy agreement, *(c)* competitive market analysis prepared by a broker, *(d)* real estate option.

104. It is against the law for a broker to do which of the following with respect to a deposit given by a buyer: *(a)* give it to the principal, *(b)* place it in escrow, *(c)* deposit it in broker's savings account, *(d)* place it in a trust account.

105. Which of the following is not a function of an exclusive listing agreement: *(a)* sets broker's commission, *(b)* states purchase price, *(c)* lists closing costs, *(d)* appointment of an agent.

106. Which of the following contracts are likely to be declared void in a court action: *(a)* purchase contract obtained by duress but signed by both parties, *(b)* purchase contract signed by a resident alien, *(c)* lease option contract not recorded, *(d)* real property installment sale contract.

107. The administrator of an estate is: *(a)* appointed by a court, *(b)* selected by decedent in will, *(c)* selected by heirs, *(d)* decedent's attorney generally selects administrator.

108. Recording a trust deed gives: *(a)* ownership interest, *(b)* equitable title to beneficiary, *(c)* constructive notice to interested parties, *(d)* none of these.

109. If Jinks, a California resident, signs his wife's name to a document relating to community property, which of the following is correct: *(a)* it must be capable of being recorded in order to be valid, *(b)* the law allows a husband to sign any document for both spouses, *(c)* it is a forgery, *(d)* none of these.

110. For an offer to be considered in a probate sale at the opening of bids, the amount of the offer must be at least: *(a)* any amount buyer wishes to offer, *(b)* 25 percent of full cash value as set by assessor, *(c)* 90 percent of court approved appraisal, *(d)* amount of existing liens.

111. Which of the following is necessary to a valid mechanic's lien: *(a)* amount must be at least $500 *(b)* recordation, *(c)* it must be filed by the property owner, *(d)* none of these.

112. Right of survivorship is a basic characteristic of: *(a)* condominium ownership, *(b)* ownership by spouses, *(c)* joint tenancy, *(d)* tenancy in common.

113. Leases are examples of: *(a)* ownership interest, *(b)* security interest, *(c)* less-than-freehold estates, *(d)* fee ownership.

114. California law requires which of the following to be recorded in order to be valid: *(a)* leases, *(b)* instruments affecting title to real property, *(c)* all classes of easements, *(d)* none of these.

115. The beneficiary, in a deed of trust, is the: *(a)* borrower, *(b)* party signing the promissory note to repay purchase money, *(c)* lender, *(d)* party holding property in trust.

116. With respect to real estate offices in California, which of the following is most common: *(a)* partnerships with two or more real estate broker licensees, *(b)* syndicates, *(c)* individual proprietorships, *(d)* corporate structures.

117. Which of the following is more likely to be found in the sale of a business opportunity than in the sale of a residential apartment building: *(a)* special tax benefits, *(b)* appraisal report submitted to savings and loan association, *(c)* sales and use tax payment, *(d)* payment of commission money to two brokers.

118. Mutual agency is most important with respect to: *(a)* escrow officers, *(b)* net listings, *(c)* partners in a real estate partnership, *(d)* agency created by court order.

119. Which of the following is incorrect as regards an attorney-in-fact: *(a)* may be able to perform same acts as principal, *(b)* appointment is written, *(c)* must hold a real estate license or special court permit, *(d)* none of these.

120. The maximum amount of commission a broker may receive is: *(a)* 12 percent, *(b)* any amount agreed to by broker and principal, *(c)* minimum is by agreement but maximum is set by civil code statutes, *(d)* NAR code of ethics sets maximum amount.

121. The most common type of subdivision found in California is: *(a)* shopping centers and industrial parks, *(b)* recreational, *(c)* standard residential, *(d)* condominium.

122. The basic rules which govern the disposition of a buyer's deposit money can be found in: *(a)* U.C.C., *(b)* Business and Professions code, *(c)* rules of the banking commissioner, *(d)* trust account statutes.

123. A buyer who inquires about the purchase of property in a subdivision must be provided with a copy of the Commissioner's Public Report and must: *(a)* bring it to any real estate broker for verification or deposit it in escrow, *(b)* sign a receipt, *(c)* use form provided in report for preparation of purchase offer, *(d)* none of these.

124. Directional growth is best described as: *(a)* number of floors in a highrise building, *(b)* flow of a waterway, *(c)* population shifts, *(d)* addition to existing building.

125. Carl applies for a loan of $85,000 and is told that the loan fee will be two points plus $200. The amount of the fee is: *(a)* $1,900 *(b)* $190 *(c)* $1,800 *(d)* none of these.

126. The best sources of secondary financing are usually: *(a)* private parties, *(b)* savings and loan associations, *(c)* commercial banks, *(d)* mutual savings banks.

127. Percolation is a term which is used with reference to: *(a)* minerals, *(b)* furnace thermostats, *(c)* water, *(d)* alluvion.

128. If a building is sold for $275,000, what commission does broker Smith receive if the commission is 7 percent up to $100,000 of sales price and 6 percent of the balance: *(a)* $1,050 *(b)* $19,025 *(c)* $1,750 *(d)* $17,500.

129. An offer is accepted and broker opens escrow. The escrow officer writes to existing lenders requesting: *(a)* appraisal, *(b)* full payment, *(c)* a demand, *(d)* loan commitment.

130. *Boot* is a term often found in connection with: *(a)* commercial leases, *(b)* residential complexes, *(c)* tax-free exchanges, *(d)* building construction.

131. If Smith, a Realtor®, and Brown, a general contractor, wish to purchase real property together, they can: *(a)* act as principals, *(b)* purchase after entering into a general partnership agreement as required by law, *(c)* purchase if Brown obtains a real estate license, *(d)* act as principals after obtaining a permit from the Real Estate Commissioner.

132. The Bulk Sales Law is encountered in connection with which of the following sales: *(a)* mineral, oil, and gas, *(b)* water rights, *(c)* business opportunities, *(d)* multiple sales in a tract development.

133. A bearing wall: *(a)* is a surveyor's marker, *(b)* supports weight, *(c)* is a term used in connection with solar energy, *(d)* always faces a view.

134. Smith accepts a selling price of $125,000. What will Smith net if closing costs are $3,250, a loan of $29,320 is due to the existing lender, and a commission of 7 percent is paid: *(a)* $83,680 *(b)* $84,930 *(c)* $92,430 *(d)* none of these.

135. A survey of A's property discloses a neighbors fence is 1½ feet on A's side of the property line. This is known as: *(a)* appurtenant easement, *(b)* gross easement, *(c)* encroachment, *(d)* prescriptive easement.

136. All of the following are required in a lease except: *(a)* property description, *(b)* lessor's signature, *(c)* term, *(d)* notary stamp.

137. Which of the following is not depreciable property for income tax purposes: *(a)* residence rented to a relative of the owner, *(b)* a commercial building leased for three years, *(c)* unimproved country property, *(d)* apartment building.

138. Which of the following statements is incorrect with respect to a real estate broker: *(a)* can purchase and sell property as a principal, *(b)* can charge a fee for an appraisal report, *(c)* may employ salesmen licensees, *(d)* must maintain a trust account.

139. Which of the following is not used in California: *(a)* tenancy in common by spouses, *(b)* fee estates, *(c)* severalty estates, *(d)* estates by entirety.

140. The ownership of the common area in a large condominium is held by owners as: *(a)* tenants in partnership, *(b)* joint tenancy, *(c)* tenants in common, *(d)* none of these.

141. Which of the following terms is most nearly the opposite of alienation: *(a)* transfer, *(b)* conveyance, *(c)* acquisition, *(d)* quitclaim.

142. To use the term *Realtor*®, a broker must belong to: *(a)* N.A.R., *(b)* M.A.I., *(c)* California Department of Real Estate, *(d)* C.P.M.

143. In actual dollars, which value gives the highest amount: *(a)* market, *(b)* loan, *(c)* assessed, *(d)* original cost to build.

144. Which of the following statements is correct: *(a)* The Real Estate Commissioner is elected by the voters, *(b)* If a broker is found guilty of commingling, his license can be subject to revocation, *(c)* Punitive action for commingling is outside the jurisdiction of the Commissioner, *(d)* transfer of business property is usually by deed of reconveyance.

145. A party wall: *(a)* is built to conceal plumbing pipes, *(b)* is used in common by adjoining owners, *(c)* is the same as a firestop, *(d)* is not allowed in California buildings.

146. A borrower paid five points for a loan. The lender sold the loan at a 3½ point discount and received $77,200. The original amount of the loan was: *(a)* $80,000 *(b)* $81,060 *(c)* $78,280 *(d)* $74,400.

147. Which of the following statements is correct: *(a)* multiple listings are exclusive listings, *(b)* multiple listings are net listings, *(c)* the use of a termination date is optional in exclusive agency listings, *(d)* a broker need not disclose the selling price to seller in an option listing sale.

148. Which of the following is most nearly the opposite of appreciation: *(a)* utility, *(b)* zoning ordinances, *(c)* depreciation, *(d)* modernization.

149. Which of the following is most often found in connection with a search of the public records regarding real property: *(a)* mechanic's lien, *(b)* judgment, *(c)* property tax lien, *(d)* original government patents.

150. The minimum age at which an applicant may take the real estate broker examination is: *(a)* 21, *(b)* 17, *(c)* 18, *(d)* 20.

ANSWERS

1.	*(c)*	26.	*(d)*	51.	*(c)*	76.	*(c)*	101.	*(a)*	126.	*(a)*
2.	*(b)*	27.	*(a)*	52.	*(a)*	77.	*(d)*	102.	*(a)*	127.	*(c)*
3.	*(a)*	28.	*(c)*	53.	*(b)*	78.	*(c)*	103.	*(d)*	128.	*(d)*
4.	*(c)*	29.	*(b)*	54.	*(c)*	79.	*(a)*	104.	*(c)*	129.	*(c)*
5.	*(c)*	30.	*(c)*	55.	*(c)*	80.	*(a)*	105.	*(c)*	130.	*(c)*
6.	*(a)*	31.	*(c)*	56.	*(b)*	81.	*(a)*	106.	*(a)*	131.	*(a)*
7.	*(b)*	32.	*(b)*	57.	*(a)*	82.	*(b)*	107.	*(a)*	132.	*(c)*
8.	*(c)*	33.	*(d)*	58.	*(c)*	83.	*(c)*	108.	*(c)*	133.	*(b)*
9.	*(d)*	34.	*(a)*	59.	*(c)*	84.	*(a)*	109.	*(c)*	134.	*(a)*
10.	*(c)*	35.	*(b)*	60.	*(d)*	85.	*(c)*	110.	*(c)*	135.	*(c)*
11.	*(b)*	36.	*(a)*	61.	*(c)*	86.	*(d)*	111.	*(b)*	136.	*(d)*
12.	*(b)*	37.	*(c)*	62.	*(d)*	87.	*(c)*	112.	*(c)*	137.	*(c)*
13.	*(c)*	38.	*(a)*	63.	*(c)*	88.	*(a)*	113.	*(c)*	138.	*(d)*
14.	*(d)*	39.	*(c)*	64.	*(c)*	89.	*(a)*	114.	*(d)*	139.	*(d)*
15.	*(d)*	40.	*(d)*	65.	*(b)*	90.	*(a)*	115.	*(c)*	140.	*(c)*
16.	*(a)*	41.	*(c)*	66.	*(a)*	91.	*(c)*	116.	*(c)*	141.	*(c)*
17.	*(c)*	42.	*(a)*	67.	*(d)*	92.	*(a)*	117.	*(c)*	142.	*(a)*
18.	*(b)*	43.	*(b)*	68.	*(c)*	93.	*(c)*	118.	*(c)*	143.	*(a)*
19.	*(c)*	44.	*(c)*	69.	*(c)*	94.	*(d)*	119.	*(c)*	144.	*(b)*
20.	*(d)*	45.	*(d)*	70.	*(a)*	95.	*(d)*	120.	*(b)*	145.	*(b)*
21.	*(c)*	46.	*(c)*	71.	*(b)*	96.	*(c)*	121.	*(c)*	146.	*(a)*
22.	*(c)*	47.	*(c)*	72.	*(b)*	97.	*(b)*	122.	*(b)*	147.	*(a)*
23.	*(b)*	48.	*(d)*	73.	*(a)*	98.	*(a)*	123.	*(b)*	148.	*(c)*
24.	*(a)*	49.	*(c)*	74.	*(c)*	99.	*(a)*	124.	*(c)*	149.	*(c)*
25.	*(c)*	50.	*(a)*	75.	*(a)*	100.	*(c)*	125.	*(a)*	150.	*(c)*

Index

WINTER   REGISTRATION   01/10/84

SSN: 571-98-0923   NAME: KIRSTINE PENNY R

                                              STUDENT STATUS UNKNOWN
                                              OK for 8+ units

SECTION COURSE   DAYS   HOURS   INSTRUCTOR   ROOM   UNITS   FEE   C/N
3078   BUSI 47   T   06:00-09:50 FORD   802   4.0   .00
                 1/03/84 TO 3/24/84
                                                         *****
                                                         4.0

                         FEES   FEES   FEES   FEES
                         *****   PAID   DEFERRED   WAIVED

                 LATE REG   2.00   .00   .00
                 TOTAL FEES   2.00   .00   .00

Please keep this receipt.
It will be REQUIRED for
you to get a REFUND !!!

Paid by CHECK
B0948

S

This book has been set VIP, in 10 and 9 point Caledonia, leaded 2 points and 1 point respectively. Chapter numbers are 20 point Helvetica Bold. Chapter titles are 16 point Helvetica Bold. The size of the type page is 40 by 55½ picas.